Novels
for Students

National Advisory Board

Novels
for Students

Presenting Analysis, Context, and Criticism on Commonly Studied Novels

Volume 18

David Galens, Project Editor

Foreword by Anne Devereaux Jordan

GALE®

THOMSON
GALE

Detroit • New York • San Diego • San Francisco • Cleveland • New Haven, Conn. • Waterville, Maine • London • Munich

Novels for Students, Volume 18

Project Editor
David Galens

Editorial
Anne Marie Hacht, Ira Mark Milne, Pam Revitzer, Kathy Sauer, Timothy J. Sisler, Jennifer Smith, Carol Ullmann, Maikue Vang

Research
Nicodemus Ford, Sarah Genik, Tamara Nott

Permissions
Shalice Shah-Caldwell

Manufacturing
Stacy Melson

Imaging and Multimedia
Dean Dauphinais, Leitha Etheridge-Sims, Mary Grimes, Lezlie Light, Luke Rademacher

Product Design
Pamela A. E. Galbreath, Michael Logusz

ISBN 0-7876-6030-2
ISSN 1094-3552

Printed in the United States of America
10 9 8 7 6 5 4 3 2 1

Table of Contents

The Informed Dialogue: Interacting with Literature

When we pick up a book, we usually do so with the anticipation of pleasure. We hope that by entering the time and place of the novel and sharing the thoughts and actions of the characters, we will find enjoyment. Unfortunately, this is often not the case; we are disappointed. But we should ask, has the author failed us, or have we failed the author?

We establish a dialogue with the author, the book, and with ourselves when we read. Consciously and unconsciously, we ask questions: "Why did the author write this book?" "Why did the author choose that time, place, or character?" "How did the author achieve that effect?" "Why did the character act that way?" "Would I act in the same way?" The answers we receive depend upon how much information about literature in general and about that book specifically we ourselves bring to our reading.

Young children have limited life and literary experiences. Being young, children frequently do not know how to go about exploring a book, nor sometimes, even know the questions to ask of a book. The books they read help them answer questions, the author often coming right out and *telling* young readers the things they are learning or are expected to learn. The perennial classic, *The Little Engine That Could, tells* its readers that, among other things, it is good to help others and brings happiness:

"Hurray, hurray," cried the funny little clown and all the dolls and toys. "The good little boys and girls in

the city will be happy because you helped us, kind, Little Blue Engine."

In picture books, messages are often blatant and simple, the dialogue between the author and reader one-sided. Young children are concerned with the end result of a book—the enjoyment gained, the lesson learned—rather than with how that result was obtained. As we grow older and read further, however, we question more. We come to expect that the world within the book will closely mirror the concerns of our world, and that the author will *show* these through the events, descriptions, and conversations within the story, rather than *telling* of them. We are now expected to do the interpreting, carry on our share of the dialogue with the book and author, and glean not only the author's message, but comprehend how that message and the overall affect of the book were achieved. Sometimes, however, we need help to do these things. *Novels for Students* provides that help.

A novel is made up of many parts interacting to create a coherent whole. In reading a novel, the more obvious features can be easily spotted—theme, characters, plot—but we may overlook the more subtle elements that greatly influence how the novel is perceived by the reader: viewpoint, mood and tone, symbolism, or the use of humor. By focusing on both the obvious and more subtle literary elements within a novel, *Novels for Students* aids readers in both analyzing for message and in determining how and why that message is communicated. In the discussion on Harper Lee's *To*

Kill a Mockingbird (Vol. 2), for example, the mockingbird as a symbol of innocence is dealt with, among other things, as is the importance of Lee's use of humor which "enlivens a serious plot, adds depth to the characterization, and creates a sense of familiarity and universality." The reader comes to understand the internal elements of each novel discussed—as well as the external influences that help shape it.

"The desire to write greatly," Harold Bloom of Yale University says, "is the desire to be elsewhere, in a time and place of one's own, in an originality that must compound with inheritance, with an anxiety of influence." A writer seeks to create a unique world within a story, but although it is unique, it is not disconnected from our own world. It speaks to us *because* of what the writer brings to the writing from our world: how he or she was raised and educated; his or her likes and dislikes; the events occurring in the real world at the time of the writing, and while the author was growing up. When we know what an author has brought to his or her work, we gain a greater insight into both the "originality" (the world of the book), and the things that "compound" it. This insight enables us to question that created world and find answers more readily. By informing ourselves, we are able to establish a more effective dialogue with both book and author.

Novels for Students, in addition to providing a plot summary and descriptive list of characters—to remind readers of what they have read—also explores the external influences that shaped each book. Each entry includes a discussion of the author's background, and the historical context in which the novel was written. It is vital to know, for instance, that when Ray Bradbury was writing *Fahrenheit 451* (Vol. 1), the threat of Nazi domination had recently ended in Europe, and the McCarthy hearings were taking place in Washington, D.C. This information goes far in answering the question, "Why did he write a story of oppressive government control and book burning?" Similarly, it is important to know that Harper Lee, author of *To Kill a Mockingbird,* was born and raised in Monroeville, Alabama, and that her father was a lawyer.

Readers can now see why she chose the south as a setting for her novel—it is the place with which she was most familiar—and start to comprehend her characters and their actions.

Novels for Students helps readers find the answers they seek when they establish a dialogue with a particular novel. It also aids in the posing of questions by providing the opinions and interpretations of various critics and reviewers, broadening that dialogue. Some reviewers of *To Kill A Mockingbird,* for example, "faulted the novel's climax as melodramatic." This statement leads readers to ask, "Is it, indeed, melodramatic?" "If not, why did some reviewers see it as such?" "If it is, why did Lee choose to make it melodramatic?" "Is melodrama ever justified?" By being spurred to ask these questions, readers not only learn more about the book and its writer, but about the nature of writing itself.

The literature included for discussion in *Novels for Students* has been chosen because it has something vital to say to us. *Of Mice and Men, Catch-22, The Joy Luck Club, My Antonia, A Separate Peace* and the other novels here speak of life and modern sensibility. In addition to their individual, specific messages of prejudice, power, love or hate, living and dying, however, they and all great literature also share a common intent. They force us to *think*—about life, literature, and about others, not just about ourselves. They pry us from the narrow confines of our minds and thrust us outward to confront the world of books and the larger, real world we all share. *Novels for Students* helps us in this confrontation by providing the means of enriching our conversation with literature and the world, by creating an *informed* dialogue, one that brings true pleasure to the personal act of reading.

Sources

Harold Bloom, *The Western Canon, The Books and School of the Ages,* Riverhead Books, 1994.

Watty Piper, *The Little Engine That Could,* Platt & Munk, 1930.

Anne Devereaux Jordan
Senior Editor, TALL
(Teaching and Learning Literature)

Introduction

Purpose of the Book

The purpose of *Novels for Students (NfS)* is to provide readers with a guide to understanding, enjoying, and studying novels by giving them easy access to information about the work. Part of Gale's "For Students" Literature line, *NfS* is specifically designed to meet the curricular needs of high school and undergraduate college students and their teachers, as well as the interests of general readers and researchers considering specific novels. While each volume contains entries on "classic" novels frequently studied in classrooms, there are also entries containing hard-to-find information on contemporary novels, including works by multicultural, international, and women novelists.

The information covered in each entry includes an introduction to the novel and the novel's author; a plot summary, to help readers unravel and understand the events in a novel; descriptions of important characters, including explanation of a given character's role in the novel as well as discussion about that character's relationship to other characters in the novel; analysis of important themes in the novel; and an explanation of important literary techniques and movements as they are demonstrated in the novel.

In addition to this material, which helps the readers analyze the novel itself, students are also provided with important information on the literary and historical background informing each work. This includes a historical context essay, a box comparing the time or place the novel was written to modern Western culture, a critical essay, and excerpts from critical essays on the novel. A unique feature of *NfS* is a specially commissioned critical essay on each novel, targeted toward the student reader.

To further aid the student in studying and enjoying each novel, information on media adaptations is provided, as well as reading suggestions for works of fiction and nonfiction on similar themes and topics. Classroom aids include ideas for research papers and lists of critical sources that provide additional material on the novel.

Selection Criteria

The titles for each volume of *NfS* were selected by surveying numerous sources on teaching literature and analyzing course curricula for various school districts. Some of the sources surveyed included: literature anthologies; *Reading Lists for College-Bound Students: The Books Most Recommended by America's Top Colleges;* textbooks on teaching the novel; a College Board survey of novels commonly studied in high schools; a National Council of Teachers of English (NCTE) survey of novels commonly studied in high schools; the NCTE's *Teaching Literature in High School: The Novel;* and the Young Adult Library Services Association (YALSA) list of best books for young adults of the past twenty-five years.

Input was also solicited from our advisory board, as well as from educators from various areas.

From these discussions, it was determined that each volume should have a mix of "classic" novels (those works commonly taught in literature classes) and contemporary novels for which information is often hard to find. Because of the interest in expanding the canon of literature, an emphasis was also placed on including works by international, multicultural, and women authors. Our advisory board members—educational professionals—helped pare down the list for each volume. If a work was not selected for the present volume, it was often noted as a possibility for a future volume. As always, the editor welcomes suggestions for titles to be included in future volumes.

How Each Entry Is Organized

Each entry, or chapter, in *NfS* focuses on one novel. Each entry heading lists the full name of the novel, the author's name, and the date of the novel's publication. The following elements are contained in each entry:

- **Introduction:** a brief overview of the novel which provides information about its first appearance, its literary standing, any controversies surrounding the work, and major conflicts or themes within the work.

- **Author Biography:** this section includes basic facts about the author's life, and focuses on events and times in the author's life that inspired the novel in question.

- **Plot Summary:** a factual description of the major events in the novel. Lengthy summaries are broken down with subheads.

- **Characters:** an alphabetical listing of major characters in the novel. Each character name is followed by a brief to an extensive description of the character's role in the novel, as well as discussion of the character's actions, relationships, and possible motivation.

  Characters are listed alphabetically by last name. If a character is unnamed—for instance, the narrator in *Invisible Man*—the character is listed as "The Narrator" and alphabetized as "Narrator." If a character's first name is the only one given, the name will appear alphabetically by that name.

  Variant names are also included for each character. Thus, the full name "Jean Louise Finch" would head the listing for the narrator of *To Kill a Mockingbird,* but listed in a separate cross-reference would be the nickname "Scout Finch."

- **Themes:** a thorough overview of how the major topics, themes, and issues are addressed within the novel. Each theme discussed appears in a separate subhead and is easily accessed through the boldface entries in the Subject/Theme Index.

- **Style:** this section addresses important style elements of the novel, such as setting, point of view, and narration; important literary devices used, such as imagery, foreshadowing, symbolism; and, if applicable, genres to which the work might have belonged, such as Gothicism or Romanticism. Literary terms are explained within the entry but can also be found in the Glossary.

- **Historical Context:** This section outlines the social, political, and cultural climate *in which the author lived and the novel was created.* This section may include descriptions of related historical events, pertinent aspects of daily life in the culture, and the artistic and literary sensibilities of the time in which the work was written. If the novel is a historical work, information regarding the time in which the novel is set is also included. Each section is broken down with helpful subheads.

- **Critical Overview:** this section provides background on the critical reputation of the novel, including bannings or any other public controversies surrounding the work. For older works, this section includes a history of how the novel was first received and how perceptions of it may have changed over the years; for more recent novels, direct quotes from early reviews may also be included.

- **Criticism:** an essay commissioned by *NfS* which specifically deals with the novel and is written specifically for the student audience, as well as excerpts from previously published criticism on the work (if available).

- **Sources:** an alphabetical list of critical material used in compiling the entry, with full bibliographical information.

- **Further Reading:** an alphabetical list of other critical sources which may prove useful for the student. It includes full bibliographical information and a brief annotation.

In addition, each entry contains the following highlighted sections, set apart from the main text as sidebars:

- **Media Adaptations:** a list of important film and television adaptations of the novel, including source information. The list also includes stage adaptations, audio recordings, musical adaptations, etc.

- **Topics for Further Study:** a list of potential study questions or research topics dealing with the novel. This section includes questions related to other disciplines the student may be studying, such as American history, world history, science, math, government, business, geography, economics, psychology, etc.

- **Compare and Contrast Box:** an "at-a-glance" comparison of the cultural and historical differences between the author's time and culture and late twentieth century/early twenty-first century Western culture. This box includes pertinent parallels between the major scientific, political, and cultural movements of the time or place the novel was written, the time or place the novel was set (if a historical work), and modern Western culture. Works written after 1990 may not have this box.

- **What Do I Read Next?:** a list of works that might complement the featured novel or serve as a contrast to it. This includes works by the same author and others, works of fiction and nonfiction, and works from various genres, cultures, and eras.

Other Features

NfS includes "The Informed Dialogue: Interacting with Literature," a foreword by Anne Devereaux Jordan, Senior Editor for *Teaching and Learning Literature* (*TALL*), and a founder of the Children's Literature Association. This essay provides an enlightening look at how readers interact with literature and how *Novels for Students* can help teachers show students how to enrich their own reading experiences.

A Cumulative Author/Title Index lists the authors and titles covered in each volume of the *NfS* series.

A Cumulative Nationality/Ethnicity Index breaks down the authors and titles covered in each volume of the *NfS* series by nationality and ethnicity.

A Subject/Theme Index, specific to each volume, provides easy reference for users who may be studying a particular subject or theme rather than a single work. Significant subjects from events to broad themes are included, and the entries pointing to the specific theme discussions in each entry are indicated in **boldface.**

Each entry may have several illustrations, including photos of the author, stills from film adaptations, maps, and/or photos of key historical events, if available.

Citing *Novels for Students*

When writing papers, students who quote directly from any volume of *Novels for Students* may use the following general forms. These examples are based on MLA style; teachers may request that students adhere to a different style, so the following examples may be adapted as needed.

When citing text from *NfS* that is not attributed to a particular author (i.e., the Themes, Style, Historical Context sections, etc.), the following format should be used in the bibliography section:

> *"Night." Novels for Students.* Ed. Marie Rose Napierkowski. Vol. 4. Detroit: Gale, 1998. 234–35.

When quoting the specially commissioned essay from *NfS* (usually the first piece under the "Criticism" subhead), the following format should be used:

> Miller, Tyrus. Critical Essay on *Winesburg, Ohio. Novels for Students.* Ed. Marie Rose Napierkowski. Vol. 4. Detroit: Gale, 1998. 335–39.

When quoting a journal or newspaper essay that is reprinted in a volume of *NfS,* the following form may be used:

> Malak, Amin. "Margaret Atwood's *The Handmaid's Tale* and the Dystopian Tradition," *Canadian Literature* No. 112 (Spring, 1987), 9–16; excerpted and reprinted in *Novels for Students,* Vol. 4, ed. Marie Rose Napierkowski (Detroit: Gale, 1998), pp. 133–36.

When quoting material reprinted from a book that appears in a volume of *NfS,* the following form may be used:

> Adams, Timothy Dow. "Richard Wright: Wearing the Mask," in *Telling Lies in Modern American Autobiography* (University of North Carolina Press, 1990), 69–83; excerpted and reprinted in *Novels for Students,* Vol. 1, ed. Diane Telgen (Detroit: Gale, 1997), pp. 59–61.

We Welcome Your Suggestions

The editor of *Novels for Students* welcomes your comments and ideas. Readers who wish to suggest novels to appear in future volumes, or who have other suggestions, are cordially invited to contact the editor. You may contact the editor via e-mail at: **ForStudentsEditors@gale.com.** Or write to the editor at:

Editor, *Novels for Students*
Gale
27500 Drake Road
Farmington Hills, MI 48331–3535

Literary Chronology

1707: Henry Fielding is born on April 22 in Somerset, England.

1749: Henry Fielding's *Tom Jones* is published.

1754: Henry Fielding dies on October 8 in Lisbon, Portugal.

1775: Jane Austen is born on December 16 in Steventon, Hampshire, England.

1811: Jane Austen's *Sense and Sensibility* is published.

1817: Jane Austen dies on July 18 in Winchester, England, after a gradual illness.

1847: Bram Stoker is born Abraham Stoker on November 8 in Clontarf, Ireland.

1885: D. H. Lawrence is born David Herbert Richard Lawrence on September 11 in Eastwood, Nottinghamshire, England.

1897: Bram Stoker's *Dracula* is published.

1900: Thomas Wolfe is born on October 3 in Asheville, North Carolina.

1900: Hal Borland is born Harold Glen Borland on May 14 in Sterling, Nebraska.

1912: Bram Stoker dies on April 20 in London, England, of syphilis.

1913: D. H. Lawrence's *Sons and Lovers* is published.

1919: Iris Murdoch is born on July 15 in Dublin, Ireland.

1925: Robert Cormier is born on January 17 in Leominster, Massachusetts.

1929: Thomas Wolfe's *Look Homeward, Angel* is published.

1929: Milan Kundera is born on April 1 in Brno, Czechoslovakia.

1930: D. H. Lawrence dies on March 2 in Vence, France, from tuberculosis.

1931: Sébastien Japrisot is born in Marseille, France.

1933: Reynolds Price is born on February 1 in Macon, North Carolina.

1938: Thomas Wolfe dies on September 15 in Baltimore, Maryland, from tubercular meningitis.

1942: Isabel Allende is on August 2 in Lima, Peru.

1949: Graham Swift is born on May 4 in London, England.

1954: Iris Murdoch's *Under the Net* is published.

1962: Reynolds Price's *A Long and Happy Life* is published.

1963: Hal Borland's *When the Legends Die* is published.

1977: Robert Cormier's *I Am the Cheese* is published.

1978: Hal Borland dies on February 22 in Sharon, Connecticut.

1983: Graham Swift's *Waterland* is published.

1984: Milan Kundera's *The Unbearable Lightness of Being* is published.

1991: Sébastien Japrisot's *A Very Long Engagement* is published.

1999: Isabel Allende's *Daughter of Fortune* is published.

1999: Iris Murdoch dies on February 8 in Oxford, England, from complications arising from Alzheimer's disease.

2000: Robert Cormier dies on November 2 in Boston, Massachusetts, from lung cancer.

Acknowledgments

The editors wish to thank the copyright holders of the excerpted criticism included in this volume and the permissions managers of many book and magazine publishing companies for assisting us in securing reproduction rights. We are also grateful to the staffs of the Detroit Public Library, the Library of Congress, the University of Detroit Mercy Library, Wayne State University Purdy/ Kresge Library Complex, and the University of Michigan Libraries for making their resources available to us. Following is a list of the copyright holders who have granted us permission to reproduce material in this volume of *Novels for Students* *(NfS)*. Every effort has been made to trace copyright, but if omissions have been made, please let us know.

COPYRIGHTED MATERIALS IN *NfS*, **VOLUME 18, WERE REPRODUCED FROM THE FOLLOWING PERIODICALS:**

College Literature, v. 1, fall, 1974. Copyright © 1974 by West Chester University. Reproduced by permission.— *Criticism: A Quarterly for Literature and the Arts*, v. VIX, summer, 1972. Copyright, 1972, Wayne State University Press. Reproduced by permission of the publisher.—*Education*, v. 120, fall, 1999. Reproduced by permission.— *ELH*, v. 66, fall, 1999. Copyright © 1999 by The Johns Hopkins University Press. All rights reserved. Reproduced by permission.— *Journal of Narrative Technique*, v. 9, fall, 1979. Reproduced by permission.—*Modern Fiction Studies*, v. XV, autumn, 1969. Copyright © 1969 by Purdue Research Foundation, West Lafayette, IN 47907. All rights reserved. Reproduced by permission of The Johns Hopkins University.—*Publishing Research Quarterly*, v. 8, spring, 1992. Reproduced by permission of Transaction Publishers.—*Queen's Quarterly*, v. LXXIX, winter, 1972 for "*Dracula*: Bram Stoker's Spoiled Masterpiece" by Royce MacGillivray. Reproduced by permission of the author.—*Renascence*, v. XXXV, summer, 1983. © copyright, 1983, Marquette University Press. Reproduced by permission.—*Review of Contemporary Fiction*, v. 9, summer, 1989. Reproduced by permission.—*Salmagundi*, n. 73, winter, 1987. Copyright © 1987 by Skidmore College. Reproduced by permission.—*South Atlantic Quarterly*, v. 63, spring, 1964. Copyright © 1964 by Duke University Press, Durham, NC. Reproduced by permission.—*Southern Humanities Review*, v. 18, winter, 1984 for "The Narrator in *Look Homeward, Angel*" by Hugh M. Ruppersburg. Copyright 1984 by Auburn University. Reproduced by permission of the author.—*Studies in the Literary Imagination*, v. XXIII, fall, 1990. Copyright 1990 Department of English, Georgia State University. Reproduced by permission.—*Twentieth Century Literature*, v. 35, spring, 1989. Copyright 1989, Hofstra University Press. Reproduced by permission.

COPYRIGHTED MATERIALS IN *NfS*, VOLUME 18, WERE REPRODUCED FROM THE FOLLOWING BOOKS:

Campbell, Patricia J. From *Presenting Robert Cormier.* Dell Publishing, 1990. Copyright © 1985, 1989 by G. K. Hall & Co. Reproduced by permission.—Wilt, Judith. From *Abortion, Choice, and Contemporary Fiction: The Armageddon of the Maternal Instinct.* The University of Chicago Press, 1990. © 1990 by The University of Chicago. All rights reserved. Reproduced by permission.

PHOTOGRAPHS AND ILLUSTRATIONS APPEARING IN *NfS*, VOLUME 18, WERE RECEIVED FROM THE FOLLOWING SOURCES:

Allende, Isabel, photograph. Archive Photos. Reproduced by permission.—Austen, Jane, illustration. © Bettmann/Corbis. Reproduced by permission.—Bus traveling up Eagle Street, photograph. © Bettmann/Corbis. Reproduced by permission.—Donegan, Lonnie, and his skiffle group, photograph © Hulton-Deutsch Collection/Corbis. Reproduced by permission.—Emma Thompson, Kate Winslet and Gemma Jones in the film *Sense and Sensibility*, photograph. The Kobal Collection. Reproduced by permission.—Finney, Albert and Diane Cilento in the film *Tom Jones*, 1963, photograph. The Kobal Collection. Reproduced by permission.—Forrest, Frederic as Tom Black Bull, Richard Widmark as Red Dillon, scene from Hal Borland's *When the Legends Die*, directed by Stuart Millar. The Kobal Collection. Reproduced by permission.—French gunners keep watch from the observation balcony of a screened trench, at Verdun, photograph. © Bettmann/Corbis. Reproduced by permission.—Gold miners, panning for gold at a river, photograph. © Hulton Archive/Getty Images. Reproduced by permission.—Group of Ute Indians in Salt Lake City, Utah, photograph. © Hulton/Archive Photos, Inc. Reproduced by permission.—Helen Chandler, as Mina Seward, with Bela Lugosi, as Count Dracula, clutching her neck, a scene from the 1931 film version of *Dracula*, photograph. The Kobal Collection. Reproduced by permission.—Henry Fielding, engraving. The Library of Congress.—Irons, Jeremy as Tom Crick, embracing Sinead Cusack, as Mary Crick, a scene from the 1992 film of Graham Swift's *Waterland*, photograph. The Kobal Collection. Reproduced by permission.—Juliette Binoche, as Tereza, with arm around Daniel Day-Lewis, as Tomas, a scene from the 1987 film version of Milan Kundera's novel, *The Unbearable Lightness of Being*, photograph. The Kobal Collection. Reproduced by permission.—Lawrence, D. H., photograph. © Hulton-Deutsch Collection/Corbis. Reproduced by permission.—Men in small boats, fishing near tall ships, in the harbor off Valparaiso, Chile, in 1851, photograph. © Corbis. Reproduced by permission.—Murdoch, Iris, photograph. The Library of Congress.—Nixon, Richard Millhous, Patricia Nixion-Cox, (Nixon at podium), Washington D. C., 1974, photograph. The Library of Congress.—Price, Reynolds, photograph by Grant Halverson. AP/Wide World Photos. Reproduced by permission.—Queneau, Raymond, photograph by Jerry Bauer. © Jerry Bauer. Reproduced by permission.—Stoker, Bram, 1906, photograph. AP/Wide World Photos. Reproduced by permission.—Student demonstrators, link arms while singing "We Shall Overcome," outside the United States Consulate, in Toronto, Canada, photograph. © UPI Telephoto/Corbis. Reproduced by permission.—Swift, Graham, holding his novel, 1996, photograph by Lynne Sladky. AP/Wide World Photos. Reproduced by permission.—Tepes, Vlad (Dracula), engraving from a painting. © Hulton Archive/Getty Images. Reproduced by permission.—Trevor Howard, as Walter Morel, sitting, watching Dean Stockwell, as Paul Morel, a scene from the 1960 film version of *Sons and Lovers*, photograph. The Kobal Collection. Reproduced by permission.—Kundera, Milan, photograph by Vera Kundera. Reproduced by permission.—Wolfe, Thomas, painting. The Library of Congress.—Worker filling sandbags to use as a barricade against the swollen waters of a river, photograph. © Hulton-Deutsch Collection/Corbis. Reproduced by permission.—Young man walking alongside marching Soviet troops in Prague, photograph. © Hulton-Deutsch Collection/Corbis. Reproduced by permission.

Contributors

Bryan Aubrey: Aubrey holds a Ph.D. in English and has published many articles on twentieth-century literature. Entries on *A Very Long Engagement* and *Waterland*. Original essays on *A Very Long Engagement* and *Waterland*.

Cynthia Bily: Bily teaches writing and literature at Adrian College in Adrian, Michigan. Entry on *I Am the Cheese*. Original essay on *I Am the Cheese*.

Joyce Hart: Hart has degrees in English literature and creative writing and writes primarily on literary themes. Entries on *Daughter of Fortune, Under the Net*, and *When the Legends Die*. Original essays on *Daughter of Fortune, Under the Net*, and *When the Legends Die*.

Diane Andrews Henningfeld: Henningfeld is a professor of English literature and composition who writes widely for educational and reference publishers. Entry on *The Unbearable Lightness of Being*. Original Essay on *The Unbearable Lightness of Being*.

David Kelly: Kelly is an instructor of literature and creative writing at two colleges in Illinois. Entry on *A Long and Happy Life*. Original essay on *A Long and Happy Life*.

Charlotte Mayhew: Mayhew is a freelance writer. Original essay on *Daughter of Fortune*.

Candyce Norvell: Norvell is an independent educational writer who specializes in English and literature and holds degrees in linguistics and journalism. Entry on *Tom Jones*. Original essay on *Tom Jones*.

David Partikian: Partikian is a Seattle-based freelance writer and English instructor. Entry on *Sense and Sensibility*. Original essay on *Sense and Sensibility*.

Ryan D. Poquette: Poquette has a bachelor's degree in English and specializes in writing about literature. Entry on *Dracula*. Original essay on *Dracula*.

Chris Semansky: Semansky is an instructor of English literature and composition. Entry on *Sons and Lovers*. Original essay on *Sons and Lovers*.

Daniel Toronto: Toronto is an editor at the Pennsylvania State University Press. Original essay on *Daughter of Fortune*.

Scott Trudell: Trudell is a freelance writer with a bachelor's degree in English literature. Entry on *Look Homeward, Angel*. Original essay on *Look Homeward, Angel*.

Daughter of Fortune

Isabel Allende

1999

Isabel Allende says of her female protagonist in *Daughter of Fortune*, Eliza, that she might well represent who the author might have been in another life. Allende spent seven years of research on this, her fifth novel, which she says is a story of a young woman's search for self-knowledge. Allende also believes that the novel reflects her own struggle to define the role of feminism in her life.

In *Daughter of Fortune*, Eliza takes a physical journey through time and space as she travels from Chile to Gold-Rush-era California. That journey also represents a spiritual quest. Eliza, as she stows away in a dark hole at the bottom of a ship, awakens to the challenge of first redefining herself in a man's world of adventure and aggression before she refines herself and returns to a new definition of what it is to be an unfettered and independent female.

Allende says that *Daughter of Fortune* did not turn out as she had planned and that during the process of composition, she often got angry with some of her characters who would not do what she wanted them to do. She also says that, while she was still writing the book, she had a dream that told her the book was finished, although she thought she still had a lot more to write. Her mother, who, at the age of seventy-eight, remains her only editor, questioned the ending as being too abrupt. However, Allende states that she knew that her dream was telling her that the story had arrived at its own natural ending. Some reviews of the book call *Daughter of Fortune* one of Allende's best.

Isabel Allende

Author Biography

In 1973, author Isabel Allende fled Chile with her husband and their two children after her uncle, Salvador Allende, then president of Chile, was forced out of office. From this experience, Isabel would go on to write her first novel, created from a series of letters that she wrote to her grandfather, who still resided in Chile.

Allende was born on August 2, 1942, in Lima, Peru, but would move with her family three years later to Chile. After completing her education, she worked ten years as a journalist for various magazines, newspapers, television shows, and movie documentaries. One of the magazines that she wrote for was *Paula*, a publication that advocated women's rights to divorce and abortion, a very radical position in Chile in the 1960s.

When she and her family escaped to Venezuela, she continued her career as a journalist but also began what would become her first published novel, *The House of Spirits* (1982)—a book that would win her much international acclaim. The novel would also mark her as one of the leaders of the Latin American feminist movement, as her characters confront the traditional, passive role of women. A movie adaptation was produced in 1993.

Allende wrote two more novels in rather quick succession, *Of Love and Shadows* (1984) and *Eva Luna* (1985), and enjoyed several whirlwind tours around the world as a novelist. In the late 1980s, Allende took advantage of a book tour to the United States to promote her newly published collection of short stories, *The Stories of Eva Luna* (1989), to take a break from the emotional stress of her recent divorce. It was during this time that she met Willie Gordon, an American man whom she would later marry. Gordon also became the model on which the character Gregory Reeves, from Allende's 1991 novel *The Infinite Plan*, was based.

Three years later, Allende's twenty-eight-year-old daughter, Paula, died after a long illness. Allende's memoir, *Paula*, was written as a long letter to her daughter, explaining the story of her family. The writing of this book, plus the effect of having to face the death of her daughter, drained Allende's creative spirit. In an attempt to rekindle her love of writing, she became involved in a project of putting together a collection of recipes. This lighthearted topic is captured in her book *Aphrodite*, the title referring to the nature of the recipes, which is food that inspires love.

Allende went on to write *Daughter of Fortune* (1999) and *Portrait in Sepia* (2000). *The City of Beasts* is a story that Allende wrote for an audience of young adults.

Plot Summary

Part 1

Isabel Allende's *Daughter of Fortune* begins with the narrator recalling the details of Eliza Sommers's arrival at the home of Rose and Jeremy Sommers. Rose and Jeremy took her in on March 15, 1832, the day celebrated as her birthday.

The Sommers live in Valparaíso, Chile. Rose and Jeremy are brother and sister. Rose takes care of household chores (with the help of Mama Fresia, a native woman who runs the kitchen) while Jeremy directs an import/export business. Rose and Jeremy's brother John is a sea captain who often visits them.

Eliza is something of a plaything for Rose, who likes to dress her in fancy clothes and provide a proper education for her. Mama Fresia, on the other hand, looks after Eliza's physical and psychological welfare. Rose teaches Eliza to play the piano and to enjoy reading. Mama Fresia teaches her to cook and to heal herself with medicinal herbs.

Jacob Todd is introduced early in the first chapter as a "charismatic redhead with the most beautiful preacher's voice." He has come to Chile on a bet, claiming that he can sell three hundred bibles. He is warmly received by the upper echelon of Chilean-British society, including Jeremy and Rose Sommers. It does not take long for Todd to fall in love with Rose, who constantly rebuffs his attentions.

As the story unfolds, Allende inserts a brief history of Chilean culture, including facts about immigration, the influence of the British Empire on society, as well as the controls placed on women, who were expected to remain largely inside the home. Agustín del Valle, a wealthy landowner, is introduced as representing the epitome of wealth, influence, and patriarchy.

Eliza enters puberty with the onset of her menstruation cycle, which Miss Rose tells her not to discuss with anyone. Jeremy, noting that Eliza is maturing, comments that "intelligence is a drawback in a woman," proffering his sentiments about the female sex in general. Rose wants to send Eliza to school, but Jeremy is against it. Rose, in retaliation, refuses to do anything in the home and locks herself away in her bedroom. Jeremy eventually submits.

Feliciano Rodríguez de Santa Cruz and the daughter of landowner Agustín del Valle, Paulina, are introduced next. Feliciano represents the newly established rich class, made so by the discovery of gold. He falls in love with Paulina, a match that her father is against. In order to prevent the two from getting together, he orders that Paulina must be taken to a faraway convent to be raised by the nuns until she comes to her senses. He also commands that her head be shaved to shame her. Todd steps in when he hears of Paulina's fate. He helps Feliciano find her. Eventually, Agustín relents, and Paulina and Feliciano are married.

Next, Todd befriends Joaquín Andieta, a very poor young man who works at Jeremy's business and preaches socialism on the side. Andieta and Todd often meet and discuss politics. Andieta believes that Todd lives "in the clouds," because he believes in a communal society. Andieta is more practical: his goal is to unionize workers and promote land reforms.

Part one closes with Todd being discovered as a fraud (the British community in Chile took him into their circle because they thought he was a preacher) and with Miss Rose trying to find an appropriate suitor for Eliza. Her attempts fail, as she introduces Eliza to Michael Steward, an English

Media Adaptations

- Books on Tape, Inc., has a recording of *Daughter of Fortune* (1999) read by Blair Brown.

---

naval officer, who turns the tables on Miss Rose and falls for her. Eliza, taking matters into her own hands, falls in love with Joaquín. In a flashback scene, the story of Miss Rose's ill-fated love affair with Karl Bretzner, a Viennese tenor, who, Rose later discovers, is married and has two children, is revealed.

Part 2

Joaquín decides that he must travel to the United States to make his fortune. He and Eliza have been meeting clandestinely, and she mourns his decision. Feliciano and Paulina are also affected by the gold rush, but through Paulina's clever business mind, they decide to invest in a steam ship, which will provide food for the hungry masses of miners in the States. They enlist John as their captain.

Mama Fresia discovers love letters that Joaquín and Eliza have written to one another, thus exposing the secret that the young couple have been involved sexually. Eliza tells her that she will clear her name by marrying Joaquín, and, toward this goal, she must follow him to California. When Mama Fresia realizes that Eliza is pregnant, she concocts a recipe to try to abort the fetus. She is unsuccessful.

John arrives in Chile and introduces Tao Chi'en, a Chinese man who has been working for him. It is through Tao Chi'en that Eliza will be smuggled aboard another ship and taken to California. At the time, Tao does not know that Eliza is pregnant. He only knows that Eliza is in love and must be reunited with Joaquín. Tao, who is suffering the loss of his wife, fully understands Eliza's emotions. He brings her aboard and stows her in the belly of the ship in a small cargo hold.

In another flashback scene, the story of Tao Chi'en is told. He is the son of a poor healer, who eventually was forced to sell Tao to a group of traveling merchants. When the merchants discover that

Tao is a healer, they sell him, in turn, to one of China's greatest acupuncturists as an apprentice. It is through this great healer that Tao receives his name as well as his education in the medicinal arts. When his master dies, Tao travels to Hong Kong, where he sets up a business. According to tradition, Tao looks for a wife who has very small feet, the sign of beauty in Chinese culture at that time. Ironically, it is because of her bound feet (which cause her health to be frail), that his wife, Lin, eventually dies. Later, during a drunken spree, Tao is kidnapped by John and taken aboard his ship.

Tao soon learns that Eliza is pregnant. She becomes seriously ill, and he must take care of her when she miscarries. He cannot be with her at all times, so he enlists the help of Azucena Placeres, a Chilean prostitute who is traveling to San Francisco to set up a business there. She helps Eliza regain her strength, and, for her efforts, Eliza gives her a jeweled necklace.

Upon arriving in San Francisco, Eliza dresses as a young boy and accompanies Tao through the town as they search for a place to stay. Although Tao was not planning on staying in San Francisco, he finds that he cannot leave Eliza. She is still too weak to fend for herself. He is not, like everyone around him, interested in finding gold. He would rather set up his medical practice. Meanwhile, back in Chile, Rose meets with Joaquín's mother and finds that he has gone to California. Rose later confides in John, asking him to search for Eliza there.

Part 3

Eliza regains her strength and begins her search for Joaquín. In her costume as a boy, she takes on the identity of Joaquín's brother. Eliza has left Tao in order to widen her search, but she often writes letters to him. She realizes how much she misses him.

It is through her travels that Eliza begins to find her courage and her independence. She sells prepared meals, writes letters for others, and offers her services in the medicinal arts. In the process, she meets new friends, such as Babalu the Bad and Joe Bonecrusher, who travels throughout the gold-mining counties offering entertainment. It is with Joe Bonecrusher's group that Eliza earns a living playing the piano.

Tom No-Tribe is introduced. Joe Bonecrusher adopted the Native American child after his tribe was massacred. Eliza takes to Tom and, when a fire breaks out in the house, saves him. In the meantime, Tao becomes established in his medical prac-

tice and becomes an advocate for the young Chinese girls who have been sent to the United States as prostitutes. The girls, some as young as eleven, rarely live more than two years after arriving. Tao eventually finds Eliza and asks that she come back to San Francisco to help him, which she does.

Back in San Francisco, Eliza hears of Joaquín's death. Before going to view his body, she realizes that she has fallen in love with Tao.

Characters

Elías Andieta
See Eliza Sommers

Joaquín Andieta
Joaquín is a very poor young man who ekes out a living at Jeremy Sommers's import business. He is a socialist at heart, much like Allende's own uncle, and works hard to try to unionize workers and protest against the government's treatment of the poor. He seduces Eliza with his intelligence and spirit, but it is unclear if he really falls in love with her. Joaquín seems rather to be in love with the idea of socialism. He leaves Chile in pursuit of gold in California. Stories about him abound, especially after Jacob (Todd) Freemont begins to mythologize him in exaggerated newspaper accounts of his activities, renaming him Joaquín Murieta. The story of Joaquín after his arrival in California is obscure. Readers never see him again, so all the details about his whereabouts and his activities are no more verifiable than gossip. He is found dead at the end of the story, having been shot by a group of mercenaries as they supposedly try to rid the West of one more notorious "Mexican" outlaw.

Señora Andieta
Señora Andieta is Joaquín's mother. She is very poor and loves her son very much. She is the one who leads Rose to assume that Eliza has gone to California when Rose visits her and discovers Joaquín's location.

Babalu the Bad
Babalu the Bad is a bodyguard for Joe Bonecrusher's girls. He is very big and said to be able to do the work of several men. He tries to make a "man" out of Eliza, whom he thinks is a bit too feminine to be a boy. He is an illiterate convict from Chicago who walked across the Midwest and the mountains to look for gold in California.

Joe Bonecrusher

Joe Bonecrusher is a very masculine woman who works as a madam in a traveling parlor of prostitutes. She and her girls are protected by Babalu the Bad. Joe befriends Eliza, letting her earn her keep by playing the piano to help entertain the men who come to visit Joe's girls.

Karl Bretzner

Karl Bretzner is an Austrian tenor who goes to London to perform several of Mozart's works for the royal family. He seduces Rose Sommers with his voice. She attends every performance, which he eventually notices and takes advantage of when he invites her to his dressing room. According to the narrator, he is built like a butcher, but his voice arouses an uncontrollable passion in Rose, and she gives in to him. Later, Jeremy Sommers guesses what is going on and investigates Bretzner, discovering that he is a married man and the father of two children.

Tao Chi'en

Tao Chi'en was born in Kwangtun Province in China to a very poor family. His father is a healer, and, before his family sells Tao, he learns many healing properties of plants, a fact that saves his life later when he is resold to a wealthy *zhong yi*, an acupuncture master, as an apprentice. The master takes Tao Chi'en in as his own son, gives him his name, and teaches him everything that he knows. When the master commits suicide, Tao inherits his money and medical instruments.

Tao then moves to Hong Kong, where he sets up his own practice and marries Lin. Then, in a totally inebriated state, Tao is kidnapped by John and taken aboard his ship to work as a cook. Tao and John become friends, which leads to Tao's being in Chile when Eliza asks for his help in smuggling her aboard a ship that is going to California.

Tao is haunted by the spirit of his wife, but he must accept the fact that his relationship with Eliza is deepening. He sets up a medical practice in San Francisco while Eliza travels through the mining towns in the California mountains, searching for Joaquín. Tao becomes involved in helping to rescue young Chinese girls who are brought into San Francisco as forced prostitutes. In the end, he and Eliza admit their feelings for each other.

Chile Boy

See Eliza Sommers

Agustín del Valle

Agustín del Valle is a character who represents the rich landowners and the power they have in Chile. He is known as a rake (a womanizer) and a severe landlord who often brutalizes his tenants. He is also the epitome of a dictatorial patriarch, as he demands that his family obey him. He rules the women in his family with an exceptionally tight rein, to the point of insisting that his daughter Pauline be taken to a distant convent after she falls in love with a man of whom he does not approve. Pauline defies him, however, demonstrating Allende's rejection of the patriarchal society.

Pauline del Valle

When Pauline del Valle falls in love with Feliciano, her father orders that her hair be cut off to shame her and then sends her to be raised by nuns, locked away in a convent. Pauline is a feisty woman, however, and defies her father by running away from the convent and into the arms of her lover. Eventually, her father relents and allows the young couple to be married. Pauline proves to be a good wife and a very intelligent and intuitive businesswoman.

Jacob Freemont

See Jacob Todd

Mama Fresia

Mama Fresia is of Mapuche Indian descent and works in the Sommers household as a cook and maid. She takes care of Eliza in ways that Rose does not. She tends Eliza's health with medicinal plants and incantations, teaches her skills in the kitchen, and tells her stories from her ancestral mythology. She also teaches Eliza how to read her dreams and how to understand nature. These skills, more than the ones that Rose teaches Eliza, help Eliza to survive during her journey into the Wild West of 1850s California.

Lin

Lin is Tao Chi'en's wife. She was brought to Tao through a matchmaker. Tao loved her for her tiny feet, which had been bound since she was a child. She and Tao fall in love upon marrying, and she eventually becomes pregnant but loses the baby. Not much later, she becomes ill. After her death, she appears to Tao and eventually tells him to move on with his life.

Joaquin Murieta

See Joaquín Andieta

Tom No-Tribe

Tom No-Tribe is the adopted son of Joe Bonecrusher. Joe found him after Tom's tribe had been massacred when Tom was only four years old. Eliza tells Tao that she wants to one day have a son as brave as Tom.

Azucena Placeres

Azucena Placeres is a Chilean woman who is on the same ship as Eliza as they go to San Francisco. Tao enlists Azucena's assistance in helping Eliza through her fever. Eliza repays her by giving her one of her necklaces. Later, John recognizes the necklace and insists that she tell him where Eliza is. Azucena lies, telling John that Eliza is dead.

Feliciano Rodriquez de Santa Cruz

Feliciano discovers gold in northern Chile. Since his money is newly found, he is not accepted into the old Chilean aristocracy and is rejected by Agustín del Valle, the father of the woman he loves. Feliciano plots to steal Pauline away from the convent where her father has sent her. Later, after they are married, Feliciano trusts Pauline's intuitive business sense and opens a bank account in her name, giving her money to invest on her own.

Eliza Sommers

Eliza Sommers is the product of an affair between John Sommers and a Chilean woman, whose name John cannot remember. She is left on the doorstep of Rose and Jeremy's house. Her development takes an interesting twist as she learns about British society through Rose and the way of the Chilean peasant through Mama Fresia. At the age of sixteen, she falls in love with Joaquín and has a clandestine love affair, which results in pregnancy. When Joaquín leaves to find gold in California, she insists on following him. To do so, she must sneak away from Rose and Jeremy and be hidden on board a sailing ship.

As she rides in the belly of the vessel in the dark recesses of the very small storage room, she loses her baby and is symbolically reborn to a new sense of self. It is through this experience that she also meets Tao, who will represent a more mature love relationship for her. When she arrives in California, she sets out to find Joaquín. In the process, she finds herself. First, she dons men's clothing and takes on a masculine identity in order to free herself from the prescribed notions of womanhood she has come to know. During this process, she takes on the name of Elías Andieta, the younger brother of Joaquín. Other people whom she meets also give

her the nickname Chile Boy. In finding her independence, she discovers that she can redefine her feminine role. In the wild, she learns to earn her own living and to see life as an adventure rather than as a boring process of following someone else's senseless rules. It is then that she realizes that the love for Joaquín was immature. At the time of his death, she realizes that she is free of all the shackles that have held her back.

Jeremy Sommers

Jeremy Sommers is the oldest sibling of the Sommers family, the brother of Rose and John. He is thirty years old and still single when Eliza is left on his doorstep. He travels to Chile, taking his sister Rose with him to escape a scandal she was involved in, and becomes the manager for the British Import and Export Company, Ltd. He is very protective of Rose and also very concerned about appearances. He tries to rule his little family like a dictator but is often thwarted by both Rose and Eliza.

John Sommers

John Sommers is the renegade of the Sommers family. He has spent all of his adult life at sea. He drinks hard and finds pleasure in a wide variety of women. He is the exact opposite of his older brother, Jeremy. He is also the father of Eliza, although he does not admit this until the end of the story.

Rose Sommers

Rose Sommers is Jeremy and John's sister. She has a love affair with the Austrian tenor Karl Bretzner, a married man, while she lives in London. She spends the rest of her life taking care of Jeremy, who remains a bachelor.

When Rose is twenty years old, she takes in a baby girl, whom she names after her mother. She suspects that the baby is a child of her brother John, but she does not confront him with this fact until the end of the story. She lives vicariously through Eliza, doing all that she can to help the young child grow up and find a successful husband. She rarely consults Eliza about her own desires.

Rose enjoys the liberty of not having to submit to the demands of a husband and brushes off several proposals, including those of Jacob Todd. Although she enjoys her semi-independence, she states that she wants Eliza to grow up and have a better fate than her own.

Michael Steward

Michael Steward is a naval officer whom Rose sees as a proper suitor for Eliza. She woos him in Eliza's name, which confuses the young man, who incorrectly assumes that Rose herself is attracted to him.

Jacob Todd

Jacob Todd is referred to as a "charismatic redhead." He comes to Chile on a bet that he can sell three hundred bibles. It is assumed that he is a preacher, a fact that he does not deny, and, eventually, he accepts money built on this assumption. Todd falls in love with Rose but is rebuffed. He later is found out to be a fraud and leaves Chile, only to reappear in the story while Eliza and Tao are in California. In San Francisco, he takes on the name Jacob Freemont and becomes a newspaper reporter who writes a series of exaggerated stories about Joaquín, building him up as an infamous rebel, which ultimately leads to Joaquín's death.

Ah Toy

Ah Toy is based on a real person, a Chinese woman who sets up a house in which men can pay to look at her. This soon leads to more promiscuous activities, which end with Ah Toy becoming a very wealthy madam. She imports young Chinese girls, whom Tao tries to rescue.

Themes

Patriarchy

One of Allende's main themes is that of patriarchy, which makes reference to a society in which men make all the rules, thus having authority over women and children. She sets this up in the first part of the story by demonstrating Jeremy's control of the Sommers household. She also emphasizes it with the creation of Agustín del Valle and his ruthless behavior toward the people who work for him and toward his daughter, Pauline, who tries to defy him. Allende does this with a purpose. In both cases, with Jeremy and Agustín, the women eventually get their way. No matter how strict the men are, the women do what they have to do in order to pursue their own interests. In parts two and three, Eliza continues to play out the rebellion against patriarchy as she searches for her identity and her independence. In order to do so, she dons men's clothing, stepping into their world and, in essence, competing with them. She is successful in doing so but realizes that she is not a man and is tired of playing the part. When she returns to her feminine self, she gains confidence and independence.

Love

There are many different types of love expressed in this novel. Several of them are paired with a contrasting form to better define each of them. For instance, Rose's love of Eliza is much different from Mama Fresia's love. Rose loves Eliza as a young child might love a doll. She likes to dress her up and show her off. She also uses Eliza in a way to improve on her own life—to discipline Eliza so she will not make the same mistakes that Rose made growing up. Mama Fresia, on the other hand, loves Eliza for herself. She wants to help mold her so that Eliza will grow up strong.

Eliza is also torn between two loves. First, there is Joaquín, whom she falls in love with upon first sight and with whom she shares her first sexual relationship. She follows him to California because of her feelings for him but realizes, in the process, that she hardly even knows him. As she matures and becomes more independent, she realizes that her strong friendship to Tao is a deeper kind of love and, upon Joaquín's death, she comments that she is free (supposedly free of her fixation on Joaquín).

Tao Chi'en also has an early love, with his wife Lin. Although the love between them appears more true than the feelings shared between Eliza and Joaquín, Tao chooses his wife because of the small size of her feet. Her feet were bound in childhood, so they would not grow to adult size, an ancient Chinese practice. Tao found out too late that this practice actually compromised his wife's health. Because of her crippled feet, Lin was more dependent on Tao. Later, Tao realizes that he enjoyed the mature relationship with Eliza, a woman who learned to fend for herself.

Rose also has two different kinds of love. She falls madly in love with Karl Bretzner. Their love was passionate but very temporary, because Bretzner was a married man. However, Rose was so consumed with this passion that she required no more love in her life, at least not from a man. She has many other suitors, but they are all rather comical in comparison to her affair with Bretzner. Jacob Todd, for instance, loves Rose for no discernible reason; and the young suitor Michael Steward is a fool whose affections Rose acknowledges with horror.

Medicine

Medicine is a topic that runs throughout the novel, but it is medicine as seen through different cultures. Mama Fresia comes from a tribe indigenous to Chile. She heals Eliza with concoctions and

Topics For Further Study

- There are many different types of fortunes discussed in Isabel Allende's novel, some made in gold mines, some made in prostitution, others made in the ownership of land. But what kind of fortune do you think Allende refers to when she titles her book *Daughter of Fortune*? She most certainly is alluding to Eliza as the daughter, but what is Eliza's fortune? Back up your answer with specific instances from the novel.

- Research the story of Ah Toy. Did she really import young girls and force them to be prostitutes? Were there no laws to protect them? Are there current laws in California that would prevent the same thing from happening today? Research the prostitute rings in Thailand that are similar to the business that Ah Toy was running. Are there any groups or laws that are trying to protect the young Thai women?

- Write a paper about the progression of rights of women in Chile from the beginning of the nineteenth century until today. How have they changed? Are there any leaders who stand out? How does the feminist movement differ from the one in the United States? Are women freer in Chile? Did they gain any rights earlier than women in the United States? What are some of the statistics of women in business in Chile? In politics?

- What were the sailing vessels like that traveled from South America to California in 1850? Find illustrations not just of the outside of a ship that would be comparable to the one that Eliza sailed on but also of the inside structure. How did all the people and animals and cargo fit in the ship? How much room did the passengers have to walk around? What would their daily routine have been like while at sea? What about the crew? What kinds of jobs would they have held? What kind of food did they eat? What are the statistics of deaths aboard such ships?

- Create a journal as if you were Eliza during the course of her sea voyage. What do you think must have been going through her mind? Imagine how you would have felt to have been enclosed in such a small cabin for so long, swaying with the waves, afraid of dying but almost equally scared to face yet another day in such dismal conditions. Remember how protected her life had been: she had hardly ever been out of her house alone, yet now she was sailing to another country. What do you think kept her alive?

---

spells. Tao learned traditional Chinese medicine and treats his patients with a combination of herbs, plants, and acupuncture. He befriends Ebanizer Hobbs, a Western-taught physician who knows more about exploratory surgery than about natural healing. Tao would like to learn more about Western techniques from Hobbs in order to broaden his skills; and thus the two world views about medicine merge.

Style

Point of View

Allende tells her story through a third-person narrator. The strength of this approach is that the narrator can relate events through various positions, following one character after another as they act out their roles. This allows the reader a broad but limited view. It is broad because the narrator sees the story, like a person with a video camera, as the story unfolds. The camera is not fixed to any one point. Thus the reader views Miss Rose, for example, as she struggles with her brothers, whether or not Eliza, the protagonist, is involved in the scene. The narrator is limited, though, because there is very little knowledge of what is going on inside the mind of any character. Thus the reader is mostly left on his or her own in drawing conclusions about the emotions and psychological challenges that the characters experience. Conclusions can be drawn on a surface level, however, through an observation of the characters' actions, the dialogues they are involved in, and occasional and general comments by the narrator. One such observation is made about Tai Chi'en: "Tai Chi'en sank into widowhood with total despair," the narrator comments, thus giving the reader a sense of Tai Chi'en's feelings about his wife's death.

Historical Account

Allende has written her novel as if she were giving a historical account about actual events. She conveys this image through many different devices. First of all, she uses specific dates. She divides her book, for instance, into three separate parts, and each one is assigned a specific time period. Part one takes place between 1843 and 1848, while part two continues through 1848 and 1849, and part three between 1850 and 1853. Allende also supplies the birth date of Eliza, the female protagonist, as March 15, 1832; and she gives the date of Joaquín's departure for California as December 22, as well as Tao and Eliza's arrival there as "a Tuesday in April of 1849."

Allende also incorporates specific historical events into her novel. The California gold rush was a real event, as was the statehood of California, which occurred in 1850. She mentions the years of great immigrations into Chile and the discovery of copper and the subsequent economic impact on Chile's economy. Furthermore, Allende refers to real historic figures such as French painter Raymond Monvoisin (1790–1870); John Marshall, who was the first to discover gold in California; and Ah Toy, a Chinese immigrant who made her fortune in houses of prostitution.

Quest

Allende keeps her readers riveted to her story by creating quests for several of her characters. As her characters passionately set out on their adventures, readers naturally want to tag along to discover what will happen to them. Eliza, for instance, enters on her quest to find her lover Joaquín while he looks for gold. Tao also is on a quest, first to become a healer, then to find a wife. Next, he enters on a new quest as he starts his life all over. Eliza's is the most prominent quest and the most transformational, as she changes from a pampered and dependent child of a well-to-do English-Chilean family to an independent woman who redefines herself.

Divided Story

Daughter of Fortune is written in two different styles. Most of part one is told in an expansive or comprehensive way with only a slight emphasis on Eliza, the protagonist. This section is filled with different characters, some who play a major role in Eliza's life and some who barely interact with her. Background material is given for the Sommers family and for Chile. Characters are allowed extensive introductions. The relationships between Rose and Jacob Todd and between Pauline del Valle and Feliciano Rodríguez de Santa Cruz are explored extensively.

However, in parts two and three, the focus of the story tightens as Allende zooms in on the details of the lives of her female and male protagonists, Eliza and Tao. The section begins with Tao helping Eliza leave Chile; then Allende creates a flashback in Tao's background. She follows them as they land in California and temporarily go their separate ways, only to reunite and realize their love.

Historical Context

Overview of Chile's Contemporary Political History

Chile is a long, narrow country that extends down the western shore of South America from Peru and Bolivia at the north to the Straits of Magellan and the base of Argentina to the south. Much of Chile's economy is based on agriculture and mining, chiefly of copper. The mines were traditionally owned by the country's elite. However, in the twentieth century, they were taken over by U.S.-based companies, a fact that ultimately affected Chile's politics.

The political atmosphere of Chile tended to be very conservative, controlled by the moneyed classes of landowners, businessmen, and mine owners who supported the National Party or *Partaido Nacional* (PN). However, this changed in the first quarter of the twentieth century, when socialist and communist parties emerged, calling for land reform, better working conditions, and a more uniform distribution of the country's wealth. This is the same time that U.S. interests in Chile's copper mines occurred.

During the 1950s and 1960s, political parties from the left and the right vied for control of the government, with conservative capitalist Jorge Alessandri winning the elections in 1958 and the Christian Democrat, or *Partido Democrata Cristiana* (PDC), candidate Eduardo Frei winning in 1964. It was during this election that Frei is reported to have received great financial assistance from the United States in his bid for office because U.S.

business interests did not want to see socialist Salvador Allende, his competitor, come into power.

In 1969, the PDC split into right-wing and left-wing factions, thus dividing their political clout. Inflation and unemployment were also rising, adding more intensity to the socialist bid to make land reforms and to redistribute the profits of the big Chilean businesses. Therefore, when the 1970 elections came around, there was a three-way race for president. On the far right was former president Alessandri. The left had two candidates: Salvador Allende, the most radical, and Radomiro Tomic, who was supported by the PDC. Allende surprised everyone by eking out a victory, thus becoming the world's first freely elected socialist president.

Allende's objective was to replace Chile's economic structure by ousting the capitalists and the large landowners. Industry would be nationalized, social programs would be created, and wages would be increased as profits were decreased; unemployment would, therefore, decline. One year after his election, general salaries had indeed risen by almost 50 percent. U.S. mines were confiscated, which ultimately caused an escalation of U.S. involvement in attempts to destabilize the Chilean economy by dropping aid programs and establishing economic sanctions. Shortly afterwards, inflation in Chile rose and production fell.

Allende sensed that he was in trouble. However, he had very few places to turn to in order to find support. He had little control over Congress and over the military (whose officers were mainly U.S. trained). The media was controlled by capitalists who did not approve of his policies.

General Augusto Pinochet seized power on September 11, 1973, bombing the presidential palace and shooting anyone on the streets who was not wearing a specifically colored shirt. Allende was later found shot to death, an event that was called a suicide. Thousands of Allende's supporters were killed, and the rest were sent into forced exile. Pinochet immediately dissolved Congress and banned all leftist political parties. Many people were reportedly tortured during his first years in office. He did, however, restore the economy but was eventually and peacefully voted out of office in 1989.

Former president Eduardo Frei coordinated human rights tribunals during the 1990s as a result of the actions of Pinochet, but the strong military power thwarted many of Frei's attempts. Pinochet stepped down as commander-in-chief of the military in 1988, but, before doing so, he created for himself a constitutional lifetime seat in Chile's Senate. He also

declared political immunity for himself in any future trials. He was, nonetheless, arrested in 1999 while visiting London. He returned to Chile in 2001, where the courts ruled that he is too ill to stand trial.

California's Gold Rush

In January 1848, John Sutter's work crew was in the process of building a saw mill on the American River in Coloma, California, a small town outside of Sacramento, when John Marshall found a handful of gold nuggets in the water. The news quickly spread, marking this event as the beginning of California's gold rush and one of the largest human migrations in history. Over one-half million people descended upon the golden state. It would also mark the birth of an industry that would last one hundred years.

The news of the gold rush reached China in 1848, and thousands of people sold everything they owned in order to sail to California. Upon arrival, most Chinese people were met with hostility. They were often resented by American-born prospectors, who tended to believe that the land belonged to them. Other miners were even more hostile if and when the Chinese stakes proved to be valuable. In these instances, several Chinese miners had their land stolen, their claims renamed, and sometimes their lives threatened.

Many women from China resorted to prostitution to pay for their voyages from their homeland, while others turned to traditional professions as doctors, restaurant and laundry shop owners, and farmers.

The Latino population in California at this time suffered greatly. Squatters were known to take over large ancestral Mexican estates, an act that was often sanctioned by the U.S. government. Anti-Mexican sentiment in California spread to include other Latino cultures. People from Central and South America were regarded as unwanted foreigners and were often driven out of their own mines by groups of angry and aggressive men. Reacting to both the hostility against individuals and the court decisions that always seemed to go against them, groups of Mexican vigilantes began to form. New laws against Latinos were quickly written, but only in English, as the legislature refused to translate them into Spanish.

Critical Overview

Allende is one of the most popular female writers from Latin America. She is also one of the leading South American feminists. Her female characters

VIEW OF THE PORT OF VALPARAISO, CHILI.

Engraving circa 1851 detailing the port of Valparaiso, Chile, the setting of part one in Daughter of Fortune

rebuke the traditional confines of patrimony and often challenge the roles that are imposed on them by their society. However, in *Daughter of Fortune*, Sophia A. McClennen states for *Review of Contemporary Fiction*, Allende has gone one step further: "… the protagonist recognizes that her identity does not depend entirely on the man she loves." McClennen also points out that, by Allende disguising her protagonist as a boy throughout the last half of the novel, she provides many interesting topics of discussion about "gendered identities."

Peter Donaldson, writing for *New Statesman*, found *Daughter of Fortune* to possibly be Allende's best novel yet. Although he feels that the second half of Allende's book seems to be diverted from the "driven clarity" of the beginning of the story, he still enjoyed the broadened scope of her work as she leaves Chile behind and attempts to illustrate the turbulent times associated with California and the gold rush.

Daughter of Fortune is more like a "television miniseries than a motion picture," proclaimed Ruth Lopez for the *New York Times Book Review*. The novel "tells a pleasurable story," writes Lopez, but there is "nothing profound in the novel's prose." Nonetheless, Lopez finds that Allende "smoothly navigates" the reader through the story. R. Z. Sheppard, in a review for *Time*, also praises Allende's storytelling skills, referring to *Daughter of Fortune* as a "riproaring girl's adventure story." Sheppard finds that Allende exemplified a new approach of feminist writers who have been "plugging late 20th century cultural attitudes into a spacious 19th century literary vehicle." Allende's writing, according to Sheppard, demonstrates a confident woman's point of view.

On the other hand, Michiko Kakutani, writing for the *Seattle Post-Intelligencer*, does not appreciate Allende's "feminist lamentations" on the state of nineteenth-century women. Kakutani finds Allende's characters to be "simplistic and trite" and refers to the book as a "bodice-ripper romance." She much prefers Allende's first novel, *The House of Spirits* over *Daughter of Fortune*.

Writing for the *Guardian*, Alex Clark also expresses disappointment with *Daughter of Fortune*, again preferring Allende's earlier works. The scope of the novel is too broad, Clark believes, and this gives Allende too little time to deepen her characters' development. However, there are moments in the narrative, especially those that concern "the enigmatic Rose," Clark writes, in which Allende demonstrates her storytelling skills and "her ear for the intriguing and bizarre."

Criticism

Joyce Hart

Hart has degrees in English literature and creative writing and writes primarily on literary themes. In this essay, Hart examines the symbolism surrounding the rebirth of Allende's female protagonist, Eliza.

Similar to the biblical story of Jonah and the whale, Isabel Allende throws her female protagonist Eliza into the darkest recesses of a sailing ship, forcing her young heroine to confront her innermost convictions. The challenge brings Eliza close to death, but she prevails and goes on to claim a new identity. Her journey, as told in *Daughter of Fortune*, takes her from South to North America as well as from adolescence to adulthood. It is a voyage rich in symbols of a developing woman who rebels against a confining patriarchy and then must fill the void with a new definition of self.

Allende is often referred to as the Latina proponent of feminism. Her stories are driven by women who defy the constraints that their society imposes. They are raised under the dictates of a strict patriarchy that wants to silence them, and they must find the courage to create their own voices. Eliza Sommers exemplifies a typical Allende feminist heroine as she is first molded by her adopted parent-figures, who believe that the best possible future for her is to be kept by a man. Although *Daughter of Fortune* ends with Eliza in love with a man, she enters that relationship as an equal partner only after she has completed a journey in which she develops self-confidence and independence.

The story begins with another subtle biblical allusion, this time to the prophet Moses, as the narrator relates the story of how Eliza, as a baby, was abandoned. The memories of that day are mixed. Eliza believes that she was lying in a soapbox, for she remembers the scent; but Rose says that she found the baby Eliza in a wicker basket, reminiscent of Moses's adoption. Although the details of her life are not significantly tied to the story of Moses, Eliza is, in her own way, a leader, demonstrating through her adventures that there is a path that women can follow which will lead to freedom.

Eliza's own oppression comes in many forms. She must first deal with Rose, who insists on dressing her in fancy clothes to impress her societal friends. Because Eliza must not dirty these expensive dresses, she is imprisoned within them, unable to romp around the house like the playful child that she is. As she grows older, she must wear a corset, a tightly strung and stiffly reinforced bodice that artificially creates a small waist and a high-rising bosom—feminine features that attract men. To encourage a so-called correct posture, Eliza is also outfitted with a metal rod that is placed down her back as she practices the piano. Although Rose herself is gladly unmarried, understanding that she is a lot freer as a single woman, she wants to raise Eliza in a way that eliminates the mistakes that she made as a young woman. She spouts feminist attitudes and enjoys her semi-independent role, but she is thrown into confusion when she takes on the role of motherhood. Eliza is named for Rose's mother, and possibly the thought of her mother makes Rose review her own life through a filter tainted by the prejudices and conditionings of an earlier generation. The result is that Rose's rebellion, which she found gratifying, is suddenly overlaid with a film of guilt. As a mother, she feels more responsible socially and therefore constrains (or attempts to constrain) Eliza's natural impulses. Upon Eliza's reaching puberty, for instance, Rose warns her that men will now be able to do with her whatever they want, suggesting that Eliza should be wary of her own sexual stirrings. Rose looks upon Eliza's menstruation as a curse, and discussions about emotions are forbidden. Just as Eliza's body is confined in rigid undergarments reinforced from time to time with unyielding metal rods, so are her heart and soul contained. The material restrictions on her body are symbolic of the encumbrances of fear and guilt placed on her emotions and on her spirit.

Fortunately for Eliza, she has Mama Fresia, who has her own limitations but who at least provides Eliza with another interpretation of reality. Mama Fresia is an earthy woman who encourages Eliza to play in the dirt, to learn the language of plants and animals, and to understand the power of her dreams. In other words, she is almost the exact opposite of Rose. She is, however, a little too concerned with superstitions and has a fear of poverty and rejection. Although she tells Eliza to trust the messages that she receives in her dreams (an outlet for the emotions), she does not approve of Eliza's fixation on the young suitor Joaquín. However, when Eliza tells her that she is pregnant, Mama Fresia attempts to help her with an abortion. Mama Fresia is not a totally independent woman, but she is an alternative to Rose, feeding Eliza's imagination with the possibility that there may be other feminine definitions to discover.

Some of these feminine definitions are also brought out through Joaquín, who arouses Eliza's sexuality. Although she has rebelled against some of the restraints placed on her by Rose and Jeremy, it is not until she meets Joaquín that she totally defies them. She sneaks out of the house and then lies to cover her tracks. She is driven with the need to explore something about herself that no one had previously ever spoken of: passion. Joaquín epitomizes passion. He is a driven man, determined to change the world; and Eliza is infected with his zeal. The two young people mate, but not for purposes of conception. The birth that will proceed from their union is not a combination of their genes but rather a symbolic rebirth of Eliza herself.

She begins her trip tenuously as she is sneaked aboard and then taken down into the bowels of the vessel: "There, in the darkest, deepest pit of the ship, in a two-by-two meter hole, went Eliza. . . . She could … cry and scream as much as she wished, because the sloshing of the waves against the ship swallowed her voice." It is here that Eliza plays out the story of Jonah and the whale. She, too, has been symbolically swallowed. It is here that she will spend the next several weeks, where she will have nothing but herself to confront. She will suffer the loss of the small fetus that resides in her womb and then will fall into a semiconscious state. She will be kept alive on a sparse diet, spiked with a hint of morphine to ease her pain. During her time in the darkness of the ship, she is stripped of her past identity, as symbolized by her miscarriage: the loss of an undeveloped self. The unconscious state of her mind, enhanced with drugs and hallucinations, represents a trip into the depths of her soul. When she recovers, she finds that one journey has ended, but, like Jonah who was finally spit out by the whale, yet another adventure is about to begin. Upon her arrival on the shores of North America, she arises, weakened not only physically but also in orientation. She is in a new land with new definitions still waiting to be tried on. She will don the clothes and identity of a man to protect herself; and it will take time before she understands in which new direction she must go.

In her male disguise, Eliza symbolically puts on the mantle of masculine traits, although this happens gradually. At first, she is too frail to fend for herself and must rely upon Tao, who continues to reinforce her health, which he does naturally through medicinal herbs and good nutrition. He also

> "The unconscious state of her mind, enhanced with drugs and hallucinations, represents a trip into the depths of her soul. When she recovers, she finds that one journey has ended, but, like Jonah who was finally spit out by the whale, yet another adventure is about to begin."

encourages her to be aggressive in her pursuit of who she is and what she wants. Eliza tries to figure it all out, but she has not fully arrived in the present. Parts of her past still haunt her; and before coming to any specific conclusions, she falls back on the training she received from Mama Fresia, who taught her everything she knows about the culinary arts. In this capacity, she serves meals to the miners around her, taking up the feminine position of nurturer. However, she soon tires of this role; and although her courage has blossomed and she is able to bid farewell (at least temporarily) to Tao, she is still influenced by her immature passions. Since she has no clear definition yet of who she will become, she again fixes her drive on Joaquín, who represents the stimulus that began her transformation. She falsely believes, though, that it is through Joaquín that she will be able to find herself.

Critics have commented that this is how most of Allende's previous novels have ended. The female protagonist rebels against the patriarchy that dominates her life only to turn to a man in order to define herself. Not so in *Daughter of Fortune*, although at this point in the story it looks as if that is exactly what Eliza is about to do. For a large portion of the remaining story, Eliza is involved in the pursuit of Joaquín, yet he is always elusive. He is represented in a rumor here, a confabulated tale somewhere else, but he never appears in the flesh. This is because Eliza's real quest is not based on finding Joaquín but in finding herself, which she does obliquely through her supposed need of him.

She makes her way through the man's world of the Wild West, where the few women that she encounters are either prostitutes, women whom the narrator describes as being men born in women's bodies, or effeminate men whom Eliza suspects are women, like herself, in male disguise. At one point in her journey, Babalu the Bad, a man who befriends her, tells Eliza that she is too weak and that he is going to make a man out of her. Shortly after this, the narrator states that Eliza "had no idea what trail to follow." The narrator is referring to Eliza's pursuit of Joaquín, but the statement also serves as commentary on the status of Eliza's thoughts. She has grown tired of searching for the elusive Joaquín. "Joaquín Andieta had evaporated in the confusion of the times," the narrator relates. He had turned into someone with whom Eliza could no longer identify, and without him Eliza feels suddenly lost. However, it does not take long for her to realize that the consequences of her quest have taught her quite a lot. She begins to realize how little she really knows about Joaquín and questions why she is looking for him. Everything about him has become confused in her mind to the point that their brief shared history appears as a fantasy. It is at this juncture that Eliza fully faces reality, one that she has conceived on her own. It is also at this point that Tao finds her and invites her to return with him to San Francisco. Eliza tells him that she is tired of dressing like a man. "It's very boring to be your stupid little brother, Tao," she says. He responds: "You won't have to dress as a man; there are women everywhere now." These statements are loaded with allusions to a change not only in Eliza but also in the relationship between Eliza and Tao. Tao wants Eliza to return with him, as if he understands that her solo journey is completed. He also implies that their relationship can now go beyond the platonic. The feminine is blossoming everywhere!

Eliza returns with Tao and discovers that she enjoys working with him, helping other pubescent girls disentangle themselves from oppression. She does not need to be with him. Rather, she has chosen to share a relationship with him. She has graduated into a much more fully developed woman. She feels so confident about her new position that she allows her more feminine traits to once again rise to the surface. She discards, at least momentarily, her masculine props and puts on one of her old dresses. When she does so, however, she refuses to constrain herself in the tight corset that she used to wear. The days of confinement are over. She neither has to enhance the physical aspects of her femininity through unnatural means nor bolster her confidence by adapting a masculine stance. She

now understands what it means to be an independent woman, a definition that she has created for herself.

Source: Joyce Hart, Critical Essay on *Daughter of Fortune*, in *Novels for Students*, Gale, 2003.

Daniel Toronto

Toronto is an editor at the Pennsylvania State University Press. In this essay, Toronto discusses Eliza's journey to becoming a free woman and its significance.

The title of Isabel Allende's *Daughter of Fortune* is *Hija de Fortuna* in the original Spanish, and while the popular English translation of the title is in no way incorrect, another translation is possible. In Spanish, a common way of expressing possession is to use the preposition *de*—or in English, "of." The phrase "David's friend" would be expressed *amigo de David*, which, when translated back into English word-for-word, is "friend of David." Along the same lines, *Hija de Fortuna* can be translated as "Fortune's Daughter." This alternative translation brings out an interesting interpretation of the title that implies the offspring, product, or results of fortune rather than the meaning that comes to mind at first glance: the female progeny of a wealthy family. Both meanings are valid in the context of the novel. Eliza, the heroine, is the daughter of a relatively well-to-do family. She also, by the end of the book, has become a new, more fully developed person, which could not have happened without the occurrence of certain unlikely events. In other words, luck was key to her growth as an individual. This is not to say, however, that she did not possess any characteristics that contributed to her maturation. She is clearly a determined and adventuresome person with an obvious free spirit that would be difficult to completely suppress in any circumstances. The course of *Daughter of Fortune* takes Eliza on a journey that leads to her becoming a developed and liberated individual, a journey that is the result of a combination of fortune as well as Eliza's strength and tenacity as she strives to realize her desires. This allows the author to present a criticism of the oppressive, and generally male-dominated, situations that Eliza is subject to while at the same time offering hope to readers who may be suffering under similar limitations.

The importance of Eliza's faculties are established immediately when the very first line of the novel reads, "Everyone is born with some special talent, and Eliza Sommers discovered early on that she had two: a good sense of smell and a good memory." Both are invaluable to her throughout the book. Her ability to detect exactly what is in a dish by smell allows her, on several occasions, to earn a living by cooking when she has no other financial means. Her memory allows her access to her past. Whether recalling the teachings of Mama Fresia, stoking her desire by thinking of Joaquín's touch, or maintaining connection with Tao Chi'en through a cognitive recreation of his scent, her memory serves on a number of occasions. Other, likely more significant virtues, contribute to her survival as well as her growth. Her obstinacy allows her to persevere in the face of many obstacles:

> "Give me your blessing, Mamita," she asked. "I have to go to California to look for Joaquín."
>
> "How can you do that, alone and pregnant!" Mama Fresia exclaimed with horror.
>
> "If you don't help me, I'll do it alone."
>
> "I am going to tell Miss Rose everything!"
>
> "If you do, I'll kill myself. And then I will come and haunt you for the rest of your days. I swear I will," the girl returned with fierce determination.

This determination serves her on many occasions. It carries her into and through her love affair with Joaquín Andieta. It leads her to make a deal with Tao Chi'en, a near stranger at the time, that will allow her to follow her lover to California. It gives her strength when she is shut up in the hull of a ship, suffering from sickness and a dangerous miscarriage. She is able to give up rules and conventions, instilled in her from a very early age, to the point that she lives and dresses as a hardworking, lower-class man in order to survive and continue the pursuit of her lover. At one point, she writes to Tao Chi'en, saying "I am finding new strength in myself; I may always have had it and just didn't know because I'd never had to call on it. I don't know at what turn in the road I shed the person I used to be, Tao."

A gift she does not posses, however, is foresight:

> She had left Chile with the purpose of finding her lover and becoming his slave forever, believing that was the way to extinguish her thirst to submit and her hidden wish for possession, but now she doubted that she could give up those new wings beginning to sprout on her shoulders.

Without her intending it, "[Eliza] fell in love with freedom." Once she has it, she does not let it go, and in fact continues to push the envelope. She finds a way to have all she desires without sacrificing her freedom. Miss Rose, her adoptive mother,

> " I do not think Allende would question that all deserve freedom. When freedom is not a given, however, Allende provides us with Eliza to lead the way, on the chance that it can still be earned."

had found "independence she would never have with a husband." However, it came at a great cost. Rose had to give up the love of her life as well as any possibility of having a lover in the future. She has given up the chance of ever having a child of her own, and, possibly the most painful of all, she is condemned to living her life under the rule of a strict brother who cringes at the idea of showing any sort of physical affection towards his sister. Eliza, on the other hand, has a romantic relationship with Tao Chi'en, a man whom she at one point looks at and "realized that she had never been so close to anyone." Eliza lives freely with Tao Chi'en, and as his equal. It is foreshadowed throughout the book that she has a long relationship with him, which, of course, allows for the possibility of her having her own children. Though initially Eliza is limited in that she must live as a man, she eventually finds the will and courage to live openly as a free woman. She is so confident of her freedom that she even tells Tao Chi'en, "I am going to write Miss Rose." Her determination in going after what she wants in combination with her love of freedom allows her to reestablish a connection to a family that she loves, despite the possibility of their making an attempt to control her again.

However, even in view of these displays of character, it is still undeniable that Eliza's journey toward freedom could not have happened without certain fortunate happenings. To begin with, Eliza would never have had the same chances at freedom that she did if she hadn't been placed on the doorstep of the Sommerses' home. To be a member of the lower class in Valparaíso, Chile, could have been too much to overcome, even for the obstinate Eliza. The example we have from *Daughter of Fortune* of a peasant-class citizen attempting

Gold miners panning for gold at a river dig circa 1850

to achieve liberation, Joaquín Andieta, ends up dying for his cause. Who knows how much more difficult it would have been for a woman in such a situation. It is also fortunate that it was Joaquín Andieta she fell hopelessly in love with:

> She regretted nothing she had shared with her lover, nor was she ashamed of the fires that had changed her life; just the opposite, she felt that they had tempered her, made her strong, given her pride in making decisions and paying the consequences for them.

This passion had clearly been important for her, and it also led her to California, where, as Eliza writes, men "bow to no one because they are inventing equality."

Eliza's miscarriage, though sad and nearly fatal, drastically increases her chances of independence and survival, judging by the examples of Joaquín's mother and the singsong girls. Joaquín's mother is driven into poverty by her family after bearing an illegitimate son; the singsong girls are left to die when they can no longer perform their services as a result of pregnancy. There is clearly no reverence for a woman pregnant with an illegitimate child in these settings.

Several instances of small, unlikely events drastically change the course of the story. Purely by coincidence, Tao Chi'en arrives at the bar in Valparaíso at the same time as Eliza and Mama Fresia and subsequently saves them from two sailors who are "clearly drunk and looking for trouble." Then there is the second chance meeting with Tao Chi'en a short time later that leads Eliza to California. Of course, neither would have happened without John Sommers' deciding to kidnap him in the first place.

By contrast, luck is not on the side of the singsong girls, the young women who are captured or sold into slavery, only a fraction of whom Tao Chi'en is able to save. More often than not, they are forced into prostitution, their pimps caring nothing for them and depositing them in empty rooms, absurdly termed "hospitals," to die when they are pregnant or too sick to serve. Sometimes even poison is used so the pimps can be rid of the bodies more quickly. Those Tao Chi'en is able to give a better life are forever scarred:

> The less fortunate, who were freed at almost their last breaths from the "hospital," never lost the fear that like a disease in the blood would consume them for the rest of their days. Tao Chi'en hoped that with time they would at least learn to smile occasionally.

Though these girls, and they are only girls, do have the chance at a better life through the generosity of Tao Chi'en, they will never be completely liberated from the trauma of their experiences. There are also the countless others that Tao Chi'en never has the chance to help.

I do not think Allende intends her readers to think that the singsong girls, if as talented or capable as Eliza, could escape their fates. Allende's harsh depictions of cruelty and injustice in *Daughter of Fortune* demonstrate that she means to criticize the occurrence of such atrocities as well as the societies that allow them to happen. She wants her audience to see that even her heroine could not contend with such adversity, that Eliza is indeed fortune's daughter. At the same time, the fact that Eliza would not have been able to complete her journey of growth through luck alone makes her a recommendation for those who are similarly oppressed, as many of her readers would be. Allende was born in Peru and raised in Chile, and according to Patricia Hart in *Narrative Magic in the Fiction of Isabel Allende*, "Practically speaking, feminism in many Latin American countries is in its infancy."

As Nora Erro-Peralta says in her essay on Allende in *Dictionary of Literary Biography*, "Despite this incredibly painful, difficult material, her works are not filled with a sense of pessimism or despair." *Daughter of Fortune* focuses on Eliza and not the singsong girls, therefore leaving the readers with a sense of hope. Eliza still overcomes incredible adversity to achieve as much freedom as any male of her society at the time, and she does so while still embracing life and her femininity. According to Hart, Allende's writing satisfies the lament of Erica Jong's character Isadora, concerning the lack of feminine role models in literature:

> ... Flannery O'Connor raising peacocks and living with her mother. Sylvia Plath sticking her head into an oven of myth. Georgia O'Keeffe alone in the desert, apparently a survivor. What a group! Severe, suicidal, strange. Where was the female Chaucer? One lusty lady who had juice and joy and love and talent too?

In *Isabel Allende: A Critical Study of Her Work*, Esperanza Granados states "... Allende's female point of view is oriented towards offering poetic solutions to many of the crises faced by Chileans and by other Latin Americans as well." The thesis was published before *Daughter of Fortune* was written, but the sentiments still clearly apply. I do not think Allende would question that all deserve freedom. When freedom is not a given, however, Allende provides us with Eliza to lead the way, on the chance that it can still be earned.

Source: Daniel Toronto, Critical Essay on *Daughter of Fortune*, in *Novels for Students*, Gale, 2003.

Charlotte Mayhew

Mayhew is a freelance writer. In this essay, Mayhew discusses the different interpretations of Isabel Allende's novel Daughter of Fortune.

Daughter of Fortune, Isabel Allende's ninth book, defies classification into a single type, or genre, of literature. Critical reviews of the novel, which was published originally in Barcelona, Spain, in 1998, offer up interpretations of Allende's work that focus on her apparent political views, the elements of magical realism in her work, and the aspects of her work that seem overtly feminist. None of these interpretations do justice to the story or to the complexity of the finished novel, which blends many elements together seamlessly to form a satisfying and complete whole.

The novel starts out by focusing on the early life and development of the female protagonist, Eliza Sommers. Eliza is a foundling who is left, shortly after her birth, in the garden of the house inhabited by Rose Sommers, an Englishwoman living with her brother, Jeremy Sommers, an executive of the British Import and Export Company, Ltd., in Valparaíso, Chile, in the 1830s. Miss Rose has no prospects of or interest in marriage herself but is thrilled at the chance to be a mother to this needy infant. Against her brother Jeremy's objections, she takes the baby in, naming her Eliza after their mother. It is revealed much later in the novel that Eliza is, in fact, the love child of their brother John. Rose knows this, though she keeps it secret, and this influences her firm stance on the treatment of Eliza throughout the novel. As Eliza is completely unaware of the family connection, she does not feel bound to the family, except emotionally. When the time comes for her to choose between facing an uncertain future in Chile and following her lover to California, she follows her lover without out a tremendous sense of guilt.

Eliza's early childhood is shaped by the influence of the housekeeper, Mama Fresia, Rose and Jeremy Sommers, their brother John Sommers, and the frequent visitors to the Sommerses' house. Eliza is taught English standards of behavior when Miss Rose has the time and inclination to pay attention to her. When Miss Rose is busy, Eliza's care falls to Mama Fresia, the Sommerses' housekeeper and a native Chilean.

Eliza grows up with a blend of two distinctly different cultures, both of which mold the person she becomes. The first is the more repressed English society, represented by Jeremy and Rose Sommers. When Eliza is an adolescent, Rose tells her,

"
Daughter of Fortune is, above all, a novel about two unlikely protagonists who come together by happenstance, eventually learning from each other as they seek their fortunes in a new land."

> I would happily give my life to have the freedom a man has, Eliza. But we are women, and that is our cross. All we can do is try to get the best from the little we have.

Rose then launches a campaign to educate Eliza in all the social niceties she will need to make a good marriage, including piano lessons. When Eliza eventually travels to California, she spends months playing the piano for a traveling brothel—hardly what Miss Rose had intended. It is a wonderful bit of irony that the one skill Eliza hated and Miss Rose insisted would be necessary does, in fact, enable Eliza to pay her way when her life takes her on a very different path than the one Rose Sommers had planned for her.

This part of the novel lends itself to feminist interpretation because of the character of Miss Rose, as it is slowly divulged. She is at first shown as a prim and proper English spinster—a rather flat character. It is revealed later that Miss Rose lives with her brother partly to escape the social ruin she faced in England after a disastrous affair with a traveling tenor who was, unfortunately, married. Towards the end of the novel, Eliza remembers Miss Rose saying to her, "A woman can do anything she wants, Eliza, as long as she does it discreetly." In her spare time and without the knowledge of her brother Jeremy, Miss Rose writes risqué novels which her brother John brings to her publisher in London. John uses some of the proceeds to buy Eliza presents and jewelry for her dowry.

Likewise, Eliza also uses the jewelry her unbeknownst-to-either-of-them father, John Sommers, has been collecting for her dowry on his voyages around the globe. Eliza bribes Tao Chi'en to smuggle her onto a ship bound for California with a pearl necklace from her dowry. When Eliza

miscarries and falls sick mid-voyage, Tao bribes Azucena Placeres, another passenger, with a turquoise-studded brooch to help care for Eliza. It is this brooch that John Sommers eventually sees Azucena wearing in California, though she lies and tells him Eliza died on the voyage.

While Eliza is still in Chile, Miss Rose's interest in Eliza waxes and wanes, depending on the other projects she is working on. This inconstant attention serves Eliza well in the future by making her self-sufficient and self-reliant. It also allows Eliza to spend more time with Mama Fresia, the Sommerses' housekeeper, who teaches Eliza the things that she values:

> That was how Eliza learned Indian legends and myths, how to read signs of the animals and the sea, how to recognize the habits of the spirits, and the messages in dreams, and also how to cook.

These skills also serve Eliza well when she journeys to California. She earns money reading letters to the illiterate miners and writing letters back to their families. She earns money to buy a horse and other supplies for her search for Joaquín Andieta by cooking and selling her excellent food; she also cooks for the traveling brothel. Eliza's imaginative meals earn her the friendship of the group's bouncer, Babalu the Bad; later, her skills at healing earn her his respect. Because of her knowledge of herbs, both for cooking and for healing, she earns the respect of Tao Chi'en. Unlike many of the other women in the novel, Eliza has been strangely well-equipped by Miss Rose and Mama Fresia for the unusual path her life has taken. As heroines go, Eliza Sommers is not run-of-the-mill. This is one of the most refreshing things about the novel. The story Allende weaves is so dense with themes that it is nearly impossible to predict the next plot twist.

In a 1991 interview with Jacqueline Cruz, Jacqueline Mitchell, Silvia Pellarolo and Javier Rangel, in response to a question about "women's" literature, Allende said:

> . . . when we speak of women's literature you need the adjective because otherwise you don't know what you are referring to, as though it were a lesser genre. It was assumed for a long time that women's literature touched only on certain themes, and women could not write about history, politics, philosophy, or economy.

Daughter of Fortune touches on all these subjects as it follows the story of Eliza Sommers in Chile, then shifts to China to begin the story of Tao Chi'en, back to Chile where Eliza and Tao meet, and finally concludes in California. In all three locations, the subject of how women earn their keep comes up. It first appears when Miss Rose worries about how Eliza will support herself. The only obvious choice open to a young bourgeois Englishwoman at the time is to make a good marriage.

The specter of dire economic consequences looms large. Eliza's love interest, Joaquín Andieta, and his mother live in abject poverty because his mother made the mistake of succumbing to the passion Mama Fresia warns Eliza about. Miss Rose has escaped this fate by the simple fact that she did not become pregnant by her lover. Miss Rose is also lucky because her brother was willing to take her away to Chile, though her life in Chile is more of a life in a gilded cage than a free life. Provided she follows the social norms of the age, Miss Rose can be a society matron, despite her single status. She hides her solitary pursuit of writing and carefully keeps her past buried. She manipulates her brother to get her way when the question of Eliza's education and dowry comes up but has little real power over the direction her own life takes. Miss Rose is also savvy enough to realize that, should she marry Jacob Todd, she would lose what little autonomy she does have.

Eliza is vaguely aware of Miss Rose's circumstances while she is growing up. Eliza does not know all her secrets, but she sees Miss Rose's unhappy spells and learns from them. Unlike Miss Rose, Eliza does not feel bound by obligation to follow the societal norms. She is a product of two cultures and can pick and choose what she wants from each. Eliza risks all for love—first in sending notes to Joaquín Andieta, later in meeting him in the room with the armoires, and still later, in following him to California.

It is during the ship voyage to California that the groundwork for a different life is laid down; while Eliza does not at that time see herself staying with Tao Chi'en, she knows no one else in California and relies on him when they first arrive. For his part, Tao feels very protective of her, despite his belief that she is unfeminine and beneath him in station. They both have started to change their feelings about the other, though neither is as yet very aware of it. Eliza's masquerade as Tao's mute brother leads them both down an unseen path; it allows Eliza the freedom to act like a man and not be bound by the conventions of a woman. And it allows Tao to overlook her gender and treat her as more of an equal. The odd arrangement allows each to grow more comfortable with the other until they are good friends who rely on each other. Eliza,

though, still feels bound to her quest to find Joaquín; it is in pursuit of this that she and Tao part ways and later come to realize how much the other meant to them. Still, Eliza pursues her quest until the bitter end. When she sees the preserved head of the bandit Joaquín Murieta, she says, "I am free." At last, she can follow a different path; her choices are wide open and not limited like those of the women around her.

The prostitutes in Chile, China, and California are presented as women with few choices. Azucena Placeres, who tends Eliza in the hold of the ship, is stuck in a dead-end line of work because she has no other marketable skills. Though, according to what she's leaving behind in Chile, Azucena's prospects in California are quite good. When John Sommers later encounters her in California, she is doing as well as can be expected, given her employment. She is not impoverished, but neither is she as well off as she had hoped to be.

In comparison to the prostitutes in China, where Tao Chi'en grows up, Azucena is doing very well indeed. In Tao's country, the prostitutes are little more than slaves. Tao, as a young man, is not disturbed by this; it is simply the way of things and he does not question this. The class system is highly structured. Tao himself is only the fourth son, less important in the family hierarchy than his three older brothers. In the confines of nineteenth-century China, women are second-class citizens at best; sons are far preferred over daughters. Allende does not shy away from presenting these facts, but they are not the main point. They are merely stepping stones readers encounter. To put extra emphasis on Allende's treatment of this part of the storyline is to miss the point. Tao as a character is immature in China. It is his exposure to other countries and other ways of living, as well as his association with Eliza, that opens his eyes to the fact that it is unfair to treat other human beings as less than human.

In California, Tao Chi'en confronts the ugliest side of the world's oldest profession when he is called on as *zhong yi* (an expert in Chinese medicine) to minister to the dying prostitutes in the house of Ah Toy. Ah Toy runs her house of prostitution in the traditional Chinese way; the singsong girls (as they are called by Eliza and Tao Chi'en) are little better than caged animals, imported for one purpose and casually discarded when they are used up. Tao Chi'en is shaken by his experience the first time he goes to treat one of Ah Toy's singsong girls; the girl is little more than a bag of bones and already dead.

What Do I Read Next?

- Allende's *Paula* (1995) is a memoir that she wrote for her daughter Paula, while the young woman was in a coma. It is a story about Allende's family and has received very good reviews. The experience, however, was exhausting for Allende, who suffered a writer's block after completing it.

- *The House of Spirits* (1982) was Allende's first and most acclaimed novel. She wrote this book while living in exile and remembering the effect that her grandfather had on her. It is written as a series of letters to him, and it tells the story of one family through three generations of women: grandmother, mother, and the narrator, who is a young woman.

- A nonfiction book by Allende, published in 2003, is *My Invented Country: A Nostalgic Journey through Chile*. In this book, Allende covers such topics as the terrorist attacks on September 11, 2001, and the Chilean coup d'état in 1973.

- Allende often credits Gabriel García Márquez as one of her major inspirations. García Márquez's *One Hundred Years of Solitude* (1967; reprinted in 1998) is one of his greatest achievements. Readers willingly follow the male protagonist along a complicated and mystifying path of unrequited love, continually hoping that he will one day find a release for his desires. García Márquez is a master at using the techniques of magic realism to tell a story.

- Laura Esquivel's novel *Like Water for Chocolate* (1990) features a young woman who has a magical influence over people through her cooking. This is a very unusual (and sometimes comical) story of forbidden love that takes place in Mexico. In 1993, the novel was made into a movie that received rave reviews.

- Tessa Bridal, born and raised in Uruguay, witnessed political upheaval in her country that was, unfortunately, similar to what had previously occurred in Chile. Her book *The Tree of Red Stars* (1997) is a fictional account of the terror that she and her friends experienced.

- *Poems, Protest, and a Dream* (1997) was written by poet Sor Juana Inés de la Cruz, who was born in Mexico in 1648 and spent her entire adult life in a convent. This dual-language collection of her works includes an essay that offers insights into her life and her times, with an emphasis on the role of women in society, an issue that continues to be of concern today.

When Tao returns to his home, he meditates all night, calling on the spirit of his dead wife to help him. It is his dead wife who challenges him to help the singsong girls. It is because of Tao's exposure to other cultures and to Eliza Sommers herself that he is able to consider helping them. When he was in China, Tao passed by them, even used them, without a thought. Now that he is more enlightened, he realizes that he must do something to counteract the suffering he has seen. Critic Patricia Hart, in her article "Magic Feminism in Isabel Allende's *The Stories of Eva Luna*," writes "Once more, the literally impossible event . . . brings us to a profound psychological truth: the burden to the souls of honorable men that the existence of prostitution imposes." In the case of *Daughter of Fortune*, the literally impossible event is the conversation Tao Chi'en holds with the spirit of his dead wife, Lin. There is no other character with whom Tao can have the discussion that brings him to his enlightened choice; he asks Ah Toy to give him the near-dead singsong girls for medical experiments. He nurses them back to health and then helps them find a new life. He finds he needs Eliza's help in this endeavor. It is this work of great compassion that brings Eliza back to him and, finally, sets Eliza herself free.

The economics of sustenance for nineteenth-century women is a running theme in this novel, as are other highly-charged political and social issues such as racism and sexism. While they are not the focus of the novel, Allende calmly uses the backdrop of these issues to provide the characters the means to grow, change, and, finally, to create a new path for themselves. *Daughter of Fortune* is, above all, a novel about two unlikely protagonists who come together by happenstance, eventually learning from each other as they seek their fortunes in a new land.

In a 1992 interview with Alberto Manguel, Allende said, "A novel is like a tapestry; the design reveals itself as it progresses, but you have to keep at it or the design vanishes, the coherence is gone." Like a tapestry, *Daughter of Fortune* works because threads of all colors blend together to form one large design. If one removed the colors one by one, what would be left would be a jumble of threads on the floor instead of a coherent work. Each thread, each piece, is necessary to create the whole tapestry, as each plot thread is necessary to render the whole story in clear, brilliant color.

Source: Charlotte Mayhew, Critical Essay on *Daughter of Fortune*, in *Novels for Students*, Gale, 2003.

Sources

Allende, Isabel, *Daughter of Fortune*, HarperCollins Publishers, Inc., 1999.

Clark, Alex, "Rags from Riches," in *Guardian*, November 13, 1999.

Cruz, Jacqueline, Jacqueline Mitchell, Silvia Pellarolo, and Javier Rangel, "A Sniper between Cultures," in *Conversations with Isabel Allende*, University of Texas Press, 1999, p. 205.

Donaldson, Peter, "Novel of the Week: *Daughter of Fortune*," in *New Statesman*, December 13, 1999, p. 57.

Erro-Peralta, Nora, "Isabel Allende," in *Dictionary of Literary Biography*, Vol. 145, *Modern Latin-American Fiction Writers, Second Series*, Gale Research, 1994, pp. 33–41.

Granados, Esperanza, *Isabel Allende: A Critical Study of Her Work*, Pennsylvania State University, 1991, p. iv.

Hart, Patricia, "Magic Feminism in Isabel Allende's *The Stories of Eva Luna*," in *Multicultural Literatures through Feminist/Poststructuralist Lenses*, University of Tennessee Press, 1993, pp. 103–36.

———, *Narrative Magic in the Fiction of Isabel Allende*, Associated University Presses, 1989, pp. 31, 177.

Kakutani, Michiko, "Allende Quits Magical Realism for a Bodice-Ripper Romance," in *Seattle Post–Intelligencer*, November 6, 1999, section C, p. 2.

Lopez, Ruth, "Left on a Genteel Doorstep," in *New York Times Book Review*, October 24, 1999, pp. 7, 17.

Manguel, Alberto, "A Sacred Journey Inward," in *Conversations with Isabel Allende*, University of Texas Press, 1999, pp. 274–75.

McClennen, Sophia A., Review of *Daughter of Fortune*, in *Review of Contemporary Fiction*, Vol. 20, No. 2, Summer 2000, pp. 184–85.

Sheppard, R. Z., "Footnotes No Longer," in *Time*, Vol. 154, No. 20, November 15, 1999, p. 108.

Further Reading

Bloom, Harold, ed., *Isabel Allende*, Chelsea House Publishers, 2002.

This book is a new collection of essays devoted to the writings of Isabel Allende, including an essay titled "The Struggle for Space: Feminism and Freedom" by Ronie-Richelle Garcia-Johnson.

Boessenecker, John, *Gold Dust and Gunsmoke: Tales of Gold Rush Outlaws, Gunfighters, Lawmen, and Vigilantes*, John Wiley & Sons, 1999.

Although Hollywood has created an image of the Wild West as encompassing all the western territories, Boessenecker demonstrates that most of the notorious characters were concentrated in the California gold rush areas, writing this fact-based account to put faces and dates on the real people who fought hard (and not always fairly) for a chance to strike it rich. This is a well-written and intriguing book.

Kaufman, Edy, *Crisis in Allende's Chile: New Perspectives*, Praeger Publishers, 1988.

This book was written a decade after the overthrow of Salvador Allende and offers another view of the official and unofficial involvement of the U.S. government in Chile's politics. It was written by the executive director of the Harry S. Truman Institute for the Advancement of Peace.

Levy, JoAnn, *Daughter of Joy: A Novel of Gold Rush California*, Forge, 1998.

Based on the life of prostitute Ah Toy, Levy's book contains an interesting fictional account of how the Chinese immigrant made her money in San Francisco's red light district. Ah Toy referred to those in her profession as "daughters of joy."

Rojas, Sonia Riquelme, and Edna Aguirre Rehbein, eds., *Critical Approaches to Isabel Allende's Novels*, P. Lang, 1991.

This is a collection of critical essays and interpretations of Allende's fictional works. It is written in both Spanish and English and is part of American University's study series on Latin-American literature.

Dracula

Bram Stoker
1897

Dracula, by Abraham Stoker—who generally published under the abbreviated first name Bram—was first published in Great Britain in 1897. Although myths and legends about vampires had existed since ancient times, Stoker's novel synthesized much of this lore and gave it a palpable feeling in the character of Count Dracula. In fact, the character of Dracula has since become so popular that many people who were first exposed to the famous vampire through film or television do not even know who Stoker is. While films, most notably the 1931 film *Dracula*, starring Bela Lugosi, have overshadowed the book, they have also helped to keep the story alive. In the last half of the twentieth century, the onslaught of *Dracula* films has added even more mystery to the legend of Count Dracula.

Stoker's inspirations for Count Dracula are heavily debated. However, most critics agree that Dracula was based in part on a historical figure, Vlad the Impaler, a fifteenth-century Romanian ruler known for his indiscriminate brutality, which included a taste for impaling people alive on wooden spikes and watching them die in slow agony. Other inspirations suggested by scholars include John Polidori's story "The Vampyre" (1819), Sheridan Le Fanu's novella *Carmilla* (1872), and Emily Gerard's Transylvanian travel book *The Land beyond the Forest: Facts, Figures, and Fancies from Transylvania*, which was published in the late 1880s, right before Stoker wrote his novel. However, while these and other sources have been

named as potential inspirations, most modern critics agree that Stoker put his own spin on the vampire myth. In fact, Stoker worked longer and harder on this novel than any of his other works, taking seven years to research and write *Dracula*.

While the character of Count Dracula was important for establishing the conventions of what would become an entire genre of horror tales, the book's plot was also very timely. In their exposure to Dracula and their attempts to catch him and destroy him, the various vampire hunters underscore the Victorian attitudes that were present at this time. The Victorian Age took place in England during the reign of Queen Victoria (1837–1901). Victorian moral and religious beliefs included the expected roles of men and women. This is most notable in the book's discussion of sexual matters, which are portrayed in both literal and symbolic ways. The student who wishes to dig deep into the historical and cultural context of the novel should check out *The Annotated Dracula* (1975), by Leonard Wolf. This edition, which is currently out of print, is available in many libraries. The edition includes extensive footnotes to the text, as well as maps, photographs, and captivating illustrations that underscore the Gothic aspects of the novel.

Bram Stoker

Author Biography

Bram Stoker was born Abraham Stoker on November 8, 1847, in Clontarf, north of Dublin, Ireland. Stoker was the third of seven children, and he was violently ill as a child. When he was sick, Stoker read many books and listened to the horror tales his mother told him. These led Stoker to start writing ghost stories, even as a child. After graduating from Trinity College, Dublin in 1868 with honors in mathematics, Stoker took a civil service position, but he most enjoyed going to the theater in his free time. In 1871, when local critics did not comment on a performance of Henry Irving—Stoker's favorite actor—Stoker offered to write an unpaid review of the performance for the *Dublin Mail*. Stoker continued to write unpaid reviews for the newspaper for several years. When Irving returned to Dublin to perform in 1876, Irving read Stoker's celebratory review of the actor's performance and invited Stoker to dinner. The two men struck up a friendship, and, in 1878, Irving leased the Lyceum Theatre in London and appointed Stoker as manager. Stoker married his neighbor, Florence Balcombe, and the two moved to England

where Stoker worked both as the theater manager and as Irving's acting manager from 1878 to 1905.

At the same time, Stoker began to publish his own works. In 1882, Stoker published his first book, *Under the Sunset*, a book of twisted children's stories. Eight years later, he published his first novel, *The Snake's Pass* (1890). However, it was not until the 1897 publication of *Dracula* that Stoker received real attention from the critics, and even then it was mixed. However, although the critics were hesitant to endorse Stoker's horror novel, it was a popular success. Despite Stoker's good fortune, he remained loyal to Irving, whose bad business practices and failing career eventually led the two men to abandon the Lyceum Theatre. Following Irving's death in 1905, Stoker—who had always been in the actor's shadow—was distraught. Stoker had a stroke shortly after Irving's death, which incapacitated him somewhat. At the end of his life, Stoker and his wife became increasingly poor, and he looked to others for assistance. At the same time, he continued to write. His works in this late stage include *Lady Athlyne* (1908), *The Lady of the Shroud* (1909), and *The Lair of the White Worm* (1911). Stoker died of syphilis on April 20, 1912, in London. However, Stoker's *Dracula* has lived on and has since overshadowed its author.

Plot Summary

Chapters 1–4

Dracula starts out with several entries in Jonathan Harker's journal, which comprise the first four chapters. These entries set the structure for the rest of the novel, which is also told mainly through journal entries and letters. This first section introduces Harker, who is a recently promoted English solicitor (a type of attorney). Harker travels eastward across Europe from London to Transylvania, where he is going to meet Count Dracula and explain to the count the particulars of his London real estate purchase. As he travels across the country to the castle, he notices the reaction of various area residents who are frightened by Dracula's name. At Harker's last checkpoint, a coach from Dracula's castle arrives for him. Harker notes the strength of the driver. When he arrives at Dracula's castle, the count, an older gentleman, opens the door, and Harker notes that Dracula is also very strong. Over the next several days, Harker notes that Dracula is never around during the daytime, there are no mirrors in the castle, Dracula has no reflection in Harker's shaving mirror, and Dracula appears to be alone in the castle. Harker realizes that he is a prisoner.

At Dracula's request, Harker writes to his supervisor and to his fiancée, Mina Murray, letting them know the count wishes him to stay for a month. Dracula warns Harker that it is unsafe to wander the castle, and especially to fall asleep in any part of the castle other than his room. Harker ignores Dracula's advice and goes exploring. On two occasions, he sees Dracula scaling the castle wall at night, like a lizard. Harker is almost bitten by three women but is saved by Dracula, who warns them to keep their hands off Harker, saying that the solicitor belongs to him. Dracula gives them a baby to eat instead. Harker watches several days later as the baby's mother stands outside the castle, demanding that Dracula give her back her child. Dracula says a few commands, and a pack of wolves comes and eats the woman. Desperate, Harker climbs down the wall of the castle and discovers Dracula in his coffin. Harker realizes that the count has no heartbeat and appears to be dead. In the evening, Dracula reappears, and Harker demands that the count let him go. However, when Dracula obliges and opens the door, a pack of wolves appears. Harker, disheartened, realizes that Dracula is not really going to let him go. Harker overhears Dracula telling the three women that they can have Harker the next night. In the morning, Harker tries

to escape but finds every way locked. Ultimately, he decides to climb down the castle wall and try to reach a train back to England.

Chapters 5–16

Lucy and Mina write back and forth to each other several times, discussing Lucy's engagement to Arthur Holmwood and her denial of two other suitors, Dr. John Seward and Quincey Morris. Seward works with his patient, Renfield, who has a penchant for trying to eat bugs in an attempt to suck the life out of them. Mina goes to Whitby with Lucy and her mother to vacation while waiting for Jonathan. She sees a mysterious ship arrive, which lost most of its crew at sea. The ship is carrying fifty boxes. Lucy begins sleepwalking and starts having nightmares. Dracula bites her, but Mina mistakes the holes on Lucy's neck for something else. Lucy starts to get weak and pale, and Mina assumes she is getting sick. Renfield is restless over the presence of his master. Mina receives word that Jonathan is in a hospital in Budapest, and she travels there to join him. They are married. Mina also writes several letters to Lucy, telling her about Jonathan's journal from Castle Dracula, which she has promised not to read since she does not wish to know the cause of her husband's madness.

Meanwhile, in Whitby, Lucy gets weaker. Holmwood asks Dr. Seward to look at Lucy. Seward does, but in turn sends for his old mentor, Professor Van Helsing, who is alarmed at Lucy's anemic state. He performs a blood transfusion, transferring some of Holmwood's blood into Lucy. Although this temporarily helps Lucy, she keeps getting worse and gets transfusions from three other men: Seward, Morris, and Van Helsing. Van Helsing also insists on making Lucy wear garlic around her neck, but her ill mother removes it. A wolf breaks through the bedroom window that night, giving Lucy's weak mother a fatal heart attack. Lucy dies two days later. Jonathan and Mina return home, and Jonathan sees Count Dracula on a street. Jonathan and Mina hear of Lucy's death from Van Helsing. They also hear of an attractive lady who has been snatching children from near the cemetery. Van Helsing speaks with Mina, who lets him read Jonathan's journal. He assures Jonathan that his experiences at Castle Dracula actually happened. Van Helsing hears about the woman in the cemetery and realizes that this is Lucy, now a vampire. He takes Seward to the cemetery at night and shows him Lucy's empty tomb. The next night, Seward, Van Helsing, Morris, and Holmwood return to the cemetery, where they encounter the vampire

Lucy. She tries to attack but is driven back by Van Helsing's cross. The following day, the four men enter Lucy's tomb, and Holmwood drives a stake through her heart.

Chapters 17–24

Seward reads Jonathan's diary, while Mina listens to Seward's account of how they killed the vampire Lucy. Mina collects all of the notes she can on Dracula from Seward's diary, Jonathan's diary, and various other sources. She and Jonathan weave it into a chronological account of the past couple of months, which they present to Van Helsing and the rest of the group. Mina visits Renfield, then the group assembles to discuss Dracula. Van Helsing gives them all some historical background on vampires, and they ultimately decide to join forces to try to find Dracula's various resting places, the boxes of earth that came over on the ship, and consecrate them so that he cannot use them. Renfield, afraid of losing his soul, makes a desperate plea to Dr. Seward to be set free. Harker leads the men to Dracula's house, Carfax, which is right next door to the asylum. They discover a little more than half of the boxes of earth. Dracula, who can only gain access to a home if he is invited, gets Renfield to let him in. He starts sucking blood from Mina every night, although she mistakes his visits for nightmares. Mina starts to get noticeably weaker and paler.

While the men hunt down the rest of Dracula's coffins, Mina rests more and more. One night, Seward is called to attend to Renfield, who has been fatally injured in an inexplicable way. By talking to him, Seward and the other men, minus Harker, find out that Dracula visited Renfield, who realized that the count had been sucking blood from Mina. Renfield tries to prevent the count from attacking Mina anymore, but Dracula overpowers him, throwing him to the floor. The men rush upstairs to Mina's room, where they see Dracula forcing her to suck his blood, while Jonathan is in a stupor. Van Helsing drives Dracula away with a eucharist wafer, but later, when he presses a wafer on Mina's forehead as a protection, it burns her. Everybody realizes that Mina is half-transformed into a vampire. The men return to Carfax to consecrate the boxes of earth. They find Dracula's other houses and split up to consecrate the other boxes. However, they only find forty-nine out of the fifty boxes and realize that Dracula still has one left. They assemble at one of Dracula's houses, waiting for the count to arrive. When he does, he tries to attack them, but Jonathan counters with his

Media Adaptations

- *Dracula* has been adapted into countless films. However, the film that helped define the cinematic image of the count was the classic 1931 version titled *Dracula*, which starred Bela Lugosi in the title role. The film, which was produced by Universal Studios and directed by Tod Browning, is available on VHS and DVD from Universal Home Video.

- In 1992, *Dracula* was adapted into a film titled *Bram Stoker's Dracula*, one of the few titles to mention the original author. Francis Ford Coppola directed the film, which was released by Columbia Pictures. The film also featured a star-studded cast, including Gary Oldman as Dracula, Keanu Reeves as Jonathan Harker, Winona Ryder as Mina Murray, Anthony Hopkins as Professor Van Helsing, and Cary Elwes as Arthur Holmwood. It is available on VHS and DVD from Columbia/Tristar Home Video.

- *Dracula* has been adapted into several spoof films. One of these is *Dracula: Dead and Loving It* (1995), released by Columbia Pictures and directed by Mel Brooks, who also played the part of Professor Van Helsing. Other actors include Leslie Nielsen as Count Dracula, Steven Weber as Jonathan Harker, and Amy Yasbeck as Mina Murray. The film is available on VHS from Castle Rock Home Video.

- *Dracula* was adapted as an unabridged audiobook in 2002. It is available from Brilliance Audio.

knife. Likewise, the other men help to drive the count off with their crucifixes.

As Mina's condition worsens, they realize that she has a psychic link to Dracula. As a result, Van Helsing starts hypnotizing her during sunrise and sunset when this link is activated, and through Mina they realize that Dracula is going to try to escape back to his castle by ship. The men plan to chase Dracula and, after some discussion, Mina goes along, too.

Chapters 25–27

The group splits up to chase Dracula in three ways. While Van Helsing and Mina travel to Castle Dracula, Seward and Morris chase the count over land, and Harker and Holmwood hire a river steamer. Although the three unnamed vampire women from Dracula's castle try to coax Mina away from Van Helsing, he thwarts them with holy items, then travels to the castle in the daytime to kill the three female vampires. Meanwhile, the two groups of men quickly catch up with Dracula, who is being transported by a group of gypsies. When Dracula is close to his castle, the group of vampire hunters arrives on the scene at the same time. In the ensuing fight, the gypsies are driven off, but not before they give Quincey Morris a fatal wound. Still, he and Jonathan are able to kill Dracula, just moments before Dracula is about to transform himself into an ethereal shape. As Jonathan's knife decapitates the count and Quincey's knife stabs him, the vampire turns into dust. Mina notes in an epilogue that she and Jonathan have named their son Quincey and that their story would seem very farfetched to others.

Characters

Count Dracula

Count Dracula is an old vampire who keeps Jonathan Harker prisoner in his castle and who ultimately tries to relocate to London and create a race of vampires. The character of Dracula was derived from many sources, including vampire lore and the historical figure Vlad the Impaler. Even before Jonathan meets the count, Dracula's reputation precedes him, and many locals try to warn Jonathan and give him items like crosses to ward off Dracula. Jonathan notes the inhuman strength of Dracula, the first of many strange traits. As Jonathan and others learn throughout the novel, Dracula has limited motion during the day, consumes only human blood, must pass over water in certain ways, has no reflection, must sleep on soil from his own land, has power over certain animals and weather, and has the power to turn others into vampires. This last trait causes considerable concern for the group of vampire hunters that assembles to fight him since Dracula bites two women—Lucy Westenra and Mina Murray—who are dear to many of the hunters. Dracula is successful in transforming Lucy into a vampire, although the vampire Lucy is killed by her own bridegroom, Arthur Holmwood, in her coffin.

Mina, on the other hand, has a better chance at survival. Because of this, the fight against Dracula becomes two-pronged. First, the group of hunters slowly gather evidence to show where Dracula's many coffins containing his native soil are located, so that they can consecrate them with a eucharistic wafer and deny Dracula all of his resting places. By doing this, they hope to pin the count in a corner and kill him before he can create a new race of vampires in London. At the same time, the group is fighting against time because Mina is slowly transforming into a vampire. These two fights culminate in a spectacular chase sequence, where Dracula realizes that most of his London resting places have been destroyed. The count flees eastward to his castle, believing that he has duped the vampire hunters. However, through the psychic link that Dracula shares with the half-transformed Mina, the group is able to predict Dracula's movements. The group overtakes Dracula before he can reach his castle, and Jonathan cuts off Dracula's head while Quincey Morris stabs the count, turning him to dust.

Lord Godalming

See Arthur Holmwood

Jonathan Harker

Jonathan Harker is the fiancé of Mina Murray and a solicitor who travels to Transylvania to assist Count Dracula with the count's purchase of a London property. Once in the castle, Jonathan notices some odd things about Dracula, including his inhuman strength, his ability to scale walls like a lizard, the lack of his reflection in mirrors, his tendency to be gone during the day, and the fact that Jonathan has never seen him eat food. As Jonathan spends more time in the castle, he realizes that he is Dracula's prisoner. After three mysterious women in the castle try to bite Jonathan when he is half-asleep, he realizes even more that Dracula and his companions are probably not human. One morning, Jonathan explores the castle and finds Dracula in his coffin, with no heartbeat. When Dracula appears that evening, Jonathan demands to be let go but is stopped by wolves that suddenly appear at the castle's front door. The next morning, after he witnesses Dracula's coffin being transported outside the castle on its way to England, Jonathan escapes the castle by climbing down the wall.

He ends up in a foreign hospital, and everybody—including Jonathan himself—assumes that he is mad. However, when he returns to London and hears about the strange happenings with Lucy

Westenra and others, he realizes that the count is real and sets about trying to destroy him. When Mina is bitten by Dracula and half-transformed into a vampire herself, Jonathan is even more desperate to kill the count, which he almost does on one occasion when he surprises Dracula. However, it is not until they have chased Dracula from London to Transylvania that Jonathan gets his chance. He decapitates Dracula with a knife.

Arthur Holmwood

Arthur Holmwood is the fiancé of Lucy Westenra and is forced to kill the vampire version of Lucy. Arthur is known as Lord Godalming after his father dies and he inherits the title. In the beginning, Arthur is Lucy's chosen suitor, winning her hand in marriage over his two friends, Dr. Seward and Quincey Morris. However, this victory is bittersweet when Lucy begins to get ill. Arthur, like the other men present, donates his blood in a transfusion to Lucy after Professor Van Helsing says that she is anemic and needs it. However, the repeated transfusions are not enough, and Lucy ultimately dies. Although Arthur does not believe it at first, he is eventually shown that Lucy has become a vampire. He assumes the responsibility of killing her in her coffin. After this, although he is distraught over her death, Godalming uses his title and influence in several ways to help the group of vampire hunters find and destroy Dracula's various coffins in London. He also uses his influence to try to detain Dracula during his escape back to his castle. Godalming and Dr. Seward help fight off the gypsies who try to prevent Jonathan and Quincey from killing Dracula.

Mina

See Wilhelmina Murray

Quincey P. Morris

Quincey Morris is the only American character in the book; he stabs Dracula but receives a fatal wound himself from gypsies. In the beginning, Quincey is one of the three suitors of Lucy Westenra. Although she denies him, he still cares for her and becomes one of several men to give her a blood transfusion when she is anemic from being bitten by Dracula. After his death, Mina and Jonathan name their son after him.

Wilhelmina Murray

Wilhelmina Murray is the fiancée of Jonathan Harker, and she is almost turned into a vampire by Count Dracula. Throughout the story, Wilhelmina

is referred to mostly by the shortened name Mina. In addition, before she and Jonathan are married, she is Mina Murray. After they are married, she is Mina Harker. Mina is worried when she does not hear from Jonathan for a long time, and she helps nurse him back to health when he is released from the foreign hospital. Mina is confused at the strange condition of her friend Lucy Westenra, whose health starts to decline after Lucy sleepwalks and encounters a strange man. As various characters start to compare notes, and Mina reads Jonathan's journal of his horrifying experiences in Dracula's castle, she realizes that the strange man was Dracula. As part of the team of vampire hunters, Mina assumes the role of secretary, taking and organizing all of their notes to try to figure out the best way to find and kill Dracula.

However, when Dracula bites Mina and makes her drink some of his blood, she starts to turn into a vampire herself. The rest of the team is initially optimistic that they can save Mina. But when a holy object burns her forehead, they all realize that she is cursed and will become a vampire if they do not kill Dracula soon. It is through Mina and her psychic link to Dracula that they are able to determine the route he is taking back to his castle. When the group of vampire hunters breaks into smaller groups to try to overtake Dracula by land or by water, Mina travels with Professor Van Helsing. When they are nearing Dracula's castle, the three female vampires try to coax Mina into joining them, but Van Helsing restrains Mina from going. When Dracula has been destroyed, the mark disappears from Mina's head, a sign that she has been cleansed of evil and is no longer in danger of becoming a vampire.

R. M. Renfield

R. M. Renfield is a mental patient in Dr. Seward's asylum; he is also the servant of Dracula. Like Dracula, Renfield has superior strength, a fact noted by Dr. Seward in his phonographic journal entries. He also has the odd habit of eating bugs in the same way that Dracula drinks blood. When Dracula arrives in England, Renfield becomes noticeably more excited and is sometimes hard to restrain. It is Renfield's escape to Dracula's London estate, which is right next door to the asylum, that ultimately leads the vampire hunters to Dracula's new home. At one point, Renfield begs to be let go, for his own salvation, but Seward refuses. When Dracula enters Renfield's cell, Renfield realizes that Dracula has been drinking Mina's blood. Renfield tries to save Mina by restraining Dracula from leaving, but Dracula overpowers Renfield, cracking his skull in the process. It is Renfield's account of all of this that makes the vampire hunters realize Mina has been bitten.

Dr. John Seward

Dr. Seward is the director of an insane asylum who realizes that one of his patients is connected to Dracula. Dr. Seward is one of Lucy Westenra's three suitors. When she turns his marriage proposal down, he is distraught but buries himself in work. When he does this, he notices the strange behavior of R. M. Renfield, a patient who eats bugs and talks about his master. When Lucy falls ill, Seward calls his friend and mentor, Professor Van Helsing, to come into town. After they try in vain to save Lucy's life by giving her blood transfusions, Van Helsing shows Dr. Seward that Lucy has turned into a vampire. Although Seward does not believe it at first, he quickly resolves to do what he can to help stop Dracula. Unlike the other characters who keep paper journals to record their thoughts, Dr. Seward uses a modern phonograph. His reliance on modern technology like this is one of the reasons why he has a hard time believing in the supernatural at first. As the story progresses, Seward realizes that Renfield's master is Dracula, and Seward joins the group of vampire hunters in seeking out and destroying Dracula's London sanctuaries. After the chase sequence at the end of the novel, Seward arrives in time to help fight off the gypsies while Jonathan Harker and Quincey Morris kill Dracula.

The Three Female Vampires

The three unnamed vampire women first appear during Jonathan Harker's stay at Castle Dracula. When they first arrive, Jonathan is not sure if he is dreaming or mad, since they materialize out of thin air. They try to bite Jonathan but are stopped by Dracula, who gives them a baby to eat instead. Near the end of the novel, they leave the castle to try to coax Mina into joining them. However, Professor Van Helsing drives them away and goes to the castle the next day, where he kills all three vampires.

Professor Abraham Van Helsing

Dr. Abraham Van Helsing is the lead vampire hunter, and the one who knows the most about Dracula. Van Helsing has heard about Dracula before and is able to let the others know about the vampire's past, strengths, and weaknesses. Van Helsing was Dr. Seward's mentor and as such taught Dr. Seward his scientific methods. However,

Van Helsing, who speaks with a thick Dutch accent, is just as versed in the supernatural. When he first sees the anemic Lucy, he realizes that she has been bitten by Dracula but keeps his suspicions to himself while he gathers evidence. He does, however, coordinate several transfusions of blood from himself and others to Lucy in an attempt to save her life. When his other methods, including making Lucy wear garlic to bed and placing a crucifix over her dead body, are thwarted by Lucy's mother and a greedy servant, respectively, Van Helsing realizes they must kill Lucy. He stakes out Lucy's tomb day and night, first with Dr. Seward and then with the other male vampire hunters, so that they can see she has been turned into a vampire and that she must be killed.

Professor Van Helsing is very fond of Mina and, like the others, is distraught when she is bitten. He is also very fond of Renfield, who reacts very warmly to Van Helsing. Van Helsing leads the group in the chase to destroy Dracula's London sanctuaries and chase him back to his castle in Transylvania. He also saves Mina's soul by preventing her from joining the three vampire women. In the end, he is one of the men who helps to fight off the gypsies when they try to prevent the group from destroying Dracula.

Lucy Westenra

Lucy Westenra is an Englishwoman who dies and becomes a vampire after she is bitten by Dracula. In the beginning, Lucy is distraught because she must choose between three suitors: Dr. Seward, Quincey Morris, and Arthur Holmwood. She chooses the latter, but her engagement is thwarted by Dracula, who bites Lucy one night while she is sleepwalking. After this first experience, Lucy has many bad dreams and is repeatedly bitten by Dracula. Although Professor Van Helsing and others try to save her by giving her blood transfusions to relieve her anemic state, she ultimately dies from Dracula's bites. After she is dead, she turns into a vampire and starts to prey on little children around London. The children are mesmerized by Lucy, who drains some of their blood before leaving them to wander back home. The newspapers pick up the story, and Professor Van Helsing realizes that it must be the vampire Lucy. He leads Dr. Seward to stake out Lucy's tomb, convincing him that Lucy is a vampire. Finally, he leads Arthur Holmwood to see the same thing, and Holmwood drives a wooden stake through his intended bride, at which point her vampiric features return to normal and her soul is saved.

Themes

Salvation and Damnation

As several characters note in the novel, a person's physical life is of secondary importance to the person's eternal life, which can be jeopardized if the person is made evil by a vampire like Dracula. Professor Van Helsing says, when he is explaining why they must kill the vampire Lucy, "But of the most blessed of all, when this now Un-Dead be made to rest as true dead, then the soul of the poor lady whom we love shall again be free." Even characters that are of questionable goodness, such as the mental patient, R. M. Renfield, realize that, although they can find immortality by being a vampire, they cannot find salvation. Renfield says, when he is begging Dr. Seward to let him go, not explaining that he is afraid of his master, Dracula: "Don't you know that I am sane and earnest now; that I am no lunatic in a mad fit, but a sane man fighting for his soul?" When Mina is distraught after realizing that Dracula has started to turn her into a vampire, Van Helsing warns her to stay alive if she wants to achieve her salvation. "Until the other, who has fouled your sweet life, is true dead you must not die; for if he is still with the quick Un-dead, your death would make you even as he is."

Roles of Men and Women

The novel underscores the expected roles of men and women in Victorian times. Women were expected to be gentle and ladylike and, most of all, subservient to men. For example, in one of her letters, Lucy notes, "My dear Mina, why are men so noble when we women are so little worthy of them?" Lucy is frustrated that she has to choose between her three suitors and does not wish to hurt any one of them by saying no. Lucy says, "Why can't they let a girl marry three men, or as many as want her, and save all this trouble? But this is heresy, and I must not say it." Women are expected to live for their husbands, so much so that Mina practices her shorthand while Jonathan is away so that she can assist him when he gets back. Mina says, "When we are married I shall be able to be useful to Jonathan."

Even more important than a woman's devotion to her husband was the idea that women, at least gentlewomen, should be pure. As part of this, men were expected to respect a woman's privacy and never burst in on her when they might catch her in an undressed state. Quincey notes this when Professor Van Helsing says they need to break down the door to Mina's room. Quincey states, "It is un-

Topics for Further Study

- Read several British newspaper articles circa 1897 to get a feel for how they are written. Imagine that you are a contemporary reporter in Victorian London and that you have found all of the notes that Mina Murray and the others kept about their vampire hunting. Write an article exposing their adventures, keeping it in the style of the newspapers of the time.

- Research the vampire lore of eastern Europe and other regions that Stoker drew upon to write *Dracula*. Find at least five other "rules" about vampires—things they can do, things they cannot—that Stoker did not include in his novel, and write a detailed description about each one. For each rule, try to find one literary work, film, or other form of media that has incorporated this rule.

- Research the medical science that Stoker incorporates in the novel, and discuss how it related to contemporary medicine in Stoker's time. Now compare the medical methods that Van Helsing and others use to try to heal Lucy and Mina to current medical methods used to treat blood-related conditions like anemia.

- Compare the courting process described in the novel with modern dating methods in England. Imagine that you are one of the characters from the novel who has been transported to modern-day England. Write a journal entry describing your perceptions of modern dating methods while remaining true to Victorian attitudes and the specific traits of the character you choose.

usual to break into a lady's room!" However, as Van Helsing notes, in situations where the woman might be in mortal danger, this rule should be broken. Van Helsing is worried, rightly so, that Dracula might be attacking Mina. So he replies to Quincey, "You are always right; but this is life and death."

In fact, the role of men as saviors of their women, which is underscored again and again in the novel, was another aspect of Victorian life.

When it came to danger, especially physical danger, women were expected to act like damsels in distress. Mina fulfills this role after she is bitten and looks to Jonathan for support. Notes Mina of Jonathan's hand, "it was life to me to feel its touch—so strong, so self-reliant, so resolute."

Reason and Madness

The novel also explores the ideas of reason and madness. In the beginning, Jonathan believes that he is going mad when he sees the three women vampires appear out of thin air. Later, he thinks that all of his experiences were the result of hallucinations brought on by madness. Seward works at an insane asylum, so he is exposed to madness every day. As a result, Seward tends to always follow his scientific reasoning, a fact that Van Helsing notes, "You are a clever man, friend John; you reason well, and your wit is bold; but you are too prejudiced. You do not let your eyes see nor your ears hear." Because of this, Seward does not believe in the vampire Lucy, even after seeing her the first time. His mind is unable to reconcile the supernatural things that he has seen, and so it simply blocks them out, at least temporarily. He is the type of man who would rather base his life on hard facts and hard science and who likes to use the newest technologies like the phonograph. His mentor, Van Helsing, is also an accomplished scientist, but he realizes that sometimes it is necessary to forget what one has been taught and believe in something else, even if it seems mad or heretical. Van Helsing says "it is the fault of our science that it wants to explain all; and if it explain not, then it says there is nothing to explain."

Style

Gothic Novel

Dracula is a Gothic novel, which is also sometimes known as a Gothic romance. Many scholars consider Horace Walpole's novel *The Castle of Otranto* (1764) to be the first Gothic novel. Like *Dracula*, Walpole's novel was wildly popular. Gothic novels generally focus on mystery and horror, and they usually have some supernatural elements. In *Dracula*, the supernatural elements are many, starting with the use of a vampire as the title character. In addition, the specific attributes given to the vampire underscore his inhumanity. Jonathan says, after witnessing Dracula scale the castle wall like a lizard, "What manner of man is this, or what manner of creature is it in the semblance of man?" Jonathan's plight in the beginning, when he is trapped in Dracula's castle, is also typical of Gothic novels, which often place their heroes in seemingly inescapable situations. Finally, the various settings—including Dracula's imposing castle, the ghostly landscape of Transylvania, and the graveyard and Lucy's tomb in London—are all settings that are found in Gothic fiction.

Epistolary Novel

In addition to being a Gothic novel, *Dracula* is also an epistolary novel, meaning that it is told through a series of letters instead of a single, connected narrative. Actually, although letters like these compose some of the plot, particularly the exchanges between Mina Murray and Lucy Westenra, the book also relies on journal entries and news articles to tell the tale. In fact, the book begins with an entry in Jonathan Harker's journal: "Left Munich at 8:35 p.m. on 1st May, arriving at Vienna early next morning." Some of these entries, like the one referenced above, contain mundane details about Harker's journey. These specific details about Harker's journey give the book a feel of realism, which is consistent with the naturalistic movement that became popular at the turn of the nineteenth century. It also helps to counterbalance the supernatural aspects of the novel by making it seem as if the book is true.

In epistolary novels like this one, the narration is all in the first person. However, in *Dracula*, which bounces around from character to character, readers receive several first-person accounts. This disjointed approach helps to disorient the reader, who must try to figure out what is going on based on several separate accounts.

Suspense

The use of multiple first-person narrators helps to increase the suspense in the book, since Stoker jumps around from character to character, building tension in a certain situation and then moving on to the next one. In this way, the reader is left to wonder what is going to happen in a specific situation or to a specific character. The best example of this is the anticipated fate of Jonathan Harker. In the first four chapters, Stoker builds suspense, starting on Harker's journey. After hearing enough warnings from the local residents, Harker starts to be concerned for his safety and notes, "I am not feeling nearly as easy in my mind as usual. If this book should ever reach Mina before I do, let it bring my goodbye." Although Jonathan later thinks he

Compare & Contrast

- **1890s:** In the Victorian Age in England, attitudes towards sex are extremely repressed and private. However, in reality, the Victorian era is teeming with pornography, prostitution, and other illicit activities—signs that human sexual desires are not fully repressed. With the advent of photography, pornography enters a new phase.

  Today: In most Western nations today, sex is a very public issue. Sex has become an integral part of many ad campaigns, television shows, and films. However, some groups, such as conservative Christian groups, still advocate the repression of sexual images and content in media.

- **1890s:** In England, Oscar Wilde is sentenced to prison for his homosexuality.

  Today: Although United States President Bill Clinton promises to champion gay rights during his presidency, many members of the gay and lesbian community are disappointed by his infamous "don't ask, don't tell" policy for the United States military. This policy allows homosexuals to remain active in the military as long as nobody knows they are homosexual.

- **1890s:** Stoker taps into the fear of damnation and unholiness with his novel *Dracula*, in which several characters' souls are put in jeopardy. If Dracula succeeds in his quest, he will convert several others into soulless humans.

  Today: The moral and ethical issues surrounding cloning come to a head when an independent company announces that it has cloned the first human. Some worry about a homogenous race of humans that is engineered to look a certain way.

- **1890s:** Citizens of London are still reeling from the crimes of Jack the Ripper, an unnamed murderer who killed at least five women in London's East End in 1888.

  Today: For more than a century, the case of Jack the Ripper has remained unsolved. However, in 2002, popular mystery author Patricia Cornwell claims that the murderer was the well-known artist Walter Sickert.

---

was overreacting, at least when he first meets the count, the seed of doubt and suspense is planted in the reader's mind. This seed continues to grow as Jonathan notices certain things about Dracula: "The mouth, so far as I could see it under the heavy moustache, was fixed and rather cruel-looking, with peculiarly sharp white teeth." As he stays at the castle, Jonathan gives readers even more information about Dracula's vampiric qualities, which help to heighten the suspense.

However, at the end of the fourth chapter, Stoker adds the most suspense of all, when he has Jonathan announce his intention to try to leave the castle, "I shall try to scale the castle wall farther than I have yet attempted. . . . And then away for home! away to the quickest and nearest train!" While readers root for Jonathan, they must wait several chapters to find out whether or not he is successful in his attempt, since the novel switches gears and starts to talk about the experiences of Mina and Lucy. The novel continues to build suspense, which culminates in the massive chase to kill Dracula and save Mina.

Historical Context

Organized Religion in the Victorian Age

The Victorian Age witnessed both a rising and falling in the popularity of organized religion. When religious activity was at its peak, it was pervasive. Morality and religion—especially the Christian religion—infused all aspects of life. Stoker's use of Christian elements such as a cross and a eucharist wafer as weapons against the evil Dracula underscores this idea. However, by the end of the century, when Stoker wrote *Dracula*, the moral compass was not as clear, and many people experienced a crisis in their religious faith. This was due in large part to the publication of several scientific works that challenged conventional notions of religion. One of the most famous of these was Charles Darwin's *Origin of Species* (1859).

Sexuality in the Victorian Age

In many ways, the Victorian Age was paradoxical. On the outside, men and women strove to appear pure and conservative. They observed proper courtship rituals, adopted an uninterested attitude towards sex, and at all times tried to act with decorum—at least in public. In private, however, it was a different story. The same time period that saw all of these restrictive rules also witnessed a booming prostitution industry. While this was generally accepted, there was one form of sex that was considered deviant and criminal: homosexuality. Through part of the Victorian Age, homosexuality was a capital offense. However, by the 1890s, the sentence had been reduced to prison time, which was the fate of noted author Oscar Wilde.

During the Victorian Age, pornography found a huge audience. In 1890, an anonymous author published *My Secret Life*, a massive autobiography that detailed the author's sexual experiences and gave an accurate portrayal of the darker side of Victorian society. While some people wrote about sex in an academic sense, studying the sociological and psychological aspects of human sexuality, some people found it hard to make a distinction between these scholarly studies and pornography that was meant only to arouse. One of people's fears about pornography was that it might lead to sexually criminal behavior, such as rape.

Jack the Ripper

In the late 1880s, when Stoker was getting ready to write his novel, London's East End was terrorized by an anonymous serial murderer known simply as Jack the Ripper. Although these crimes did not include sexually deviant acts like rape, most of the Ripper's victims were prostitutes, which has led some to believe that the murderer's motivation may have been sexual in nature, perhaps a consequence of sexual repression.

Health and Medicine in the Victorian Age

Victorians were extremely worried about their health, especially in London, where crowded and unsanitary city conditions often led to widespread disease. Medicine in the nineteenth century was largely undeveloped, and medical education was not yet regulated. As a result, many doctors were inexperienced and did their patients more harm than good. In the novel, the characters' health is referred to often. Lucy requires many blood transfusions in an attempt to keep her alive; other characters fall ill throughout the novel; when Jonathan escapes from Dracula's castle, he makes it to a hospital and eventually gets nursed back to health by Mina. However, even after he is healthy, Mina is very careful to keep an eye on Jonathan, concerned that he might have a relapse. Both Lucy's mother and Arthur Holmwood's father suffer from illnesses during the novel. In addition, after giving Lucy their transfusions, the male characters have to rest up to save their strength and avoid getting sick.

Critical Overview

When *Dracula* was first published, critics found little literary merit in the novel. A reviewer for the *Athenaeum* wrote in 1897, "*Dracula* is highly sensational, but it is wanting in the constructive art as well as in the higher literary sense." However, even those critics who did not believe that the novel was literary acknowledged it as a horror work that would appeal to its audience. The *Athenaeum* reviewer says, "Isolated scenes and touches are probably quite uncanny enough to please those for whom they are designed." In fact, some reviewers admitted that, although their Victorian sensibilities instructed them to reject the base qualities of the novel, they were drawn to it. For example, the *Bookman* reviewer notes, "we must own that, though here and there in the course of the tale we hurried over things with repulsion, we read nearly the whole with rapt attention." This mixed attitude—praising the horror aspects while denying the work's literary merit—continued throughout most of the twentieth century. For example, in his 1918 book *The Vampire: His Kith and Kin*, Montague Summers notes this dubious distinction. Summers explains, "the reason why, in spite of obvious faults it is read and re-read—lies in the choice of subject and for this the author deserves all praise." So, despite its widespread popular appeal, *Dracula* did not share the literary distinction of other Gothic novels like Mary Shelley's *Frankenstein*.

However, as was also true of Shelley's novel, Stoker's novel exploded onto the screen in the twentieth century and has enjoyed more than one hundred adaptations in several languages. Partly

Helen Chandler as Mina Seward and Bela Lugosi as Count Dracula, in the 1931 film adaptation of Dracula

due to this attention, critics began to review the novel once again in the latter half of the twentieth century. Royce MacGillivray says, in his 1972 essay in *Queen's Quarterly*, "Certainly without the films it is hard to believe that Dracula would be one of the few proper names from novels to have become a household word." Many of these reviewers focused on the sexual aspects of *Dracula*. For example, in his 1959 essay "The Psychoanalysis of Ghost Stories," Maurice Richardson notes that the novel "provides really striking confirmation of the Freudian interpretation." In fact,

Richardson is so enamored of this idea that he says the story does not make sense unless it is viewed as Freudian. Richardson says, "it is seen as a kind of incestuous, necrophilous, oral-anal-sadistic all-in wrestling match." Other reviewers agree, although most note that Stoker, who was very moral himself, probably did not realize that he was embedding sexual symbolism in his work. C. F. Bentley says, in his 1972 essay in *Literature and Psychology*, "In common with almost all respectable Victorian novelists, Stoker avoids any overt treatment of the sexuality of his characters."

This was one of many essays in the 1970s, a time when critics experienced renewed interest in the novel. As Stephanie Moss notes in her 1997 entry on Stoker for *Dictionary of Literary Biography*, "The critical revival of *Dracula* in the early 1970s turned a trickle of literary criticism into a deluge." As Moss notes about modern critics, "The most frequently mentioned psychological aspect is the madonna/whore schism within Victorian perceptions of women, seen most clearly in Lucy's transformation from aristocratic female to vampire." This trend has continued to the present day.

Criticism

Ryan D. Poquette

Poquette has a bachelor's degree in English and specializes in writing about literature. In this essay, Poquette discusses Stoker's use of time in Dracula.

Right from the start, *Dracula* is a novel obsessed with time. Jonathan Harker's first journal entry notes, "Left Munich at 8:35 p.m. on 1st May, arriving at Vienna early next morning; should have arrived at 6:46, but train was an hour late." From this rather plain beginning, the reader is drawn into a suspenseful tale in which the clock starts to tick faster and faster as the fates of the characters are determined. However, Stoker is subtle in his use of time, so that the reader does not even realize that it, while not a main theme, gives the story its structure. This structure is organized in a way that increases the suspense and disorientation of the reader as the novel progresses.

Although Jonathan's diary starts out mundane, it quickly becomes terrifying. As he travels across the country to the castle, he notices the reaction of various area residents, who are frightened by the name of Dracula, and one woman even begs Harker not to go to Dracula's castle and gives Harker a cross. Harker is unnerved by these warnings but pushes on. Harker translates some of the language of the villagers, including *Satan*, *hell*, and other words that denote evil. These evil signs, which grow to include the inhuman activities of the count himself, help to polarize the plot, turning the story into a classic fight between good and evil. Both sides offer immortality, or timelessness, but there are strong differences between the two. The Christian version of immortality is endless time lived in spirit form. This eternal salvation is the goal of Christian religion, and good Christians will sacrifice anything to preserve this, even their lives, as the men risk their lives to try to save Mina's soul.

By chasing Dracula, the men risk being sentenced to an immortal life as a vampire. This immortality is endless time lived in physical form. Unlike Christian immortality, which is based upon the soul, eternal life as a vampire means living in a soulless body. When the men are called upon to kill the vampire Lucy, Van Helsing notes that they have saved her soul and released her from endless damnation. Van Helsing says, "For she is not a grinning devil now—not any more a foul Thing for all eternity. No longer is she the devil's Un-Dead. She is God's true dead, whose soul is with Him!"

Besides large-scale versions of time like heavenly immortality and eternal damnation as a vampire, Stoker also uses smaller, more contained images in his novel. For example, from the beginning, the story quickly organizes itself around a day-night pattern. Jonathan arrives at Castle Dracula during the night. However, while he was used to knowing the time down to the minute as he was traveling, times seems to float once he gets to Castle Dracula, where he only knows roughly what time it is. This sense of disorientation is increased by the fact that Dracula keeps Jonathan up all night talking, so that Jonathan will sleep during the day when Dracula sleeps. Jonathan says, "I had finished my meal—I do not know whether to call it breakfast or dinner, for it was between five and six o'clock when I had it." These inexact times are a far cry from the ultra precise times that Jonathan was used to on his trip and which he has come to rely on in his daily job as a solicitor, which requires a precise attention to details like time.

Because of this "strange night-existence," as Jonathan calls it, he starts to think that he might be losing his mind or hallucinating. Jonathan soon learns that Dracula leaves the castle on many nights, scaling the castle walls in the process. This makes Jonathan realize that he can use the daytimes to explore the castle for a way out. However, while exploring one afternoon, he becomes tired and falls asleep in a different part of the castle. When he wakes up, it is nighttime, a dangerous time for him in Dracula's castle. In fact, as one of the female vampires gets ready to bite him, Jonathan sits waiting, "with beating heart." However, Dracula saves Jonathan from the women, at least temporarily, and Jonathan realizes that if he is going to plan an escape, it must be at a certain time, preferably in the morning when he has a whole day to climb down the castle wall and try to reach a city.

Just as the day and night system of time poses serious issues for Jonathan's safety while at Castle Dracula, time quickly becomes an issue for the others as soon as Dracula arrives in London. When Dracula starts to feed off Lucy, she becomes increasingly more weak and pale. Although Van Helsing and Seward try to ward off Dracula's advances, their efforts are thwarted. Finally, Van Helsing says that they are running out of time. "There is no time to be lost. She will die for sheer want of blood to keep the heart's action as it should be." Although it takes two more transfusions to help Lucy, she appears to be getting better. Lucy notes that she has gone several days without incident, which makes her think that she is in the clear: "Four days and nights of peace. I'm getting so strong again that I hardly know myself." However, despite all of these efforts, a telegram from Van Helsing telling Seward to watch after Lucy arrives late. This mistake proves to be nearly fatal, as Dracula sends a big wolf to break Lucy's window, which gives Lucy's mother a fatal heart attack and greatly weakens Lucy. As Seward notes, Van Helsing works frantically, trying to beat the clock and save Lucy's life: "I never saw in all my experience the Professor work in such deadly earnest. I knew—as he knew—that it was a stand-up fight with death."

However, Stoker's most spectacular use of time is the revelation that Mina has been half-transformed into a vampire, which sets off the final chain of events. Once they realize this, the men, who have already been rushing around to try to stop Dracula from converting London into a town full of vampires, realize that the stakes are even higher and the timeline is even shorter. The realization comes not when they burst in upon Mina, being forced to suck the vampire's blood but when Van Helsing's eucharist wafer burns Mina's forehead: "it had seared it. . . . My poor darling's brain told her the significance of the fact as quickly as her nerves received pain of it." Up until now, the men did not realize the severity of Mina's having been bitten and having the chance to turn into a vampire. However, since the holy symbol is burning her flesh, this is a sign that they are all running out of time. If Mina is not to become one of the immortal undead, they need to find Dracula and kill him. Van Helsing says of Dracula, "he can live for centuries, and you are but mortal woman. Time is now to be dreaded—since once he put that mark upon your throat."

This fact gives the men the motivation they need to chase Dracula from London to Transylva-

> In the end, the battle between good and evil, spiritual immortality and eternal physical damnation, the vampire hunters and Dracula comes down to just a few moments of time."

nia, risking their own lives and salvation. However, they are aided in their quest, ironically, by time. Although Dracula has the power of immortality, he is limited in his movement during the day and must rely on the help of other, mortal men. Because of this fact, Dracula panics and takes the surest and safest way of passage out of London, by boat. However, this gives the vampire hunters a timely advantage, since they can reach their destination much faster by land and cut Dracula off before he reaches his castle. In addition, since Mina has always been obsessed with time in an effort to help Jonathan in his business, she has learned how to memorize train timetables, which comes in handy when trying to thwart Dracula. Mina says, "I knew that if anything were to take us to Castle Dracula we should go by Galatz, or at any rate through Bucharest, so I learned the times very carefully."

In the end, the battle between good and evil, spiritual immortality and eternal physical damnation, the vampire hunters and Dracula comes down to just a few moments of time. Mina notes that the capture of Dracula takes place near the end of the day, right before Dracula is about to be free of his daytime prison: "As I looked, the eyes saw the sinking sun, and the look of hate in them turned to triumph." However, time is ultimately on the hunters' side, since Jonathan lunges at Dracula just in time, his "great knife" decapitating Dracula. As Mina continues, she realizes that even Dracula was human once. With Jonathan's act, the human part of Dracula—which has lived an immortal physical damnation for hundreds of years—finally finds peace as his soul is delivered into spiritual eternity: "there was in the face a look of peace, such as I never could have imagined might have rested there."

Source: Ryan D. Poquette, Critical Essay on *Dracula*, in *Novels for Students*, Gale, 2003.

> "
> It was this carefully-processed research which produced the archetype of all modern literary vampires, determining their appearance, their abilities and their limitations (especially, of course, the fatal flaws which permit their destruction)."

Brian Stableford

In the following essay, novelist and sociologist Stableford examines the history behind Stoker's novel.

Bram Stoker's *Dracula* completed the set of three 19th-century horror stories which were to create modern myths in alliance with Hollywood. Like Mary Shelley's *Frankenstein* and Robert Louis Stevenson's *Strange Case of Dr. Jekyll and Mr. Hyde* it owed its origin to a nightmare, but it took Stoker many years of research and forethought to get himself to the point of beginning an actual draft. Even then he encountered difficulties, eventually dropping the opening sequence that was later published separately as "Dracula's Guest." What remains is untidy, although the presentation of the story as a patchwork of documents helps to sustain the pretence that the untidiness is merely superficial. In fact, it could hardly be more deep-seated; the novel is shot through with loose ends, unsettled questions, inept transitions and dramatic changes of emphasis. Such conundrums and confusions are part of the book's very essence. Had Dracula not been such a changeable and paradoxical character he could not have been half so fascinating; nor could he have been qualified to become the central monster of 20th-century folklore, celebrated as much by humour as by horror schlock, and as often redeemed—at least in recent times—as re-damned.

Stoker borrowed some of the inspiration for *Dracula* from John Polidori's "The Vampyre" and J. Sheridan Le Fanu's "Carmilla"—Stoker and Le Fanu were both graduates of Trinity College, Dublin—but when he went in search of an aristocratic model for the "king-vampire" of his night-

mare he found a new one, as different from its predecessors as Carmilla Karnstein was from Lord Byron. This was the 15th-century Voivode Vlad Tepes, "the Impaler," who was also nicknamed Dragul ("Dragon" or "Devil"; Dracul in the Latinized version) but whose scribes often signed him Dragulya, meaning "son of Dragul," to distinguish him from his similarly-nicknamed father. In re-characterizing Dracula Stoker borrowed extensively but selectively from the rich Eastern European vampire folklore popularized by Dom Augustine Calmet. It was this carefully-processed research which produced the archetype of all modern literary vampires, determining their appearance, their abilities and their limitations (especially, of course, the fatal flaws which permit their destruction). Every modern vampire which violates this template does so consciously and deliberately; it cannot simply be ignored. No other novel of any kind has ever stamped out an image so firmly and so decisively.

Stoker's *Dracula* is supposed to be an incarnation of pure evil, but this role is confused even in the original text—a confusion which has paved the way for a vast range of calculated variations. In the dream which provided the seed from which the story grew the "king-vampire" appeared only at the end, interrupting the female vampires who posed a more immediate threat to the dreamer—as they do, in the text, to Jonathan Harker. Harker therefore owes his life to the creature he subsequently determines to destroy. The main threat which Dracula subsequently poses is that of conferring extraordinary sexual attractiveness and a kind of immortality on the novel's two main female characters, Lucy and Mina. Stoker dutifully declared such a fate to be far worse than death, but he must have known that it had already been viewed in a more ambiguous light in works by John Keats, Théophile Gautier and others.

Like "Carmilla," *Dracula* is among the most strikingly erotic works published in Britain during the Victorian era, but if its conscientious representation of female "voluptuousness" and sexual appetite as a manifest disgrace is not consciously hypocritical it must surely be reckoned severely neurotic. Had such hypocrisies and neuroses died with Victoria Dracula would not have become so astonishingly promiscuous in his more recent seductions, but they did not—and all the heroic Draculas of the 20th-century *fin de siècle* have not yet succeeded in staking the unnaturally-beating hearts of those hypocrisies and neuroses, nor in reducing them to ashen dust with bright Enlightenment.

Stoker had always suffered the effects of a morbid imagination and had made earlier efforts to turn its produce to useful effect. His collection of allegorical fairy tales *Under the Sunset*—which does not seem to the modern eye to be very suitable for children—includes such dark pieces as "The Invisible Giant," about the ravages of plague, and "How 7 Went Mad." When *Dracula* became a runaway bestseller Stoker tried to follow it up with something similar but he had no idea how he had worked the trick and his attempts to copy it ranged from the feeble to the fatuous. There is an element of supernatural horror in the treasure-hunt story *The Mystery of the Sea*, but it remains fugitive and the story itself fizzles out. *The Jewel of Seven Stars* employs the then-fashionable motif of a revivifiable mummy of a lovely but accursed Egyptian queen, but the action comes to an abrupt conclusion just as the story proper seems to be about to begin. The original ending was, in fact, so brutally opaque that another (perhaps by another hand) was substituted in later editions, but the revamped version fails dismally to save the plot from cringing self-destruction. *The Lady of the Shroud* is an old-fashioned political Gothic in which vampirism plays a very peripheral (and probably illusory) role.

The Lair of the White Worm is one of the most spectacularly incoherent novels ever to reach print; the only excuse for its existence one can suggest is that it must have been based on another actual nightmare, which the aging and ailing Stoker had not time to gather into an organized plot. On the other hand, its lurid portrayal of the *femme fatale's* doppelgänger as a great White Worm has offered intriguing fuel for thought to critics interested in sexual symbolism. The other short pieces collected in *Dracula's Guest* are not handicapped by Stoker's incapacity for organizing novel-length texts but they are mostly very weak. "The Judge's House" is a tolerable pastiche of Le Fanu and "The Secret of the Growing Gold" is effective even though the gold in question is only blonde hair, but the remainder are trivial. Attempts by Peter Haining and others to locate "lost" Stoker stories that had not been previously reprinted have produced nothing of any real interest.

At the end of the day, it seems as if the inspiration that led Bram Stoker to write *Dracula* was an unrepeatable accident of fate owing more to luck than judgment—but that should not detract from the credit due to its author. Nobody else ever wrote a book like *Dracula*, and it certainly has not been for want of trying.

Source: Brian Stableford, "Stoker, Bram," in *St. James Guide to Horror, Ghost & Gothic Writers*, edited by David Pringle, St. James Press, 1998, pp. 573–75.

Vlad Tepes, also known as Vlad the Impaler, *a fifteenth century Romanian ruler who was one of the inspirations for Stoker's Count Dracula*

Rebecca Stott

In the following essay, Stott discusses the decadent gothic genre and how the qualities of Dracula *place the novel in that genre.*

When Bram Stoker wrote *Dracula* in 1897 he was able to draw upon a century-long tradition of interest in vampirism, firmly associated with the exotic fantasies of romanticism and with the theme of seduction and evil. By 1913 the book was in its 10th edition. After its first stage production in 1930 the sales of the book doubled and by the 1930's the first vampire films began to emerge. With the extraordinary number of subsequent films produced this century, Dracula has become a 20th-century myth of unparalleled resonance.

Stoker's text has been the focus of renewed critical interest in the last few decades, as the subject of a plethora of critical readings and interpretations: Marxist, Freudian, feminist, and Darwinian. As fantasy, drawing on one of the most ancient Eastern European superstitions, it invites and stimulates such diverse and interesting speculations.

Those familiar with the film myth of Dracula are often surprised by the density and literary quality of

> "*Dracula* is a novel which insists on protecting (and patrolling) women as much as it insists on patrolling the Empire."

Stoker's text. Film versions are rarely loyal to it to any degree. It insists, like so many fantastic texts, on its own authenticity. In the tradition of Wilkie Collins it claims authenticity by narrating events through the diaries and letters of the characters involved. But Stoker goes much further than Collins by mobilising almost any form of information: ship's logs translated from the original Russian, newspaper cuttings, doctors' reports, telegrams, memoranda, even transcribed verbal accounts from a phonograph.

The text needs contemporary testimony to provide a scientific account of the movements, habits, and history of the central threat of the novel—Dracula—and it relies on the constant production of such information. Van Helsing (a Dutch Catholic "scientist"), the principle vampire hunter, supported by his team of assistants—Seward (a medical man specialising in the treatment of the insane), Godalming (an aristocrat), Harker (a lawyer), and Quincey Morris (an American), insist on a flow of information within the band of hunters. "Good women tell all their lives," Van Helsing tells Mina. *Dracula* is a confessional novel: without confession there would be no text.

The central action of the novel is defensive. Dracula is planning to invade England, to create an empire of "semi-demons." Harker travels to Transylvania as lawyer to the Count and it is in this opening "gothic" section of the novel that we are first introduced to the vampire superstition and its Eastern European origins. The second section of the novel jolts us back to England and the domestic complacency of the central characters. In the background, unseen, Dracula is invading the country. Invasion stories of many kinds were reaching a peak around the turn of the century, exacerbated by real fears of political instability in Europe. *Dracula*, for all its gothic and fantastic characteristics, dramatises this fear.

Lucy Westenra, the innocent and beautiful young heroine, is the first victim of the invading Count. Van Helsing is brought in to study the strangely anaemic state of the fading heroine. With Mina Harker, the heroine with a "man's brain," the defenders band together to protect England from the advancing threat, now identified by Van Helsing as vampirism. They are too late to save Lucy despite a series of major blood transfusions from four men. Now dead, but Undead, she stalks Highgate cemetery preying on young children, and she must be staked in a violent and ritualistic ceremony which critics have identified as a kind of gang rape. The novel is packed with scenes of erotic power which have invited sexual readings in the late 20th century, but which went apparently unnoticed by the novel's 19th-century audience.

It has been observed that the vampire hunters not only doubt their own sanity (much of the novel takes place in a lunatic asylum) but actually mirror the sadism and violence of Dracula. The instability of narrators and the problematising of vision are characteristics of fantastic literature from Poe onwards, as is the compulsion to exorcise the demonic "other": the Not-I. The band of vampire hunters enact many sadistic rituals, such as the staking of Lucy, in the name of the protection of the Empire.

Dracula is a novel which insists on protecting (and patrolling) women as much as it insists on patrolling the Empire. The men are forever placing protective circles of Holy Wafer and garlic flowers around the women. Dracula will invade through any gap. It is a novel which expresses fears of Dracula's effect upon women—their sexualisation. While the central threat of the novel is the seducing Dracula, the novel is populated with *female* vampires—four of the five central female characters are vampires. Dracula attacks only women.

The novel forms part of a late 19th-century genre which David Punter has identified as decadent gothic. The four great novels of this genre are Stevenson's *Dr. Jekyll and Mr. Hyde*, Wilde's *The Picture of Dorian Gray*, Stoker's *Dracula* and Wells's *The Island of Dr. Moreau*. All these novels enact fears of regression and degeneration stimulated by the discoveries of evolutionary theory. All are concerned in some ways with "the liberation of repressed desires." Dracula can be seen as the beast within, so precariously contained. He must be tracked down and eliminated. While the novel moves towards his final elimination—he crumbles into dust once staked—the hunters do not observe the elaborate rituals of staking. The ending is ambiguous: Mina (who has herself sucked

Dracula's blood) gives birth to a child on the anniversary of Dracula's death—a male child who bears the names of all the band of men involved in the tracking of Dracula. Moreover, the hunters are thrown back again on their own uncertainty. They are left with their only record of the dramatic events as a "mass of typewriting."

Source: Rebecca Stott, "*Dracula*: Novel by Bram Stoker, 1897," in *Reference Guide to English Literature*, 2d ed., edited by D. L. Kirkpatrick, Vol. 3, St. James Press, 1991, pp. 1554–55.

Carol A. Senf

In the following essay, Senf steps outside of the usual readings of Dracula *as a battle between Good and Evil to explore the unreliability of the story's narrators and the moral ambiguity hidden in the tale.*

> The fault, dear Brutus, is not in our stars,
> But in ourselves, that we are underlings.
> *Julius Caesar*, I, ii, 134–135

Published in 1896, *Dracula* is an immensely popular novel which has never been out of print, has been translated into at least a dozen languages, and has been the subject of more films than any other novel. Only recently, however, have students of literature begun to take it seriously, partially because of the burgeoning interest in popular culture and partially because *Dracula* is a work which raises a number of troubling questions about ourselves and our society. Despite this growing interest in Bram Stoker's best-known novel, the majority of literary critics read *Dracula* as a popular myth about the opposition of Good and Evil without bothering to address more specifically literary matters such as style, characterization, and method of narration. This article, on the other hand, focuses on Stoker's narrative technique in general and specifically on his choice of unreliable narrators. As a result, my reading of *Dracula* is a departure from most standard interpretations in that it revolves, not around the conquest of Evil by Good, but on the similarities between the two.

More familiar with the numerous film interpretations than with Stoker's novel, most modern reader are likely to be surprised by *Dracula* and its intensely topical themes; and both the setting and the method of narration which Stoker chose contribute to this sense of immediacy. Instead of taking place in a remote Transylvanian castle or a timeless and dreamlike "anywhere," most of the action occurs in nineteenth-century London. Furthermore, Stoker de-emphasizes the novel's mythic qualities by telling the story through a series of journal extracts, personal letters, and newspaper clippings—the very written record of everyday life. The narrative technique resembles a vast jigsaw puzzle of isolated and frequently trivial facts; and it is only when the novel is more than half over that the central characters piece these fragments together and, having concluded that Dracula is a threat to themselves and their society, band together to destroy him.

On the surface, the novel appears to be a mythic re-enactment of the opposition between Good and Evil because the narrators attribute their pursuit and ultimate defeat of Dracula to a high moral purpose. However, although his method of narration doesn't enable him to comment directly on his characters' failures in judgment or lack of self-knowledge, Stoker provides several clues to their unreliability and encourages the reader to see the frequent discrepancies between their professed beliefs and their actions. The first clue is an anonymous preface (unfortunately omitted in many modern editions) which gives the reader a distinct warning:

> How these papers have been placed in sequence will be made manifest in the reading of them. All needless matters have been eliminated, so that a history almost at variance with the possibilities of later-day belief may stand forth as simple fact. There is throughout no statement of past things wherein memory may err, for all the records chosen are exactly contemporary, *given from the standpoints and within the range of knowledge of those who made them.*

Writers of Victorian popular fiction frequently rely on the convention of the anonymous editor to introduce their tales and to provide additional comments throughout the text; and Stoker uses this convention to stress the subjective nature of the story which his narrators relate. The narrators themselves occasionally question the validity of their perceptions, but Stoker provides numerous additional clues to their unreliability. For example, at the conclusion, Jonathan Harker questions their interpretation of the events:

> We were stuck with the fact, that in all the mass of material of which the record is composed, there is hardly one authentic document; nothing but a mass of typewriting, except the later notebooks of Mina and Seward and myself, and Van Helsing's memorandum. We could hardly ask any one, even did we wish to, to accept these as proofs of so wild a story.

The conclusion reinforces the subjective nature of their tale and casts doubts on everything that had preceded; however, because Stoker does not use an obvious framing device like Conrad in *Heart of Darkness* or James in *The Turn of the Screw* or employ an intrusive editor as Haggard does in *She* and because all the narrators come to similar conclusions about the nature of their opponent, the reader is likely to forget that these documents are subjective records, interpretations which are "given within the range of knowledge of those who made them."

While Stoker's choice of narrative technique does not permit him to comment directly on his characters, he suggests that they are particularly ill-equipped to judge the extraordinary events with which they are faced. The three central narrators are perfectly ordinary nineteenth-century Englishmen: the young lawyer Jonathan Harker, his wife Mina, and a youthful psychiatrist Dr. John Seward. Other characters who sometimes function as narrators include Dr. Van Helsing, Seward's former teacher; Quincy Morris, an American adventurer; Arthur Holmwood, a young English nobleman; and Lucy Westenra, Holmwood's fiancée. With the exception of Dr. Van Helsing, all the central characters are youthful and inexperienced—two dimensional characters whose only distinguishing characteristics are their names and their professions; and by maintaining a constancy of style throughout and emphasizing the beliefs which they hold in common, Stoker further diminishes any individualizing traits. The narrators appear to speak with one voice; and Stoker suggests that their opinions are perfectly acceptable so long as they remain within their limited fields of expertise. The problem, however, is that these perfectly ordinary people are confronted with the extraordinary character of Dracula.

Although Stoker did model Dracula on the historical Vlad V of Wallachia and the East European superstition of the vampire, he adds a number of humanizing touches to make Dracula appear noble and vulnerable as well as demonic and threatening; and it becomes difficult to determine whether he is a hideous bloodsucker whose touch breeds death or a lonely and silent figure who is hunted and persecuted. The difficulty in interpreting Dracula's character is compounded by the narrative technique, for the reader quickly recognizes that Dracula is *never* seen objectively and never permitted to speak for himself while his actions are recorded by people who have determined to destroy him and who, moreover, repeatedly question the sanity of their quest.

The question of sanity, which is so important in *Dracula*, provides another clue to the narrators' unreliability. More than half the novel takes place

in or near Dr. Seward's London mental institution; and several of the characters are shown to be emotionally unstable: Renfield, one of Dr. Seward's patients, is an incarcerated madman who believes that he can achieve immortality by drinking the blood of insects and other small creatures; Jonathan Harker suffers a nervous breakdown after he escapes from Dracula's castle; and Lucy Westenra exhibits signs of schizophrenia, being a model of sweetness and conformity while she is awake but becoming sexually aggressive and demanding during her sleepwalking periods. More introspective than most of the other narrators, Dr. Seward occasionally refers to the questionable sanity of their mission, his diary entries mentioning his fears that they will all wake up in straitjackets. Furthermore, his entries on Renfield's condition indicate that he recognizes the narrow margin which separates sanity from insanity: "It is wonderful, however, what intellectual recuperative power lunatics have, for within a few minutes he stood up quite calmly and looked about him."

However, even if the reader chooses to ignore the question of the narrators' sanity, it is important to understand their reasons for wishing to destroy Dracula. They accuse him of murdering the crew of the *Demeter*, of killing Lucy Westenra and transforming her into a vampire, and of trying to do the same thing to Mina Harker. However, the log found on the dead body of the *Demeter*'s captain, which makes only a few ambiguous allusions to a fiend or monster, is hysterical and inconclusive. Recording this "evidence," Mina's journal asserts that the verdict of the inquest was open-ended: "There is no evidence to adduce; and whether or not the man [the ship's captain] committed the murders there is now none to say." Lucy's death might just as easily be attributed to the blood transfusions (still a dangerous procedure at the time Stoker wrote *Dracula*) to which Dr. Van Helsing subjects her; and Mina acknowledges her complicity in the affair with Dracula by admitting that she did not want to prevent his advances. Finally, even if Dracula is responsible for all the Evil of which he is accused, he is tried, convicted, and sentenced by men (including two lawyers) who give him no opportunity to explain his actions and who repeatedly violate the laws which they profess to be defending: they avoid an inquest of Lucy's death, break into her tomb and desecrate her body, break into Dracula's houses, frequently resort to bribery and coercion to avoid legal involvement, and openly admit that they are responsible for the deaths of five alleged vampires. While it can be argued that *Dracula* is a fantasy and therefore not subject to the laws of verisimilitude, Stoker uses the flimsiness of such "evidence" to focus on the contrast between the narrators' rigorous moral arguments and their all-too-pragmatic methods.

In fact, Stoker reveals that what condemns Dracula are the English characters' subjective responses to his character and to the way of life which he represents. The reader is introduced to Dracula by Jonathan Harker's journal. His first realization that Dracula is different from himself occurs when he looks into the mirror and discovers that Dracula casts no reflection:

> This time there could be no error, for the man was close to me, and I could see him over my shoulder. But there was no reflection of him in the mirror! The whole room behind me was displayed; but there was no sign of a man in it, except myself. This was startling, and, coming on the top of so many strange things, was beginning to increase that vague sense of uneasiness which I always have when the Count is near.

The fact that vampires cast no reflection is part of the iconography of the vampire in East European folklore, but Stoker translates the superstitious belief that creatures without souls have no reflection into a metaphor by which he can illustrate his characters' lack of moral vision. Harker's inability to "see" Dracula is a manifestation of moral blindness which reveals his insensitivity to others and (as will become evident later) his inability to perceive certain traits within himself.

Even before Harker begins to suspect that Dracula is a being totally unlike himself, Stoker reveals that he is troubled by everything that Dracula represents. While journeying from London to Transylvania, Harker muses on the quaint customs which he encounters; and he notes in his journal that he must question his host about them. Stoker uses Harker's perplexity to establish his character as a very parochial Englishman whose apparent curiosity is not a desire for understanding, but a need to have his preconceptions confirmed. However, instead of finding someone like himself at the end of his journey, a person who can provide a rational explanation for these examples of non-English behavior, Harker discovers a ruined castle, itself a memento of bygone ages, and a man who, reminding him that Transylvania is not England, prides himself on being an integral part of his nation's heroic past:

> ... the Szekleys—and the Dracula as their heart's blood, their brains and their swords—can boast a record that mushroom growths like the Hapsburgs and the Romanoffs can never reach. The warlike days are over. Blood is too precious a thing in these days

> *In fact, Stoker reveals that what condemns Dracula are the English characters' subjective responses to his character and to the way of life which he represents."*

of dishonourable peace; and the glories of the great races are as a tale that is told.

To Harker, Dracula initially appears to be an anachronism—an embodiment of the feudal past—rather than an innately evil being; and his journal entries at the beginning merely reproduce Dracula's pride and rugged individualism:

> Here I am noble; I am *boyar*; the common people know me, and I am master. But a stranger in a strange land, he is no one; men know him not—and to know not is to care not for . . . I have been so long master that I would be master still—or at least that none other should be master of me.

It is only when Harker realizes that he is assisting to take this anachronism to England that he becomes frightened.

Harker's later response indicates that he fears a kind of reverse imperialism, the threat of the primitive trying to colonize the civilized world, while the reader sees in his response a profound resemblance between Harker and Dracula:

> This was the being I was helping to transfer to London, where perhaps for centuries to come he might . . . satiate his lust for blood, and create a new and ever-widening circle of semi-demons to batten on the helpless. The very thought drove me mad. A terrible desire came upon me to rid the world of such a monster. There was no lethal weapon at hand, but I seized a shovel which the workmen had been using to fill the cases, and lifting it high, struck, with the edge downward, at the hateful face.

This scene reinforces Harker's earlier inability to see Dracula in the mirror. Taken out of context, it would be difficult to distinguish the man from the monster. Behavior generally attributed to the vampire—the habit of attacking a sleeping victim, violence, and irrational behavior—is revealed to be the behavior of the civilized Englishman also. The sole difference is that Stoker's narrative technique does not permit the reader to enter Dracula's thoughts as he stands over his victims. The reversal of roles here is important because it establishes the subjective nature of the narrators' beliefs, suggests their lack of self-knowledge, and serves to focus on the similarities between the narrators and their opponent. Later in the novel, Mina Harker provides the following analysis of Dracula which ironically also describes the single-mindedness of his pursuers:

> The Count is a criminal and of criminal type . . . and *qua* criminal he is of imperfectly formed mind. Thus, in a difficulty he has to seek resource in habit . . . Then, as he is criminal he is selfish; and as his intellect is small and his action is based on selfishness, he confines himself to one purpose.

Both Mina and Jonathan can justify their pursuit of Dracula by labeling him a murderer; and Mina adds intellectual frailty to his alleged sins. However, the narrators show themselves to be equally bound by habit and equally incapable of evaluating situations which are beyond their limited spheres of expertise. In fact, Stoker implies that the only difference between Dracula and his opponents is the narrators' ability to state individual desire in terms of what they believe is a common good. For example, the above scene shows that Harker can justify his violent attack on Dracula because he pictures himself as the protector of helpless millions; and the narrators insist on the duty to defend the innocents.

The necessity of protecting the innocent is called into question, however, when Dr. Van Helsing informs the other characters about the vampire's nature. While most of his discussion concerns the vampire's susceptibility to garlic, silver bullets, and religious artifacts, Van Helsing also admits that the vampire cannot enter a dwelling unless he is first invited by one of the inhabitants. In other words, a vampire cannot influence a human being without that person's consent. Dracula's behavior confirms that he is an internal, not an external, threat. Although perfectly capable of using superior strength when he must defend himself, he usually employs seduction, relying on the others' desires to emulate his freedom from external constraints: Renfield's desire for immortality, Lucy's wish to escape the repressive existence of an upper-class woman, and the desires of all the characters to overcome the restraints placed on them by their religion and their law. As the spokesman for civilization, Van Helsing appears to understand that the others might be tempted by their desires to become like Dracula and he warns them against the temptation:

> But to fail here, is not mere life or death. It is that we become as him; that we henceforward become foul things of the night like him—without heart or conscience, preying on the bodies and the souls of those we love best.

Becoming like Dracula, they too would be laws unto themselves—primitive, violent, irrational—with nothing to justify their actions except the force of their desires. No longer would they need to rationalize their "preying on the bodies and souls of their loved ones" by concealing their lust for power under the rubric of religion, their love of violence under the names of imperialism and progress, their sexual desires within an elaborate courtship ritual.

The narrators attribute their hatred of Dracula to a variety of causes. Harker's journal introduces a being whose way of life is antithetical to theirs—a warlord, a representative of the feudal past and the leader of a primitive cult who he fears will attempt to establish a vampire colony in England. Mina Harker views him as a criminal and as the murderer of her best friend; and Van Helsing sees him as a moral threat, a kind of Anti-Christ. Yet, in spite of the narrators' moral and political language, Stoker reveals that Dracula is primarily a sexual threat, a missionary of desire whose only true kingdom will be the human body. Although he flaunts his independence of social restraints and proclaims himself a master over all he sees, Dracula adheres more closely to English law than his opponents in every area except his sexual behavior. (In fact, Dracula admits to Harker that he invited him to Transylvania so he could learn the subtle nuances of English law and business.) Neither a thief, rapist, nor an overtly political threat, Dracula is dangerous because he expresses his contempt for authority in the most individualistic of ways—through his sexuality. In fact, his thirst for blood and the manner in which he satisfies this thirst can be interpreted as sexual desire which fails to observe any of society's attempts to control it—prohibitions against polygamy, promiscuity, and homosexuality. Furthermore, Stoker suggests that it is generally through sexuality that the vampire gains control over human beings. Van Helsing recognizes this temptation when he prevents Arthur from kissing Lucy right before her death; and even the staid and morally upright Harker momentarily succumbs to the sensuality of the three vampire-women in Dracula's castle:

> I felt in my heart a wicked burning desire that they would kiss me with those red lips. It is not good to note this down, lest some day it should meet Mina's eyes and cause her pain; but it is the truth.

For one brief moment, Harker does appear to recognize the truth about sexual desire; it is totally irrational and has nothing to do with monogamy, love, or even respect for the beloved. It is Dracula, however, who clearly articulates the characters' most intense fears of sexuality: "Your girls that you all love are mine already; and through them you and others shall yet be mine—my creatures, to do my bidding and to be my jackals when I want to feed." Implicit in Dracula's warning is the similarity between vampire and opponents. Despite rare moments of comprehension, however, the narrators generally choose to ignore this similarity; and their lack of self-knowledge permits them to hunt down and kill not only Dracula and the three women in his castle, but their friend Lucy Westenra as well.

The scene in which Arthur drives the stake through Lucy's body while the other men watch thoughtfully is filled with a violent sexuality which again connects vampire and opponents:

> But Arthur never faltered. He looked like a figure of Thor as his untrembling arm rose and fell, driving deeper and deeper the mercy-bearing stake, whilst the blood from the pierced heart welled and spurted up around it. His face was set, and high duty seemed to shine through it; the sight of it gave us courage so that our voices seemed to ring through the vault . . . There in the coffin lay no longer the foul Thing that we had dreaded and grown to hate that the work of her destruction was yielded as a privilege to the one best entitled to it, but Lucy as we had seen her in life, with her face of unequalled sweetness and purity.

Despite Seward's elevated moral language, the scene resembles nothing so much as the combined group rape and murder of an unconscious woman; and this kind of violent attack on a helpless victim is precisely the kind of behavior which condemns Dracula in the narrators' eyes. Moreover, Lucy is not the only woman to be subjected to this violence. At the conclusion, in a scene which is only slightly less explicit, Dr. Van Helsing destroys the three women in Dracula's castle. Again Dr. Van Helsing admits that he is fascinated by the beautiful visages of the "wanton Un-Dead" but he never acknowledges that his violent attack is simply a role reversal or that he becomes the vampire as he stands over their unconscious bodies.

By the conclusion of the novel, all the characters who have been accused of expressing individual desire have been appropriately punished: Dracula, Lucy Westenra, and the three vampire-women have been killed; and even Mina Harker is ostracized for her momentary indiscretion. All that remains after the primitive, the passionate, and the individualistic qualities that were associated with the vampire have been destroyed is a small group of wealthy men who return after a period of one year to the site of their victory over the vampire. The surviving characters remain unchanged by the events in their lives and never come to the realization that their commitment to social values merely masks their violence and their sexuality; and the only significant difference in their condition is the birth of the Harkers' son who is appropriately named for all the men who had participated in the conquest of Dracula. Individual sexual desire has apparently been so absolutely effaced that the narrators see this child as the result of their social union rather than the product of a sexual union between one man and one woman.

The narrators insist that they are agents of God and are able to ignore their similarity to the vampire because their commitment to social values such as monogamy, proper English behavior, and the will of the majority enables them to conceal their violence and their sexual desires from each other and even from themselves. Stoker, however, reveals that these characteristics are merely masked by social convention. Instead of being eliminated, violence and sexuality emerge in particularly perverted forms.

Recently uncovered evidence suggests that Bram Stoker may have had very personal reasons for his preoccupation with repression and sexuality. In his biography of his great-uncle, Daniel Farson explains that, while the cause of Stoker's death is usually given as exhaustion, Stoker actually died of tertiary syphillis, exhaustion being one of the final stages of that disease. Farson also adds that Stoker's problematic relationship with his wife may have been responsible:

> When his wife's frigidity drove him to other women, probably prostitutes among them, Bram's writing showed signs of guilt and sexual frustration . . . He probably caught syphilis around the turn of the century, possibly as early as the year of Dracula, 1896. (It usually takes ten to fifteen years before it kills.) By 1897 it seems that he had been celibate for more than twenty years, as far as Florence [his wife] was concerned.

Poignantly aware from his own experience that the face of the vampire is the hidden side of the human character, Stoker creates unreliable narrators to tell a tale, not of the overcoming of Evil by Good, but of the similarities between the two. *Dracula* reveals the unseen face in the mirror; and Stoker's message is similar to the passage from *Julius Caesar* which prefaces this article and might be paraphrased in the following manner: "The fault, dear reader, is not in our external enemies, but in ourselves."

Source: Carol A. Senf, "*Dracula*: The Unseen Face in the Mirror," in *Journal of Narrative Technique*, Vol. 9, No. 3, Fall 1979, pp. 160–70.

Royce MacGillivray

In the following essay, MacGillivray exposes weakness in Stoker's characterization in Dracula *but maintains nevertheless that the work has serious literary merit.*

Bram Stoker's *Dracula* has never been much praised for its literary merits. Yet this horror novel, first published in May 1897, survives today, after more than seventy years of popularity, as one of the little group of English language books from the nineties still read by more than scholars. Because of the succession of horror films based on it, whether *Dracula* would have achieved this success solely through its intrinsic merits is uncertain. Certainly without the films it is hard to believe that Dracula would be one of the few proper names from novels to have become a household word, known even to people who have never heard of the novel. Stoker created a myth comparable in vitality to that of the Wandering Jew, Faust, or Don Juan. This myth has not, so far, been crowned with respectability by its use in great literature, yet is it too much to suggest that in time even that may be achieved? Such a myth lives not merely because it has been skillfully marketed by entrepreneurs but because it expresses something that large numbers of people feel to be true about their own lives.

In the following pages I want to examine *Dracula* with more attention than is usually given to it. Since the novel will probably have readers for many years to come, it is best that it be read with understanding. This understanding can be best achieved by scholarly debate, to which the following is a contribution. While the idea of scholarly study of a horror novel may initially seem ridiculous, I think I can show that *Dracula* is substantial enough to deserve the attention of scholars. Even if the novel should seem to most others less impressive than it has seemed to me after a number of readings, I suggest that the historian and sociologist will find it worthwhile to pay attention to the contents of a novel that has been so influential in our century.

As the original Dracula story of Stoker's novel has been distorted by the Dracula films deriving from it and is known in variant forms to readers who have never read the novel, it is perhaps useful to establish common ground by giving an outline of the plot.

As the novel opens, Jonathan Harker, a young English lawyer, is travelling in Transylvania and enjoying himself as the scenes about him grow ever wilder and stranger. His destination is the castle where Count Dracula, who is the client of Harker's superior, has requested his attendance on matters of business. When Harker reaches the castle, the count, a tall old man, welcomes him warmly, but Harker soon finds that he is a prisoner and that the count is a vampire or an evil spirit of some undefined kind. Stoker is very painstaking in instructing his readers about vampires, which were not as familiar to Victorian readers as they became to later generations, and it is not clear whether Harker as yet knew enough about them to identify the count as one. We only know that he manages, through horrified observation, to put together a reasonably complete picture of Dracula's way of life. Dracula is planning to emigrate to England and needs Harker to improve his knowledge of the life and language of England. At last Dracula sets off for England with fifty large boxes of earth from the castle chapel; these will serve as the graves which he needs for his resting places. Harker is left behind in the castle to be the victim of three female vampires. We are not told precisely how Harker escapes—Stoker has a sure sense of the advantages of *not* telling his readers everything they want to know—but apparently he carries out his intention of climbing down the castle wall. After a spell of hospitalization in Budapest for brain fever, the result of his ordeal, he arrives safely back to England.

There the threat posed by Dracula calls into existence a band determined to outwit him: Harker and his newly married wife; Dr. Seward, a psychiatrist and head of a private lunatic asylum; Arthur Holmwood who becomes Lord Godalming in the course of the novel; Quincey Morris, an adventuresome American of the Teddy Roosevelt sort; and a celebrated Dutch scientist and physician, Seward's old teacher Abraham Van Helsing. Under the guidance of Van Helsing, they track down as many as they can find of Dracula's lairs, the boxes of earth, and make them uninhabitable for him by placing in them pieces of the consecrated wafer of the Eucharist. Reduced at last to the refuge of a single box, Dracula flees back to the continent. The pursuers follow, and in a dramatic scene on the snow before the castle, just as the sun is about to set and so give the vampire the supernatural powers that will enable him to kill or elude his pursuers, he is destroyed in the prescribed manner, by the piercing of his heart and the severing of his head.

Stoker, who sets his narrative uncompromisingly in the framework of the technologically advanced and modern-minded Victorian civilization, weaves into it the commonplace details of everyday life precisely where we expect them least. It is absurd, and yet convincing, to find that Dracula has a sizeable library in his vampire castle, from which he has been quarrying information about the customs, laws, and so forth of England. Coming into the room one evening, Harker finds him lying on a sofa reading Bradshaw's railway guide. In the castle, where no servants are ever seen, Harker glimpses Dracula making Harker's bed and setting his table. As we read of the meals which Harker was served ("an excellent roast chicken," "an excellent supper") we wonder, as Stoker probably intends we should, whether Dracula also did the cooking. It is touching that when the pursuers break into the house Dracula has bought in Piccadilly they find his clothes brush and brush and comb there—necessary implements, it seems, even for someone who lives in a coffin. While they wait at his house, Mrs. Harker, with pleasing impudence, sends them a telegram there to warn them that Dracula may be approaching. When Dracula, intent upon fleeing from England, meets a sea captain to commission him to ship his one remaining box of earth out of the country—the captain of course does not know that the stranger who is addressing him is a vampire and will be hiding in the box—Dracula is seen to be wearing a straw hat, which, as Van Helsing remarks in his imperfect English, "suit not him or the time." Perhaps this element of the incongruous in the novel is intended only as a gentle form of self-parody, or of mockery at tales of the supernatural. I think, however, that it plays a rather more important role than this. We live daily, Stoker seems to say, with the incongruous, with the ironies, contradictions, and wild absurdities of life. We have no reason then to be surprised if the most preposterous events should come upon us at the very moment when life seems most sober, rational, and humdrum.

Stoker created in Dracula a towering figure who dominates the novel and appears utterly convincing. It was unfortunate for Stoker that he did not live early enough to write his novel at the beginning rather than the end of the nineteenth century. Had Dracula come to literary life in the age of Romanticism and the Gothic novel, one imagines that he would have been received rapturously into the literary tradition of western Europe instead of being sternly restricted, as he has been, to the popular imagination. In view of the extraordinary pains Stoker took to make the geographical and social background of the novel as accurate as possible—his description of Whitby, where Dracula landed in England in the midst of an immense storm, is a reliable guide for tourists today—it is not surprising to find that he selected for his vampire a real historical figure, Vlad the Impaler, also known as Dracula, who was voivode or prince of Wallachia from 1456 to 1462, and again in 1476. In real life Dracula was known for his horrifying cruelty, but Stoker, who wanted a monster that his readers could both shudder at and identify with, omits all mention of the dark side of his reputation and emphasizes his greatness as a warrior chieftain. As Dracula entertains young Harker in his castle, he cannot refrain from reminiscing about the campaigns in which he took part. Though he pretends to be merely talking about the history of his part of Europe and conceals all personal involvement, a telltale sign appears: "In his speaking of things and people, and especially of battles," Harker notes, "he spoke as if he had been present at them all." When Van Helsing has had a Budapest correspondent make enquiries into the identity of the historical figure whose living corpse they are pursuing, he is able to report:

> He must, indeed, have been that Voivode Dracula who won his name against the Turk, over the great river on the very frontier of Turkey-land. If it be so, then was he no common man; for in that time, and for centuries after, he was spoken of as the cleverest and the most cunning, as well as the bravest of the sons of the "land beyond the forest." That mighty brain and that iron resolution went with him to his grave, and are even now arrayed against us. The Draculas were ... a great and noble race, though now and again [there] were scions who were held by their coevals to have had dealings with the Evil One. They learned his secrets in the Scholomance, amongst the mountains over Lake Hermanstadt, where the devil claims the tenth scholar as his due. In the records are such words as "stregoica"—witch, "ordog," and "pokol"—Satan and hell; and in one manuscript this very Dracula is spoken of as "wampyr," which we all understand too well. There have been from the loins of this very one great men and good women, and their graves make sacred the earth where alone this foulness can dwell. For it is not the least of its terrors that this evil thing is rooted deep in all good; in soil barren of holy memories it cannot rest.

Fixing himself on this biographical basis, Stoker gives his vampire story an unexpected and, in view of later exploitations of the Dracula theme in films, a remarkably sophisticated psychological interest, and even a degree of pathos. Anyone who compares Stoker's portrait of Dracula with the lore that Montague Summers has collected in his two volumes on vampires will find that Dracula, a polished and eloquent gentleman as well as a wily antagonist, is untypical. In their non-fictional existence, as described by tradition, vampires tend, it seems, to be squalid and animal-like. But for the superiority of Dracula there is a reason beyond that of his superiority in life. Dracula, we are led to believe, has been slowly recovering his faculties since the time of his death, when they were partly destroyed. While the execution of his elaborate project for transferring himself to England, where multitudes exist to be his prey, is the highest achievement that his process of self-development has yet yielded, there are possibilities that if he survives he will become more dangerous still. "What more may he not do," Van Helsing asks, "when the greater world of thought is open to him?" Dracula's power to grow intellectually is, however, barren. No matter what he grows into, he must remain painfully and utterly separated from the surrounding world of men and all its values.

Dracula, though at a lower level of literary achievement, is—like *Steppenwolf*, *L'Etranger*, and *La Chute*, a novel of alienation. The depiction of Dracula as an alienated figure derives from the traditional vampire legends, the Gothic novels, and the idea of the romantic hero, as well as from Stoker's psychological acumen. When we have seen Dracula in this light, we can grasp the double irony of his statement to Harker in the castle that "I long to go through the crowded streets of your mighty London, to be in the midst of the whirl and rush of humanity, to share its life, its change, its death, and all that makes it what it is." This touching sentimentality, which masks the fact that he wants to be among these people to prey on them, also masks his defeat. Though he has retained and recovered some human characteristics, he can no more share the people's "whirl and rush" and life and change than he can ever see again the armies he commanded so long ago. Dracula's disastrous expedition to England can even be seen as unconsciously suicidal, as his attempt to extinguish his anguish in a lasting death.

Besides being an alienated figure, Dracula is, as Maurice Richardson has said in his remarks on the novel, "a father-figure." The theme of Dracula as a father figure is less overt than the theme of alienation, and one feels that in inserting it in the novel Stoker was not fully conscious of his own feelings. Dracula is the patriarch of his castle, for

as a little sifting of the evidence will show, the three female vampires who share it with him are his wife and two daughters, perhaps by another marriage, or his wife and two sisters. Rather more importantly for the emotional undercurrents of the novel, Dracula even aspires to be, in a sense, the father of the band that is pursuing him. Because he intends, as he tells them, to turn them all into vampires, he will be their creator and therefore "father."

This only means that they will become a different kind of "family": as a little examination will show, they are already a "family." They even participate in a kind of group marriage—one is tempted to say a kind of group sex—when four of them give blood by transfusion from their own veins to Dracula's victim Lucy Westenra. The significance of the blood transfusion is pointed out for any reader who might have missed it when Arthur, who mistakenly supposes that he alone has given blood to Lucy, speculates that the blood transfusion has made Lucy his wife in the sight of God. Somewhat ludicrously, no fewer than three of them had previously proposed to Lucy all in one day. At the end of the novel this closely knit band of pursuers even manages to produce a baby in the form of the Harkers' child Quincey, whose "bundles of names" we are told, "links all our little band of men together." Van Helsing, the guide of this family, is, Richardson says, a good father figure. While Van Helsing actually seems more a kindly elder brother than a father, his nearness to the father role is one of the things that make him faintly resemble Dracula and thus tinge him slightly with moral ambiguity. (Perhaps the reason why he is so thin as a character is that too much of him consists of materials left over from creating the vast figure of Dracula.)

The theme of Dracula as father figure gains psychological interest from the framework of references to the death or murder of parents in which it is inserted. One of Dracula's earliest victims in the novel is a mother who comes to the castle to demand the return of her abducted child. In a horrifying scene which Harker watches from a castle window she is torn to pieces by the wolves who are at Dracula's call. An old man, another father figure, is found dead with a broken neck in the churchyard at Whitby shortly after Dracula's landing at that port. Then there are the deaths from natural causes of Arthur Holmwood's father; of Harker's employer and patron, who had been a father to him and to Mrs. Harker; and of the mother of Lucy Westenra. It is suggestive of the emotional significance the patricide theme seems to have had

What Do I Read Next?

- Although many people wrote vampire stories after *Dracula*, Anne Rice is generally acknowledged as the first writer to put some major twists on the vampire conventions made famous by Stoker's novel. Rice's *Interview with the Vampire* (1976) is the first book in a series of books about vampires, which has been collected into a single volume titled *Vampire Chronicles*. This collection has influenced many later writers of vampire stories.

- Like *Dracula*, Mary Shelley's *Frankenstein; or The Modern Prometheus* (1811) is widely different from most of its screen adaptations. The story details Dr. Frankenstein's scientific experiments that galvanize his mismatched corpse into life and the struggle to catch the monster after it gets loose.

- For an overall reference to vampires that is both academic and fun, *The Complete Idiot's Guide to Vampires* (2002), written by English professor Jay Stevenson, provides an intelligent overview of the legends, history, and culture of vampires, including the impact on modern media like films and television.

- Although Stoker is best known for *Dracula*, he wrote other horror books, including *The Lair of the White Worm* (1911). In this book, the main character's neighbor is a vampiric being who transforms herself into a serpent.

- In *Dreadful Pleasures* (1993), James B. Twitchell examines the lure of horror throughout human history, through media as primitive as cave paintings to those as advanced as the modern feature film.

- H. G. Wells's *The War of the Worlds* (1898) features an invasion by an advanced race of beings that survive on the blood of their victims, particularly human blood.

---

for Stoker that the last three of these deaths are incidental to his narrative, which would be improved by their omission. Even Quincey Morris, who is killed at the end of the novel in the final struggle against the vampire, becomes a retrospective father when the Harkers' baby, Quincey, is born on the anniversary of his death and perpetuates his name.

The counterpart to this theme of parricide is the theme of the murder of children by their parents. Stoker introduces anecdotally the story of a hunchbacked son who committed suicide in revenge for his mother's hatred. We are led to believe that the mother of Lucy Westenra was partly responsible for her daughter's death by failing to follow the instructions laid down by Van Helsing for Lucy's protection from the vampire. Dracula himself appears in the role of murderous parent: to turn people into vampires, in effect to make them his children, he must first kill them. In a dialogue with overtones of incest, it is hinted that Dracula, in accordance with the rule that vampires begin their careers by preying first on their nearest kin,

has made his daughters or sisters into vampires. The sequence of birth and infanticide is represented by the scene in the castle in which Dracula, who has been out hunting, produces a child from a sack and hands it over to the female vampires to be their victim.

The theme of parent-child conflict reaches its culmination at the end of the novel with the destruction of Dracula himself at the hands of his intended children, his pursuers. As Richardson reminds us, what Stoker has described is similar to the destruction of the father of the primal horde by his offspring as imagined by Freud in *Totem and Taboo*.

A recent biography of Stoker is called *A Biography of Dracula: The Life Story of Bram Stoker*, but the book does not try to substantiate the claim of its title about the connection between Stoker and Dracula. When I suggest that there is indeed reason to suppose that Dracula was partly based on Stoker, I am not attacking Stoker's character. The popularity of the Dracula myth in this century suggests that many persons find a resemblance between

> " It is hard to believe that anyone who has observed the power Stoker shows in *Dracula* of setting a scene and developing its action with a maximum of conciseness and vividness could dismiss him as a mere writer of thrillers."

themselves and Dracula and between themselves and vampires in general. It is hard not to suggest that vampire stories, including *Dracula*, reflect, in a sensationalized but recognizable form, the truth that the close association of any two persons is almost certain to involve, however faintly, some "vampirish" exploitation, be it economic, intellectual, or emotional, of one of them by the other.

Who was Bram Stoker? He was born in Ireland in 1847, and began his career by following his father into the Irish civil service. Some years later he gave up his civil service employment to migrate to England as the acting-manager of the great actor, Henry (later Sir Henry) Irving. Meanwhile, he had dabbled in journalism and unpaid dramatic criticism and laboured on his first book, a legal manual on the duties of clerks of petty sessions in Ireland. For well over a quarter of a century he served Irving diligently. Besides managing the actor's London theatre, he accompanied him on a number of American tours. He also found time, despite the heavy duties of his position, to write novels and short stories and to qualify as a barrister. Though hampered by ill-health, he wrote industriously in the years after Irving's death, urged on now by the need to earn a living by his pen. His two volume *Personal Reminiscences* of Irving, a product of this period, is still well known. When he died in 1912, six years after Irving, it was an indication of his extraordinary exertions that the word "Exhaustion" appeared on his death certificate.

Described in *A Biography of Dracula* as a "genial, red-bearded giant," Stoker seems to have been the very reverse of sinister or exotic. At least one of the writers on Stoker has suggested that there is a surprising contrast between this paragon of Victorian manhood and normality and *Dracula*, with its concentration on morbid subjects. One can see, however, certain parallels between Stoker's life and the fictional Dracula's which must have assisted him in creating his hero-villain. After a sickly childhood in which he was unable to leave his bed and stand on his own feet until he was in his eighth year, Stoker became a champion athlete at Trinity College, Dublin, and grew to the size that made his biographer call him a "giant." In his own development Stoker must have found clues for his depiction of Dracula as someone who developed in the tomb, slowly groping his way toward the full mastery of the possibilities open to him. Similarly, Stoker's migration from Dublin, where he must have felt isolated with his youthful literary ambitions, to London, the intellectual capital of the British Isles and the hub of a vast empire, parallels Dracula's migration from his thinly populated Transylvanian feeding-grounds to the same city and its teeming human life. In his isolation in Dublin and in his later role as an Irishman in England, Stoker must have picked up clues for his depiction of Dracula as an alienated figure. Even the cumbersome train of baggage that Irving and his acting company carried with them as they toured the provinces and America may have been in his mind when he described Dracula's movements with his boxes of earth.

One of the defects of the novel is the Victorian emotionalism which occasionally makes the modern reader wince. A far graver defect, however, is its weakness of characterization, a rule whose only exception is the magnificent and convincing figure of Dracula. This weakness is especially evident in all six of the little band of heroes pursuing Dracula. Harker is the most convincing, principally because Stoker has not tried to give him a distinct character but has been content to let him be a transparent object through which events are viewed. Part of the reason why the first fifty or sixty pages of the novel, which deal with Harker's experiences in Transylvania, are so much better than the remainder of the work is that no characters but the superior Dracula and Harker appear in them, except briefly. After these first pages, in which he is introduced in great detail, Dracula is removed almost completely from the direct view of the reader. In this way Stoker maintains in the reader a sense of the ominous—not, be it noted, a sense of the mysterious, which is little awakened because the approach which the heroes of the novel take to the reemergence of vampires in modern society is severely practical and rationalistic—but he deprives himself of the full use of his strongest creation.

The only character in the novel who comes close to being boring is, oddly enough, slightly better developed than most of Stoker's characters. This is Renfield, the zoophagous patient in Dr. Seward's lunatic asylum. Renfield's repulsive desire to eat flies, birds, and other small living creatures, and all the other details of his malady and daily life are described with surprising relentlessness. Eventually he is allowed to play a feeble part in the action by admitting Dracula into the asylum when his prospective victim, Mrs. Harker, is visiting there; according to the rules which tradition tells us govern a vampire's actions, he cannot enter a house until one of its occupants has admitted him, but thereafter he can come and go as he pleases. As Stoker is a story teller par excellence, it is strange that he does not enliven the sections which deal with Renfield by including more action, perhaps in the form of a subplot based on Renfield's past life. But if the treatment of Renfield is unsuccessful, that is not because he is irrelevant to the novel. I suggest we should regard him as a good idea which does not quite succeed. His simplest function is to tie together disparate parts of the narrative through his presence. Stoker may also have felt the need of a sluggishly unfolding account of Renfield to contrast with the usual swift pace of his narrative. But most importantly, Renfield joins Dracula and his pursuers in a triangular relationship in which he heightens our awareness of their character and position.

As we seek to define the most important role he plays in this relationship, it becomes evident that he is the sad anti-Dracula of the novel. Along with his desire to feed on living things, he has dim hopes of becoming a vampire. Meanwhile, his madness and his prison walls confine him as much as Dracula is confined by his alienation and the rules that restrict the actions of a vampire. We are constantly aware of Renfield's exclusion from the band of pursuers and thus see in him an echo of Dracula's alienation. In the same way, it may be mentioned in passing, Dracula's alienation is mocked by the clubbiness and family feeling of the pursuers. The anti-Dracula may at the same time be seen as a participant in a parent-son conflict of unusual sterility. He plays the role of son and Dr. Seward of father, but the age relationship of father and son is reversed, with the doctor being younger than his "son." In this way, just as Dracula is a kind of super-father, Renfield is a father broken and made harmless—so much reduced from his rightful fatherhood that when he is murdered by Dracula it is hard to be sure whether we are even entitled to count him as another of Stoker's murdered parents. Since the quest of the vampires

for blood seems often to be in some undefined way a sexual quest, it is tempting to see Renfield, the would-be vampire, as suffering from sexual frustration, and it is not only tempting but plausible to suggest that sexual frustration was one of the elements that Stoker drew on in creating him.

Dracula is a thoroughly unpolitical novel. This statement is true both in the sense that Dracula ignores the party issues of the day and in the more general sense that it ignores the strains of the class society of late Victorian England. To the historically minded, however, it is interesting for its expression of certain attitudes belonging to Stoker's part of the Victorian period, and for its anticipations of the intellectual climate of our century. The alienation theme in the novel is especially relevant to the twentieth century—indeed, is brought out in the novel with a sharpness which seems almost anachronistic and which deserves close examination by the historians of the development of the English novel—but the novel expresses also the disquiet of many Victorian intellectuals about the atomizing and dehumanizing effects of their own time. While the novel's parent-child conflicts are presumably rooted in Stoker's private feelings, one can see interesting parallels with the twentieth-century revolt against the Victorian father and the whole Victorian heritage as expressed, for instance, in Butler's *The Way of All Flesh* and Gosse's *Father and Son*. The novel also reflects the foreboding with which some Victorians faced the new century. Surely some ill-fortune would take away the good things which had been so unstintingly poured upon Victorian England? Dracula may have partially symbolized for contemporaries this nameless threat. The vampire theme has special relevance, too, to the Victorian problem of loss of faith. The abandonment of traditional Christianity reopened the whole question of what becomes of a person after death. In our time *Dracula* probably gains part of its impact from the intense fears which have clustered, more in this century than in any other, about the problem of growing old, a problem which vampires, who are capable of living forever, have solved.

But of all that is historically interesting in *Dracula*, nothing is more curious than its combination of the Victorian preoccupation with death and an almost twentieth-century preoccupation with sex. This combination is found, for example, in the hunting activities of the vampires, who belong to the dead but pursue the living in what often seems to be a spirit of blatant sexuality, and in the destruction of beautiful female vampires by driving stakes through their hearts as they sleep in their tombs.

I must not allow my remarks on the faults of this novel to conceal the remarkable skill with which it is written. It is hard to believe that anyone who has observed the power Stoker shows in *Dracula* of setting a scene and developing its action with a maximum of conciseness and vividness could dismiss him as a mere writer of thrillers. It is even harder to believe that anyone who has examined this novel's extraordinary richness of detail and Stoker's ability to subordinate this richness to a severely disciplined plot could regard him as deficient in inventiveness, intellectual power, or a sense of literary design. The long passage I quoted earlier shows that his language rises at times to a kind of poetry. Had stoker been able to overcome the single problem of his weakness in characterization, there is no reason why *Dracula* should not have been one of the minor masterpieces of English fiction. Even in its imperfect form it deserves to be known to scholars as more than a source of sensational films.

Source: Royce MacGillivray, "*Dracula*: Bram Stoker's Spoiled Masterpiece," in *Queen's Quarterly*, Vol. 79, No. 4, Winter 1972, pp. 518–27.

Sources

Bentley, C. F., "The Monster in the Bedroom: Sexual Symbolism in Bram Stoker's *Dracula*," in *Literature and Psychology*, Vol. 22, No. 1, 1972, pp. 27–34.

MacGillivray, Royce, "*Dracula*: Bram Stoker's Spoiled Masterpiece," in *Queen's Quarterly*, Vol. 79, No. 4, Winter 1972, pp. 518–27.

Moss, Stephanie, "Bram Stoker," in *Dictionary of Literary Biography*, Vol. 178, *British Fantasy and Science-Fiction Writers Before World War I*, edited by Darren Harris-Fain, Gale Research, 1997, pp. 229–37.

"Novel Notes: *Dracula*," in the *Bookman*, Vol. 12, No. 71, August 1897, p. 129.

Review of *Dracula*, in the *Athenaeum*, No. 3635, June 26, 1897, p. 235.

Richardson, Maurice, "The Psychoanalysis of Ghost Stories," in the *Twentieth Century*, Vol. 166, No. 994, December 1959, pp. 419–31.

Stoker, Bram, *Dracula*, edited by Maurice Hindle, Penguin, 1993.

Summers, Montague, "The Vampire in Literature," in *The Vampire: His Kith and Kin*, 1928, reprint, University Books, 1960, pp. 271–340.

Further Reading

Belford, Barbara, *Bram Stoker: A Biography of the Author of "Dracula,"* Knopf, 1996.

In this compelling biography, Belford examines the life of Stoker, who has always been less famous than his greatest creation, *Dracula*. As Belford shows, this trend was true in Stoker's life, overshadowed as he was by his employer, the actor Henry Irving.

Gerard, Emily, *The Land beyond the Forest: Facts, Figures, and Fancies from Transylvania*, AMS Press, 2001.

This travel book was originally published in the late 1880s, and many believe that it was one of Stoker's references for the Transylvanian portion of the novel. The book also talks about the vampire legends of the area.

McNally, Raymond T., and Radu Florescu, *In Search of Dracula: A True History of Dracula and Vampire Legends*, Little, Brown, 1975.

This famous Dracula reference explores the real-life links between Stoker's title character and the historical Dracula, Vlad the Impaler.

Pool, Daniel, *What Jane Austen Ate and Charles Dickens Knew: From Fox Hunting to Whist—The Facts of Daily Life in Nineteenth-Century England*, Touchstone Books, 1994.

This highly informative reader's companion is ideal for those who wish to learn more about the language, culture, and customs of nineteenth-century England, including courtship rituals and Victorian attitudes towards sex. As such, it serves as an indispensable guide to Stoker's novel.

I Am the Cheese

Robert Cormier
1977

I Am the Cheese, published in 1977, was Robert Cormier's second young adult novel. It tells the story of a teenaged boy who discovers that his family is part of a witness protection program and that his parents have been keeping secrets from him all his life. As he tries to determine who and what he is, he is threatened and finally overcome by the terrifying forces of a government that is more interested in preserving its own power than in protecting one small boy. The idea for the book grew out of Cormier's reading a magazine article about the then-new federal witness protection program and his fascination with the idea of individuals struggling against an unjust society.

The book has sold consistently well since its publication, but it has also attracted controversy. Some have felt that the book's complicated structure and pessimistic ending are inappropriate for young people, and the novel has occasionally been challenged and banned in school libraries. Nonetheless, it has been recognized for excellence by several influential organizations, including the American Library Association and the Children's Literature Association. It was named an Outstanding Book of the Year by the *New York Times* and a Best Book of the Year by *School Library Journal*, among other recognitions.

Author Biography

Robert Cormier was born on January 17, 1925, in Leominster, Massachusetts, the town that served as

the model for Cormier's fictional Monument, Massachusetts, the setting for several of his novels. He was one of eight children of Lucien Cormier, a factory worker, and his wife Irma. Growing up in the Great Depression, Cormier enjoyed the inexpensive means of recreation available to him, especially going to the movies and reading books from the public library. When he was about thirteen, he read Thomas Wolfe's novel *The Web and the Rock*, about a boy who wants to be a writer. As an adult, Cormier remembered this novel as the most important influence on his own decision to become a writer.

After graduating from high school in 1942, Cormier tried to join the military and help fight World War II, but his poor eyesight kept him out. Instead, he took a factory job and enrolled in college classes. When one of his professors submitted a story of his to a magazine without Cormier's knowledge, he became a published author for the first time. Newly confident in his writing skills, he left college and took a job writing radio commercials. Soon after, he met, courted, and married Constance Senay. They had four children.

Cormier's next job was as a newspaper reporter, a job he sought because it would enable him to both write and support a family. He worked as a journalist for more than thirty years and won several awards for his work. Meanwhile, in his spare time he turned again to fiction in the late 1950s and published his first novel, *Now and at the Hour*, in 1960. He established a routine of writing fiction late at night, when the rest of the family had gone to bed.

Cormier's fourth novel, based on the experience of one of his teenaged sons at school, was *The Chocolate War* (1974). His first novel for and about young adults, the book has been both popular and controversial; it has sold nearly a million copies, and has occasionally been banned or challenged in schools and libraries because of its gloomy realism. In 1977, Cormier published his second young adult novel, *I Am the Cheese*, which was also popular with young readers but criticized by some adults because of its pessimistic ending. This was followed by nine more novels, a collection of short stories, and a collection of newspaper columns.

Some critics have speculated that Cormier might have become more famous if he had traveled more or moved to a big city, but he liked staying near his family in his hometown. His marriage to Constance lasted until his death—more than fifty years—and he worked with the same literary agent for more than forty years. Cormier was still living

in Leominster, the town where he was born, when he suffered his last illness. He died of lung cancer in a Boston hospital on November 2, 2000.

Plot Summary

Chapter 1

I Am the Cheese opens with the words "I am riding the bicycle and I am on Route 31." These words are important for several reasons: they introduce the novel's protagonist, they establish the first-person point of view and present tense that will characterize one strand of the novel, and they begin a paragraph that will be repeated later in the novel. In this first chapter, one of fifteen in the present tense, the narrator is a teenage boy riding an old bicycle from Monument, Massachusetts, to Rutterburg, Vermont, to bring a securely wrapped gift to his father.

The boy, Adam, appears to have decided on this trip rather abruptly: he did not tell anyone at home or at school that he was leaving, he did not call "Amy," and he did not take his pills. He quietly wrapped up his father's gift, grabbed an old cap to keep his ears warm in the October wind, and took his savings of thirty-five dollars and ninety-three cents. Now, as he bikes along, he looks over his shoulder to see whether he is being followed. Only four or five miles into the seventy-mile trip he is getting tired, but a long downhill lets him coast for a while.

Chapter 2

The second chapter begins with code letters ("TAPE OZK001"), followed by a transcript of an interview between "T" and "A." T identifies himself as Brint, and asks questions to help A remember "that night." It seems that A is unable to remember anything clearly, although he has been given some sort of medication to relax him or to help him remember. After a few exchanges on the interview tape, the writing shifts to a prose narrative in the past tense, told by a third-person limited narrator with insight into the mind of one character, who appears to be Adam at an earlier time. A young boy, lying in bed with his Pokey the Pig stuffed animal, overhears an urgent whispered conversation between his parents. He realizes they are trying to keep him from hearing. This past-tense narrative is interrupted by another transcription from the tape, as Brint urges Adam to remember exactly what he heard.

These three strands—the present-tense sections narrated in the first person by Adam, the present-tense transcripts of interview tapes, and the past-tense memories of Adam presented in the third person—are interwoven throughout the remaining thirty-one chapters of the novel. No strand contains direct references to the others, but characters and plot elements overlap to create a mysterious but unified story in the reader's mind. Perhaps the easiest way to understand how the plot unfolds is to trace each strand separately to the end of the novel.

The Tapes

The sixteen transcriptions of Brint's interrogation of Adam form a plot of their own, as Brint tries to see what Adam can remember of his past. In the first few tapes, Brint appears kind and sympathetic as he gently encourages Adam to see just one more thing. He occasionally suggests topics for discussion (for example, the person Paul Delmonte), but he quickly and calmly backs off whenever Adam resists.

In the fourth tape, Adam asks whether Brint is a doctor and if they are in a hospital. The reader will notice, though Adam does not appear to, that Brint does not answer these questions but deftly turns the conversation in another direction. From this point on, Brint takes a more active role in the interviews, steering the interviews toward topics of his choosing. His tone becomes edgier as he presses Adam to remember every detail of a phone call between his mother and aunt, a conversation between his father and Grey, or the contents of his father's desk drawer. It becomes clear that Brint is not interested in Adam's well-being; rather, Brint's goal is to determine whether Adam remembers any information about the corruption his father uncovered.

The last tape, TAPE OZK016, contains Brint's summary report of his third annual series of interrogations of Adam. He reports that Adam shows no memory of any information his father uncovered and speaks coldly of the earlier "termination of Witness #599–6 and affiliate (spouse)"—Adam's parents. He recommends that Grey (Personnel #2222) be reinstated since it cannot be proven that he aided in their murders. Finally, he recommends that Adam remain in confinement until "termination procedures are approved" or until he "obliterates."

Adam's Memories

Under Brint's interrogation, Adam remembers several key incidents from his past. He remembers walking to the library with his father one day when

Media Adaptations

- *I Am the Cheese* is available as an unabridged audiobook from Recorded Books, LLC. It was produced in 1994 and narrated by J. Woodman and J. Randolph Jones.

- *I Am the Cheese* was adapted as a commercial motion picture in 1983. Directed by Robert Jiras, the film stars Robert Wagner as Brint.

he was nine years old and his father's suddenly taking a detour through the woods. Adam was not sure why his father abruptly changed course but felt his father had seen or sensed danger.

At other times, Adam remembers Amy Hertz, his only friend. The two met at the library when they collided and dropped their books, and Amy soon became the person who drew Adam out of his isolation. She enjoyed pulling elaborate practical jokes that she called "Numbers," tricks like filling and abandoning grocery carts, or setting car radios in a parking lot on high volume. Amy inadvertently added to Adam's growing suspicions when she told him that she had met a man from Adam's hometown and that this man had never heard of Adam's family. As Adam's suspicions grew, however, something kept him from sharing his questions and his discoveries with Amy.

When Adam was fourteen, he became curious enough to look in his father's locked desk drawer. There he found two different birth certificates in his own name, listing two different dates of birth. Soon he discovered that, contrary to what his parents had always told him, he had a living relative, his mother's sister, whom his mother phoned once a week. Finally, this told him everything: The family's real name was not Farmer but Delmonte; Adam's birth name was Paul. David Delmonte, Adam's father, had been a newspaper reporter who had uncovered evidence of a link between organized crime and the government. After he testified before Congress, the family was given a new identity and moved to Monument, Massachusetts, where the mysterious Mr. Grey had kept an eye on them ever since.

Shortly after Adam/Paul learned the truth about his family, Mr. Farmer received instructions from Mr. Grey to take the family on a vacation. Adam and his parents headed for Vermont, singing and enjoying being together. When they stopped at a scenic overlook, another car deliberately ran into them, killing David's mother instantly. Adam's last memories were of his father running away and of Mr. Grey looking at his mother's body.

Adam's Bike Ride

In the present-tense sections of the novel, Adam continues his bike ride toward Rutterburg, Vermont, to bring his father a gift. He is lonely and frightened as he bikes along, but he bolsters his courage by singing "The Farmer in the Dell," the song his father used to sing on family outings, and by thinking about phoning Amy when she is home from school. Along the way, Adam encounters various hazards: a cold rain, two young men who chase and threaten him, another boy who steals his bike. At a pay phone he calls Amy's number, but a strange man answers. Puzzled, Adam keeps going. When he gets to a motel where he plans to spend the night, he is told that the motel has been closed for years—another mystery, since he recently stayed there with his parents.

Finally, Adam reaches Rutterburg, where he comes to a hospital and a doctor who calls him "Paul" and escorts him to his room. Apparently, Adam's bike trip has been mostly in his imagination—he has only been circling the hospital grounds. The package turns out to be Pokey the Pig, Adam's only source of comfort, and he is grateful to have it back in his arms. Lying in bed, Adam sings the last verse of "The Farmer in the Dell," in which "The cheese stands alone" and concludes, "I am the cheese." Chillingly, the last chapter of the novel occurs after Brint's last tape. It is just a paragraph, and it begins where the first chapter began: "I am riding the bicycle and I am on Route 31."

Characters

Brint

The man known only as Brint interrogates Adam on the interview tapes. At first he appears to be a psychiatrist, helping Adam remember his past. His tone is gentle and kind, and he encourages Adam to take his time. Gradually, it becomes clear

that he has his own agenda and that discovering what Adam can remember is perhaps more important to Brint than it is to the boy. As the reader begins to distrust Brint, so does Adam, and he resists answering Brint's questions. When Adam voices his mistrust or asks Brint a direct question about his intentions, Brint cleverly changes the subject, and Adam, in his drugged state, does not notice the deception. In the end, it appears that Brint is not a psychiatrist at all but a government investigator attempting to determine whether Adam ("Subject A") remembers anything incriminating.

Adam Farmer

Adam Farmer is the main character of the novel; he narrates one strand of the story in the first person and is the center of the action in the other two strands. Adam is a pleasant but shy and nervous boy who has few friends and little confidence. He is often afraid—of dogs, open spaces, closed spaces, "a thousand things." He wants to be a writer, like Thomas Wolfe. As he enters his teen years, he falls in love with Amy, who draws him out of his shell, and he begins to notice that his parents seem to have a secret. Slowly, he discovers that he was born with a different name (Paul Delmonte) and that he and his parents were relocated and given new identities by the government. In the "present" strands of the novel, Adam is riding his bike to visit his father in Rutterburg, Vermont, a town seventy miles away. In another strand of the novel, he is interrogated by a man named Brint, who wants to know what Adam remembers of his past. Gradually, it becomes clear that Adam/Paul is being held in some sort of mental institution, continually drugged. His bike trip, as is revealed at the end of the novel, occurs mostly in Adam's imagination. In fact, his father and his mother are dead. Remembering "The Farmer in the Dell," the song his father used to sing, Adam is the one who says to himself near the end of the novel, "I am the cheese"—the cheese that stands alone.

David Farmer

David Farmer, Adam's father, was born Anthony Delmonte, and until Adam/Paul was a toddler he was a newspaper reporter. When he discovered a connection between organized crime and government officials, he testified before Congress, was threatened, and had his wife and son relocated and renamed, along with himself, by the U.S. Department of Re-Identification. Since then, he has gone by the name Mr. Farmer, worked as an insurance agent, and kept in touch with the mysterious Mr. Grey. The relationship between Adam and his father is warm and close; they enjoy spending time together, and their love and respect is obvious. Adam's happiest memories are of his father leading the family in an off-key rendition of "The Farmer in the Dell." When Adam begins to unravel the family secret, Mr. Farmer tells him about the relocation but assures his son that the government is keeping them safe. Shortly afterward, however, the family is lured out of town and deliberately hit by a car. Adam's last memory is of his father running away from the scene of the accident, but Brint's final tape reveals that Mr. Farmer is dead.

Louise Farmer

Louise Farmer, Adam's mother, is a reclusive and frightened woman who keeps to the house most of the time. Until Adam begins to learn about the family's secret, he does not understand his mother's condition, but he is protective and loyal toward her. Mrs. Farmer, previously Louise Nolan Delmonte, has entered the witness protection program with her husband and son, but, unlike her husband, she has never trusted Mr. Grey or the government's promise to keep them safe. The product of an unhappy childhood and a life of struggle, she does not trust easily. She clings to her Catholic faith and attends Mass regularly. Occasionally she defies Mr. Grey in small ways, but the thought of putting her family in danger terrifies her. Her only relief from fear comes during the weekly phone call she is allowed to make to her sister, Martha, a cloistered nun. Her fears prove warranted at the end of the novel, when she is murdered in front of Adam.

Mr. Grey

The man Adam thinks of as Mr. Grey at first appears to be Mr. Farmer's boss in the insurance business. He visits Adam's father periodically, and the two men disappear into Mr. Farmer's basement office to talk business. In fact, Grey's name is really Thompson, and he is the government man responsible for keeping the Farmer/Delmonte family safe. It is Mr. Grey who tells them where to live, where and when to take a vacation, and when to be extra cautious. Adam's mother does not trust him, and her suspicions appear to be justified when Adam recognizes Mr. Grey at the scene of his mother's death. Brint also suspects that Grey ("Personnel #2222") may have had a hand in Adam's parents' deaths but concludes that there is no hard evidence to prove it.

Amy Hertz

Amy Hertz, daughter of the local newspaper editor, is confident where Adam is uncertain, cynical where he is trusting. She takes delight in breaking the rules by doing the mostly harmless practical jokes she calls "Numbers." Amy is important to Adam, first as his only real friend and later as his girlfriend. When Adam gets discouraged during his bike trip, the thought that he will be able to phone Amy gives him hope. When he does call her number, however, the man who answers does not know Amy—an early clue that the bike trip itself may not be what it seems. Amy, however, is above suspicion, the only person in Adam's life who is exactly who and what she appears to be.

Martha Nolan

Martha Nolan is Mrs. Farmer's older sister and only living relative, a cloistered nun living in Portland, Maine. After the family's relocation, Mr. Grey allows Mrs. Farmer to make one phone call per week to Martha, since Martha has no contact with the outside world and could not accidentally give anyone information about the Farmers. These Thursday phone calls are the only joy in Mrs. Farmer's week. When Adam eavesdrops on one of the phone calls, he learns for the first time that he also has a living relative, an aunt.

Themes

The Individual against Society

Like the central character of Cormier's earlier work, *The Chocolate War*, Adam Farmer confronts forces that are stronger than he is, and he ultimately faces them alone and loses. These forces in *I Am the Cheese* are all the more sinister because they are housed where Adam should be able to expect protection—in his own government and his psychiatrist—and because the danger arose only after Mr. Farmer committed a courageous and moral act.

For fourteen years, Adam's parents do their best to keep him safe. Mr. Farmer at first refuses the government's offer of a new identity, accepting only when he realizes that his wife and child are also in danger. In hiding, the Farmers seem in some ways to have a relatively normal life, and the scenes of the family laughing and singing "The Farmer in the Dell" are lighthearted and warm. However, their safety is in isolation. Mrs. Farmer does not join committees and make friends as Mrs. Hertz does; in fact, she almost never leaves the house. Mr. Farmer is cut off from his work as a writer. The family appears to have no living relatives, no friends, no neighbors to chat over the fence with.

Topics for Further Study

- If you were making a film version of *I Am the Cheese*, whom would you cast to play the part of Brint and how would you tell him to behave during his interrogations of Adam? Would you have him look menacing, or completely innocent? Would you make him clearly evil or kind, or would you leave room for the audience to wonder about his intentions?

- When *I Am the Cheese* was first published in 1977, some parents and teachers worried that the unhappy ending would be frightening and inappropriate for young adult readers. They also felt that the language and violence were inappropriate. Compare the novel to other books you have read or to movies or television shows you have seen. What age group do you think the book is best suited for? Explain your reasoning.

- *I Am the Cheese* is considered a novel specifically for young adults. What parts of the book make it especially appropriate for this audience? How do you think adults would respond to the novel?

- Research the psychological concept of repression. Why might Adam have a hard time remembering what happened to his parents? What kinds of medicine and other treatments might he be receiving to help him recover?

This isolation becomes a part of Adam's personality. Although he does not share his parents' fear of discovery, he is a frightened and shy child. Amy Hertz seems to be his first close friend, but, even as he comes to love her, he never confides in her. He and his parents are alone, with only Mr. Grey to protect them and connect them to the outside world.

Of course, as Mrs. Farmer suspects all along, Mr. Grey cannot (or will not) protect them. Although it is unclear whether Grey arranged the car accident or was trying to prevent it, he is there at the moment that Adam is finally separated from his parents. Now Adam is on his own, in the hands of a man who may or may not be a doctor, in a build-

ing that may or may not be a hospital, being given drugs that may help or harm him. No one is going to rescue Adam from his confinement because no one knows who or where he is. He will stay a prisoner until he either is "terminated" or he "obliterates." The idea of a teenage boy held prisoner by ruthless adults is made even more shocking by the mention of his only companion: Pokey the Pig. When the individual stands alone against a society this cruel, a serious question is raised about whether or not it is possibile for the individual to prevail.

Innocence and Experience

In many ways, *I Am the Cheese* is a typical coming-of-age story. During the course of the story, Adam ages from nine years old to about seventeen, and he begins to understand who and what he is. At nine, Adam walks with his father to the library and sees his father frightened for the first time. He also sees his father act bravely to fight off a dog. Typical for a nine-year-old, Adam accepts his father's explanation for the detour and does not challenge his father's plan for escaping the dog. At the corner of his mind, however, is the smallest doubt, which he later labels as his first "clue" that all is not as it appears to be. He is beginning to think of his parents as people who might have emotions, who might make mistakes. Adam is growing up.

When he is fourteen, Adam takes new strides toward adulthood. He befriends Amy Hertz and even falls in love with her, enjoying the sensations of kissing her and touching her breasts. For the first time, he feels a bit embarrassed about his mother's isolation. He dares to look in his father's locked drawer and then begins spying on his parents to learn their secrets. These are natural steps toward independence, as his father acknowledges: "It's your right to know. You're not a child anymore."

Style

Separate Threads

The most challenging element of *I Am the Cheese* is its three-part structure. Three separate threads, or strands, run side by side through the novel, and there is no omniscient narrator or author's note to explain the connections between them. First-time readers must be patient and allow the separate pieces to sort themselves out.

The book opens with an unnamed boy riding his bicycle toward his father in the hospital. Who is the boy? Why is his father in the hospital? There are no answers in this section, but there are two clues: the boy lives in Monument, Massachusetts, and he loves Amy Hertz. The next section is an interview between "T" and "A." "A" might be a clue to the boy's name, but then again it might not: the man identified as "T" calls himself "Brint," so the letters are not initials. The third section is a memory of a young boy lying in bed and overhearing a conversation between his parents. The young boy seems to be "A" from the interview, but is this the same boy who is riding a bike?

Gradually, the pieces come together. For the first four chapters the boy on the bike in the present tense is known only as "I" and the boy in the past tense is known only as "he." In the fourth chapter, Brint asks "A" if he would like to discuss Paul Delmonte, but "A" does not recognize the name. In the fifth chapter, the boy in the past-tense strand is identified as Adam Farmer, and it soon becomes clear that Adam Farmer is also the boy on the bike. Each chapter now brings new revelations and seems to offer new understanding until a later chapter shows that some of what seemed clear before is untrue. Adam Farmer does know Paul Delmonte. Mr. Grey is really Mr. Thompson. Mr. Farmer is not in a hospital. Adam is not riding his bike from Massachusetts to Vermont.

This complicated structure (which Cormier himself assumed was too complex for young readers to follow) serves at least two functions in the novel. Adam is given three separate voices: the present-tense first-person narrator voice, the voice on the tapes, and his voice in dialogue during the past-tense sections. These three voices are a testament to Adam's insanity: in his own mind, the three voices speak in turn, out of his control. He cannot control his own thoughts, his own memories. He has forgotten his identity. The three narratives also place the reader at a disadvantage. Like the Farmers, the reader is constantly off balance, unsure what to trust. This is Cormier's message, as spoken by the old man with the map: "Don't trust anybody." As the reader picks her way through the three narratives, she gathers clues and tries to interpret them, but she is frequently deceived. The structure of the novel echoes the structure of modern society: disjointed, deceptive, and beyond individual control.

Historical Context

New Realism

With works including *The Chocolate War* and *I Am the Cheese*, Cormier became associated with

a movement in young adult literature called new realism. Prior to the mid-1960s, most books written for young adults (that is, for readers in approximately grades six through twelve) had several elements in common: they featured protagonists who were white and from the middle class, mostly living with both parents in suburban neighborhoods; they dealt with themes of growing up and feeling alienated, but they ended with the conflicts resolved and young people feeling safe within their families; they avoided issues such as divorce, drug use, sexual exploration and orientation and other issues that teenagers deal with.

Many fine books that are still considered classics were written during the first half of the twentieth century, but in the 1960s a different kind of book began to appear. These books were categorized as a fresh movement called new realism, which dealt with controversial issues that previous books had avoided, spoke in an edgier tone, and maintained the undecorated approach of realism. Often, they did not end happily.

The idea of a literature intended for young adults is a relatively new one; in fact, the arrangement that teens would still live a protected life within their families and devote their energies primarily to education did not exist in the United States until the early twentieth century. As children stayed in school longer, instead of marrying or working in the factories to help support their families, teachers looked for literature that would address their particular concerns. As modern life brought with it new challenges and technologies for young people, including divorce, drugs, and contraception, books geared toward adolescents began exploring ways to confront contemporary life. Finally, as an awareness spread throughout the country that not all Americans are white, or well-off, and heterosexual, a wider range of protagonists and settings began to appear.

I Am the Cheese includes many of the features of new realism: a lonely protagonist with a difficult life, his growing awareness of both his sexuality and his independence, adults who cannot be relied on, language that reflects the way young people really spoke in 1977, a complex structure, and a decidedly dark tone and gloomy ending. Some felt at first that young people would be confused or harmed by these new approaches, but new realism has, according to most critics, brought refreshing changes to young adult literature.

Losing Faith in Government

The stereotypical image of the United States in the 1950s is of a land where all citizens were

Compare & Contrast

- **1970s:** The federal Witness Protection Program is new, and not many citizens have factual information about it. Its workings are mysterious, and the program itself seems more the material of fiction than of real life.

  Today: The witness protection program is frequently depicted in novels and films. Although most people still do not have any real knowledge of the program, the fact that it exists does not seem remarkable or frightening.

- **1970s:** Because of the Vietnam War and the Watergate incident with its revelation of deceit at the highest levels of government, the American people are distrustful of their government in a way that they have never been before. Cynicism like that experienced and described by Robert Cormier reaches new levels.

Today: Many people assume that politicians and government leaders are not completely honest, but this dishonesty does not frighten them as it once did. Surveys reveal that this lack of trust creates feelings of disengagement rather than fear.

- **1970s:** The technology of the day makes it easier for the Farmers to keep their secret. Mr. Farmer keeps his secret documents in a locked drawer, not on a computer, and there is no Internet to help Adam look up old records. As he bikes along, Adam knows he must wait for the next town with a pay phone to call Amy.

  Today: Computers, cell phones, mini cameras, and other technologies are found in many middle class homes like that of the Farmers.

---

happy and well fed and patriotic, and for many people this was true. With World War II over, there was an increased prosperity and a heightened sense that Americans had united and won over the enemy. The years just after the Vietnam War, however, created a different feeling in many Americans. That war did not end gloriously for the United States, and as journalists and activists investigated government documents, they revealed that the American people had been deceived in many ways about the conduct and results of the war. In 1972, when only a small number of U.S. troops remained in Vietnam, the Watergate burglary was discovered; this incident eventually led to President Richard Nixon resigning in disgrace and the imprisonment of several members of his staff. J. Edgar Hoover, the former head of the Federal Bureau of Investigation (FBI), died, and evidence began to surface that the FBI had for years used its powers illegally to harass and threaten U.S. citizens. A memo was discovered that showed that the Justice Department had traded a lawsuit settlement for campaign contributions. These and other events were at first shocking to the American people, but

gradually they became more cynical and distrusting of their government.

Robert Cormier was no exception. A journalist for over three decades, he knew very well that elected officials are not immune from corruption by money and power. He also witnessed small ways that the government has begun to intrude on our lives. In an interview with Geraldine DeLuca and Roni Natov, he describes his own paranoia about government intrusion, and explains "I wanted to portray the kind of fear that I think is in our lives today."

Critical Overview

Although *I Am the Cheese* has sold well and received several awards since its publication over twenty-five years ago, it was initially resisted by a significant number of teachers, librarians, and parents who felt that the book was unsuitable for young readers. Some objected to small elements in the novel, including a reference to Amy Hertz's breasts, which seemed at the time to be out of step with what was generally available for middle- and high-school readers. The biggest controversy, however, was over the tone of the novel and the decidedly unhappy ending. Believing that young readers should be protected from negative messages, many called for the book to be removed from classrooms and school libraries. The controversy over the relatively recent trend toward darker novels for young people is explained in Rebecca Lukens's essay "From Salinger to Cormier: Disillusionment to Despair in Thirty Years." Lukens, comparing three Cormier novels to J. D. Salinger's *The Catcher in the Rye*, shows that Salinger's central character "finds that he is his own best hope" and that "Cormier's characters come to no such faith." She concludes that "unlike Salinger who offers discovery, Cormier offers only despair."

Most critics, however, acknowledge the novel's dark vision but find redeeming qualities in it. In a 1977 review for the *Horn Book Magazine*, Paul Heins calls the book "a magnificent accomplishment" and "truly a novel in the tragic mode, cunningly wrought, shattering in its emotional implications." Clearly Heins, like many others, did not believe that young readers needed to be shielded from unpleasantness. Roger Sutton, in a 1982 review for *School Library Journal*, wrote that "under the grim, no-win surface lies a very conventional, respectable morality: wrong may triumph over right, but the reader is certainly shown which is which." Robert Bell, writing in 1978 for the *School Librarian*, admired the book greatly but issued one caveat: "Sixteen is young enough, I feel, for the harrowing experience of encountering this remarkably powerful book. Very strongly recommended, for any age beyond that."

Criticism

Cynthia Bily

Bily teaches writing and literature at Adrian College in Adrian, Michigan. In this essay, Bily examines the motif of the doppelgänger *in Cormier's novel.*

When Robert Cormier published *The Chocolate War* in 1974, and then *I Am the Cheese* in 1977, he was heralded (and scolded) for being part of a new trend in literature. This movement, which came to be known as new realism, was in fact new in many ways: it depicted life the way it really is for many people, with its struggles as well as its

Former U.S. President Richard Nixon, involved in Watergate, a scandal that caused Americans to lose faith in their government

joys, and it presented issues and ideas that had not been offered specifically to young readers before.

But like all literature that seems bound to last, *I Am the Cheese* was not entirely new. Literature is a conversation across the centuries and across cultural borders, and many of the ideas and motifs that most resonate with readers recur in new works, echoing the themes of past works. The idea, for example, that as readers of *I Am the Cheese* we feel pity for Adam and his fear and despair was first described more than twenty-three hundred years ago by the Greek philosopher Aristotle, who called works that elicit these feelings tragedies. In writing his tragedy, Cormier created a new character in a new setting, but one who follows an ancient path to destruction. Another motif that connects *I Am the Cheese* with literature from the past is the use of the *doppelgänger*, or the double.

The word *doppelgänger* is a German word, meaning "double walker." The experience of meeting one's double is found in folk tales and fairy tales from around the world, but it was German writers of the nineteenth century who gave us the term. The *doppelgänger* as a literary motif was especially fascinating to writers in the nineteenth

> In Western literature, the appearance of the *doppelgänger* is never a happy occurrence; it is a sign that calamity, usually death or insanity, is near."

century, even before modern psychological theories argued that what we think of as the self is really made up of several selves. The most well-known example is Robert Louis Stevenson's 1886 novel *The Strange Case of Dr. Jekyll and Mr. Hyde*, in which a scientist succeeds in separating his own impulses for good and evil into two distinct personalities. Edgar Allan Poe's 1839 short story "William Wilson" features a man who is tormented by his *doppelgänger* in the form of another man, who reappears throughout his life—unless he is only imagining it. Often, meeting one's double is a sign that death will soon follow, but in Charles Dickens's 1859 novel *A Tale of Two Cities*, Charles Darnay is saved by his double, Sydney Carton. Other examples include Fyodor Dostoyevsky's *The Double* (1846) and Joseph Conrad's "The Secret Sharer" (1912). All of these writers used the *doppelgänger* to depict in a concrete way the complex psychological divisions within one character.

In *I Am the Cheese*, nearly every character has a double, and several characters cross paths with multiple versions of themselves. Because of the witness relocation program, every member of the Farmer family has two identities, or two selves: Adam David Farmer is also Paul Delmonte; Louise Holden Farmer is also Louise Nolan Delmonte; David Farmer is also Anthony Delmonte. The Delmonte selves are like and unlike the Farmer selves. Louise Delmonte loved her small town and the people in it. She was happy and young, and she laughed frequently. Louise Farmer is a very different person. Adam wonders sometimes what has happened "to transform his mother from the laughing, tender woman to whom the scent of lilac clung into the pale and subdued and antiseptic woman who seldom left the house, who lurked behind window curtains." Louise Farmer is a mirror image of Louise Delmonte. She looks just like her other self, but she is her own opposite. David Farmer is similarly a

reflection of Anthony Delmonte. Instead of his beloved career as a journalist, he earns his living now as an insurance agent, doing work he does not find satisfying. Whereas he was once brave enough to stand up to the government, he is now afraid of strangers on the street.

Each of Adam's parents also has another double, a person living in Monument who seems to demonstrate what life could have been like. Amy's father works for the town newspaper, doing the work that Mr. Farmer wishes he could return to, and his only mention in the novel is when he entertains another newspaperman from the town where Adam supposedly was born. At the time, Adam does not realize the cruel irony of the situation. Amy's mother has the kind of active life Adam's mother gave up. When Adam first meets her, she is on the phone arranging a committee meeting and then running out the door to another meeting. Mr. and Mrs. Hertz are minor characters whose absence would not have changed the overall plot of the novel. Cormier seems to have included them primarily to serve as *doppelgängers*, to emphasize what might have been, and to heighten our pity at what Adam's parents have lost.

Adam also has an old identity as Paul Delmonte When he first learns about his old name, it casts into doubt his entire sense of self:

> . . . a small part of him was isolated and alone, a part that was not Adam Farmer any longer but Paul Delmonte. I am Paul Delmonte, a voice whispered inside of him. . . . Then who is Adam Farmer? Where did he come from?

For a while he is uneasy and has to reassure himself that "I am the same person I have been for fourteen years." At times, however, he finds his secret exciting, something to brag about. He is afraid that he might place Amy in danger by telling her his secret, by announcing, "Look, Amy, I'm not just shy and awkward Adam Farmer, but a fugitive on the run, leading a double life. I am Paul Delmonte."

Like his parents, Adam also has another *doppelgänger* living in Monument: Amy Hertz. Amy is in some ways just like Adam and in some ways his opposite. The first time they meet, it is as though Adam bumps into a mirror: "She was going into the Monument Public Library and he was coming out and they collided at the door. The books they held in their arms spilled all over the place." In a Gothic horror story, we would never be sure whether Amy was a figment of Adam's imagination, but this Amy seems quite real. Still, Adam could not invent a better alter ego: she likes books, as he does, but she is brave where he is timid, full of laughter where he is withdrawn. Only once he meets Amy, his double, does he find the confidence and the brashness to become a spy in his own home.

The first-time reader of *I Am the Cheese* is not aware of it, but nearly every person Adam meets on his bike ride also has a double. When he finally arrives at the "hospital," he encounters people who are strangely reminiscent of people he meets on his trip, and it gradually becomes clear that he has imagined most of what we assumed happened to him during the journey. The nice old man with the map who helps Adam think through his route is really Mr. Harvester, the maintenance man at the hospital. The dog who chases Adam's bicycle, "a German shepherd, sleek and black, a silent sentinel guarding the driveway of a big white house," is Silver, the dog who lives on the hospital grounds and who "delights in chasing people and knocking them down." In a "small restaurant, a lunchroom really," Adam is harassed by three tough boys, Whipper, Dobbie and Lewis, until Luke the counterman puts down the phone and intercedes; in fact, Whipper, Dobbie, and Lewis are also among the "troubled people" who live at the hospital, and Luke is the switchboard operator who sometimes helps serve meals. And so on. Like the Farmers, and like Mr. Grey, none of the people Adam meets is who she or he appears to be.

It seems clear that Adam has created these *doppelgängers*, these dual identities, to serve a psychological need of his own. He has repressed the memories of the car accident that was not an accident, and though he is sure that his mother is dead, he cannot remember how he knows this. He wants to believe that he is riding to see his father and bringing something of value to him. So he gets on his bike with his own most valued possession, Pokey the Pig, and rides around and around the hospital grounds. And he creates another reality and other identities to make his life less painful. In Western literature, the appearance of the *doppelgänger* is never a happy occurrence; it is a sign that calamity, usually death or insanity, is near. As the last chapters of the novel show, Adam is very close to the end, either through termination or obliteration, when his world of *doppelgängers* is revealed.

But answering the question of why Adam imagines or creates doubles for the people around him raises another, fascinating question: What else has he created? If the entire bike trip happened only in his imagination, what reason is there to believe that the events in the novel's other strands actually happened?

The doctor at the hospital calls the boy "Paul." Could the boy have created the identity of Adam Farmer out of his imagination? Poe's "William Wilson" is also told by a first-person narrator, and by the end of the story there is great doubt as to whether he has actually met another man who is his double or whether his insanity has only led him to think so. Could the same be true of Adam/Paul?

The fact is, we can never know. Was Adam Farmer created by Mr. Grey or by Paul Delmonte? ("Who is Adam Farmer? Where did he come from?") Are the tapes verifiable documentation that something actually occurred to Subject A, perhaps at the hand of Personnel #2222 (also known as Mr. Grey and as Thompson), or is the sly reference to *The Wizard of Oz* in the "OZK series tapes" a hint that, like Dorothy's experiences, it has all been a dream? Cormier has layered so many levels of duplicity and deceit that it is impossible to tell. Either the government agencies in charge of protecting the Delmonte family are so intrusive and so false that nothing that touches them can be trusted, or the entire novel is the result of the wandering imagination of an insane child. Neither is a comforting thought. With the motif of the *doppelgänger*, Cormier participates in a long literary tradition, even as he locates his novel in the terrifying double world of modern society.

Source: Cynthia Bily, Critical Essay on *I Am the Cheese*, in *Novels for Students*, Gale, 2003.

Maia Pank Mertz

In the following essay excerpt, Mertz discusses how I Am the Cheese *can be used to study literary style and structure.*

I am the Cheese is consistently one of the most difficult novels for my college students, yet also one of their favorite works for analysis. Cormier's novel is particularly appropriate for dealing with two concepts that inexperienced readers seem to find particularly elusive: *style* and *structure*. Because a number of essays have analyzed Cormier's work, and this novel in particular, I will try to avoid repeating what has been stated elsewhere. The most recent study of Cormier is Patricia J. Campbell's *Presenting Robert Cormier* (1990), one of the books in the Laurel-Leaf Library of Young Adult Authors. In her chapter on *I am the Cheese*, Campbell states that the "triple strands that are braided together to make the story, the three alternating levels on which the narrative progresses, are an intricate but internally consistent device." According to Campbell, these are the three levels of narrative:

> It speaks to readers of all ages about the loss of innocence and the pervasive nature of evil in current society. But only through an analysis of its literary elements is it possible for young readers to understand why it is a powerful work."

The bike ride is told in first-person present tense. The tapes, as dialogue, have neither person nor tense (but we assume they are happening in the present), and the revelation of Adam's past that grows out of these tapes proceeds chronologically and is in third-person past tense.

Structurally, then, there are three levels of story, and three points of view. As Campbell notes, this is extremely confusing when the novel is read for the first time. Only in subsequent readings does it become possible to see the relationships that exist among the various levels of story. Campbell describes the novel as a mosaic. My students compare it to a jigsaw puzzle, a puzzle that is extremely difficult to put together because the pieces are so varied. In fact, one student noted that even when the last piece is in place, the "picture" is still not clear. But good novels, like good puzzles, became easier to "put together" the more we work with them.

Although the internal structure of the novel is complex, the external structure—the juxtaposition of the "tapes" with the bike journey and the past—provides a means to start discussions of structure. After reading the first two chapters, readers can begin to understand how the writer is using the different levels and points of view to move the story forward. What emerges, then, is a structure or form that is integral to the story. In effect, form and content merge. The way the story is told is essential to the content of the story. A clear example of how the structure relates to the story is that the opening lines of the novel are repeated at the end. The story is cyclical. Like Adam's interrogations, it begins anew.

If structure is the overall form of the story, the design that the author has used, *style* constitutes the manner of expression that the writer has chosen to tell the story. Young readers seem to understand the term best when it is simply described as *how* the writer tells the story. Consistently, Cormier's style captures the pace and intensity of the events in the story. For example, the opening is extremely powerful.

I am riding the bicycle and I am on Route 31 in Monument, Massachusetts, on my way to Rutterburg, Vermont, and I'm pedaling furiously because this is an old-fashioned bike, no speeds, no fenders, only the warped tires and the brakes that don't always work and the handlebars with cracked rubber grips to steer with. A plain bike—the kind my father rode as a kid years ago. It's cold as I pedal along, the wind like a snake slithering up my sleeves and into my jacket and my pants legs, too. But I keep pedaling, I keep pedaling.

The first sentence parallels the "furious" pace of the boy pedaling the bike. There is an urgency in the tone, an urgency that couches something overtly evil—"like a snake slithering up my sleeves." The alliteration of that phrase—when read out loud it sounds ominously like hissing—presents even to the most inexperienced reader a sense of foreboding. Throughout the novel, Cormier is able to capture the mood of a scene by his powerful use of language. For example, he conveys the cold, clinical, almost mechanistic tone of the taped interviews through brief, abrupt dialogue.

A: It's hazy—just a series of impressions.
T: Let the impressions come.
(5-second interval)
A: That night—
T: Tell me about that night.

These clinical interviews are juxtaposed against vivid descriptions of Adam in the clinic: "He was in bed and the sheets were twisted around him and his body was hot, his eyes like raw onions, head aching. He cried out once or twice, softly, tentatively." Early in the novel the inhumanity toward Adam becomes apparent.

Throughout the novel, Cormier is able to enhance our knowledge of *what* happens by his vivid descriptions. One of the most memorable is the description of the car accident.

Into them. Into his father, his mother, himself. The car smashing, shattering. A flash of steel, sun glinting, and he felt himself, crazily, moving through the air, no feeling, no pain, no sense of flight, but actually in the air, not flying but moving as if in slow motion, everything slowed down, tumbling now and twisting and in the tumbling and the twisting he saw his mother die. Instantly.

The one-word sentence, "Instantly," punctuates the almost dreamlike slow motion of the accident itself. It is final. As he says at the end of this passage, "He looked at his mother, her head at the wrong angle, a rag doll tossed away." His mother's lifeless body is like a child's toy—limp, with eyes that are "sightless, vacant." The horror of the accident is conveyed by altering the pace of the description and by evoking parallels that all readers can understand. By comparing the dead mother to a rag doll, Cormier assures a strong emotional response from readers.

Although the novel is complex both structurally and thematically, it has some very simple and obvious literary elements that are worthwhile noting. The use of names, for instance, is relatively easy for students to analyze. The name "Grey," for example, embodies the ambiguities of good and evil; he also represents the unknown, the "grey" areas of life. "Adam" is the symbol of innocence because of the biblical allusion and also because children traditionally represent innocence in fiction. "Farmer," the name given Adam's family to replace their real name, Delmonte, also evokes purity. Throughout the American literary tradition, the country, embodied in the farmer, has epitomized innocence because to work with the earth is to be in contact with God.

The analyses that this novel has received since its publication attest to its power and sophistication. Adults as well as adolescents are challenged by its structure, style, and theme. It speaks to readers of all ages about the loss of innocence and the pervasive nature of evil in current society. But only through an analysis of its literary elements is it possible for young readers to understand why it is a powerful work.

Source: Maia Pank Mertz, "Enhancing Literary Understandings through Young Adult Fiction," in *Publishing Research Quarterly*, Vol. 8, No. 1, Spring 1992, pp. 23–33.

Jean W. Ross

In the following Contemporary Authors (CA) *interview, Ross presents an interview with Robert Cormier that was conducted by telephone on April 13, 1987.*

CA: After three novels and many short stories for adults, The Chocolate War *was a resounding success and placed you solidly as a writer for young adults. It wasn't a label you'd consciously sought. How do you feel about it now, and how much does it influence the actual writing?*

Cormier: Sometimes I'm of two minds about it. On the one hand, this label has gained me a terrific audience of young people, and I know the success of my career has turned on that audience. I

> " I don't have to simplify stories. I write as if the audience didn't exist, really. I've aimed for the intelligent reader and have often found that that reader is fourteen years old."

hear from them all the time, letters and phone calls, and I do a lot of speaking at schools and libraries, which I enjoy very much doing. So it has been very good. The only qualm I do have is that I think the label does limit my audience. I really don't feel that I write young adult books, and I think a lot of adults who might read them stay away from them because of the label. But that is the only detrimental effect I can come up with.

In terms of my own writing, the beautiful part of it is that I can still write and have this audience and yet not limit my plots or my subtleties. I don't have to simplify stories. I write as if the audience didn't exist, really. I've aimed for the intelligent reader and have often found that that reader is fourteen years old.

CA: You told Victoria Irwin for the Christian Science Monitor *that you enjoy writing about young people because you feel an affinity for them. Did that come primarily from having your own children?*

Cormier: Yes, I think it definitely did. First of all, it comes from memories of my own teenage years. If I have total recall of anything, it's not facts and figures but the way those years were, and not ever wanting to go through them again. Then when my own children became teenagers, I saw them going through the same things I'd gone through and realized that they were universal and timeless. Seeing my own children renewing those adolescent years did lead me to start writing about them—but not for them. The short stories prior to *The Chocolate War* in which I dealt with young people were inspired by that same combination of my children's experiences and my memories of my own.

CA: Yes. You explained in the introductions to the stories collected in Eight Plus One *how things that happened to your children played a part in your writing, and* The Chocolate War *grew out of an experience your son Peter had. How have your children responded to your books?*

Cormier: They're very supportive. One thing that makes a parent feel good is doing something that makes his children proud of him. They've all been avid readers, so my having achieved a reputation as a writer has made them very proud. And it's always been a family affair anyway. While they were growing up, I was writing all the time. They shared the bad times, the rejections, as well as the good times when a sale would come along and we'd go out and have a family dinner to celebrate, or go shopping and buy gifts. They've always been very much a part of the writing.

CA: And you've more than once spoken of the support your wife has given.

Cormier: Oh yes. In fact, I've always thought my wife would have made a great editor, because she has a very discerning eye. She reads my work before anyone else sees it. It's terrific to have a built-in editor, and someone that you trust. She does the final manuscript typing, and then I usually circulate it among my children prior to publication.

CA: In what ways have you found your newspaper work helpful in writing fiction?

Cormier: The main thing, I think, is the discipline it establishes. In newspaper work you write to a deadline; you write every day, when you don't feel like writing. You have to write economically, and sometimes to order. You may cover a lengthy story and then be told to cut it down to two pages. I think a lifetime of doing that carries over to my own work. I find that discipline seems to be such a problem, not only with myself, but with other people. I know a lot of talented people who never seem to get around to writing something. I have always been able to do this on weekend and nights. Besides the discipline I've gotten from the newspaper work, there's that direct journalistic style, which I still use to some extent. I use a lot of similes and metaphors, figures of speech, but essentially my style is very direct, and I strive for clarity. I think that comes out of my newspaper work, making the story real to the reader without any embellishment. In fiction, though, you can embellish somewhat and be more creative.

CA: The subconscious plays a great part in your writing, as you've described it. Are there ways you can aid and abet that faculty so that it can keep working at its best for you?

Cormier: I think why I like novel writing in contrast to short story writing is that your charac-

ters are developed, and then they're sort of with you all the time, the way friends would be with you. And sometimes the best idea of what a character should do in the plot comes when I'm driving the car downtown or something like that. In terms of a schedule, I don't think of what I have to write on a given day. For instance, when I sat down this morning at the typewriter, I wasn't thinking in terms of having to write five pages or ten pages, but of what the characters were going to do. That's how they become real and stay with you.

I think the subconscious works in another way. I usually look at the writing late at night before I go to bed and begin writing again in the morning. I have a feeling something happens while I sleep. This night-morning habit sets up a continuity and a momentum, and I'm sure the subconscious has a part in that. It's hard to trace it, but I know that if I'm away from the work for a while, like on an extended trip, it's harder getting back in the swing of things, because the characters start fading in my mind.

In an interview with Paul Janeczko for English Journal *you said that you write to communicate the emotions of your characters. How emotionally involved with them do you become in the writing?*

Cormier: Very emotionally involved, really. Often things happen to them that upset me, that I don't want to happen. I was greatly affected by Kate's death in *After the First Death*, and the death of the little boy, Raymond. When I realized that the situation was set up so that a child would have to be murdered in cold blood, I really was aghast that I'd written myself in to that kind of corner. Knowing what had to happen when I saw Kate's fate developing, knowing that she would ultimately and ironically do something that would cause her death, really bothered me. You do get involved with your characters, which is sometimes a hard thing for people who don't write to understand. I've said this at symposiums, and people look at me strangely. It doesn't bother me as much as if real people die, not to that extent. But it does affect me.

CA: Is your own emotion during the writing a measure of how well a story is working?

Cormier: Yes, definitely. In fact, I abandoned a novel a couple of years ago because of that. I thought it was a very clever plot, and I still think it's a very clever plot, with a couple of great psychological twists. My protagonist was a middle-aged man, and frankly I was not emotionally involved with him. So he began to bore me, and I just abandoned the novel. Because I wasn't emotionally involved with the character in that novel, it was more or less hack work, being clever. I think writing is more than that.

CA: I Am The Cheese *is a difficult book not only emotionally, but also in terms of plot. Patricia J. Campbell discussed it quite intelligently in* Presenting Robert Cormier. *Do readers have a hard time with it?*

Cormier: Yes, they do. I receive an awful lot of mail, and a good deal of it concerns *I Am the Cheese*. A typical letter from a fourteen-year-old might say, "Dear Mr. Cormier: I just read *I Am the Cheese*. I read it twice. Will you please answer the following questions ..." Then there's a long list of questions. And it's difficult for adults as well. There is a degree of ambiguity in it in the first place; all the questions aren't answered in the story. It's a funny thing about the writing. I wonder sometimes how I might have written a book if I had known the effect it would have on people. Writing is so private; even though you're writing for publication, at the time you're doing it you're not thinking of people reacting in a certain way. So when I see these questions come in, I wonder whether I might have clarified it a bit more. I'm not sure whether I would or not.

CA: What do you hope readers will get from the books?

Cormier: I really try to affect them emotionally, to get some kind of reaction. I hope a book will linger with the reader. I'm not writing to make people feel good, and I think indifference would be the worst of all. I'd rather have a critical review than no review. I'm happy to have people put down the book and say, "Yes, that's the way it could happen. I don't *like* what happened, but that's the way it *could* happen.

CA: There's so much dishonesty between adults and young people, as you've said yourself. Adults like to say, "These are the happiest years of your life," and that's usually not true.

Cormier: Yes. Kids are told that all the time. I was told that. I thought, something's got to be wrong, because these are terrible years. They had their peaks and pits, but there were so many pits! And you're not in control of your life. There's no perspective. They tell you they want you to be responsible people, and then they tell you to be in at eleven o'clock. There are all these dichotomies at work. I think some of the dishonesty comes from adults wanting to protect their children from certain realities, to sugar-coat what's going on. I used

to be told, "You won't remember this on your wedding day." It didn't help at the moment, when I was really lacerated by something.

CA: No. And once you begin to get smart, you just think you're being lied to a lot.

Cormier: Yes. I think kids are being lied to so much. In fact, they become accustomed to the lies, like the television lie that the good guy wins at the end of the program, the heroes of "Miami Vice" go on forever. They're even lied to in the commercials. Everybody knows that buying the right deodorant is not going to win you love. There's a continual lying going on, and they're adjusting to that. So when they read a realistic book, they cling to it and think, here's someone telling the truth. This is reflected in the letters I get from young people. So many readers say, "You tell it the way it is." That's very gratifying, because I get so many complaints from adult would-be censors.

CA: Speaking of television, one criticism that's made constantly of young people is that they watch television instead of reading. Do you consider television a competitor with your books?

Cormier: It is such a visual world, it's so hard to avoid it. But somebody's reading out there, because kids are reacting. I know a lot of my books are in the classroom, so kids are getting them from teachers. I'd say yes, obviously the kids are watching television, and they can't be reading a book at the same time. We are creating a visual need. On MTV, they're aiming for an attention span of about three minutes. It is having an effect. But thank goodness there are still young people who love to pick up a good book at the library and rush home with it. And there are a number of them around, according to the mail I get.

CA: Do troubled young people call or write for help?

Cormier: Not very often. When it does happen, it really shakes me up emotionally. I received a phone call last year from a girl in a psychiatric clinic in Connecticut who got a great deal of comfort out of *I Am the Cheese* because she felt that she was without identity, much like Adam, in a world she hadn't made. We spoke for probably a half-hour. Occasionally I'll go into a school and someone will mention a problem. But it's rare. Most of the letters I get are from kids who just want to touch base, and probably want to be writers, so they don't bring up problems. They may say there's a situation in their school something like one I've written about, but they really don't ask my advice about personal problems.

CA: You were reluctant to do a sequel to The Chocolate War, *but* Beyond the Chocolate War *apparently kept tugging at you. After the second book, do you feel through with the characters and the story?*

Cormier: I thought I was! I wrote *Beyond the Chocolate War* after being badgered by young people for years and years asking what happened to the characters from *The Chocolate War*, and I wanted to find out. I thought I had closed the door on them; by the time I had finished the second book, I was kind of weary of Archie Costello and company. But again they're asking questions. And I'm kind of intrigued with Archie; I sometimes wonder what he would be like a few years into the future—say at twenty-eight. And Jerry Renault still intrigues me. He seemed to develop more for me in the sequel than he did in the original book. It's been on my mind. Who knows? It took me ten years to get around to *Beyond the Chocolate War*. I have no immediate plans for another book on the topic, but I must say those characters are pretty much alive to me. But then some of the characters from the other books are alive to me even now, and I haven't felt any compulsion to write about them.

CA: Maybe that's a sign that they're good characters, they're real.

Cormier: I hope so. There was a very minor character in *The Chocolate War*, Tubs Casper, who appeared for one scene. The kids invariably asked about him and what happened to him, almost to the point of being angry with me for introducing him and not bringing him back. And in a way, even though I felt bad that I hadn't brought him back, it delighted me that the character became so real from that one simple scene. It's great when your characters really have life.

CA: How do you feel about Anne Scott MacLeod's definition, in Children's Literature in Education, *of your novels as "at bottom, political," because you are "far more interested in the systems by which society operates than . . . in individuals"?*

Cormier: First of all, I'm always conscious of being a storyteller, and stories turn on creating real characters. I have themes or issues that I'm interested in as an individual, and if I can bring them into play, fine. Even writing about a chocolate sale in high school, I suddenly realized that I was exploring the abuse of power, intimidation, things like that. But those aren't my primary concerns. I'm always most concerned with the story itself and the people, creating people who really live and affect the reader. A story doesn't work at all unless the

character are real. I don't think of myself as a thematic writer or as writing primarily to explore current issues or to expose things going on in the world. This is secondary. And while I hope it's there on a secondary level and can be explored and communicated, I think of myself primarily as a storyteller.

CA: Do you think criticism in the field of young adult literature is generally good?

Cormier: I think there are some very good things being done now. The Twayne series of biographies of young adult writers, of which mine is one, I think is a good step ahead. The *ALAN Review*, which concentrates on young adult books, has some great articles. *VOYA (Voice of Youth Advocates)* does a fine job. Slowly but surely, I think, the critical writing is becoming much more widespread and better than it was a few years ago. I think the best critical writing is the kind that illuminates the work for the subject. Patricia Campbell did that in her Twayne book; she made some links that surprised me. That kind of criticism is valid, but sometimes I read something I'm very puzzled about, because it wasn't anything that I had in mind. Often critics look for symbolism in things that really don't exist. And yet I think there are some subconscious things that get into the books that I'm probably not even aware of.

CA: Much of the critical writing on your work has dealt with its bleakness, and you have countered the criticism in various ways, depending on the specific circumstances. How would you respond to the charge now, considering the body of your work at this point?

Cormier: I guess my attitude hasn't changed. I've never let the criticism affect my writing. I think there are values in my work that go beyond the bleakness. I'm so used to hearing that criticism, I really don't give it much thought. If I feel I'm doing my job honestly, being faulted for other things doesn't bother me. And I didn't set out to explore a whole bleak landscape in a body of work. When I wrote *The Chocolate War*, I wasn't aware that I was going to write *I Am the Cheese*. I didn't feel the books were that similar when I was writing them. The thing I've always been afraid of is rewriting the same novel; that's why I hesitated to do a sequel to *The Chocolate War*. That's one of the reasons why Jerry was such a problem: I didn't want to bring him back to Trinity, because I thought then I would just be writing *The Chocolate War* all over again. So I've been careful about that, even though people have looked at my writing as a body of work and seen similarities. I try to make each novel as different as possible. But maybe I haven't. It's always how the reader sees it.

The novel that I'm now working on is different from the work that is recent, at least. It's not because I was trying to strike out in any particular direction; it's something that took hold of me emotionally at a particular time in my life. I just go to the typewriter every day, and characters come to life for me to write about.

Source: Jean W. Ross, "Interview with Robert Cormier," in *Contemporary Authors New Revision Series*, Vol. 23, Gale Research, 1988, pp. 87–94.

Patricia J. Campbell

In the following essay, Campbell explores how subsequent readings of I Am the Cheese, *while not involving the surprise of a first reading, allow readers to recognize clues and appreciate the literary structure of the novel.*

TAPE YAK 001

P: Stop.

R: You mean stop reading?

P: Yes. You, the reader. Right here. First, before you go on, you must answer one question.

R: What do you want to know?

P: Have you read *I Am the Cheese* yet?

R: No. I thought I'd read this chapter first.

P: That would be a great pity. It would spoil things for you—the suspense, the intriguing perplexities, the myriad shocks of discovery, the false leads—in a word, the fun. I would emphatically advise that you make the journey with Adam before you cover the same ground a second time with me.

R: All right.

P: Excellent. We shall continue afterwards. Let us suspend now.

END TAPE YAK 001

And so, having finished the book, the reader is irresistibly compelled to turn back to the beginning and, like Adam, begin all over again. The story circles back on itself, revolving like the wheels of a bicycle, like children in a ring playing "The Farmer in the Dell." But for the reader, unlike Adam, each time the experience is different.

The first time through, we know only what Adam knows. Our blank spaces are his, and the truth comes to us—and to him—in a series of disorienting jolts. As the *New York Times* said, "the book is assembled in mosaic fashion: a tiny chip here, a chip there, and suddenly the outline of a face dimly begins to take shape. Everything is related to something else...." But this is far too simple a description. Perry Nodelman, in his incisive article "Robert Cormier Does a Number," has attempted to analyze the complex and unsettling experience of a first reading of *I Am the Cheese*.

A reader's first impulse, Nodelman observes, is to approach the story as a logical, detached detective. The key, it seems, is in understanding the events of the mysterious past. But this leads to anxiety, disorientation, and confusion—"that uncertainty we call suspense"—because the events of the present are not clear. "Since we do not know what effects the mysterious past we are trying to understand led to, we act less with the cool certainty of mystery novel detectives than with the anxiety of confused people asked to think logically about incomplete information. That sounds uncomfortable—and it is. Cormier cleverly makes us accept and enjoy our confusion by providing *one* genuine past ... and what appear to be *two* different presents that that past led to. ... With our attention focused on sorting such things out, looking for clues and making guesses, we accept our uncertainty about present circumstances as part of the pleasure of the mystery."

The one possibility that never occurs to us, continues Nodelman, is that both presents are happening at once, that Adam is at the same time on a journey to Rutterburg and being interrogated by Brint. "Cormier cannot allow us to consider it, for it depends on our knowledge that the bike trip is a fantasy, knowledge that is the key to the entire mystery. He deflects our attention from the literal truth of the novel, the impeccably chronological ordering of events that seem to have no chronology, by making them seem to have no chronology. How Cormier manipulates readers into believing the wrong things and ignoring the right ones is fascinating to explore."

A close look at the two opening chapters, first as a novice and then as an experienced reader of *I Am the Cheese*, will illustrate this process. In the beginning we know only that someone is riding a bicycle from Monument to Rutterburg. Who? Why? A young person, evidently, who has been close enough to his father still to want to use an old bike like his, even though it makes him pedal "furiously"—a strangely intense word. The rhythm of the paragraph suggests the steady pumping of his legs. Then the first tiny hint of something sinister: "the wind like a snake slithering up my sleeves."

In the second paragraph we learn that the sight of a hospital reminds the rider of his father in

Rutterburg. Is he ill there? Is the journey to visit him? Whatever it is, it must be urgent because the cyclist accelerates his pedaling at the thought. Then another hint of chill—the rotten October. The love of Thomas Wolfe that the cyclist has shared with his father confirms our guess about their relationship, and the elderly phrase used to describe a teacher—"he regarded me with suspicion"—tells us that the person is a student, young but bookish and probably solitary. And he is kind—he waves when he passes a child who looks lonesome. But why does he think someone might be following him? Now he tells us he didn't wave good-bye to anybody when he left on this trip. Why not? Where were they? This is not the kind of person who skips school and goes away without at least telling someone. It doesn't fit. We begin to feel puzzled.

Immediately, Cormier gives us what seems to be an explanation of sorts: the irrational fears, and later, the pills, tell us that the bike rider has emotional problems. But why? Other questions come fast now. What is the gift? Why are his father's clothes in the cellar? If he has money, why doesn't he take the bus?—his reasons ring a bit hollow. Why is it so important that he go on his own power? And why must he do it this way "for his father"? The intensity of his determination seems inappropriate—but perhaps it is a sign of his unbalanced state.

Then another character is introduced: Amy Hertz. She, we know immediately, is a very different kind of person. "What the hell, as Amy says, philosophically." A tough, cocky, self-assured sort of person. The fact that such a girl is the object of the bike rider's love tells us more about his needs (and also confirms that he is a young *man*). But his reasons for not phoning her before he leaves seem logical. When he dumps his pills into the garbage disposal he seems "reckless and courageous" to us as well as to himself, and when a car howls its horn at him "for straying too far into the roadway" we think it is a result of that recklessness. It becomes apparent that the journey is going to be long and grueling, and as the boy struggles through, breaks free, and is off on his way, we are too busy exulting with him to notice that we have been left with a double handful of unanswered questions.

The second chapter clarifies nothing; indeed, it adds a second layer of perplexities. The preceding chapter was in the present tense, and so is this one, at first. Has the boy been in some sort of an accident that has put him here in the hands of a doctor? Or is this even the same boy? Is one of the chapters a flashback to the other? Which? The form

is even more puzzling. It seems to be some sort of official record of a tape recording, but for what possible reason can the date have been deleted? Why is the questioner labeled "T" when his name is Brint? Does it stand for "tape"? Or "therapist," perhaps? (Cormier himself has said that he used "T" because it is the *last* letter of Brint's name—but, then, can that statement be part of the Number?) Even for a psychiatrist his speech is strangely stilted and formal: "shall," "I have been advised," and that ominous phrase from the torture chamber, "the better it will be for you." But when the questioning turns to the boy's earliest memories we are on familiar ground again. Isn't that how people always begin with a therapist? Even the sense of menaced flight that pervades the boy's story could be explained by his mental illness, as could his perception of Brint as threatening. Except for two disquieting details: the cigarettes that his father never again smoked, and the way Brint pounces on the word *clues*. When the boy dissolves in panic, almost, but not quite, we believe in Brint's benevolence when he says, " Everything's going to be all right." But there have been no answers to some basic questions, nor will there be any until many, many pages later. As Nodelman says, "novelists usually make us ask such questions at the beginnings of novels, in order to arouse our interest. But they usually quickly answer them, and then focus our attention on new developments . . . In keeping us in the dark . . . Cormier extends throughout most of *I Am the Cheese* the disorientation we usually stop feeling a short way into other novels."

"A second reading . . . is a different experience. Now the novel seems filled with clues, with obvious evidence of what seemed incomprehensible before, and with huge ironies." All of Adam's forgotten past is still available to us, and we can see his buried knowledge at work on the fabric of his fantasy. As he goes about his preparations for the journey to Rutterburg, we also at the same time see him preparing for the ride around the hospital grounds, and we know that the road he will travel in his imagination is the same route he and his parents took on the fatal "vacation" trip, in a different Thomas Wolfe October. This time we know why he doesn't wave good-bye to anyone and why he talks himself out of calling Amy. It is his own loneliness that stands on the sidewalk in the form of a child and his own fear of Them that follows behind invisibly. His fear needs a face, so he tells himself that he is afraid of elevators, exposed open spaces, rooms without windows, dogs—all animals, in fact, plus snakes and spiders ("they are not rational," he explains later, cryptically). He knows there is good reason for terror, but he dare not give it its true name.

Even though he has money, he must talk himself into pedaling the bike because he is going nowhere there are buses, and he "travels light" because he needs no "provisions or extra clothing" for that trip inside the fence. His father's jacket and cap are, to him, in the basement because that is where he last saw them in his past, even though Dr. Dupont has brought them to him here in the hospital. And Pokey the Pig, who represents the safe comfort of childhood and will be gift-wrapped, is in "the cabinet in the den" where Adam searched for and found the first terrible evidence of his own nonexistence. He dresses in his father's clothes and looks in the mirror as if to bring him back to life. But he must justify it to his conscious mind by remarking how good the cap is for the cold. It is the hospital that has provided him with the mind-clouding green and black capsules that he pours into the sink. And it is the memory of the car that killed his mother that blares past as he leaves the driveway. Only his thoughts of Amy are fresh and clear and not overlaid with anything else.

Now when Adam tells Brint the story of his parents' escape we know why "their voices scratched at the night," why Adam's father never smoked again, why there were purple half-moons under his mother's eyes. The slightly inappropriate word *clues* has, of course, been implanted in his mind by Brint during earlier investigations. When Adam says, "It's as if I was born that night," we appreciate the irony, and when he wants to tell Pokey how brave and clever he has been, we recall with poignance that in the end—and now—there is no one *but* Pokey to listen sympathetically to such confidences. Even the number of the tape—OZK001—is significant. It reminds us of *The Wizard of Oz* and Dorothy's return to Kansas where she, like Adam, is reunited with the real people who appear as fantasy characters in her dream. But Cormier is still not through playing games with us. Adam associates the lilac perfume with his mother—but in the last chapter of the book he has noticed that fragrance in the hallway of the hospital. And we still don't really know why Brint is recorded as "T."

The triple strands that are braided together to make the story, the three alternating levels on which the narrative progresses, are an intricate but internally consistent device. The bike ride is told in first-person present tense. The tapes, as dialogue, have neither person nor tense (but we assume they

> All of Adam's forgotten past is still available to us, and we can see his buried knowledge at work on the fabric of his fantasy."

are happening in the present), and the revelation of Adam's past that grows out of the tapes proceeds chronologically and is in third-person past tense. A slightly confusing factor is that in the early phases of the bike ride Adam enjoys some memories of the warm, safe times of his childhood—and these fit into the chronology of the memories he is sharing with Brint. This is all perfectly clean-cut and clear the second time around, but a first-time reader feels that the events of the story have been scrambled intriguingly.

Of all the sinister characters Cormier has created to embody his ideas about evil, Brint is perhaps the most chilling. Indeed, it is tempting at first to jump to the conclusion, because of his stiffly formal speech, that he is a machine, perhaps some kind of interrogation computer. Tempting, because the worst thing about Brint, the most appalling realization, is that he *is* (or *was*) a human being, but he has been so corrupted by his immersion in evil that he can sit year after year across from Adam, calmly herding him through lacerating self-discoveries and feeling not one flicker of pity or mercy. Only twice does he seem human, but in both cases it is immediately clear that the pose is a trick. At one point he exclaims about the beauty of the weather—but only to jolly Adam out of a deep withdrawal. Later, when Adam is remembering his father's distrust of Grey, he suddenly sees something in Brint's expression that makes him suspect that he is "one of those men who had been his father's enemy." Brint, realizing that he has almost given himself away, covers quickly. "I am sorry that you were disturbed by the expression on my face. I, too, am human. I have headaches, upset stomach at times. I slept badly last night. Perhaps that's what you saw reflected on my face" But Adam is not entirely convinced. "It's good to find out you're human," he grants uncertainly. "Sometimes I doubt it."

What Do I Read Next?

- *The Chocolate War* (1974) was Cormier's first novel for young adults. With its disturbing ending in which the lone hero does not win against evil forces, it caused a controversy similar to that caused by *I Am the Cheese*.

- In *Fade* (1988), Cormier presents another three-part structure and another story of hidden identity. The first third of the novel is based on Cormier's own life as a small-town New England boy in the 1930s.

- Chaim Potok's *My Name Is Asher Lev* (1972) is a novel about a Hasidic Jewish boy growing up in Brooklyn. A loner who shares Adam Farmer's desire to become a writer, Asher finds that his artistic impulses put him in conflict with his family and his community.

- *Where the Lilies Bloom* (1969), by Vera Cleaver and Bill Cleaver, is a novel about a family of orphan children in Appalachia who keep their father's death a secret so they will not be split up. The second-oldest child, the young teen Mary Call, struggles to keep her family together against challenges posed by the adults in her life.

- *WITSEC: Inside the Federal Witness Protection Program* (2002) is written by Pete Earley and also by Gerald Shur, the federal attorney who created the program. Through the examples of many people who have been relocated through the program, the book reveals some cases gone awry and also many successes, but none of the duplicity hinted at in *I Am the Cheese*.

Much of the content of the dialogue portion of the tapes is the progress of Adam's reluctant realization that Brint is his enemy. He wants so much to believe in him as a benevolent father-figure, who has his welfare at heart, that sometimes he even tries to prompt Brint into this role. He wonders aloud why Brint never asks him about his mother, and another time he is a bit hurt when Brint interrupts his reminiscences, and he says plaintively, "You sound impatient. I'm sorry. Am I going into too much detail? I thought you wanted me to discover everything about myself." Later he finally cannot avoid noticing that it is only certain kinds of information that interest his interrogator, although he repeatedly protests that he has only Adam's welfare at heart. But Adam really does know the truth about Brint, and he cannot entirely hide it from himself, even at the beginning. In the second tape he says, "He had a kindly face although sometimes his eyes were strange. The eyes stared at him occasionally as if the doctor—if that's what he was—were looking down the barrel of a gun, taking aim at him. He felt like a target." Adam is completely in Brint's power, both physically and mentally. The windows of the interrogation room are barred; the shots and the pills control his feelings and his mind. To recognize his captor as the enemy is unbearable, and so he pushes away the knowledge as long as he can and tries to find goodness in Brint. And so does the reader. It is this blurring of the distinction between good and evil that gives the tapes their peculiar horror, and that points to the larger theme of the book.

Cormier has had some revealing things to say about Brint. He chose the name, he says, to suggest someone bloodless and cold, to rhyme with *flint* and *glint*. At first he was not sure whether the character was a psychiatrist or not. "But I thought this would be the way it would sound if a character were using a slight knowledge of psychology to take advantage of a situation." Brint's knowledge may be "slight," but he has certainly learned the superficial tricks of the trade, as when he turns Adam's suspicions back on himself by accusing him of attacking his therapist to create a diversion whenever certain buried information is approached. In the Brint/Adam interchange there is a hint of a theme that Cormier was to explore more thoroughly in *After the First Death:*. "Adam comes to him completely innocent in his amnesia, and Brint corrupts that. That's what evil is, the destruction of in-nocence." Although Cormier emphasizes Brint's machinelike quality by never giving us any de-scription or background, he claims he has a home life in mind for him. "I picture Brint in a two-car garage, a family, belongs to the Elks. . . . He has this job in an agency where he's got to keep ques-tioning all these people, but at night he leaves the area and goes home and has a regular life. . . ." Somehow the idea of Brint presiding over a sub-urban household seems like part of the Number. Has Cormier forgotten that Brint is instantly avail-able to Adam in the night? Obviously he sleeps nearby in the hospital, probably in a spartan room where he hangs his impeccable suit neatly in the closet. Then he lies rigidly on a narrow cot all night without rumpling the covers, stretched out on his back with folded arms. He does not allow himself to dream.

At a crucial point in the narrative, Brint lays out some priorities. "Permit me to summarize. The first landmark was that day in the woods with the dog. The second landmark was that call from Amy." The Dog, as both symbol and event, recurs often in Adam's narrative. In the first chapter, the very thought of "all the dogs that would attack me on the way to Rutterburg, Vermont," almost keeps him from setting out on the journey. He keeps an eye out for dogs when he does get on the road, and sure enough, soon he is threatened by one. As soon as we know that the bike trip is unreal, it is clear that this is a dream dog. The breed is German shepherd, a kind of animal associated with official power, po-lice, Nazis. He is black, and, like Brint, he looks at Adam silently "with eyes like marbles." And, con-trary to the normal behavior of dogs, he is guard-ing an empty house where there is no owner to defend. As in a dream, the direct attack is deflected to the tires. The beast tries "to topple the bike, send it askew and have me crashing to the roadway, his victim," just as Brint with his persistent questions tries to topple the delicate structure of defense that allows Adam to delude himself with the imaginary escape of the trip to Rutterburg. Even when Adam has eluded this animal, he has a prophetic feeling "that the dog will pursue me forever."

In the tape immediately following, Adam of-fers a startling remark. "Maybe the dog is a clue," he says tentatively. It sounds as if he is referring to the dog he has just escaped in the preceding chapter. Is this a link finally between the two sep-arate narrative streams? But the idea is aborted as soon as Adam clarifies his statement: "I thought of the dog when I looked out this morning and saw a

dog on the grass." Brint assumes that he is talking about Silver, the dog that experienced readers know is kept on the hospital grounds, and that Adam has been wary of as he returned to reality from the end of his trip. But Silver is the third dog evoked in this conversation, not the second. The dog Adam is re-calling is the animal that attacked his father in the woods, a dog that first-time readers have not yet met, except through Adam's fears. Here Cormier achieves an extraordinary effect. The question of which dog is reflection and which dog is real be-comes multiplied and confused, and the image is of dogs, single and several, reflected endlessly in a trick mirror. This moment plants a subliminal suggestion that the three strands of narrative are one story, returning to the now double meaning of Adam's casual "Maybe the dog is a clue."

The dog in the woods is, of course, the central dog. This episode has a surreal tone, although it is part of the memories retrieved by Brint's ques-tioning, and therefore true. The battle of the father and the dog is unnecessary to the story line, strictly speaking, but as a metaphor it is a compelling side-trip for Cormier. The key is Adam's description of the growling dog: "the way it stood there, im-placable, blocking their path. There was something threatening about the dog, a sense that the rules didn't apply, like encountering a crazy person and realizing that anything could happen, anything was possible." Implacable, no appeal, like the forces that have trapped Adam—and in memory he savors his father's courage in battle and his victory.

And finally, it is a dog that brings the whole complex narrative structure down to one focus. As Adam returns sadly and quietly from his long trip, he wheels through the grounds of "the hospital" and is met by a kindly doctor. Has he at last broken free and come to a safe place? But as soon as he meets Silver in the hall, the momentary hope is blasted. We have seen Silver before, through the window of Brint's office, and we know now without a doubt that Adam has never left the place of interrogation.

Brint's second landmark is the call from Amy. The reader, like Brint, suspects that there was more to this incident than met Adam's ear. "Was Amy part of the conspiracy?" is a frequent question in Cormier's mail. The letter writers wonder shrewdly if she was prompted by the enemy to probe Adam's past, or if perhaps the name "Hertz" is meant to suggest that she "hurts" him. This Cormier denies emphatically. Amy is innocent and, as Adam wished, quite separate from the structure of in-trigue, and the reason she is no longer there after three years is not that the enemy got her, but simply that her family moved away. Actually, Amy is the opposite of hurtful to Adam. She, as he says, "brought brightness and gaiety to his life." Cormier introduced her out of compassion for his protagonist: "I was conscious that Adam was leading a very drab life—his father a shadow, his mother withdrawn, and he was introverted—and I thought, this is getting pretty dull. So I introduced her to liven up the book, to give him a little love and affection, and, of course, instantly I fell in love with her." As Cormier's female characters often do, Amy led her creator pages and pages out of the way into episodes that had to be discarded later.

Amy, with her quick imagination, her antic sense of humor, her tender toughness and her nonchalance, is truly a charming creation. But what lies behind that toughness? Does her mother's preoccupation with committee work have something to do with it? We see her only through Adam's adoring eyes, but actually all is not well with Amy's soul. Amy, like Adam, is an outsider, a loner. Her Numbers have more than a little anger in them; they are not funny to the victims. Sometimes they have a strained quality, like the caper in the church parking lot, or depend for their effect on an enigmatic quirk of thought, like the cartful of baby-food jars left in front of the Kotex display in the supermarket. She really needs Adam to laugh with her. There is nobody else in the audience.

To Adam, the Numbers are "heady and hilarious but somehow terrible." To defy authority is foreign to his nature. But through his participation in the Numbers he gains the courage to investigate the mysteries about his past. "I, too, am capable of mischief," he thinks as he eavesdrops on his father and Mr. Grey. Thoughts of Amy give him courage on the bike ride, too. "What the hell, as Amy would say," he tells himself. Her last real words to Adam are a casual "Call me," and throughout his eternal bike rides he tries. Or thinks he tries. He makes excuses, or he calls at the wrong time, or he hangs up because the wise guys are approaching. He really knows that after three years Amy Hertz has disappeared from his life, and there is no comfort to be found at 537-3331. When he does finally make the connection with that number the Number is over, and it is the beginning of the end of his illusion.

Adam is to some extent based on Cormier himself as a boy. Not only his fears and phobias and migraines, but his personality and ambitions recall Cormier at fourteen. He is shy and book-loving,

and home is a warm, safe retreat from a hostile world where wise guys lie in wait at every corner. Like Jerry in *The Chocolate War*, he knows only too well the scenario that begins "You lookin' for trouble?" Cormier betrayed in the operating room is vividly evoked when Adam says, "I don't like to be confined or held down. My instinct, then, is to get up on my feet, flailing my arms at anything that might try to hold me down, confine me." When Adam explains the writer inherent in his attitude toward life, it is also the young Cormier speaking: "Anyway, his terrible shyness, his inability to feel at ease with people, had nothing to do with his mother. He felt it was his basic character; he preferred reading a book or listening to old jazz records in his bedroom than going to dances or hanging around downtown with the other kids. Even in the fourth or fifth grade, he had stayed on the outskirts of the school-yard watching the other kids playing the games—Kick the Can was a big thing in the fourth grade—anyway, he had never felt left out: it was his choice. To be a witness, to observe, to let the events be recorded within himself on some personal film in some secret compartment no one knew about, except him. It was only later, in the eighth grade, when he knew irrevocably that he wanted to be a writer, that he realized he had stored up all his observations, all his emotions, for that purpose." And there is poignance for Cormier in the closeness and deep affection Adam feels for his parents, especially the warm glow of love at the last supper at the Red Mill—just before his father's death.

Between creator and creation there is an ironic contrast in one respect. "I'm not built for subterfuge and deception," says Adam. It is this quality that makes him a too-perfect subject for interrogation. Because he is so guileless, they—who are so complex in evil that they cannot comprehend simple honesty—persist in thinking he must be hiding something. Again and again he willingly turns the pockets of his mind inside out for them, but they still suspect he has something up his sleeve. It occurs to him to hold back, but he always ends by telling all.

His resistance has been channeled in other directions. The fantasy bike ride is Adam's gesture of defiance in the face of the Implacable. This explains the fierce intensity of his determination to make the journey "for my father," and the inevitability he feels in the beginning about his decision to go—"I knew I would go the way you know a stone will drop to the ground if you release it from your hand." Like Jerry, his gesture is stubborn and half-aware, not the grand, controlled action of a hero. "I am a coward, really," he admits, but in the refrain "I keep pedaling" there is persistent courage. Adam must repeatedly overcome obstacles and break through his fears, but each time he does he can soar for a moment and he finds new hope and strength.

As in dreams real emotions are translated into fantasy people and events, so as the bike ride progresses Adam's hidden awareness of the menace all around him begins to come to the forefront of his mind and take on personification, shape, and form as Whipper and the wise guys, as Fat Arthur and Junior Varney, as snarling dogs and the terrible ferocious vomit-pink car with the grinning grille. Meanwhile in the interrogations he is bringing to consciousness memories that bleed their terror into his secret life of the mind so that he is less and less able to sustain the fantasy. As he approaches the final truth, his newly discovered knowledge of the amount of time that has passed intrudes into the dream in a collision of logics. When he gets to the motel where he and his parents spent a safe night "last summer" he finds it "feels as if it has been neglected for years and years." The effect is eerily disorienting. One last time he tries to call Amy, but the gruff man on the phone and his own mind tell him she is gone; he is no longer able to delude himself with hopes of her comfort or with the defiant illusion of escape. He wants to wake up—"I would give anything to be folded into bed, the pills working their magic, soothing me"—and in a moment he does. The dream begins to smear and waver like the woman's face through the wet wind shield. Everything slows down; sounds are distorted, like a movie in a disintegrating projector. The darkness gathers him. Yet still—on a first reading—still we believe this is reality.

Like Amy, Cormier "always withholds information about the Numbers until the last possible moment, stretching out the drama." Even here at the end, there is one last tiny gleam of false hope. We think Adam has arrived in Rutterburg at last. Then he turns the corner and sees the hospital, and as he greets one by one the people from his fantasy the shattering truth crashes down. For the first time he sings the *last* verse of "The Farmer in the Dell." The cheese stands alone, and he is the cheese.

The final tape, with its cold, bureaucratic verdict, has been the subject of much speculation. With a little study, a key can be puzzled out:

Subject A—Adam

Personnel #2222—Thompson, or Grey

File Data 865-01—the record of Adam's father's testimony and subsequent official events related to it,

OZK Series—the interrogation tapes between Adam and Brint

Department 1-R—the government agency to which Adam's father testified

Tape Series ORT, UDW—the tapes of Adam's two previous interrogations

Witness #559-6—Adam's father

Policy 979—a rule that "does not currently allow termination procedures by Department 1-R"

And Department 1-R, notice, is the agency to whom Adam's father gave his witness, presumably the good guys, but it is *they* who have imprisoned Adam, and they who are being asked to "obliterate" him. Who, then, are the Adversaries? And Grey? Up to now, it has seemed that it was Grey's legs that Adam saw as he lay on the ground after the crash, but was that just because that person wore gray pants? And Grey, remember, did not "necessarily" wear gray clothes.

Even Cormier's own words from the answer sheet he mails to questioners do not completely clear up the ambiguity: "Grey was not part of the syndicate. He was not a double agent in the usual sense, although he double-crossed Adam's father, setting him up for the syndicate and the accident. He was present at the scene to clean up afterward, but hadn't counted on Adam's survival—an embarrassment to the agency." So whose side is he on? In terms of Adam's future, it matters not at all. As Anne MacLeod puts it, "the two systems are equally impersonal, and equally dangerous to the human being caught between them. What matters to the organization—*either* organization—is its own survival, not Adam's." In the third chapter the old man at the gas station has asked Adam, "Do you know who the bad guys are?" He doesn't and neither do we. What is so overwhelming here is not just that evil is powerful, but that the good guys and the bad guys turn out to be—probably—indistinguishable. It is not a matter of good against evil, but of the cheese standing alone against everything, his whole world revealed at last as evil. Where now is Cormier's imperative for collective good? There is nobody left to come to his rescue. This is not a metaphor. MacLeod says, "This stark tale comments directly on the real world of government, organized crime, large-scale bureaucracy, the apparatus of control, secrecy, betrayal, and all the other commonplaces of contemporary political life." We could all be the cheese.

"A magnificent accomplishment," said *Hornbook*. "Beside it, most books for the young seem as insubstantial as candyfloss," said the *Times Literary Supplement*. "The secret, revealed at the end, explodes like an H-bomb," said *Publishers Weekly*. "A masterpiece," said *West Coast Review of Books*. The *New York Times Book Review* and the Young Adult Services Division of the American Library Association both included it on their respective lists of best books of the year for young people. But Newgate Callendar wondered in the *New York Times* if the book might turn out to be "above the heads of most teen-agers." Cormier, too, was afraid that he was in danger of losing his newfound young adult audience.

The book had begun as a time-filler. "Sometimes when there's nothing that's compelling, I do exercises. So I put a boy on a bike and had him take off on a Wednesday morning with a box on his bike. Then right away I wondered, what's he doing out of school on a Wednesday morning, where's he going, what's in the package? . . . I started to give him a lot of my own fears, phobias . . . And I wrote virtually all of the bike part without knowing where it was going." For a while he searched for a second level among religious themes of pilgrimage, the Stations of the Cross, death and resurrection. Then one day, "across my desk at the newspaper . . . came this thing about the Witness Relocation Program. This was at a time when very little was known about it." He began to wonder about the hardships of giving up a past, and "then it struck me, . . . how much harder for a teen, who doesn't even know who he is yet!" He knew he had found his second level. He went back to the bike ride to make it fit. The creation of *I Am the Cheese* was a very intense experience for him. "During the time I was writing the book, no one saw any part of it. I felt like the mad doctor in a laboratory, because I didn't think it would ever work, yet I felt compelled to write it. It was coming out at breakneck speed." "I still picture Adam riding that bike around the institution grounds, as real now as the day I discovered him."

To those who wonder if there have been political repercussions Cormier says, "I know it's critical of government, yet I think the strength of our government is that you *can* be critical of it, because there are so many good things about it, like the very fact that I can write this book." "Believe me, if we did not have a good government, I might have been

jailed or my book censored before it ever hit the stores."

Or perhaps the CIA and the Mafia don't read young adult literature.

Source: Patricia J. Campbell, "*I Am the Cheese*," in *Presenting Robert Cormier*, Dell Publishing, 1985, pp. 80–95.

Sources

Bell, Robert, Review of *I Am the Cheese*, in the *School Librarian*, September 1978, p. 281.

DeLuca, Geraldine, and Roni Natov, "An Interview with Robert Cormier," in the *Lion and the Unicorn*, Vol. 2, No. 2, Fall 1978, pp. 125–26.

Heins, Paul, Review of *I Am the Cheese*, in the *Horn Book Magazine*, August 1977, pp. 427–28.

Lukens, Rebecca, "From Salinger to Cormier: Disillusionment to Despair in Thirty Years," in *Webs and Wardrobes*, edited by Joseph O'Beirne Milner and Lucy Floyd Morcock Milner, University Press of America, 1987, p. 13.

Sutton, Roger, "The Critical Myth: Realistic YA Novels," in *School Library Journal*, November 1982, p. 35.

Further Reading

Keeley, Jennifer, *Understanding "I Am the Cheese,"* Lucent Books, 2001.

> Part of Lucent's Understanding Great Literature series, this volume is geared toward a younger audience than the Twayne volumes. This book includes an illustrated biography, a plot summary, character sketches, analysis, excerpts from reviews, and an annotated bibliography.

Nodelman, Perry, "Robert Cormier Does a Number," in *Children's Literature in Education*, Summer 1983, pp. 94–103.

> Nodelman offers a reader-response analysis of *I Am the Cheese*, tracing his own reactions to unfolding elements in the novel. He shows how Cormier intentionally tricks the reader into misinterpreting what is going on until the horrible truth is revealed at the end.

Silvey, Anita, "An Interview with Robert Cormier," in the *Horn Book Magazine*, March/April 1985, pp. 145–55, and May/June 1985, pp. 289–96.

> Spread over two issues, much of this interview focuses on Cormier's fifth young adult novel, which is *Beyond the Chocolate War* (1985). Along the way, it offers a detailed look at Cormier's writing process and includes reproductions of several manuscript pages showing Cormier's editing and revising marks.

Sutton, Roger, "Kind of a Funny Dichotomy: A Conversation with Robert Cormier," in *School Library Journal*, June 1991, pp. 28–33.

This interview was conducted soon after Cormier
was announced as the winner of the third Margaret
A. Edwards Award for young adult authors. Cormier
discusses the contrast between the pessimism in his
books and the optimism that was a cornerstone of
his own life, and he explains how his Catholic faith
shaped his world view.

A Long and Happy Life

Reynolds Price

1962

Upon its first publication in 1962, *A Long and Happy Life* announced the arrival of a major literary talent. Reynolds Price's first novel, published just a few years after his graduation from college, is a tale told in the southern Gothic tradition, regarding the sorrows of a young woman, Rosacoke Mustian, who tries to find love in an obscure rural town. Her long-term boyfriend, Wesley Beavers, is mysterious to her, showing Rosacoke enough interest to make her feel that they might have a true bond but also flirting with other women and ignoring her to such an extent that she often wonders if he knows her at all. Price tells this story with an exacting eye for detail and a firm control of his characters' emotions as they come to grips with the births and deaths that control the courses of their lives. He creates a very specific geographical location, a countryside where whites and blacks, poor and rich, know each other and live together as neighbors, and where the surrounding forest is still wild enough to raise the sense of wonder in people who have known it all their lives. Since the publication of *A Long and Happy Life*, Reynolds Price has distinguished himself as a poet, fiction writer, essayist, and playwright. While all of his works have been important to the American literary scene, this novel remains one of his most significant contributions.

Author Biography

Reynolds Price was born on February 1, 1933, in Macon, North Carolina. His father, William, was a

traveling salesman; his mother, Elizabeth, was a homemaker with a quirky, eccentric personality that came to play a direct influence on the focused sense of storytelling that Price was to develop. The author spent his childhood in small North Carolina towns, a fact that shows clearly in his fiction, which is most often concerned with the lives of characters from the Carolina backwoods. His talent as a writer manifested itself early, and it opened doors for him that would change the course of his life. He attended Duke University in Durham, North Carolina, on a scholarship and was awarded a Rhodes Scholarship to attend Oxford University in England. After graduating from Oxford in 1958, Price became an instructor at Duke, and he has remained with Duke ever since then, rising from the level of instructor to chair of the Department of English.

A Long and Happy Life was Price's first novel, published in 1962. It was critically acclaimed, winning several awards for a first novel, and established the author as a major American literary voice. Since then, he has published frequently in a range of genres: novels, plays, poetry, short stories, memoirs, and essays.

A major event in Price's life occurred in 1984, when he was diagnosed with astocytoma, or cancer of the spinal cord. Tests determined that there was a tumor on his spinal cord that had been there a long time, possibly all his life. The subsequent operation to remove it left Price paralyzed in both legs. This change in his lifestyle created a change in his writing style, as he outlined in 1995 in his book *A Whole New Life*. For one thing, having limited mobility left him more time to write. In addition, his works became more introspective and focused more on religious themes. In 2001, Price published *A Great Circle: The Mayfield Trilogy*, a collection of three novels—*The Surface of the Earth*, *The Source of Light*, and *The Promise of Rest*—spanning almost two hundred years in the history of one North Carolina family.

Reynolds Price

cently the two young women had not seen much of each other. Mildred died giving birth to a baby, having never told anyone who the child's father was. Rosacoke is embarrassed to ride to the church on a loud motorcycle, but Wesley sees "no reason to change to a car for a Negro funeral." During the ceremony, he stays outside the church, tuning the motorcycle loudly. Rosacoke is the only white person at the ceremony. Wesley rides away during the funeral, and when Rosacoke leaves she has to walk home.

In the woods, she stops at a clear water spring that she recalls finding when she and Mildred and others were playing as children. Wesley finds her there, thinking about her life, and convinces her to go to the church picnic with him.

Rosacoke's family is at the picnic by Mason's Lake. Her brother Milo swims with Wesley and with Willie Duke Aycock, a buxom beauty contest winner who has had a crush on Wesley since childhood; Milo's wife Sissie, pregnant with their first child, feels sick and is cared for by Rosacoke's mother; Baby Sister, the youngest of the clan, pretends to baptize the many children of another family, the Guptons; and Macey Gupton's wife, Marise, tends to the couple's fourth child. Wesley explains that he will be going to Norfolk, Virginia,

Plot Summary

Chapter 1

A Long and Happy Life takes place in rural North Carolina. It begins in July, with the novel's protagonist, Rosacoke Mustian, riding to a funeral on the back of a motorcycle driven by Wesley Beavers, her on-and-off boyfriend of six years. The funeral is for Mildred Sutton. Mildred played with Rosacoke's family when they were all little, but re-

Media Adaptations

- *A Long and Happy Life* is one of five novels that Price reads from on *Reynolds Price Reads*, an audio collection published from the American Audio Prose Library and available online at www.audible.com.

- Price discussed the use of his North Carolina as a bonding force in his fiction in "Reynolds Price," a 1989 entry in the Public Broadcasting System's *Writer's Workshop* series, released on video by PBS.

where he was in the navy, to sell motorcycles. He jokes around about other women he has known. Milo jokes that Rosacoke could keep Wesley committed to her by becoming pregnant.

After everyone leaves the picnic and night is falling, Wesley lures Rosacoke into the woods, pretending that he is looking for a spring to drink from. He tells her that Willie Duke Aycock will be going to Norfolk when he does because she has a job there. In the woods, he tries to convince Rosacoke to have sex with him, but she refuses.

For a few weeks, Rosacoke writes letters to Wesley, and he responds with flighty, noncommittal post cards. Willie Duke returns in November with a new, wealthy boyfriend. It is a few days before Rosacoke finds out that Wesley came back to town with them.

Chapter 2

At church, Willie Duke introduces Rosacoke to Heywood, her boyfriend. She says that they are leaving that afternoon in Heywood's small airplane. Later, when Rosacoke and her mother are looking at a picture of her father, who died thirteen years earlier, Baby Sister bursts in and announces that the airplane just flew over with three people in it. Rosacoke assumes that Wesley has gone back to Norfolk without stopping to see her.

She takes her camera and goes to the house of Mildred's mother because she had promised to take

a picture of Mildred's baby for her relatives. When she arrives, it is too late in the day and, therefore, too dark to take a picture. It is also too dark to walk home, so she decides to walk further on to the Beavers' house to phone her brother Milo for a ride. There she finds, to her surprise, Wesley standing on the front porch.

He is as evasive as ever when she asks about their relationship. As he is driving her home, they see some deer crossing the road and follow them into the woods to see if they will go to the watering hole. Wesley takes her to an open field that she was not aware of, and there they have sex. During the passion, Wesley says, "I thank you, Mae," which he does not remember saying afterward. Rosacoke immediately regrets having given in to his pressures, and wants to go home. After he goes back to Norfolk, they exchange a few letters. Rosacoke wants to know how he feels about her, but she tears up the letters that approach this subject.

One of her letters is a long, detailed account of how her sister-in-law, Sissie, went into labor, and of the disappointment at finding that the baby died during childbirth. Milo, the baby's father, becomes distant from Sissie and the rest of the family. Rosacoke vows to stay beside her brother and help him through his grief, but, when they pick up the mail in town, she finds a letter from Wesley asking her if "the coast is clear"—a way of asking whether she is pregnant. The question upsets her so much that she has Milo drop her off at home, unable to go on with him.

On December 15, Rosacoke writes a letter to Wesley saying that she is in fact pregnant but that she does not expect any action from him. She is willing to bear the responsibility for the baby by herself. Before sending the letter, she tears it up.

Chapter 3

The third section begins three days before Christmas. Rato, who is the brother of Milo, Rosacoke, and Baby Sister, comes home from the army, bringing presents. Rosacoke goes off to the house of Mr. Isaac, the dying rich man who owns much of the land in the area. A series of strokes have reduced him to being like an infant. His assistant, Sammy Ransom, has to feed him and clean him and prop him up in his chair, and the old man's only pleasure is sucking on candy. Wesley comes to Mr. Isaac's house to get Rosacoke and tell her that she has to be in the church pageant that her mother has planned, since Willie Duke has eloped and will not be available. Outside, she tells Wesley about her pregnancy, and he reluctantly offers to elope with her that night. Rosacoke rejects his offer.

In the Christmas pageant, Rosacoke plays Mary. She leans over the manger where a baby, Frederick Gupton, lies. During the performance, the baby seems poised to cry. Rosacoke's first reaction is to turn him over to his real father, Macey Gupton, who is playing Joseph, but she realizes that it would look strange for the show. She picks the baby up and he gnaws at her breast until he is tired out. As different characters approach the manger scene, Rosacoke realizes that only one of them, Wesley Beavers, truly knows her, and she decides that she will, after all, marry him, and she whispers her decision to the sleeping baby, wishing him "a long and happy life."

Characters

Landon Allgood

Landon is a helpless man who is addicted to paregoric, a tincture of opium. He has no toes because once, long ago, he fell asleep in a road one Christmas and they fell off. On the day of Mildred's funeral, he is found sleeping in the church. On the day of the Christmas pageant, Rosacoke finds him stealing decorations from the church, which he explains are for his sister, Mary, who is Mildred's mother and is raising her baby, Sledge. Mary promised to give him a hot meal if he would bring her Christmas greens. Landon's name is brought up during the Christmas pageant when Rosacoke smells paregoric on the breath of the baby, Frederick, and realizes that it is being used to keep him narcotized.

Mr. Isaac Alston

"Mr. Isaac," as he is called, is the rich landowner whom the people in Rosacoke's life look up to. The forest around them is referred to as "Mr. Isaac's forest," implying that nature belongs to him, making him godlike. He is eighty-two years old and has lost most of his mental faculties due to a series of strokes. His one interest in life is horehound candy. The people in the county look to Mr. Isaac as a trusted benefactor: for instance, when Rosacoke's father died, Mr. Isaac came to the house and gave her mother fifty dollars. As a measure of their esteem, they all pitch in together to buy him a new wheelchair, even though Sammy, who takes care

of Mr. Isaac, tells them that he probably would not appreciate the gesture because he is so mentally unaware.

Willie Duke Aycock

A local beauty pageant winner—she won a Dairy Queen Contest the previous summer—Willie Duke has had a crush on Wesley Beavers for a long time. She goes to Norfolk when he does because she has a job curling hair, causing Rosacoke to assume that they are having an affair until she comes home a little later with a new boyfriend, Heywood Betts. Soon after, she and Heywood go to Florida to be married.

Wesley Beavers

Wesley is the boyfriend of the novel's protagonist, Rosacoke Mustian. They have been dating for about six years. At the start of the novel, Wesley is back home just briefly, having spent three years in the Navy, stationed at Norfolk, Virginia, fixing radios. He is leaving soon to return to Norfolk to work in a motorcycle dealership. He drives Rosacoke to a funeral on his motorcycle, then stays outside, gunning the cycle's engine, tuning it and polishing it, oblivious to the distraction that he is causing to the ceremony. When he takes Rosacoke to a church picnic, he and her brother Milo joke about sex, and he flirts with another girl, Willie Duke Aycock. He later teases Rosacoke with the fact that Willie Duke is going to Norfolk at the same time that he is, implying that they might have an affair. Wesley tries hard to convince Rosacoke to have sex with him, mostly by hinting flirtatiously about other women with whom he has been involved, but she holds out.

After they finally do have sex one night, Wesley returns to Norfolk. He is distant and cheerful when he writes, signing his one letter "Your friend, Wesley" and asking her if "the coast is clear" (his playful way of asking if she has become pregnant). When he finds out that she has in fact become pregnant, he stalls, asking why she took so long to tell him and whether she has had any other lovers, before he asks her to run off to South Carolina with him and be married that night.

Heywood Betts

Heywood is a pilot who owns his own airplane ("scrap metal is my work," he tells Rosacoke, "—flying's just a hobby"). He comes home with Willie Duke Aycock in November, after she has been away to Norfolk for a few weeks. By Christmas, they are engaged.

Macey Gupton

Macey is the father of four children. When Sissie Mustian is in labor, Macey offers to help out, using his extensive experience in childbirth. As a result, he is there when the doctor pronounces the baby dead. Later, Mama Mustian wants to call him to find Milo, who has run away in his grief, and Rosacoke tells her, "Don't call in the Guptons for any more Mustian business." During the Christmas pageant at the end of the book, Macey plays Joseph, standing by while Rosacoke, as Mary, takes care of his eight-month-old son playing the infant Jesus.

Marise Gupton

The sister of Willie Duke Aycock and wife of Macey Gupton, she has had four children already and, by the end of the novel, is pregnant with the fifth.

Baby Sister Mustian

Baby Sister is thirteen years old. Her father committed suicide before she was born. She occupies herself playing with dolls, pretending to be a mother to them, and leading the smaller children in games.

Emma Mustian

"Mama" is the mother of Milo, Rosacoke, Rato, and Baby Sister. She serves as a reminder of love in vain: for thirteen years, she lived with their father, who was a terrible drunk and an abusive husband. When Rosacoke is upset about Wesley's leaving, Mama brings her a picture of her father, one of the very few fond reminders she has of him. At the end of the book, Rosacoke feels required to participate in the Christmas pageant because Mama is the one who organized it.

Milo Mustian

Milo is Rosacoke's brother. He is married to Sissie, and throughout the first half of the book, while she is pregnant with their first child, he makes jokes about women "catching" men with sex. Later, when the baby dies during childbirth, Milo is so distraught that he will not even talk to Sissie. Rosacoke promises to stay with him and give him someone to share his grief with, but a letter from Wesley upsets her and she has to abandon him. He takes all of the baby clothes they bought and gives them to Mildred Sutton's mother, who is raising Mildred's baby. Milo later returns home and resumes a strained relationship with his wife.

Rato Mustian

Horatio "Rato" Mustian is Rosacoke's brother, named after their father. For most of the novel, he

is away in the army. He returns at Christmas with presents, including one for Milo and Sissie's baby, not knowing that it died.

Rosacoke Mustian

Rosacoke is the main character in the novel. She was born in 1937 and is about twenty-one years old at the time the novel takes place. She is a serious woman who is not sure whether the great love of her life is in fact true love or if her mind is just grasping at some potential for excitement and escape from small community life.

Rosacoke lives with her family in a small house in rural North Carolina, where they have lived all of their lives. At the start of the book, she and Wesley Beavers have dated for six years and are so close that people around town assume that they are going to be married someday. She is constantly irritated with Wesley because he flirts with other women and jokes about all of the girlfriends he has had. When he tries to have sex with her before leaving to take a job in another town, she turns him down. In the letters that she exchanges with him after that, she asks Wesley if he loves her, and he writes back about superficial matters.

After Wesley has come back to town she does give in and has sex with him. She regrets it immediately when he calls her by another woman's name during intercourse.

Rosacoke finds that she is pregnant and resolves to keep the news to herself, to keep Wesley from feeling a sense of responsibility, just as Mildred Sutton, who died during childbirth, never revealed the name of her child's father. She changes her mind, though, after visiting Mr. Isaac, an old man who is, mind and body, like a child. She tells Wesley about the baby, and he somewhat reluctantly agrees to marry her, but she refuses his offer until, during the annual Christmas pageant, Rosacoke (playing the Virgin Mary) comes to understand the baby that is representing the infant Jesus. She decides to marry for her child's sake, despite her own prospect for unhappiness.

Sissie Mustian

At the beginning of the novel, Milo's wife Sissie is pregnant with their first child, and she feels sick in the July heat. Later, when the baby dies during childbirth, she becomes severely depressed.

Sammy Ransom

Sammy takes tender care of the aging Isaac Alston, to such an extent that he is often referred to as

"Mr. Isaac's Sammy." The rumor that Milo spreads, and that Rosacoke is convinced of later on, is that Sammy is the father of Mildred Sutton's child.

Mildred Sutton

This novel begins with Mildred's funeral. She was a childhood playmate of the Mustians. Seeing Mildred when she was pregnant gave Rosacoke the feeling that Mildred had somehow become wiser than she. Mildred died soon after her twenty-first birthday, giving birth to her son, Sledge, without telling anyone who the child's father was. One of Rosacoke's clearest childhood memories is of finding a clearing deep in Mr. Isaac's woods with Mildred and several other children. A deer suddenly appeared, causing Mildred to blurt out, "Great God A-mighty!"

Themes

Love

Central to Rosacoke Mustian's dilemma in this book is the question of whether Wesley Beavers truly loves her. On one hand, his focus when he is home is on her. He escorts her to picnics and drives her places that she needs to go, such as Mildred's funeral. People kid him about when they are going to be married, and late in the book Sammy Ransom says that he just assumed that they already had plans. Despite their social situation, though, Wesley is distant to Rosacoke in private. He hints at relations with other girls, teasing her with talk of skinny-dipping and dancing with them. (Rosacoke eventually finds out that his hints are probably real when he blurts out another girl's name during sex.) He does not tell her when he is coming to town or when he is going. He has never asked for a picture of her, and the only one he has is one that she insisted he take. He writes seldom, and only about inconsequential things. When she asks in a letter, "are we in love?" he responds, "You are getting out of my depth now."

At the same time, Rosacoke is not sure whether what she feels for Wesley is love or not. She has been compelled by him since their first meeting six years earlier, but she does not know why. At one point she thinks of the things that she has kept from their relationship, letters and mementos, as being no more to her than the reminders of her dead father. The book can be read in terms of Rosacoke's exploration of other relationships—Milo and Sissie, Macey and Marise, Mildred and Sammy, her parents, and even Willie Duke and Heywood Betts—in terms of what they can tell her about love. In the end, she decides to marry Wesley because "After all Wesley knows me," even though she says that it is the baby, not Wesley, who knows about love.

Identity

One of the reasons that Wesley is able to make Rosacoke accept his casual attitude toward their relationship is that she does not know who she is and what she can rightfully expect from life. He, on the other hand, is full of self-confidence. When she asks why he acts as he does, he responds, "Because I am Wesley." When she is upset with him, Rosacoke has one request of him: "Do me a favor. . . . Say *Rosacoke*." She needs Wesley to acknowledge her individuality.

She looks back to her childhood fondly as a time when life was full of adventure, when finding a new area of forest or seeing a deer unexpectedly could open up new possibilities. She is growing up, though, a fact that is highlighted in the novel by the contrast between Rosacoke, who is the kind of person willing to take responsibility for attending her friend's funeral, and Baby Sister, who, at thirteen, is lost in a fantasy life with her dolls.

But the onset of adulthood is not appealing to her as she looks at the models of adult behavior around her. No one has the sane, kind, and respectful life that Rosacoke wishes for herself. When she finds herself pregnant, she realizes that all of the people around her spend their lives serving their babies or, in the case of Sammy and Mr. Isaac, serving an old man who has reverted to infancy. Her mother, for instance, has nothing good to say about devoting her life to a drunken and abusive man. Macey and Marise Gupton's lives are overrun with the children they keep producing. Mildred loses her life to childbirth. Milo and Sissie are devastated by the loss of their child. Rosacoke resists all assumptions that she and Wesley will become just another rural couple, that she will be just another of his sexual conquests and then just another young mother. Cradling the infant Frederick in her arms, he reaches out to her as he would to his mother, and she rejects the mother role, telling him, "Frederick, I ain't who you think I am."

In the end, though, Rosacoke does assume the identity of wife and mother. Her one thin hope of identity is hung on Wesley, on the fact that "he knows me," even though he has already shown little ability or willingness to distinguish her from the rest of his women.

Topics for Further Study

- The people in this novel live in a rural area with electric lights and telephones, but they possess not much more in the way of modern conveniences. Write an essay explaining how the story would have been different if they had the technology available today.

- Explain the leech that attaches to Wesley's leg when he is swimming in Mason's Lake. What kind of leeches are found in North Carolina? What are their habits? What other species are found around the country?

- At the Christmas pageant, Rosacoke smells paregoric on the baby's breath. Research various potions and elixirs that people have given babies throughout history, including at least one currently popular method for quieting them.

- Research some of the songs of mourning that you think may have been sung at Mildred Sutton's funeral and play them for your class.

Birth

It is of no small importance that *A Long and Happy Life* begins with the funeral of Mildred Sutton, who has died while giving birth to a baby. Mildred represents the camaraderie of Rosacoke's childhood and the mystery of approaching adulthood: having run into her once when she was pregnant, she reflects on how "Mildred knew things that Rosacoke didn't know." Her initiation into adulthood kills Mildred, and throughout the book there are other episodes of birth that are just as significant.

Baby Sister's situation reflects Mildred's. The Mustians' father died after his wife, Mama, was pregnant for the fourth time but before Baby Sister's birth. Being born of just one parent makes Baby Sister infantile herself, for she occupies herself with games and dolls, oblivious to the world around her.

When Rosacoke's sister-in-law Sissie gives birth, it is the baby, not the parent, who dies. The

parents are left in despair, their relationship with each other damaged, probably forever.

Finally, there is the situation of Mr. Isaac Alston. Having once been a powerful man in the county, he is regressing toward the womb. Mr. Isaac is in his eighties and expects to live to ninety like all the men of his family. Due to a series of strokes, he is unable to dress himself, comb his own hair, or sit up by himself, and he needs an assistant to do these things for him in the same way that a baby needs its mother. His one joy in life, the only thing that he constantly recognizes, is candy. Rosacoke's visit to his house late in the book reminds her of his wealth and generosity when he was a younger man and that idea of human potential overcoming human frailty is one of the key factors in her resolve to do what she can for the baby she is carrying.

Style

Point of View

A Long and Happy Life is told from a third-person limited point of view. It is third person because the narration refers to all characters as "he" or "she," as opposed to "I" or "you." It is limited because almost all the action described is seen from Rosacoke Mustian's perspective. Events are relayed as Rosacoke remembers or experiences them. Once in a while, the narrative breaks this pattern and gives readers the thoughts of other characters, such as when, after Wesley has sex with Rosacoke in a field, his thoughts are given: "Not knowing whether she would wait or walk on home, Wesley took his time." Instances of points of view other than that of Rosacoke are extremely rare in this book.

Setting

Setting is usually important to novels, but it is especially crucial to this one. The rural North Carolina that Price presents to his readers in this and in other books is a quiet place where people lack the distractions of the modern electronic age and are, therefore, more focused on the lives of the people around them. Births and deaths are the high points of their lives; jobs and education have little to do with them. An airplane coming to town is big news, and people stand out on their porches to see its arrival or departure. When Wesley leaves North Carolina for Virginia, the distance is so considerably far that Rosacoke can only send off letters and hope that he might respond; when he suggests that

Compare
&
Contrast

- **1962:** The space race is going ahead with full force. The first American orbits around the earth this year.

  Today: Space travel is taken for granted and is hardly noted in the news. The international space station has humans in orbit around the earth at all times.

- **1962:** Infant mortality—the number of children who die before they reach one year of age— averages 26 out of 1000 in America. This number is even higher in rural areas and for children born outside of hospitals.

  Today: Modern medical procedures have the infant mortality rate below 8 in 1000.

- **1962:** A wealthy aviation enthusiast, like the novel's Heywood Betts, might have a small,

propeller-driven biplane, with passengers' heads exposed in the open breeze.

  Today: A wealthy aviation enthusiast would own a Cessna or Piper private jet.

- **1962:** Popular music is dominated by white artists. In the coming years, black musicians will begin to directly influence the American music scene through white artists like Elvis, the Beatles, and the Rolling Stones—who take old blues musicians as their inspiration—and by the Motown sound.

  Today: Black musicians are at least as celebrated as white musicians, although there are still separate stations for predominantly black music, referred to as "urban" or "R&B."

---

they elope to Florida, it is like suggesting a trip to another country.

This situation results in making the lives of all the characters intertwine, so that the Mustians know all about the Guptons and the Ransoms and the Suttons and the Allgoods. It is also, however, a major source of Rosacoke's discontent, as she struggles against the role of motherhood that all young women in her little world are expected to adopt.

Historical Context

The Segregated South

Contemporary readers might be surprised to find the casual friendships between blacks and whites portrayed in this novel. Throughout much of American history, races were segregated in the southern states, including North Carolina, where this novel takes place. Most histories of that region in the 1960s tend to focus on the growing violence between blacks and whites as the Civil Rights movement heated up.

Segregation followed from the end of slavery in 1865 and was made into law when the Supreme Court, in 1896, declared that it would not be unconstitutional to treat blacks and whites differently as long as both sides were offered "separate but equal" accommodations. Throughout the first half of the twentieth century, many southern states adhered to that policy in theory, although the railroad cars, hotels, housing, etc. that were assigned to blacks were clearly worse than those allowed whites. This situation could not be changed democratically because laws were passed to keep blacks from voting, blocking their way with requirements about land ownership and I.Q. tests that were usually given selectively, excluding uneducated blacks but not uneducated whites.

After World War II, the Civil Rights movement took hold in this country. Black Americans who had been treated as equals in Europe were not content to be treated as second-class citizens in the country they had fought to defend. The 1950s brought a fierce conflict against segregation in the South. In 1954, the Supreme Court struck down the "separate but equal" doctrine in schools, ordering

During a Civil Rights demonstration in 1965, students unite in front of the U.S. Consulate and sing "We Shall Overcome"

them to find a way to let black students attend the same schools that white students attended. In 1955, Rosa Parks made a significant statement against segregated transportation by refusing to move from the "whites only" section of a Montgomery, Alabama, bus. As the courts found more and more segregationist practices to be illegal, white supremacists became increasingly violent against blacks who crossed the racial lines. Over two hundred black homes and churches in the South were bombed between 1947 and 1965. Governors of southern states, such as George Wallace of Alabama and Ross Barnett of Mississippi, supported their white constituents' desire to keep the racial status quo, even if it meant violence; federal troops were called in when local or state agencies could not be trusted to protect black citizens.

By the early 1960s, white students from northern colleges had been mobilized by southern civil rights groups, such as Reverend Martin Luther King Jr.'s Southern Christian Leadership Conference, to help with desegregation. The presence of liberal-minded whites at voter registration drives and sit-ins against businesses that refused to serve blacks gave the Civil Rights movement more public attention than it had before. More media outlets started covering violent demonstrations during this period, raising public concern across the country. As a result, a new generation of northern black activists arose, espousing militant slogans and, in some cases, phrasing the fight for civil rights as a war between blacks and the United States government.

Today, the racial situation in the South in the 1960s is remembered for news coverage of violence. The novel's depiction captures a truer image of day-to-day race relations: blacks clearly held a disadvantage, but they also socialized with their white neighbors, albeit in a guarded fashion.

Critical Overview

From its first publication, *A Long and Happy Life* has been recognized as the start of a major literary career, showing a promise of talent that Reynolds Price has continued to make good on to this day. Robert Drake, writing in the *Southern Review*, noted that the book "stood out like a beacon of light, or, at the least, a breath of fresh air" among other works of the time that were more programmatic or that relied on sexuality to be interesting. Noted literary critic Granville Hicks told readers, "I have seldom read a first novel that had such sustained lyric power as Reynolds Price's *A Long and Happy Life*: not pretty, pseudo-poetic prose but a vigorous, joyful outburst of song."

As Price's career progressed, his works were well-received, but critics continually return to his first novel as being, if not his best, then among his best. Theodore Solotaroff began a 1970 review of Price's career by observing that "Eight years ago Reynolds Price, then twenty-nine years old, published a first novel . . . which immediately established him as the legitimate heir of the great southern writers of the past generations." He went on to characterize the writer's career up to that point as "complex," with novels and plays of varying quality, though always interesting.

The characters in *A Long and Happy Life* were continued by Price in two more novels and a play, none of which impressed critics as much as the original novel.

Criticism

David Kelly

Kelly is an instructor of literature and creative writing at two colleges in Illinois. In this essay, Kelly shows an appreciation for Price's skill at raising references and insinuations in A Long and Happy Life *that never need to be explained.*

There are many reasons to recommend Reynolds Price's 1962 debut novel, *A Long and Happy Life*, and most of them have to do with the way that Price makes his characters and their situation real and convincing. The world that surrounds the book's protagonist, Rosacoke Mustian, is vivid, rich, and varied, so much so that, as in the real world, there are issues and actions that can never be fully understood. It starts with a mystery—who is the father of Mildred Sutton's baby?—and continues to drop one open-ended suggestion after another. Who is the younger boy in the photo of Rosacoke's father, and what is he shouting? What happens between Milo, Wesley, and Willie Duke beneath the surface of Mason's Lake, that the men would carry her back to the shore "like a sack of dry meal" and then would race back to swim the whole lake twice? Where does Rosacoke work? Like life, the novel offers glimpses of things that an observer might hope to find out more about but that, as often or not, are left to sheer guesswork.

This effect is, of course, achieved by omission. Price raises issues, implies things, that he never fol-

lows through on. The credit he deserves is due to how difficult a feat this is. There is a constant struggle in any piece of fiction between the writer's attempt to imitate the world's unevenness and the possibility that a work that does in fact look too "real" will come out looking like a sloppy piece of writing. Handled well, as it is in *A Long and Happy Life*, the technique of leaving questions unanswered will leave readers with a sense of wonder. When handled poorly, as it is in the overwhelming majority of fiction that consciously tries to arouse curiosity, readers end up not feeling challenged or curious but only that the writer has done a poor job of proofreading the novel for continuity. That the right balance is achieved in this novel is commendable, especially in light of the fact that it is the writer's first novel. Readers do not feel impatient about what they do not know, and they tend to have confidence that everything will have some relevance in the end.

Not all of the unresolved issues are of the same level of importance, of course. Some have answers that can be reasonably inferred by readers who are willing to take the time to think about the context for a moment. For instance, the actions beneath the lake's surface already questioned here will fall into that category, as readers can guess, even without the specifics, that they are something fairly sexual. Other questions, such as Rosacoke's job, may be curious, but they really do not have to be answered, even after Price has teased his audience by having Rosacoke's mysterious, unnamed boss beg her to hurry back after she calls in sick. Another writer might be kind to his audience in such a case and satisfy their curiosity, but Price is secure enough to not feel pressured into giving information that is really not necessary for the story to go on. Still other mysteries, like the truth of the situation in the picture from 1915, seem central to the question of who the Mustians are. For the book to raise crucial issues like this and then abandon them might approximate the way that such unfinished pieces of information present themselves in real life, but they are nonetheless maddening to readers who are, after all, on a search for the deepest corners of their protagonist's identity.

Perhaps the finest example of information that Price withholds from his readers, which another writer would spell out for them, is the question of what, exactly, might be in the poem that Rosacoke once wrote for the "What I Am Seeking in an Ideal Mate" contest. The book mentions this poem only once, with the explanation that it was "never sent in as it got out of hand." The possible contents of

> "Leaving the poem out of *A Long and Happy Life* might give readers a vague sense of dissatisfaction, as if an unfulfilled promise has been made, but in that way it serves to make them feel the discontentment Rosacoke must feel."

this poem are intriguing, and they represent the balance that the novel strikes consistently. On one hand, readers would find it to be terrifically helpful to have Rosacoke's romantic ideal spelled out for them, given that the main focus of the entire book is her effort to match the flawed reality of Wesley Beavers to the image in her mind of what he ought to be. Her poem would say a lot about why she is discontent throughout the whole story. On the other hand, though, is it really necessary to have Rosacoke's ideal mate spelled out? She is a uniquely gifted and sensitive character on most matters, but there are plenty of good reasons to assume that her idea of love is not particularly unique. The fact that she even thought about entering such a poetry competition implies in itself that what she thinks of as proper "mate" material probably covers the sort of ideas that are ordinary for a small-town girl who has more experience in preparing for love than she actually has in love. Her requirements for such a mate undoubtedly include caring, friendliness, devotion, romantic thinking, etc.—in short, all of the characteristics that Wesley does not have. Price is shrewd to realize that the importance of Rosacoke's poem lies not in the items she names but in the sheer number of them, indicating just how many desires she has that have gone unfulfilled. Leaving the poem out of *A Long and Happy Life* might give readers a vague sense of dissatisfaction, as if an unfulfilled promise has been made, but in that way it serves to make them feel the discontentment Rosacoke must feel.

The story treats things having to do with the body as the greatest mysteries of all: Mildred dies during birth, and Sissie's baby does not make it through the birthing process. These facts would not have been all that unusual for a small country town some forty years ago, but it is interesting that the narrative asks no questions about what happened in either case. Each death is accepted as just the sort of thing that can happen. Even the pregnancy which results from Rosacoke's first and only sexual encounter is compared to the miraculous virgin birth of the Bible when she is dressed up like the Virgin Mary in the Christmas pageant and given a child to hold. The cause of her pregnancy is clear enough, but Rosacoke still carries the attitude of a virgin, accepting the consequences of sex without ever directly accepting the fact that she has experienced it. Price never explains her decision to give in to Wesley's pressures for sex, only that it comes just after she realizes that Wesley will never change his ways. In effect, her pregnancy is treated as a natural and unavoidable event once she gives in and decides to not fight against the mysteries of the world.

This is the hidden dynamic that remains for readers to consider without being told by the author what they should think. Rosacoke's expectations from love are unstated but easily assumed; what Wesley expects of love can never be understood, and the novel ends when Rosacoke quits trying. The difficult thing, for both Rosacoke and the readers, comes from trying to determine how much his evasions are done on purpose and how much they are done because evasion is just his nature. His method of flirting with her is to make her jealous by insinuating events that he refuses to tell her about. In one case, he brings up the idea of "skinny dipping" but not who he swam naked with. (She can tell that he is not just pretending to be worldly, though, by the lack of tan lines around his bathing suit.) During sex, he calls her by the name "Mae" but offers no explanation. Caught in a lie when he tells her that he has been ill from the air flight and has not been out since his arrival, when Rosacoke has already spoken with someone who saw him out the night before, he "tightened his lips, not as if he had made a joke but as if he had ridden that track as far as he intended and wouldn't she like to throw the switch?" Rosacoke accepts what she does not know about Wesley's life when she comes to the realization that it does not matter whether he is intentionally misleading her or is telling the truth to the best of his limited ability: either way, he is what he is.

In this sense, *A Long and Happy Life* is itself like Wesley Beavers, teasing its readers with its secrets, drawing their curiosity, and, ultimately, making them live comfortably with the fact that some things will always remain mysteries. It is a rare author who can make readers take a book on its own terms, but Price shows himself with this novel to know his characters and their environment well enough that there is never a question that unanswered questions are anything but intentional. In his first novel, he achieved one of the most difficult tasks a fiction writer can attempt: making readers feel comfortable with what they do not understand.

Source: David Kelly, Critical Essay on *A Long and Happy Life*, in *Novels for Students*, Gale, 2003.

William J. Schafer
Roger Thompson

In the following essay, Schafer and Thompson give an overview of Price's career and writings.

Reynolds Price has moved from detailed examination of North Carolina rural life to an intense concern with the artist's vision of reality. Beginning with the tragicomic saga of the Mustian family (the novels *A Long and Happy Life* and *A Generous Man*, and the story "A Chain of Love," now collected in *Mustian*), he has come in *Love and Work* and *Permanent Errors* to wrestle with narrative forms closer to the bone. In the preface to *Permanent Errors* Price described his work as "the attempt to isolate in a number of lives the central error of act, will, understanding which, once made, has been permanent, incurable, but whose diagnosis and palliation are the hopes of continuance."

This applies to all Price's fiction. *A Long and Happy Life* is the inside story of Rosacoke Mustian, a country girl seeking a conventional life with an unconventional young man, Wesley Beavers. Her error is that she conceives "a long and happy life" only in the clichéd terms of romance, of settled-wedded-bliss tradition. She reviews her life, her family's life, is discontent, becomes pregnant by Wesley and finally comes to see him and herself in larger terms, terms of myth, in a Christmas pageant which shows her the complete (and divine) meanings of motherhood, birth, and love.

Myth becomes the vehicle of self-understanding more overtly in *A Generous Man*, which shows the Mustian family several years earlier. It describes an allegorical search for an escaped circus python, a giant serpent named Death, and the discovery of a lost treasure. Milo Mustian describes the stifling forces of convention which circumscribe their lives: "it's what nine-tenths of the humans born since God said 'Adam!' have thought was a life, planned out for themselves—all my people, my

> Reynolds Price has moved from detailed examination of North Carolina rural life to an intense concern with the artist's vision of reality."

Mama, my Daddy (it was what strangled him), Rosacoke. . . ." Only by transcending the everyday, by seeing human life in larger terms, can the individual escape the slow strangulation of "permanent errors" and find direction and meaning in existence.

Good Hearts updates and completes the saga of Rosacoke Mustian and Wesley Beavers, who have reached married middle age and the wisdom of accumulated domestic experience. Wesley, after 28 years of marriage to Rosacoke, suddenly leaves home. Both Wesley and Rosacoke learn about their unique needs and natures, especially their sexual temperaments, in this separation. By the end of the story they are reunited after realizing essential truths about the evolving physical and spiritual demands of love.

Price's fiction has become increasingly abstract and complex as he has moved to a more inward vision. From the first he has used sets of images and metaphors to suggest a mysterious or magical reality beyond his pastoral settings. He has deepened this metaphorical (and psychological) interest in *Love and Work* and *Permanent Errors*, where the protagonists are no longer the eccentric pastoral figures of the Mustian clan but are closer to Price's own viewpoint. Price's fiction has always dealt with confusion of the heart and alienation of the mind, but the recent work draws its images and symbols from Price's own experience—his family, a visit to Dachau prison camp, the writer's situation. The grotesqueness and unfamiliarity of the Mustian clan are replaced by more familiar and universal facts of contemporary life.

In *The Tongues of Angels*, Price creates a memoir-like *bildungsroman,* a story of adolescent initiation and adult epiphany, set in a Smoky Mountain summer camp. The novel explores directly the spiritual springs of art and the religious meaning of experience as an artist renders it. This is Price's most overt and effective disquisition on profound religious experience and memory as the basis of art.

In two large novels, *The Surface of the Earth* and *The Source of Light*, Price is most ambitious. The narratives deal with a family saga encompassing the first half of our century and drawing from Price's own experience. The novels detail through letters, conversations, and lyrical soliloquies the Mayfield family and its cycle of birth, maturity and death as viewed by Rob Mayfield, who focuses the narratives. The family is more genteel than the Mustians, and these novels detail a world of important things and social valences. The search by Rob Mayfield for a sense of himself and for a peaceful reconciliation with his father's memory is an important mirror image of Rosacoke Mustian's growth into adulthood.

Love and death are polarities in Price's work— how to save life from death, how to prevent life from becoming deathly, stale, void of myth and magic. The theme appears most clearly in *A Generous Man*, when the Mustians set out to find and kill Death, the great serpent, and are finally told, "Death is dead." In the course of this magical hunt, Milo Mustian comes to understand what he must do to save himself from the slow death of a clichéd life; Rato Mustian, the wise fool, grapples with Death and escapes its coils through his cunning folly; Rosacoke moves from complete innocence to the dawn of maturity. In his later fiction Price has moved from symbols of external life to more internalized ones: sleep, dreams, a writer seeking a relationship between love and work, self and others, private life and shared life. Price's fiction describes the individual's perceptions of himself and of the realities around him, the uses of imagination. His characters travel on a quest for the potency of myth and the ability to transcend a closed vision of everyday reality. They move toward permanent truths through "permanent errors."

Blue Calhoun is, in essence, another story of permanent errors, the novel being an extended letter written by Blue to his granddaughter through which he hopes for penance. Blue has seen his life crumble: a relapsing alcoholic, his decline begins with an affair with sixteen-year-old Luna. For Blue, these errors move inexorably to tragedies for which he feels responsible, including the death of his wife and his daughter by cancer. The feeling of guilt pervades Price's work, as does the desire for absolution, and both center on the interweaving of death and love.

Any understanding of love in Price's work is necessarily connected to grief, loss, and death, so

that in *The Promise of Rest*, just as in *Blue Calhoun*, Price draws to the center of his work a man whose life of errors works to uncover the truths offered by love even in the shadow of death. While *The Promise of Rest* details the final days of Wade Mayfield, the novel is more the unburdening of Wade's father Hutch and parallels Blue's unburdening of his past to his granddaughter. Hutch's mission to rescue Wade from isolation as he dies of AIDS is more a mission to revisit his own bisexual past and to understand the crumbling of his marriage and his disavowal of his African-American relationships.

Wade's gay relationship with an African American causes, literally and metaphorically, Hutch to reconnect with his past, with his errors, and to reconcile them with the fact of the death of his son. Hutch's various loves are at the center of the work, and each of those loves ends in a death: Hutch fails to reunite with Straw, his African-American friend with whom he had a gay relationship; Hutch's marriage to Ann ends in divorce; Wade, Hutch's only child, dies of AIDS. Each of these deaths are explorations of the love that once gave them life, of the relationships Hutch nurtured with different people in his life.

In *Roxanna Slade*, Price returns to a female narrative voice for the first time since *Kate Vaiden*, but the story, which reads variously as advice manual and extended elegy, parallels *Blue Calhoun*'s life narrative of love and death and the awful connections forged in the dark corners of the South. Indeed, Roxanna's life as told in the book literally begins with the death of Larkin Slade. Roxanna marries Larkin's brother, Palmer, and the two have a child, who is named after Larkin. The novel, told in the rambling, but forceful, narrative voice of Roxanna Slade, centers upon the complex relationships between black and white, male and female, and how those relationships affect others around them.

Palmer's illegitimate daughter, born by a poor African-American woman, becomes in almost Dickensian fashion the helpmate of Roxanna, and through the connections, Roxanna's life is laid bare. The narrative of Roxanna is self-consciously concerned with "telling it straight," and in large part, that purpose undergirds Price's work as a whole. While by no means a realist, Price uncovers the complexity that governs relationships and how love and death compete in a structuring reality. Price's works increasingly focus on the intensity of the relationships that govern lives, and how those relationships essentially change the realities of the world.

Source: William J. Schafer and Roger Thompson, "Price, (Edward) Reynolds," in *Contemporary Novelists*, 7th ed., edited by Neil Schlager and Josh Lauer, St. James Press, 2001, pp. 817–19.

Jean W. Ross

In the following Contemporary Authors (CA) *interview, Ross presents an interview with Reynolds Price that was conducted by telephone on January 18, 1991.*

CA: You've had both the discipline and the good fortune to explore your world in several forms: novels, short stories, poetry, essays, memoir, plays. Is there something to say, starting out, about the benefits and maybe the difficulties of examining your material in these different ways?

Price: Apart from the normal difficulties of trying to do anything well, I don't think any particular form or genre has presented more difficult problems than another. Obviously the novel requires much the most sustained application of energy. Certainly in the beginning of my career I found it considerably easier to write shorter things—poems, essays, short stories. But I think the longer I've continued to write the novel, the more I have felt that it has gone from being a difficult kind of application to being a job that has the joys of steady work that I feel good about.

I've enjoyed working in the different forms. One of the real problems in having a "literary career" is that, if you go on doing it for as long as I have, which is since I was twenty-one years old, part of what you're trying to do is keep yourself interested. And even more important than that, you're keeping yourself alert. You're trying continually to discover ways to clean your spectacles so that you can go on watching the world with a depth and freshness that anyone past the age of thirty-vie knows are difficult to maintain.

CA: You might have become an artist, like the first-person narrator of your 1990 novel The Tongues of Angels, *but before you were out of high school you came to feel your painting skills were insufficient for a career, as you said in the 1989 memoir* Clear Pictures. *Do you think some part of your experience in painting and drawing has helped you as a writer?*

Price: I think it has, tremendously. I think it trained my powers of witness, if you will. I talked in *Clear Pictures* about the fact that both my par-

ents were especially watchful people, my mother perhaps most of all. That may well have come from the fact that she was an orphan. both her parents had died when she was young, and she had to grow up in someone else's family. Though it was in fact the family of her loving sister, she was still a bit of an outsider, an outlaw, in her childhood. And I think outlaws and the excluded of the world do very much tend to be the keen watchers of the world. They'd better be. I think perhaps the years I spent drawing and painting intensified what was probably a kind of acquired bent from my mother.

CA: Do you still draw and paint?

Price: I have spasms of it. I haven't done anything now for several years. I might pick up an occasional pad and sketch, but nothing sustained. I had my first spinal surgery in 1984, and as a result of the surgery and the radiation I was unable to write for four or five months. During that period I did a tremendous amount of drawing. Once it all ended, after about a year, it became clear to me that part of what I was apparently doing was repeating the whole pattern of my beginning to be involved in writing, which was to start out with the painting and drawing and somehow let that segue into another form in mimesis, another form of portraying the visible world. What I'd been working on before the surgery was *Kate Vaiden*. Afterwards, the book broke down completely on me, and it was four or five months before I could get back to work on it. Painting turned out to be the bridge that got me across the ravine.

CA: Do you feel your illness changed the course of that book in any way?

Price: I suspect that it did. Strangely enough, I had literally written the last sentence of Part One of the three parts of the book the day that I went into the hospital. So I had come to a natural stopping point in the story. That was both good and difficult. The difficulty was in making a leap from Part One to Part Two. I think if I had stopped in the middle of a scene, I might have been able to pick it up immediately and write the answer that the other character gives to what had just been said. But I had to get her across the gap between Part One and Part Two, and I couldn't do it for a long time. Once I did start, the novel moved with tremendous rapidity for me. I think I must have recommenced around December of '84 or January of '85, and I had finished by June.

I don't think there can be any doubt that there were changes in the book that are attributable to the events that I had gone through in recent months, but because I never plan novels in fine detail I couldn't say how I might have veered off an

> " There's very little conscious planning in the way my books come to me. They just arrive, and I try to have the sense to get them down."

original plan. I never had a detailed outline. I had only a general knowledge that Kate would discover her lost son at the end of the book and that we would leave the novel with the thought that she was trying to make contact, but we shouldn't' know what the nature of that contact would be. Otherwise the details invented themselves. So perhaps a detail such a Kate's discovering that she has cancer may well be directly a result of my own surgery. I certainly didn't feel driven to put in something about cancer because I'd just had it. But who knows? It very likely turned up for that reason.

CA: I was fascinated to read after I read the novel that your mother had been the inspiration for Kate.

Price: She was. Again, the events of the novel have almost no resemblance to the events of my mother's life. And Kate's a lot younger than my mother: My mother was born in 1905. But the atmosphere of Kate, of this person who's undergone an awful domestic tragedy early in her life, was the atmosphere of my mother's life. Her mother died when my mother was five, and her father died when she was fourteen.

CA: Like so many of your characters, Kate is someone the outsider might not take a second look at, the "ordinary" person whom you always show not to be ordinary.

Price: That's something I've consciously wanted to do from the beginning of my career. I think it's partly because I came from a family in which people were gentle and civilized but not highly literate. Only one or two members of either side of my family ever attended the university. So all my life I've felt a desire to make those generally inarticulate people articulate in fiction.

CA: Many readers knew you first as the author of A Long and Happy Life, *which told the early story of Rosacoke Mustian and Wesley*

Beavers. *Rosacoke has first surfaced, though, in a story you write in 1955, "A Chain of Love." Mustians appeared in other books and stories, and Rosa and Wesley reappeared in 1988 in* Good Hearts. *What kept you interested in the family over a span of more than thirty years?*

Price: It would be hard to say. As I said in the preface in the book called *Mustian*, which brings together the existing Mustian stories up to 1983, they started when I was a senior in college and had to produce a short story for a creative writing class. I came up then with this story about Rosacoke, which I talked a good deal about in that preface. I simply can't say why.

In the winter of 1964, after the very appalling weeks and months that surrounded the assassination of John Kennedy, I was trying to write the novel that ultimately became *The Surface of the Earth*, but it seemed too depressing and too difficult for me to focus on at such a low ebb in our national life. I suddenly found myself thinking about a kind of rural comedy, and the character of Rosacoke's brother Milo came to hand as the most available character to be the center of this story. *A Generous Man* fairly quickly built itself around the character of Milo, though of course it backdated him to his early teens, earlier than *A Long and Happy Life*.

If you had asked me about the Mustians a year after I finished *A Generous Man*, I probably would have said, I'm sure I'm through the with Mustians. But in the early '70s I thought maybe I should look at them again. I made some notes and then I thought, No, that's it; let's leave them alone. So I got down to about 1985 or 1986, right after I'd finished *Kate Vaiden*, and I thought I was going to write a novel in the male first person, a novel that, though it would have direct connection with the plot or the characters of *Kate Vaiden*, would be a sort of male companion to the female point of view in Kate. But I couldn't write it. I wasn't ready to happen in 1986. Then all of a sudden I found myself thinking about the possibility that Wesley was going to run away from home and leave Rosa alone and that a disaster would happen to her. The next thing I knew, I was writing what turned out to be *Good Hearts*. There's very little conscious planning in the way my books come to me. They just arrive, and I try to have the sense to get them down.

CA: Do you think Wesley and Rosa might come back?

Price: I'm not going to say no this time! But I have absolutely no plans or ideas for that. If they come back, they'll come knocking at the door in their own time.

CA: At one time you expressed strong feelings for The Surface of Earth *and* The Source of Light, *both of which failed to get widespread critical acceptance at the time they were published. Do you think those books will get another look from at least academic critics because of the publicity your more recent work has gotten?*

Price: They do get a lot of attention; I'm always being sent articles that people have written about them. I think it's impossible to calculate what further attention they'll get. As for how I feel about them, those books constitute a single long novel which comes in two parts, and those nearly thousand pages of fiction certainly constitute to this point the largest attempt that I've made. And large doesn't mean the greatest number of pages; it means the most sustained attempt to look at the most of human life, the largest piece of time and character. In that sense I have a special fondness for the books. But there's really nothing I've written that I'm ashamed of or wish I could make disappear. I certainly don't go back and reread my own work. Not that I think it's bad, but it's sort of like going back and looking at old photographs of one's self and thinking, Oh, look at my haircut!—which of course I thought was wonderful at the time. I'm not a narcissist about my own work, but I'm glad I wrote it all.

CA: The hypnosis therapy you undertook to help you control pain gave you the heightened memory of childhood experiences that was part of the impetus to write the memoir Clear Pictures. *Does that kind of recall continue to happen?*

Price: No, not in the same way. After I had that series of what I call hypnosis lessons at Duke Hospital, memory was coming back in a kind of tumble that was abnormal for me. I've always had what I thought was a good memory, but that was a fairly phenomenal adventure for just those few months. In fact, the first great rush of memory I got as a result of the hypnosis was the material that became *The Tongues of Angels.* It was a lot of memory about my working as a camp counselor in the mountains of North Carolina when I was twenty years old; that all started flooding back over me in great detail. Then I began to make notes for those memories; I thought, Someday I'll write a book based on that summer of mine in the mountains near Asheville. But memories about my family and the towns in which I grew up were tumbling in simultaneously. For whatever unknown reason,

I began writing the family memories first. Once *Clear Pictures* was finished, I turned back and got out my notes about old Camp Sequoia and began working on what became *The Tongues of Angels.*

CA: That book was the second novel you'd written in the first-person voice, Kate Vaiden *having been the first. How did you make that choice in the two novels, and what significance might be attached to its coming late in the sequence of your work?*

Price: I had done an occasional short story in the first person, and in my second volume of stories, *Permanent Errors*, there was a novella in the male first person. I'm trying to finish a novel now which is also in the male first person, and it may be the result of this hope that I've had to write a companion novel to *Kate.* I think I was a bit allergic to the first person early in my career. I was always quoting to my students something that Hemingway had said, which was that anybody can write a novel in the first persons. I sort of know what he meant: If you have the normal novelist's gift for mimicry, you can just say, I am this person, and start talking as that person. In many ways that's easier than saying he or she did so-and-so. But why I've had this explosion of three first-person novels in recent years I couldn't say. I've enjoyed it tremendously, but I wouldn't hesitate to write a third-person novel tomorrow. In fact I have been writing a lot of short stories the last couple of years, and most of those are third-person stories.

CA: What accounts for the increase in short stories?

Price: For the first time in my life, I've made myself a member of my short-story class. I teach a senior graduate class in short-story writing, and this semester I'm teaching a long-story class. I've made myself a contributing member: I do the assignments when the students do, and that's resulted in my coming up with the first new batch of stories I'I've had since 1970, when my second volume of stories was published. I put my stories out on the table and urge the students to be as honest with the teacher as he is with them. Of course, they probably aren't quite as candid as they ought to be, but with a little encouragement, they dig in pretty well.

CA: The titles of your 1985 poetry collection, The Laws of Ice, *and your 1990 one,* The Use of Fire, *make me think of Robert Frost's poem "Fire and Ice." Would you talk about how those opposites figure in your titles and in the collections?*

Price: I haven't counted, but I think the majority of the poems in *The Laws of Ice* come after the cancer surgery I had in the summer of '84. The title poem is very much about the experience of being totally ambushed at a particular moment in one's life by an enemy so enormous that even if one survives, one is going to become a new person as a result of that encounter. The laws of ice are the laws of death and affliction to which we are all subject from the moment we're born. *The Use of Fire* contains a great many poems which are based in the second and third surgeries I had and the wonderful period of recovery I've had since the fall of '86, when the most recent surgery occurred. There's a kind of spaciousness and relaxation and a sort of serene retrospection in *The Use of Fire* which I don't feel in *The Laws of Ice* at all. There's literal fire and ice then—literal terror and great warmth.

CA: Being sensitive to the frustration and real damage book reviewers can cause writers, how do you approach doing reviews and criticism of other people's work?

Price: In the very beginning of my career, I wrote one or two snooty reviews of the "I could do better than this" sort. But I think I very quickly realized that just wasn't worth doing, that there were plenty of people out there who were ready to take care of the "beat 'em up in the alley" detail, and I decided that since my time and energy were limited anyway, I wasn't going to review books that I didn't already know I liked. Since then, whenever anyone has asked me to review a book, I've always said that I would look at it and give them a quick answer, but I wouldn't do it sight unseen because I don't feel any necessity to beat up on people's writing.

There was one book I reviewed years ago, a book of short stories for children that I profoundly felt should be kept out of the hands of children. They were stories very much about violence and sexual abuse, and it seemed to me that for the age group they were being aimed at, they were a very bad idea. But that's the only case I can think of that I've written a review saying, "Do not buy this book—or at least, do not give it to your child." Other than that I've reviewed books that I knew in principle I was going to like and that I wanted to praise. I think the whole premise of book reviewing is so unexamined. A mediocre novel is not at all likely to damage the world or to damage anyone else's soul. At the very most it might set their pocketbook back fifteen or twenty dollars. I never

have understood the passion that highly negative reviewers like to take in their line about movies and books. To be a profession reviewer seems very strange, in any case.

CA: You've taught for most of your adult life. What's made it worth the doing?

Price: I worked out a wonderful relationship in 1963 whereby I teach one semester a year. For the last few years that's been the spring semester. I teach two courses; I teach two days a week and usually come in part of another day for conferences. Since college terms have gotten so short, I'm really teaching under four months a year. I put most of my energy during that four months into the teaching. It's been sort of like crop rotation: teaching fourth months, writing for eight, then teaching four. But since I've now made myself a member of the short-story class, I continue writing during my teaching semesters.

I get a tremendous sense of reward from the students I work with. I generally teach the poetry of Milton, and I have about forty-give people in that class. In the writing class, ideally I have about twelve—this semester I have fifteen, which is a little bit larger than I wanted, but there were that many good people. I wanted to be a teacher as far back as I wanted to be a writer, and i know that my wanted to be a teacher was a result of my having such disciplined and demanding teachers in my childhood. I came along in the last great age of the old-made schoolteacher, and i was tremendously responsive to those women. It's one of my great joys now that I'm still in touch with some of them.

CA: It's widely felt that students don't come to college with the background in reading that students used to bring to college—back in the days of those old-maid schoolteachers. How do you deal with that in teaching?

Price: I was an undergraduate at Duke from 1951 to 1955, and partly I try to remind myself that among my own contemporaries there were lots of boys who'd never read the daily paper, much less Tolstoy. So we may be looking back at the past with much too rosy spectacles. But there's very little one can do for the student who's eighteen or twenty-one and comes in saying he's never read anything. You can hand him basic lists of whatever books you think are indispensable for whatever kind of work he hopes to do—and I've known the rare students who have actually taken off a couple of years and worked at a pizza restaurant or whatever to read their way through the books they'd never read.

But it's unfortunate if people don't read those books while they're young. I know the reading I did before I was sixteen or so sank into me in a way that nothing ever has since—partly, I guess, because our minds aren't nearly as full of stuff when we're children as they are later. Our files get so crowded as we get older. I'm really thrilled that, sort of by accident, I read *Anna Karenina* when I was fourteen or fifteen, and *Madame Bovary*. I can see now what great books they are, but they don't take the top of my head off the way they did when I first read them. I remember the moment in which I finished the scene of Emma Bovary's death, and it was as though a tornado had hit the house. Now I read it and I think its' a very great novel, I'm glad it exists, but I'm not swept off to Kansas on my bicycle.

CA: North Carolina seems an uncommonly fertile and nurturing ground for writers. Do you have any thoughts on why this is so?

Price: I think with all its woes and with all its insistence on sending Jesse Helms to the Senate, North Carolina has a gentler brand of Southern life than most of the deeper Southern states. It's a more welcoming place. It's more prepared to tolerate the kinds of people that writers generally are—prickly customers, gadflies on the hide of society. But I think we owe the present bonanza of fine novelists and poets and dramatists to the existence of wonderful universities and colleges in the state; that's the ultimate reason. There's a nexus of Duke and Chapel Hill and North Carolina State all within twenty miles of one another. And a great many of the people who went to those universities have decided to continue to live here because it is such a good place.

CA: Unlike some major writers born in the South, you stayed in the South, without a rebellion or an apology. For people who haven't read what you've written on the subject, would you talk about that choice and how you think it has affected your writing?

Price: In my childhood and adolescence, aside from a few bad experiences with my childish contemporaries, I had a very good experience in the South. I wasn't aware that I was in the South; I was aware that I was in a loving family in towns that I mostly liked. So I never felt, "Oh my God, get me out of Dixie" and caught the Silver Meteor to streak out of Raleigh to Penn Station, which a lot of my contemporaries and slightly older people did. I will, though, have to be honest and say that my return to the South after I'd spent three years in graduate

What Do I Read Next?

- The history of the Mustian family begins several years earlier than the setting of *A Long and Happy Life*. Milo is fifteen in *A Generous Man*. This is available in the collection *Rosacoke and Her Kin*, which includes *A Generous Man*, *A Chain of Love*, *A Long and Happy Life* and *Good Hearts*. It is published by Scribner Paperback Fiction.

- The story of Price's 1984 bout with crippling spinal cancer, his interaction with the medical profession, and his recovery are examined by the author in *A Whole New Life: An Illness and a Healing*, published by Plume in 1995.

- Many critics have pointed out the resemblance between Price's characters and the characters of fellow Southerner Carson McCullers in her 1940 classic *The Heart Is a Lonely Hunter*, a story about the residents of a Georgia mill town who labor under a sense of isolation.

- Eudora Welty was considered one of America's finest fiction writers, certainly one of the finest writers about Southern values and customs. She was also a friend of and collaborator with Reynolds Price. Her novels are all meticulously crafted, but readers can find echoes of *A Long and Happy Life* most clearly in her story "First Love," found in *Collected Stories of Eudora Welty*, published in 1982 by Harvest Books.

school in England was fortuitous. I'd been in my last year at Oxford thinking I had to try to get a job from three or four thousand miles away, and I suddenly got a letter from Duke, my alma mater, asking if I'd accept a three-year contract to come back and teach freshman English. It seemed the easiest way on earth to solve the problem of getting a job from that far away. So I came back in 1958 and began teaching at Duke. One thing led to another, the way it can do in life, and I've simply stayed here because it turned out that I never wanted to go anywhere else. I don't know what would have happened if I'd been offered a good job at Swarthier. Or at Dartmouth—I might have wound up living in New England. I had not passionately planted my banner on Southern soil and said, "I proclaim this my homeland forevermore." But that's the way it turned out, and I have no regrets, far from it.

CA: Are there movies under way now from any of the novels?

Price: Movies in my career have been under way forever. *A Long and Happy Life* was sold to the movies about ten minutes after it was published. Now it's had literally about a dozen movie options on it. *Kate Vaiden* seems very close to becoming a film, and a very fine artist has bought *The Tongues of Angels*, which is presently having a screenplay written—not by me. I hope that's going to be done. I did one television play on request for American Playhouse, a play called "Private Contentment," which they produced beautifully. That was very satisfying. But so far I've had no feature films. I'd love to see one. I've loved movies since I was old enough to be carried into them, and I'd be delighted to see what someone would make of a book of mine. I hope I'll get to eventually.

CA: You mentioned earlier the novel that you're working on now. Do you have plans beyond that, or long-range goals for your writing?

Price: No. I just want to keep doing more of the same. I have a book of three long stories coming out this spring from Atheneum. It's called *The Foreseeable Future*. And I've just had *New Music* published, a trilogy of plays produced last year in Cleveland. They cover over forty years in the life of a family. And I'm about to finish this new novel. That's what's on my plate at the moment, and I don't have specific plans for anything else. But that doesn't worry me, because I almost never have plans from one book to the next.

Source: Jean W. Ross, "Interview with Reynolds Price," in *Contemporary Authors New Revision Series*, Vol. 37, Gale Research, 1988, pp. 358–66.

Sources

Drake, Robert, "Coming of Age in North Carolina," in the *Southern Review*, Vol. 3, No. 1, Winter 1967, pp. 248–50.

Hicks, Granville, "Country Girl Burdened with Love," in *Critical Essays on Reynolds Price*, edited by James A. Schiff, G. K. Hall, 1998, pp. 53–55.

———, "A Generous Man," in *Saturday Review*, March 26, 1966.

Levinger, Larry, "The Prophet Faulkner," in the *Atlantic Monthly*, June 2000, pp. 76–86.

Price, Reynolds, "An Awful Gift and a Blindness," in the *Southern Review*, Vol. 36, No. 2, Spring 2000, pp. 385–94.

Rooke, Constance, "Chapter One: Christian Solitary," in *Reynolds Price*, Twayne Publishers, 1983, pp. 1–14.

———, "Chapter Two: A Long and Happy Life," in *Reynolds Price*, Twayne Publishers, 1983, pp. 15–39.

Schiff, James A., *Understanding Reynolds Price*, University of South Carolina Press, 1996, pp. 11–38.

Solotaroff, Theodore, "The Reynolds Price Who Outgrew the Southern Pastoral," in *Saturday Review*, September 26, 1970, pp. 27–29.

Further Reading

Kaufman, Wallace, "Notice I'm Still Standing: Reynolds Price," in *Conversations with Reynolds Price*, edited by Jefferson Humphries, University of Mississippi Press, 1991, pp. 5–29.

>   Kaufman, a personal friend and collaborator with Price, combines two conversations with the author, from 1966 and 1971. Much of the focus of the earlier interview is on *A Long and Happy Life*.

Rooke, Constance, *Reynolds Price*, Twayne Publishers, 1983.

>   This is one of the few overviews of Price's career and it contains extensive and interesting background about *A Long and Happy Life*.

Schiff, James A., *Understanding Reynolds Price*, University of South Carolina Press, 1996.

>   Schiff's chapter on the Mustian novels traces Price's history of Rosacoke's family, from the first short story in which they appeared in 1958 to the 1988 novel that catches up with Rosacoke and Wesley's marriage nearly thirty years after the publication of *A Long and Happy Life*.

Look Homeward, Angel

Thomas Wolfe
1929

A thinly disguised autobiography and a portrait of the early twentieth-century American South, *Look Homeward, Angel* is the most famous book of an author who used to be regarded as an equal of Ernest Hemingway, F. Scott Fitzgerald, and William Faulkner. Published in New York in 1929, Thomas Wolfe's novel was considered striking and important—a work by a genius with a grand, compelling personality. It is a novel in the American romantic tradition, meant to contain Wolfe's own "American experience" as represented by his alter ego, Eugene Gant.

In the seventy-four years since it was published, the novel has received steadily less critical attention. Wolfe's initial editor, Maxwell Perkins, cut sixty thousand words from its original text to make it more readable, but many recent critics and readers continue to find *Look Homeward, Angel* a hugely sprawling text that is sometimes clearly bombastic. Some are also offended by what it says about race and gender. These elements have led to a decline in Wolfe's reputation and a reevaluation of his importance to the literary movement of his time.

Nevertheless, Wolfe's first novel remains very important to the twentieth-century American tradition, and Wolfe generally retains his contemporary reputation as a unique genius. The best critical approach to his work is one that understands it firmly within its time and place. It is a novel with a strong sense of autobiography, a *Bildungsroman* (novel of development), an attempt at a comprehensive display of life in the American South from 1900 to

Thomas Wolfe

1920, and a response to the modernist movement of American writers who were living and writing in Europe.

Author Biography

Born October 3, 1900, in Asheville, North Carolina, Thomas Wolfe was the youngest of eight children, two of whom died when they were very young. His father, William Oliver Wolfe, traveled around the northern United States, married twice without having children, and then moved to Asheville, where he married Julia Elizabeth Westall. When her youngest son was seven, Thomas's mother bought and moved into a boarding house called "The Old Kentucky Home." The children shuffled between the two homes, and Thomas became interested in the private school he attended at age eleven.

Wolfe entered the University of North Carolina when he was only fifteen. He eventually excelled there, and after he graduated he moved to Boston to complete a master of arts program at Harvard. By this time, he had begun writing plays and short stories, declaring in letters to his mother that he wanted to put "the American experience"

on paper. Wolfe traveled to Europe several times, and on the ship back after one journey, he met Aline Bernstein, with whom he began a long relationship. Bernstein supported Wolfe while he worked on *Look Homeward, Angel*, which Scribner published in 1929 after making some significant cuts to the autobiographical novel.

Wolfe then set out on an ambitious project for a six-part novel series on American themes. Pressure from his publisher contributed to the hurried completion of his second novel, *Of Time and the River*, in 1935. Wolfe then postponed his large project and began work on a novel about another autobiographical hero, the innocent George Webber. In May 1938, Wolfe gave a draft of this novel to his new editor at Harper's and went on vacation. Days later, he was hospitalized in Seattle with a brain infection from pneumonia. He was taken to Baltimore, where he died after an unsuccessful operation on September 15, 1938.

By the time of this death, Wolfe had become a somewhat legendary American figure. Over six and a half feet tall, he was described as passionate and often moody, and he made a lasting impression on those that knew him. His editor published three posthumous novels out of his unfinished manuscript: *The Web and the Rock*, *You Can't Go Home Again*, and *The Hills Beyond*, which describe George Webber's family history and adventures, including his love affair with Esther Jack (Aline Bernstein).

Plot Summary

Part 1

Look Homeward, Angel begins with the journey of Englishman Gilbert Gaunt to Pennsylvania; there he marries a Dutch woman. One of his sons, Oliver Gant (the name was changed upon Gilbert's immigration), becomes a stonecutter and travels through the South until settling with his first wife, Cynthia. After her death, Gant thinks he is dying of tuberculosis and travels west until he reaches the small mountain-valley town of Altamont.

Gant sets up a stonecutting shop and recovers from his restless illness when spring comes. He then meets Eliza Pentland, whom he marries. Then he builds a grand house. Oliver Gant and Eliza have nine children (six of whom survive). Gant begins to go on severe drinking binges, which Eliza vehemently tries to temper.

In 1900, when Gant turns fifty, the conflict between Gant and Eliza comes to a climax. Eliza tries sending him to sanitariums and forbidding saloon owners to serve him drinks, but this only infuriates Gant. One night, he comes home violently drunk. It takes two neighbors, a doctor, and Eliza's brother, Will, to help his daughter, Helen, calm him down. Eliza gives birth that night to her youngest son, Eugene. Gant begs forgiveness from her.

Even as a small child, Eugene thinks deeply about the isolation and loneliness in the world. When he is two, he wanders into his aristocratic neighbors' estate and is almost killed by a horse. His older brother Grover's death from typhoid saddens him deeply. This death causes Eliza to move home from St. Louis, where she was attempting the first of her moneymaking adventures.

Gant continues to grow further from his wife and closer to his daughter Helen. When he is fifty-six, Gant takes a "last great voyage" to California. When he finally returns, he continues his habits of building gigantic fires and making his family eat huge amounts of food.

Eugene discovers his love of books and begins his vibrant inner life at age six. He has several adventures playing with his friends from school (including racist pranks against Jews, African Americans, and poor whites), and once he is almost beaten by the principal for writing insults about him. Eugene's parents make him start a job selling the *Saturday Evening Post*, like his brothers Ben and Luke.

Before Eugene turns eight, Eliza takes him on her next big project—to purchase and run a boarding house called "Dixieland." Eugene still spends much of his time at Gant's house with Helen. But he has his first major crush at Dixieland, on a married woman who has an affair with Eugene's oldest brother, Steve.

Part 2

Eugene grows up rapidly. One day he wins the composition contest the new principal, John Leonard, holds. Margaret Leonard convinces Eliza to send Eugene to their new private school. Mr. Leonard teaches the boys rudimentary Latin and his sister Amy teaches math and history. Mrs. Leonard (whom Eugene idealizes) teaches the boys English, a subject she is passionate about.

Eugene becomes closer with Ben and grows to hate Steve more. Luke and Ben hate Steve too. One night, after Steve has been yelling drunkenly at Eliza and has given Luke a bloody nose, Ben angrily beats him up. Helen tours the South singing but moves back to Altamont after her partner, Pearl,

Media Adaptations

- *Look Homeward, Angel* was adapted as a three-act comedy/drama by Ketti Frings, first produced in New York at the Ethel Barrymore Theatre in 1957. It was published by Scribner in 1958, won the Pulitzer Prize, and was adapted by Gary Geld and Peter Udell as the musical comedy *Angel*, performed on Broadway in 1978.

- John Chandler Griffin's *Memories of Thomas Wolfe: A Pictorial Companion to "Look Homeward, Angel"* (1996) is a very helpful companion piece to Wolfe's novel, both as a source of contextual information and as a way of bringing the events to life.

gets married. Luke does a lot of hustling and tries to pay his way through school, but he drops out and gets a factory job.

Gant sells Eliza his precious stone angel for a poor woman's grave. He takes Eugene to early movies and visits Dixieland more often, but he is "dying very slowly" of prostate cancer. Gant has a very brief affair with a Dixieland tenant and sexually harasses an African American cook but is rapidly and visibly decaying of old age.

Eugene gets a paper route through the African American section of town and grows wilder, harrying subscribers for payments. He nearly has sex with a mulatto (mixed race) prostitute, Ella Corpening. Eliza goes on a trip to Florida, while Eugene stays with the Leonards and continues reading a great deal of literature.

With the beginning of World War I, Eugene wants to join the navy and Ben tries to join the army, but neither actually does so. Eugene goes on a trip to Charleston, where he has a fling with an older girl named Louise. When he returns, he wins a medal for an essay on Shakespeare and acts in a pageant as Prince Hal (from Shakespeare's *Henry IV* cycle). After Helen gets married and moves away, Gant decides inflexibly to send Eugene (at only sixteen) to the state university.

Part 3

Eugene's first year at university is "filled for him with loneliness, pain, and failure." Although he enjoys the education itself, other students mock him frequently. One of them, Jim Trivett, says he will make a man of Eugene and takes him to see a prostitute. When he goes home for Christmas, Eugene only feels better after he has admitted his exploits to Ben and Dr. McGuire.

After a slightly less painful second semester, Eugene goes home again and meets twenty-one-year-old Laura James at Dixieland. One night, after Eugene cuts his hand while trying to subdue his drunken father, she kisses him and he falls rapidly in love with her. They go on a picturesque walk through the mountains and make promises to never leave each other.

At the end of June, however, Laura leaves Altamont, telling Eugene she will be gone for a few days. But she never returns. She writes him a letter informing him that she will be married the next day, and Eugene goes through a savage despair—until Ben once again makes him feel better.

Back at college, Eugene becomes popular and joins a great deal of clubs. When he comes home again for Christmas, his family lets him try a drink for the first time. After he pours more secretly, he becomes extremely drunk. He wanders to town. After his friends bring him back, his family finds him drunk in bed. They all bemoan the curse of drink.

In the spring, Eugene goes on a trip to Virginia in search of Laura. He is still in love with her. When he gets there, he cannot bring himself to seek her out and instead squanders all of his money until he has no choice but to find a job. After working hard all summer, he sends Laura a bitter letter and returns to Altamont.

Eugene returns home from college in October because Ben is deathly ill with pneumonia. The family places the blame on Eliza, whose stinginess may have stopped Ben from getting the proper care, and they bicker with each other while they watch Ben die. When Ben can no longer order her away, Eliza holds his hand and watches Ben's last moments with Eugene.

Luke and Eugene have a burst of energy when Ben is dead, and Eliza tells them to make arrangements in town for an expensive funeral. Eugene breaks into ironic laughter when the undertaker, Horse Hines, is very proud of how he has made up the corpse. Eugene finds the funeral superficial and listens to Helen complain about wasting her life taking care of Gant (who is still alive, if barely). That night, Eugene visits Ben's grave, where he has an eerie discussion with Miss Pert, Ben's companion from Dixieland. Eliza had thrown her angrily from their house during Ben's illness, although Miss Pert was the only person who took care of Ben when he was becoming very sick.

Eugene has a busy and proud final semester at college. After a conversation with his favorite teacher about Harvard, he goes back to Altamont for the last time. Eliza has become completely obsessed with her real estate ventures, but Eugene's anger makes her agree to pay for a year at Harvard. Before Eugene leaves home forever, he visits the town square and sees Ben's ghost. They talk about why Eugene is leaving, and the experience becomes more mystical, with images of the past and of fantastical visions appearing all over the square. Then Ben disappears "without an answer," and Eugene prepares to leave.

Characters

Principal Armstrong

Armstrong, a fat, "delicate" man, is Eugene's first school principal.

Hugh Barton

Hugh is Helen's husband, an eloquent salesman ten years older than she. Although he takes her to Sydney, where Gant lived during his first marriage, Hugh eventually moves back to Altamont, where Helen can once again take care of Gant. Hugh complains that Gant takes advantage of his closest daughter, but eventually he is silent in response to Helen's strong will.

Miss Brown

Although this is unlikely to be her real name, "Miss Brown" is a tenant of Dixieland from the Midwest who sleeps with Eugene. Eugene does not have any money, so she accepts his medals from Leonard's school as payment.

Dr. J. H. Coker

Coker is the doctor who comes, too late, to deal with Ben's pneumonia. He is always smoking a cigar and is characterized by a profound weariness.

Ella Corpening

Ella is a poor mulatto resident from the African American section of Altamont. Eugene comes very close to losing his virginity to her when collecting for his paper route.

Guy Doak

Guy is Eugene's roommate at the Leonard's school during Eliza's trip to Florida. He is one of the few northerners in the book and has "a sharp, bright, shallow mind, inflexibly dogmatic."

Ben Gant

Ben is Eugene's closest brother, who dies of pneumonia at the end of the novel. He is a scowling and independent child not very close with anyone in the family except Eugene. His success at the newspaper office makes him money, with which he is generous, and he always disparages Eliza for being cheap. The family is devastated that Eliza's hesitation in spending the money for medical attention may have been responsible for Ben's death.

Although he wants to join the army, Ben is never allowed to because of his ill health, and this makes him more cynical and frustrated about the purpose of his life in Altamont. Ben is always making the comment, "Listen to this, will you," to an imaginary witness (an "angel") that understands the ridiculous situation he believes himself to be in. His closest companion is Miss Pert, who nurses him when he starts to become very sick.

Eugene feels so close to Ben partly because he is outside the dynamic of the family. Ben teaches his younger brother a great deal and always looks out for him despite masking this feeling in cynicism. He buys Eugene presents, gives him far more money than Eliza or Gant, and thinks in broader terms than most people in Altamont. He does not answer Eugene's tortured questions at the end of the novel, but his scowling honesty about the purpose of life is very important to how Eugene grows up.

Bessie Gant

Bessie is Gant's cousin, who grimly nurses Ben during his pneumonia.

Daisy Gant

A "timid, sensitive girl, looking like her name," Daisy is Eugene's oldest sister. Since she is much older than Eugene and gets married when he is still young, he never becomes very close to her.

Eliza Pentland Gant

Eugene's mother, Eliza, is a stubborn woman who manages her family through many difficult years. An extremely hard worker, able to organize the family's finances much better than her husband,

Eliza is also characterized by her stinginess and property hoarding. She almost always pretends not to have very much money, and this is a constant source of regret and annoyance for her family. At the same time, this determination helps her drive herself and the family through years of conflict.

Her relationship with her husband is a huge battle, one that she eventually seems to win. Gant frequently launches tirades against her for having ruined his life and tied him down, but at certain points he becomes very tender towards her; for example, when he sells her his sacred stone angel. They often do not live together and cannot reconcile the profound antipathy of their natures, but they and the family have a lasting bond nonetheless.

Eugene has mixed feelings for his mother. He is repulsed by her stinginess, yet he feels very strongly drawn to her and ultimately finds it extremely difficult to leave her. Her youngest son is particularly important to her; they have an inexplicable bond, and through the novel she always insists that he live with her no matter where she moves. Eliza has very high expectations of Eugene that he means to fulfill, and ultimately she is the one to pay for all of his schooling.

Eugene Gant

Eugene is the protagonist of the novel, an autobiographical version of Wolfe himself. He is drawn as a very dramatic and self-conscious hero, a "dreamer," who changes drastically through the overview of his first twenty years. One of the main subjects of the novel is how Eugene is formed by his family and by Altamont in general, and what of the wide experience of growing up there he wants to take with him as an adult. For example, the conflict between Gant and Eliza also takes place within Eugene: how much to push forward rashly as a "lost" adventurer (like his father) and how much to dwell conservatively at home with his mother.

A lanky child with no athletic ability, Eugene's talent is in reading and writing literature. Margaret Leonard is so important to his development because she teaches him the classics of English literature and a love for writing that will presumably continue throughout his life. At college, Eugene is very awkward at first, which is why he is ridiculed. He eventually compensates for this lack of social grace with overconfidence in his intellect. He is sometimes babied within his family and is often treated as the "last hope" of success; Gant wants him to be a politician, and the others have less defined ideas of money and fame.

The development of Eugene's sexuality is a very important theme in the novel. He has no relationships with girls of his own age but many with older women, including prostitutes. His only feelings of love are directed towards Laura James and his mother, but Eugene feels betrayed and shameful when Laura leaves to get married, and it is clear she has deceived him. In general, he is only capable of becoming boundlessly romantic, as with Laura, or of detaching sex from emotion entirely, as with any of the older prostitutes.

Eugene has some friends, but his closest and most lasting relationships are with adults, including Ben, who is quite a bit older. He is a lonely child who goes out of his way to prove himself and maintain his pride. When Ben dies, Eugene reaches the height of being alone and no longer feels bound to Altamont.

Grover Gant

Ben's twin, Grover is Eugene's "gentlest and saddest" brother. When he dies of typhoid at only twelve years old, Eliza moves back to Altamont from St. Louis, profoundly saddened.

Helen Gant

Her father's daughter, Helen has an "insatiable" and tireless motherly impulse. She has always been close to Gant. She takes care of many men, especially Gant, but also her husband, Hugh, and her brothers, by taking complete control of the situation and babying them to the point of stifling them with food, comfort, and warmth. Often she erupts in anger when they seem to fall out of line—when Gant becomes recklessly drunk or Eugene displays "Pentland queerness"—but after she releases her anger, Helen goes back to her controlling motherly impulse.

Like her father, Helen is an alcoholic, but she does not admit this to herself and finds her alcohol in various, more dangerous, medicines and tonics. She goes on singing tours and toys with various men but ultimately marries a safe choice, a salesman ten years older named Hugh Barton. Hugh loves her deeply but eventually begins to feel jealous of Helen's consuming affection for her father. When the Bartons move back to Altamont, Helen complains more frequently of wasting her life away taking care of Gant, but she continues to do so through to the end of the novel. Helen competes with Eliza to be the true mother of Eugene and ultimately loses, although her youngest brother does find her to be a sort of "goddess" of the home.

Luke Gant

Luke, closest to Eugene in age, is the town's favorite among the children. He is not a good student, but his social skills are excellent and he has a talent for selling and hustling in a variety of contexts. He has a stutter but still manages to order around younger boys and win the affection of older people. After dropping out of college and finding a successful job, Luke joins the navy and is stationed at different bases around the country. When Ben dies, Luke and Eugene take care of many of the arrangements.

Steve Gant

Eugene characterizes his brother Steve as a heartless outcast from the family. Steve drops out of school at fourteen and travels around without a job, occasionally coming home, where he is grudgingly received, sometimes with fighting among the brothers. Gant has always hated his eldest son, and Eliza is the only one in the family who thinks he is a good person.

William Oliver Gant

Gant is the tall, grandiose, passionate father of the family. Known to everyone, even his wife, as "Mister Gant," Eugene's father is a somewhat mysterious figure as well as a constant and important presence throughout the novel, even when he is sickly with old age. *Look Homeward, Angel* follows his steady degeneration from a violent, powerful, intimidating man with an unquenchable thirst for adventure into a senile and ineffectual old man stricken with cancer and on the brink of death.

When Eugene is young, Gant is characterized as a master of loud rhetoric, often directed against his wife, who eats huge amounts and constantly creates mammoth fires. An often unreliable and brutal alcoholic, he epitomizes excess and limitless desire, and he provides a complete opposite to his overly frugal, property-hoarding wife. Gant loves his house, but he hates the idea of accumulating property and blames all of his problems on Eliza, in part because this is her obsession. He is much closer to his eldest daughter Helen, who eventually comes to resent him for requiring that she take care of her father all his long life.

Gant wants Eugene to become a senator or president, and he insists that Eugene go to college at only sixteen. He instills in his son a boundless desire for new experiences. Gant begins to get sick early in Eugene's life and gradually loses his energy (with occasional alcoholic releases) for opposing Eliza. By the time Eugene is ready to leave home, Gant has faded from the main thrust of the novel and the family is waiting for him to die.

Gilbert Gaunt

Gant's father, Gilbert Gaunt, is an Englishman who comes to America before the Civil War begins. He marries a Pennsylvanian woman after immigration authorities change his name to "Gant."

Horse Hines

Horse is a friend of the family and is the undertaker who dresses Ben for burial. He takes his craft very seriously, and the pride he takes in the "natural" job he has done on Ben's corpse makes Eugene laugh with "pity" and disgust.

Pearl Hines

Pearl is Helen's friend and singing companion. When Pearl gets married to a man from Jersey City whom she met during their travels, Helen moves back home.

Laura James

Laura is Eugene's first love, whom he meets at Dixieland. She is not a pretty girl, and Eugene does not realize he loves her right away, but soon he falls for her subtlety and aristocratic charm. Although she says she meant all of the vows they made to each other, Laura had been engaged for a year before she met Eugene, and this sparks a great deal of resentment.

Eugene sees Laura as a paradox of virtue and deception. Although he writes her two letters and follows her to Virginia, Eugene never sees Laura after she returns home to get married. Nevertheless, Laura is the only woman with whom Eugene falls in love and is one of his only opportunities to avoid being, as he says, "alone."

Jannadeau

Gant's large and muscular close friend, Jannadeau is the family's Swiss neighbor.

Lily Jones

Lily is the owner of a brothel near Eugene's college, and he loses his virginity to her during his first year.

Sinker Jordan

Sinker, an adventurous wartime worker, is Eugene's only friend and fellow money-waster during his adventure in Norfolk, Virginia.

Miss Amy Leonard

Miss Amy, John Leonard's sister, is a large, "powerful" woman who teaches mathematics and history.

John Dorsey Leonard

Leonard is a strong, somewhat dull but "honorable" man who runs Eugene's private school. Formerly the principal of the public school, he teaches athletics and Latin, but Eugene learns little from him as compared with what he learns from Leonard's wife.

Margaret Leonard

Margaret is Eugene's frail teacher with a vast knowledge of literature that she teaches passionately. She is the one who chose him to be in the Leonards' school, and he feels very close to her even when he is regularly misbehaving. Eugene idealizes both Margaret and the literature she finds so important, and she thinks of him as a son.

Louise

Louise is Eugene's first romantic partner. A "plump" twenty-one-year-old waitress, she meets Eugene on a school trip to South Carolina when he is fifteen.

Miss Irene Mallard

An "elegant" woman "mixed of holiness and seduction," Miss Mallard teaches Eugene to dance. Like Miss Brown, except without any physical relationship, she is a tenant of Dixieland to whom Eugene turns after Laura James leaves.

Mrs. Morgan

A tenant of Dixieland whom Gant says is a Cherokee Indian, Mrs. Morgan receives the rare benefit of Eliza's generosity because she is struggling and pregnant.

Will Pentland

Will, Eliza's entrepreneurial brother, represents the "insatiate love of property" that characterizes the Pentland family.

Miss Pert

Nicknamed "Fatty," Miss Pert is Ben's closest companion, and he visits her room at night in Dixieland for many years. Although their relationship is obscure, it is clear that she was the only person to help Ben in the early and dangerous stages of his pneumonia. Eliza kicks her out of Dixieland while Ben is dying, and Ben's death leaves her somewhat incoherent. At the end of the novel, she

Topics For Further Study

- Thomas Wolfe was a legendary figure in his time. Read some primary source historical material to examine how his contemporaries viewed him. For example, read *The Journey Down* by Aline Bernstein, which remembers their passionate relationship from her point of view. How do you think Wolfe's personality affected his reputation?

- What do you think *Look Homeward, Angel* says about race relations? Did the novel's treatment of African Americans offend you? What do other critics say about Wolfe's racial views? Do some reading about the African American experience in early twentieth-century North Carolina and discuss how accurately the novel portrays these circumstances.

- One of Wolfe's intentions in writing his first novel was to create a new tradition of southern literature. Did he succeed? Read some other books classified as "literature of the South," such as William Faulkner's novels. What kind of tradition do these books follow? Do you think recent books by Toni Morrison, such as *Beloved*, follow Wolfe's idea of a southern tradition?

- Wolfe was obsessed with the idea of "the American experience." What would Walt Whitman or Henry David Thoreau say about this idea? Read some of their writings to find out. Compare and contrast Wolfe and these American romanticists to a current writer like Phillip Roth and his version of the American experience in his novel *American Pastoral*.

---

meets Eugene by Ben's grave and tells him she is moving back with her granddaughter in Tennessee.

"Pap" Rheinhart

"Pap" is one of Eugene's closer friends from the Leonards' school. He has a kindly look and partakes in many of Eugene's wandering adventures through Altamont.

Mrs. Selborne

Mrs. Selborne is a married tenant of Dixieland who sleeps with Steve. She is also a friend of Helens and briefly a "living symbol of desire" for Eugene.

Jim Trivett

Jim is the student who lives near Eugene's college boarding house and takes him to a brothel. Resentful because Eugene will not write a paper for him, Jim says he will make a man out of the sixteen-year-old student and brings him to the prostitute Lily Jones.

Vergil Weldon

An old philosopher who enjoys having Eugene in his class, Mr. Weldon is Eugene's most important teacher at college. He encourages Eugene to study further at Harvard.

W. O.

See William Oliver Gant.

Themes

The American Experience

Wolfe is interested in portraying a representative American experience and an allegory of American youth in his novel. Although Wolfe is often associated with expatriate American writers such as Hemingway and Fitzgerald, and made several long trips to Europe while he was writing *Look Homeward, Angel*, the author saw himself within the American tradition. Wolfe would not have deemed his writings "modernist" in the international sense of the term. He is better classified as an American romantic.

This is not to say that Wolfe's first novel is not innovative or daring; indeed, no one would publish it except Charles Scribner's Sons (a firm famous for publishing innovative modernist works). Even though Wolfe worked within the American tradition and was compared to writers such as Walt Whitman and Henry David Thoreau, he was attempting to establish a new form of American romantic writing in a modern context.

Much of *Look Homeward, Angel* is frankly sexual in nature, and much of it relies on a concept of a stark break with the past to achieve a radical new understanding of the truth of the world. These concepts would be associated with modernism. Simultaneously, however, the aching desire to return home and to elaborately establish a vision of the traditional South are common romantic themes. There are also naturalist tendencies in certain long and seemingly disjointed passages about life in Altamont. Wolfe and his contemporaries would have understood him as using characteristics of the new style to develop a traditional American form.

Bildungsroman

This German term for "novel of development" is popular among critics, such as Richard S. Kennedy, in describing the form of *Look Homeward, Angel*. The opposing forces of adventurous departure and conservative return to the home, represented by Gant and Eliza, the northern man and the southern woman, reveal the struggle in Eugene's growing process. Indeed, the theme of growth is important not only to Eugene's character; it serves as a metaphor for the "American experience" discussed above. Wolfe is interested in the ways America develops through the first decades of the twentieth century, and his novel details the rise to maturity of the South in particular.

Born in 1900, Eugene is an appropriate symbol for the infancy of the South in a new century. Wolfe spends a considerable amount of time discussing old southern values, including racial superiority, Confederate patriotism, and landowning. In the novel, these ideas develop and change based upon Eugene's understanding of them, and their compatibility with such drastic political events as World War I. After Ben dies, Eugene finds that he must leave, although not without a certain affection, and go to the North. Wolfe seems interested, as displayed in his long passages about the way southern life is changing, in bringing the South itself along on this journey of modernization while still retaining a certain amount of tradition. A break is ultimately necessary, however, as the division grows sharper and Eugene can no longer idealize his home.

Although Eugene needs to break away from his home in order to develop into an adult, Wolfe does not make it clear that a break from southern values is the single key to successful maturation. The idea of development in the novel also requires an understanding of and even a longing for the past. While Eugene seems to have reached a certain kind of maturity when he is ready to depart for the North, he is perhaps not so far away from the romantic tradition of the southern experience and the "look homeward" of the title.

Style

Romanticism

Wolfe's style has often been called "romantic," both because of the emotional extremes of its sprawling style and because of the American tradition it is not entirely outside. American writers like Walt Whitman, who among other achievements captured a broad sense of American life, were very influential over Wolfe's authorial intentions. Wolfe frequently wrote that he loved America and wished to represent its "grandness"; part of this process in *Look Homeward, Angel* consisted of melding traditional American and modern European techniques, similar to his melding some of their important themes (discussed above).

This results in a unique and varied style. Often Wolfe goes on at great length in what seems to be a "stream of consciousness" style, something present in modernist writers such as James Joyce, and sometimes he exhibits some of the frankness about sexuality that is common in modernist style. But his work simultaneously reads like a southern epic, with involved natural description and even invocations of dramatic verse such as the "O Lost" refrain. These styles sometimes conflict, and in particularly melodramatic passages such as a description of Helen and Gant preparing food, for example, are unrestrainedly romantic. This allows Wolfe a certain dexterity in describing certain events by the technique he finds most suitable; and it suggests what Wolfe would have liked to create: a new stylistic tradition in southern writing that melds old and new methods.

Historical Context

By the beginning of the twentieth century, America was rapidly developing into a modernized country with a consumer economy. Southern towns, like their northern counterparts, were quickly expanding, and new jobs and industries were resulting from the continued growth of the leisure class. A

Compare & Contrast

- **1900–1920:** The infant mortality rate in the United States is 140 per 1,000 live births.

  Today: Infant mortality has shrunk dramatically to below 8 per 1,000 live births.

- **1900–1920:** The races in the American South are notoriously unequal. Segregation and discrimination are widespread, and most blacks live in poverty. During these two decades, there are 1,413 recorded lynchings of African American males, compared with 156 of whites.

  Today: All races are equal under the law. There is increasing effort made to address economic inequities among African Americans and other non-whites in the South, and segregation is generally unacceptable.

- **1900–1920:** Real estate and investment is becoming very popular among those who can afford it, given the rapid expansion of American cities.

  Today: Buying property and real estate has once again become a popular way to get rich. Investment has taken on many new forms, and it is not so clear that the economy is expanding at any given moment, but developers and investors continue to try to exploit the market.

---

resort town such as Asheville, North Carolina (the double for Wolfe's Altamont), was a popular site for investment during these years. Successful careers in real estate and property management were not uncommon during this time of expansion.

World War I was a key drive to American production. America's entry into the war in 1917 marked the beginning of an unprecedented period of production and economic prosperity. The Roaring Twenties continued until the massive stock market crash of 1929. Meanwhile, in the North, a cultural upheaval had been occurring since the war; "flappers" challenged the domestic constraints of women, while jazz and modernist literature were drastically changing artistic tradition.

In general, the South was much slower to adopt these new ideas. Race relations were extremely poor; lynching remained a frequent occurrence from 1900 well through the publishing of *Look Homeward, Angel*, and discrimination was overt and debilitating throughout the South. Although the long Reconstruction period after the Civil War had finished by the turn of the century, southerners retained their traditional values well into the twentieth century.

American writers, such as Fitzgerald and Hemingway, frequently traveled to Europe in the 1920s, where they joined an expatriate literary movement known as modernism. Characterized by its rejection of the previous generation's value system and its experimentation in form, modernism was the cutting-edge style of the era. Modernism is generally considered to have begun around the beginning of World War I in 1914, because of the connotation of a rupture from the past that the Great War signified; but Americans came somewhat later upon the scene.

Wolfe lived in Europe for some time during the writing of *Look Homeward, Angel*, and he certainly employed some modernist ideas. But his interest in the American tradition of romanticism lay outside the mainstream goals of his contemporaries. Other American authors diverted from the course of modernism, but most either continued in the naturalist tradition of Edith Wharton or experimented in new forms entirely. Wolfe was somewhat unique in his desire to form a neo-romantic tradition.

Critical Overview

Although it sparked some resentment in Asheville, North Carolina, *Look Homeward, Angel* received a considerable amount of praise in the both the North and the South when it was published in 1929. As

Asheville, North Carolina, hometown of Thomas Wolfe and the basis for the fictional town of Altamont in Look Homeward, Angel

John Earl Bassett writes in his essay "The Critical Reception of *Look Homeward, Angel*": "Four favorable articles in important New York newspapers were instrumental to the success that *Look Homeward, Angel* did have."

Some critics, most notably Bernard DeVoto in his 1936 article from the *Saturday Review*, argued that Wolfe has a tendency towards "bombast, and apocalyptic delirium." This group tends to disparage "romantic" American novels generally. But even DeVoto writes that parts of *Look Homeward, Angel* show "intuition, understanding, and ecstasy, and an ability to realize all three in character and scene, whose equal it would have been hard to point out anywhere in the fiction of the time." In 1951, William Faulkner rated Wolfe the highest (the only person above himself) among contemporary American writers.

Look Homeward, Angel remains Wolfe's most popular and respected work, but it has gone through a significant decrease in critical attention. This is partly due to the novel's views on race and gender and partly due to what John Hagan calls "the still prevailing notion that Wolfe's first novel, though undeniably powerful in some respects, is mere 'formless autobiography,' the product of a *naïf* who had no 'ideas' and only a rudimentary technique."

The majority of criticism on Wolfe is strongly biographical; John Lane Idol Jr. writes in *A Thomas Wolfe Companion* that the "tallest heap would be labelled 'The Life and Legend of Thomas Wolfe,' since it focuses on his reputation as a kind of American giant." Idol suggests that many critics are interested in psychoanalytical reading of Wolfe's works because his novels are only understood after "seeing him in his time and place." Critics such as Richard S. Kennedy, on the other hand, are interested in how Wolfe's life and its relation to art represent the early twentieth-century American experience.

Criticism

Scott Trudell

Trudell is a freelance writer with a bachelor's degree in English literature. In this essay, Trudell discusses the sexual and racial symbolism in Wolfe's novel.

Throughout *Look Homeward, Angel*, Eugene displays a somewhat worried attitude toward sexuality. Whether it is the feeling that his loins are "black with vermin" after the frequent visits to Lily Jones's brothel or the deception by Laura James

> Wolfe is not casually racist, or racist as a product of his time and place; the allegory of his first book actively advocates an urgent program of racial superiority."

that undermines his extreme passion, Eugene has almost uniformly unhealthy relationships with women. His romance with Louise, the first of his many brief affairs with older women, marks the beginning of a tendency either to unrealistically idealize women or to degrade them, and this habit continues through Eugene's dramatic break from his mother at the end of the novel.

A psychoanalytical reading of *Look Homeward, Angel* would partially account for this tendency by revealing Eugene's massive and unresolved Oedipal complex. Wolfe, who practiced some dream therapy himself and was certainly aware of the pervasive influence of Freudian theory at the time, seems to acknowledge this quite explicitly in passages such as, "every step of that terrible voyage which his incredible memory and intuition took back to the dwelling of her womb." Freud wrote that degradation of sexual partners was a common by-product of an unresolved Oedipal complex, and he would have seen Eugene as a classic case. The feeling of "incestuous pollution" with Miss Brown is perhaps the clearest example of Eugene's attempting to live out the incest taboo in a different context, and in a more general way, this may account for the vast age differences in all of Eugene's affairs.

Wolfe develops this idea in a variety of contexts. The relationship of Helen and Gant, also clearly Freudian, arouses an outwardly jealous battle between mother and daughter that ultimately results in Eliza's firmer hold on Eugene. And Wolfe connects Eliza's bond with her youngest son inextricably with his other relationships. Eliza is actively jealous of Laura James and Miss Brown in particular; Eugene must confront his mother and kiss her four times before he can finally sneak away to sleep next to Laura for the first time.

Indeed, it is clear that Wolfe is conscious of the Oedipal complex and that he uses it for much of his most important romantic symbolism. The refrain itself, "O Lost," employs the "exile" from the "dark womb" as a metaphor for the human experience, and it is clear that this is a fundamentally important image for Wolfe when he connects it to his grandest and most universal themes: "our earliest ancestors had crawled out of the primeval slime; and then, no doubt, finding the change unpleasant, crawled back in again." Wolfe seems to be developing an idea of the womb as an ambiguous mix of messy slime and uncorrupted perfection, in line with the Freudian concept that the incest taboo is often merged with idealized romantic desire.

Wolfe is very interested in the interdependency between universal and local themes, and, as C. Hugh Holman writes in his essay " 'The Dark, Ruined Helen of His Blood': Thomas Wolfe and the South": "this universal experience was for him closely tied up with the national, the American experience." Since these political and symbolic areas are so connected for Wolfe, it is not surprising that personal or even Oedipal connections are so frequently tied to political ideas; this is why Gant represents the North, and Eliza is a fixed symbol of the American South.

This basic association has some interesting consequences. Underneath Eugene's surface conflict—that he must eventually tear himself away from the South (his mother) he loves and wander to the firm intellectual land of the North—there is a complex web of desire. For example, Eliza's obsession with property represents a variety of ideals for her son. Although Eugene finds his mother stingy and petty, and the Pentland family seems to be more of a lowborn "clan" than an established or elitist family, Eliza's obsession with hoarding property is nevertheless connected to Wolfe's notion of the majestic, traditional, southern aristocracy.

It is no coincidence that the name of Wolfe's hero means "well born"; the fantastical and romantic vision of the book seeks to ascribe the traditional superior values of the upper class to Eugene's character while he leaves his home. It turns out to be difficult or impossible for Eugene to retain these values; he seemingly must reject the South altogether by the time he leaves Ben's ghost. But the desire and the idealization of establishment and property remain; indeed, the best example comes from the allegorical story of the Hilliards' estate during Eugene's infancy. While attempting to move towards the aristocratic house which is "crudely and symbolically above him," Eugene is punished with "the mark of the centaur"; Wolfe is clearly implying some nobility of nature in Eugene that is suppressed by circumstance.

In this example, the aristocratic ends happen to be thwarted by a "slovenly negress" and a "God-damned black scoundrel," two African Americans whose laziness and dirtiness seem to place them at blame for the situation. Since the episode is so highly allegorical, it seems quite unlikely that this is a coincidence. Poor whites and African Americans seem to curse Eliza and her son's search for established wealth. A quick search through the text finds a number of supporting examples; the poor, unreliable African American section of town makes Eugene's paper-collecting route notoriously difficult, prostitutes and degenerates make Dixieland an extremely difficult place to run, and Eliza is constantly having problems with the African American girls who work at Dixieland—eventually none of them will work for her because she is so cruel. Indeed, Eugene's subverted desire for aristocratic privilege sullied because of the "inferior" classes.

Returning, then, to the theme of subverted sexual desire towards the Oedipal symbol for the South, it begins to become clear how exactly this works out in a political and social allegory. The aristocratic, traditional South, represented by Eugene's mother, is continually in danger of sexual, economic, and social degradation. Wolfe finds a suitable allegory here because, by its very definition, the desire for the mother is an incestuous, unclean taboo. Eugene cannot possess his mother, or the South, in its pure form, so he finds a series of older women (reminiscent of his mother) whom he must degrade, according to Freud's formula, in order to have them as sexual partners.

In the process of this symbolism, however, Wolfe continually returns to his most convenient and overt symbol of sexual impurity and incestuous danger. African Americans are associated in *Look Homeward, Angel* not only with laziness and dirtiness; they are characterized as a disease of poverty and incest that endangers the pure white race. When Eugene rides on his paper route, "past all the illicit loves, the casual and innumerable adulteries of Niggertown," he is depicted as a romantic hero on the brink of an abyss of despair, gathering money from a black menace in service to an idealized white paradise. The novel is extremely invested in developing this idea of an incestuous and forbidden threat to the pure South and the white mother. Wolfe is not casually racist, or

racist as a product of his time and place; the allegory of his first book actively advocates an urgent program of racial superiority.

Eugene's encounter with Ella Corpening, whose name resembles the Latin word for "body" (*corpus*), is perhaps the best example of the base physical and sexual threat that African Americans pose to Wolfe's idea of white purity. Seemingly a prostitute of sorts, whose moaning makes her appear completely crazy, Ella seems to inspire a desire in Eugene that he sees as forbidden and evil to a romantic extreme. But what is particularly significant about Ella is her "mulatto," or mixed African and Caucasian, blood. It is precisely this (to Wolfe) deceptive mix of purity and impurity that constitutes the allegorical danger in the situation. Wolfe is careful to highlight "the rapid wail of sinners in a church" after this near brush with racial mixing that, in the allegorical logic of the novel, is even more dangerous than the consummated encounters with poor white prostitutes.

The dense web of Eugene's submerged desire for the South seems to be rejected by the end of *Look Homeward, Angel*. Eugene breaks with his mother in an episode of emergence from the Oedipal complex and moves north, and Wolfe seems to abandon the type of racist allegory described above. But a deep longing remains for the values of the South, including racial superiority and purity from incestuous or "slovenly" sexual ideas represented by African American women. The title itself commands the pure white, "lost" soul to look homeward, back towards a mythical purity in constant threat of what Wolfe represents as pollution by racially mixed sexual desire.

Source: Scott Trudell, Critical Essay on *Look Homeward, Angel*, in *Novels for Students*, Gale, 2003.

Nancy Carol Joyner

In the following essay, Joyner discusses the popularity and merits of Look Homeward, Angel.

"Genius is Not Enough," the catchy title of Bernard De Voto's negative review of Thomas Wolfe's essay *The Story of a Novel*, was not written of *Look Homeward, Angel: A Story of the Buried Life*. Ever since the publication of Wolfe's first and unarguably best novel, it has been a target for critical attack and encomium. But the severest attacks Wolfe suffered were in reaction to his subsequent work. If Wolfe had never written anything else, *Look Homeward, Angel* would have more stature today. It has been dismissed as a "novel of youth," attractive only to teenagers; it has been excoriated

> These traits of lyricism and realism, along with a Joycean complexity and exuberant good humor, are the most compelling qualities of the work."

as formless, verbose, shallow, and altogether too personal. While there is some truth in all of those accusations, the novel stands as a unique, perdurable monument of American literature. Richard Walser has called it "the most lyric novel ever written by an American," while Wolfe's principal British champion, Pamela Hansford Johnson, finds it the most "clear-sighted" of his novels, portraying his world "with an objectivity altogether remarkable." These traits of lyricism and realism, along with a Joycean complexity and exuberant good humor, are the most compelling qualities of the work.

An unabashedly autobiographical *Bildungsroman*, the book recounts the inner and outer life of the first twenty years (1900–20), of Eugene Gant. Eugene is the youngest of seven children of W. O. and Eliza Gant, a couple who live in the mountain village of Altamont. W. O., a Pennsylvanian with a penchant for rhetoric, alcohol, and prostitutes, owns a stonecutter's shop; his wife is a native of the area with a well-developed head for business and an interest in real estate. After a brief stint in 1904 in St. Louis, where one of her twins dies, she opens a boarding house in Altamont named Dixieland. The precocious Eugene starts school, aged five, against his mother's wishes. He spends his high school years in a private academy and at 15 enrolls in the university at Pulpit Hill. On his first summer vacation he has a brief romance with Laura James, a boarder at Dixieland. During the next summer he works as a laborer in Norfolk and that fall his favorite brother, Ben, dies of influenza. He graduates from college and leaves Altamont to study in the north.

All of the events of the preceding paragraph are exactly parallel to Thomas Wolfe's life. Only the names of the living characters and some place names have been changed. Altamont is the fictitious name for Asheville, North Carolina; Pulpit Hill is Chapel Hill. Floyd C. Watkins, after identi-

fying 250 or 300 names of characters and places in *Thomas Wolfe's Characters*, maintains that there is not a single entirely fictional character or incident in the novel.

Anticipating negative reactions from the easily identifiable characters he portrays, Wolfe explains in a prefatory note that "all serious work in fiction is autobiographical" and that "he meditated no man's portrait here." Many of his readers did not accept that disclaimer, however, and were enraged when the book appeared (coincidentally in the same month as the stock market crash). That reaction is incorporated into his later work in two ways: fictionally in *You Can't Go Home Again* and factually in *The Story of a Novel*.

In *The Story of a Novel* Wolfe observed that "the quality of my memory is characterized . . . in a more than ordinary degree by the intensity of its sense impressions, its power to evoke and bring back the odors, sounds, colors, shapes, and feel of things with concrete vividness." Wolfe's special talent, then, is not a reportorial one but one which exercises almost total recall of sensory images. It is important to remember that he produced the bulk of his enormous manuscript, originally 350,000 words, while he was living in London during 1926–28. That he was far removed in space and time from the events he describes makes the sense of immediacy in his writing all the more impressive.

In spite of charges of formlessness, *Look Homeward, Angel* is carefully constructed. It attains unity and shape through the focus on Eugene, the chronological sequence of events, the preservation of the theme of the search for identity, and the balance, in Chapters 5 and 35, of the death scenes of the twins.

The tombstone in the form of an angel is a significant unifying device. "An angel poised upon cold phthisic feet, with a smile of soft stone idiocy" is first mentioned on the second page of the novel. It is the focus of Chapter 19, "The Angel on the Porch," an excellent vignette published in slightly different form in the August 1929 issue of *Scribner's Magazine*. A similar angel is present in the last scene of the book when Eugene has a conversation with his dead brother, Ben. As all symbols must, this one holds a multitude of meanings: death, remembrance, existence on a spiritual plane, W. O. Gant, and the stone-like quality of people in their inability to communicate with each other. When the original title of the novel, *O Lost*, was changed to the inspired borrowing from Milton's "Lycidas," the angel imagery was further strengthened.

Finally, one should not overlook the pervading humor of the novel. Bruce R. McElderry, Jr., in fact, has found it to be the funniest book in American literature since *Huckleberry Finn*. One manifestation of the humor may be seen in the comedic appeal of the characterizations—W. O.'s bombast, Luke's stuttering, Eliza's habit of pursing her lips and nodding her head. Another element of humor is found in the tone and timing. One instance involves the scene early on when the baby Eugene's face is stepped on by a dray-horse, Eugene having escaped from his yard into an adjoining alley and the driver of the encroaching wagon having fallen asleep. A physician is called: "'This looks worse than it is,' observed Dr. McGuire, laying the hero upon the lounge. . . . Nevertheless, it took two hours to bring him round. Everyone spoke highly of the horse."

Look Homeward, Angel was published in the same year as William Faulkner's *The Sound and the Fury* and Ernest Hemingway's *A Farewell to Arms*. While it does not currently enjoy the prestige of those other landmarks of American letters, it has never been out of print and continues to attract popular and critical attention. If Wolfe's genius was not enough to sustain a universally acclaimed writing career, it was ample for the creation of a genuine literary achievement.

Source: Nancy Carol Joyner, "*Look Homeward, Angel*: Novel by Thomas Wolfe, 1929," in *Reference Guide to American Literature*, 4th ed., edited by Thomas Riggs, St. James Press, 2000, pp. 1015–16.

Hugh H. Ruppersburg

In the following essay, Ruppersburg examines narration in Look Homeward, Angel, *concluding that it "is a first-person novel, narrated retrospectively by a narrator who clearly sympathizes and identifies with the young protagonist."*

The authors of such semiautobiographical novels as *Remembrance of Things Past* and *A Portrait of the Artist as a Young Man* relied on narrative point of view to maintain a critical, objective distance from their text. Thomas Wolfe, another autobiographical novelist, did the same. Though often criticized for his apparently narcissistic inability to remain separate from his story, Wolfe used point of view in *Look Homeward, Angel* (1929) to exploit the experiences of his own life for artistic rather than merely egotistical purposes. As a significant component of narrative form and meaning, point of view in Wolfe's first novel thus merits careful examination.

Curiously, critical opinion on the subject has been sparse and divided. Expressing the traditional attitude, Richard S. Kennedy describes the novel's point of view as third person. C. Hugh Holman believes the narrator is "some unidentified person— not Eugene Gant (unless he is telling the story in the third person)." In contrast, Louis D. Rubin observes that readers "come to identify the authorial personality with that of Eugene when older, . . . recreating the events of his childhood in order to understand them." Joseph Millichap calls the narrator an "older and wiser" Eugene, while Carl Bredahl suggests that the narrator is Eugene metamorphosed from his old, cast-off self into an artist. Fortunately, this divergence in opinion can be resolved. The novel provides sufficient evidence to support a specific identification of the narrator and his role in the narrative process.

Look Homeward, Angel reflects many of the typical characteristics of third-person narrative. Physically uninvolved in the action, the presiding external narrator calls little attention to himself. Instead he focuses on Eugene, the Gants, and Altamont. Eschewing the indifference of most third-person narrators, however, he often seems so interested in telling the story that many readers identify him with Wolfe, widely known to have based the novel on events and people from his own life. Such an identification is incorrect. The narrator possesses an existence and personality distinct from the author's—so distinct that we can regard him as a "third person" only with difficulty. Gérard Genette argues that third-person narration is physically impossible to begin with. Every narrative is, he writes, "by definition, to all intents and purposes presented in the first person . . . The real question is whether or not the narrator can use the first person to designate one of his characters." Accordingly, Genette would regard Wolfe's novel as narrated by a physical being who speaks it aloud or writes it down—a "first-person" narrator. But is this theoretical being an actual character?

Concrete evidence in the published text and the "O Lost!" typescript reveals that he is a character, a first-person speaker, and an actual participant, of one sort or another, in the story he tells.

The strongest such evidence is the narrator's occasional habit of referring to himself with first-person pronouns. Singular and plural first-person pronouns occur throughout the book in literary allusions, stream-of-consciousness passages, and indirect discourse. The antecedents of these pronouns are usually clear. In at least five instances, however, the antecedent of the pronoun "I" proves to be none other than the narrator himself. These self-references occur on pp. 4, 29, 204, 223, and 522.

In each case the narrator uses the "I" while explaining or qualifying something he has said. In Chapter 1, he interrupts an account of W. O. Gant's life in Baltimore by remarking: "—this is a longer tale. But *I* know that his cold and shallow eyes had darkened with the obscure and passionate hunger that had lived in a dead man's eyes, and that had led from Fenchurch Street past Philadelphia" (my emphasis). In Chapter 18, he describes the emotions of Eugene and his brothers after they have fought among themselves: "They were like men who, driving forward desperately at some mirage, turn, for a moment, to see their footprints stretching interminably away across the waste land of the desert; or *I* should say, they were like those who have been mad, and who will be mad again, but who see themselves for a moment quietly, sanely, at morning, looking with sad untroubled eyes into a mirror." A similar metaphor concludes the novel: "as [Eugene] stood for the last time by the angels of his father's porch, it seemed as if the Square already were far and lost; or, *I* should say, he was like a man who stands upon a hill above the town he has left, yet does not say 'The town is near,' but turns his eyes upon the distant soaring ranges." These self-conscious first-person references reveal the narrator's undeniable presence and establish his relationship to the narrative. They show that he knows a great deal, for with self-confident omniscience he relates the thoughts and feelings of the people he describes. More importantly, they show his desire to explain the events of the story according to his own knowledge of time and human nature.

The narrator also occasionally refers to himself with objective and possessive case pronouns, and with the first-person plurals "we," "us," and "our." The latter often simply indicate a narratorial we (like the royal we, or the narrator of many nineteenth-century British novels) which does not differ significantly from the five singular references. An example occurs as the narrator begins to discuss Eugene's infancy: "*We* would give willingly some more extended account of the world his life touched during the first few years" (my emphasis). Aside from indicating his presence, the narrator uses these plural pronouns to evoke in the reader a sense of kinship with the protagonist, whose experience becomes metaphorically representative of all human experience. He also uses them to confirm his own kinship to the reader, whom he groups with himself and the protagonist in the mutually inclusive category of the human race. The novel's proem introduces the kinship, which the opening paragraphs of the first chapter emphasize: "Each of us is all the sums he has not counted . . . The seed of our destruction will blossom in the desert, the alexin of our cure grows by a mountain rock, and our lives are haunted by a Georgia slattern, because a London cutpurse went unhung." The narrator further cements the relationship by habitually addressing the reader as "you." The plural "we" and pointed "you" literally compel the reader's identification with the narrative, Eugene, and the narrator. They invest the reader with a sense of participation in, and commitment to, events he is only reading about. They likewise denote the narrator's active presence in the novel.

A number of the narrator's self-references were evidently edited from the "O Lost!" typescript by Scribner's editor Maxwell Perkins. According to Francis Skipp, Perkins deleted twenty-two cases of what he considered inappropriate "authorial comment" (which were really narratorial comment), a total of 442 lines. In a description of these cuts, Professor Skipp has identified at least four instances of the plural "we" (for example, "We believe, reader, we told you some time ago that Julia [Eliza] had begun to think of Dixieland") and one of the singular "I" ("But pardon, reader, I diverge"). In other deleted passages the narrator expresses his opinions (he calls "The Rime of the Ancient Mariner" the "greatest romantic poem that has ever been written in the English language," for instance, and attributes the lynching of Negroes for rape to the hypocrisy of the "deacon retreating up the alley towards his black wench").

Similar expressions of opinion occur in the published novel. Despite them, the narrator generally assumes an objective attitude towards the story. His first-person singular references are rare; first-person plural pronouns usually occur only in the most lyrical passages. He also tends to distance himself from the main characters by focusing a semiomniscient viewpoint most often on Eugene, less frequently on such characters as W. O. and Eliza. Within these restrictive perspectives, the narrator speaks with insight and intimacy about the characters' feelings, thoughts, and reactions to the world. As a result, we come to believe that we know a great deal about Altamont, though we see it only through the eyes of a few inhabitants. Because of the contrast between the limited perspectives of characters and the narrator's more broadly encompassing view, the novel gives the impression of being related by an omniscient voice, when in fact it is told mainly through its characters.

The narrator is also distanced from his story by time. In several instances he notes what the protagonist will think or remember "years later." Commenting on Eugene's zealous loyalty to Southern tradition, he explains: "Years later, when he could no longer think of the barren spiritual wilderness . . . he still pretended the most fanatic devotion." When Eugene notices Margaret Leonard's deformed index finger, the narrator observes that "it was years before he [Eugene] knew that tuberculars sometimes have such fingers." Skipp cites three similar examples in the material cut from the "O Lost!" typescript. One even describes a trip which Eugene makes to Europe well after the time of the last chapter. Thus, the narrator tells the story retrospectively, and he remains acquainted with what Eugene thinks and does long after the novel's conclusion.

At times, however, the narrator abandons his objectivity and involves himself emotionally in the narrative. His separation from the protagonist then seems to vanish almost entirely. One such moment occurs at the end of Chapter 30, the climax of the Laura James episode. In a lyric eulogy to lost youth and love, the narrator exclaims, "Ghost, ghost, come back from that marriage that *we* did not foresee, return not into life, but into magic, where *we* have never died, into the enchanted wood, where *we* still lie, strewn on the grass" (my emphasis). The eulogy first appears to employ another example of the universalizing "we," inviting the reader to compare his own memories of lost youth and love with Eugene's. Repeated examination, however, suggests that the narrator has given this particular "we" a special ambiguity. Taken literally, the passage foreshadows Laura's revelation of her engagement. The narrator calls her marriage one "*we* did not foresee." His reference in this context to a specific event in the protagonist's life implies unmistakably that he is describing his own grieving memories of lost love. Indeed, circumstantial evidence suggests that the narrator is an older, more mature Eugene, that the "we" refers both to his older and younger selves.

The argument for this identification merits review: the first-person narrator reveals intense emotional involvement with what he describes, though he remains physically separate from the action. He speaks from a future vantage point in time, often sympathizing strongly with his protagonist. When he comments on what Eugene will remember in later years, he draws an implicit comparison between the past-time character and what he became in the future. First-person pronouns not only imply

> **The argument for this identification merits review: the first-person narrator reveals intense emotional involvement with what he describes, though he remains physically separate from the action."**

that the narrator is a character but also reveal at rare moments that both he and Eugene have the same experiences in common. Finally, in several scenes Eugene remarks pointedly, "I shall remember"—as if to remind himself and the reader that in narrating the novel he has done just that, preserving his memories in the story he relates, confirming his life's significance in the reflexive structure of a narrative which bends ever back towards a past that itself moves steadily towards the future moment when he begins to remember.

The narrator-protagonist's role fits smoothly into the structure of *Look Homeward, Angel*. To the chronicle of a young man's life and society it adds the story of the narrator's, and the protagonist's, self-discovery. It also imbues the book with a certain symmetry: in the final chapter Eugene sets out towards his destiny. Years later, he tells his life story in order to rediscover the events and people who made him what he was then, what he has now become. The lyrical dithyrambs of Chapters 30, 35, and 37 thus dramatize the older Eugene's emotions as he remembers his younger self. His identity also explains the predominant use of Eugene's perspective in narrating the novel. An uninvolved third-person narrator's reliance on a single character's perspective would require no justification. But with a narrator who pronounces himself a character—a limited, fallible inhabitant of a world governed by natural laws—we inevitably must question how he knows what he knows. Who but a narrating Eugene could better remember, describe, and analyze his own experiences?

Unfortunately, Eugene's role as narrator does not explain his ability to reveal the innermost thoughts of such individuals as Eliza and W. O., or to give the description of town life in Chapter 14 (during which Eugene is asleep). Perhaps these apparent inconsistencies point to a structural flaw in the novel. Or maybe Eugene learned about what they describe from family members and townspeople. Yet such contrived explanations only partially satisfy, and they fail to recognize the narrator's motives for telling Eugene's story. *Look Homeward, Angel* is no dry, historical chronicle whose narrator must document his every statement with footnote and bibliographical entries. It is art, literary fiction, an excursion into the buried lives of its characters—and the narrator's quest to discover his past by remembering and reconstructing it.

The narrator seems most interested in discovering and understanding his father. Chapter 19, for instance, records in detail the thoughts and feelings of W. O. Gant during his talk with the prostitute Queen Elizabeth. Eugene does not witness this encounter, and it may never have actually occurred. But no factual biography could so vividly illuminate an aging man's inner being, his awareness of impending senescence "in a world of seemings." Though such a scene does not present known facts, it nonetheless uncovers reality—the truth which transcends fact—as the narrator succeeds in reconstructing it. Discovery through creation also occurs in the seventh chapter, a "stream-of-consciousness" narrative focused on W. O. Gant's half-formed thoughts, feelings, and perceptions as he walks through town. Here again the narrator recreates his father, attempting to view hint objectively, yet also with the subjective prejudice and admiration of a son. By explaining Gant to the reader, he simultaneously explains the man to himself. Discovery through creation (or recreation) is the fundamental force which compels the narrator-protagonist to tell his story in the first place.

Eugene's narratorial role thus provides an appropriate vehicle for exploring the effects of the past—one's individual past, his family heritage, and world history—on the present. The continuity of linear time links the present moment to all others. In his opening "Note to the Reader," Wolfe introduces this theme: "we are the sum of all the moments of our lives—all that is ours is in them." The theme's structural metaphor lies in the novel's reflexive narrative structure, which moves inevitably towards the final chapter's climax and Eugene's decision to leave Altamont and seek "in the city of myself, upon the continent of my soul" the "forgotten language, the lost world, a door where I may enter, and music strange as any ever sounded." Chapter 40 marks the critical moment of the narrator-protagonist's life. The destiny towards

which Eugene embarks the narrator achieves in his narration. The consequences of this episode ultimately enable his telling of the story, hence the creation of the novel itself.

Additional evidence for the narrator's identity lies in his relationship to the author. Wolfe made his book in his own image, modeling the protagonist on his younger self. Yet he found significance in Eugene's life not became it was his own but because he saw it as the metaphoric embodiment of every human life. Not possessed of the compulsion for impersonality prominent in the fiction of Conrad, Joyce, and Faulkner, Wolfe wanted to insure that his readers understood him, that they shared his vision. He thus makes his personality everywhere apparent in his novel. The narrator is his persona, through whom he can dispassionately relate the protagonist's life, and who at rare moments allows him to participate directly in Eugene's experience. Both Wolfe and the narrator-protagonist undergo the same contemplative process of remembering as they produce the novel. The narrator evaluates the impact of his early life on his present. Through the narrator, Wolfe does the same. Yet in no sense does he narrate. The narrator is his alter-ego, the authorial personality who narrates for him. If the narrator is an older version of the young Eugene, and Eugene a fictional version of the young Wolfe, then it seems logical to regard the narrator as a fictional version of the author. Wolfe himself never speaks, and the illusion of fiction is never violated. What Max Perkins took for intrusive "authorial commentary," what critics mistake as Wolfe's voice, is actually the voice of the narrator, Wolfe's fictional counterpart and persona.

Perhaps because of the close link between Wolfe and his protagonist-narrator, the narrative source of the emotional lyrical passages has often puzzled readers. C. Hugh Holman speculates that they are produced by "a person located in the time of writing rather than the time of action yet intimately bound up with the action of an intense emotional bondage," but he implies that this person is Wolfe, speaking through the veil of third-person narrative. Richard S. Kennedy suggests that in one instance, the apostrophe to Laura James in Chapter 30, Wolfe speaks unabashedly in his own voice: "You who were made for music, will hear music no more: in your dark house the winds are silent. Ghost, ghost, come back from that marriage that we did not foresee, return not into life, but into magic, where we have never died, into the enchanted wood, where we still lie, strewn on the grass." Kennedy believes these lines "refer to death and the grave. The marriage that we did not foresee is death. Since there is nothing in *Look Homeward, Angel* about Laura James' death, . . . it seems evident that Wolfe has reference to Clara Paul [his model for Laura James], who really did die in the influenza epidemic a year or so after young Tom Wolfe knew her." Professor Kennedy properly identifies the episode from Wolfe's life which exerted a major influence on the diction and intensity of the passage, but the novel's preoccupation with memory and the past suggests another interpretation: the narrator-Eugene is remembering his first romance. He recalls it as clearly as if it had just ended, but he realizes painfully that it belongs to the lost and dead past. Laura James is a "ghost," a ghost of his past, a memory. Her "marriage" is simply that—the marriage which ended her romance with Eugene. His wish to return "into magic, where we have never died, into the enchanted wood" is his desire to return to the past and resurrect the love affair dead for so long. Knowing that Clara Paul died a few years after her summer romance with Wolfe may enrich our appreciation of the episode, but in no way is that knowledge necessary: the episode makes complete sense without it. Narrative structure suggests a far more likely voice for the episode than Wolfe's—Eugene Gant's. Wolfe obviously used some of his own memories to write this chapter, but he did not grant them precedence over his primary interest in Eugene.

Intense, emotional moments such as the conclusion of Chapter 30 form the poetic center of *Look Homeward, Angel*. Almost always they mourn the irrecoverable past, as in the apostrophe to Laura James, Gant's vision of the town square in Chapter 19, and Ben's death. Plural first-person pronouns fuse the perspectives of the protagonist, narrator, and author and invite the reader to share their sense of loss. The most effective lyrical passages merge all four viewpoints into one cathartic, cohesive vision of the world. In this way narrative point of view reinforces the universality of Eugene Gant's experience.

Despite proof of a first-person narrator and abundant evidence of his specific identity, Eugene's role as narrator must remain only speculative. The novel's structure, the narrator's emotional involvement, Wolfe's desire to make art from his life—all strengthen its likelihood. But the novel offers no proof more substantial than the evidence I have cited. In my opinion, however, this was the book Wolfe was trying to write, the book for which his nature suited him, for which he had spent years of preparation: a young man's story, told retro-

spectively by that young man grown older. Wolfe's desire to be an artist in the modern sense, his awareness of methods used by such modern writers as Joyce, whom he admired, convinced him to resist his impulses and attempt a different sort of work. To a great extent he succeeded, but the narrative form to which he was instinctively drawn remains evident in his novel's point of view, the narrator's personality, and the interrelationship between past and present.

Look Homeward, Angel, then, is a first-person novel, narrated retrospectively by a narrator who clearly sympathizes and identifies with the young protagonist. Evidence in the text further suggests that the narrator and his protagonist are the same person, that the narrator of Thomas Wolfe's first novel tells the story of his own life.

Source: Hugh H. Ruppersburg, "The Narrator in *Look Homeward, Angel*," in *Southern Humanities Review*, Vol. 18, No. 1, Winter 1984, pp. 1–9.

Richard S. Kennedy

In the following essay, Kennedy examines how Wolfe's literary style in Look Homeward, Angel *brings a richness and variety that elevates the story and its characters to a higher level.*

The German term, *Bildungsroman*, which can best be translated as "novel of development" or "novel of growth" has never, to my knowledge, been adequately defined or characterized as a subcategory of the novel. We recognize in the term itself the core of its meaning. It refers to a novel which has as its subject the story of a young man or young woman who goes through the struggles of growing up and in the end reaches maturity, a point at which he has sufficient understanding of life that he can bring his career somewhat under control, free from the mistakes of the past. This kind of novel has a very strong appeal for readers because the experience is common to us all and is important to us all. The appeal is not only to young people but to everyone, for we are always, all our life long, going through the process of maturing. We are always learning from experience, we are always seeking to understand the life around us, we are always wrestling with problems that affect our destinies. I would even venture to say that the reader who is tired of stories about the process of maturing is tired of life.

The theme of passing from innocence to knowing is found in many short stories which treat of a climactic episode that changes the way the central character looks at life. Katherine Mansfield's *The*

> "By various devices, Wolfe enlarges his scene beyond the family circle and beyond town life to make us aware that Eugene is part of a very large and complex world and that he is one of the participants in the history of man."

Garden Parts, for instance, brings Laura to the point at which she has a new insight into the complexity and strangeness of the world around her. After viewing the dead body of the young working man and offering apologies for her hat, she can declare to her brother, "Isn't life——?" and she, wordless at this point, lets us supply the many words that can fit—fascinating, bewildering, enigmatic, surprising, and so on. A novel, however, will have a whole series of these illuminating experiences. The usual sequence is to bring the hero or heroine from birth up through adolescence. But the important point is that the struggle toward understanding must be dominant and the movement must be from confusion toward control. Thus *The Red Badge of Courage*, although it begins at the point the hero is going into the army, would be properly called a novel of development because the hero is put through many tests until at last he achieves manliness and courage. Wouk's *The Caine Mutiny*, which covers about the same age span for the hero and places him in the military service, does not fall in the category of the *Bildungsroman*. The great bulk of the book is devoted to questions of authority and justice. Dickens' *Great Expectations* has a complicated mystery which winds through its plot, yet it is a good example of the novel of development. Pip goes through moral floundering from which he gradually emerges toward the end of the book. On the other hand, Dostoevsky's *Crime and Punishment*, which deals with a young man and his moral groping, cannot be called a novel of development because its focus is on a social theme and a religious theme which arise out of the misapplication of a theory that has led to murder. The first half of Dreiser's *An American Tragedy* follows the

pattern of the novel of growth but the last half does not. The defining characteristic, then, of the *Bildungsroman* is a series of ordeals and learning experiences through which the hero passes as if going through initiation rites at the brink of manhood.

The thematic pattern itself is very old. For example, the maturing of Telemachus is an important part of Homer's *Odyssey*. But the pattern does not turn up often until the Romantic Movement when self-consciousness became common practice in literature. Most of the great examples of the *Bildungsroman* appear in the nineteenth and twentieth centuries: Thackeray's *Pendennis*, Meredith's *Ordeal of Richard Feverel*, Melville's *Redburn*, Maugham's *Of Human Bondage*, Lawrence's *Sons and Lovers*. The list could be very long.

Thomas Wolfe's *Look Homeward, Angel* is almost a classic example. Indeed Thomas Wolfe was very perceptive about the features of the *Bildungsroman* because it was the kind of book he could handle best. He recognized, for instance, that the novel of development was actually another form of the journey novel—with life as the journey and a certain psychological geography as the ground to be covered. In the manuscript of *Look Homeward, Angel*, he placed at the beginning of his narrative the word "Anabasis," which mean in Greek "a going up." He took the term from Xenophon's account of the journey "up-country" of Cyrus the Persian in pursuit of the Greeks. Wolfe recognized, too, the sense of quest in the reaching out toward maturity. When he began work on his book *Of Time and the River*, he decided that the theme would be the search for a father—it was to be a symbolic search for a figure of authority. In his last book, *The Web and the Rock*, he intended that it would be about "the innocent man discovering life." He planned to put on the title page a quotation from *War and Peace*, "Prince Andrei looked up at the stars and sighed; everything was so different from what he thought it was going to be."

Look Homeward, Angel contains all the experiences that the apprentice-hero usually passes through, except the religious ordeal. The story presents the struggle of young Eugene Gant to free himself from his environment and particularly to break free of a possessive mother. He passes through common childhood experiences in conflict with his brothers and sisters. He opens up his imagination through the world of books. He develops sexual curiosity. He reaches out for wider horizons under the guidance of sympathetic teachers in school. He gets his first job. He finds new intellectual freedoms and bewilderments in college. He undergoes sexual initiation. He is introduced to alcohol (the sacred brew of twentieth-century initiation rites). He faces the problem of death when his favorite brother is swept away in the influenza epidemic. He falls in love and endures loss of love. He makes the break from home, and, as the book comes to a close, he reaches an interpretation of life and finds a way of life that he can follow.

But the mere presence of this subject matter (or this archetypal pattern, as one may call it) is no demonstration of the literary value of the work. A novel like *The End of Roaming* by Alexander Laing or one like *A Tree Grows in Brooklyn* by Betty Smith would have this pattern too, for any autobiographical novelist or any commercial novelist can adopt the pattern and, for his ephemeral purposes, draw upon the appeals which the pattern offers. A work must have something more if we will class it as a work of art worthy of being read more than once or worthy of being studied and of being discussed. The something more will be philosophic breadth, perhaps the kind of treatment that turns the hero into Everyman (or, one should say, Every Young Man). Or to put it another way, the something more will be the handling of the material in such a way as to create an intricate and harmonious literary complex which will enhance the significance of the book as well as provide the aesthetic pleasure of the successful work of art.

In another place, I have discussed the complexity of ideas that provide a framework for the story of Eugene Gant in *Look Homeward, Angel*, and I have also tried to show how, by means of symbol and structural arrangement, Wolfe created a full and ordered world for his hero to operate in. Now I would like in this study to take just one other element of Wolfe's literary endeavor and point out how it makes its contribution to the richness of this work. I want to talk about Wolfe's style. I will begin with a reminder that the American writer has a good knack for taking lowly materials and surrounding them with an aura of the great and important. Melville takes a rough crew and an odoriferous whaling vessel and by means of style and structure creates a prose epic. Tennessee Williams takes a nymphomaniac and a thug and with symbol and technical manipulation creates a profound and moving tragedy. Wolfe takes the story of a lower-middle-class boy who lives in a Southern town and creates a novel of development that transcends its restricted lineaments. By various devices, Wolfe enlarges his scene beyond the

family circle and beyond town life to make us aware that Eugene is part of a very large and complex world and that he is one of the participants in the history of man. Style is one of the means by which he creates a sense of variety and abundance in the book for Wolfe has a variety of styles that he employs.

One of the narrative styles may be described as rich, sometimes overflorid, arranged in long, loose sentences, frequently made up of elements piled in a series:

> Eugene was loose now in the limitless meadows of sensation: his sensory equipment was so complete that at the moment of perception of a single thing, the whole background of color, warmth, odor, sound, taste established itself, so that later, the breath of hot dandelion brought back the grass-warm banks of Spring, a day, a place, the rustling of young leaves[;] or a page of a book, the thin exotic smell of tangerine, the wintry bite of great apples; or, as with *Gulliver's Travels*, a bright windy day in March, the spurting moments of warmth, the drip and reek of the earth-thaw, the feel of the fire.

When the diction is concrete, as it is in this example, the style is very effective, particularly for communicating an atmosphere of plenitude—of a world that has so much in it that because of abundance itself it must be very good.

At times, Wolfe's prose takes on some of the qualities of the poetry of the Imagists. There are passages which are simple, metaphorical, and rhythmical in which an impression in the mind of Eugene is carried vividly to us—as, for example, when the boy thinks of his brother:

> My Brother Ben's face, thought Eugene, is like a piece of slightly yellow ivory; his high white head is knotted fiercely by his old man's scowl; his mouth is like a knife, his smile the flicker of light across a blade. His face is like a blade, and a knife, and a flicker of light: it is delicate and fierce, and scowls beautifully forever, and when he fastens his hard white fingers and his scowling eyes upon a thing he wants to fix, he sniffs with sharp and private concentration through his long pointed nose.

The effect of passages like this is to create the impression that life is full of vivid little moments of illumination which can be responded to and experienced intensely.

I have called passages like these poetic because they have rhythm and highly charged language, but they are just one of Wolfe's characteristic ways of saying things. There are times, however, when he is consciously being "poetic": that is when he writes short, set pieces (he later called them dithyrambs) that have an elevated manner and a

What Do I Read Next?

- William Faulkner's *The Sound and the Fury* (1929) is perhaps the most well-known book by this famous Southern novelist. Its experimentation with point of view and the stylization of the past in the novel represent a radical approach to storytelling.

- *Of Time and the River* (1935) is the second installment in Wolfe's autobiographical narrative of Eugene Gant. Covering the years from 1920 to 1925, the novel begins with Eugene's journey to Harvard and ends after a series of adventures in Europe, when he falls in love with Esther Jack (a character based on Wolfe's former mistress).

- *The Rebuilding of Old Commonwealths: And Other Documents of Social Reform in the Progressive Era South*, (1996) edited by William A. Link and part of The Bedford Series in History and Culture, provides a series of primary source historical documents which address the issue of social change in turn of the century Southern America.

- Ernest Hemingway's novel *A Moveable Feast*, published in 1964, contains the author's memories about what it was like living in the expatriate modernist writing community in 1920s Paris.

formality of address and of arrangement in his sentences. We find these inserted in various places in the book. Here is one which Wolfe has placed at the end of a scene about Eugene's first love-affair:

> Come up into the hills, O my young love. Return! O lost, and by the wind grieved, ghost, come back again, as first I knew you in the timeless valley, where we shall feel ourselves anew, bedded on magic in the month of June. There was a place where all the sun went glistering in your hair, and from the hill we could have put a finger on a star. Where is the day that melted into one rich noise? Where is the music of your flesh, the rhyme of your teeth, the dainty languor of your legs, your small firm arms, your slender fingers, to be bitten like an apple, and the little

cherry-teats of your white breasts? And where are all the tiny wires of finespun maidenhair? Quick are the months of earth, and quick the teeth that fed upon this loveliness. You who were made for music, will hear music no more: in your dark house the winds are silent.

When a prose lyric like this elegy is very personal to Wolfe, it is an intrusion, but one would never want to banish it. It becomes a memorable passage. It remains a beautiful excrescence on the work. Its general function then is only its presence as part of the encyclopedic profusion of the book. More often, such passages are formal apostrophes, and the effect is rather of oratory than poetry. The reader has a feeling that a public spokesman is giving voice to a communal emotion or attitude. Again there is a sense of a larger world which surrounds the hero and with which he must come to terms.

There are other passages in which the style combines both the grand and the commonplace. The effect is to elevate or to ennoble the commonplace. When old Mr. Gant returns from a trip and looks over the home town, Wolfe begins the whole section with an epic style, even employing epithet: "How looked the home-earth then to Gant the Far-Wanderer?." The verbal contrasts that Wolfe plays with are many: he combines the rich and the spare; he exaggerates and then follows up with understatement; he joins the majestic and the Vulgar, the formal and the colloquial. The effects are varied. Sometimes he is highly comical. At other times, he makes ordinary details seem to be recurrences in the endless cycles of time. For example, here is a passage which makes use of mythological allusion and high flown language about the coming of spring—when little boys play games in the street:

> Yes, and in the month when Proserpine comes back, and Ceres' dead heart rekindles, when all the woods are a tender smoky blur, and birds no bigger than a budding leaf dart through the singing trees, and when odorous tar comes spongy in the streets, and boys roll balls of it upon their tongues, and they are lumpy with tops and agated marbles; and there is blasting thunder in the night, and the soaking millionfooted rain . . .

In *Look for Homeward, Angel* style is used for depth as well as for breadth. Wolfe uses the stream-of-consciousness style quite frequently in the book—usually a series of phrases and images that are supposed to represent the thought-stream of the characters. Here is an example. But I will spell out the movement of thought before quoting it. Old Mr. Gant is riding through Altamont. He thinks of some of the chamber of commerce booster slogans about the town. His thought jumps to Los Angeles and its growth. He thinks then of Mr. Bowman who lives in

California and who used to be in love with Mrs. Gant. This makes him think about himself and an experience with a woman in New Orleans. This then makes him remember a time long ago in New Orleans when he was robbed in a hotel room. He thinks of prostitutes in New Orleans. He then thinks of fictional heroines in stories about New Orleans. This makes him spin out a fantasy in which he plays a heroic part.

> America's Switzerland. The Beautiful Land of the Sky. Jesus God! Old Bowman said he'll be a rich man some day. Built up all the way to Pasadena. Come on out. Too late now. Think he was in love with her. No matter. Too old. Wants her out there. No fool like—— White bellies of the fish. A spring somewhere to wash me through. Clean as a baby once mort. New Orleans, the night Jim Corbett knocked out John L. Sullivan. The man who tried to rob me. My clothes and my watch. Five block, down Canal Street in my nightgown. Two A. M. Threw them all in a heap—watch landed on top. Fight in my room. Town full of crooks and pickpockets for prizefight. Make good story. Policeman half hour later. They come out and beg you to come in. Frenchwomen. Creoles. Beautiful Creole heiress. Steamboat race. Captain, they are gaining. I will not be beaten. Out of wood. Use the bacon she said proudly. There was a terrific explosion. He got her as she sank the third time and swam to shore.

Stream-of-consciousness passages amplify the characterizations in a book. But the general impression of the excursions through the minds of the characters in *Look Homeward, Angel* is that the hidden life of the psyche, the buried life as Wolfe calls it, is teeming with activity and that human life, such as that developing in Eugene, is a mysterious but wonderful thing.

These are some examples of the narrative styles. The presence of many different dialogue styles, of course, increases the stylistic variety, particularly because most of the characters are quite distinctive in the way they speak: W. O. Gant is full of exaggeration and rhetorical flourish; Mrs. Gant carries on in the rambling, interminable manner of free association; Ben is sharp and laconic; Luke stutters. In addition there are the currents and eddies of talk in the town—the words of clerks, servants, loafers, politicians, gatherers at the lunch counters. Much of this town talk, seemingly insignificant, is like that in Wilder's *Our Town:* it reflects the rhythms of life, comings and goings, deaths and entrances. Moreover, it is good talk, with a marked colloquial flavor. Here, for example, is Gant on the streetcar:

> "Jim Bowles died while you were gone, I reckon," said the motorman.

> "What!" howled Gant. "Merciful God!" he clucked mournfully downward. "What did he die of?" he asked.

> "Pneumonia," said the motorman. "He was dead four days after he was took down."

> "Why, he was a big healthy man in the prime of life," said Gant. "I was talking to him the day before I went away," he lied convincing himself permanently that this was true, "He looked as if he had never known a day's sickness in his life."

> "He went home one Friday night with a chill," said the motorman, "and the next Tuesday he was gone."

Beyond this, *Look Homeward, Angel* has a number of other evidences of Wolfe's linguistic interest such as parodies of pulp fiction stories with Eugene as the hero—like the one about Bruce-Eugene Glendenning, international vagabond, who fights off the dangerous natives and keeps back two cartridges for himself and the beautiful Veronica Mullins; or Eugene's fantasies when he comes from the motion picture theater—Eugene Gent, the Dixie Ghost, who shoots it out with Faro Jim in the Triple Y Saloon. In this book, Wolfe plays with language in dozens of ways.

What I have been trying to establish is that by means of style Wolfe has done two important things. First, he has provided a swirl of experience around his hero and made the whole experience of life and of growing up seem exciting and valuable. Second, the linguistic variety has contributed to the complexity of the little universe in which Wolfe has placed Eugene Gant and which the boy is trying to understand. In his search for understanding, Eugene has been impelled to look to the city and its crowded streets and to the multiplicity of social experience that travel and wandering seem to offer. But at the end of the book, the ghost of his brother Ben, returned from the dead, tells Eugene that he is wrong. Eugene should look inside himself for the way to understanding. "*You* are your world," says Ben. The quality and the amplitude of that world has been partly conveyed to us by means of style.

Source: Richard S. Kennedy, "Wolfe's *Look Homeward, Angel* as a Novel of Development," in *South Atlantic Quarterly*, Vol. 63, No. 2, Spring 1964, pp. 218–26.

Sources

Bassett, John Earl, "The Critical Reception of *Look Homeward, Angel*," in *Critical Essays on Thomas Wolfe*, G. K. Hall, 1985, pp. 21–26.

DeVoto, Bernard, "Genius Is Not Enough," in *Thomas Wolfe: Three Decades of Criticism*, edited by Leslie Field. University of London Press, 1969, pp. 131–38, originally published in the *Saturday Review*, April 25, 1936.

Hagan, John, "Structure, Theme, and Metaphor in Thomas Wolfe's *Look Homeward, Angel*," in *Critical Essays on Thomas Wolfe*, G. K. Hall, 1985, p. 32.

Holman, C. Hugh, "'The Dark, Ruined Helen of His Blood': Thomas Wolfe and the South," in *Thomas Wolfe: Three Decades of Criticism*, edited by Leslie Field, University of London Press, 1969, pp. 17–36, originally published in *South: Modern Southern Literature in its Cultural Setting*, edited by Louis D. Rubin Jr. and Robert Jacobs, Doubleday, 1961.

Idol, John Lane, Jr., *A Thomas Wolfe Companion*, Greenwood Press, 1987, pp. 63–73.

Wolfe, Thomas, *Look Homeward, Angel: A Story of the Buried Life*, 1929, reprint, Charles Scribner's Sons, 1952.

Further Reading

Donald, David Herbert, *Look Homeward: A Life of Thomas Wolfe*, Harvard University Press, 2003.

This new edition of Wolfe's biography gives a thorough overview of the mystique surrounding the author.

Ensign, Robert Taylor, *Lean Down Your Ear upon the Earth, and Listen: Thomas Wolfe's Greener Modernism*, University of South Carolina Press, 2003.

Ensign's critical study identifies the modernist elements of Wolfe's work but stresses the naturalism and romanticism of the author's technique.

Field, Leslie A., ed., *Thomas Wolfe: Three Decades of Criticism*, University Press of London, 1969.

This collection of critical essays provides a broad spectrum of analytical context for Wolfe's work.

Wolfe, Thomas, *O Lost: A Story of the Buried Life*, edited by Arlyn Bruccoli and Matthew Joseph Bruccoli, University of South Carolina Press, 2000.

This new version of Wolfe's first novel is based on the original manuscript, from which Maxwell Perkins cut about sixty thousand words. Although similar to *Look Homeward, Angel*, the new version has sparked a debate about what should be the standard text as well as about the current value of Wolfe's work generally.

Sense and Sensibility

Jane Austen

1811

Sense and Sensibility was first published in 1811, sixteen years after Jane Austen began the first draft, titled "Elinor and Marianne." Financed by Austen's brother and attributed only to "A Lady," it was the first of her novels to be put into print.

Austen is particularly known for her sharp portraits of early-nineteenth-century upper-class English society and for her remarkable talent in creating complex, vibrant characters. *Sense and Sensibility* is no exception. It is the story of two sisters, Elinor and Marianne Dashwood, who, as members of the upper class, cannot "work" for a living and must therefore make a suitable marriage to ensure their livelihood. The novel is a sharply detailed portraiture of the decorum surrounding courtship and the importance of marriage to a woman's livelihood and comfort.

The novel is also, as is most evident in its title, a comparison between the sisters' polar personalities. The eldest sister, Elinor, exemplifies the sense of the title—she is portrayed as a paragon of common sense and diplomatic behavior—while her younger sister Marianne personifies sensibility in her complete abandonment to passion and her utter lack of emotional control. In upholding Elinor's levelheaded and rational behavior and criticizing Marianne's romantic passions, Austen follows the form of the didactic novel, in which the personalities of two main characters are compared in order to find favor with one position and therefore argue against the other. Although rich in character development and wit, *Sense and Sensibility* is viewed

Jane Austen

lege. Their delight in language, puns, and witticisms is evident in Austen's works.

Except for brief stints at boarding schools, Austen was schooled largely at home, benefitting from her father's extensive library. She and her sister Cassandra, who remained her closest friend throughout her life, were given a proper girls' education in that they learned to play the piano and draw, but unlike their brothers, who attended Oxford, they were not afforded a formal, extended education.

Austen's novels often focus on the necessity of women of her society to marry for security. Although Austen did have several suitors throughout her early adulthood, she never did marry, either because of a lack of money on both sides or because of a lack of compatibility.

As a teenager, Jane wrote plays and stories, mostly satires and parodies of contemporary work, for the amusement of her family. She began the manuscripts for her serious novels in her early twenties, but she was hard-pressed to find publishers for any of them. Sixteen years after first beginning *Sense and Sensibility* as "Elinor and Marianne," a publisher finally agreed to take the manuscript—but the printing was done at the expense of Austen's brother. To avoid developing a scandalous reputation, for it was still frowned upon for women to indulge in literary endeavors, Austen published her first book anonymously. *Sense and Sensibility* proved to be successful: Austen netted 140 pounds. Encouraged, she went on to publish three more novels: *Pride and Prejudice* (1813), *Mansfield Park* (1814), and *Emma* (1816). However, even after her work gained in popularity and demand, her brother Henry did not reveal his sister's identity until after her death.

Austen died in Winchester on July 18, 1817, after a gradual illness. Henry went on to publish Austen's final novels in 1818. They were *Northanger Abbey* and *Persuasion*.

as one of Austen's lesser works because of this formulaic approach, which Austen abandons in her more mature novels.

Author Biography

Jane Austen, a nineteenth-century English novelist, is considered one of Britain's most important writers. Her talent has been compared to that of Shakespeare, and her work remains an integral and important part of what is commonly accepted as the canon of classic English literature.

Austen was born December 16, 1775, in Steventon, Hampshire, the seventh child and second daughter of Rev. George Austen and his wife Cassandra. As a clergyman's daughter, Austen was a member of the professional class. As she lived her entire life in the country, she wrote about her society and her surroundings, and she would become famous for her insightful portrayals of upper-class English country life.

The Austens, though plagued by debt, were a learned family of book lovers. Her mother wrote light poetry, and her brothers, in early adulthood, aspired to literary endeavors while they were at col-

Plot Summary

Chapters 1–2

Elinor and Marianne, the Dashwood sisters and main characters of the novel, are introduced. The novel opens with a description of the line of inheritance of the Dashwood estate. Mr. John Dashwood, the half brother of the Dashwood sisters, is left controlling virtually the entire inheritance. He promises his father that he will take care of his half sisters.

Mrs. John Dashwood shrewdly convinces her husband that his promise need not include any significant financial obligation to his sisters. Mr. and Mrs. John Dashwood take over the residence in Norland after inheriting the estate, leaving Mrs. Henry Dashwood and her daughters feeling like visitors in their home. Elinor, Marianne, and the younger Margaret will have to rely on their charms in securing a husband for their future comfort and security.

Chapters 3–5

Edward Ferrars, the brother of Mrs. John Dashwood and a man due to inherit a significant fortune, is introduced as a love interest of Elinor. The temperaments of Elinor and Edward suit each other perfectly. Both are practical and not inclined to passionate outbursts. Marianne is not impressed with Edward. However, Mrs. Dashwood, recognizing the necessity of her daughters to marry well, is pleased with the developing intimacy between the two. Mrs. Dashwood, accepting the offer of a relation, moves with her daughters to a cottage in Barton. The move separates Edward and Elinor.

Chapters 6–8

The Dashwoods get settled in their new home and make the acquaintance of Sir John Middleton, the relation who made the cottage available to them. The sisters are invited to the Middleton's home for a social gathering. There they meet Lady Middleton, Mrs. Jennings, who is Lady Middleton's mother, and Colonel Brandon, a friend of Sir John. Marianne plays the pianoforte and Colonel Brandon silently listens. Marianne thinks that Brandon, a man of thirty-five, is old, jaded, and has outlived his usefulness in enjoying life. Later, Mrs. Jennings, a gossip and matchmaker, believes that Brandon is interested in pursuing Marianne.

Chapters 9–10

While out walking with Margaret, Marianne falls and twists her ankle. She is rescued by the dashing John Willoughby. Later, the Dashwoods learn that Willoughby has a good reputation and is due to come into a fortune. Willoughby and Marianne have similar, romantic outlooks on life and share the same opinions on art. Marianne, in tune with her romantic notions about life, falls head-over-heels in love with Willoughby.

Chapters 11–12

Elinor believes that the relationship between Marianne and Willoughby is too intimate and that it has crossed the boundaries of decorum; they are

Media Adaptations

- *Sense and Sensibility* was first adapted for television in 1985. This version starred Irene Richards and Tracey Childs.

- A movie adaptation was produced in 1995 by Columbia/Tri Star Studios and directed by Ang Lee. The film starred Emma Thompson (who also wrote the Oscar-winning screenplay), Hugh Grant, and Kate Winslet.

- Several abridged audio recordings of the novel have been produced, most notably a version read by Kate Winslet, produced by Highbridge.

- An unabridged audio version, 900 minutes long and performed by Jill Masters, is available from Blackstone Audiobooks.

too open with each other. The gift of a horse to Marianne is viewed as unacceptable and extravagant. Elinor, unlike her sister, finds Brandon a likeable character. The theory that humans are destined to have only one love is broached. Brandon has had his heart broken. Elinor can forgive this because she is sensible. Marianne, with her romantic notions, believes this a fatal flaw.

Chapters 13–15

Brandon gets bad news in a letter, which Mrs. Jennings conjectures must contain news about an unfortunate Miss Eliza Williams. Brandon departs, and Willoughby makes mocking comments about his serious nature. Marianne and Willoughby become more and more of an item of gossip and speculation. Willoughby shows Marianne the house he is to inherit. The assumption is that Marianne will one day be mistress of this house as the future Mrs. John Willoughby. However, there is no formal engagement announcement, and Elinor and her mother are left to speculate about the true nature of the relationship. Willoughby's dialogue further unmasks his romantic notions. He is just like Marianne. They are romantics who behave according to sensibility and not sense. Willoughby suddenly breaks the news to Marianne that he must depart for London.

Chapters 16–18

Marianne sulks over the sudden, unexpected departure of Willoughby. It is in her nature to suffer openly. Edward Ferrars appears at Barton for a short visit. The further portrayal of Edward's sensible character illustrates his suitability for Elinor. Elinor suspects that the lock of hair Edward has in a ring was stealthily taken from her during their time together in Norland.

Chapters 19–21

Elinor handles Edward's departure with stoicism, in marked contrast to Marianne pining for Willoughby. The Palmers, relatives of Mrs. Jennings, appear at a social gathering. Various allusions about the unreliability of gossip as an information source are made in these chapters; for example, Mrs. Palmer "heard" from Brandon's "look" that Marianne and Willoughby are to wed. The Steele sisters are introduced during a social gathering. Elinor does not like Lucy Steele, but her sensible diplomacy forbids her from making this apparent.

Chapters 22–24

Elinor learns that she has been grossly mistaken about Edward's sentiments. Lucy Steele admits that she, Lucy, is engaged to Edward, and that the lock of hair is hers. Elinor, who Lucy has taken into her confidence, bears this news silently for the sake of propriety.

Chapters 25–26

The daughters agree to accompany Mrs. Jennings to London. Marianne is completely self-absorbed during the journey. She wants to meet Willoughby in London. Upon arrival, she writes him a note, which remains unanswered.

Chapters 27–30

Brandon appears in London. Gossip abounds regarding the relationship between Marianne and Willoughby. However, Marianne is increasingly perturbed over Willoughby's failure to contact her. Finally, she meets him at a party. Willoughby, who is there with another woman, treats her rudely. Marianne is devastated. The next day, Marianne receives a cruelly cool letter from Willoughby and becomes hysterical with grief.

Chapters 31–32

Brandon appears and relates to Elinor the true character of Willoughby, revealing that he seduced

Eliza Williams. Brandon and Willoughby fought a duel over the incident. The reader learns, incidentally, that Willoughby has married Miss Grey, a woman of considerable circumstance. Marianne remains completely despondent.

Chapters 33–36

John Dashwood appears in London. Mrs. Ferrars, the mother of Edward, also appears. Edward finds himself in the uncomfortable position of being in a room alone with Elinor and Lucy. Marianne is still so self-absorbed that she cannot discern that there is no relationship between Edward and Elinor.

Chapters 37–41

The engagement of Lucy and Edward is unwittingly made public. Mr. and Mrs. John Dashwood and Mrs. Ferrars are all greatly upset by the socially unsuitable match. Marianne finally learns that her sister, too, has a broken heart. Mrs. Ferrars disinherits her eldest son, leaving Edward in serious financial difficulties. The good-hearted Brandon offers, in a conversation with Elinor, to provide Edward with a living. Elinor relates the offer to Edward.

Chapters 42–44

The Dashwood daughters leave for Cleveland and then home to Barton. After a long walk in the rain, where Marianne goes to look on Cum Magna (the estate in which Willoughby lives), she catches a cold and soon becomes feverish. She is quite ill and there is concern as to whether she will survive. Elinor asks Colonel Brandon to send word to the girls' mother to rush to Cleveland. Willoughby appears uninvited and makes a startling confession to Elinor: he needed to marry for money and regrets treating Marianne the way he did. The final letter jilting Marianne was actually dictated under orders of his fiancé. Marianne slowly recuperates.

Chapters 45–50

Mrs. Henry Dashwood arrives. Brandon admits to her his feelings for Marianne. Mrs. Henry Dashwood realizes that Brandon would be perfect for Marianne. Marianne realizes that her behavior has been bad and that her romantic philosophy is flawed. When Marianne learns of Willoughby's visit, she holds her composure; she has learned to behave like her sister. Elinor mistakenly believes that Edward has wed. She is truly wounded. Then, Edward appears. As in so much of the book, the gossip is wrong: Edward's brother Robert is the one who married Lucy, after Lucy changed her affection to Robert due to Edward's financial despondency. Edward now pursues his true feelings and asks Elinor to marry him. Edward's penitence towards his mother gradually allows him to get back in her good graces. Mrs. Ferrars gives grudging consent to their marriage, which occurs in the autumn. The marriage of Brandon and Marianne becomes inevitable. Elinor and Edward end up near Barton, on Brandon's estate in Delaford. The book ends with a description, alluding to life being a sensible, practical compromise.

Characters

Colonel Brandon

Colonel Brandon is the affluent suitor and eventual husband of Marianne Dashwood. Although reserved and not passionate, he has a very good heart and helps out those in distress. His charitable behavior toward Eliza Williams and Edward Ferrars makes him the unnoticed knight in shining armor. Upon first meeting, and throughout most of the book, Marianne considers Brandon much too old (thirty-five) and sensible. He has clearly already had his heart broken, and the romantic Marianne believes that everyone is fated to only love once; she prefers the young, handsome, and spontaneous Willoughby, who eventually jilts her. Proving that patience is a virtue, Brandon remains on the perimeter until Marianne gets over being jilted. Brandon's character and temperament conform to Austen's and Elinor's idea of sense rather than sensibility.

Miss Elinor Dashwood

Elinor Dashwood is the eldest daughter of Mrs. Dashwood. At nineteen years of age, she is quite mature. She personifies the sense in the title of the work; she is practical and concerned with diplomacy. She values coolness of judgment more highly than rash surrender to emotional whims. In spite of the fact that she has strong feelings and artistic talent (she draws), a sense of prudence governs her actions. She puts the concerns and well-being of others above her own. She sees Edward Ferrars, a man who comports himself much like she does, as a future spouse. When this match briefly fails, she copes privately, never letting on to others how much she is wounded. She is the glue that holds the family together during times of stress; she often counsels her mother and sisters to behave

with restraint. Throughout the book, Austen holds up Elinor as a paragon of virtue.

Mrs. Fanny Dashwood

Fanny Dashwood is the wife of John Dashwood. She is manipulative and greedy and convinces her husband that he need not concern himself with the financial comfort of his half sisters. Her arguments in chapter 2 show that she is both shrewd and selfish. Her thoughts, much like her husband's, revolve around the family wealth and social standing. Mrs. Henry Dashwood and her daughters dislike Fanny. When Fanny installs herself as mistress at Norland, Mrs. Dashwood and her daughters accept an offer to leave for Barton. Austen never gives a flattering description of Fanny, displaying a marked scorn in all depictions of her.

Mr. Henry Dashwood

Henry Dashwood is the father of Elinor, Marianne, and Margaret. His untimely death, when coupled with the provisions in his uncle's will, leaves his wife and daughters in a financial predicament. Henry Dashwood's wish that his son John provide for his half sisters is not fulfilled to the extent of his intentions.

Mrs. Henry Dashwood

Mrs. Henry Dashwood is the mother of Elinor, Marianne, and Margaret. After the death of her husband, she leaves the estate in Norland because she cannot stand Mrs. John Dashwood, her stepson's wife, who has abruptly replaced her as the lady of the estate. She accepts an invitation from a relative, Sir John Middleton, to live with her daughters in a cottage in Barton. Her temperament is closer to the sensibility, or passionate nature, of Marianne than the sense, or sensible nature, of Elinor. Elinor must often keep her mother from acting imprudently.

Mr. John Dashwood

Mr. John Dashwood is the half brother of Elinor, Marianne, and Margaret. He is coldhearted and selfish. His wife easily manipulates him and brings him around to her way of thinking. He falls prey to his wife's cunning, in chapter 2, when she convinces him that his father never intended for him to help his half sisters financially. Constantly obsessed with money and social standing, he neglects to take care of his sisters as his father had wished. He wants to see his sisters marry well so that he is not bothered by a bad conscience. Austen never describes him in flattering terms.

Margaret Dashwood

Margaret is the younger sister of Elinor and Marianne. As she is not yet old enough to court suitors, she is used mainly as a character through which other characters in the novel discern information about Elinor and Marianne.

Miss Marianne Dashwood

Marianne is the middle Dashwood sister. She is considered the "catch" of the Dashwood family by those who gather at Sir Middleton's parties. Marianne personifies the sensibility in the title of the book. Marianne is a girl whose "sorrows, her joys, could have no moderation." She is all passion and romantic notions; this is typified in her playing the piano. While living out her passions, she is totally self-absorbed and unconcerned with the poor impression that she often makes on others. It is often up to her sister, Elinor, to smooth over her behavior. Marianne believes that it is only in the nature of the human spirit to love once. Her obsession with Willoughby, a man who jilts her, as her one true love, leads to a long period of despondency in which she must gradually reassess her values and philosophy. She ends up marrying Colonel Brandon, a man of whom she once spoke derisively. Nevertheless, she is content because she comes to respect the wisdom of sense over sensibility. The transformation of Marianne's values and behavior is a crucial theme in the book.

Dr. Davies

Dr. Davies often drives the Miss Steeles around in his coach.

Edward Ferrars

Edward Ferrars is the love interest of Elinor Dashwood. He is the eldest son of a man who died very rich. However, he must marry a woman of his mother's approval to come into his fortune. Austen writes, "He was not handsome, and his manners required intimacy to make them pleasing." Edward is not pretentious and prefers a simpler life than the one his mother has planned for him. His practical nature and moderate character are similar to Elinor's. The two end up together as the book comes to a close.

Mrs. Ferrars

Mrs. Ferrars is a meddlesome, vindictive woman who attempts to control her sons by holding their inheritance as ransom. She wants to see Edward marry the rich and socially connected Miss Morton. When Edward makes public his plan to marry Lucy Steele, a woman of low social and financial standing, Mrs. Ferrars disowns her eldest son.

Robert Ferrars

Robert Ferrars is Edward's younger brother. A coxcomb, he becomes the beneficiary of his mother's anger at Edward. When his mother disinherits Edward, she makes Robert the main beneficiary, although Robert ends up marrying the very woman, Lucy Steele, who caused the strife.

Miss Sophia Grey

Miss Grey is the woman whom Willoughby eventually marries. She forces Willoughby to write the letter that causes Marianne's despondency.

Dr. Harris

Dr. Harris is the doctor who tends to Marianne when she falls deathly ill.

Mrs. Jennings

Mrs. Jennings is the mother of Lady Middleton and Mrs. Charlotte Palmer. She is merry, fat, and rather vulgar. Obsessed with gossip and matchmaking, she is intent on marrying off the Dashwood sisters. She makes jokes often and has a good heart.

Sir John Middleton

Sir John Middleton is a relative of Mrs. Dashwood who offers her and her daughters a small cottage at Barton in Devonshire. He often gives large dinner parties to which the Dashwood daughters are always invited. John is forty years old, good-humored, and solicitous. He is, however, somewhat of a bore; his conversation is often restricted to hunting.

Lady Middleton

Lady Middleton is the wife of John Middleton. In her mid-twenties, she is handsome and elegant. However, she is somewhat cold and reserved. Obsessed with her children, she talks of virtually nothing else. The Dashwood sisters find her and her husband good-natured but boring.

Mrs. Charlotte Palmer

Charlotte Palmer is Mrs. Jennings's other daughter. She is in her early twenties, pregnant, and not quite as elegant as her sister. She is good-natured, optimistic, and happy. The Dashwood sisters consider her rather silly and boring.

Mr. Thomas Palmer

Thomas Palmer is the husband of Charlotte. He is about twenty-six, grave, and with an air of self-importance. He does not say much, is rather taciturn and brooding, and is considered rather boring by the Dashwood sisters.

Mrs. Smith

Mrs. Smith is an elderly relative of Willoughby's who controls his future wealth.

Miss Anne Steele

Miss Anne Steele is the older sister of Lucy. She is not as good-looking as her sister. Nearly thirty, she is destined to be an old maid.

Miss Lucy Steele

Lucy Steele is the girl to whom Edward Ferrars proposes during his education at Mr. Pratt's (who is her uncle). When Edward is disinherited, Lucy feels no remorse in switching her interest to Edward's brother, Robert. Lucy is not well educated. Austen includes many grammatical errors and inconsistencies in Lucy's conversations.

Miss Eliza Williams

Eliza Williams is the illegitimate daughter of the first love of Colonel Brandon. Although not her father, Brandon provides for Eliza, even after she is seduced and abandoned by Willoughby.

Mr. John Willoughby

John Willoughby is the dashing and handsome romantic interest of Marianne Dashwood. He conforms exactly to her idea of love and, at twenty-five, is much younger than Colonel Brandon. He appears out of nowhere to rescue her from distress and then proceeds to sweep her off her feet. He has impassioned views on art that conform with Marianne's exactly. However, he is also a callous womanizer who left one woman in a dire predicament and who immediately begins to see other women after separating from Marianne. He must also rely on a good marriage to procure his fortune. Willoughby jilts Marianne in a most cruel manner with a callous letter, leaving her to wallow in the misery of rejection for much of the book. He remains rather a villain until he confesses to Elinor that he resents having married for money and was forced to write the letter at his future wife's dictation.

Themes

Sense

The sense of the novel's title refers to the rational, sensible nature of Elinor, which Austen holds up as exemplary. Elinor suffers through various trials and tribulations, particularly after being jilted by Edward. However, she never abandons herself to her emotions and never lets her own disappointments affect her behavior toward others. In fact, she strives to keep her heartbreak to herself for the sake of social propriety and for the sake of her own family's ease. She always remains sensitive to others' feelings, even if she does not particularly like them, and strives to behave with social graciousness. She keeps the secret of Lucy's engagement to Edward to herself. En route to London, while Marianne indulges her obsession with Willoughby and ignores her hostess, Elinor holds polite conversations with Mrs. Jennings. Austen, in making Elinor the heroine of the book, shows that the sensitive approach to social interactions is superior to a selfish abandon to emotions.

Sensibility, or Passion, and Romanticism

The sensibility in the novel's title can be read as passion and refers to Marianne's emotional, romantic nature. *Sense and Sensibility* is largely seen as a criticism of romanticism, of which freedom of passion and emotion is an important tenet. The romantic sensibility of Marianne is portrayed by Austen as selfish and is gradually unmasked as weak and unrealistic when compared to Elinor's diplomatic and sensible beliefs. Austen's view is that a person who lives for passion is bound to be disappointed by the harsh realities of life. Marianne falls victim to her romantic notions after Willoughby jilts her. Her hysterical, inconsolable behavior is largely a result of her romantic nature. Marianne becomes physically and emotionally weak while her sister, who has suffered a similar fate but has a more sensible philosophy, can still function on a day-to-day basis. When Marianne recovers from a near-deadly illness brought on by her hysteria, she resolves to control her emotions, abandoning her more naïve romantic philosophies and adopting an outlook more akin to Elinor's—illustrating Austen's prevailing view of the inferiority of romanticism to rationality and emotional control. Marianne's eventual marriage to Colonel Brandon is practical, based on sense, not passion.

Marriage and Courtship

Sense and Sensibility describes the courtship of Elinor and Marianne Dashwood by their suitors. The importance that many families place on the wealth of a potential partner is a significant theme that runs throughout the book, playing a major part

Topics For Further Study

- In *Vindication of the Rights of Women*, a classic feminist work published during Austen's lifetime, Mary Wollstonecraft argues that because women are enslaved to their weaker sensibilities, they must become completely dependant on the more rational men to survive. Wollstonecraft believes that women can only gain their independence through the complete rejection of their sensibility in favor of a strict course of rational education. Based on your reading of *Sense and Sensibility*, how do you think Jane Austen would respond to this argument? Do you think she was a supporter of Wollstonecraft's views?

- One of the major political movements of the eighteenth century was taking place in France during the time that Jane Austen began her writing career. The Jacobins had just taken over France from the aristocracy; their cry for individuality and personal freedom, or sensibility, was revolutionary at the time and would come to profoundly impact all of European politics. How do you see the political events in France affecting Austen's writing of *Sense and Sensibility*? Does she side with the Jacobins' cry for individual freedoms, or do you think Austen was more conservative and would have wanted to retain the status quo?

- *Sense and Sensibility* is often described as a "didactic" novel, that is, a novel that pits two opposing viewpoints against each other. Didactic novels were popular at the time Austen was writing and were known for being formulaic: one view point always won over the other. The opposing viewpoints in this novel are obviously

sense and sensibility. Do you consider *Sense and Sensibility* to be didactic in the classic sense of the word? In other words, is there a clear winner and loser in the struggle between sense and sensibility?

- One of the curious characteristics of *Sense and Sensibility* is the almost complete absence of father figures from the main action. The father of nearly every adult child in the novel who has to make a decision about matrimony is either dead or absent, and for some it is the mother who has sole authority over them. In fact, mothers play a leading role in the upbringing and education of many of the novel's leading characters. Can you discern Austen's view of motherhood from your reading of *Sense and Sensibility*? How are the mothers in the novel represented, and what point do you think Austen is attempting to make?

- *Sense and Sensibility* very much centers around a small minority of the English population at the beginning of the nineteenth century, namely, the upper class. There is little mention of workers or farmers, yet agrarian reform and the earliest stages of the Industrial Revolution were having a profound affect on these lower classes and, in turn, were affecting the upper classes that Austen was writing about. Research the class structure of England at the time of the publication of *Sense and Sensibility*. Describe the reforms that were affecting farmers at the time and discuss the ways the working classes were being affected by changing technologies. How did these changes come to impact the classes represented by the characters in *Sense and Sensibility*?

---

in the characters' conversations and preoccupations. Willoughby cannot consider Marianne as a spouse because she is not wealthy enough. Mrs. Ferrars pressures her sons, unsuccessfully, to marry wealthy women. The sisters' different attitudes toward love are contrasted in how they fall in love and deal with rejection. Romantic, passionate love, exemplified

by Marianne's philosophies, is contrasted with the more sensible reasons for choosing a spouse, which are illustrated by Elinor's more rational approach.

Role of Women

Austen's portrait of the Dashwood sisters is an excellent example of the plight of upper-class English women without an abundance of family wealth in the late eighteenth and early nineteenth centuries. These women had to marry well to remain comfortable financially. Working was not a viable option; a woman's fate was largely contingent on her husband and his standing in society, or else she remained completely dependent upon the generosity of her male relatives. Lucy Steele, the most uncouthly ambitious of all the female characters, blatantly jilts her longtime fiancé, Edward Ferrars, when he loses his inheritance, and she marries his newly rich brother. Though both Elinor and Marianne are interested in their respective men not for their fortunes but for their compatibility, they are well aware that a "suitable match" not only means finding a man of compatible nature but also of enough means to support a marriage and family.

Ideal Love

The romantic notion of one ideal, passionate love is critiqued and parodied through the behavior and views of Marianne. She criticizes Brandon for having already loved. However, after she is jilted by Willoughby, she must come to realize that human beings adapt to disappointment and learn to feel strong emotional attachments again. Marianne's fate in marrying the very man she initially belittled is further evidence of Austen's skepticism concerning the notion of ideal love.

Social Classes and Hierarchies

Austen's novel gives an accurate portrait of the professional class (Austen's own) and the landed gentry (the social class one above her own) in eighteenth- and nineteenth-century England. The landed gentry characters have estates and are idle (they do not have careers and jobs in the modern sense). Many of the women in the professional class marry upwards into the landed gentry. This happens to Marianne. Wealth is passed down through inheritance and the concept of primogeniture, where the eldest son becomes the legal heir of his parents' estate. John Dashwood inherits the Dashwood estate and is left to dole out funds to his sisters as he chooses. Edward, Mrs. Ferrars's eldest son, is to be the primary heir until the scandalous announcement of his engagement to the socially inferior Lucy Steele. None of the characters in the professional or landed gentry class worry where their next meal is coming from. The "cottage" at Barton that Mrs. Henry Dashwood moves into with her daughters has quite a few rooms. Although the Dashwoods' financial situation is not bright, they are not members of the working class.

Style

Original Conception and the Didactic Genre

Sense and Sensibility was first drafted as an epistolary novel—that is, a novel in the form of letters between characters. It is likely that Austen was imitating the format of Samuel Richardson, an author whom she grew up admiring who presented heroine-centered domestic fictions. At some point in her writing, Austen dismissed the idea of an epistolary novel and instead drafted what would eventually become the didactic novel, a form that was popular in the 1790s. Critic Marilyn Butler explains: "The didactic novel which compares the beliefs and conduct of two protagonists—with the object of finding one invariably right and the other invariably wrong—seems to have been particularly fashionable during the years 1795–1796." Seen in this light, Austen's first published novel, right down to the duality in the title, is a perfect example of the didactic novel. In fact, it is so much so that critics are apt to dismiss it as formulaic in comparison with Austen's later, more mature works. Butler asserts that *Sense and Sensibility* is "unremittingly didactic," and she adds, "All the novelists who choose the contrast format do so in order to make an explicit ideological point."

Presentation of Dichotomous Ideologies

The duality that Austen presents is the contrast between Elinor's sense and Marianne's sensibility. This duality implies much more than the mere definitions of the two words; the sisters personify conflicting philosophies and ideologies. Critics have grappled with one another to define and redefine exactly what Elinor's sense and Marianne's sensibility signify. Various critics have attributed Elinor's sense to humble Christian values and a conservative nature. Austen's portrayal of Marianne, conversely, is often viewed as an indictment against various literary and political philosophies then in style. The two most obvious targets in the negative portrayal of Marianne are romanticism and the egocentric philosophy of the revolutionaries in France. Much like German author Johann Wolfgang von Goethe did in *The Sorrows of Young Werther*, Austen presents a character with a weak, romantic philosophy who becomes unhinged by strictly adhering to its precepts. Seen in this light, Marianne's oversensitive, passionate nature is a criticism of the egotistical nature of romanticism (while it may not have been deliberately so, romanticism as a movement was still ill-defined, it certainly encompasses the weaknesses of the developing movement), especially when contrasted with Elinor's classical nature. Elinor's behavior also alludes to the weaknesses in the individualistic philosophy of Jean Jacques Rousseau, whose work influenced the French Revolution.

Butler feels that Austen eventually grew bored with the didactic nature of the work. The novel advances according to a strict formula. The heroines are courted and jilted by men who they see as indicative of their corresponding philosophies. However, late in the novel, after the sisters have accompanied Mrs. Jennings to London, Austen's authorial talents loosen the constrictions of the didactic novel; she presents events more ambiguously, and minor characters like Lucy Steele play increasingly important roles, particularly after Marianne, jilted and hysterical, is removed from the central action of the novel. The categorical assumption implicit in the didactic genre that one philosophy is right and the other is wrong is weakened by Austen's allowing Marianne to live. Butler writes that "it is remarkable how the harsh outlines of the ideological scheme are softened. Often the changes are small ones, such as turning the jilted heroine's near-obligatory decline and death into a feverish cold caught, plausibly, from staying out to mope in the rain." In short, Austen's talents are too abundant and her observations too precise to be restricted by the formula she chose. Critics feel that the work is more stunted and constrained than her later writings, which were not hindered by this genre choice.

Narrative Voice

In order to portray the contrasting ideologies, Austen employs the third-person narrative technique; the narrator is not part of the action in any way. However, the tone of the narrator is closely aligned with Elinor's beliefs and value system. Elinor is constantly described in flattering terms, while Marianne's behavior is presented in an unflattering light. So, although the narrative is presented in the third person, it is not exactly neutral. There is a scathing quality to this narrative voice that, although it preaches moderation and diplomacy in behavior, is quick to describe greedy, vacuous, insipid minor characters in blunt, terribly unflattering terms. One need only look at a description of Mrs. John Dashwood (Fanny), Mrs. Ferrars, Lady Middleton, or Robert Ferrars to realize that the narrator is often not acting with the same restraint that she preaches.

Language

John F. Burrows writes, "Jane Austen's letters make it clear that she and her family were keenly interested in the niceties of usage and amused by solecisms [grammatical mistakes] of every kind." Austen delights in conveying the dialogue of Lucy Steele verbatim, with plenty of grammatical errors alluding to her poor social standing and lack of education. However, in spite of this exception, dialogue is not an important aspect of the work. This is because, as Butler writes, "the heroine is not so much in doubt about the nature of external truth, as concerned with the knowledge of herself, her passions, and her duty." *Sense and Sensibility* is an introspective novel that need not rely on dialogue to convey Elinor and the narrator's convictions.

Historical Context

Social Classes in the English Eighteenth and Early Nineteenth Centuries

Jane Austen was a member of the professional class. The men in the professional class were expected to pursue a profession, either the army, navy, clergy, law, or medicine. The women were excluded from these professions and were expected to marry. Elinor and Marianne are representative examples of young ladies of the professional class. In *Sense and Sensibility*, they socialize with and marry into the landed gentry, the next higher social class. Social assimilation and upward mobility of this sort is a major theme in many of Austen's works.

Members of the landed gentry were largely idle. They lived off the wealth of their estates. For leisure, the men hunted and the women gathered in the parlor. They lived in country estates and were completely separated from any squalor of the big city, London, and remained unaffected by economic hardships caused by the war with France. In order to ensure that a family's wealth did not diminish by being split up excessively, the concept of primogeniture was obeyed: the eldest son inherited the majority of the estate and the younger sons were left to join the professional class, in which they actually needed to earn a living in a profession. Although Colonel Brandon is not the eldest son, his brother died early, leaving him in the position of the eldest. When she learns that her son, Edward, intends to marry a woman beneath him in social rank, Mrs. Ferrars disinherits her eldest son in favor of the younger fop, rake, and coxcomb, Robert.

Austen rarely mentions aristocratic characters in her work. Members of the lower social classes

Compare & Contrast

- **1800s:** Women in the class to which Jane Austen and the Dashwood sisters belong are not allowed to work. They depend upon suitable marriages or the generosity of their male relatives for financial support and have virtually no economic freedom.

  Today: While women still face discrimination in the workplace, such as unequal pay, women are free to enter any profession they desire and can be found in leadership roles both in the business world and in the government.

- **1800s:** As well as being denied economic freedom, women are also not allowed much social freedom. They are not allowed to travel alone even a short distance from their homes, and unmarried women cannot keep unchaperoned company with men who are not their relatives for fear of ruining their reputation and thus their chances of a suitable marriage.

  Today: Because of economic independence, women have the freedom to purchase property, to live alone, to travel alone, and to move about freely without fearing for their reputations.

- **1800s:** English society at the time of Austen's writing is sharply divided between the working class and the upper-class, landed gentry.

  Today: Thanks to industrial developments of the nineteenth and twentieth centuries and the economic changes they brought, the middle class in Western countries, such as the United States and Britain, now makes up a significant part of the population.

- **1800s:** It is uncommon and frowned upon for women to undertake serious artistic endeavors such as writing. Jane Austen, though her work is received warmly, maintains her anonymity until her death for fear of developing a scandalous reputation because she writes novels.

  Today: Women, though still facing an uphill battle for equal recognition across the arts, are now recognized as major contributors to literature. For example, although the majority of Nobel Prizes for Literature have been awarded to men, women such as Toni Morrison (1993) and Wislawa Szymborska (1996) have recently been recognized.

- **1800s:** The protection of an unmarried woman's chastity is of utmost importance in making a suitable marriage. Women such as Miss Eliza Williams in *Sense and Sensibility*, who become pregnant out of wedlock, are doomed to a life of shame and economic hardship, as are their children.

  Today: With the development and acceptance of a variety of birth control methods, women today can have complete, independent control of their sexuality. Also, an increasing number of women are opting to have children outside of marriage.

---

are only mentioned in passing. An important exception is Eliza Williams, the unfortunate woman who is seduced by Willoughby. Otherwise, the lower classes are represented by the servants, who do not play an important role in the work.

The French Revolution

The political and social unrest in France had a major effect on England. War was declared on France in 1793, resulting in economic hardship and sacrifices among the lower classes. Ivor Brown writes that "the poverty of the masses was aggravated by the long struggle with France and the scarcity of food inevitable in war-time." The landed gentry was largely immune, living the life of leisure on country estates. Officers were chosen from the professional class.

The war with France and other conflicts are not mentioned in *Sense and Sensibility*. Although the events in the novel take place in a very specific time, Late Georgian and early Regency England, the characters and plot are free of politics. However, although the French Revolution is not explicitly mentioned, critics like Marilyn Butler have pointed out that Marianne's "Sensibility" is an implicit criticism of the individualistic, revolutionary philosophy taking root in the era. Butler, in "Sensibility and Jacobinism" (Jacobins being the most radical French revolutionaries) writes that

> Austen's version of 'sensibility'—that is, individualism, or the worship of self, in various familiar guises—is as harshly dealt with here as anywhere in the anti-Jacobin tradition. Even without the melodramatic political subplot of many anti-Jacobin novels, Mrs. Ferrars's London is recognisably a sketch of the anarchy that follows the loss of all values but self-indulgence. In the opening chapters especially, where Marianne is the target of criticism, 'sensibility' means sentimental (or revolutionary) idealism, which Elinor counters with her sceptical or pessimistic view of man's nature.

Contemporaries of Austen

Austen lived through one of the most renowned periods of English poetry, which brought us the romantics, John Keats and Lord Byron. Percy Bysshe Shelley was also a contemporary, but his work was not recognized until after his death. The poetry of these writers came to symbolize the romantic movement. Although it was not yet a movement as such in Austen's lifetime, aspects of the philosophy, including Shelley's anarchism, are criticized through the portrayal of Marianne's "sensibility."

The Position of Women

Women of Jane Austen's social class were not allowed to work, a circumstance that allowed them little economic freedom. Nor were women allowed social independence; they could not travel alone or make unchaperoned visits to men who were not their relatives. Much of *Sense and Sensibility*, as well as Austen's other novels, is centered around the household and parlor life, and indeed she wrote on the subject of domestic life because, as a woman without the economic or social freedom to venture very far from the home, it is the realm that she knew best.

When Austen was writing in the early 19th century, it was uncommon for women to write; indeed, it was still largely frowned upon in society. Austen had a great deal of trouble getting *Sense and Sensibility* published (it was her first book to see print). Its first printing was paid for by her brother, and the author was listed as "A Lady." Although the novel enjoyed success and Austen went on to publish several more novels to warm reception, her identity remained unknown to the public. Claire Tomlin, in her biography, quotes Austen, illustrating her anxiety toward public notice: "To be pointed at . . . to be suspected of literary airs—to be shunned, as literary women are . . . I would sooner exhibit as a rope dancer." She would rather not receive public credit for her talent than develop a "reputation."

Religion

Austen, like the majority of her contemporaries, belonged to the Church of England, the Anglican Church. The theology is a compromise between Roman Catholicism and non-Calvinist Protestantism. Members of Austen's social class, the professional class, and the landed gentry were likely to benefit from the status of conferred positions and patronage connections. Edward Ferrars plans to "take orders" after being disinherited by his mother. Brandon, a member of the landed gentry, then offers him a rectory. Positions within the church hierarchy are often based on who one knows rather than what one's religious convictions are.

Critical Overview

Sense and Sensibility, Austen's first published work, was initially attributed to "A Lady." Considering her desire to remain anonymous and a tendency for criticism of the age to merely include a plot summary, there were few reviews of *Sense and Sensibility* in Austen's lifetime. Although he only mentioned *Sense and Sensibility* in passing, renowned Scottish novelist Sir Walter Scott wrote of his admiration for *Emma*, a later work of Austen's, a year before Austen's death in 1816. As for so many important writers, acclaim was to come slowly and posthumously. Later recognition did not single out *Sense and Sensibility*; all of Austen's works began to gain a wider audience and appreciation in the years following her death, particularly following a collected volume of her works which appeared in 1833. After Scott, critics started taking measure. As noted by editor Graham Handley in his 1992 compilation of Austen reviews, the *Edinburgh Review* in January of 1843 compared her admirably to Shakespeare, noting that her characters are "all as perfectly discriminated from each other as if they were the most eccentric of human beings." Handley also quoted G. H. Lewes's words from 1847: "[Henry] Fielding and Miss Austen are the greatest novelists in our language." However,

(From left) Emma Thompson, Kate Winslet and Jemma Jones star as Elinor, Marianne, and Mrs. Dashwood, in the 1995 film adaptation of Sense and Sensibility

noted Handley, Charlotte Brontë was not so impressed; she preferred George Sand to the "only shrewd and observant" Austen.

It was not until her nephew, J. E. Austen-Leah, wrote *Memoir* (1870) that Austen's reputation began to really take off. As her reputation grew, so did the need for more biographies and biographical information. The letters between Austen and her sister Cassandra appeared in 1884. Various other personal studies appeared, trying to give a broader perspective than that of her nephew in the memoir. Finally, in 1938, Elizabeth Jenkins's landmark biography, *Jane Austen: A Biography* appeared.

By the twentieth century, Austen's reputation was so well established that she could not be ignored. Henry James, G. K. Chesterton and Virginia Woolf, among many others, sang praises of Austen. Graham Handley, in *Criticism in Focus: Jane Austen*, quotes Woolf from a passage that originally appeared in the *Times Literary Supplement* of May 1913, in which Woolf lauded Austen as one of the top three English novelists.

While nineteenth-century criticism tended to focus on Austen's work as a whole, by the twentieth century, criticism on Austen had become highly specialized; critical works addressing *Sense and Sensibility* apart from the other novels became the norm. Much of the criticism dealt with the portrayal of Marianne and her romantic sensibility. W. A. Craik's study of Austen's novels, as put forth by Graham Handley, include the now widely accepted view concerning Marianne: "Marianne has been found more attractive than Elinor by most readers, which Jane Austen clearly did not intend." Other studies illustrated the historical ideologies implied in the conflicting personalities of Elinor and Marianne. Marilyn Butler compared Elinor's demeanor to that of humble Christians of the era. "The most interesting feature of the character of Elinor," Butler wrote, "and a real technical achievement in *Sense and Sensibility*, is that this crucial process of Christian self-examination is realised in literary terms." Conversely, Marianne has all the characteristics of the Jacobins, a radical party who played a part in the French Revolution. Feminist studies also appeared; for example, Claudia Johnson's work that criticizes the patriarchy that the heroines must endure. By 1994, critical editions and study guides appeared that were dedicated largely to *Sense and Sensibility*. These studies examined the minutiae of courtship in Austen's era, the influence of the French Revolution on Austen's philosophy, and feminist interpretations that regarded Austen's conformity, concerning the portrayal of Marianne in *Sense and Sensibility*, with skepticism.

Criticism

David Partikian

Partikian is a Seattle-based freelance writer and English instructor. In this essay, Partikian addresses the question of whether Jane Austen is a political writer based on the fate of her heroines.

Austen, lauded as one of England's most important writers of the nineteenth century, is known for her astute social and psychological observations of the world in which she lived: middle-to-upper-class nineteenth-century England. Her first novel, *Sense and Sensibility*, centers closely on the domestic lives of a close circle of well-to-do friends and relatives. The narrative action and dialogue in the novel, however, is completely separated from political and historical events of the era; the action appears to occur in a hermetically sealed bubble. The countryside of Barton, where the Dashwood sisters live, and the London of Mrs. Jennings and other landed gentry seems to be far removed from the poverty of slums, class disenfranchisement, and any talk of political or social reform that characterized the political climate of the England in which they lived. Thus, Austen has not been widely viewed—both to her credit and to her criticism—as a political writer.

It is evident, however, after examining the political landscape in which Austen was writing, that the intent of the novel seems to be politically motivated, even though she does not explicitly mention politics. *Sense and Sensibility* has traditionally been viewed as a largely formulaic, didactic novel—a popular format in Austen's time, in which two philosophies are pitted against each other. In *Sense and Sensibility*, as the title suggests, Austen pits romantic notions (sensibility) against rationale (sense) by comparing the socially proper Elinor Dashwood with her romantically-inclined sister Marianne. Through this comparison, and the subsequent condemnation of Marianne's romantic philosophy, Austen takes on the biggest political controversies of her day, namely, the ideologies of revolutionary France and the growing cry for the equality of women.

Although it is not apparent from the polite conversation at the Middleton's social gatherings, the action in *Sense and Sensibility* takes place in an England that is increasingly unstable. The country is fighting a war with France where the individualistic philosophy of the revolutionary Jacobins rules the day. (The Jacobins were the revolutionaries who overthrew France's monarchy to replace it with a republic; they executed many of the aristocracy, including the king and queen, by the guillotine.) This revolutionary sentiment was perceived as a threat to the status quo and economic hierarchy within the upper classes in England. Additionally, social and economic changes in the form of agrarian reforms and industrial capitalism were also gradually transforming English society; they posed a specific threat to the landed gentry, whose comfortable lifestyles were becoming less and less secure. Critic Mary Poovey writes, "By the first decades of the nineteenth century, birth into a particular class no longer exclusively determined one's future social or economic status, the vertical relationships of patronage no longer guaranteed either privileges or obedience, and the traditional authority of the gentry, and of the values associated with their life-style, was a subject under general debate." In light of such changes, the beliefs of moralists and the gentry, who their opinions represented, were coming under increasing scrutiny. Although Austen did not outwardly confront these issues, many other writers of her era did.

Another revolution that was seeing its beginnings in England was the fight for equality of women. In the early nineteenth century, the period in which *Sense and Sensibility* takes place, women had no rights: they could own no property, they could not enter into professions, and they had to depend entirely upon men for their economic welfare. Mary Wollstonecraft, a "radical" who fought for egalitarianism, wrote her seminal *A Vindication of the Rights of Woman* in 1792, only a few years before Austen began her early drafts of *Sense and Sensibility*. Wollstonecraft's work called for the equal education of women and condemned the "delicacy" that women were taught to conform to for the sake of becoming proper wives and mothers. This notion of "delicacy," though not specifically mentioned by Austen, equates loosely with Elinor's "sense," or her conviction of the importance of social propriety and demureness.

Thus, the unromantic, socially proper Elinor, whom Austen makes the heroine of her novel, directly contradicts the reformist and revolutionary sentiment that was taking root in England.

The first critic to broach the subject of politics in the work of Austen was Marilyn Butler. Butler's seminal work *Jane Austen and the War of Ideas*, which first appeared in the mid-1970s, compares Austen's castigation of Marianne's sensibility with Austen's own disapproval of the rabid individualism of the Jacobins, the radical group that had gained control of France during her lifetime. While some critics, as critic Robert Clark notes, blanched at this new criticism that "discovered politics in a realm naturally free of such sordid matter," it is rather difficult to read *Sense and Sensibility* without realizing that, whether intentional or not, Austen left a text rife with political sentiment. To enjoy Austen or to dismiss her because she only represents a narrow class of society in her works is to miss out on the novel's many subtle political allusions and social criticisms. The bickering between critics should not concern whether Austen's book is political, but rather just what political and social philosophy Austen may be endorsing.

Austen's championing sense over sensibility can certainly be read as her disapproval of writers espousing the Jacobin sentiment and even feminist reformers such as Wollstonecraft. While this approach is certainly valid, the fact that Elinor's sense prevails in the end should not necessarily be taken as a tacit endorsement of the society in which Austen lived. While Austen may have disagreed with those outwardly clamoring for a change in the status quo, she subtly acknowledges that the status quo does indeed have flaws. Just as it is an oversimplification to claim that Elinor's personality is bereft of sensibility—after all, the stoical Elinor is greatly affected by the false news that Edward has wed Lucy Steele—it is likewise an oversimplification to claim that Austen wholeheartedly endorses Elinor's diplomatic, prudent philosophy of sense.

In a traditional, formulaic fairy tale like those of the Grimm Brothers, the hero lives "happily ever after" while the villains are duly punished. Snow White and Cinderella both marry their perfect princes while Snow White's wicked stepmother is tortured to death and Cinderella's sisters have their eyes pecked out by crows. *Sense and Sensibility* begins like a fairy tale; it appears to be a formulaic work, as a fairy tale is formulaic. It starts out as a didactic novel, a format that was popular during Austen's era, in which two seemingly contradictory philosophies are pitted against one another.

However, it is clear that Austen, while writing *Sense and Sensibility*, felt constrained by the formula of the didactic novel; otherwise, she would have killed off Marianne with the fever, much like German writer Johann Wolfgang Goethe, in perhaps

> Perhaps the Christian doctrine of modesty is just a strategy to help Austen cope with a repressive social system and a male-dominated, patriarchal hierarchy that other writers, like Wollstonecraft, shouted against. Austen's artistry and subtle prose, with all its ironic implications, make it possible for her to whisper rather than shout."

the most famous novel of the eighteenth century, killed off his Werther, a character who adheres to "sensibility" just as stubbornly as Marianne. This would have been the fitting demise to a character who stubbornly persisted with her romantic philosophy to the very end. But Austen deviates from this didactic approach and tempers her ending; it is more ambiguous in what it signifies or endorses. Marianne lives but must modify her beliefs.

The book's ultimate "happily ever after" is rather lukewarm: the less amenable and more acquisitive and greedy characters—the "villains"— like Mr. and Mrs. John Dashwood, Lucy Steele, and Robert Ferrars, escape unscathed. There are no Prince Charmings in *Sense and Sensibility*, just husbands who represent mediocre compromise. Austen, in her description of Elinor's future spouse writes, "Edward Ferrars was not recommended to their good opinion by any peculiar graces of person or address. He was not handsome, and his manners required intimacy to make them pleasing." Marianne ends up marrying Major Brandon, an arthritic man eighteen years her senior who she once mocked and who, throughout the novel, does not have the forthrightness to address her directly. Thus, the ending is ambiguous in that there are no clear winners or losers. The categorical extremes of right and wrong or good and evil are less clearly delineated in Austen's work than they are in the typical didactic novels of the era.

In the much-quoted summation, Austen writes:

> Between Barton and Delaford, there was that constant communication which strong family affection would naturally dictate; and among the merits and the happiness of Elinor and Marianne, let it not be ranked as the least considerable, that though sisters, and living almost within sight of each other, they could live without disagreement between themselves, or producing coolness between their husbands.

Austen's ironic tone and use of negatives in describing the happy ending and the future spouses of the sisters betray a sense of dissatisfaction with the prevailing social system. Sense is perhaps the only viable option in a world that has become vaguely distasteful. This is not exactly a glowing endorsement of the fate of the heroines. Rather, it beckons the notion of Christian tolerance and endurance in the midst of a world that is anything but the Garden of Eden. While Marianne's sensibility is refuted, her stubborn beliefs do not earn her death; Austen allows her to live. Marianne's marriage to Brandon is but a mediocre compromise in a world bereft of Prince Charmings. Meanwhile, Elinor, because she aspires to more humble goals, attains exactly what she had desired. The lukewarm fate of the heroines can, on one level, be read as an endorsement of the tenets of the Anglican Church to which Austen belonged: Elinor's philosophy is akin with traditional Christian values of prudence, modesty, and silent endurance. However, it is difficult to read the novel today and not feel a sense of the author's discontentment with the society in which she lived.

Perhaps the Christian doctrine of modesty is just a strategy to help Austen cope with a repressive social system and a male-dominated, patriarchal hierarchy that other writers, like Wollstonecraft, shouted against. Austen's artistry and subtle prose, with all its ironic implications, make it possible for her to whisper rather than shout. And, almost two hundred years later, critics still listen carefully and debate whether or not Austen subtly weaves a radical tone in her texts.

Source: David Partikian, Critical Essay on *Sense and Sensibility*, in *Novels for Students*, Gale, 2003.

William W. Heath

In the following essay, Heath discusses the ideas of "sense" and "sensibility" in the context of Austen's world and her prose.

Jane Austen's first novel to be published, *Sense and Sensibility* was developed from a sketch in letters ("Elinor and Marianne") begun some 15 years earlier. Its title seems to locate it firmly in a neoclassical, dualistic moral world where the values of reason and restraint, embodied in Elinor's good sense, will finally triumph over the impulsive, romantic sensibility of her sister Marianne. Yet even by its second chapter, any readerly security in such terms as "justice" and "good sense" is immediately put at risk as John Dashwood and his wife Fanny use rational calculation and prudent self-interest to hide their greed from themselves as they "sensibly" persuade one another that the intent behind the father's deathbed legacy of £3000 to his daughters, John's stepsisters, can be satisfied by an occasional gift of fish and game. Just as the novel's first scene shows how Sense can become a screen for coldness and cruelty, so too the novel as a whole dramatizes the gaps that occur between language and behavior, feeling and action: gaps that the unscrupulous exploit, the naive are trapped by, and the wise must use every resource of imagination to repair, or at least understand.

In this deceptively expressible world the two elder Dashwood sisters (Margaret, the youngest, is largely forgotten by the reader, and the author) try to work out their destinies, discover and narrate their own stories, by very different models. Like all of Austen's young women, both implicitly acknowledge that financial security and social stability, let alone enhancement, depend on marriage. Yet Marianne assumes that that relation should found itself on the unmediated openness of one freely expressive heart to another; her sister, that marriage is first a social contract, mediated by a language that, in turn, preserves a rational and decorous civilisation as a stay against humankind's baser instincts. Both sisters choose, and apparently are chosen by, men of appropriate character: Elinor's Edward Ferrars (brother of her stepbrother's wife) is a man all of whose works "centered in domestic comfort and the quiet of private life" and who is "too diffident to do justice to himself"; Marianne's Willoughby, conversely, with his "lively spirits," "open affectionate manner," and "natural ardour" is "exactly formed to engage Marianne's heart."

Each sister, however, is deceived: following Willoughby to London after his sudden and unexplained removal from Devonshire, Marianne is cruelly cut by him, in the novel's most powerfully dramatic scene ("'Good God! Willoughby, what is the meaning of this?'") at a party they attend with their cousin Lady Middleton; Elinor, ministering to her distraught sister (who has been rejected in favor of an heiress), supresses her own recent and painful discovery that Edward has been secretly engaged for four years to Lucy Steele, a vulgar, scheming climber. Both sisters also soon learn that Willoughby had previously seduced and abandoned, pregnant, the 16-year-old ward of their taciturn friend Colonel Brandon. Much confusion is brought about by (among other events) Edward's being disinherited for his unsuitable engagement to Lucy, his initial refusal to break off the engagement (out of a strict sense of honor) even after Lucy wants her freedom when she realizes he will be an impoverished clergyman, and comic confusions involving Edward's foppish brother Robert, who takes his brother's place in Lucy's affections and ambitions. Marianne, never fully recovered from the illness brought about by unrequited love, collapses again with fever en route home to Devon. Willoughby, rushing to what he assumes will be her deathbed, makes a confession and apology to Elinor, who is passionately moved by his distress, and by her sympathy for his economic impotence. After recovering, Marianne comes to see virtue in Brandon, who offers a living to Edward, and the sisters marry prudently at last: Elinor and Edward, in the Parsonage at Delaford, "had in fact nothing to wish for, but the marriage of Colonel Brandon and Marianne, and rather better pasturage for their cows," while Marianne, "born to an extraordinary fate ... to discover the falsehood of her own opinions, and to counteract, by her conduct, her most favourite maxims ... found herself at nineteen, submitting to new attachments, entering on new duties, placed in a new home, a wife, the mistress of a family, and the patroness of a village."

Though the novel's final paragraphs seem to celebrate happiness and power ("patroness of a village") gained through submission and accommodation to society and the taming of impulsive vitality, the narrator's sly ironies ("better pasturage," "extraordinary fate") point toward a level of awareness no character in the novel is allowed, and the author herself partly suppresses. Together, Elinor and Marianne represent the sort of disciplined imagination later found in such complex characters as Elizabeth Bennet (*Pride and Prejudice*) or Anne Elliot (*Persuasion*), but much of *Sense and Sensibility*'s depth exists in implication: in the erotic energy of Willoughby and its devastating effect on Marianne (nearly fatal) and Elinor (who decides not to tell her sister the full truth of Willoughby's confession); and in the complex representation of power relations, whereby men ruthlessly dominate and manipulate women, women have only their sexual marketability as defense, and both sexes are imprisoned in a structure that denies

> " ... the narrator's sly ironies ('better pasturage,' 'extraordinary fate') point toward a level of awareness no character in the novel is allowed, and the author herself partly suppresses."

most people (except perhaps for clergymen and gentleman farmers) useful work as a source either of wealth or personal worth.

Source: William W. Heath, "*Sense and Sensibility*: Novel by Jane Austen, 1811," in *Reference Guide to English Literature*, 2d ed., edited by D. L. Kirkpatrick, Vol. 3, St. James Press, 1991, pp. 1841–42.

P. Gila Reinstein

In the following essay, Reinstein explores how Austen renders complex and various manifestations of sense and sensibility in her characters and their situations.

In *Sense and Sensibility* Jane Austen ostensibly opposes practicality and sensitivity, praising the former and censuring the latter. Further examination of the novel, however, reveals a subtler, more significant moral opposition between selfishness and unselfishness. Although the title of the novel suggests a simplistic approach to values, Austen's characters and moral discriminations are, in fact, complex, reflecting the complexity of life itself. The qualities of sense and sensibility are embodied by characters in the novel in many gradations and with different shades of definition. Neither consistent, unmitigated sense nor thorough-going sensibility is, finally, acceptable in the novel, for both tend to lead to selfish, even destructive behavior. Moderation, the mixture of prudence and decorum with warm emotions and aesthetic enthusiasm, seems to be the ideal presented in *Sense and Sensibility*.

Austen skillfully portrays the tensions between sense and sensibility, selfishness and selflessness through the characters she creates, both in their actions and in their patterns of speech and thought. Norman Page, in his excellent study, *The Language of Jane Austen*, suggests that this novel "evinces an alert interest in language as an aspect of social

> " Austen skillfully portrays the tensions between sense and sensitivity, selfishness and selflessness through the characters she creates, both in their actions and in their patterns of speech and thought."

behavior," and establishes his point by analyzing the syntax of the chief characters, especially Elinor and Marianne. I would like to extend his study by utilizing the techniques of stylistic analysis to explore the language patterns of various significant characters both major and minor, and to relate the results to a thematic analysis in the tradition of what might be called the "morality school" of Austen criticism.

The most important characters to consider are the heroines, Elinor and Marianne Dashwood. In the course of the novel, each grows to be less one-sided and more like her sister. On this point I disagree with Robert Garis, who asserts that *Sense and Sensibility* fails because Elinor neither learns nor changes, and is "emphatically praised for not needing to." It seems to me that one of Austen's central points is that both sisters need to change, and the novel is a comedy because both are able to. When the novel opens, Elinor is prudent, judicious, and self-controlled to the point of stiffness, whereas Marianne abandons herself to quivering passions and irrational intuitive judgments. Elinor is conscious of her duties to family and society; Marianne rejects all outside claims and lives according to her own personal standards. Neither, to be sure, is a pure caricature of sense or sensibility, even initially. Austen clearly indicates that both possess good qualities of mind and feeling, but exercise them differently. When Austen first introduces the heroines, she tells us that Elinor has "strength of understanding and coolness of judgment," but also "an excellent heart;—her disposition was affectionate, and her feelings were strong; but she knew how to govern them." Marianne, in turn, "was sensible [here meaning intelligent] and clever; but eager in everything; her sorrows, her joys, could have no moderation ... she was everything but prudent."

At the beginning of the novel, the reader learns that each sister has constructed a self-image which she tries to realize completely and use as a standard in everyday affairs. Elinor determines to be judicious; Marianne, sensitive. The girls are innocent and inexperienced, and therefore believe that they will be able to control their lives and their reactions to the lives of those around them by merely choosing to do so. Marianne expresses their complacent sense of self control: "At my time of life opinions are tolerably fixed. It is not likely that I should see or hear anything to change them." Life, however, does get in the way. A self-image is very easy to preserve under circumstances that do not challenge it beyond its limits. Elinor and Marianne are taxed beyond their control and find themselves shaken by feelings and occurrences they cannot dominate. A similar set of events happens to them, and they are both educated and matured through their experiences. Both fall in love with a man who is not able or willing to get attached, but who, despite himself, reciprocates the affection. The young women suffer a trial of waiting while their lovers' worth is tested: the men have to uphold or break a previous decision. Both seem to have lost their loves and endure intense pain. Finally all is explained, and Elinor triumphs by consummating her romantic attachment, while Marianne grows wiser, learning that love can have many manifestations. It is an ironic touch that prudent Elinor marries Edward, her first and only love, despite family opposition, on the verge of poverty, and then only by a quirk of fate—Lucy Steel's sudden shift. Marianne, on the other hand, is forced to retract her youthful, ignorant assertions about romantic first love. She makes a rational, practical match for esteem and comfort, with a man whom she learns to love slowly, in a mild and quiet way, altogether unlike her earlier images of what satisfactory love must be. At the end of the book, both young women are more mature and less one sided; Marianne makes a conscious effort toward self-control and propriety, and Elinor is so overwhelmed by emotions that she shows her feelings openly and spontaneously.

The plot gives some idea of the way in which the girls change, but language reveals far more. Austen's use of syntax is "a medium for communicating, by imitation rather than summary or analysis, the outline of a passage of experience, and the structure of the sentence forces upon the reader ... a miming of the heroine's experience." Consider Elinor. At the beginning of the book she speaks of her regard for Edward.

"Of his sense and his goodness," continued Elinor, "no one can, I think, be in doubt, who has seen him often enough to engage him in unreserved conversation. The excellence of his understanding and his principles can be concealed only by that shyness which too often keeps him silent. You know enough of him to do justice to his solid worth. But of his minuter propensities as you call them, you have from peculiar circumstances been kept more ignorant than myself."

Elinor's prose is balanced, and sentences frequently divide neatly into two equal parts joined by a coordinating conjunction. Her use of the formal sentence reflects her sense of the importance of self control, discipline, and duty. "Her syntax is thus an index of her temperament," according to Norman Page. Elinor's sentences are heavy with nouns and substantives (participles, gerunds, and infinitives used as nouns) such as "sense," "goodness," "conversation," "excellence," "to do justice" and so on, which give the sentences a weighted, static tone. Notice her concern for judging and evaluating, which here she expresses in terms of "solid worth." She seems deliberately hesitant to use adjectives and adverbs, and she avoids colorful phrasing. Her verbs are most often "state of being" words or passive voice or impersonal constructions or verbs of intellectual activity such as seeing, knowing, thinking. Instead of describing Edward in bold terms, Elinor uses limiting, qualifying words and negatives which repress emotional intensity and put a distance between Elinor and her own opinions: "*no one* can, *I think*, be *in doubt*, who has seen him *often enough*," and so on. She seems to put her most private feelings and thoughts into the third person, as if that were the only way to justify them.

Contrast Marianne's "autumn leaves" speech, which also appears early in the book.

"Oh!" cried Marianne, "with what transporting sensations have I formerly seen them fall! How have I delighted as I walked, to see them driven in showers about me by the wind! What feelings have they, the season, the air altogether inspired! Now there is no one to regard them. They are seen only as a nuisance, swept hastily off, and driven as much as possible from the sight."

Her sentences are asymmetrical; instead of balancing clauses, Marianne piles up phrases of increasing intensity which come to a climax. Jane Austen uses a great variety of rhetorical devices to heighten Marianne's style. In the quoted passage, an interjection sets the tone of excitement. Marianne's speeches are typically graced with rhetorical questions, apostrophe, personification, and hyperbole. Elinor speaks in a static prose of nouns and colorless verbs; not so Marianne. Marianne's

verbs are active, and her adjectives, participles, and adverbs evoke lively pictures: "walked," "driven," "have inspired," "hastily swept," and so on. By assigning such a style to Marianne, Austen brings to life, rather than merely tells about, a girl of strong feelings, susceptible to beauty in her environment and prone to exaggerated modes of expression. Elinor, in contrast, keeps in abeyance all those feelings not strictly permitted by the social code. She takes an amused, mildly critical view of Marianne's excesses. After the latter concludes her nostalgic outburst, Elinor dryly remarks, "It is not every one . . . who has your passion for dead leaves."

These are the heroines at the beginning of the novel, before life steps in to overturn their self images. When Elinor first learns she has lost Edward to Lucy Steele, she is still in relative control of herself, but her balance begins to break down, in speech as well as in behavior.

"Engaged to Mr. Edward Ferrars!—I confess myself so totally surprised at what you tell me, that really— I beg your pardon; but surely there must be some mistake of person or name. We cannot mean the same Mr. Ferrars."

And yet, for all the dashes, and disjointed and fragmentary sentences, Elinor exerts herself to maintain politeness to Lucy, and by so doing, keeps herself from falling apart. She spares herself humiliation, and Lucy, triumph. Later, alone, she weeps more for Edward's mistake than for her own disappointment. Because her sense of duty sustains her—duty to Lucy's confidence and duty to spare her mother and sister unnecessary and premature suffering—she manages to conceal the painful information for months.

Marianne's reaction to the sudden collapse of her hopes is characteristically different. When Willoughby returns her letters and informs her that he is engaged to Miss Grey, Austen contrasts Elinor's long-suffering, unselfish control with Marianne's self-centered emotionalism.

"Exert yourself, dear Marianne," she cried, "if you would not kill yourself and all who love you. Think of your mother; think of her misery while *you* suffer; for her sake you must exert yourself."

"I cannot, I cannot," cried Marianne; "leave me, leave me, if I distress you; leave me, hate me, forget me! but do not torture me so. Oh! how easy for those who have no sorrow of their own to talk of exertion! Happy, happy Elinor, *you* cannot have an idea of what I suffer."

"Do you call *me* happy, Marianne? Ah! if you knew!—And can you believe me to be so, while I see you so wretched?"

Elinor urges Marianne to fulfill her responsibility to those who love her. Her own sense of duty sustains her, but Marianne's is insufficient to the task. Marianne bursts out with intense, illogical hyperboles and exclamations. Elinor, of course, has been rejected in the same way by her beloved—indeed, in a more irritating manner, by nasty Lucy Steele in person. Elinor here almost slips and reveals her own sorrow when Marianne accuses her of being happy, but quickly covers up her momentary lapse with a credible, if self-righteous excuse. Elinor's discipline is strong to a fault, for she denies herself the sympathy of those who love her and refuses them the chance to give, which is, after all, half of the act of loving. Both young women are suffering, both are deeply touched, but one selfishly wallows in misery while the other tries to carry on her life as usual.

Thus far, the self-images hold up rather well, with only minor deviations. When life becomes more complicated, however, the over-sensitive Marianne is chastened, while the self-negating Elinor loses control and pours out repressed feelings despite herself. Illness frightens Marianne and then allows her time to meditate. She recovers, a reformed young woman, and her speech pattern reflects her new attempt to control herself and observe decorum. For the first time she concerns herself with rational judgment, moral responsibility, and propriety. Of the Willoughby affair she says, "I *can* talk of it now, I hope, as I ought to do." Austen assigns to Marianne the stylistic quirks of Elinor, such as qualifying statements with apologetic phrases, to show us Marianne's newly reflective nature. Marianne, realizing the resemblance between her own and her sister's misfortunes, is doubly humbled when she compares their reactions to pain.

> "Do not, my dearest Elinor, let your kindness defend what I know your judgment must censure. My illness has made me think—it has given me leisure and calmness for serious recollection. Long before I was enough recovered to talk, I was perfectly able to reflect. I considered the past; I saw in my behaviour since the beginning of our acquaintance with him last autumn, nothing but a series of imprudence towards myself, and want of kindness to others."

Here her sentences are balanced and symmetrical, turning on carefully polished antitheses and parallels. Verbs are static or describe mental, rather than physical, action. The new pace of Marianne's sentences is slow and dignified, not impulsive and irregular as before. Marianne's maturation/reformation is reflected by her use of Elinor-like sentences.

Elinor has an opposite development. She, through long tension and disappointment, begins to let emotional, bitter words escape, as her carefully guarded propriety cracks. Under stress she occasionally repeats, accumulates phrases for emphasis, and conveys the breathless, impulsive tone originally characteristic of Marianne. Speaking of Lucy's engagement to Edward, she says,

> "It was told me,—it was in a manner forced on me by the very person herself, whose prior engagement ruined all my prospects; and told me, as I thought, with triumph. . . . I have had her hopes and exultations to listen to again and again."

Although here Jane Austen opens Elinor's heart and has the character show some of the turmoil it contains, Elinor is still able to express herself verbally. There is one further step in her education to womanhood: she must be so deeply moved that she is speechless and unable to depend on the polite formulas with which society usually provides her. This final chastening experience happens when Edward suddenly returns after Elinor has, presumably, lost him forever. In this scene, she is at first able to make small talk, to "rejoice in the dryness of the season," but then is forced to put her head down in "a state of such agitation as made her hardly know where she was." When the truth of Lucy's marriage to Robert Ferrars comes out, Elinor completely loses control of herself, can no longer sit in her place, but dashes out of the room and bursts "into tears of joy, which at first she thought would never cease." Elinor is overcome by sensibility.

Why do Elinor and Marianne both need to change in the novel? What is it that each has that the other must learn? Is it simply that Marianne must correct her irresponsible freedom and adopt Elinor's stifling prudence? Are warmth and sensitivity frowned upon? Are practical concerns set above personal ones? It seems to be more complicated than that. Neither sense nor sensibility by itself is attacked; neither, unqualified, is sufficient. The focus of Austen's criticism seems to be elsewhere.

The true opposition in the novel is between selfishness and selflessness. Marianne's relationship with Willoughby errs, not in its warmth, but in its self-centeredness. In public they have words and glances only for each other. Their imprudent display of attachment, their lack of reserve in company and between themselves comes from belief in a personal morality which cuts them off from the rest of the world. Their relationship flourishes for their own pleasure, independent of the demands of society and family. Since they feel superior to everyone else in sensitivity and candor, they judge others without honest reflection and continually mock their friends. Their love is exclusive and smugly self-centered; when the relationship collapses, Marianne is left with the bitter residue of those feelings. In her suffering, she believes herself to be unique and inconsolable; instead of trying to pull herself out of misery, she remains "equally ill-disposed to receive or communicate pleasure." The illness, which she cannot call up or dismiss by whim, cures her of her exclusive concern for her own pleasures and pains.

Elinor's relationship with Edward is something rather different. Although his family objects to a marriage between them, their friendship is acceptable to their society. Their behavior is decorous and inoffensive. In public they are active members of whatever group they find themselves in; to Elinor's immediate family, the friendship brings comfort and delight, because everyone is welcome to share in the affection of the couple. Their love, unlike Marianne and Willoughby's, turns outward.

Marianne is sensitive and absorbed in herself, while Elinor is practical and concerned primarily with her duty to others. Neither is a caricature of either extreme, and as the book develops, they grow toward a golden mean. To Jane Austen, neither sense nor sensibility is all-good or all-bad. Her judgment upon all the characters, including the heroines, depends on whether they use their sense or sensibility for selfish satisfaction or for the general comfort.

Austen seems to use Elinor as a voice for her own opinions, and is altogether less critical of her than of Marianne. Elinor, for example, is the ear into which Lucy, Colonel Brandon, Willoughby, and Marianne confess. Elinor advises and lectures the others how to behave properly under their difficult trials. For these reasons it seems as if Austen's principal approval lies on the side of sense rather than sensibility. This imbalance of emphasis is really caused by the fact that sensibility is inclined to individual satisfaction at the expense of general happiness, whereas sense tends toward the opposite.

As if to underscore this point, the novel includes several secondary characters who speak for greater extremes of sense or sensibility, with differing amounts of selfishness and unselfishness. The John and Fanny Dashwoods, for example, are prime instances of people abounding in hard, cold sense and very little else. Austen condemns them

beautifully in the second chapter of the first volume, which contains the discussion of John's promise to his dying father. Fanny, exercising brilliant logic and playing on selfish rationalizations, pares down the aid John is to give his sisters from three thousand pounds to nothing. Their language is almost a parody of Elinor's balanced, reflective, polished sentences.

> "Well, then, *let* something be done for them; but *that* something need not be three thousand pounds. Consider," she added, "that when the money is once parted with, it never can return."

The repetition of phrases, the symmetry, and the careful concern for cause and effect, is the style of sense. Or again, consider this passage:

> "Indeed, to say the truth, I am convinced within myself that your father had no idea of your giving them any money at all. The assistance he thought of, I dare say, was only such as might be reasonably expected of you."

Notice the apologetic, qualifying phrases that give a weighted, judicious tone to the inexcusably greedy sentiments. Austen lets us know that these people are practical, but laughably self-centered.

Mrs. Dashwood, the girls' mother, is at the opposite extreme. She, because she is older, is fully confirmed in her imprudent, impractical ways. To be sure, she is often able to comfort her daughters in the abundance of her warmth, but she is also able to inflict pain from her want of caution. She "valued and cherished" Marianne's excesses of sensibility. She persistently pushes Marianne and Willoughby, and Elinor and Edward together, by assuming and letting it be spoken of, that the couples are about to be engaged. Her injudicious, misplaced affection is an agent of unintentional destruction; her unguarded, hasty statements or guesses cause suffering precisely where she means to soothe and strengthen. Trusting feeling, rather than thought, she blinds herself to whatever does not suit her purposes. One notable instance is the letter she sends to Marianne praising Willoughby, which reaches London after Willoughby's engagement to Miss Grey has been announced. Her letter, instead of supporting Marianne and leading her to wise self-government, cuts her so deeply that she falls apart. After Marianne's illness, Mrs. Dashwood is somewhat more sympathetic to Elinor's pleas for prudence, but she has not really learned: she is, for example, carried away by Colonel Brandon's love for Marianne, and invents and exaggerates to suit her fancy. Her impractical, sensitive self-absorption is shown to be sometimes dangerous, always foolish.

Perhaps an ideal combination of sense and sensibility on a lower level of education and refinement than that of the heroines', is Mrs. Jennings. She is a mother-substitute for them during most of the story, and therefore can be contrasted reasonably with Mrs. Dashwood. Mrs. Jennings' speech is occasionally ungrammatical and coarse, and she is addicted to gossip and teasing. Norman Page notes that, "She is exceptional in Jane Austen's gallery in being given dubious linguistic habits which nevertheless carry no overtones of moral censure." Despite her language, she functions properly in society, like Elinor, and communicates affection in her family circle, like Marianne. Most significantly, toward the end of the novel she evaluates situations more justly than any other adult.

Austen first introduces Mrs. Jennings in the role of a buffoon—fat, merry, loquacious, even boisterous and vulgar. She retains the character of a foolish jokester until the sisters accompany her to London. There, in her own home, Austen develops Mrs. Jennings into a truly worthy woman. She is genuinely kind and solicitous for the happiness of her guests, although surrounded by superficial, egotistical people. Unlike her daughter, Lady Middleton, Mrs. Jennings is not a snob. She is loyal to her "old city friends" who seem distastefully unfashionable to her elegant children. Her town house, her friends, her way of life are described as handsome and not at all insipid. Full of life, Mrs. Jennings is able to laugh at herself as well as at others, and her jokes are good-humored, without barbs. What is possibly the most impressive of Mrs. Jennings' qualities is that, while she knows the world and understands the call of money, she holds people and their feelings to be more important. Her nature is warm like Mrs. Dashwood's, but she is neither tremulously sensitive nor blind to the realities of society. Although her mind is acute, she is neither cold nor reserved. When all the adults suddenly turn against Edward, after his engagement to Lucy is made known, she defends him and his spirit. She approves of his loyalty and willingness to sacrifice material comfort for what is, as the reader must agree, a high and unselfish end. Mrs. Jennings delights in the youth and joy of the couple although there is no question of any personal gain for her. When events turn so that Elinor wins Edward, she does not become sour or resentful that her happy predictions were mistaken. It is enough for her generous heart that a bit of happiness is advanced in the world.

Mrs. Jennings' style of speech is an amusing mixture of controlled balance and effusive disorder. At some points she speaks evenly weighted prose with parenthetical expressions to slow the pace and formalize the tone. Her words are never ponderous, because her lively mind undercuts any heavy seriousness.

> "Upon my word I never saw a young woman so desperately in love in my life! *My* girls were nothing to her, and yet they used to be foolish enough; but as for Miss Marianne, she is quite an altered creature. I hope, from the bottom of my heart he won't keep her waiting much longer, for it is quite grievous to see her look so ill and forlorn. Pray, when are they to be married?"

This combination of logic (or semi-logic), of comparison and contrast, of affectionate catch phrases ("Upon my word," "from the bottom of my heart"), of unlabored, yet approximately symmetrical structure, is typical of Mrs. Jennings at her best. Much of her language, however, is fragmented, disjointed, and relatively chaotic in form. She overflows with the breathless wordiness of a fat, merry, middle-aged woman to whom meanness or hardness of any sort is foreign.

> "Poor soul!" cried Mrs. Jennings, as soon as she [Marianne] was gone, "how it grieves me to see her! And I declare if she is not gone away without finishing her wine! And the dried cherries too! Lord! nothing seems to do her any good. I am sure if I knew of any thing she would like, I would send all over the town for it. Well, it is the oddest thing to me, that a man should use such a pretty girl so ill! But when there is plenty of money on one side, and next to none on the other, Lord bless you! they care no more about such things!—"

Although she sees the cruel pursuit of wealth and position around her, it does not corrupt her judgment of how things ought to be. Mrs. Jennings is free of what Jane Nardin calls "Ambition … the farthest extreme of mercenary 'sense' and it characterizes all the really bad people in the novel …" She may be an incorrigible chatterer, but she is also a faithful friend in all her attitudes and actions. She talks a lot, but she does more and does it gladly, without complaint. In a way, Jane Austen explains Mrs. Jennings by putting these words in her mouth: "And what good does talking ever do you know?" Her noisiness does little good, as she herself knows, but neither does it do any harm, for it is always light in tone. Her actions, her steady, honest giving of warmth, encouragement, and spirit, help Elinor through the hard days, and set an example of mingled good sense and sensibility, unmarred by selfishness.

Willoughby is another character whose actions demonstrate that neither sense nor sensibility is implicitly frowned upon, but that both are evil when

What Do I Read Next?

- *Pride and Prejudice* (1813), the second of Jane Austen's novels to be published, is perhaps her most famous work. Much like *Sense and Sensibility*, the action in this novel centers on upper-class English society, in particular the courtship of the Bennet sisters. Elizabeth Bennet, a spitfire of a character, and her equally spirited beau Mr. Darcy are one of literature's most famous pairs.

- *Mansfield Park* (1814), by Jane Austen, tells the story of Fanny Price, an insecure girl who is brought up by her rich aunt and uncle and examines the questions of morality of the time. It has been described as unique among Austen's work in its more somber and moralizing tone.

- *Emma* (1815), the last of Austen's novels to be published before her death, is a lighthearted story of upper-class courtship, featuring a charming heroine but nevertheless displaying Austen's razor-sharp wit and observation of her society. Emma has much in common with Marianne of *Sense and Sensibility* in both her spirited naïveté and her eventual growth into a more mature wisdom, an act which exhibits Austen's views of the necessity of social propriety.

- *Jane Austen's Letters* (1997), a new edition edited by Deirdre Le Faye, is a compilation of Austen's witty and sharp correspondence, which give insight into her daily life and the inspiration she had for her novels.

- *A Vindication on the Rights of Woman*, by Mary Wollstonecraft, was published in 1792. While Austen was busy writing novels that portrayed the domestic and economic situations of upper-class women, the women's rights movement in England was coming into full swing. Mary Wollstonecraft, a radical of the time, composed this most significant work to call for the equal education of women across the social strata. A shocking and controversial work during its time, it is today considered a classic of women's literature.

- *A Room of One's Own* (1929), written by British author, literary critic, and feminist Virginia Woolf, outlines Woolf's groundbreaking analysis of the position of women in English literature, including Jane Austen.

- Percy Bysshe Shelley, a nineteenth-century poet, was one of the key figures of the romantic movement. Romanticism places great importance on passion, emotion, and the self, which Austen is thought to criticize in her portrayal of Marianne in *Sense and Sensibility*. Shelley's most famous long poems are "Prometheus Unbound" (1820) and the highly controversial "Laon and Cythna" (1817), which was banned during his life because of its sexual references and its negative portrayal of the church.

- John Keats was also a key poet of the romantic movement. Poems such as "The Eve of St. Agnes" (1819) and "Ode on a Grecian Urn" (1819) concentrate on the sensuality of both natural and artistic beauty.

---

selfishly applied: Willoughby acts both parts, but is always consummately self-centered. His life is guided solely by what will bring him maximum pleasure at minimum expense of wealth or emotional effort. He becomes involved with Marianne mostly because she is a convenient distraction to fill the idle time he must spend in the country with Mrs. Smith. Charmed by Marianne's beauty and vivacity, he falls into her pattern of self-indulged, exclusive sensitivity. That Willoughby follows Marianne's lead, Austen makes clear by her wry, afterthought inclusion of Willoughby's beliefs.

> But Marianne abhorred all concealment where no real disgrace could attend unreserve; and to aim at the restraint of sentiments which were not in themselves illaudable, appeared to her not merely an unnecessary effort, but a disgraceful subjection of reason to commonplace and mistaken notions. Willoughby thought the same....

He is a weak, drifting character, willing to change himself, if the change will assist him in his pursuit of pleasure. "He acquiesced in all her decisions, caught all her enthusiasm." Typical of his flabby morality is the way in which he excuses himself for the dreadful affair with Eliza Williams, Colonel Brandon's ward; he lays the blame on her, calling her wild and ignorant, rather than castigating himself for taking advantage of her.

A comparison of Willoughby's actions and speeches with those of his fellow-suitor, Edward, brings to light some curious parallels. Willoughby, like Marianne, superficially represents the "sensible," and Edward, like Elinor, the "sense." As the book develops, however, Willoughby acts more for selfish, practical motives, and Edward for unselfish, emotional, even romantic ones. Both men have prior attachments when they meet the Dashwood sisters, and both want only an innocent friendship, without complications. Edward is so involved with Lucy that he feels himself safe from serious emotional attachment. Willoughby, deeply in debt, has prior plans of marrying a lady with a fortune, and uses Marianne as a means to remove the summer tedium, as well as to gratify his vanity by winning her affection. Both men, contrary to their intentions, fall in love and find themselves in a dilemma. Willoughby takes the cold, mercenary way out—he chooses the selfish "sense" of Fanny and John Dashwood, of Mrs. Ferrars, of Lucy Steele. Edward, on the other hand, determines to stand by his rash, youthful promise. He refuses to compromise his honor and cannot bring himself to inflict pain where he thinks he is trusted and long loved. Elinor's extreme reserve keeps him ignorant of her love, and he has no real sense of hurting her by his loyalty to Lucy. Willoughby makes a money match and regrets it; Edward stands by one love match until free to make a second, and is rewarded for his choice.

The language of the two men is as markedly different as that of the sisters. Most of the time Willoughby speaks wittily, twisting Elinor's logically structured sentences into clever jests by using anti-climax, surprise antithesis, and nonsensical pseudo-logic. Answering Elinor's defense of Colonel Brandon,

"Miss Dashwood," cried Willoughby, "you are now using me unkindly. You are endeavouring to disarm me by reason, and to convince me against my will. But it will not do. You shall find me as stubborn as you can be artful. I have three unanswerable reasons for disliking Colonel Brandon: he has threatened me with rain when I wanted it to be fine; he has found

fault with the hanging of my curricle, and I cannot persuade him to buy my brown mare."

His flippant sentences balance, turn neatly on polished constructions, and have many of the other characteristics previously attributed to Elinor's more serious prose. He does occasionally speak in the language of enthusiasm borrowed from Marianne:

"And yet this house you would spoil, Mrs. Dashwood? You would rob it of its simplicity by imaginary improvement! and this dear parlour . . . you would degrade to the condition of a common entrance, and everybody would be eager to pass through the room which has hitherto contained within itself, more real accommodation and comfort than any other apartment of the handsomest dimensions in the world could possibly afford."

The sentence structure rambles asymmetrically, accumulates phrases, uses extreme, hyperbolic words and superlatives altogether out of place with the normal amount of energy given to discussions of household improvement, and generally takes on the traits of "sensibility." Willoughby's language vacillates between the two styles, depending on whom he is with and what kind of impression he wants to make. His vacillation differs from Mrs. Jennings' in that he seems able to manipulate his style to curry favor: his fickle, insincere point of view matches his glib talk.

When he comes to confess to Elinor, that stormy night when Marianne lies deathly ill, he uses the vocabulary of a Lovelace. He scourges himself verbally, but in his melodrama, he seems as insincere as ever. He cannot simply admit to himself that he did wrong and caused pain. Instead, he must convince himself of his remorse by using high flown diction: "Oh God! what an hard-hearted rascal I was!"; "*I* was a libertine"; "Thunderbolts and daggers!," and so on.

Contrast this carrying on with Edward's more modest, but no less interesting, words. Throughout the novel, Edward's speeches are self-effacing, even mildly self-mocking. He has an excellent sense of humor, which is always directed against himself. Discussing the countryside around the Dashwood cottage, in response to Marianne's lyric excitement, he says:

"You must not inquire too far, Marianne—remember I have no knowledge in the picturesque, and I shall offend you by my ignorance and want of taste if we come to particulars. I shall call hills steep, which ought to be bold; surfaces strange and couth, which ought to be irregular and rugged; and distant objects out of sight, which ought only to be indistinct through the soft medium of a hazy atmosphere. You must be satisfied with such admiration as I can honestly give."

His prose is smooth and even, like Elinor's, and has a similarly slow, reflective pace, because Austen uses many of the same stylistic devices for both. He judges himself by strict standards, but is not self-righteous. He maintains the same style of speech, regardless of his audience: he is consistent, unlike the hypocritical Willoughby. Edward's sense of his own worth is very small; he does not believe that anything is owed to him because of his personal merits or birth. His under-estimation of his own worth leads to a certain amount of trouble, causing him to attach himself to Lucy originally, though he was worthy of far better. That is also how he failed to see Elinor's growing love—someone who esteems himself so lightly and judges himself so sternly is unlikely to assume that a young woman is falling in love with him, especially without encouragement.

When he finally returns to Barton to explain his new freedom and express his love for Elinor, he chooses simple, characteristically modest phrases. After the few broken sentences which constitute the scene that dramatically reveals Lucy's duplicity, Edward comes back to make a full confession of his mistakes. Unlike Willoughby, he does not accuse himself of grand and dastardly deeds, but of a natural stupidity based on inexperience and insecurity. His words are halting, qualified by apologetic phrases: "I think," "what I thought at the time," "at least I thought so *then*, and I had seen so little of other women," and so on. The conclusion and climax of his speech are in negatives of reasonable self-censure, not at all hyperbolic or artificially intensified by diction or imbalanced structure—but the intensity, although suppressed, is evident:

> "Considering everything, therefore, I hope, foolish as our engagement was, foolish as it has since in every way been proved, it was not at the time an unnatural, or an inexcusable piece of folly."

He concerns himself with judgment, with the standards of society, and does not exclude himself from humanity because of his guilt, as Willoughby tries to do. And yet, Edward's remorse and chagrin are clearly conveyed, and the passage is charged with restrained emotion of a more convincing sort than that professed by Willoughby.

Edward and Willoughby, Elinor and Marianne, more than extremes of sense and sensibility, represent extremes of ego-negation and ego-centrism. In the course of the novel, Edward's modesty wins him rewards after much suffering. Willoughby reveals himself to be pitifully cold and selfish under his facade of sensibility. The sisters grow to be refined, elegant young women, following the excellent moral example of Mrs. Jennings. Overwhelming sense is criticized in the persons of John and Fanny Dashwood; and overwhelming sensibility, in the character of Mrs. Dashwood. Both poles inflict pain by self-willed blindness to the feelings of others or to the consequences of their actions. *Sense and Sensibility* is a novel describing the education of two young women into the world of mature responsibility, the world in which compromises are necessary when circumstances get out of control. The sisters learn to look to others instead of being engrossed in themselves; they learn to accept the love and help of others instead of assuming that they can manage alone; they learn to combine warmth and intensity with prudence and judgment. Elinor and Marianne, when the novel closes, are prepared to add to the pleasure and happiness of those immediately around them as well as to their society in general. *Sense and Sensibility* presents a complicated and compelling morality through an excellent story.

Source: P. Gila Reinstein, "Moral Priorities in *Sense and Sensibility*," in *Renascence*, Vol. XXXV, No. 4, Summer 1983, pp. 269–83.

Sources

Brown, Ivor, *Jane Austen and Her World*, Henry Z. Walck, 1966.

Burrows, John, "Style," in *The Cambridge Companion to Jane Austen*, edited by Edward Copeland, Cambridge University Press, 1997, pp. 170–88.

Butler, Marilyn, "Sensibility and Jacobinism," in *"Sense and Sensibility" and "Pride and Prejudice,"* by Jane Austen, edited by Robert Clark, St. Martin's Press, 1994, pp. 38–52.

Clark, Robert, "Introduction: Closing (with) Jane Austen," in *"Sense and Sensibility" and "Pride and Prejudice,"* by Jane Austen, edited by Robert Clark, St. Martin's Press, 1994, pp.1–25.

Handley, Graham, *Criticism in Focus: Jane Austen*, Bristol Classical Press, 1992.

Poovey, Mary, "Ideological Contradictions and the Consolations of Form," in *"Sense and Sensibility" and "Pride and Prejudice,"* by Jane Austen, edited by Robert Clark, St. Martin's Press, 1994, pp. 83–100.

Tomlin, Claire, *Jane Austen: A Life*, Alfred A. Knopf, 1997, p. 217.

Further Reading

Armstrong, Isobel, *Jane Austen: "Sense and Sensibility,"* Penguin Group, 1994.

Armstrong provides a comprehensive criticism and examination of *Sense and Sensibility*, including the novel's social constructs and the philosophical beliefs of the characters.

Gilbert, Sandra, and Susan Gubar, *The Madwoman in the Attic*, New Haven, 1979.

Gubar and Gilbert are two of the most important feminist literary theorists of recent times. This seminal work brings to light the psychological anxieties faced by women writers throughout the history of English literature, caused by their inferior status in society.

Harding, D. W., *Regulated Hatred and Other Essays on Jane Austen*, edited by Monica Lawlor, Althone Press, 1998.

Harding, a significant literary critic of the twentieth century, considered Austen one of his favorite authors. Written over a span of sixty years, the essays in this collection examine a range of aspects of Austen's writing, from its historical context to the psychology of her characters.

Jenkins, Elizabeth, *Jane Austen*, Farrar, Straus and Cudahy, 1949.

Jenkins provides a seminal biography of Jane Austen.

Monaghan, David, ed., *Jane Austen in a Social Context*, Macmillan Press, 1981.

This collection of essays examines Austen's contemporary social context and the way it is exhibited in her writing.

Neill, Edward, *The Politics of Jane Austen*, St. Martin's Press, 1999.

This contemporary collection of essays on Austen's major work defends the position that Austen was a subtle political writer.

Sons and Lovers

D. H. Lawrence
1913

Initially titled "Paul Morel," *Sons and Lovers*, published in 1913, is D. H. Lawrence's third novel. It was his first successful novel and arguably his most popular. Many of the details of the novel's plot are based on Lawrence's own life and, unlike his subsequent novels, this one is relatively straightforward in its descriptions and action. The story recounts the coming of age of Paul Morel, the second son of Gertrude Morel and her hard-drinking, working-class husband, Walter Morel, who made his living as a miner. As Mrs. Morel tries to find meaning in her life and emotional fulfillment through her bond with Paul, Paul seeks to break free of his mother through developing relationships with other women. The novel was controversial when it was published because of its frank way of addressing sex and its obvious oedipal overtones. The novel was also heavily censored. Edward Garnett, a reader for Duckworth, Lawrence's publisher, cut about 10 percent of the material from Lawrence's draft. Garnett tightened the focus on Paul by deleting passages about his brother, William, and toning down the sexual content. In 1994, Cambridge University Press published a new edition with all of the cuts restored, including Lawrence's idiosyncratic punctuation.

Sons and Lovers is also significant for the portrait it provides of working-class life in Nottinghamshire, England. Lawrence's disgust with industrialization shows in his descriptions of the mining pits that dot the countryside and the hardships and humiliation that working families had to endure to survive.

D. H. Lawrence

A prolific writer, Lawrence published four novels, a play, a collection of poems, and a collection of stories before he turned thirty. His first real success came with the publication of his third novel, *Sons and Lovers* (1913), a fictionalized autobiography of his relationships with his mother and Jessie Chambers, a love interest from his youth, and a social portrait of provincial life in Nottinghamshire. The novel describes Paul Morel's fixation on his mother, and how that fixation informs his other relationships. Much of Lawrence's writing addresses the intersections between sexual desire and class identity and the consequences of denying the wants of one's animal self. Subsequent novels and criticism cemented his reputation as an enemy of bourgeois morality. Some of his better-known works include *The Rainbow* (1915); *Women in Love* (1920); *Psychoanalysis and the Unconscious* (1921); *Fantasia of the Unconscious* (1922); *Studies in Classic American Literature* (1923); *St. Mawr* (1925); and *The Plumed Serpent* (1926). Lawrence's most controversial novel, *Lady Chatterly's Lover* (1928), was accused of being pornographic, and its publishers were taken to court.

Lawrence's restless, peripatetic existence—he and Freida traveled constantly—came to an end on March 2, 1930, at Vence, in the south of France, when he finally succumbed to tuberculosis, which had plagued him for most of his life.

Author Biography

David Herbert Richard (D. H.) Lawrence was born in Eastwood, Nottinghamshire, England, on September 11, 1885, the son of coal miner Arthur Lawrence and schoolteacher Lydia Beardsall. A novelist, critic, and poet known for writing about the conflicts between men and women, Lawrence derived much of his material from his childhood, which was fraught with tension. His mother resented his father's hard drinking and lack of ambition, and the two bickered and quarreled regularly. Lydia Beardsall eventually succeeded in turning her five children against their father, and she developed an especially close bond with David, after having nursed him back to life from a bout of double pneumonia during childhood. When she died in 1910, Lawrence's illness returned and almost killed him. After recovering, he quit his teaching post at the Davidson School in Croydon, terminated his romantic relationships, and flung himself headlong into his writing career, abandoning his middle-class desires and adopting a bohemian lifestyle. In 1912, he eloped with Frieda von Richthofen Weekley, the wife of a professor at the University of Nottingham, who left her husband and three small children to be with Lawrence.

Plot Summary

Chapter 1: The Early Married Life of the Morels

The first chapter of *Sons and Lovers* introduces the Morel family and describes the story's setting, a neighborhood called "The Bottoms," where the miners live. Mrs. Morel is pregnant with her third child, which she does not want because she has fallen out of love with her husband and because the family is poor. When her husband comes home from working at a bar, the two argue over his drinking.

This chapter also contains a flashback to the time when Mrs. Morel met Walter at a Christmas party. She was twenty-three, reserved, and thoughtful; he was twenty-seven, good-looking, and outgoing, and very different from Mrs. Morel's father. They are married by the following Christmas. Less than a year into their marriage, however, Mrs. Morel discovers that Walter is not the man she thought he was. He does not own his house as he said he did, and he is in considerable debt.

Two key events occur in this chapter. The first is when Walter cuts his son's hair while his wife is sleeping. Mrs. Morel views this as a betrayal, and the image of William, her favorite child, standing in front of his father with shorn locks on the floor, stays with her. The second event occurs when Walter comes home drunk late one night and fights with his wife. Walter locks his pregnant wife out of the house, letting her in later, after he has slept off part of his alcohol.

Chapter 2: The Birth of Paul, and Another Battle

With the help of Mrs. Bower, a midwife, Mrs. Morel gives birth to a son. Walter arrives home, immediately asks Mrs. Bower for a drink, has his dinner, and then goes upstairs to see his wife. The arrival of Paul increases the tension in the house, as the couple continues to bicker and fight. Walter does not like to be around his family, and the estrangement between the two adults grows. In one scene, Walter drunkenly pulls out a drawer and throws it at his wife, hitting her and cutting her above the eye. He is ashamed of his actions, but tells himself it is her fault. He spends the next few days drinking at a bar. Toward the end of the chapter, Walter steals money from his wife's purse, and then denies it when she confronts him. He stalks out of the house with a bundle of his belongings saying that he is leaving, but he returns home that night.

Chapter 3: The Casting off of Morel— The Taking on of William

In this chapter, Walter falls ill, but his wife nurses him back to health. Mrs. Morel, however, is devoting more and more of her attention to the children. She tolerates her husband, but does not love him. In the period after Walter's illness, the couple conceives another child, Arthur, who is born when Paul is one and a half years old. Arthur becomes Walter's favorite child and is like him both physically and temperamentally.

Walter and his wife fight over how to discipline their children and plan for their future. Mrs. Morel vetoes her husband's suggestion that William work in the mines; she finds him a job at the Co-operative Wholesale Society instead. At nineteen, William takes a job in London, much to his devoted mother's chagrin.

Chapter 4: The Young Life of Paul

This chapter focuses on Paul's childhood, and all of the events narrated are in relation to his character. Mrs. Morel and her husband still fight, and

Media
Adaptations

- The most acclaimed film adaptation of Lawrence's novel is the 1960 film *Sons and Lovers*, directed by Jack Cardiff and starring Trevor Howard, Dean Stockwell, and Wendy Hiller. The film was nominated for seven Academy Awards. Many libraries and video stores carry the video.

- In 1995, Penguin Audiobooks released an audiocassette of Lawrence's novel with Paul Copley narrating.

Walter drifts further away from the family, even though they have moved from "The Bottoms" and into a new house. There are also moments when the family bonds, and Mrs. Morel encourages the children to share the events of the day with their father. But overall, Walter is more alienated than ever from his wife and children, especially Paul. A significant event occurs when Paul breaks his sister's doll and then experiences hatred for the doll. This echoes his father's own behavior toward his mother.

Chapter 5: Paul Launches into Life

In this chapter, Walter injures his leg, causing anxiety in his family and guilt in Mrs. Morel, who is concerned for her husband's health but guilt ridden because she no longer loves him. Paul, now fourteen, hunts for work and lands a position with Thomas Jordan, a manufacturer of surgical appliances, as a junior clerk. William, still in London, is now dating, and sends his mother a photograph of his girlfriend, Lily Weston. His mother is not impressed.

Chapter 6: Death in the Family

In this chapter, Arthur leaves home to attend school in Nottingham, where he lives with his sister, Annie. Paul visits the Leivers's farm where he meets Miriam Leivers. The "Death" in the chapter title refers to William's death. He dies after a short illness, and his mother is devastated. Paul falls ill with pneumonia, but his mother nurses him back to health, and the two develop an intense emotional bond.

Chapter 7: Lad-and-Girl Love

Paul develops a close relationship with Miriam, who aspires to transcend her working-class roots through education. She takes care of Paul when he is sick and falls in love with him. Paul, however, remains ambivalent about the relationship and struggles to define what he feels toward her. Mrs. Morel does not like Miriam, because she believes that Miriam is taking Paul away from her.

Chapter 8: Strife in Love

The key events in this chapter include Arthur's enlistment in the army and events illustrating Paul's struggle to define his feelings for Miriam while at the same time remaining emotionally faithful to his mother. Paul also sees Clara Dawes, whom he tells Miriam he likes.

Chapter 9: Defeat of Miriam

This chapter details Paul's recognition that he loves his mother more than Miriam and would never marry and leave her. Compounding his love for his mother is his awareness that she is old now and not well. He breaks off his relationship with Miriam, who remains angry with him for being so influenced by his mother. However, Paul continues to visit the Leivers's farm, where he later meets Clara again, but he tells Edgar, Miriam's brother, that he does not like Clara because she is so abrasive. He is both attracted to and repelled by Clara's dislike of men.

Annie marries Leonard, even though neither of them have much money, and Mrs. Morel buys Arthur out of the army. Arthur returns home and promptly marries Beatrice Wyld.

Chapter 10: Clara

One of Paul's paintings is sold for twenty guineas to Major Moreton. Paul discusses his success with his mother, who expresses her desire that he settle down with a woman and make a better life for himself. Paul visits Clara and meets her mother. He revises his opinion of Clara and secures a job for her. The two grow closer, and Clara discusses her failed marriage with him.

Chapter 11: The Test on Miriam

Paul returns to Miriam, convinced that the "problem" between them stems from the lack of sexuality in their relationship. He tells her that he loves her, and the two sleep together. However, the relationship deteriorates when Miriam tells him that she feels they are too young to marry. Once again, Paul breaks off the relationship, and the two become bitter toward each other.

Chapter 12: Passion

Paul spends more time with Clara, telling her that he has split up with Miriam. The two are extremely passionate with each other, and Paul invites her to meet his mother. Paul later invites Clara and her mother on a trip to the seaside.

Chapter 13: Baxter Dawes

In this chapter, Paul encounters Clara's husband, Baxter Dawes, numerous times, and the two fight once, with Dawes injuring Paul. Paul remains torn between his love for his mother and his desire to bond with other women. He realizes that he will not be able to marry while his mother is still alive. At the end of the chapter, Paul discovers that his mother is ill with a tumor.

Chapter 14: The Release

In this chapter, Gertrude Morel dies, after Paul—who cannot bear to see her suffer—and his sister give her an overdose of morphine in her milk. Paul befriends Baxter Dawes, who is ill with fever, and eventually facilitates his reconciliation with Clara.

Chapter 15: Derelict

Paul is despondent after his mother's death and contemplates suicide. Miriam meets him for dinner and proposes that they marry, but Paul turns her down. Clara returns to Sheffield with her husband, so she is also now out of Paul's life. Walter Morel sells the house, and he and Paul take rooms in town. The novel ends with Paul's recognition that he will always love his mother, and he decides to stay alive for her sake.

Characters

Baxter Dawes

Baxter Dawes is thirty-two years old and a big handsome man. He is Clara Dawes's estranged husband. He is a smith at the same factory as Paul, with whom he fights when Paul begins to spend time with Clara. Dawes is moody, argumentative, and defiant and is fired from his job after fighting with his boss, Thomas Jordan. Later, Dawes falls ill with typhoid fever. Paul visits Dawes in the convalescence home, and the two become friends. Later, Paul tells Dawes that Clara has always loved him, and he helps Baxter and Clara reconcile.

Clara Dawes

Clara Dawes, the estranged wife of Baxter Dawes, is a childless, full-figured, blonde-haired, and sensuous woman, and a friend of Miriam Leivers. She is proud and haughty, a supporter of women's rights, and is attracted to Paul's animality. Clara and Paul have a passionate love affair, but she eventually returns to her husband, nursing him back to health after he falls sick with typhoid fever. Although she was deeply attracted to Paul, she never felt truly connected to him.

Mr. Heaton

Mr. Heaton is the Congregational clergyman who visits with Gertrude Morel after Paul is born. He is Paul's godfather and tutor.

Thomas Jordan

Thomas Jordan owns the factory where Paul and Clara and Baxter Dawes work. A strong-willed capitalist, he fires Baxter Dawes after fighting with him. He eventually takes Paul under his wing and introduces him to middle-class social life.

Miriam Leivers

The daughter of the family at Willey Farm, Miriam meets Paul when she is sixteen. She is serious, self-conscious, somewhat spiritual, and does not like sex, though she sleeps with Paul, hoping that it will make him love her. Miriam is like Paul's mother in that both of them are morally prudish and strong-willed. Even though Paul makes it clear he will not marry her, Miriam believes that their souls will always be together.

Annie Morel

A bit of a tomboy, Annie is Paul's older sister, and the two spend much time together in childhood. She becomes a junior teacher at the Board School in Nottingham, and marries her childhood friend, Leonard. When their mother lies dying, she helps Paul give her an overdose of morphine.

Arthur Morel

Arthur is Paul's younger brother and the favorite of Walter Morel, whom he resembles both physically and temperamentally. He joins the army but hates it. After his mother buys him out of the army, he returns home and marries Beatrice.

Gertrude Morel

Gertrude Coppard Morel is the first protagonist of Lawrence's novel. Refined, intellectual, and deeply moral, she comes from a family of professionals. Her father was an engineer and her family long-time Congregationalists. She marries Walter Morel when she is twenty-three years old, attracted to his swarthy good looks, humility, and animated personality. After the birth of her first child, she falls out of love with her husband and begins to actively despise him, looking for fulfillment in her relationships with her children, particularly her sons, William and Paul. The intensity of her emotional bond with these two makes it difficult for them to develop romantic relationships. She dislikes William's girlfriend, Lily Weston, and is jealous of Paul's friend, Miriam Leivers. After William dies, she pins her hopes for the future on Paul. She wants him to be successful and to escape a working-class miner's life. Though she is deathly ill, she hangs onto life, because she cannot bear to part from her son. Paul eventually helps her die by giving her an overdose of morphine.

Paul Morel

Paul Morel is the protagonist in the second half of the novel. Although his mother regrets being pregnant with him because she does not believe the family can afford another child, she grows to love and protect him after he is born. Paul is frail, sensitive, and artistic and develops a very close bond with his mother, hating to disappoint her. The women he courts, Miriam and Clara, can never replace the bond he feels with his mother, and when she dies, Paul feels their souls will be forever bonded. Paul's search for identity is tied up in his capacity to separate himself from his mother, and to understand the extent with which he is shaped by his family and community life.

Walter Morel

Walter Morel is Gertrude's husband and a coal miner. He is rugged, handsome, sensuous, and very practical, deriving much of his joy in life from working and being with his fellow miners. Although he pledges not to drink, he begins to after the birth of their first child. The Morels quarrel regularly, often over Walter's drinking. Gertrude grows to loathe not only Walter's drinking but his crude and unsophisticated behavior as well, and she enlists her children in hating their father. After his wife dies, he becomes a broken man, full of regret and fear.

William Morel

William Morel is the first son, and Gertrude Morel's favorite child. He is smart, beautiful, and popular with other children. When he turns 13, his father suggests that he work in the mines, but his mother finds an office job for him. Later, he moves to London, where he finds a good job with a good salary. Like Paul, he cannot develop a satisfying relationship with a woman because he is so close to his mother. He dates and then breaks up with Lily Weston, a pretentious and helpless woman. When William dies, in his early twenties, his mother becomes withdrawn and reclusive.

Jerry Purdy

Jerry Purdy is Walter Morel's best friend and drinking buddy and is very much disliked by Mrs. Morel.

Mrs. Radford

Mrs. Radford is Clara Dawes's mother. She is refined and stately-looking, yet pushy. She convinces Paul to find a job for Clara at Jordan's.

Louisa Lily Denys Weston

Lily is an attractive yet intellectually-limited girl whom William courts in London. She acts helpless and makes many demands on William, but she behaves as if she were royalty. Williams grows to dislike her, and she forgets all about him shortly after he dies.

Beatrice Wyld

Beatrice is a flirtatious girl who marries Arthur when he returns from the army.

Themes

Free Will

Lawrence addresses the issue of free will in his novel, asking to what extent his characters' environment influences their characters' choices. Lawrence makes this explicit in his descriptions. For example, when Paul begins to look in the newspapers for work, the narrator writes, "Already he was a prisoner of industrialism . . . He was being taken into bondage. His freedom in the beloved home valley was going now." The modern industrial world, specifically as it manifests itself in the effect mining culture has on the Morel family, shapes the characters' desires. Mrs. Morel, who believes she is morally better than the miners, is dis-

gusted by what mining has made of her husband, and she pushes her children away from that work. She finds jobs for both Paul and William so that they will lead better lives than their father. The sons have difficulty making choices of their own. They are so driven to please their mother that they sacrifice their own pleasure and needs to satisfy hers. Neither can develop emotionally healthy relationships with women, and both struggle to balance their own wants with those of their mother. Another character who suppresses her will for the needs of another is Miriam Leivers, who sleeps with Paul to please him, even though she feels little sexual passion for him.

Sexuality

By explicitly depicting human sexuality in his novel, Lawrence flouted the moral conventions of the genre and of society, and his notoriety grew. At least one publisher refused *Sons and Lovers* because of its sexual content. Lawrence's theories about human behavior revolved around what he called "blood consciousness," which he opposed to "mental and nerve consciousness." Lawrence contended that "blood consciousness" was the seat of the will and was passed on through the mother. This is obvious in Paul and William's bond with their mother and in Paul's tenacity and emotional volatility, which his mother also shares.

Lawrence argued that modern society had somehow come to be dominated by mental consciousness and so was largely unconscious of its own desires. He wrote about his theories of human behavior in *Psychoanalysis and the Unconscious* (1921) and *Fantasia of the Unconscious* (1922), along with his theories about male-female relationships. His controversial novel, *Lady Chatterly's Lover* (1928), was accused of being obscene and pornographic, and its publishers were taken to court. Lawrence also flouted moral conventions in his personal life, eloping with Frieda von Richthofen Weekley, the wife of a professor at the University of Nottingham.

Some critics have argued that Paul's relationship to his mother illustrates Freud's Oedipus complex and have characterized both Paul and Lawrence as being sexually tortured and repressed by the degree of their emotional intimacy with their mother.

Class

Lawrence's characters illustrate the class contradictions at the heart of modern industrial society. Capitalism pits classes against one another and even pits individuals of the same class against one an-

Topics For Further Study

- Compare Lawrence's novel to the film adaptation made of it in 1960 which was directed by Jack Cardiff. How does Cardiff adapt Lawrence's episodic telling of the story to the screen? What information does Cardiff leave out of the film, and what effects do these omissions have on the story? Discuss as a class.

- Make a chapter by chapter timeline of the novel, detailing major events and shifts in point of view. Hang the chart in the classroom, and make any necessary changes to it while discussing the novel.

- Gather in groups and draw a portrait of Paul's brain, marking off sections according to the thoughts and people that preoccupy him during the novel. How much space would you give to Miriam? How much to his mother? How much

to his father? Present the portrait to the class and explain your labeling choices.

- In explaining his theory of the oedipal complex, Freud claimed that between two and five years old, during the phallic stage of their development, boys fantasize about being their mother's lover. The boy's sexual interests, however, are soon met with the threat of castration from the father, and the eventual successful resolution involves identification with the father and assuming an active and aggressive social role in a patriarchal society. Discuss how the relationship between Paul and his mother does *not* illustrate or echo the Oedipus complex.

- Write a summary of what might happen in a sixteenth chapter. What happens to Paul once he reaches the "faintly humming, glowing town"? Take turns reading your summaries to the class.

other. Lawrence develops this theme by depicting conflicts among various groups and characters. For example, William feverishly climbs the social ladder, only to discover that he is more alienated from his family the further up he climbs. His girlfriend, Lily, a pretentious and snobbish Londoner, holds herself above the working class and condescends to the Morels, treating them as "clownish" people and hicks. Even Mrs. Morel, a former teacher, has contempt for the work of her own husband and is disgusted by her miner friends, whom she considers lowly. The starkest contrast between classes, however, is illustrated in the relationship between Thomas Jordan, the capitalist factory owner, and his workers, whom he patronizes and quarrels with.

Style

Episodes

Sons and Lovers is structured episodically. This means that the novel consists of a series of

episodes tied together thematically and by subject matter. Structuring the novel in this manner allows Lawrence to let meaning accumulate by showing how certain actions and images repeat themselves and become patterns. This repetition of actions and images is part of the iterative mode. By using this mode, Lawrence can blend time periods, making it sometimes difficult to know whether an event happened once or many times. Lawrence is using the iterative mode when he uses words such as "would" and "used to."

Point of View

Point of view refers to the perspective from which the narrative is told. *Sons and Lovers* is told mostly from a third-person omniscient point of view, as the narrator has access to the thoughts of the characters and moves back and forth in time while telling the story. The first half of the novel focuses on Gertrude Morel and the second part focuses on Paul. However, although Lawrence strives to create a narrator that is impartial and presents material in an objective manner, the narrator occasionally

Compare & Contrast

- **1900–1920:** In 1912, Sigmund Freud delivers a speech before the London Society of Psychical Research detailing for the first time his theories on the unconscious as a repository of thoughts repressed by the conscious mind. Over the next few decades, psychoanalysis grows in popularity, with thousands of psychiatrists undergoing and then practicing Freudian psychoanalysis.

  Today: Though academic interest in Freud remains strong, very few practicing Freudian psychoanalysts remain.

- **1900–1920:** World War I is fought between 1914 and 1918, resulting in tens of millions of casualties.

  Today: In 2001, terrorists kill more than 3,000 people by flying jet airplanes into the twin towers of Manhattan's World Trade Center, and President George W. Bush of the United States declares war on terrorism.

- **1900–1920:** In 1917, the world's first mass-produced tractor, the Fordson, is introduced, and farmers quickly produce crop surpluses.

  Today: Governments of the United States and Britain regularly offer subsidies to their farmers to *not* grow crops.

makes editorial comments on the action, as he does in the first part of the novel after Mrs. Morel has been thinking that her life will be one of continued drudgery. The narrator intrudes, saying, "Sometimes life takes hold of one, carries the body along, accomplishes one's history, and yet is not real, but leaves oneself as it were slurred over." Lawrence alternates between showing and telling in the novel. When he shows, he simply describes the characters' action and lets them speak for themselves. When he tells, he summarizes scenes and sometimes comments on them. The narrator's presence is most evident in the latter instance.

Historical Context

1885–1910: England

Lawrence's novel begins in 1885 and ends in 1911, roughly following the outline of Lawrence's own life. During that time, British miners battled their capitalist bosses for better pay and safer working conditions. However, large swings in demand for coal contributed to industry instability, and it was common for miners' unions to be rewarded a raise one year and presented with a cut in salary

the next. As the rate of industrialization increased, so did the gap between rich and poor. Nowhere was this gap more apparent than in the difference between how the miners lived and how the owners of the mines lived. Lawrence's father, on whom Walter Morel is based, began working in the mines when he was ten years old. A typical week for him consisted of six twelve-hour days, with only two paid holidays a year. One way out of the danger and poverty of the mining life was through education. The Education Act of 1870, which attempted to provide elementary education for all children, gave hope to the parents of many working-class children. The act allowed local school boards to levy and collect taxes. Elementary schooling, however, was not entirely free until the 1890s, when "board" schools could stop charging fees. Before that, parents were expected to pay between one and four pence per week per child. William, Paul, Clara, and Miriam all went to school, which significantly increased their chances of finding better work.

At this time, there was also a difference between public and private schools. Public schools were more expensive than private schools, as private schools often received their funding from an endowment or from a corporation, which ran them or hired a board of governors to do so. Social class was, and remains, intricately entwined with education. Schools not only provided students with the basic skills to obtain jobs, but they also offered students the chance to form friendships and alliances with other students and their families. Gaining admission to the better schools, however, depended on the student's family's resources and connections.

As a result of the Education Act, industrialization, and urbanization, more positions in skilled and semiskilled labor became available during the last quarter of the nineteenth century. The number of clerks, for example, quadrupled between 1850 and 1900, with the British government, particularly the Post Office, employing the bulk of them. Vocational schools gradually replaced apprenticeships, and quasi-professional fields such as photography, bookkeeping, and librarianship emerged, providing additional choices for those with the desire or wherewithal to make better lives for themselves. There were more opportunities for men; however, women, especially unmarried women, found work as typists, secretaries, and telephone operators.

While Lawrence was lambasting industrialization and the loss of humanity's bond with the land, rural people were pouring into cities throughout the nineteenth century, seeking a better life. The agricultural depression of the 1870s further depleted the number of farmers, and by the turn of the century more than 80 percent of Britain's population lived in cities. The "faintly humming, glowing town" toward which Paul walks at the end of the novel is full of telephones and buses, trams, automobiles, and subway trains.

Trevor Howard as Walter Morel and Dean Stockwell as Paul Morel in the 1960 film adaptation of Sons and Lovers

Critical Overview

In general, reviewers praise *Sons and Lovers*, though when doing so, they just as often point out its shortcomings. A writer for the *The Saturday Review*, for example, gives the novel this backhanded compliment: "The sum of its defects is astonishingly large, but we only note it when they are weighed against the sum of its own qualities." A reviewer for the *New York Times Book Review* has reservations with the novel's style, writing in an essay titled "Mother Love," "It is terse—so terse that at times it produces an effect as of short, sharp hammer strokes." However, the same writer calls the book one of "rare excellence." Writing almost a decade later in 1924, in her essay "Artist Turned Prophet" for *The Dial*, Alyse Gregory asserts that Lawrence is at his very best in *Sons and Lovers*,

The Rainbow, and *Twilight in Italy*. In these works, Gregory argues, Lawrence's "febrile and tortured genius flows richly and turbulently. Every passing stir upon his sensitiveness is passionately or beautifully recorded."

Predictably, the novel also caught the attention of the psychoanalytic community. In his essay "*Sons and Lovers*: A Freudian Appreciation" written for *The Psychoanalytic Review*, Alfred Booth Kuttner uses Freud's psychosexual theory of the oedipal complex to explain the choices Paul Morel makes. This approach, like many of Freud's theories themselves, was later widely attacked as being reductive. More recent criticism of the novel has drawn on the theories of Jacques Lacan, among others. Earl Ingersoll, for example, in his essay, "Gender and Language in *Sons and Lovers*," argues that a Lacanian approach to the novel is more productive than the Freudian psychoanalytic approach critics such as Kuttner have taken. Exploring the relationship between language and the characters' interactions, Ingersoll charts Paul's maturation as a movement from "the text of the unconscious associated with the mother to the empowerment of metaphor associated with the Name-of-the-Father."

Ingersoll links highbrow English with the mother and lowbrow with the father.

Criticism

Chris Semansky

Semansky is an instructor of English literature and composition. In this essay, Semansky considers Lawrence's novel as a Bildungsroman.

Sons and Lovers is an example of a *Bildungsroman*, an autobiographical novel about the early years of a character's life, and that character's emotional and spiritual development. The term derives from German novels of education, such as Johann Wolfgang von Goethe's *Wilhelm Meister's Apprenticeship*, which details the experiences of an innocent young man who discovers his purpose and passion in life through a series of adventures and misadventures. Lawrence offers up a rendering of his own first twenty-five years of life in more or less chronological order, showing how Paul Morel must negotiate the pull of family and culture to cultivate his individuality.

By writing a novel that is predominantly based on people and times from his own life, Lawrence implicitly invites readers to treat the work as non-fiction. This has often led to confusion, however, as some of the events in *Sons and Lovers* have no factual basis in Lawrence's life but rather are symbolic dramatizations of his key emotional struggles. The character in the book that has occasioned the most controversy is Miriam Leivers, whom Lawrence based on Jessie Chambers, a friend from his youth. Chambers encouraged Lawrence to rewrite the novel after he had sent her a draft. She was disappointed in the revision as well, because she felt it did not accurately portray their relationship. Chambers attempted to tell the "real" story of her relationship with Lawrence in her own memoir, *D. H. Lawrence: A Personal Record*.

The relationship between Paul and Miriam that Lawrence describes fulfills the conventional criteria of the *Bildungsroman*, which often includes a detailing of the protagonist's love affairs. Critic Brian Finney is even more specific in his description of the genre's criteria in his examination of the novel *D. H. Lawrence: Sons and Lovers* when he writes, "Normally, there are at least two love affairs, one demeaning, and one exalting." In this scheme, Miriam, of course, represents the "de-

meaning" relationship. Although she gives herself to Paul sexually, she does so reluctantly, sacrificially, and without passion.

Finney describes other criteria of the *Bildungsroman*:

The child protagonist is usually sensitive and is constrained by parents (the father in particular) and the provincial society in which he or she grows up. Made aware of wider intellectual and social horizons by schooling, the child breaks with the constraints of parents and home environment and moves to the city where his or her personal education begins—both in terms of discovering a true vocation and through first experiencing sexual passion.

Paul certainly fulfills the criterion of being sensitive. Lawrence describes him as "a pale, quiet child" who "was so conscious of what other people felt." However, the primary constraint on his development is his mother, rather than his father. It is Mrs. Morel that Paul resembles and loves and who forms the psychological barrier that Paul repeatedly comes up against in his drive to know himself. Mrs. Morel, though, is also a facilitator in Paul's development, as she attempts to shield him from her husband's vulgar habits and rescues him from a life in the mines.

Mrs. Morel also attempts to mitigate the effects that the society in which they live have on her children. Bestwood, a thinly-veiled version of Eastwood, where Lawrence was born, is the setting of the novel, and in the opening chapter Lawrence recounts the history of the Midlands countryside, Mrs. Morel's childhood, and the time when she met and married Walter Morel. This narrative strategy of describing the factors that contributed to Paul's conception allows Lawrence to foreground the influence of Paul's environment and family life on the development of his character. Paul was born in "The Bottoms," a six-block area of housing for miners. Life in "The Bottoms" is largely one of on-going despair. After a day in the mines, the men drink and cavort, while their wives tend to domestic chores such as cooking and cleaning. Mrs. Morel is unlike the other wives in that she comes from a higher social station and had expectations for a better life. In *The Dictionary of Literary Biography*, Kinglsey Widmer describes Mrs. Morel primarily as a destructive figure in Paul and William's lives, writing:

Her Protestant ethos of self-denial, sexual repression, impersonal work, disciplined aspiration, guilt, and yearning for conversion-escape, not only defeats her already industrially victimized coal-miner husband but also contributes to the defeat of several of their sons.

Paul's "defeat," however, is only possible because Paul knows the difference between success and failure. Without his mother's sour but demanding presence and her daily disillusionment with the world, Paul might not have developed his love for painting or his desire to transcend his provincial roots. Paul's tortured relationship with his mother actually allows him to develop his own ideas about the meaning of individuation and fulfillment. By having to balance his need to please her with his need to have a healthy sexual and emotional relationship with a woman, Paul arrives at an understanding about himself and what he can and cannot control.

This self-understanding, a crucial phase of character development in a *Bildungsroman*, entails the knowledge that there is less in life that Paul can control than his mother has taught him. Mrs. Morel believes that through hard work, will power, and self-denial one could move up the social ladder and find contentment. What she does not grasp is the extent to which the self suffers from such desires. Paul discovers through his relationship with Clara that the temperament he has inherited from his mother is destroying him. He comes to realize that attempts to deny passion or to manage the contents of his consciousness are doomed to fail. Critic Helen Baron claims that Lawrence embeds his own understanding about human consciousness not only in Paul's character but also in the very style of the writing. In her essay, "Disseminated Consciousness in *Sons and Lovers*," Baron writes that Lawrence tests readers' assumptions that the will can control what the body feels and the mind thinks, claiming Lawrence represents consciousness as something that cannot be contained. "Lawrence's exploration of consciousness," Baron writes, "is so strongly embedded in the narrative tissue that the very words themselves are treated as cells with permeable boundaries."

In addition to Paul's "education" in the ways of love and human consciousness, he also developes his talent for painting, even selling a few paintings. Paul's passion to paint stands in for Lawrence's own passion to write, and, by describing Paul's growth as an artist, Lawrence participates in the literary tradition of the *Kunstlerroman*, which is a novel that describes the early years and growth of an artist. James Joyce's *Portrait of the Artist as a Young Man* is another such novel that is both *Bildungsroman* and *Kunstlerroman*.

The nature of these two subgenres almost demands that they follow the literary tradition of re-

> "Without his mother's sour but demanding presence and her daily disillusionment with the world, Paul might not have developed his love for painting or his desire to transcend his provincial roots."

alism, which Lawrence does as well. Realistic novels portray character, setting, and action in a recognizable and plausible way. They are located in a specific time or historical era and in a specific cultural milieu. Authors of realistic novels often rely on the use of dialect and concrete details of everyday life to compose their stories, and they make clear the motivations of characters' actions, emotions, and thoughts. Often, such novels depict the working class. Although written just a decade into the twentieth century when literary modernism was emerging, *Sons and Lovers* belongs to the tradition of nineteenth-century realism in its attention to detail and locale, and its attempt to accurately depict a way of life.

Because it has straddled the border between fiction and fact, *Sons and Lovers* has become a lightning rod for a number of Lawrence critics seeking insight into the writer's growth as an artist. As a *Bildungsroman*, the novel offers clues as to how Lawrence viewed his emotional and aesthetic maturation. Like Lawrence, Paul has to overcome the death of his mother and enter a world he has to remake in order to survive. Fighting the impulses to destroy himself, Paul sets his mouth tight and marches off to town to start anew.

The year after this novel was published, Lawrence married Frieda von Richthofen Weekley, the upper-class ex-wife of a university professor; Lawrence had been involved with her since 1912. Like Paul's mother and Lawrence's own mother, Lawrence chose a mate outside of his own class. The two would remain together until Lawrence's death.

Source: Chris Semansky, Critical Essay on *Sons and Lovers*, in *Novels for Students*, Gale, 2003.

> " ... the novel succeeds because it records not only minute shifts in the mood of its personae but also because, by locating the action on the level of human interactions, it traces the vicissitudes and motivates the development of Paul's spirit."

David Hayman

In the following essay, Hayman discusses what makes Sons and Lovers *a successful novel.*

D.H. Lawrence's first and most conventional novel, *Sons and Lovers*, is already the work of an accomplished writer. Grounded in the novelist's autobiography, it is in the fullest sense a sentimental education. Unlike his other works, this novel has a fully integrated plot, relatively little sermonizing, and characters with firm flesh over their analogized bones. If they stand for something, as Lawrence's characters always do, we are not told what. On the other hand, many of the qualities we have learned to associate with this writer are already present: the lavish descriptions of natural phenomena; the use of epic tags as a powerful rhythmic device to establish the resonances of the personae; the erotic thrust of the language; the tendency to refresh images by inverting their conventional charge; the quirky psychology; and the nervous episodic shifts. Add to this the writer's occasionally embarrassing use of naive hyperbole.

Most striking is Lawrence's use of the double or interlace plot so reminiscent of Tolstoy's *Anna Karenina*, though here the pattern is far less mechanical than it is elsewhere. The novel's basic plot line concerns the powerful oedipal attachment developed by Paul Morel's clever, sensitive, frustrated mother, a coal miner's wife tied to a coarse, strong-willed, and occasionally brutal man. A major strand relates to the story of that marriage and her attempts to achieve fulfillment through, first one, and then a second son. Significantly, the novel begins with a full treatment of the pre-Paul experience, her courtship and early disillusionment, the nurturing of her first two children in the dingy miner's house and the devolution of Morel into what is too readily perceived to be a drunken brute. Lawrence is too subtle to indulge in crude typing here. Both the disappointed wife and her husband emerge as complex figures at once internally consistent and capable of surprising shifts in mood and behavior. Her story dominates, however, delineating among other things her efforts to raise her children above the life imposed by the miners' existence.

The mother's life is poised against the well-articulated maturation or *Bildung*, of her physically fragile and sensitive second son, Paul. It is this boy who, after the death of his brother William, captures his mother's imagination and becomes the focus for her affections and ambitions. The novel recounts how the boy gradually extricates himself from his engagement with her. To accomplish this Lawrence resorts to a complex shifting perspective, brief scenes, and frequent bald statements of attitude. This enables him to give appropriate time and the right valence to each of the many protagonists and, more importantly, to phase out the mother as the center of Paul's creative and amorous life.

Anything but reticent, Lawrence combines the flat statement of emotion and attitude with a vividly impressionistic system of reactive prose vignettes. Thus we have the astonishing moments of affinity through nature which characterize some of the more vivid scenes: e.g., Paul's communion with his mother over some flowers and the painful botanical encounters with his first girl, Miriam. Though generally grounded in physical circumstances, the action of this "psychological" fiction is detailed with extraordinary clarity and mood-making precision. It is developed precisely through personal encounters that tend to be highly formulaic, conveyed through the reciprocal awareness of two dueling or communing characters: "[Miriam] suddenly became aware of his keen blue eyes upon her, taking her all in. Instantly her broken boots and her frayed old frock hurt her." If, on occasion, this laying bare of nerve endings grates, in the long run, the novel succeeds because it records not only minute shifts in the mood of its personae but also because, by locating the action on the level of human interactions, it traces the vicissitudes and motivates the development of Paul's spirit. Only Tolstoy has been willing and able to do this on so broad a scale, though Tolstoy is capable of more objectivity than Lawrence.

If at times we may feel that less would be more (as it is in Joyce's *Portrait of the Artist*), we may still find Lawrence's slow accretion of poignant detail and his rhythmic reiteration of personality and physical traits effective. Furthermore, the short scenes enable the writer not only to shift mood and pace, but also to move from emotional intensity to analysis. What makes this tale of a man and three women convincing and engrossing is undoubtedly Lawrence's ability to convince us that shadings of attitude, the minimal signals to which characters respond, are indeed important. Lawrence make us sensitive to the impact of casual remarks, glances, gestures, their capacity to signal turning points in a relationship.

Ultimately it is the anti-oedipal thread wound by Mrs. Morel's two younger rivals that saves Paul, that and his mother's pathetic death. In Miriam, he finds a generous but unsatisfactory surrogate, a young woman willing to sacrifice herself on the altar of his sensibility. This is the rival his mother forcefully rejects. By contrast, the older and more self-reliant Clara Dawes, for whom Paul must battle the brutal Dawes, defines Paul's sexual and emotional freedom without challenging his mother's role. Together, these women set him on the road to the "faintly humming glowing town" of his maturity.

Paul's relationships are all tense and experimental, and though he is clearly the focus of much of the action, neither he nor any of the women is unambiguously admirable or even completely adequate to the moment. It is to this excruciating balance of tensions set against the everyday world of a working-class family that *Sons and Lovers* owes its success, to this and to its meticulously honest and painfully engaging chronicle of Paul's identity crisis.

Source: David Hayman, "*Sons and Lovers*: Novel by D. H. Lawrence, 1913," in *Reference Guide to English Literature*, 2d ed., edited by D. L. Kirkpatrick, Vol. 3, St. James Press, 1991, pp. 1862–63.

Richard D. Beards

In the following essay, Beards examines Sons and Lovers *within the context of the* Bildungsroman, *finding this approach best suited to understand the novel's literary aspects and theme of alienation.*

There are two traditional approaches to *Sons and Lovers*, one of which treats the novel as a psychological study, emphasizing particularly Paul's Oedipal complex; the second of which focuses on the autobiographical, exploring the many passages where Lawrence seems to be retelling his own experience fictionally (the scenes of family life, the mining background, Paul and Miriam's relationship.) While the first approach risks reducing the novel to a case history, the second has the danger of undermining *Sons and Lovers'* effectiveness as fictional vision, turning it instead into a confessional autobiography, and vitiating Lawrence's achievement with plot, symbol, dramatic scene, and invented character. Moreover, these two approaches often join forces, so that autobiography is used to support the claims of psychological analysis, psychological generalizations cited to strengthen the autobiographical critique—especially where there are gaps in what we know of Lawrence's life. An example of the latter treatment is the attempt to clarify the at best hazy identity of the original for Clara Dawes (Louie Burrows? an unidentified Nottingham mistress? Frieda, later Lawrence's wife?) by referring to what psychology calls "the reaction formation," in particular Lawrence's attempt to escape his mother's domination by drawing close to an opposite. Both of these approaches, the autobiographical and the psychological, lead to interesting questions and cruxes in the novel, offering the student opportunity to consider two kinds of critical literature. On the one hand he gets to study a literary rendering—and a superb one—of the Oedipus complex; on the other, he can absorb the facts of Lawrence's life as they are recorded in his letters, in autobiographical sketches and in memoirs about his "Sons and Lovers" period.

It is my contention in this essay that seeing *Sons and Lovers* against the pattern of the traditional *Bildungsroman* illuminates many of the literary aspects of the novel about which neither the psychological nor the autobiographical approach cares and that this view does justice to one of Lawrence's best artistic achievements. In addition, because the *Bildungsroman* emerges in the nineteenth century and continues into our own, its focus on the conflict between an alienated individual and the cultural forces (family, neighborhood, class, religious and ethical milieu) against which this individual seeks to establish himself relates directly to the lives of our students. Moreover, the kind of conflict I have outlined comprises the real plot of *Sons and Lovers*, expressed jointly in Paul's struggle to free his soul from his mother and to become an artist where economic necessity all but rules out such a possibility. Paul's movement toward self-realization is expressed symbolically in his rejection of adjustment to the everyday (an adjustment made by his brother Arthur and sister,

Annie) in favor of the starry night in which he finds hope at the novel's end; in his attraction to cities (first Nottingham, then London, and ultimately perhaps even Paris) instead of "The Bottom" or, later, the houses on Scargill Street; and in his refusal to make life for himself in terms of provincial possibilities. But before an examination of the specific details of *Sons and Lovers*, it would be wise to review some of the general characteristics of the *Bildungsroman*.

The *Bildungsroman* ("novel of self-development" or "apprenticeship novel" are the best English equivalents) features a protagonist, an apprentice to life, whose goal is to master it so that he can achieve an ideal or ambition, fulfillment of which will heighten his sense of self. A look at related types of fiction may serve to clarify the *Bildungsroman* itself. Close to the confession and the autobiography, the *Bildungsroman* is often a first or second novel which fictionalizes its author's growing up. It is also similar to the picaresque novel, though in the *Bildungsroman* the journey through life has been internalized; adventures are important principally for their effect on the protagonist's psychological development and sense of self. The *Bildungsroman* protagonist is usually more passive, reflective, intellectual and artistic than his picaresque counterpart, probably because the author, himself introverted and creative, has fashioned his character out of himself. Still another type of related fiction is the initiation story or novel, though here the focus is a single moment of vision where the protagonist accepts either the code of his elders or the hard facts of life itself, or both (e.g. Faulkner's "The Bear," James' "The Lesson of the Master," Crane's "The Red Badge of Courage"). Compared to the initiation novel, the *Bildungsroman* compounds the choices which the central character is called upon to make, forcing him to define separately but in a continuous process his values in regard to four crucial concerns: vocation, mating, religion, and identity.

All of these decisions must be made without the aid of formal education, for whenever schooling is depicted in novels of self-development it is shown to be sterile and hopelessly anachronistic, if not downright farcical (e.g. *Pendennis, Great Expectations, The Ordeal of Richard Feverel*). One sometimes suspects that the impetus for a fictional sub-genre which shows protagonists designing and shaping their own lives is the need to respond to a culture where the educative institutions (schools, churches, family and class traditions) are in chaos. While the college teacher understandably will feel

a bit defensive pointing out the *Bildungsroman's* typical assessment of formal education—*Sons and Lovers* doesn't even bother to mention Paul's schooling—it should be noted this decision results from wider forces than mere pedagogical incompetence. It is no accident that the *Bildungsroman* emerges strongest in the nineteenth century, for it is during this epoch that the traditional class society and its heavily class-weighted institutions and values, in effect since the Renaissance, undergo pressure and serious erosion. It is in this century too that for the first time a young man who was not born a gentleman could choose to ignore the social status and even the particular work of his father without necessarily facing near-suicidal odds (see, for example, Robinson Crusoe's regrets and guilt over ignoring his father's advice). While large numbers of the more intelligent and energetic members of the lower and middle classes sought to rise above their inherited stations in life, the educational system continued to reflect an outmoded society where class determined the content and quality of one's education. Hardy's *Jude the Obscure* illustrates perfectly the disparity between its stonecutter hero's ambitions and the educational opportunities available to one of his class. In *Sons and Lovers* Paul Morel's education is casual rather than institutional; he is tutored in French and German by the local minister, Mr. Heaton; coached in composition by his brother William; encouraged in his art by his mother; and self-taught when it comes to literature, Miriam serving in both of the last two instances to inspire Paul to his best.

The same independence which characterizes Paul's education helps to prevent his capitulation to the economic and social outlook of his elders and peers, though his mother's distaste for her husband and the way of life he stands for certainly stiffens her son's resistance. Like many of his nineteenth-century predecessors, Paul shows considerable pluck, resilience and idealism in pushing his way toward an artist's future, though the usual stress laid by critics on his Oedipal conflict undermines our sense of Paul's consistency and force of character. Persistent belief in his future as an artist accounts for Paul's refusal to accept provincial goals and expectations. Surprisingly, economics plays a much larger role in *Sons and Lovers* than is often recognized, partly because it bears little if any relationship to Paul's psychological emergence, nor much more to Lawrence's own personal experience (though his letters reveal considerable concern over his finances, Lawrence never allowed making a living to interfere with his writing).

Simply expressed, the economic question in *Sons and Lovers* sets earning against creating. Four times in the novel the reader gets detailed accounts of the coal miner's finances: how pay is divided in the family, pp. 17–18, pp. 69–72 (collecting wages at the company office), p. 87 (compensation when Morel is injured) and pp. 198–201 (dividing the pay among four butties). Obviously, Lawrence is recalling these details from his own experience and such scenes help to establish the realistic depiction of turn-of-the-century life among Midlands miners for which *Sons and Lovers* is justly famous. But beyond this relationship to realism, these scenes fit the money or wage motif of the novel on the whole, a motif which sounds a relentless and unavoidable bass note against which Paul's lyric fantasies of artistic fruition must compete. Each time Paul receives a raise at Jordan's or moves up in the hierarchy there, we are told about it. Likewise, William's mercurial rise to something like gentleman's status in London law office circles stands both as exemplum and warning to Paul; William's record is more than merely that of an older sibling, for he was Mrs. Morel's first son—and "lover"— though he has escaped only to die prematurely. Later in the novel, when Paul seems to believe he can have art and money too, imagining himself a popular and therefore well-to-do artist, the alliance between art and income seems a romantically founded and improbable one. In a scene which follows a passage where Mrs. Morel angrily denounces her husband for leaving her too little money for the week ("a measly twenty-five shillings!"), Paul shows Miriam his designs for " decorating stuff, and for embroidery." "With a touch of bitterness" he explains, "I did it for my mother, but I think she'd rather have the money." Later, in the first paragraph of Chapter XII, "Passion," we are informed that Paul is beginning to earn a living through his textile and ceramic designs, while "at the same time, he laboured slowly at his pictures." Furthermore, Paul's integrity as an artist (he has to accept less money for a commissioned painting because he will not paint what is demanded of him) and the peculiar subject of his painting, luminous figures "fitted into a landscape," don't promise the kind of success Paul imagines for himself. Regardless, however, of his probable future, Paul here faces a problem which confronts all protagonists in self-development novels—how to make a living. If we fail to consider the vocational and economic issue in Paul Morel's development, we thin out and over-simplify his struggle toward self-realization. Knowledge of the typical *Bildungsroman* protagonist alerts us to this aspect of Lawrence's novel.

A second characteristic of all *Bildungsromane* is that their protagonists must always decide on a suitable mate or at least define the ideal who waits in the near-distant future; the central figures in self-development novels are thus, among other things, apprentice lovers. This aspect of *Sons and Lovers* has received close attention from critics of all persuasions; if the plot of mother-son love itself is not enough, Lawrence's treatment of Gertrude, Miriam, and Clara, and their respective relationships to Paul have aroused heated debate, charge and counter-charge. The way in which the novel appears to blame Gertrude for dominating and almost destroying Paul and to indict Miriam for her near-frigidity and squeamishness has given rise to a great deal of angry discussion almost from the day the novel appeared. In our own time by far the most provocative attack on this aspect of *Sons and Lovers* has been Kate Millett's in *Sexual Politics*. Writing from a Marxist-feminist perspective, Millett accuses Paul (and by implication, Lawrence) of using the three women in his life, then discarding them when they no longer serve his self-centered interests. Millett describes Paul as the "perfection of self-sustaining ego" and states, "the women in the book exist in Paul's orbit and cater to his needs: Clara to awaken him sexually, Miriam to worship his talent in the role of disciple and Mrs. Morel to provide always that enormous and expansive support...." Despite the bluntness and even crudeness of her critique, and the fact that in regard to Gertrude, Millett seems to contradict herself (elsewhere in her discussion she calls the novel "a great tribute to his mother and a moving record of the strongest and most formative love of the author's life"—one must admit some truth to the charge.

Students today are especially sensitive to the treatment of female characters in fiction, particularly where, as in *Sons and Lovers*, there is sufficient development to assess a life pattern or unachieved potential in these lives. Undeniably, Gertrude's life is laid before us; we know enough of her history to see the sources of her aspirations, first for herself, then for herself and her husband, finally for her successive sons. Her sense of entrapment in a dead-end marriage to Morel, her envy of Mrs. Leiver's life, her vicarious participation in life through her children—these and other details allow us to know her predicament. And when, in her final illness, Paul administers a fatal dose of morphine, her victimization—by unavoidable pregnancies which

What Do I Read Next?

- Lawrence's novel *The Rainbow* (1915) follows three generations of a Nottingham family, detailing their love affairs, marriages, and family relationships. This is the first of Lawrence's novels to describe sexual situations in an open manner, and its publication stirred controversy.

- Lawrence was also a poet. His first collection, *Love Poems and Others* (1913), contains some of his best-known poems.

- Lawrence's idiosyncratic study of American literature, *Studies in Classic American Literature* (1923), has itself become a classic.

- Sophocles's *Oedipus Rex* tells the story of the banished king of Greek mythology who killed his father and married his mother. A number of critics refer to the Oedipus myth when discussing *Sons and Lovers*.

- Daniel Weiss's *Oedipus at Nottingham* (1962) explores the oedipal themes in Lawrence's fiction.

bind her tighter to her despised mate and which sap her strength and by a culture which discourages women from working in the world—is made final by her son. Likewise, Clara and Miriam, opposite as they are in character, seem purposeless and incomplete unless they can join in a vitalizing relationship with a male. Clara—listless, cynical and cold (several scenes show her kneeling before a fire, presumably trying to imbibe its warmth)—drifts until she consummates her relationship to Paul, who, when he realizes their relationship is merely physical, brings Clara and her estranged husband Baxter back together again. Miriam's faith that Paul will ultimately return to her, that his spiritual and idealistic side will triumph over his need for sex, seems pathetic finally, in view of her sacrificial sexual surrender to him, her compulsive chapel going when Paul is involved with Clara, and his final dismissal of her: "'Will you have me, to marry me?' he said very low . . . 'Do you want it?'"

she asked very gravely. 'Not much,' he replied, with pain."

The tradition of the *Bildungsroman* itself provides an explanation for this apparent male bias, for fiction with a developmental focus always slights characters not of the protagonist's sex, and for that matter, *all* the other characters. One of the distinguishing traits of the apprenticeship novel is the strong central figure for whose experience and development the lesser figures exist, and from whose process of self-realization the novel receives one of its principal unifying elements. Futhermore, the novel of self-development generally is written from a narrowly omniscient point of view, the author standing beside his character, as it were, and most often interpreting experience through his character's mind, senses and emotions. Thus the *Bildungsroman*'s customary point of view adds to a sense of the protagonists egoism and lends emphasis to his seeming exploitation of the novel's other figures.

Because mating plays such a significant part in maturation—and thus in apprenticeship fiction—protagonists, whether male or female, will inevitably use and exploit at least several members of the opposite sex. Thackerary's Pendennis, for example, eponymous hero of the novel sometimes called the first *Bildungsroman* in English (1849–1850), is involved several times (with Fotheringay, an Irish actress; with Fanny Bolton, a "poor but honest" girl from the lower classes; and with Blanche Amory, a continental adventuress in the manner of George Sand and her heroines) before succumbing in marriage to his mother's ward, companion and protege, Laura, whom he has all but ignored through most of the novel. Similarly, in Lawrence's *The Rainbow*, Ursula Brangwen, a typical *Bildungsroman* heroine, rejects two men who want to marry her, Anthony Schofield and Anton Skrebensky, because, as she thinks to herself after rejecting Anthony, "ultimately and finally, she must go on and on, seeking the goal that she knew she did draw nearer to." Thus Millett's account of Paul's position at the conclusion of *Sons and Lovers* ("Having rid himself of the two young women, . . . Paul is free to make moan over his mother's corpse, give Miriam a final brushoff, and turn his face to the city) is hardly very convincing when one has in mind fictional tradition, in particular, the *Bildungsroman*'s tendency to adopt the protagonist's point of view, to maximize for the reader the central figure's sense of self-concern, to give other characters instrumental rather than independent functions.

Ursula Brangwen's goal in *The Rainbow*, "to be oneself ... a oneness with the infinite," realized in botany lab as she peers down a microscope after her professor had denied any mystical dimension in life, brings us to both of the remaining concerns of the *Bildungsroman* protagonist: his quest for identity and for the right relationship to the transcendent and non-human in the universe. Admittedly, some apprenticeship novels (*Pendennis*, *Pere Goriot*), in their intensive treatment of social reality, largely ignore supernatural and intangible realities. Yet from Carlyle's *Sartor Resartus* (1833–1834) on, the religious crisis and the more general search for the transcendent meanings of life have typified novels of self- development. For Paul Morel as for Ursula, religious sense and identity are deeply intertwined; this interrelationship has become, of course, a hallmark of Lawrence's mature fictions, where a knowledge of oneness is brought about by an interfusion of the individual and the natural world via sex or a "lapsing out" of consciousness. It is quite easy to misread symbolic scenes in *Sons and Lovers*—and I think Millett and others are guilty of this—through failing to take into account Lawrence's idea of one's relationship to the infinite. It is possible for instance to interpret Paul's vision of Clara bathing—he sees her as "not much more than a clot of foam being blown and rolled over the sand ... just a concentrated speck blown along, a tiny white foam-bubble, almost nothing among the morning"—as his belittling of her, preparatory to his terminating their relationship. In fact, Millett evaluates the scene as follows: "Paul converts himself into a species of god in the universe before whom Clara dwindles to the proportions of microscopic life." Other critics have judged Paul lost and despondent in the final paragraphs of the novel because he feels like "so tiny a spark" being pressed into extinction. Both assessments are wrong, for they ignore the implicit paradox in Lawrence's definition of self, where real being requires this feeling of tininess, of being infinitessimal. Millett, in her eagerness to indict Paul's self-centeredness, ignores this essential of the world-view Lawrence establishes in *Sons and Lovers*. An opposite view to Millett's, one which venerates Lawrence's mystical vision where Millett only scorns it, has been recently expressed by Joyce Carol Oates. Acknowledging the irritating challenge of Lawrence's love ethic, Oates declares Lawrence to be, not as Millett would have it, a sexual reactionary, but "too

radical for us even today." Lawrence, Oates continues, "goes back beyond even the tradition women are rebelling against, today, to a mystical union based upon the primitive instincts of our species, but carrying us forward into pure spirit." He may well be abrasive, "yet one comes to believe that Lawrence is absolutely right."

Still another recent critic, Calvin Bedient, has effectively argued that for Lawrence the fusion of soul which the author himself felt with his mother transcended the Oedipal, giving Lawrence—and therefore his fictional projection Paul—the sense of a mystical oneness next to which other relationships to women seem ordinary, flat, and merely personal. Only at the peak of physical or sexual exhilaration does Paul experience the infinite; such moments occur when he is swinging in the Leiver's barn, riding his bicycle recklessly home after a strained evening at the farm, making love with Clara on a steep clay river bank or with Miriam in a pine grove. As Paul expresses it after the latter experience, "the highest of all was to melt out into the darkness and sway there, identified with the great Being." Bedient is convincing when he suggests that although Lawrence wasn't aware of it in *Sons and Lovers*, the work conveys rather fully its author's vision of the highest state of being and how that state can be obtained.

In counterbalance to those scenes where Paul lapses out of consciousness, often outdoors and frequently at night, *Sons and Lovers* furnishes occasional comments on its protagonist's changing relationship to traditional religious life and practice; Paul's fall from orthodoxy coincides with the growth of his mystic awareness and his ability to summon it, while, on the literal level, it evidences his growth away from the Morel family's habitual and easy chapel going. At twenty-one, we are told, "he was beginning to question the orthodox creed;" the following spring "he was setting now full sail towards Agnosticism, but such a religious Agnosticism that Miriam did not suffer badly." The term "religious Agnosticism" indicates, I think, the growth in Paul of the mystical sense I have been describing, "agnostic" both because Lawrence speaks of God only metaphorically and because Paul's "religion" has nothing to do with any institutional faith.

Later in the novel Paul clarifies the nature of his religious belief in an argument with Miriam: "It's not religious to be religious ... I reckon a crow is religious when it sails across the sky. But it only does it because it feels itself carried to where it's going, not because it thinks it's being eternal.' The crow's lack of consciousness, its utter passivity—"it feels itself carried to where it's going"—corresponds to Paul's (and Lawrence's) sense of the religious as opposed to Miriam's.

What *Sons and Lovers* depicts in the way of identity for the protagonist, then, is two-fold; there is the Paul who is second son to the Morel family, a Bestwood provincial aiming for the artist's life, the one whose personal history and day-by-day development the novel charts, and there is the Paul who is increasingly opened up to manifestations of a living natural universe, a speck of which he is and in whose dark precincts his mother exists "intermingled." It is this mystical level of identity that Lawrence illuminates so effectively, for the first time in *Sons and Lovers;* it is indeed hard to think of another novelist who conveys this dimension so convincingly. Thus Lawrence is able to contribute to the *Bildungsroman* and to English fiction generally a deeper interpenetration of the human and the vital natural world than had been previously envisioned—or than has been created fictionally since.

Paul's two-level identity is further clarified by his symbolic association with several biblical and mythological figures. When he is an infant, his mother imagines him a Joseph, though later in the same scene she suddenly declares "I will call him Paul." When he is courting Miriam, Paul himself assumes a special relationship to the constellation Orion: "Orion was for them [Paul and Miriam] chief in significance among the constellations." These connections to astrological and biblical mythology in themselves suggest both the everyday and the vitalistic identities of Paul, the individual myths containing, moreover, details pertinent to all the typical self-developing protagonists in general and to Paul Morel in particular. Paul's similarity to his apostle namesake comes out most clearly in his relationship to Miriam; to her he is a stern moralist and rule-giver, whose irritability presages radical growth, though the principles of Paul's ultimate ethic come close to inverting his biblical predecessor's.

Pauls' connections to Joseph are perhaps more obvious; like Joseph, he is a younger and favored son who leaves his father and homeland, and, after a period of bondage, is proclaimed a genius among a foreign people. (The biblical story of Joseph, is, in fact, a prototype of the novel of self-development.) When Walter Morel is injured in the pits, Paul is forced to give up his painting

and his fantasies of where his art might take him—"His ambition . . . when his father died [was to] have a cottage with his mother, paint and go out as he liked . . . And he thought that *perhaps* he might also make a painter, the real thing." The scene in which the news of his father's injury reaches home captures beautifully Paul's intense devotion to his art in the midst of family catastrophe; while Mrs. Morel bustles about preparing to see to her despised yet needing mate, Paul continues with his painting. "Bondage" for Paul is explicitly related to the laboring world; forced by his father's mishap to seek a job, he reflects: "Already he was a prisoner of industrialism . . . He was being taken into bondage. His freedom in the beloved home valley was going now." Later, on his way to be interviewed at Jordan's surgical appliance factory, Paul passes through the company yard, which Lawrence describes as being "like a pit," recalling the pit in which Joseph is abandoned by his brothers. Whereas Joseph ultimately triumphs as the Pharaoh's dream interpreter, Paul's victory is to be an artistic one.

Orion, third of the mythic figures with whom Paul is associated, symbolizes perfectly the progressive, self-achieving element in the *Bildungsroman* hero. Sword raised, feet in bold stride, Orion represents the battle-ready hunter in the process of his quest. It is important to recognize the disparity between the reserved, even diffident Paul and his mythological inspiration in the northern night sky; Orion, like Paul's mother, is, as the novel concludes, a source of inspiration, permanently fixed and shining, not a symbol of the already-achieved. Whatever wounds the death of his mother aggravates in Paul, he imagines her star-like and ever-present, like Orion, the hunter, an encouragement to go on.

The concluding pages of *Sons and Lovers* present several difficult but ultimately answerable question as to Paul's probable future which the apprenticeship novel can help clarify. In an interesting article entitled "Autobiograph in the English *Bildungsroman*," Jerome Buckley argues that because the novel of self-development is highly subjective, commonly fictionalizing the author's own experience, "the novel has frequently an inconclusive or contrived ending," its creator being too close to the experience being retold "to achieve an adequate perspective on (it)." "*Sons and Lovers*," he adds, "scarcely persuades us that Paul Morel at last finds the release from his fixation that Lawrence apparently won, perhaps in the very act of writing the novel." Commenting on the final paragraph of *Sons and Lovers*, Buckley asserts that "nothing has prepared us for so positive a resolution. If Paul is at last free and whole, his victory is not inherent in his story; it is imposed upon it from without." Even with the added weight of Lawrence's own judgment on the ending ("Paul is left in the end naked of everything, with the drift toward death") I would maintain that Paul's triumph *is* "inherent in his story" and that a knowledge of the *Bildungsroman*, precisely in those characteristics I have been discussing, helps us to see the rightness of the final affirmation.

Paul's trajectory all through *Sons and Lovers*, like that of many other *Bildungsroman* protagonist (Ursula Brangwen, Wilhelm Meister, and Augie March among them) has been away from pressure to conform—whether social, familial or economic—and toward the accomplishment of his own ideal. Paul's brother, first William, then Arthur, are foils to his aspiration; William prostitutes his attractive personality for social and business success; Arthur, initially rebellious and impulsive, capitulates to provincial expectations: "He buckled to work, undertook his responsibilities, acknowledged that he belonged to his wife and child." William's life, presented in far more detail than Arthur's, forms a compressed *Bildungsroman* in itself, wherein his mercurial rise to social and financial success, his quick movement from the provinces to London, and his absurd romance with Gypsy Western come close to forming a grim parody of apprenticeship fiction. William's rapid and thoughtless climb contrasts dramatically with Paul's slow, painful, self-conscious struggle toward freedom and self-realization. The dramatic contrast between the two brothers serves to support the promising view of Paul's future suggested by the final paragraph of *Sons and Lovers;* Paul's values are nothing like his older brother's, and Paul consciously rejects a business career and the social approval and circumstances William is so desperate to gain. Lawrence reflects this difference symbolically when Paul goes to Nottingham to receive first prize for his painting. Dressed in William's altered evening suit, Paul "did not look particularly a gentleman." Moreover, Paul argues vigorously against his mother's advice that he ought "in the end to marry a lady." Having refused to follow William's ambitions, condemned by Lawrence's tone and treatment as well as by the obvious pattern of self-destruction and folly implicit in the older brother's choices, Paul is freed from William's fate.

> " Paul's trajectory all through *Sons and Lovers*, like that of many other *Bildungsroman* protagonist . . . has been away from pressure to conform—whether social, familial or economic—and toward the accomplishment of his own ideal."

Further proof that Paul's victory is not as Buckley maintains, "imposed . . . from without," is the evolution in Paul's mystical sense of self, which I've touched on earlier. From those early occasions when we see Paul in a state of natural exhilaration to later scenes when he expresses his positive sense of lapsing out of consciousness after making love to Miriam ("the highest of all was to melt into the darkness and stay there, identified with the great being,") the alert reader is readied for the final vision when Paul sees his mother as "intermingled" with the night: "she had been one place, and was in another; that was all." Even if we discard this momentary hope as rationalization, there is additional evidence—besides the final paragraphs "but no, he would not give in"—to substantiate Paul's vision and final confidence. It is misreading Lawrence to see mere tininess as indicative of weakness and failure; Paul and his mother may, like the stars, be mere grains or sparks, yet they do not disappear. By relating his mother to the stars, Paul is admitting their special separation but not their mystical one; like Orion to Paul and Miriam in an earlier scene, Mrs. Morel is a fixed source of inspiration, the sign to her son of his own divine connection. And certainly, though much has been made of Mrs. Morel's destructive hold on her son, it is important to recognize her role in encouraging and fostering her son's talents as a painter. Few artists in fiction (and probably in life) have had more effective and more positive nurturing than Paul gets from Mrs. Morel (compare, for example, Stephen Daedelus' situation), and therefore it seems reasonable to see this maternal encouragement as ultimately sustaining rather than ruinous.

Paul's movement in the final sentences of the novel toward the "city's gold phosphorescence ... the faintly humming, glowing town" fits perfectly the province-to-city pattern of most *Bildungsromane*. All through the nineteenth century and into our own time, the city has been the place where the ambitious have sought their challenge, have striven to define themselves. Jude, Pip, Augie March, Eugene Gant, Julien Sorel, Martha Quest. Ernest Pontifex—all seek out the city in search of their imagined and idealized selves. The glow that Lawrence here ascribes to Nottingham symbolizes its hopefulness, for throughout the novel gold and flames have stood for the vital impulse of life. In the opening pages of *Sons and Lovers*, to cite an early example, we learn of Paul's mother's attraction to Arthur Morel, epitomized by the "dusky, golden softness of this man's sensuous flame of life, that flowed off his flesh like the flame of a candle...."

It is undeniably true that Paul's life is still in process when *Sons and Lovers* concludes, yet all the signs of ultimate success and of a promising independence are there; Lawrence's next novel, also a novel of self-development, ends with its heroine Ursula, having lived through a traumatic love affair, a pregnancy and a miscarriage, understanding the rainbow to promise, like the sign of the covenant, new life in a recreated world. Like her, Paul Morel, Whose trauma is his mother's death, perceives a vision of unity between the night and the stars, his mother's spirit and his own, which sends him back into the fight—fist clenched—after his temporary depression and withdrawal. Even Kate Millett, openly hostile to Lawrence's art, recognizes Paul's movement toward the world of men, evidenced by her description of him as wishing "to be rid of the whole pack of his female supporters so that he may venture forth and inherit the masculine world that awaits him"; Paul is, she asserts, "in brilliant shape when the novel ends."

More importantly, when we consider, as I have tried to do here, the four distinct trials which the *Bildungsroman* protagonist must traditionally master—vocation, mating, religion and identity—Paul's future, though Lawrence's tone is typically equivocal, seems assured. He knows what he wants to do in life; has realized the dimensions of sexual relationship, even if he hasn't found his ideal mate; has forged a new religious sense; and knows, largely because he's defined these other questions, who he is, and, equally important, what "selves" he has left behind.

Source: Richard D. Beards, "*Sons and Lovers* as Bildungsroman," in *College Literature*, Vol. 1, No. 3, Fall 1974, pp. 204–17.

Sources

Baron, Helen, "Disseminated Consciousness in *Sons and Lovers*," in *Essays in Criticism*, Vol. 48, No. 4, October 1998, pp. 357–78.

Finney, Brian, *D. H. Lawrence: "Sons and Lovers,"* Penguin, 1990, p. 14.

Gregory, Alyse, "Artist Turned Prophet," in the *Dial*, Vol. LXXVI, No. 1, January 1924, pp. 66–72.

Ingersoll, Earl G., "Gender and Language in *Sons and Lovers*," in the *Midwest Quarterly*, Vol. 37, No. 4, Summer 1996, pp. 434–48.

Kuttner, Alfred Booth, "*Sons and Lovers*: A Freudian Appreciation," in the *Psychoanalytic Review*, Vol. III, No. 3, July 1916, pp. 295–317.

Lawrence, D. H., *Sons and Lovers*, New American Library, 1960, pp. 14, 61, 92.

"Mother Love," in the *New York Times Book Review*, September 21, 1913, p. 479.

Review of *Sons and Lovers*," in the *Saturday Review*, Vol. 115, No. 3008, June 21, 1913, pp. 780–81.

Widmer, Kingsley, "D. H. Lawrence," in *Dictionary of Literary Biography*, Vol. 36, *British Novelists, 1890–1929: Modernists*, edited by Thomas F. Staley, Gale Research, 1985, pp. 115–49.

Further Reading

Cowan, James C., *D. H. Lawrence's American Journey: A Study in Literature and Myth*, Press of Case Western Reserve University, 1970.

Using Lawrence's experience in America, Cowan produces a psychological profile of the writer. Cowan links Lawrence's deteriorating health with his increasingly dark literary vision.

Goodheart, Eugene, *The Utopian Vision of D. H. Lawrence*, Chicago University Press, 1963.

Goodheart describes Lawrence's social and spiritual development in the context of the times in which he lived. Goodheart's study is focused, engaging, and useful for students of Lawrence's writing and life.

Paglia, Camille, *Sexual Personae*, Yale University Press, 1990.

In this controversial study of sex and celebrity, Paglia explores the sexual impulses of Lawrence's characters, showing how they illuminate the myths surrounding Dionysus, the Greek god of wine and orgies.

Salgado, Gamini, ed., *D. H. Lawrence: "Sons and Lovers": A Casebook*, Macmillan Press, 1969.
    This casebook on Lawrence's novel contains early reviews, critical essays, background material, and a select bibliography of works on Lawrence.

Squires, Michael, and Lynn K. Talbot, *Living at the Edge: A Biography of D. H. Lawrence and Frieda von Richthofen*, University of Wisconsin Press, 2002.

This fascinating biography of Lawrence and his wife draws compelling parallels between the couple's romantic life and Lawrence's novels.

Wood, Jessie Chambers, *D. H. Lawrence: A Personal Record*, Jonathan Cape, 1935.
    Jessie Chambers is the person on whom the character Miriam Leivers is based. In this book, she presents her view of her relationship with Lawrence.

Tom Jones

Henry Fielding
1749

Tom Jones, Henry Fielding's third novel, was first published in England in 1749 and was an immediate best-seller. It is a comedy in both senses of the formal definition: it is amusing and all ends well.

Originally entitled *The History of Tom Jones, A Foundling*, the book tells the story of the title character from infancy through his marriage to the beautiful and virtuous Sophia Western, the pursuit of whom takes up much of the tale. Along the way, Fielding relentlessly satirizes the hypocrisy and vanity of most of his supporting cast. He shows that the lusty rascal Tom is, in fact, an infinitely better human being than the vicious pretenders who surround him and scheme against him while camouflaged in a thin veneer of artificial virtue. The hero overcomes not only all external plots and obstacles but, most importantly, his own weaknesses of character, to win both love and fortune.

Author Biography

Henry Fielding was born April 22, 1707, at his grandparents' estate in Somerset, England. He was the first of seven children born to Edmund Fielding, a career military officer, and Sarah Gould Fielding, daughter of a wealthy judge.

Fielding spent his childhood on his parents' large farm in Dorset and was tutored at home. His mother died when he was ten, and his father sent the children to live with their maternal grand-

mother, Lady Gould. Edmund Fielding soon married a widow and set about squandering his children's inheritance. Lady Gould filed suit for legal custody of the children and won. In the course of these events, Henry became willful and defiant. His father sent him to Eton in 1719, where he studied Greek, Latin, and the classics. He remained there until 1724 and later briefly attended the University of Leyden in Holland.

Fielding began his writing career as a playwright; his first play, *Love in Several Masques*, was performed in London in 1728. He soon became a successful playwright and also published poems and essays.

In 1734, Fielding married Charlotte Cradock, a beautiful woman who would later be the inspiration for Sophia Western in *Tom Jones*. They had five children, four of whom would die quite young, before Charlotte died in 1744.

Fielding's play *The Historical Register*, performed in 1737, satirized Prime Minister Sir Robert Walpole so acutely that the government shut down the theater where Fielding was working. It became impossible for him to earn a living writing plays, so he went to law school and was admitted to the bar in 1740. In addition to practicing law, Fielding cofounded a political and cultural journal called *Champion*.

The year 1740 also saw the publication of *Pamela*, a novel by Samuel Richardson that soon became the first bestseller of all time. Fielding felt so strongly that the novel was overrated that he wrote a parody of it, *Shamela*. This launched his fiction career. Another, more ambitious parody of the same novel, *Joseph Andrews*, appeared in 1742.

In 1747, Fielding married Mary Daniel, who had been his first wife's maid and who was pregnant with Fielding's child. They would have five children together.

Fielding continued a successful law career as he also continued to write popular novels. He was appointed magistrate (a government position similar to that of judge) for Middlesex in 1749, the year *Tom Jones* was published and became a bestseller. His last novel, *Amelia*, was published in 1751, but he continued to write for a daily newspaper and nonfiction treatises such as *Proposal for Making an Effectual Provision for the Poor* (1753).

In early 1754, Fielding became very ill, resigned as magistrate, and sailed for Portugal, where he hoped to recover. Although he did seem to be regaining his health and began planning to write a

Henry Fielding

history of Portugal, he died in Lisbon on October 8, 1754.

Plot Summary

Book I

The narrator introduces Squire Allworthy, telling readers that he "once lived (and perhaps lives still)" in Somerset and that he was not only one of the richest men in England but also kind and intelligent. His wife had died, and their three children had all died as infants, so the squire lived with his sister, Bridget, who had never married.

The narrator further relates that on one occasion the squire was away from his estate on business for three months and, on the day he returned, found a baby in his bed. Squire Allworthy had a servant, Deborah Wilkins, take care of the baby. The next morning, he told his household that he would rear the foundling as his son. He put Bridget in charge of the baby boy and sent Mrs. Wilkins out to find out the identity of his mother.

A servant named Jenny Jones, who had recently worked both for the local schoolmaster and as a nurse to Bridget, is quickly accused and admits to being the child's mother. Squire Allworthy, who is the local magistrate, lives up to his reputation for kindness. Instead of sending her to jail, as he could do, he arranges for her to move away to a place where no one will know of her past. He even accepts her refusal to name the baby's father. She does tell him that someday he will know the father's identity. Allworthy names the baby Tom Jones.

The local physician, Dr. Blifil, introduces Bridget to his brother, Captain Blifil. Since Bridget is desperate to marry and the captain is eager to be rich, the two marry within a month. The doctor would have married her himself—for both love and money—but is already married. The Blifil brothers begin to antagonize each other, and the doctor goes off to London and dies "of a broken heart."

Book II

Bridget gives birth to a son eight months after her marriage. This boy, Master Blifil, is Allworthy's heir. Master Blifil and Tom Jones are to grow up together, in spite of Captain Blifil's objections to his son growing up with a bastard.

Mrs. Wilkins becomes convinced, through local gossip, that the schoolmaster, Mr. Partridge, is Tom's father. When Partridge is tried on the charge, his own wife testifies against him, as she is ever suspicious of him. Found guilty, Partridge loses his job. His wife soon dies of smallpox, and Partridge leaves the area.

Bridget and Captain Blifil begin to argue about everything. As Blifil dislikes Tom, Bridget shows him more and more affection just to irritate her husband. Then Blifil dies suddenly of apoplexy. Allworthy builds a monument to his virtues, which were well hidden in life.

Book III

Years have passed; Tom is in his early teens. Tom is something of a rogue and has lost the affection of all in the household. While Tom has been caught stealing three times, two of these crimes involved taking food for the family of the estate's gamekeeper, who is Tom's one ally. When the gamekeeper, Black George, joins Tom in some mischief at Tom's insistence, Master Blifil eventually reports this (although Tom has steadfastly refused to do so), and Black George is fired.

The boys' tutors, Thwackum and Square, are always ready to punish Tom but are fond of Master Blifil, who curries their favor shamelessly. In addition, both tutors have designs on marrying Bridget (for her money) and assume that favoring her son will help their cause. Not only does she have no intention of marrying either of them, Bridget actually hates her son (because she hated his father) and loves Tom.

Tom nearly prevails upon Allworthy to rehire Black George, but Master Blifil ruins things by revealing that George killed a rabbit on the estate of a neighbor, Squire Western. Tom has warm friendships with the squire and his daughter Sophia, and he is determined to try to get George a job on their estate in spite of his poaching.

Book IV

At Tom's request, Sophia persuades her doting father to hire George.

Tom falls in love with George's daughter, Molly, and Molly is soon pregnant. When this is discovered, Allworthy, the magistrate, sentences her to prison. Before she is imprisoned, Tom admits that he is the baby's father and begs Allworthy to commute her sentence, which he does.

Sophia, though distressed by all this, still loves Tom. It happens one day that Tom is on the scene when Sophia's horse bucks, and he saves her, breaking his arm in the process. He convalesces at the Western estate, where he is something of a hero.

Book V

During his recovery, Tom and Sophia's love is kindled. Tom, feeling sorry for Molly, decides to offer her money in place of his love, but when he goes to her house, he discovers the tutor Square in her bedroom with her. He later discovers, also, that Molly's baby is most likely not his. He is happy to be free to pursue Sophia.

Allworthy becomes very ill and is expected to die. He tells the assembled household that Master Blifil will inherit most of his estate, but he leaves Tom an annuity. Tom is more than satisfied; all the others complain about what they have been given.

A messenger arrives with the news that Bridget has died in transit from Salisbury. In spite of this sad news, Allworthy makes a sudden recovery. Tom is so happy that he goes out and gets drunk. Blifil is offended at this behavior in the face of his mother's death, and the two fight. Afterward, Tom meets Molly on the road. The two make love in the bushes and are discovered by not only Blifil and Thwackum but also Squire Western and Sophia.

Book VI

Squire Western's sister realizes that Sophia is in love and, genuinely mistaken, tells her brother that Blifil is the object of Sophia's affections. He is happy, and the two squires, consulting Blifil but not Sophia, agree that their offspring will marry. Blifil agrees only because of Sophia's wealth and because he knows that the marriage will make Tom miserable.

When Sophia protests her match with Blifil, her father asks Tom to persuade her to marry Blifil. Tom agrees, but of course does just the opposite. When Squire Western learns that Sophia loves Tom, he explodes; Tom, a bastard, is no match for his beloved daughter. Western tells Allworthy to keep Tom away from Sophia, and Blifil takes the opportunity to tell Allworthy about Tom's recent meeting with Molly.

Allworthy gives Tom five hundred pounds and tells him to leave the house and never return. Tom loses the money on the road and then meets Black George, who helps him search for it. George, however, has found and pocketed the money.

Tom writes Sophia a love letter, which is delivered by her servant, and Sophia responds by sending Tom all the money she has.

Book VII

Tom decides to go to sea but longs for Sophia.

The squires decide that their children will wed immediately. When Sophia is told, she and her maid, Honour, conspire to run away to the home of an understanding relative in London.

Tom, meanwhile, meets up with some soldiers fighting in a rebellion against the king and joins them. At dinner, he toasts Sophia, but one of his comrades, Northerton, says that he knows her and that she is a tramp. Tom and the soldier fight, and Tom receives a gash to his head. Northerton is imprisoned but escapes.

Book VIII

The barber who is called to dress Tom's wound is none other than Partridge, the schoolmaster convicted of fathering Tom. Partridge, who has changed his name to Little Benjamin, tells Tom that he is not his father. The two decide to travel together.

At a home where they plan to spend the night, robbers attack the man of the house, and Tom fights them off. This man, known as The Man of the Hill, tells Tom his life story.

Book IX

Out for a walk, Tom and The Man of the Hill hear a woman screaming. Tom rescues her from

Media Adaptations

- Three film versions of *Tom Jones* have been made in Britain. A silent film made in 1917 was directed by Edwin J. Collins and starred Langhorn Burton as Tom. A 1963 version was directed by Tony Richardson and starred Albert Finney as Tom and Susannah York as Sophia; it is available on videotape. A 1976 film entitled *The Bawdy Adventures of Tom Jones* was directed by Cliff Owen and starred Nicky Henson as Tom and Madeline Smith as Sophia; it, too, is available on video.

- A television miniseries entitled *The History of Tom Jones, a Foundling*, also made in Britain, appeared in 1997. It was directed by Metin Hüseyin and starred Max Beesley as Tom and Samantha Morton as Sophia. This version is also available on video.

- Penguin Books released an unabridged audio version of the novel in 1997, with Robert Lindsay as reader. Abridged versions are available from Highbridge Classics (1998, John L. Sessions, reader) and Media Books (1999, Edward Fox, reader).

the violent advances of a man who turns out to be Northerton. He tries to capture Northerton, who escapes again.

Tom takes the woman, Lady Waters, to an inn to recover. There, she seduces him.

Book X

While Tom is with Lady Waters, Sophia and Honour arrive at the inn. Sophia finds out that Tom is, once again, with another woman and swears that she is finished with him. She has the inn's maid leave her muff on Tom's (unoccupied) bed and leaves.

Tom finds the muff and plans to pursue Sophia. Squire Western arrives at the inn, and he, as well as Tom and Partridge, sets off to find Sophia.

Book XI

On the road, Sophia meets her cousin, Harriet Fitzpatrick, and her maid. The two women once lived together with their aunt and are happy to see each other. They go to an inn and begin to tell each other why they are traveling. A gentleman arrives at the inn and offers Sophia and Harriet his coach to complete their trip to London. This gentleman is the same man who, as Harriet had just been telling Sophia, recently helped her escape from her tyrannical husband.

In London, Sophia stays with a distant relative, Lady Bellaston. Harriet stays in rented quarters paid for by her gentleman benefactor.

Book XII

Squire Western is diverted from his pursuit of his daughter by the sound of a pack of hunting dogs. He joins the hunt and gives up the idea of finding Sophia.

Tom and Partridge meet a beggar who offers to sell them a book he has found. It turns out to be Sophia's. The book contains her signature, and later a one hundred-pound note falls out of it. In spite of this evidence that he is on Sophia's trail, Tom soon gives up on Sophia and decides to join the army. But he then meets a boy who has seen Sophia and sets out after her again. He and Partridge pursue her from town to town, never quite catching up.

Book XIII

Tom has had reports of Sophia's traveling companions and her destination. In London, he finds Harriet Fitzpatrick, who refuses to tell him where Sophia is. Lady Bellaston has heard so much about Tom that she is eager to meet him, and Harriet introduces her to Tom the next time he calls on her.

While at his rooms, rented from a widow named Mrs. Miller, Tom rescues a gentleman, Mr. Nightingale, who is being attacked by his footman. Tom and Mr. Nightingale become friends.

Tom receives a package containing a mask and an invitation to a masquerade party. Tom thinks this is from Harriet. At the party, he finds a person who he thinks is Harriet and asks her to tell him where Sophia is. Instead, the lady leads him to a private room, where she reveals that she is Lady Bellaston and seduces him. Tom and Lady Bellaston have frequent assignations in the coming days, and the lady provides Tom with generous financial favors.

Upon arriving at Lady Bellaston's home one evening, Tom meets Sophia there. She had returned earlier than expected from a play. Tom and Sophia are both speechless at seeing each other. When Lady Bellaston arrives, she pretends not to know Tom, and Tom pretends that he is there to return Sophia's book and money.

Book XIV

Lady Bellaston goes to Tom's lodgings late that night to let him know that she wants to continue their affair. Sophia, meanwhile, sends Tom a letter saying that he should not come to Lady Bellaston's house again as it might cause suspicion.

The next day, Mrs. Miller tells Tom that he must not have female visitors late at night. Tom agrees not to repeat the offense. Mr. Nightingale tells Tom that his father has arranged a marriage for him and that he is leaving, even though he loves Mrs. Miller's daughter, Nancy.

The following day, Mrs. Miller tells Tom that Nancy is pregnant and has tried to kill herself and that Nightingale has disappeared. Tom, of course, says he will try to help. He finds Nightingale, who says he wants to marry Nancy but cannot displease his father. Tom goes to see Nightingale's father and tells him that his son has already married Nancy. He meets Nightingale's uncle, who returns with him to see Nightingale. The uncle tries to dissuade Nightingale from marrying Nancy.

Book XV

Lady Bellaston schemes to have her acquaintance Lord Fellamar rape Sophia, whom he loves. She thinks that Sophia will feel obliged to marry Fellamar, leaving Tom for herself. The deed is prevented when Squire Western, directed by Harriet Fitzpatrick, arrives. He demands that Sophia return home and marry Blifil, which suits Lady Bellaston as well as her original plan. Honour goes to Tom's lodgings to tell him these things.

The next day, Nancy Miller and Nightingale are married. Nightingale, having seen Lady Bellaston at Tom's rooms the night before, tells Tom that she is dishonorable in every way. Tom decides to end their affair, and Nightingale says that the best way to do this is to propose marriage. Tom sends the lady a letter proposing marriage and gets the desired result.

Mrs. Miller receives a letter from Squire Allworthy stating that he and Blifil are on their way to London and would like to lodge with her. Tom, Nightingale, and Nancy move to new lodgings to make room for them.

Mrs. Arabella Hunt, a wealthy neighbor of Mrs. Miller's, has gotten to know Tom and now proposes marriage. Tom declines, although he is tempted by her money.

Although Squire Western has locked up Sophia, Tom manages to get a letter to her, vowing his love. It is Black George, whom Squire Western has brought to London, who delivers this letter.

Book XVI

When Sophia's aunt, Mrs. Western, arrives to take charge of her, Sophia is able to respond to Tom's letter.

Allworthy and Blifil arrive in London. They talk with Squire Western about how to bring about the marriage of their children.

Lady Bellaston, meanwhile, tells Mrs. Western of Lord Fellamar's love for Sophia, and Mrs. Western agrees to support this match. Further, Lady Bellaston takes two actions against Tom. First, she asks Lord Fellamar to have Tom conscripted into the navy. Second, she gives Mrs. Western the letter containing Tom's marriage proposal, knowing that Mrs. Western will show it to Sophia.

Tom goes to visit Harriet Fitzpatrick, and, as he is leaving, Mr. Fitzpatrick arrives and assumes the worst. Mr. Fitzpatrick demands a duel. Tom lands a blow that all assume will be the death of Mr. Fitzpatrick, and as a result he is jailed. In jail, he receives a letter from Sophia in which she tells him that she knows about his proposal to Lady Bellaston and never wants to hear his name again.

Book XVII

The next morning, Blifil tells Allworthy that Tom is in jail, and why. Mrs. Miller jumps in to defend Tom, relating all the kindness and good character she has seen in him. Squire Western comes in and says that he will force Sophia to marry Blifil immediately. Allworthy rejects this idea and prefers to call off the entire affair.

Meanwhile, Mrs. Western, now a strong supporter of Lord Fellamar, urges Sophia to see him.

Mrs. Miller visits Tom in jail and takes a letter from Tom to Sophia. Mrs. Miller also sings Tom's praises to Sophia.

Tom learns that Fitzpatrick has not died after all and that he has admitted demanding the duel in which Tom wounded him. He learns this from Mrs. Waters, the woman he first rescued from Northerton and then slept with at the inn en route to London. Mrs. Waters is now Fitzpatrick's mistress.

Book XVIII

Partridge visits Tom and tells him in horrified tones that Mrs. Waters is Tom's mother, Jenny Jones. Tom immediately sends for her.

Allworthy discovers, through some information innocently shared with him by a third party, Black George's theft of the bank notes Allworthy gave to Tom on the night he left the estate. Allworthy consults a lawyer, Dowling, about taking action against George. Allworthy knows Dowling because the latter was with Bridget when she died and was in charge of settling her estate.

Mrs. Miller tells Allworthy that Tom committed no wrong in his duel with Fitzpatrick. The same day, Allworthy gets a letter from the tutor Square. Near death, Square repents of all the bad things he said about Tom, admitting that much of it was exaggeration and outright lies.

Allworthy decides to ask Partridge what happened during his travels with Tom. Patridge tells Allworthy that he is not Tom's father but that Tom has slept with his own mother, Jenny Jones, who is now known as Mrs. Waters. Mrs. Waters arrives and tells Allworthy that his sister, Bridget, was actually Tom's mother. Tom's father, she says, was a clergyman's son who died before the baby was born. Mrs. Waters agreed to say she was Tom's mother in return for money that Bridget gave her. Allworthy accepts her word.

Allworthy learns that Blifil is a villain. Dowling tells Allworthy that Blifil has been scheming against Tom in various ways. For one thing, Blifil bribed the police to charge Tom in connection with the duel with Fitzpatrick. Dowling tells Allworthy of other schemes, as well, including Blifil's interception of a letter Bridget wrote to him on her deathbed.

Allworthy visits Sophia and tells her that he is glad she refused to marry Blifil. The squire hopes she will favor Tom, but Sophia refuses to consider it. Western arrives, learns that Allworthy has turned against Blifil, and realizes that Tom will be his heir. Immediately, he wants Sophia to marry Tom.

Tom and Allworthy meet and are reconciled to each other.

Mrs. Miller tells Tom that Nightingale has talked to Sophia, explaining to her that Tom's proposal to Lady Bellaston was only a scheme to get rid of her. Sophia, though, does not soften toward Tom.

Tom, when fully informed of Blifil's villainy and of George's theft of his bank notes, asks

Allworthy to show them both mercy, and Allworthy is astounded.

Tom and Allworthy go to visit the Westerns. Sophia is persuaded to marry Tom, and the wedding takes place the next day.

The narrator tells the fates of all. All are happy except the villain, Blifil, and even he, though he was expelled from the family, was granted an annuity to live on. Tom had overcome his vices at last. He and Sophia had children, to whom Squire Western was a devoted grandfather.

Characters

Bridget Allworthy

Squire Allworthy's sister, Bridget, takes care of the infant Tom at her brother's direction. She is unmarried when the story opens but later marries Captain Blifil and has a son, Master Blifil.

At the end of the story, long after Bridget has died, it is revealed that Bridget was not as virtuous as she appeared. In fact, she was Tom's mother; to hide her shame, she bribed Jenny Jones to say the child was hers.

Squire Allworthy

Squire Allworthy's kindness extends to all, from Tom's supposed mother, Jenny Jones (to whom he, in his role as magistrate, gives the lightest possible sentence) to Sophia, whom he is unwilling to force into a marriage she does not want.

When all is said and done, Allworthy chooses to make Tom his heir over the villainous Master Blifil in spite of Tom's illegitimate birth. In doing so, he gives more weight to individual character than to the strictures of society.

Lady Bellaston

Lady Bellaston is a relative of the Western family to whom Sophia flees when she runs away from home. While Sophia is staying at Lady Bellaston's London home, the lady seduces Tom, and the two have an affair.

Lady Bellaston is self-centered and vindictive, as well as promiscuous. When her affair with Tom ends, she goes to great lengths to bring about his unhappiness, from trying to have him drafted into the navy to trying to make Sophia marry someone else.

Little Benjamin

See Mr. Partridge

Mrs. Honour Blackmore

Honour is Sophia's servant. When Sophia decides to run away on the eve of her forced wedding to Blifil, Honour is loyal enough to purposely get herself fired so that she can pack Sophia's belongings along with her own. She then accompanies Sophia on her flight and is a dependable servant and messenger to Sophia throughout the tale.

Captain Blifil

The captain is a self-serving hypocrite who marries Bridget for her money and fathers one son, Master Blifil, before he dies suddenly of apoplexy.

Master Blifil

The son of Bridget and Captain Blifil, Master Blifil is hypocrisy personified. He takes great pains to pretend to be virtuous and shamelessly curries favor with anyone who is in a position to do him good. In reality, however, he is completely unprincipled. Most of his villainy is directed at Tom. He lies about Tom to cause him trouble and often bribes others to join him. He will do anything to keep Tom out of Allworthy's favor and to keep him from becoming the squire's heir. He wants to marry Sophia for two reasons: first, because he knows that she and Tom love each other; and second, for her money.

At the end of the story, readers learn that Master Blifil has known for a long time that Tom is his half-brother. When Bridget was dying, she sent a letter to Allworthy telling him the truth about Tom's parentage, but Blifil intercepted this letter and kept it from the squire. The knowledge that Tom actually had some legitimate claim to Allworthy's fortune made Blifil all the more determined to ruin Tom.

All of Blifil's schemes fail in the end, when Allworthy sees the truth about him as well as about Tom. Allworthy makes Tom his heir and exiles Blifil from the manor, giving him a small annuity to live on.

Mr. Dowling

Dowling is a lawyer. He is with Bridget Allworthy when she dies and is responsible for settling her estate. Bridget gives Dowling a letter for Allworthy revealing that Bridget is Tom's mother. Master Blifil intercepts the letter, however, so that Allworthy does not discover Tom's true parentage until the end of the novel.

Master Blifil on several occasions engages Dowling to cause difficulty for Tom, making Dowling believe that the orders to do so are originating with Squire Allworthy.

Lord Fellamar

Lord Fellamar is a friend of Lady Bellaston. He falls in love with Sophia and tries to rape her as a way of forcing her to consent to marry him. At Lady Bellaston's request, he tries to have Tom drafted into the navy to keep him away from Sophia.

Mrs. Harriet Fitzpatrick

Harriet is Sophia's cousin; the two spent some part of their childhood together in the care of Mrs. Western. They meet en route to London when Sophia is running away from her father and Harriet is running from her abusive husband.

Mr. Fitzpatrick

Mr. Fitzpatrick is Harriet's husband. He acts the part of a loving suitor but marries her for her money and, as soon as the marriage is made, becomes so harsh toward her that she takes flight.

Fitzpatrick is suspicious and rash, and when he arrives one day at his home (to which his wife has returned) and finds Tom leaving his house, he insists on a duel. Tom wounds him gravely and is sent to jail. Fitzpatrick is not all bad, however, because when he recovers, he admits that he was the one who forced Tom to duel. This information brings about Tom's release from jail.

Mrs. Arabella Hunt

Mrs. Hunt is a wealthy widow who lives next door to Mrs. Miller and comes to know something about Tom as he comes and goes there. She sends Tom a formal letter proposing marriage, and Tom is briefly tempted to accept because the woman's fortune would be a help to him. When he turns down her proposal, Tom is highly pleased with his virtue.

Jenny Jones

As the novel opens, Jenny works as a servant for the schoolmaster and his wife and also has recently been a nurse to Bridget during an illness. Jenny is very smart, and the schoolmaster has taught her Latin and other subjects. The schoolmaster's wife and others in the village are very jealous of Jenny because of her education.

When Mrs. Wilkins sets out to find out who is Tom's mother, the schoolmaster's wife accuses Jenny, and others are happy to see Jenny brought low. Jenny admits that she is Tom's mother, and Squire Allworthy metes out a light punishment: He

arranges for her to go away to a place where she can get a new start.

At the end of the book, it is revealed that Jenny is not, in fact, Tom's mother. She was willing to say she was in return for money paid to her by Bridget, the child's real mother. In her new identity as Mrs. Waters, she has an affair with Tom and, ultimately, reveals to Squire Allworthy Tom's true parentage.

Tom Jones

The novel's hero, Tom first appears as an infant left on Squire Allworthy's bed. He begins life with the good fortune to be taken in by the wealthy and kind squire, who develops real affection for Tom. The boy becomes something of a rascal, though. Not only is he imprudent and mischievous, he is, unfortunately, surrounded by people who are eager to magnify his failings and bring about his downfall.

All in all, Tom's vices, while they cause him substantial trouble and nearly cost him his beloved Sophia, are not equal to his virtues. He is several times caught stealing, but more often than not it turns out that he stole food for the family of his friend Black George. He is always ready to help anyone in any kind of trouble; many episodes feature some hapless person screaming and Tom leaping to his or her aid. When his landlady is distraught because her pregnant daughter, Nancy, has attempted suicide and Nancy's lover has absconded, Tom, as always, saves the day.

Tom is also forgiving to a rare degree. After Master Blifil has spent his entire life trying to ruin Tom, Allworthy finally sees Blifil for what he is and sends him away. Tom's response is to urge Allworthy not to be too harsh with Blifil, and he even secretly increases the annuity that Allworthy gives Blifil.

Throughout the novel, Squire Allworthy, usually with great patience and kindness, admonishes Tom that he must be more prudent and wise in his actions. It takes years and many misadventures for Tom to learn the lesson, but he does learn it.

Mrs. Miller

Mrs. Miller is a kind widow who runs the London boardinghouse where Tom stays. Tom goes to her house because Allworthy has stayed there on his own visits to London.

Tom is compassionate toward Mrs. Miller and her daughter, Nancy. When Tom's friend Nightingale is about to abandon the pregnant Nancy for a marriage arranged by Nightingale's father, Tom talks Nightingale into marrying Nancy and even tries to reconcile Nightingale's father to the marriage. In return, Mrs. Miller is a true friend to Tom. At crucial moments she comes to his defense and corrects others' mistaken views of him. She has occasion to intercede for Tom with both Sophia and Allworthy.

Nancy Miller

Nancy is the daughter of Mrs. Miller. She falls in love with her mother's boarder Mr. Nightingale. Eventually, with Tom's help in overcoming obstacles, the two marry.

Northerton

Northerton is one of the soldiers in the group of rebels Tom joins briefly. When Tom gives a toast to Sophia, Northerton, insisting that he knows her, assaults her character. In the ensuing fight, Northerton gashes Tom's head with a wine bottle. He then escapes from the guard assigned to hold him. Later, when Tom hears a woman screaming in the woods and goes to her rescue, he finds Northerton assaulting Mrs. Waters and rescues her. Tom assumes that he has interrupted a rape, but it is later revealed that Mrs. Waters had regular assignations with Northerton and was screaming because on that occasion he was trying to rob her.

Mr. Partridge

Mr. Partridge is the local schoolmaster at the beginning of the novel. Once Jenny is accused of being Tom's mother, Mr. Partridge, who is her employer, is accused of being the father. Mr. Partridge's wife testifies against him, and he is ruined. He leaves the area, changes his name to Little Benjamin, and becomes a barber.

Tom meets Little Benjamin after being ejected from Allworthy's home. The two discover each other's identities and decide to travel together. Partridge remains with Tom throughout the story, and the narrator tells readers in his epilogue that Tom has given Partridge an annuity to allow him to start another school and that Sophia is engineering Partridge's marriage to Molly Seagrim.

Mrs. Partridge

Mrs. Partridge is the schoolmaster's suspicious, mean-spirited wife. She testifies against him when he is accused of being Tom's father, although she has no real evidence of his guilt. As a result of this, she and her husband are both reduced to poverty, and she soon dies of smallpox.

Black George Seagrim

Called Black George because he has a black beard, George begins the story as the gamekeeper at Allworthy's estate. When all the other members of Allworthy's household turn against Tom, Black George is his only friend. Tom, in turn, is a friend to George, going so far as to steal food for his family.

George loses his job with Allworthy because of some mischief that Tom had encouraged him in. Tom takes all the blame himself and begs Allworthy to retain George, but fails to help his friend. Later, though, Tom succeeds in getting Squire Western to hire George, and George accompanies Western to London.

George rewards Tom's loyalty by stealing the money Squire Allworthy gives Tom the night he leaves Allworthy's house. When Tom discovers this near the end of the novel, George flees, and Tom allows George's family to keep the money.

Molly Seagrim

Molly is Black George's daughter. Tom sleeps with her and considers abandoning Sophia for her when Molly becomes pregnant and Tom thinks the child is his. He decides, finally, to give Molly money instead of his love. When he goes to her house to tell her this, he finds the tutor Square in her bedroom and then learns from her sister that Molly's pregnancy is most likely the result of her encounter with yet another man. Tom finds all of this amusing and is relieved to be free of obligation to Molly.

At the end of the novel, the narrator relates that Sophia is doing her best to arrange Molly's marriage to Mr. Partridge.

Mr. Thomas Square

Square is one of Tom and Master Blifil's two tutors. Like his counterpart, Thwackum, Square is an adversary of Tom and an ally of Master Blifil in all things. Near the end of the novel, Square, on his deathbed, writes a letter to Allworthy in which he repents of his ill treatment of Tom and even details some occasions on which Tom was falsely blamed.

Square is a deist, while Thwackum is an Anglican, and the two are constantly engaged in philosophical and theological debate. This ongoing debate mirrors that which was occurring throughout England at the time Fielding wrote.

Rev. Roger Thwackum

Thwackum, one of Tom and Master Blifil's tutors, is also an Anglican clergyman and a self-righteous bigot. Like his fellow tutor, Mr. Square,

Thwackum looks for any excuse to punish or denigrate Tom (he has a special fondness for corporal punishment), while he favors Master Blifil, who appears to be Allworthy's heir.

Mrs. Waters

See Jenny Jones

Mrs. Western

Mrs. Western is Squire Western's sister, Lady Bellaston's cousin, and Sophia's aunt. She is not married and acts as a surrogate mother to Sophia and in some ways as a surrogate wife to the squire. She is more concerned with appearances and social status than with Sophia's happiness, and, in the brawl over whom Sophia will marry, Mrs. Western supports the lewd Lord Fellamar.

Sophia Western

Sophia is the beautiful daughter of Squire Western and a friend of Tom's from childhood. Tom's pursuit of her is the central thread of the story. Sophia loves him but is understandably put off by his lusty adventures. Although she cuts him off more than once, she is finally convinced of his readiness to love only her. When all other obstacles to their union have been overcome, Sophia finally agrees to marry Tom.

Scholars generally believe that Fielding based Sophia on his own beloved and beautiful wife, who died before he wrote the book.

Squire Western

Western is Allworthy's neighbor and Sophia's father. While he loves his daughter, he shows that he loves other things more, especially money and hunting, and quite possibly liquor. When Sophia runs away from home to avoid marrying Blifil, Western goes after her but gives up his search for her when he runs across a hunting party and decides that it is too nice a day to forgo a hunt. He is determined to marry Sophia off to Master Blifil as long as Blifil is Allworthy's heir, in spite of her understandable dislike for him. As soon as Tom becomes the heir, Western changes his alliance.

In the end, Western gives his estate to Sophia so that she and Tom can live there, and he himself moves to a place where the hunting is better. He is, however, a doting grandfather to Sophia and Tom's children.

Deborah Wilkins

Deborah is Bridget's lady-in-waiting. She sees herself as the manager of Allworthy's household.

It is Deborah whom Allworthy sends out into the village to discover the identity of Tom's mother, and Deborah wastes no time in catching up on the local gossip and in using it to reach a conclusion about Tom's parentage.

Themes

Virtue and Vice

The overarching theme of *Tom Jones* is virtue and vice. The highlighted virtue is prudence, and the featured vices are hypocrisy and vanity.

Prudence, one of the time-honored cardinal virtues of Western culture, essentially means thinking ahead, considering the likely consequences of one's actions, and acting accordingly. The failure to do this is Tom's downfall over and over, until the very end of the story. Although Tom has many virtues—he is kind, good-hearted, generous, brave, loyal, and forgiving—his lack of prudence gives his adversaries opportunities to harm him and drives away his beloved Sophia, nearly for good.

Tom's imprudence often manifests in his behavior with women. In spite of his love for Sophia, he falls into one dalliance after another with unsavory women. He continues this pattern of behavior even though he knows that it is hurtful to Sophia and counterproductive to what he really wants, which is to be with her.

The standard-bearers of hypocrisy and vanity are Captain Blifil and his son, Master Blifil, but they lead a large army of followers. Bridget Allworthy, Squire and Mrs. Western, the tutors Thwackum and Square, Black George, Lady Bellaston, Mr. Fitzpatrick, Lord Fellamar, and others portray the twin vices in many different forms. They all engage in misrepresentation, outright lies, disloyalty, slander, and more in attempting to get what they want, which is money and social status. By displaying these vices in so many characters, Fielding makes clear that he imputes them to the entire society he depicts; they are the rule, not the exception.

Fielding also deals with the relative seriousness of various vices. His hero is far from perfect. Tom is blatantly promiscuous and lets his enthusiasm for fun lead him beyond the borders of good behavior and even beyond the law, as when he talks Black George into joining him in poaching on a neighbor's land. At intervals throughout the novel, Squire Allworthy is often distressed by

Topics for Further Study

- Make a list of Tom's virtues and vices. Do you think that virtue or vice is dominant in his character? Does this change in the course of the story? Explain your answers.

- In what ways is Tom like young people today? In what ways is he different? What similar challenges does he face, and what challenges of his are very different from today's?

- Do some research to learn about country life and life in London in the mid-1700s. Then decide how realistic *Tom Jones* is in its portrayal of life in England. Write an essay in which you discuss some realistic aspects of the novel and some aspects that are not historically accurate.

- Do you think that Sophia made a good choice in marrying Tom? Why or why not?

- Choose the names of ten characters in *Tom Jones* and tell why each one is appropriate. Consider such things as the meanings and the sounds of the names and how these relate to the characters' traits.

Tom's behavior and talks to him about the need for prudence and morality. Yet, until the end, Tom goes away from these talks and returns to his old ways.

In spite of the fact that Allworthy knows Tom's faults very well, he concludes at the end of the novel that Tom is a good man, whereas Blifil is a hopelessly bad one. The kinds of obvious, public vices Tom has—the very ones that society often judges most harshly—are really less serious than the hidden vices of vanity, hypocrisy, selfishness, and greed that lie at the core of Blifil's character.

Redemption

Proceeding from Allworthy's judgment that Tom's vices are less damning than Blifil's is the idea that Tom is redeemable, whereas Blifil is not. In fact, Tom is redeemed at the end of the novel. He finally sees the error of his ways and changes

them. As a result, his "sins" are forgiven, and Tom is granted Allworthy's fortune and the love of both Allworthy and Sophia. Blifil, on the other hand, is cast out of the family.

The idea that Fielding is making a point about redemption that applies beyond the scope of his story is bolstered by the fact that Allworthy's character is God-like. He is a father figure to both Tom and Blifil. He is also a magistrate and therefore is in a position to pass judgment on people and their failings. Throughout the book, he exercises this authority with compassion and restraint. He shows mercy to the powerless (such as Jenny Jones) and forgiveness to the repentant. It is easy to conclude that through Allworthy, Tom, and Blifil, Fielding is declaring that those who are good at heart will be forgiven normal human weaknesses if they are willing to learn from their mistakes.

Style

Epic, Picaresque, and Epistolary

Fielding melds elements of several traditional literary forms in *Tom Jones*. First, the novel borrows some elements of epic poems, such as Homer's *Odyssey*. In fact, in the novel itself, Fielding, as narrator, calls the book a "prosai-comi-epic," meaning a comic epic written in prose.

An epic has a strong protagonist who does heroic deeds and has a broad scope of action; that is, the events take place over a wide range of time and place. *Tom Jones* fulfills all these requirements of an epic.

Second, *Tom Jones* incorporates elements of the picaresque novel, which originated in Spain. A picaresque features a roguish hero (*picaro* in Spanish) and is episodic and more loosely structured than an epic. A picaresque is literally "one thing after another," and the only unifying thread may be that all events befall the central character. Many picaresques center on a journey, and most satirize the society in which the story takes place.Tom is certainly a roguish character, and *Tom Jones* certainly satirizes the society in which he moves. The section of the novel that relates Tom's trip to London is the most strongly rooted in the picaresque tradition.

Finally, *Tom Jones*, to a lesser extent, borrows the form of the epistolary novel, or novel of letters. Fielding's first novel, *Shamela*, was written entirely in the epistolary form, as was the novel it parodied, *Pamela*. The form was popular throughout the eigh-

Compare & Contrast

- **Mid-1700s:** England is a largely agricultural nation and is making great advances in agricultural productivity. Farmers are discovering the value of crop rotation, and better farming tools, such as ploughs and seed drills, are being developed.

  Today: England is largely industrial and commercial and imports most of its food. The economy is based on transportation, communications, and the production of steel, petroleum, coal, and electricity.

- **Mid-1700s:** England is ruled by King George II and his appointed prime minister, Sir Robert Walpole. The king rules a far-flung empire that includes not only colonies in America, India, and elsewhere but also parts of Germany, where he spends much of his time. Walpole, therefore, has great power and authority in England.

  Today: England is ruled by Queen Elizabeth II and Prime Minister Tony Blair, leader of the Labour Party. The role of the monarch has shrunk over the centuries, and England's prime minister is effectively the country's leader.

- **Mid-1700s:** With the spread of the Enlightenment, many people question religious teachings that had long been considered above question. Increasingly, people believe that reason is a better guide than blindly accepted doctrines. Some reject Roman Catholicism and other forms of organized religion in favor of deism, a doctrine that God exists but that organized religion is not a source of truth. In *Tom Jones*, the two tutors personify the division between traditional religion and deism: Thwackum is an Anglican, whereas Square is a deist.

  Today: In September 2001, Cardinal Cormac Murphy-O'Connor, the Roman Catholic cardinal for England and Wales, tells the National Conference of Priests that Christianity is nearly a dead religion in Britain, having been replaced by materialism, sensuality, selfishness, and "New Age" beliefs.

teenth century. In *Tom Jones*, Fielding has many opportunities to advance his story through letters written by his characters, who are often separated by geography, intrigue, or both.

Allegory

An allegory is a story with a double meaning; each character or event represents some other person or occurrence. John Bunyan's *Pilgrim's Progress* is a very well-known allegory in which the main character, Christian, represents "everyman," and his journey from the City of Destruction to the Celestial City represents the journey from a worldly existence to heaven.

Some scholars see *Tom Jones* as an allegory of everyman's quest to attain wisdom. This view is bolstered by the fact that the name Sophia is the Greek word for wisdom. Tom's long and difficult quest for Sophia, therefore, can be seen as the quest for wisdom, which he wins at last.

Historical Context

The Enlightenment

The Age of Enlightenment dawned in the late seventeenth century and strongly colored the entire eighteenth century in Europe and America. The era was so named because the intellectuals who nurtured it believed that the ideas it promoted were bringing humanity out of a period of darkness in which it had been bound by superstition and ignorance. The most prominent of these ideas was that human reason—not blind faith in religious doctrines or authorities—was the path to wisdom in all areas of life.

The Age of Enlightenment, or Age of Reason, as it was sometimes called, was sparked by new scientific discoveries (Newton's law of gravity, for example) and by new directions in philosophy as set out by John Locke, Thomas Hobbes, and others. Human reason was penetrating the mysteries of the physical world and imagining new kinds of societies. It seemed, therefore, that reason, freed from age-old superstitions, could lead humanity to a new golden age.

The shift from faith to reason was a major turning point that affected not just religion and philosophy but science, politics, economics, and other disciplines. The new philosophy was that understanding and knowledge, rather than being inborn or handed down from the past, emerge from observation and experience. This meant that every person had the ability to learn and was a strong argument for universal education. The idea that all could attain knowledge and wisdom led to the idea of equality. If all had the potential to learn and to act wisely, then all should have the opportunity to vote, to improve themselves socially and economically, to govern themselves, and so on. Not surprisingly, the Age of Reason led directly to the Age of Revolution in Europe and America.

By the time Fielding wrote *Tom Jones*, the Enlightenment was more than half a century old. Its ideas can be clearly seen in Fielding's handling of his story. Tom's maturity and his understanding of how to live are not imposed upon him by religious teachings or by religious or secular authorities; instead, they come through Tom's own experiences and his observations of the law of cause and effect in his life. While Squire Allworthy often urges Tom to be more prudent, Tom does not really understand what this means, or why it is so important, until he has broken the law of prudence many times and has seen the results. He wins wisdom through his own experiments.

Similarly, the fact that Tom becomes Allworthy's heir is a sign of the times. In former times, the heir would have been chosen according to societal rules, without regard for the individual traits of the persons involved. Blifil, though despicable, would have been Allworthy's heir without question because he was Bridget's only legitimate son. Tom's illegitimate birth would have put him out of contention. The individualism of the Enlightenment meant that social classes gradually became less rigid and that social conventions were more often broken. Of course, the change was not absolute. Fielding shows the ongoing conflict between the old ways and the new through characters such as Squire Western, who only consents to Sophia's marrying Tom after it is known that at least one of Tom's parents was from the upper class and that he will inherit Allworthy's money.

The Jacobite Rebellions

The Jacobites were British citizens who sought to restore the exiled Catholic Stuart dynasty to the British throne. Their name is from the Latin for "James"; their original goal was to make James Stuart, half-brother of Queen Anne (who ruled from 1702 to 1714), the ruler of Britain in place of the Protestant George I. The unsuccessful First Jacobite Rebellion took place in 1715, after Queen Anne died and George I ascended the throne.

In the 1740s, Britain was at war with France on several fronts—in Europe, in America, in India, and at sea. The Jacobites saw the government's distractions as an opportunity to try again to recapture the British throne for the Stuarts. Prince Charles Edward, who was the grandson of Queen Anne's predecessor, James II, and who was known as Bonnie Prince Charlie, led Scottish soldiers in the capture of Edinburgh and marched south toward London. He hoped to gather enough English support to place his father on the throne in place of George I. He did not win widespread support in England, however, and was soon defeated.

It is the Second Jacobite Rebellion of 1745 that Tom briefly joins in book VII of *Tom Jones*, when he has been ejected from Allworthy's home and despairs of finding Sophia.

Critical Overview

Tom Jones was an immediate success with readers. Periodicals and, therefore, published critics, were far fewer in number then than they are now, but most who wrote about the novel, for publication or in private letters, received it with some enthusiasm. One exception was Samuel Richardson, author of the recent best-seller *Pamela*, which Fielding had twice parodied. In a letter to the daughters of a friend, Richardson panned *Tom Jones* while admitting that he had not read it. Claiming that he had been warned by "judicious friends" not to do so, Richardson continued:

> I had reason to think that the author intended . . . to whiten a vicious character and to make morality bend to his practices. What reason has he to make this Tom illegitimate? Why did he make him . . . the lowest of all fellows? Why did he draw his heroine so fond, so foolish, and so insipid? But perhaps I think the worse of the piece because I know the writer and dislike his principles, both public and private.

The recipients of the letter, Astraea and Minerva Hill, disagreed with their correspondent. "We

Albert Finney as Tom Jones and Diane Cilento as Molly Seagrim in the 1963 film adaptation of Tom Jones

went through the whole six volumes," they wrote, "and found much merit in 'em all: a double merit, both of head and heart." The sisters were impressed at the way Fielding tied up all the loose ends of the plot "in an extremely moving close, where lines that seem'd to wander and run in different ways meet, all in an instructive center." Contradicting Samuelson's presumption that the novel must elevate immorality, the sisters wrote, "Its events reward sincerity and punish and expose hypocrisy; show pity and benevolence in amiable lights, and avarice and brutality in very despicable ones."

Although some critics (notably William Forsyth, writing in 1871) have continued to object to *Tom Jones* on moral grounds, few have found fault with it on literary ones. Later opinion has been more with the sisters and less with Richardson. In 1836, the author Samuel Taylor Coleridge wrote:

> What a master of composition Fielding was! Upon my word, I think *The Oedipus Tyrannus*, *The Alchemist*, and *Tom Jones* the three most perfect plots every planned. And how charming, how wholesome, Fielding always is! To take him up after Richardson is like emerging from a sickroom . . . into an open lawn on a breezy day in May.

In his preface to the Norton Critical Edition of *Tom Jones*, Sheridan Baker wrote of the novel, "It makes the English novel thoroughly literate for the first time. It marries comedy and romance, by the grace of the classics, to produce a peculiarly fresh and ironic wisdom."

Criticism

Candyce Norvell

Norvell is an independent educational writer who specializes in English and literature and holds degrees in linguistics and journalism. In this essay, Norvell examines Fielding's portrayal of teachers in Tom Jones.

Among the significant characters in *Tom Jones*, three are teachers. In a story of multi-layered and intertwined ironies, these characters, individually and collectively, are especially rich. While Fielding makes clear that all of his characters point beyond themselves, he draws the teachers in such a way that they point obviously—and unflatteringly—to certain groups. This is especially true of the tutors Thwackum and Square.

Teachers, of course, are supposed to be wiser than most, since they are entrusted to instruct

> " . . . while the young student Tom has gained wisdom and corrected his course, those who should have been to him a font of wisdom continue in their folly."

others. Fielding's teachers, however, are not wise, nor are they ethical. Therein lies one of the book's many ironies.

Mr. Partridge, the wrongly accused schoolmaster, is the first of the three to appear. He is no worse a person than the average man or woman, but he is no better and no smarter. In fact, his lack of mental sharpness is his downfall. Fielding tells readers that Jenny Jones, the servant whom Partridge instructs in Latin, soon has more facility with the language than he does. This is certainly a clue to his limited intellect. On the other hand, the fact that he teaches her is to his credit; not only is she a mere servant, but she is a woman. She is not even an attractive woman, which would have given Partridge a selfish motive to spend time with her. He seems to have taught her purely out of recognition of her abilities.

If teaching Jenny was kind, though, it was not wise. Partridge's mean, suspicious wife objects to it. When the schoolmaster is foolish enough to exchange words with Jenny in Latin while she is serving dinner, Mrs. Partridge jumps to conclusions about what has passed between them and soon uses these conclusions as an excuse to destroy her husband.

Partridge also does not excel in morality. When he takes up with Tom en route to London, he does so because he hopes for an opportunity to clear his name and re-establish his reputation. Therefore, while he, unlike many others, has no desire to harm Tom, if Tom is harmed in Partridge's effort to redeem himself, Partridge will not mind and may not even notice. When Squire Allworthy approaches Partridge near the end of the book to find out what all transpired as Tom and Partridge traveled together to London, Partridge, if he thought for a moment, would realize that what he

says may be critical in determining Tom's fate. Partridge thinks only of himself, however; he takes the occasion to tell Allworthy not only that he is not Tom's father but also that Tom has just committed incest with his mother. This added information (which turns out to be wrong) does not help Partridge's cause, but it certainly hurts Tom's until it is corrected. That Partridge speaks out of foolishness rather than hatred does not change the impact of his words.

The schoolmaster, then, is often either foolish or incorrect and is master of nothing—not even of himself. The best that can be said about him is that he is the least reprehensible of the three educators.

Thwackum and Square, the two men who tutor Tom and Master Blifil, seem to have more knowledge than does Partridge—although not enough to get what they want—but they definitely have even less moral fiber. Like Partridge, they are self-serving; unlike him, they are purposely destructive and just plain mean.

The tutors are in many ways twin characters; they share many attributes and goals. Both are pretentious and self-righteous, always eager to punish Tom (on a trumped-up charge, if necessary) while indulging themselves in hypocrisy and lies. Both eagerly absorb Master Blifil's flattery; his kind of artificial virtue is exactly their cup of tea. Both covet Allworthy's fortune, and both scheme to marry his sister, Bridget, to get their hands on it. To that end, they are doubly happy to conspire with her son, Master Blifil, against Tom at every turn. This is where their understanding, if not their villainy, falls short, however. In the first place, Bridget sees through them and has no intention of marrying either of them. In the second place, they have miscalculated in thinking that fawning over her son will endear her to them. They have failed to notice that Bridget despises her son, just as she despised his father.

Fielding writes of Thwackum that it is his practice to "regard all virtue as a matter of theory only." This is a good summation and applies equally to Square. The only difference between the two men is that they fail to practice opposite theories of virtue. Fielding uses this difference to ridicule both of the two leading philosophies of his time.

Thwackum is the traditionalist of the two, an Anglican reverend who starts from the premise that all humans are evil at the core and need to have their badness quite literally beaten out of them. Square takes the newer view, popularized by the Enlightenment, that people are inherently good and that when they do evil, they have merely strayed off their normal course and need to be helped back onto the straight and narrow. While he does not share Thwackum's enthusiasm for corporal punishment, he is not opposed to placing blame and accusation wherever he thinks it will further his own interests, justice be damned.

These two men spend much more time and energy arguing philosophy with each other than they do attending to their students. Both are pompous, verbose, and ridiculous, and both are deeply immoral. Through them, Fielding skewers Christian and deist alike. The message personified in Thwackum and Square is clear: actions, not words, constitute true morality.

If Fielding thinks that one camp is less depraved or less silly than the other, he does not give himself away. He brings both Thwackum and Square back onto the stage at the end of the book, allowing them to demonstrate that, unlike Tom, they have not been improved by time and experience. Each man sends a letter to Allworthy. Square is on his deathbed and, to his credit, does repent of the wrongs he did to Tom. However, he also proves to be a coward, confiding to Allworthy that, in fear of death and subsequent "utter darkness forever," he has abandoned his former philosophy and has become "in earnest a Christian." In short, everything in Square's letter adds up to one final attempt to ensure his own eternal comfort. He is incapable of loyalty, even to the beliefs for which he argued all his life.

Thwackum, in his letter, regrets only that he did not whip Tom enough to whip the devil out of him, calls Square an atheist, chastises Allworthy for being too easy on Tom, and, finally, says that if the local vicar should die ("as we hear he is in a declining way"), he hopes that Allworthy will appoint him as successor. Thwackum is self-righteous and self-serving to the end.

Partridge, too, receives his final dispensation from the author's hand; the reader learns that Sophia is working to arrange a marriage between Partridge and the slatternly Molly Seagram. The match is a fair one, as neither is dastardly, but both are fools.

And so, while the young student Tom has gained wisdom and corrected his course, those who should have been to him a font of wisdom continue in their folly.

Source: Candyce Norvell, Critical Essay on *Tom Jones*, in *Novels for Students*, Gale, 2003.

George A. Drake

In the following excerpt, Drake examines the manners of Fielding's characters in Tom Jones.

History remembers places as well as times, and the space of history is profoundly social rather than purely phenomenal or material. It is not produced wholly by individual psychology and yet cannot be reduced to abstract or natural space. Literary realism tends to be measured by one or the other of these extremes, as psychological realism or realism of naturalistic detail. Thus placing Fielding in the realist pantheon requires considerable exertion, if not outright violence. His scenes are starkly devoid of naturalistic detail, and he is far less concerned with accumulating the minutiae of psychological response than is his rival Richardson. But Fielding makes no claim to be a realist: his aim is to describe "not Men, but Manners." And yet it is precisely by describing manners—by turning to the realm of the *social* rather than the psychological or the natural—that Fielding is able to represent historical space. In what follows, I will look at Fielding's construction of scenes, and at the theory of history that informs his representation of manners. Ultimately, Fielding's conception of *scene*—and of space—is a function of his theory of history: he rejects both the great man theory of history that relies on individual psychology, and the naturalistic detail of "mere topographers." For Fielding, history is best explained by the social structures and strategies that constitute manners.

I.

At what is very nearly the precise textual center of *The History of Tom Jones* (Book 9, chap. 2), Jones and the Man of the Hill view the prospect from "Mazard-Hill," a fictitious peak of the Malverns. Rather than admiring "one of the most noble prospects in the World"—which Fielding coyly declines to describe—Jones is instead "endeavouring to trace out [his] own Journey hither." By omitting a description, Fielding foregrounds the responses of Jones and the Man of the Hill to the prospect. The Man of the Hill, who has seen the "wondrous Variety of Prospects" in Europe and its "Beasts, Birds, Fishes, Insects, and Vegetables," but almost nothing of its cultures and people, is interested only in the prospect itself, and indeed will shortly show his indifference to the screams of Mrs. Waters. Jones, on the other hand, invests the prospect with personal meaning by reading his own history in the landscape and measuring his distance from Sophia. By responding instantly to Mrs. Waters's screams, he

"While it is not altogether clear whether Tom is a more moral character at the end of the novel . . . he is certainly more experienced and better able to thrive."

gives priority to social space over natural or psychological space, whereas the Man of the Hill, though armed with a gun, observes the struggle with the dispassionate interest of a natural historian. What becomes clear is that while the two share a physical location, and, to a considerable extent, occupy similar social positions, they inhabit wholly different kinds of space.

The prospect from Mazard-Hill merges three kinds of history: the novel itself as a history; Jones's personal history; and, through the Man of the Hill's recital of his part in Monmouth's rebellion, the history of the Stuarts leading to the 1745 rebellion. It is a particularly revealing example of Fielding's representation of space. Despite the "noble prospect," the scene follows his typical construction—it is short on description, contains only significant characters, and is shaped primarily by the attitudes and actions of those characters. Such a scenic economy is by no means unique to Fielding—the very solid walls of *Clarissa's* rooms are not shaped by the density of Richardson's descriptions, but by Clarissa's fears, by the oppression of Lovelace and her parents, and by the very limited possibilities for free action possessed by a minor female. What is unique to Fielding is his play with the possibilities of representing space through his own self-conscious theatricality. For example, he opens the prospect scene with a parody of heroic landscape description:

> *Aurora* now first opened her Casement, *anglicè*, the Day began to break, when *Jones* walked forth in Company with the Stranger, and mounted *Mazard-Hill*; of which they had no sooner gained the Summit, than one of the most noble Prospects in the World presented itself to their View, and which we would likewise present to the Reader; but for two Reasons. *First*, We despair of making those who have seen this Prospect, admire our Description. *Secondly*, We very much doubt whether those, who have not seen it, would understand it.

While not as dramatic a reminder of the difference between representation and reality as his mock concern about "how to get thee down without breaking thy neck" after raising the reader to the height of the prospect from Allworthy's estate, Fielding's translation and apology serve a similar purpose: revealing the literary prospect as a convention.

At the same time, he suggests that the prospect itself—not just its literary representation—is a construction, and not simply an *individual* construction shaped wholly by Tom Jones or the Man of the Hill. It is, in Henri Lefebvre's terms, a *representational space*, a space with both symbolic and real dimensions that exist for more than the individual consciousness. At first, it appears curious that Fielding chooses a fictitious hill to make a point about imposing conventions on the landscape, especially as it seems, according to Martin Battestin's footnote, to be based on a real peak, the Worcestershire Beacon. Since Fielding does not hesitate to introduce other very real places like the Bell Inn into his narrative, it might be assumed that he has a purpose for disguising this one. While he may simply want to avoid too specific a location for the Man of the Hill's residence, it seems more likely that he wants to preclude the possibility that readers who *have* seen the prospect from the Worcestershire Beacon will too quickly write their own prospect, and thus miss his point.

Fielding was well aware that landscapes are mentally constructed, though he does not regard them as purely subjective. The few landscapes he describes appear to be collectively constructed, as a matter of previous convention, rather than created by an individual consciousness. The *Journal of a Voyage to Lisbon* provides a useful gloss on the prospects of *Tom Jones*. Fielding writes:

> Here we past that cliff of Dover, which makes so tremendous a figure in Shakespear, [sic] and which, whoever reads without being giddy, must according to Mr. Addison's observation, have either a very good head, or a very bad one; but, which, whoever contracts any such ideas from the sight of, must have, at least, a poetic, if not a Shakespearian genius. In truth, mountains, rivers, heroes and gods owe great part of their existence to the poets; and Greece and Italy do so plentifully abound in the former, because they furnished so glorious a number of the latter; who, while they bestowed immortality on every little hillock and blind stream left the noblest rivers and mountains in the world to share the same obscurity with the eastern and western poets, in which they are celebrated.

Poets half create not only what they see, but what their culture sees. Fielding is not simply concerned with the perception of the poet in Wordsworthian solitude, but with the shaping influence of poetry. By classing "heroes and gods" with mountains and rivers, Fielding makes landscape description into a kind of myth-making, though his comparison of "little hillock and blind stream" with "the noblest rivers and mountains in the world" suggests that landscape features possess qualities like nobility prior to being poeticized. And yet those noble rivers remain blind streams precisely because they are celebrated by poets obscured from sight. The perception of nobility, then, derives from the poets.

But Fielding was nonetheless able to gesture toward the ineffable real in his own description of natural scenes. Later in the *Voyage* he describes a sunset:

> We were entertained with a scene which as no one can behold without going to sea, so no one can form an idea of any thing equal to it on shore. We were seated on the deck, women and all, in the serenest evening that can be imagined. Not a single cloud presented itself to our view, and the sun himself was the only object which engrossed our whole attention. He did indeed set with a majesty which is incapable of description, with which while the horizon was yet blazing with glory, our eyes were called off to the opposite part to survey the moon . . . Compared to these the pageantry of theatres, or splendor of courts, are sights almost below the regard of children.

Fielding invokes the sublime by suggesting the scene is unrepresentable. And yet it is closer to what Marshall Brown has called the "urbane sublime" than the Burkean sublime. He carefully situates the conditions of observation: he is not a solitary poet, but among a group, "women and all"—when the women had been seasick, Fielding found his hours of solitude "the most disagreeable" that had ever "haunted" him. The weather is so pleasant "that even my old distemper perceived the alteration of the climate," and after weeks of waiting for a wind they have "flown" at ten knots an hour, and see a prospect of reaching Lisbon soon. Had a favorable wind not preceded, had the company been worse, had Fielding been less comfortable, the sunset would surely have been less majestic. In the passage on the cliffs of Dover, Fielding comments explicitly on the construction of landscape; in the second passage, he merely notes the coincidence of mood, circumstance, and natural setting without having to resolve whether the sunset is real. In both cases, however, the social predominates. The cliffs of Dover are not so much created by Shakespeare as by the cultural impact of Shakespeare. And Fielding is only able to experience the sunset fully among reunited company.

In *Tom Jones*, Fielding suggests that different perceptions of landscape correspond to particular groups within society, defined not so much by social rank as by sensibility. He contrasts "Taste and Imagination," which can see beauty even in "objects of far inferior note," with business travelers who simply measure abstract space:

> Not so travels the Money-meditating Tradesman, the sagacious Justice, the dignified Doctor, the warm-clad Grazier, with all the numerous Offspring of Wealth and Dulness. On they jogg, with equal Pace, through the verdant Meadows, or over the barren Health, their Horses measuring four Miles and a half *per* Hour with the utmost Exactness; the Eyes of the Beast and of his Master being alike directed forwards, and employed in contemplating the same Objects in the same manner.

"Taste and Imagination" can be taken to personify an imaginary community of sensibility typified by Lord Lyttleton (one of the models for Squire Allworthy), a community of which the family-proud but inheritance-poor Fielding could feel himself a member, but from which he could exclude a fellow "sagacious Justice."

Socioeconomic class alone, then, does not determine how Fielding's characters respond to the landscape; it is determined as well by a hierarchy of taste and judgment. Both Jones and the Man of the Hill are dispossessed country sons, exiled in the sense of being removed from their proper places, their family land. To be sure, there are important differences—the Man of the Hill is merely a younger son while Jones is a bastard; the Man of the Hill is a hermit by choice whereas Jones is only by necessity a wanderer. Yet we are clearly to see parallels: the Man of the Hill is what Jones could become; he represents, in J. Paul Hunter's words, "roads not taken, analogues in a different tone." Both are in a situation where, as Pierre Bourdieu observes of the bastard and the younger son, "minimum objective distance in social space can coincide with maximum subjective distance." Indeed, what both read in the landscape is precisely their own distance: while the Man in some sense owns the prospect from his hill, he has no living connection to it, and while Jones may trace his journey in the landscape, he reads only his distance from Sophia and Paradise Hall. But the Man of the Hill has generalized his own distance from humanity by severing humanity from the natural world. His habitual strategy is not avoidance but detachment; as a frequent traveller he has not so much been a hermit as a solitary. Echoing Defoe's *Serious Reflections of Robinson Crusoe*, the Man of the Hill claims that he "could hardly have enjoyed a more absolute

Solitude in the Deserts of the *Thebais*, than here in the midst of this populous Kingdom." Jones, on the other hand, sees his separation as merely a local rupture; he is as averse to solitude as Fielding himself.

The difference between Tom Jones's and the Man of the Hill's constructions of the world is not simply a matter of temperament or life choices. The Man of the Hill is, after all, a kind of time traveller: he says that his own "History is little better than a Blank" since the time of the Glorious Revolution, and knows nothing of subsequent public history, including both Jacobite rebellions. He is a product of another time, believing in the possibility of a fully rational world with a certainty that was becoming more tenuous in Fielding's time. He invokes the Great Chain of Being as evidence of rational order in the universe, but like the post-Houyhnhnm Gulliver, regards humanity as the one irrational link— for him "Human Nature is everywhere the same, everywhere the Object of Detestation and scorn." Both his rationalism and his misanthropy stem from the same period, the age of Locke and the Royal Society, when a more rational form of government and a scientifically ordered world seemed possible, but stymied by human failings. His misanthropy, he tells Jones, arises from the contrast between his hopes for humanity and his observations of human beings. Indeed, he claims his solitude is a result of "great philanthropy":

> For however it may seem a Paradox, or even a Contradiction, certain it is that great Philanthropy chiefly inclines us to avoid and detest Mankind; not on Account so much of their private and selfish Vices, but for those of a relative Kind; such as Envy, Malice, Treachery, Cruelty, with every other Species of Malevolence.

Unlike Thwackum and Square, the Mail of the Hill is well versed in both philosophy and scripture, but the mixture has not produced the balance Fielding thought those characters lacked. His failure to act when Mrs. Waters screams stems not so much from hypocrisy or quietism as from a kind of paralysis brought on by contradiction.

When the Man of the Hill refuses to be "imposed upon to credit so foolish a Tale" as Jones's report of the Jacobite rebellions, Fielding seems to be using him as a conventional wanderer from afar to sharpen the anti-Jacobite satire. But the Man of the Hill's misanthropy is too particular for a stock character. Personal vices do not trouble him, but vices "of a relative Kind" do, a distinction which suggests a kind of extreme individualism for which only active malevolence toward others is vicious. Yet in his own story, the two kinds of vice are in-

extricably entwined. His education is marked by extremes; he is either completely withdrawn in study or completely abandoned to personal vices that lead to relative vices like theft. No doubt Fielding has in mind here a moral lesson in moderation, and yet it is worth pursuing the Man's own explanation and excuses. He speaks, for example, of the "Contagion" that he avoids by living alone, and clearly regards Oxford and London, the sites of his own crimes, as places of disease. While he does not explicitly blame others, like his corrupt friend Sir George Gresham, for his failings, neither does he see them as arising from himself, and his detestation of human nature reflects this inverted causality. But he has in fact never lived *in* the world, he has only found alternate modes of self-absorption. His inability to negotiate social space has left him in an abstract space of *things*—indeed, he has no name but the Man *of the Hill*.

During the Man of the Hill episode Partridge constructs the world in yet another way, and through him Fielding invokes an even earlier historical period. Partridge is the only Jacobite we really see in *Tom Jones* (Squire Western, despite toasting the "King over the Water," is more properly an anti-Hanoverian than a Jacobite rebel, not willing, like Partridge, to join the rebellion), and what distinguishes him is his superstitiousness and credulity in interpreting events. He suspects witchcraft from the beginning, interrupts the Man of the Hill's life history twice with supernatural stories, and finally runs from the hill in fear. While representing Jacobites as superstitious was commonplace, Fielding explores Partridge's superstition at greater depth than might be expected. Partridge is associated not just with the Stuarts, but specifically with James I: when Partridge fears that the Man of the Hill's servant is a witch, Fielding observes that "if this Woman had lived in the Reign of *James* the First, her Appearance alone would have hanged her, almost without any Evidence." By implication, Partridge's superstition places him in that earlier epoch. If the Man of the Hill sees a landscape in which people are insignificant, and Jones a landscape only made significant by the people in it, Partridge sees a world permeated with spirits. Paradoxically, the material is for him evidence of the spiritual: he asserts that a story about the devil carrying off an adulterer must be true because "I've seen the very house where it was done," as if the reality of the setting were proof of the event. Partridge is an empiricist of sorts; when he hears of the Man of the Hill's "slight wound" during Monmouth's rebellion, he wants to know where the wound was. But his relationship to visible objects is different from the Man of the Hill's. His fixing on an insignificant detail like the location of the wound emphasizes his inability to understand narrative, to understand a history (indeed, he sleeps through much of the Man's story). Partridge's understanding of the world is essentially emblematic; what he sees in the wound and the house is not physical evidence but signs and portents. Confusion in telling and understanding narratives is a typical class marker throughout eighteenth-century literature, but Partridge's particular confusion is a historical marker as well.

We have, then, not simply three ways of constructing the world, but three sedimented layers of history. Partridge's superstition is not simply the result of ignorance—however imperfect his Latin, he does possess some education—but of an outlook constructed in an earlier period. The Man of the Hill dates from a time when a rational world might have looked more possible than it does for Fielding in 1745. Whether Jones represents a thoroughly modern individual whose space is historical is not yet clear, but before answering that question, and analyzing Jones's encounter with another time traveler, the King of the Gypsies, it will be helpful to look more closely at Fielding's use of space and his theory of history. . . .

IV.

Fielding's two interpolated episodes—the visit to the Gypsy camp and to the Man of the Hill— have close parallels. Both precede examples of Jones's imprudence—the incidents at Upton and his entanglement with Lady Bellaston—but also, more immediately, incidents of his benevolence— the rescue of Mrs. Waters and his assistance to the would-be thief. Both occur when Jones and Partridge are lost, and both are marked, through Partridge's fear, by a sense of the uncanny; just as the light from the Man of the Hill's house had seemed to him supernatural, Partridge sees the light of the gypsy camp as a certain sign of "Ghosts or Witches." In the first episode, Fielding associates superstitious fear with the reign of James I, and in the second reminds us again that such superstition belongs to the past:

> Had this History been writ in the Days of Superstition, I should have had too much Compassion for the Reader to have left him so long in Suspense, whether *Beelzebub* or *Satan* was about actually to appear in Person, with all his Hellish Retinue; but as these Doctrines are at present very unfortunate, and have but few if any Believers, I have not been much aware of conveying any such Terrors. To say Truth, the whole Furniture of the infernal Regions hath long been ap-

propriated by the Managers of Playhouses, who seem lately to have lain them by as Rubbish, capable only of affecting the Upper Gallery; a Place in which few of our Readers ever sit.

That such theatrics do continue to affect the Upper Gallery is clear from Partridge's subsequent reaction to a staging of *Hamlet*, when he believes the ghost is real. Fielding's digression on superstition before introducing the gypsies does more than mock the foolishness of the past, or of such survivals as Partridge. It suggests that manners change unevenly, moving from society in general to a few holdouts in the upper gallery. Before introducing another kind of survival, then, Fielding is at considerable pains to remind us of history's sedimentation.

Peter Carlton has observed that "the utopian nature of the gypsy Kingdom is matched by its geographical setting: Jones and Partridge . . . stumble across the gypsy camp in the middle of nowhere." Indeed, Jones and Partridge seem to cross a threshold by entering the camp, entering another kind of space, which Fielding's delaying digression emphasizes. But while Fielding's gypsies are without a home, they are not without a history; he traces their lineage to Egypt. As Battestin has shown, Fielding's use of Egyptian history, his presentation of a rogue society as utopian, and even his comparison of Egyptian absolutism to Jacobitism have analogues among his contemporaries. But Fielding's choice of a gypsy camp in particular, given the theme of homelessness and exile throughout the work, must surely have a larger purpose than a conventional inversion of social norms.

Fielding's Gypsy King would seem to be the epitome of wise governance. He judges Partridge not by his act—adultery—but by the circumstances of the act—the husband's apparent desire to trick Partridge into paying amends. And yet, having opened up the possibility of an ideal absolute monarchy, Fielding appears anxious to close it down. First, in an uncharacteristically hortatory tone, he suggests that only "two or three" monarchs have ever had sufficient moderation, wisdom, and goodness to rule absolutely, and traces the origin of *jus divinum* to the "original Grant to the Prince of Darkness." Then, as if realizing that the apparent success of the gypsy monarchy for "a tousand or two tousand Year" contradicts his argument, he relegates the gypsy utopia to nowhere because the gypsies differ in a "material respect":

> Nor can the Example of the Gypsies, tho' possibly they may have long been happy under this Form of Government, be here urged; since we must remember the very material Respect in which they differ from

all other People, and to which perhaps this their Happiness is entirely owing, namely, that they have no false Honours among them; and that they look on Shame as the most grievous Punishment in the World.

In the first instance, Fielding's tone may derive from his model, a sermon by Bishop Hoadly. In the second instance, however, Fielding reverts to irony and his usual form of causality. Whereas Hoadly's argument locates the problem of *jus divinum* in the corruptibility of the Great Man who becomes a tyrant, Fielding's afterthought attributes it to "false Honours" in general. The "material Respect" in which the gypsies differ, then, is largely a question of *manners*. But Fielding's apparent discomfort with giving the gypsy utopia any real historical existence is evident in his need to provide two different—and not entirely consonant—arguments against absolutism. He does not appear to be fully in control of his materials.

But Fielding's discomfort may arise from more than the spectre of absolutism. If Fielding's "useful and uncommon doctrine" is the necessity of judging a *situation*, then the Gypsy King would seem to have applied it in his judgment of Partridge. That kind of judgment, perhaps, seems unattainable to him; it is certainly questionable whether Tom Jones has attained that level. Fielding's ambiguous use of the word "prudence" may reflect his ambivalence about the real possibilities of true prudence and judgment, as would his coyness in enunciating the doctrine. Prudence and judgment seem to be limited by the existing state of *manners*; thus he argues that the Gypsy King's perfection is owing to the absence of "false Honours" and the efficacy of "Shame." The "nowhere" of the Gypsy utopia is essentially outside of historical space; the Gypsy King has no need of calculating the effects of changing manners. But Prudence for Tom Jones must be both the art of life and the art of thriving because his actions take place within real and changing historical spaces.

While it is not altogether clear whether Tom is a more moral character at the end of the novel than when he first falls in love with Sophia, and this has been the subject of much critical debate, he is certainly more experienced and better able to thrive. He is now a fully modern individual—and he had not been one on Mazard-Hill—precisely because he now has a competent understanding of manners and the space of modernity. His "feel for the game" has improved to the point that, rather than being subject to Blifil's machinations, he is ultimately able—though not without setbacks—to manipulate the outcome of Nightingale's romance

with Nancy, and to turn the tables on Lady Bellaston. But his moral improvement we have only on self-report. He informs Allworthy near the end of the work that his "Punishment hath not been thrown away upon me" and that he will make it "the whole Business of my future Life to deserve that Happiness you now bestow on me." But this declaration bears a striking resemblance to earlier repentances, both to Allworthy and to Sophia. It suggests no remarkable insight into his own actions; his basic moral outlook is little altered from the time that he attempted to protect Black George for illegally shooting a partridge. He remains essentially good hearted, only somewhat less impetuous.

But his manners have changed. He has gained, in Fielding's terms, experience, and if he has also gained prudence, it is as a result of becoming acquainted with the manners of others. His teachers as a youth were Square and Thwackum, and the also good hearted but easily manipulated Allworthy, and if his education was limited, it was not so much by Square and Thwackum's hypocrisy, or even by their one-sidedness toward religion or philosophy, but instead by their excessive theoretical bias. Even Allworthy is unable to give him the lessons of experience, since Allworthy seems not to have learned them himself. Tom's worldly teachers then, are characters like Partridge and Lady Bellaston, who teach him how to negotiate unfamiliar territory. As a child, for example, his failure to observe polite deference had gotten him into trouble, but Lady Bellaston teaches him how to dissemble politely. The Man of the Hill and the Gypsy King teach him largely negative lessons—they teach him what is not possible in the modern world. However, such moral lessons are not inconsistent with a view of morality that is less concerned with individual actions than with the larger chain of circumstances surrounding social interactions. Jones's moral education, then, consists not simply in learning *how* to act, but to recognize *where he is acting*.

Source: George A. Drake, "Historical Space in the 'History of': Between Public and Private in *Tom Jones*," in *ELH*, Vol. 66, No. 3, Fall 1999, pp. 707–37.

Douglas Brooks-Davies

In the following essay, Brooks-Davies discusses the intersections of the character of Tom Jones, the political context of the work, and the development of the novel by Fielding.

The History of Tom Jones, A Foundling is generally acclaimed as Henry Fielding's masterpiece in its combination of dazzlingly virtuoso plot

(Coleridge described it as one of "the three most perfect ever planned"), comic range, irony, variety of moods, and emotional and psychological intensity. It was Fielding's third major novel, born of mature reconsideration of the formula of the "comic epic poem in prose" which he had pioneered in *Joseph Andrews* and of deeply disturbing experiences, both public and domestic. The public experience was the threat to the Hanoverian monarchy and the constitution that it represented by the Jacobite rebellion of 1745; the domestic one was the death of his wife, Charlotte, whom he remembers explicitly in the opening chapter of Book 13 and upon whom the character of the novel's heroine, Sophia Western, is loosely based.

Brilliant intricacy of plot is matched in *Tom Jones* by corresponding intricacy of formal structure, for Fielding still believed, along with such conservative contemporaries as Pope, in the symbolic value of literary structure as a model of providential order (a notion inherited from Renaissance neo-Platonism). Its 18 books—the total alludes to the number of books in the first edition of Archbishop Fénelon's influential prose epic *Télémaque* (1699), a moralised "continuation" of Homer's *Odyssey*, and thus marks Fielding's novel, too, as a journey novel in the Odysseyan tradition—are arranged in a system of complex symmetries in accordance with ancient epic practice: three sets of six books deal respectively with Tom's upbringing in the country and expulsion by his Uncle Allworthy; his journey to London; and his experiences in London and return home. Within this broad symmetrical array the reader is led to detect further symmetries: the first and last books both have 13 chapters, and there are explicit cross-references between them; the most complicated (and celebrated) episode in the novel in which all the travellers' paths cross, that at the Upton inn, occupies the centre of the novel (Books 9 and 10); interpolated stories correspond to each other exactly: the Man of the Hill's long tale in Book 8 (the second book of the central section of six books) is answered by Mrs. Fitzpatrick's in Book 11 (second from the end of the central block); this block opens with the Quaker's tale of his daughter (Book 7, chapter 10) and concludes with the thematically relevant puppet show (Book 12, chapter 5).

Such elaborateness marks a refinement on the structural complexities of *Joseph Andrews* and *Jonathan Wild*; but whereas in *Joseph Andrews* especially structure had obviously reinforced the work's comic affirmation of an essentially benevolent universe, in *Tom Jones* it seems, in its hectic

> " Brilliant intricacy of plot is matched in *Tom Jones* by corresponding intricacy of formal structure, for Fielding still believed, along with such conservative contemporaries as Pope, in the symbolic value of literary structure as a model of providential order (a notion inherited from Renaissance neo-Platonism)."

over-determinateness, to be almost as mocking as the symmetries and coincidences of a late Hardy novel. For it is a curiously dark and anxious work. Unlike any other novel of its century which claims to be about lost, foundling, or wandering heroes, it explores loss and displacement in an almost existential way. Tom's foundling status isn't just a plot *motif* but, rather, the *meaning* of the novel; and it isn't merely a device for exploring human benevolence (or lack of it) in relation to the underprivileged (something Fielding was deeply committed to): it is, instead, a way into areas of considerable psychological complexity. For one thing, the novel generates a double for Tom in the form of the legitimate child Blifil, whose father soon dies and who is, in fact, Tom's half-brother. He is born in Book 2 and spends the rest of the novel blighting Tom's life. The question the novel raises is, who (or what), exactly, *is* Blifil? Is he metaphysical evil? Is he a psychological double for Tom? For it is clear that he is no mere rogue, and the prefatory essays to each of the novel's books in which Fielding discusses his theory and practice of writing are designed to implicate us as readers in the varieties of the novel's self-questioning.

Then again, Tom is offered various reputed and symbolic fathers and mothers (Allworthy himself, Partridge, Jenny Jones, Lady Bellaston), so that the question the novel raises seems to be not so much who are (or were) Tom's parents? but, rather, what is the significance of parents for the child's sense of identity? The incest motif—Tom jumps into bed at Upton with Jenny Jones (now known as Jenny Waters) and is later told that he has made love to his own mother—suggests, as do several plot parallels, that we are in the territory of Sophocles's *Oedipus*: like Sophocles, Fielding suggests that there is some necessary relationship between paternal absence and the discovery of maternal identity through sexual knowledge.

The profundity of the novel's questioning of the foundling's status (its working title had been simply *The Foundling*) is evident even from names. Blifil is known by his father's surname: he has nominal legitimacy but is morally illegitimate. Tom is always known by his supposed mother's surname, Jones. But in fact his mother was Bridget Allworthy, and his father was a passing visitor called Will Summer. His is a haunting name, but he, described in a couple of sentences only, turns out to be the non-discovery of the book. For it is the psychological journey to the parent (or so this text tells us) that is more important than parental identity itself. And why should Tom retain his mother's name? At the very least, this fact questions the status of inherited patronymics.

And it is here that the psychological plot implicates political discourse. For while Tom quests for his parents, Bonny Prince Charlie has invaded and the constitutional monarchy is threatened. Tom enlists on the side of the Hanoverians; his companion Partridge is a Jacobite, believing firmly in the divine right of the ejected Stuarts. The constitutional monarch is a benevolent father; the Stuarts, accused of tyranny by their opponents, regarded themselves as the fathers of their country. Tom's quest for his father raises questions about our perception and acceptance of kingship in the realm. The Man of the Hill irrupts into the action in Books 8 and 9 to tell of the expulsion of James II in 1688 and to draw the parallel with the invasion of 1745.

Tom's persecution and quest are paralleled by Sophia Western's. She, daughter of Allworthy's Jacobite neighbour Squire Western, is intended for Blifil but loves Tom. Imprisoned by her father (Fielding is influenced here by Richardson's monumental text of female persecution, *Clarissa*, 1747–48), she escapes, and their journeys shadow each other until, finally, misunderstandings cleared away, they marry. The significance of her name (Sophia = Wisdom in Greek) is relevant but not primary; for as her cousin and travelling companion Harriet Fitzpatrick reveals in her autobiographical

tale in Book 11, woman's (and women's) history is to a large extent a story of domestic persecution, oppression, violence, and loneliness. Its message is, do not marry if you wish to remain in control of your destiny. Her tale, too, reveals parallels between domestic and constitutional politics. Sophia's part of *Tom Jones* conveys clear signals of female freedom: Tom cannot marry her until he recognises the woman's right to freedom from male hegemony; the Stuarts cannot reinherit the realm because they refused to negotiate their absolutist hegemony. It is in its working out of such perceptions that *Tom Jones*'s brilliance lies.

Source: Douglas Brooks-Davies, "*Tom Jones*: Novel by Henry Fielding, 1749," in *Reference Guide to English Literature*, 2d ed., edited by D. L. Kirkpatrick, Vol. 3, St. James Press, 1991, pp. 1893–94.

Charles A. Knight

In the following essay, Knight looks at the structure of Fielding's Tom Jones.

Mingled admiration and bewilderment at the plot of *Tom Jones* is a recurrent motif in the history of criticism on that novel, and one returns from reading each critical essay to the novel itself with a sense that the insights one has gathered, however valuable, remain inadequate to the rich texture that the novel possesses. Perhaps one of the criteria of a masterpiece is its refusal to be pinned down by any critical formulation of it, yet that same sense of wonder and joy at the work itself leads critics again to attempt to account for their perception of its richness and coherence. A similar motif in *Tom Jones* criticism has been complaint at precisely the failure, despite numerous and notable attempts, to explain the role of the plot in unifying the novel. At times the blame for this has been thrown on Fielding himself, at times on his critics. Even those who share Coleridge's famous view of the perfection of plot in *Tom Jones* have either dismissed it with a mechanical nod to its excellence or have tended to find it, in one way or another, insignificant.

The critique is variously articulated: for some the plot seems contrived and mechanical; the events fall into place too neatly, and a balanced sense of realism is lost. Thus David Goldknopf has recently claimed that the digressive elements of the novel and the author's intervening role as a commentator "as a *systematic procedure* for upgrading the applicability and stature of his work, . . . signalize his failure to integrate intelligence and imagination." Similarly, Irvin Ehrenpreis suggests that such repeated appearances as those of Sophia's pocketbook and muff, or the attorney Dowling "imply that the main line of action has insufficient energy of its own to contain the numerous episodes of the story." Because of the symmetrical structure of the book, Ehrenpreis suggests, "one stops expecting development and tries to feel satisfied with a line of action that does not, in a cause and effect sense, lead anywhere." Ehrenpreis attempts to account for the plot by suggesting that it be regarded not in terms of "physical deeds" but in terms of "insight." "As in *Clarissa*, the dramatic moments in *Tom Jones* are moments of sudden understanding." The revelation of Tom's ancestry is, of course, the culmination of this process. I find this argument unconvincing, for unlike *Clarissa*, *Tom Jones* does not work through internal dramatization or psychological analysis of discovery, and the process of discovery itself merely throws us back to the patterns of coincidence, parallel, and symmetry that result in the discovery. Even Ehrenpreis finally suggests that "one can properly handle the complete design of *Tom Jones* as a fable illustrating the author's views of hypocrisy and candour, malice and benevolence." Plot, in *Tom Jones*, is not, then, Goldknopf and Ehrenpreis imply, satisfying in itself, but sustained by the lively mind and healthy morals of the author. Robert Alter, to cite another critic who writes incisively about Fielding, sees "virtually all of the action and dialogue, as well as the authorial comment" as referring to "one or another of a set of interrelated moral themes." Here again, the appreciation of plot, despite Alter's excellent discussion of the novel's structure, seems basically to come through an escape from the plot itself—not, in this case, through projecting the plot upon a person (the narrator) but through abstracting from it its thematic content and explaining it in terms of these abstractions. Though it would be inaccurate to deny the importance of theme in *Tom Jones*, such an explanation of plot does not seem entirely to answer the charge that it is too circumscribed, too confined to action or manners, too intent, to use Dr. Johnson's analogy, on showing us the brilliance of the dial rather than the true springs and inner workings of the watch itself. "Perfect for what," Ian Watt asks of the plot, and answers, "Not, certainly, for the exploration of character and personal relations, since ... the emphasis falls on the author's skillfully contrived revelation of an external and deterministic scheme."

This essay is an attempt to suggest that a way of accounting for the coherence of *Tom Jones*, particularly in the complex middle or "journey" books of the novel, lies in seeing and responding to mul-

tiple structures, distinguishable in their principles of organization, rather than viewing the novel through an Aristotelian concept of action, reading the novel in terms of a single concept of plot, or explaining it in terms of a moral view so large that, however well it may serve an abstract consideration of the novel, it fails to serve our specific sense of the novel itself.

In considering structure in *Tom Jones*, I shall be concerned primarily with the arrangement of events, rather than with such aspects as the narrator's role, verbal structures, and irony, aspects which can in themselves be considered intrinsic to structure but which have been the subjects of much previous study. In developing the notion of multiple structures in the arrangement of events and their significance for the perception of *Tom Jones*, it will be necessary to review some aspects of the structure of the first and last sections of the novel and then to concentrate in more detail on the middle section. I recognize that this survey covers some territory that has been explored, but some important elements of structure have been overlooked, others inadequately emphasized, and my conclusions depend upon what can be uncovered.

I

At the outset Fielding describes the clear structure of the novel in terms of basic locale and its moral implications: the novel, Fielding claims, is based on a Horatian country-city antithesis, with the values of wholesomeness and honesty seated in Somerset, in contrast to the "French and Italian seasoning of affectation and vice which courts and cities afford." But the context for this moral categorization lies in the narrator's concern for human nature as his subject (it is human nature itself which is thus "dressed" by the setting) and in his emphasis on providing a description of the relation of his subject to the interests of his reader. He thus leaves out of his "Bill of Fare" the central third of his novel, the journey from Somerset to London. His description itself implies the more static nature of the beginning and end of the novel, and this is, in fact, the kind of structure we find—a structure which analyzes a specific environment, like a microcosm, in terms of its salient moral characteristics.

Yet one of the major jokes of Fielding's initial description is that its antithesis is really not true. Affectation and vice are no more a characteristic of the town than of the country, and natural goodness is no more easily discovered by a country justice than a city magistrate. Fielding thus compares two life-styles in order to reveal their basic unity, and it is ironically in the city rather than the country that the ultimate discoveries of the novel take place.

Fielding's basic technique of structure is also similar in the first and last thirds of the novel. Fielding develops his characters, as most critics have empasized, through contrast—Jones against Nightingale, Jones against Blifil; Sophia and Lady Bellaston, Sophia and Molly Seagrim; Western and Nightingale's father, Western and Allworthy. The list can be prodigiously extended, but Fielding's method of comparison is more complicated than this. His primary comparisons are not directly between characters so much as between ideas of or attitudes towards a pair of characters in the mind of a third who must work out his relation to them both. Thus Tom's great choice in the first third of the novel, a choice that perhaps does more to determine his identity and station than any further choice, is between Molly and Sophia, while Allworthy's choice is between Jones and Blifil. And in the last section, Sophia, who loves and fears she cannot have Tom, is rescued from Lord Fellamar only to be subjected to Blifil (and her father, who rescues her from Fellamar, continues to reject him for reasons of political prejudice rather than parental solicitude). Such comparisons and their implicit value thus become dramatized in terms of choice, though there are other specific kinds of comparison, such as that between Old Nightingale and Western, which do not derive meaning primarily from dramatic choice so much as from large parallel movements of action. One of the major characteristics of this device of structure is that it is self-extending: the reader becomes aware of its importance as a dominant organizing device of the novel and thus begins to read character and incident in terms of comparison. As he does so, the reader becomes himself an organizer of the plot of the novel. The importance of Fielding's "bill of fare" approach becomes evident, for the relationship between the reader and the material becomes woven into the structure of the novel as a unifying device.

In the first and last sections of the novel, Fielding develops his larger contrasts and his causal plot through the judicious introduction of character. Thus in the first book he introduces Allworthy's household, moving towards the marriage of Bridget and Captain Blifil, which he develops further in the second. In book III he develops the contrast between Tom and Blifil, as well as the secondary contrast between Thwackum and Square. Book IV begins with the introduction of Sophia and continues with the contrasting introduction of Molly Sea-

grim. Tom's choice between the two is resolved in book V, but book VI begins with the introduction of Mrs. Western, whose presence complicates the relationship between Sophia and Jones. The introduction of these characters is an element of the author's manipulation of the action, but the plot of the novel develops naurally in relation to their appearance.

The last third of the novel follows a similar pattern, in which the arrival of characters in London is a central organizing element. Tom arrives at the beginning of book XIII, and his attempts to deal with Mrs. Fitzpatrick and, through her, to find Sophia, put him in touch with Lady Bellaston, while at the same time his friendship with Nightingale and the Millers develops. The movement of this plot, through Tom's chance meeting with Sophia and Lady Bellaston's jealousy of her, is natural until Chapter 5 of Book XV, when Lord Fellamar's attempts upon Sophia are interrupted by the sudden introduction of Western, whose presence is explained, in terms of the plot which has developed in London, in the following chapter. Western's arrival reshapes the plot (as, to a lesser degree, does the arrival of his sister in Book XVI), but the action intensifies towards the apparent ruin of Jones as, in book XVI, Blifil and Allworthy arrive. By Book XVII, all the characters who know something of Tom's history are in London, and the plot moves to unravel his past. Thus the last books of the novel are based on the comic entanglement of a plot whose essential features are changed in their basic relation to one another by the arrival of further important characters. To a far greater degree than in the first section, the natural development of the plot through entrances is complicated by Fielding's use of coincidence in resolving the novel. But in this context, coincidence is itself appropriate and revealing, for each of the characters brings to his role at a given time in the course of the novel everything we know (and much we do not know) about him and his relation to Jones. Thus the activity of the reader in making connections, observing points of comparison, and drawing conclusions, is paralleled by the activity of the narrator in bringing his plot to a conclusion, and both stand as moral observers of the comic scene.

If the beginning and end of the novel are thus tightly organized in clear and natural ways, the same cannot be so immediately said for the middle. Instead of analyzing the moral implications of a static environment which connotes, however deceptively, a definite meaning, the scene shifts, both in time and place. While in the rest of the novel, the major events move clearly from the previous events, from the introduction of characters, and from the relationships between them, the middle third of the novel seems anecdotal and digressive. Events are not so clearly related to each other. It seems to make no difference that Tom meets the soldiers after his meeting with the Quaker rather than before. Moreover, comparisons of the sort that, earlier or later in the novel, are resplendent with potential meaning seem on the surface to be specious. Thus the reader can do little with much of the material, for its derivation from causal relations in plot or from the thematic development of character is unclear—and anyway, who really cares about the Quaker, or Northerton, or the much discussed Man of the Hill? They appear and disappear without doing much more than revealing Jones as a reactor to external events and advancing him appropriately further towards London. The problem of explaining coherence in *Tom Jones* becomes largely, then, the problem of explaining structure in books VII through XII.

II

In terms of Fielding's initial explanation of the novel, the middle third clearly acts, as most critics have noted, as a bridge between the Somerset and London scenes. The road section is loaded with comic incidents involving mistaken identity—scenes which, though not clearly related to one another, develop the novel's early concern for the perception of virtue and the relation between virtue and prudence. Indeed, they provide an expansion of this thematic material, for instead of the limited world of Somersetshire, Tom is perceived by and in turn perceives a number of quite different characters. As the scope of his perception and judgment widens, Tom's experience broadens and his character develops. Thus, in fact, the development of comparable events tends to move from Tom's Somersetshire experience towards anticipation of London. This arch-like structure itself focuses, as Digeon first noted, on the Inn at Upton as its keystone, the central event of the middle books which provides the "turn" given to the plot of the novel.

The analogy of an arch is both important and exact as a description of the middle books, for it implies several dimensions of movement that proceed simultaneously to arrive at a point that is different in distance but similar in height. In order to perceive more clearly the function of different structures in the middle third of *Tom Jones*, it is necessary to examine them separately within the general notion of this archlike structure.

Most obviously, perhaps, the structure of the middle books is geographically organized. We are aware at all times that the characters are "on the road," and both their actual and intended geographical positions are an index to their status as characters. But looked at more immediately, the geographical movement of the central books is not as orderly as the "arch" image implies. Tom's initial intention on leaving Allworthy's is to go to sea but his intention is thwarted by the ignorance of his guide, who takes him away from, rather than towards Bristol. Tom then meets the company of soldiers and changes his plans, thus setting his course more clearly on land but not towards London. He thus arrives at Gloucester and then at Upton. From Upton on, his purpose becomes clear: he sets forth "in quest of his lovely Sophia, whom he now resolved never to abandon the pursuit of." Sophia's arrival at Upton is, of course, the result of her determination to follow Jones. The geographical progression of the middle books thus depends on a basic definition of purpose in the travelers, and as the motives of each in approaching London become clearer, the resultant adventures in London begin to take shape. Thus the path to London represents, both internally and externally, a linear movement in the novel, from one point to another. The geographical movement of the novel is, then, a close analogue to the causal development of the plot (though distinguishable from it) and tends to focus, from among the complex of long-range and hidden relations, on the linear element of causality, in which the immediate cause leads to certain actions which themselves cause still further effects.

But once this linear emphasis is recognized, it becomes apparent that it cannot account for many of the events of the middle books. Certainly one can trace various links leading from the novel's central chain of events and essential to it, but there are also events, particularly in Book XII, that do not fit into a causal pattern, even the long-range pattern that is resolved at the end of the novel, but which gather meaning from other kinds of pattern governing the novel.

The linear progression—both geographical and causal—is nonetheless so dominant a feature of the middle books that it tends to veil the fact that the temporal progression of the novel and the focus of its point of view are not linear, not moving in a continuous way towards a specific point. Thus the first two chapters of Book VII (after the introductory chapter) focus on Tom's predicament after leaving Allworthy's, while the next seven chapters turn to Sophia and bring her to the point of leaving her

What Do I Read Next?

- *Pamela* (1740), by Samuel Richardson, is said to have been the first best-selling novel in history. It is the story of a virtuous servant girl and her valiant efforts to escape the relentless advances of her employer. The story is told through the girl's letters. Fielding thought the novel was highly overrated, and his first two novels were parodies of it.

- *Shamela* (1741) is the first of Fielding's parodies of *Pamela*. Fielding, too, structured his story as a series of letters, but his heroine, far from being an innocent, is lusty and manipulative.

- *Joseph Andrews* (1742) is another, more ambitious, parody of *Pamela*. This time, Fielding has changed the protagonist to a male servant—the brother of Pamela—and the predatory employer is Lady Booby. This novel is considered the forerunner of *Tom Jones*.

- *Don Quixote de la Mancha*, by Miguel de Cervantes Saavedra, was first published in Spanish in two parts in 1605 and 1615 and in English in 1612 and 1620. The hilarious tale is one of the most loved novels of all time. *Tom Jones* shares some of its picaresque elements, and its plot centered on a symbolic journey.

- *Moll Flanders* (1722), another picaresque novel, was written by Daniel Defoe, who, along with Fielding, is considered one of the important originators of the English novel. Defoe's novel, too, is the story of a character who grows up without parents. Defoe's Moll Flanders, though, is handed very different circumstances than is Tom Jones and takes a very different route in life.

- *Vanity Fair*, by William Makepeace Thackeray, was published almost exactly one hundred years after *Tom Jones*, in 1848. Thackeray's classic novel deals with some of the same issues and human vices as Fielding's—vanity and hypocrisy, especially as they are encouraged by society—but his characters are more reprehensible and his novel is darker, though far from humorless.

- *Twentieth-Century Interpretations of "Tom Jones"* (1968), edited by Martin Battestin, is a collection of essays by modern critics who have differing views of the novel.

---

father's. The story then takes up Jones's journey and stays with him. Yet there are frequent interpolations: the story of the Lieutenant in VII, xii; the mutual self-revelations of Jones and Partridge in VIII, v and vi; the story of the Man of the Hill in VIII, xi–xv; and the account of how Mrs. Waters came to be attacked by Northerton in XI, vii. After the scene at the Upton Inn (during which Jones is seldom the center of revelation), the narrative moves backward in time for a summary of the events bringing Sophia to Upton (X, viii–ix), and the narrative then stays with Sophia through Book XI and the interpolated story of Mrs. Fitzpatrick. After XII, ii, where Western goes hunting, the story again turns to Jones and brings him to London. The general narrative movement of the central books is not, then, progressive and linear but follows instead a balanced pattern, alternating from Sophia to Tom and

set around the Upton scene. This pattern is itself mingled not only with the progressive pattern of causation and geography but also with the reversal of roles that takes place at Upton. Before Upton, Sophia was the pursuer of Tom, but after she leaves the inn, he becomes her pursuer, and the nature of the switch is ironically reinforced by Western's insistence on hunting (an example, in the Upton section, of imagistic patterns emerging onto the level of plot—further examples include the dinner of Tom and Mrs. Waters, as well as Sophia's leaving of her muff on Tom's bed). The overwhelming patterns of what I would call external symmetry (that is, symmetry of events) organized around the Upton scenes has been well summarized by other critics. It is important, in an analysis of multiple structures, to emphasize that mathematically there are two such patterns of symmetry. The book is divided into halves by the Upton section and into thirds according to geographical locale, and symmetrical repetition gains complexity by its appearance within these two systems. But the relation of such external symmetry to patterns in the handling of time and in the use of both Sophia and Tom as centers of revelation has not, I think, been sufficiently noted.

Such critics as Dorothy Van Ghent and V. S. Pritchett have made much of Fielding's use of summary and his ability to achieve dramatic immediacy of scene. In that respect the narrative of the middle books provides brilliant focus on the Upton scene. In Book VII, for example, the reader is sufficiently informed of Sophia's intentions to understand her sudden appearance at Upton, and at the end of Book X Fielding adds information from the past, in two summary chapters, which puts in perspective her behavior at Upton and focuses on her progress, the subject of Book XI.

The relation of the past to the present is perhaps the major comic feature of the scene at Upton. Jones is involved in an affair of the present when his real love emerges from the past (a past recent in time but remote in terms of events). The situation is complicated by the comic mistakes of Mr. Fitzpatrick and Squire Western, and these lead coincidentally to the revelation to Sophia of still another figure from her own past, Mrs. Fitzpatrick. But these interrelationships of past and present are themselves ironic in terms of later revelation—Partridge's misapprehension that Mrs. Waters, or Jenny Jones, is Tom's mother, and the final unravelling of Tom's birth. The past forms an almost inexhaustible pattern, enveloping the characters and their actions, and at the inside of this Chinese box arrangement of discovery rests Tom's true heritage. Thus one general element of the symmetry of the novel is its progressive movement both forward and backward in time. But this balancing of past and present rests upon a rather different sense of movement than a causal sequence of events, for behind these events rest their analogues in the past, as well as their hidden causes, and these reveal, once they are known, the true significance of the present. But these analogues are not the only kind of comparison focused by Fielding's use of symmetry in the middle section of the novel.

One element of this symmetry is the parallel development of Tom and Sophia. Indeed, the accidents of chance that throw their paths together—such as Sophia's encounter with Jones's guide and Jones's discovery of Sophia's wallet (two happenstances which themselves balance symmetrically at

either end of the middle section)—ultimately work in the structure of the novel as they reflect on one level comparisons that are valid at deeper levels. Similar balances on either side of the Upton fulcrum are clear in focusing attention on similar aspects of Tom and Sophia: the comparable stories of the Man of the Hill and Mrs. Fitzpatrick have been frequently noted and analyzed, but in addition Sophia's incomplete revelation to Mrs. Fitzpatrick recalls Jones's similar revelation to Partridge; the landlord's supposition that Sophia is Jenny Cameron echoes Partridge's false impression of Jones's politics; and Sophia's loss of 100 pounds corresponds to Jones's loss of Allworthy's gift (and Jones's supposed honesty contrasts with Black George's supposed dishonesty, just as his purposelessness at finding himself virtually penniless contrasts to the purpose he finds along with Sophia's pocketbook). In themselves these and other such parallels have different values: some merely suggest interesting similarities, others can be analyzed in detail. Taken together, they reveal the richness of texture in the central books, and a single chapter, looked at in some detail, can indicate the pervasiveness of these parallels and their functions in relating the stories of Tom and Sophia to each other.

Chapter viii of Book XI, for example, deals with two major events—Mrs. Honour's violent reaction to the discovery that her landlord has mistaken Sophia for Jenny Cameron ("that nasty stinking wh—re that runs around the country with the Pretender") and the arrival of a "noble peer," a friend of Mrs. Fitzpatrick who offers room in his coach to take the ladies to London. Both of these episodes have slight significance in the causal sequence of the novel, but both strongly recall Sophia's relation to Jones. Honour's language to the landlord ("'My lady!' says I," . . . is meat for no Pretenders. She is a young lady of as good fashion, and family, and fortune as any in Somersetshire," . . .) is reminiscent of her anger at the landlady who had earlier carried on about Tom's proclaimed love for Sophia ("'What saucy fellow,' cries Honour, 'told you anything of my lady?' 'No saucy fellow,' answered the landlady, 'but the young gentleman you enquired after, and a very pretty young gentleman he is, and he loves Madam Sophia Western to the bottom of his soul.' 'He love my lady! I'd have you know, woman, she is meat for his master.'" . . .). Fielding extends this comparison by explaining Honour's motives in terms of a footman who fought for the honor of Nell Gwynn, but the analogy has reference to Sophia as well as Honour because the comparison to Jenny

Cameron is symbolically appropriate to Sophia. Like Jenny Cameron, she is beautiful and ladylike, but furtive and fearful of discovery; and Jones is a metaphoric equivalent to the Pretender, at least insofar as he is a pretender to the love of Sophia and all that means in terms of social position and moral rectitude. But the reader learns, from the arrival of the "noble peer," that the landlord's suspicion of the ladies' romantic situation, though inaccurate in specific detail, is accurate in other respects which Sophia is unaware of. Harriet's description of her relationship to this gentleman echoes Sophia's incomplete account of her escape from her father, as well as the similar Jones-Partridge exchange in VIII, v and vi, while the peer's conclusion that Sophia, like Mrs. Fitzpatrick, is also escaping the tyranny of a husband recalls both the landlord's mistake and the several mistakes at Upton. The culmination of the chapter comes in Harriet's comment that the peer, a married man, is

> entirely constant to the marriage bed. "Indeed," added she, "my dear Sophy, that is a very rare virtue amongst men of condition. Never expect it when you marry; for, believe me, if you do, you will certainly be deceived."
>
> A gentle sigh stole from Sophia at these words, which perhaps contributed to form a dream of no very pleasant kind; but as she never revealed this dream to anyone, so the reader cannot expect to see it here.

The chapter ends, then, by reinforcing Tom's relevance to the incidents of the chapter, themselves parallel in nature, by the strongest parallel in Sophia's mind.

Such a specific analysis reveals two essential kinds of comparison. Fielding's approach to character, here as elsewhere, is indirect in revealing the inner life of his characters. Thus he playfully does not "tell" us what Sophia's dream is, though the context makes its nature fairly clear. Some of the comparisons focus indirectly on the inner life of character, revealing what the narrator conceals or the characters do not wish to articulate. Other comparisons fill the more conventional function of providing frames of reference in terms of which we can perceive the moral situations of the characters at given points in the novel. Thus the Jenny Cameron-Sophia comparison broadens to include Nell Gwynn and Mrs. Fitzpatrick until Mrs. Fitzpatrick's mendacious remarks on male chastity bring both Tom's and Sophia's intentions into clearer focus, both in Sophia's mind and the reader's.

But beyond this specific sense of the richness of texture in the comparisons of the novel, the larger symmetrical comparisons that arch across the Upton scenes suggest the significance of Sophia's development as a secondary narrative line, parallel to Tom's development. The external parallels of Jones and Sophia in the central books are fairly straightforward elements of the novel's plot, and both characters move, in parallel fashions shaped by Fielding's handling of his centers of revelation, from country to city—both books XI and XII pointing towards the London episodes. But both Jones and Sophia journey as well towards their own marriage and ultimate return to Somersetshire. For both characters the journey embodies the problem of learning to express their inner feelings in a world of convention dominated by quite different values than those associated with these feelings. The journeys of both involve encounters with this world of convention, both personally and vicariously. Moreover, Sophia is accompanied by Honour, Jones by Partridge, and both companions distort the nature and motives of their masters.

Thus both face a double problem of perception and action—of how to behave in a corrupt society and how to perceive and reveal their own goodness within the conventions of that society. Their eventual accommodation to these conventions, particularly in terms of sexual and family life, makes possible their marriage and the conclusion of the novel. (Sophia's final acceptance of Jones is a satisfying example of her ability to use convention in order to express her own feeling. In the fashion of a prudent heroine of romance, guarded by "Daunger," she tentatively accepts Jones, but only after insisting on a year's period of probation and good conduct. When her father insists on her marrying immediately, however, she happily gives way to the convention of filial duty.) Fielding's symmetrical handling of point of view in the middle books of the novel and his use of comparable incidents on either side of the Upton scene thus widen the significance of Tom's moral progress to include that of Sophia and thereby to achieve a clearer picture of both.

The preceding discussion of structures in the middle section of *Tom Jones* reveals, then, four distinguishable patterns: 1) the linear pattern of causal sequence, analogous to the geographical movement of characters in the central books; 2) a non-linear pattern of causation, concerning the hidden causes of events, implicit in the enveloping pattern of time, and resolved, finally, as the various characters emerge in London to reveal Tom's story; 3) a symmetrical pattern of narration, based on the alteration of Tom and Sophia as central characters and on the reversal of hunter-hunted roles after the inn at

Upton; 4) a symmetrical pattern of corresponding events, arranged around the Upton scenes and pointing backwards and forwards towards the Somerset and London scenes. These methods are in themselves controlled and ordered within the general structure of the novel. But an accurate view of the complexities of the middle books must recognize further kinds of structure as well. Among these are a number of *ad-hoc* parallels which focus on specific aspects of character without functioning structurally in the large movements of the novel. Some of the comparisons I noted in XI, viii work this way, and in this way we can regard the Northerton-Jones parallel. (Tom replaces Northerton as Mrs. Waters' lover, and, although Northerton's jesting about Sophia is the initial cause of their fight, Tom's own indiscreet use of her name is also improper and injurious to her reputation. Thus Tom, the novel's sympathetic hero, is briefly seen to share qualities with one of its least sympathetic characters.)

In addition to *ad-hoc* parallels are such devices of "rhythm" (in E. M. Forster's sense) as Sophia's muff, which are important single patterns but do not otherwise fit into an ordered arrangement of parts (playing, therefore, an intermittent rather than regular role in the structure of the novel); important also are the similar recurrent patterns of imagery—such as those of eating, clothing, and hunting—and recurrent literary allusions, particularly to epic and chivalric works. The importance of the developing relation of the narrator to the reader as an element of structure in the novel has frequently been commented upon.

Thus, in addition to the four major structuring patterns I have noted, there are a variety of different subsidiary devices of structure to which the reader must respond. Taken together, as I have suggested in my analysis of XI, viii, they constitute a rich texture of allusions—forward and backward in time, back and forth in the linear structure of the novel, towards the inner state of characters, towards external judgments by the author and reader, and towards the novel itself as a literary type analogous in structure and purpose to other literary types. Though these allusions may point, as Alter, Sacks, and others have suggested, towards theme, the complexity of structure is not echoed in an analogous complexity of theme.

III

One attempt to explain the complexity of these structures has been to speak of *Tom Jones* as a battleground for conflicting forces of literary mode or

> *Fielding's use of multiple structures enabled him to create a kind of novel unusually broad in scope; and in terms of the history of the novel, Tom Jones was a remarkable achievement."*

literary history. David Goldknopf claims that "Fielding was trying to bring both the picaresque exuberance which was his natural bent and the new, aggressive empiricism of his age under a discipline fundamentally unsympathetic to both, the neoclassical canon." But if we see the picaresque and empiricist elements of the novel as reflected in its dynamic, linear movement and the neo-classical elements as functioning in its symmetry—admittedly a somewhat simplified account of the middle books—the primary conclusion to be drawn is not that this conflict is a failure on the author's part but that it is a tension that is itself structured into the novel, an aspect of conscious design rather than unconscious impropriety. Nor is it, I think, valuable to consider "the neo-classical canon" as implying a sterile and rigid order. Seen as an aspect of structural technique, it is a method of putting certain elements of experience into particular kinds of relationship to one another. But rather than providing merely a static form, such juxtaposition of events insists, as I have suggested in the case of Fielding's comparisons, on the active participation of the reader in discovering and puzzling over the connections. The "narrator" is not, then, in total control of the novel as perceived by the reader, for he remains silent about, and ostensibly unaware of, a variety of these connections.

If the novel is regarded as a thing to be read, the common architectural, Palladian image of *Tom Jones* becomes insignificant: the reader of a novel, unlike the viewer of a building, must make his connections in the medium of time, depending not only upon observation but upon memory and his ability to generalize and hence to perceive the basis of comparison. The reader is thus left with a variety of structural devices which he must perceive and classify, and to which he must respond, always revising his perceptions and responses as new evidence in the novel comes into play. In this respect the process of reading *Tom Jones* never ends, for new possibilities become apparent on each rereading. One of the delights, then, of the diverse multiple structures of *Tom Jones* lies in the reader's sense of his own paradoxical position: he is engulfed in the formal structures of the novel, yet these formal structures are so diverse that they are beyond his ability to control at any one point in time; he repeatedly encounters balanced configurations, yet the stasis of these balances continually works against elements of surprise and the progressive movement of causality in the plot itself. The reader is thus perpetually in the process of discovering a form that extends beyond him, and his progress in achieving that discovery parallels the discoveries of the characters and the ordering of the author. Thus, though the novel ends, one's reading of the novel does not, and unity, in this context, becomes not something the novel "has" in the sense that a picture "has" composition, but a quality that is always in the process of creation.

The concept of unity thus seems less important than the experience of totality. Fielding's use of multiple structures enabled him to create a kind of novel unusually broad in scope; and in terms of the history of the novel, *Tom Jones* was a remarkable achievement. Fielding's concerns for the nature of social morality, for the experience of maturation, for the relation of sex to love, for the way people think and draw conclusions or make judgments, for the relation of motive to act, of appearance to reality, of art to human nature—all these are encompassed in the novel and viewed complexly, often in relation to one another, through an encompassing multiplicity of structures. As Sheridan Baker has pointed out, the effect of the contrived aspects of plot in *Tom Jones* is to distance us from the material, thereby achieving a comic, even ironic detachment. But the comic view plays against our involvement in the novel as process and mingles with the richness of the fic-

tive world revealed in the novel and embodied in the brilliant, multi-faceted movement of its form.

Source: Charles A. Knight, "Multiple Structures and the Unity of *Tom Jones*," in *Criticism*, Vol. XIV, No. 3, Summer 1972, pp. 227–42.

Sources

Baker, Sheridan, ed., *Tom Jones: A Norton Critical Edition*, 2d ed., W. W. Norton, 1995, p. vii.

Paulson, Ronald, and Thomas Lockwood, *Henry Fielding: The Critical Heritage*, Barnes and Noble, 1969, pp. 172–75.

Shedd, W. G. T., *Samuel Taylor Coleridge: The Complete Works*, Vol. VI, London, 1856, p. 521.

Further Reading

Battestin, Martin C., and Ruth E. Battestin, *Henry Fielding: A Life*, Routledge, 1990.
> This book is considered the definitive biography of Fielding.

Dudden, Homes, *Henry Fielding: His Life, Work, and Times*, Oxford University Press, 1952.
> A comprehensive two-volume work, this book examines Fielding's writing in the contexts of his society and his personal life.

Waller, Maureen, *1700: Scenes from London Life*, Four Walls, Eight Windows, 2000.
> This book presents a huge amount of detail about daily life (and death) in eighteenth-century London, focusing on where people lived and worked, how they behaved, what they wore and ate, and how they suffered from illness and injury. The book is made up of vignettes drawn from the author's research and by excerpts from contemporary diarists, novelists, and commentators.

Watt, Ian, *The Rise of the Novel: Studies in Defoe, Richardson, and Fielding*, University of California Press, 1957.
> This volume looks at the early development of the novel and the roles played by Fielding and his contemporaries Defoe and Richardson.

The Unbearable Lightness of Being

Milan Kundera
1984

First published in 1984 in both Paris and New York, Milan Kundera's *The Unbearable Lightness of Being* is a rich and complicated novel that is at once a love story, a metaphysical treatise, a political commentary, a psychological study, a lesson on kitsch, a musical composition in words, an aesthetic exploration, and a meditation on human existence. As an expatriate Czechoslovakian writer, Kundera draws upon his firsthand experience of the 1968 Prague Spring and subsequent Soviet occupation of his country to provide the backdrop for the story of four people whose lives are inextricably enmeshed. Because the work is so complex, there are many themes that intertwine throughout the novel, just as a theme in a musical composition will be introduced only to reappear later in a different key. Indeed there are several critics who focus their entire analysis on the way Kundera uses musical structure to put together his novel. At its most fundamental level, *The Unbearable Lightness of Being* is about the ambiguity and paradoxes of human existence, as each person teeters between lightness and weight; between the belief that all is eternal return and Nietzsche's concept that life is an ever-disappearing phenomenon; and between dream and reality.

Author Biography

Milan Kundera was born April 1, 1929, in Brno, Czechoslovakia (now the Czech Republic), the son of Ludvik and Milada Kundera. He studied music

Milan Kundera

with Paul Haas and Vaclav Kapral and attended Charles University in Prague. He studied film at the Academy of Music and Dramatic Arts in Prague, where he later held a position as assistant professor from 1958 to 1969. He was a member of the central committee of the Czechoslovak Writers Union from 1963 to 1969.

In 1962 Kundera began writing his first novel, *The Joke*. The book caused problems with the national censors, and consequently it was not published until 1967 (the English edition was first published in 1969). Kundera's frustration with the censors climaxed with a speech he gave at the Fourth Czechoslovak Writers Congress. However, Kundera and others who followed his lead were subjected to even more oppression.

For a brief period in 1968 known as the "Prague Spring," the government eased restrictions on its writers and citizens. The Soviet Bloc countries, led by the Soviet Union, were nervous about the relaxation of the regime in Czechoslovakia, and in August 1968, Russian tanks and Soviet Bloc soldiers took control of Prague. The Soviets deposed Czech leader Alexander Dubcek and put Gustav Husak in his place, instituting a repressive regime that lasted for twenty-one years. During this time, Kundera's books and plays were banned, and his works could not be sold in bookstores or read in libraries. Kundera was forbidden to publish in Czechoslovakia, and he lost his teaching position.

In 1975 Kundera received permission to immigrate to France, where he became a professor. His 1979 novel *The Book of Laughter and Forgetting* (first published in English in 1980) led the Czech government to revoke his citizenship. In 1981 Kundera became a French citizen.

Although by 1984 Kundera was internationally respected as a writer, his novel *The Unbearable Lightness of Being* secured his place in world literature. Since that time, Kundera has published widely, including the novels *Immortality*, published in French in 1990 and English in 1991; *Slowness: A Novel*, published in French in 1995, and English in 1996; *Identity: A Novel*, published in French in 1997 and in English in 1998; and *Ignorance*, published in English in 2002. Kundera's work has been well-received by critics and readers alike, and he has been awarded many prizes, including the Czechoslovak Writers Union prize in 1968 for *The Joke*; the Commonwealth Award for distinguished service in literature in 1981; a 1984 *Los Angeles Times* Book Prize for *The Unbearable Lightness of Being*; and the Academie Francaise critics prize in 1987.

Plot Summary

Part 1: Lightness and Weight

The novel opens with a meditation on philosopher Friedrich Nietzsche's idea of the eternal return, contrasted with the notion of *einmal ist keinmal*; that is, "what happens but once ... might as well not have happened at all." According to Nietzsche, eternal return is the "heaviest of burdens." The absence of this burden, however, renders life inconsequential. The binary opposition of weight and lightness continues throughout the book.

Kundera next introduces Tomas, a surgeon who has fallen in love with a young woman named Tereza. Tomas has many mistresses, engaging in what he terms "erotic friendships." When Tereza discovers Tomas's many mistresses, she is distraught. It is this contrast between the weight of Tereza's love and the lightness of Tomas's love that provides much of the material for the book.

Eventually Tomas marries Tereza. He also buys Tereza a puppy they name Karenin. Although married, Tomas does not give up his mistresses. Notable among them is Sabina, an artist. Sabina clearly understands Tomas and even becomes a close friend of Tereza's.

In 1968 the Russian occupation of Czechoslovakia begins. Sabina immigrates to Switzerland, and Tomas begins receiving calls from a Swiss doctor who wants him to immigrate to Switzerland as well. Tomas and Tereza do well in Zurich for six or seven months, until Tereza learns that Tomas is once again seeing Sabina. Tereza returns to Prague, and within days Tomas follows her.

Part 2: Soul and Body

The story returns to the beginning, this time from Tereza's point of view. This section allows the reader to understand the family background and psychology that drive Tereza. Her father was a political prisoner who died in jail, and her mother is an abusive, vulgar woman who takes great delight in humiliating Tereza. Kundera reiterates Tereza's meeting with Tomas and her decision to go to Prague. Also in this section the reader learns of Tereza's troubling dreams, which often involve Tomas. Finally, the friendship between Sabina and Tereza grows; it is Sabina who has secured a position for Tereza at the magazine where Sabina works. In one particularly intense scene, Sabina and Tereza photograph each other nude at Sabina's studio.

Part 3: Words Misunderstood

In this section the reader meets Franz, a university professor in Geneva who is having an affair with Sabina. Franz is married to a woman named Marie-Claude, whom he does not love. Throughout this section, there are brief chapters of "misunderstood words" that illustrate the differences between Sabina and Franz. For example, in a section titled "Music," Franz tries to explain his love of music to Sabina. Kundera writes, "For Franz music was the art that comes closest to Dionysian beauty in the sense of intoxication." For Sabina, however, music is noise. Her early years at the Academy of Arts ruined her feelings for music, as the school played loud, cheerful music on speakers from early morning until night. While for Franz music is a liberating force, for Sabina music is an unpleasant reminder of her life in the totalitarian state. Likewise, in a short section titled "Light and Dark," the reader discovers that Franz is drawn to darkness and that he closes his eyes when he makes love to Sabina. For Sabina, however, "living . . . meant seeing."

Given the distance between the two lovers in their understanding of reality, it is not surprising that Franz chooses to tell his wife of their affair,

Media Adaptations

- *The Unbearable Lightness of Being* was adapted as a film in 1988. The film was directed by Phillip Kaufman, and stars Daniel Day-Lewis and Juliette Binoche. The film is available on DVD from Home Vision Entertainment.

- *The Unbearable Lightness of Being* was recorded on audiocassette in 1988 by Books on Tape (Newport Beach, CA). Christopher Hurt is the reader.

the very thing Sabina does not want to happen. Consequently, Sabina leaves Franz and Switzerland, settling first in Paris and later in the United States. She receives a letter while in Paris from Tomas's son, informing her that Tomas and Tereza have been killed in a car accident. Franz becomes involved with a student and begins taking an active role in political dissension.

Part 4: Body and Soul

Tomas is working as a window washer in this section, having lost his position at the hospital. Tereza tends bar. Their schedules are very different from each other, and, by the time Tereza returns home from work each night, Tomas is asleep. When she crawls into bed beside him, she is aware of an odor coming from his hair, an odor she finally identifies as coming from the genitals of another woman. This weighs heavily on her, and she eventually has a sexual encounter with an engineer she meets at the bar. Only later does she realize that the engineer is probably a spy for the state. The atmosphere of this section is sad and heavy throughout, and the pressure of living in a totalitarian state, where there is little or no privacy, permeates the events. Perhaps the most moving part of this section is a dream Tereza has in which Tomas instructs her to go up Petrin Hill, which she does, only to find men with rifles killing those who want to die. It must be their choice, the men tell Tereza. At the last minute she says that being killed is not her choice. Although this is how the dream ends, it seems that Tereza truly does want to die.

Part 5: Lightness and Weight

In this section, the reader discovers why Tomas has been let go from his job at the hospital. It seems that he wrote a letter to an editor of a journal during the brief Prague Spring. Now, with the reinstatement of a more oppressive regime, he is called upon to recant. He refuses to do so and must consequently resign from his job. His friends and family think he is protesting the new regime. Thus, he is approached by his son Simon and the editor of the journal who published his letter. They want him to sign a petition demanding the release of Czech political prisoners. He refuses to sign this document. Finally, to get away from the intrigue and anxieties of the city, Tomas and Tereza move to a collective farm in the country, believing that this move will put them so far down on the social ladder that the state will no longer be concerned with them, since they have little else to lose.

Part 6: The Grand March

In this section Kundera explores the notion of kitsch, particularly communist kitsch. The story also returns to Franz, who decides to go to Thailand with a group of intellectuals to protest human-rights violations in Cambodia. While there, he is senselessly mugged by some street thugs and ends up dying in a hospital shortly after his return to Switzerland.

Part 7: Karenin's Smile

In this final section, the reader learns more about Tomas and Tereza's life on the farm. Their dog Karenin is very old and dying of cancer. This death affects both of them deeply. At the collective, Tomas has finally given up womanizing, and Tereza asks for forgiveness for her role in his unhappiness in life. Tomas replies that he has been happy these last years at the farm. Thus in the hours before their deaths, Tomas and Tereza are happy together.

Characters

Franz

Franz is a professor who lives in Geneva, Switzerland. He enters the book in the third part, where he is introduced as Sabina's lover of nine months. Franz is married to Marie-Claude, a woman he does not love but whom he married because she

loved him so much. He also has a daughter, Marie-Anne, who is the carbon copy of her mother. For twenty-three years, Franz has been a loyal, if unhappy, husband. Now, however, he finds he is in love with Sabina. Throughout the months of their affair, he has taken trouble to separate his lover and his wife, refusing to make love to Sabina in Geneva, choosing rather to take her on trips all over the world. He is constantly unsure of Sabina, however, and always seems to expect she will leave him. As the narrator informs the reader, for Franz love "meant a longing to put himself at the mercy of his partner.... love meant the constant expectation of a blow."

Thus, although Franz is a physically strong man, he is an emotionally weak man. He places no demands on Sabina, nor does he use his strength against her. Instead he chooses to be weak. Sabina does not find this quality attractive.

A turning point in Franz's life occurs when his wife holds a gallery opening and invites Sabina, whose pictures have been shown in her gallery. When Marie-Claude insults Sabina by telling her that her pendant is ugly, Franz decides he must tell Marie-Claude about the affair in order to protect Sabina. The situation backfires: Marie-Claude throws Franz out of the house but will not grant him a divorce, and Sabina leaves him.

This turn of events underscores a fundamental quality in Franz, namely his inability to understand women—particularly Sabina. The chapters of the book that involve Franz and Sabina are written like a dictionary, with definitions of "misunderstood words." Ultimately, it becomes clear that Franz is more in love with the idea of Sabina than with Sabina herself, and, thus, her physical absence is less of a problem than one might expect. Throughout the rest of his life, Franz always imagines Sabina is watching him, although he never sees her again.

In the sixth part of the book, Franz decides to join a group of Western intellectuals who travel to Thailand to protest Cambodian human rights violations. In an utterly senseless act, he is killed by muggers in the streets of Thailand, yet another indication of Franz's fundamental misunderstanding of humankind and reality. The final irony is that "in death, Franz at last belonged to his wife.... Marie-Claude took care of everything: she saw to the funeral, sent out the announcements, bought the wreaths, and had a black dress made—a wedding dress, in reality. Yes, a husband's funeral is a wife's true wedding! The climax of her life's work! The reward for her suffering!" Franz's death serves to underscore the futility of his life.

Sabina

Sabina is a Czech painter and one of Tomas's many lovers. The product of the Communist system of education, she is an artist who detests kitsch, noise, social realism, and music. It is through Sabina that Kundera comments on the influence of politics on art and music, as well as on the life of the political exile.

Ironically, Sabina is the character that has relationships with all of the other characters, although she is by far the most distant and distancing of all of the characters. Her affair with Tomas in Prague is a good representation of the kind of relationship she desires, one of sex and friendship without emotional commitment. When Sabina and Tomas meet in Switzerland to make love, it is their last such encounter. She wears nothing but her lingerie and a bowler hat that belonged to her grandfather, someone she never actually knew. The scene is both emotionally and sexually charged and clearly touches Sabina emotionally in a place where she does not want to be touched.

Likewise, Sabina enjoys being with Franz so long as there is little commitment. As soon as Franz tells his wife he is having an affair with Sabina, Sabina disappears from Franz's life. However, it is Sabina's scene with Tereza which is perhaps the most sexually and emotionally charged scene of the book. Tereza comes to take photographs of Sabina in her studio and suggests that she photograph Sabina nude. Sabina, for all her sexual libertinism, cannot comply immediately. Rather, Sabina first drinks three glasses of wine and talks about her grandfather's bowler hat. It is not until Tereza distances herself by picking up her camera and looking through the lens that Sabina throws open her robe. After both women take pictures of each other and find themselves enchanted by the situation, Sabina "almost frightened by the enchantment and eager to dispel it . . . burst[s] into loud laughter." Clearly the situation with Tereza is fraught with emotional content, something Sabina will not allow herself to feel.

Tereza

Tereza is a young woman from a small village who, through a whole series of coincidences, becomes Tomas's lover and later his wife. Tereza's father was a political prisoner who died in jail, leaving Tereza in the care of her vulgar, loud mother, who took great delight in embarrassing Tereza. This abuse led to Tereza's radical split between body and soul; as much as possible she rejects everything about her body. It is her soul she gives

to Tomas, and thus she represents heaviness in the burden of love she places on Tomas.

Tereza loves Tomas ferociously and, although she cannot tolerate his philandering, she cannot leave him. It seems as if her role in the book is to bear suffering. Her dreams are particularly painful. In one, she must parade nude around a swimming pool with other nude women. Tomas sits on a high chair and shoots any woman who does not perform proper knee bends. Later in the book, Tereza dreams that Tomas takes her to Petrin Hill, where he has arranged for men with guns to shoot her if she so chooses. When Tereza shares these dreams with Tomas, he finds himself ever more deeply enmeshed with his wife. Although through much of the book the two of them make each other unhappy, they nonetheless are unable to part from each other.

A turning point comes for Tereza when she returns home from work one night and smells another woman on her sleeping husband. In an act of rebellion, she ends up having a one-time sexual encounter with an engineer. Later she comes to believe this engineer is really a member of the secret police sent to entrap her for prostitution. After this event, Tereza tries to persuade Tomas to move to a collective farm in the country. When Tomas asks Tereza what has been bothering her these past months, she tells him of the odor his hair has been emitting. This revelation is enough to convince Tomas they must move to the country. Tereza finally achieves what she wants—Tomas's fidelity.

Tomas

Tomas is a successful Czech surgeon who lives in Prague. In addition to being a fine surgeon, Tomas is also an inveterate womanizer. He has many affairs and has constructed a set of rules for preventing these affairs from becoming anything other than occasions for sex.

While on a conference to a small town, he meets Tereza, a barmaid. He tells Tereza to look him up if she is ever in Prague, which she does. Tomas finds himself in love with Tereza when she comes down with influenza during her visit. However, he also finds these feelings "inexplicable." He ponders the question, is this love? Or, he wonders, "[Is] it simply the hysteria of a man who, aware deep down of his inaptitude for love, [feels] the self-deluding need to simulate it?" Tomas does not have the answer to this question, but nonetheless he feels drawn to marry Tereza. Marriage, however, does not stop Tomas from pursuing affairs with a variety of women.

For Tomas, sexual intercourse and love are not necessarily connected. He discovers this when he realizes how much he loves to sleep with Tereza, something he never does with his lovers. Tomas concludes, "Making love with a woman and sleeping with a woman are two separate passions, not merely different but opposite. Love does not make itself felt in the desire for copulation (a desire that extends to an infinite number of women) but in the desire for shared sleep (a desire limited to one woman)."

Tomas's career suffers after the Soviet occupation of Prague. When he is offered the opportunity of immigrating to Switzerland, he takes it. In Switzerland he takes up with one of his former lovers, Sabina, who has also immigrated there. However, after just a few months in Switzerland, Tereza leaves him to return to Prague. Tomas chooses to follow her after a few days, and, from the time of his return to Prague, his career goes downhill. In the repressive atmosphere of the new government, he loses his job and begins working as a window washer. Even as a window washer, however, he finds opportunities to make love to many women.

Tomas is, in many ways, an enigma. Although he loves Tereza with all his heart, he is unable to put an end to his philandering in spite of the pain it causes his wife. If he feels strongly the idea of *es muss sein* (it must be) applies to his relationship with his wife, he feels likewise about his relationship with other women. It is not until confronted with the odor emanating from his hair that he realizes he must give up all other women. He moves to the country with Tereza.

Of all the characters in the book, Tomas is the one who undergoes the most radical change from beginning to end. Just hours before his death, he dances with Tereza and tells her that he has been happy with her in the country, a happiness that seemed to have eluded him for much of his life.

Themes

Love and Sex

For all of its other concerns, *The Unbearable Lightness of Being* is first an exploration of the many facets of love. In his or her own way, each of the four main characters confronts and wrestles with the notion of love. Tomas, for example, never equates sex with love. Before Tereza comes into his life, he is very happy with his "erotic friendships." Because these affairs do not pretend to be "love" affairs, he is able to move among many

women without betraying any of them. When Tereza arrives at his apartment and becomes ill, he realizes that he feels compassion for her, and that compassion itself is love. In spite of his many affairs, he does not leave Tereza, nor is there any doubt he loves her deeply.

For Tereza, however, love carries a very different connotation. While she does not equate love and sex, when she offers her body to Tomas, she does so out of love. Indeed for Tereza love is an offering of everything. That Tomas does not reciprocate in kind is a source of bitter sorrow to Tereza. Her love is of the "heavy" kind, a burden for both Tomas and Tereza herself.

Sabina, like Tomas, has many affairs and refuses to commit to one person. Of all the characters in the book, she is the one who seems least able to love and connect emotionally with another human being. Kundera is connecting her emotional damage to her upbringing within the Soviet system. As a child, Sabina found herself constantly under the barrage of the state, in the form of the music that was played all day at the Academy for Fine Arts; the parades in which the students were forced to march; and the strict aesthetic rules of social realism. To be an artist in Soviet-controlled Czechoslovakia required complete compliance with state doctrine. For an artist, it also required a complete dampening of the creative forces and emotional responses, creating an individual who is always wary of revealing what is under the surface.

Franz too is emotionally incompetent and unable to engage in a loving relationship, although he believes himself to be in love with Sabina. As the book continues, it becomes clear that Franz loves his idea of Sabina, not Sabina herself. Tellingly, Franz closes his eyes as he makes love to Sabina, effectively erasing the woman in bed with him and substituting his own idea of Sabina in her place. In addition, when Franz misguidedly chooses to tell his wife about his affair with Sabina, he demonstrates how poorly he knows either woman. His wife does not respond at all as he imagines she will. Even worse, Sabina leaves him. After Sabina's departure, Franz in many ways is happier than when she was present. Because his idea of Sabina is somehow stronger in her absence, Franz no longer needs to square his idea of Sabina with the physical reality of Sabina.

Politics and Government

The Unbearable Lightness of Being is a political novel. It not only describes politics within the Soviet bloc, it takes as its subject political and gov-

Topics For Further Study

- In part six of *The Unbearable Lightness of Being*, Kundera writes at length about the notion of "kitsch." Define kitsch. Find examples in magazines of kitsch from twenty-first-century American culture. Create a collage using these images that gives the viewer insight as to the role of kitsch in the United States.

- Reread the sections of *The Unbearable Lightness of Being* that describe Tereza's dreams. Read several entries on dreams from psychology textbooks or reference works. What do these books indicate that Tereza's dreams reveal about her?

- Research the literary history of Czechoslovakia in the twentieth century. Who are some notable writers and their subjects? Create a timeline to locate these writers historically and to connect them with important events of their time. On your timeline, be sure to include illustrations, note major works, and identify important historical events.

- Define social realism. Using art-history books, encyclopedias, and reference works, identify the underpinning principles of social realism. Write a report explaining what you have discovered. Use images you find on the World Wide Web to illustrate your points.

- Research the lives of Alexander Dubcek and Vaclav Havel. What roles did these two important Czechs play in the history of their country?

---

ernmental oppression. None of the characters in the book can escape from the tentacles of totalitarianism that threaten to strangle each one. When Tomas, for example, during the brief Prague Spring writes an essay critical of the Communist Party, he opens himself to a series of damaging responses. After the Soviet invasion and the reinstitution of a repressive regime, Tomas is asked to recant his statement in order to keep his job as a surgeon. Tomas refuses, a stance that signals to his countrymen that he is a dissident himself. Tomas chooses to resign from the hospital and take a job as a window washer, thinking that in this way he can escape from governmental observation. However, when his son and the editor of the journal that published his essay ask him to sign a petition calling for the release of political prisoners, Tomas refuses. What both the government and the dissidents miss about Tomas is that he is largely apolitical; that is, he is someone who wants to carry on his life as a doctor without the intrusion of either government or politics. Such a stance is completely untenable, however. As a public figure, the government uses its strength to attack Tomas in the public sphere, by not allowing him to pursue the one thing at which he excels—practicing surgery.

In contrast, Tereza is a very private person, and the claustrophobia of totalitarianism affects her in a very private way. She finds herself working as a barmaid as the result of Tomas's published essay. The bar is both seedy and disreputable; even so, there are patrons who try to bring the power of the state down on Tereza. Most notably, when she has a brief affair with an engineer, she does not consider until later that, in all likelihood, the engineer is really a member of the secret police. For Tereza, the worst kind of governmental intrusion would be into her sexual life. She imagines that photographs have been taken of her with the engineer and that these pictures will later be used against her. Thus, for the private Tereza, the invasion of her personal space signifies the ultimate victory of the state over the person.

Just as the state intrudes on Tomas's public work life and Tereza's private sex life, the state intrudes on Sabina in her most vulnerable area—her art. In response to the Soviet invasion, Sabina leaves Czechoslovakia. She has already experienced what the state can do to art and has no desire to experience it again. Ironically, the tentacles of the state follow her into exile. She finds herself uncomfortably lumped together with all exiled Czech intellectuals; her work receives notice and praise not for the work itself but for her status as a dissident. Even within the émigré community, she finds herself surrounded with politics that will destroy her by forcing her to conform to some ideal other than her own. As Sabina wanders farther and farther away from her homeland, the political situation she left behind continues to shape her.

Kitsch

Kundera spends considerable energy to define, describe, and investigate the role of kitsch in communist society. "Kitsch" is a German word that loosely means inferior, sentimental, and/or vulgar art. Although kitsch claims to have an aesthetic purpose, it tends to simplify complicated ideas and thoughts into stereotypical and easily marketable forms. Kitsch appeals to the masses and to the lowest common denominator. It is the world of greeting-card poetry and velvet Elvis. For kitsch to be kitsch, it must be able to evoke an emotional response that according to the book "the multitudes can share."

Kitsch then is essential for the emotional and intellectual control of a populace in a totalitarian culture. In a system that requires all people to feel the same way about a particular event or state of being, kitsch works its magic. As Kundera writes, "Those of us who live in a society where various political tendencies exist side by side and competing influences cancel or limit one another can manage more or less to escape the kitsch inquisition: the individual can preserve his individuality; the artists can create unusual works. But whenever a single political movement corners power, we find ourselves in the realm of *totalitarian kitsch*." Kitsch, according to Kundera, is devoid of irony, since "in the realm of kitsch everything must be taken quite seriously."

Understanding kitsch brings the reader to an understanding of Sabina: it is not communism that repels her; it is communist kitsch such as the May Day parades and the art of social realism. And those who criticize kitsch, or for that matter call it kitsch, must be banned for life because it is the expression of individualism that poses the greatest threat to the totalitarian regime. Kundera concludes, "In this light, we can regard the gulag as a septic tank used by totalitarian kitsch to dispose of its refuse."

Style

Narrator

One of the most interesting devices that Kundera uses in *The Unbearable Lightness of Being* is his creation of a narrator. When the book opens, the reader encounters a meditation on the ideas of German philosopher Friedrich Nietzsche and classical

Greek philosopher Parmenides. What soon becomes clear is that there is a narrative voice undertaking this meditation, a voice that is creating and participating in the story while remaining somehow outside the story: "Not long ago, I caught myself experiencing a most incredible sensation. Leafing through a book on Hitler, I was touched by some of his portraits: they reminded me of my childhood. I grew up during the war; several members of my family perished in Hitler's concentration camps; but what were their deaths compared with the memories of a lost period in my life, a period that would never return?" Many readers will conclude the narrator is Kundera himself. Later in the story, the narrator tells the reader he has "been thinking about Tomas for many years," implying it is the author-as-narrator who has given Tomas his fictional existence. Likewise, the narrator tells the reader that Tereza began as a rumbling in his stomach.

However, while it may be easy to make the assumption that the "I" in the story is Kundera, it also does not take much of a stretch to consider the narrator as yet another character in the story itself, somehow a part of Kundera yet also separate from him. This technique is not new; Geoffrey Chaucer uses it in *The Canterbury Tales*, the famous fourteenth-century classic, when he creates a persona for himself as one of the pilgrims.

Why would a writer do such a thing? Kundera's narrator serves the function of setting up the philosophical structure of the novel. Because he is separate from the story, he is able to comment on each of the characters outside the knowledge of the characters themselves. This distance allows the reader to share privileged knowledge with the narrator that is hidden from the characters. It also leads the reader to trust that the narrator is reliable.

A second reason Kundera may choose to create a narrator is as a device to continually remind the reader that what he or she is reading is fiction, not reality. Authorial intrusions such as those made by the narrator serve to place the story in the realm of fiction, while making the author seem more present to the reader. It seems that the author is speaking directly to the reader in a kind of conversation.

However, a closer examination of this second purpose complicates the role of the narrator even further. While it may *seem* that the author is engaging the reader in conversation, what is *really* happening is that the reader is looking at black marks on paper, black marks the writer set down a number of years ago. The words on the page, no matter how much they recall the spoken voice, remain carefully

Compare & Contrast

- **1960s:** Czechoslovakia is firmly part of the Warsaw Pact, a military alliance that includes the Soviet Union and the Eastern Bloc countries.

  Today: The Czech Republic has joined the North Atlantic Treaty Organization (NATO), a military alliance that includes the United States and western European Nations.

- **1960s:** Beginning in 1962, the Czechoslovakian government begins to make movements toward reform, easing the restrictions on its citizens. In 1968, during what is known as the Prague Spring, several writers and artists speak out against totalitarianism. Within months, Soviet tanks invade Czechoslovakia, and the country is forcibly brought back within Soviet domination. It is a time of great repression.

  Today: The Czech Republic, after a period of economic reform, applies for membership in the European Union in 1996 and expects to be granted admission in 2004. At the same time, the country has maintained its close ties with some of the former Warsaw Pact nations. The Social Democratic party, under the leadership of Vladimir Spidla, wins the general election in June 2002.

- **1960s:** Writers and artists in Czechoslovakia are forced to submit their work to state-sponsored censors. All works are subjected to the aesthetic of "social realism." Works that do not conform are banned. Nevertheless, there is an active underground of writers and artists who continue to produce high quality work, although it cannot be published or shown in Czechoslovakia. Many writers and artists are forced to leave their homes and are subjected to severe oppression in their homeland.

  Today: Works by dissident Czech writers now circulate in Czechoslovakia. Vaclav Havel, himself a noted dissident writer who spent four years in prison under the old regime, is elected president of the Czech Republic in 1993. Many exiled Czech writers are able to return to their homeland for visits.

---

crafted traces of some human creator. When the reader is forced to confront the essential artificiality of fiction itself, the narrator out of necessity becomes a character himself. While the words revealing his thoughts about the characters and about human existence may indeed coincide with Kundera's own thoughts, once Kundera has chosen to write himself into the book, he has created a fictional persona who will tell the story as best he is able.

Setting

The Unbearable Lightness of Being is set during the 1960s in Czechoslovakia. The fact that Kundera himself experienced the Prague Spring as well as the Soviet takeover lends special poignancy to the story. Kundera uses his setting for several important purposes. *The Unbearable Lightness of Being* is a love story and juxtaposing the love affairs of the four main characters with the upheaval of the Russian invasion throws the issues of love into sharp contrast with the issues of hate. In addition, it is the setting that allows Kundera to use his novel as a vehicle for a consideration of the effects of the totalitarian regime on the creation of art and, by extension, on the creation of life itself.

Historical Context

The History of Czechoslovakia

The land that became Czechoslovakia was actually separate regions within the Austro-Hungarian Empire until the end of World War I. The Czech people made their homes in Bohemia and Moravia, parts of Austria, while the Slovaks resided in Slovakia, part of Hungary. While quite different in their interests, concerns, and industrialization, after World War I the two regions declared independence as the Republic of Czechoslovakia. They were briefly democratic in the years between the two world wars; however, in 1938 Adolph Hitler invaded the new nation, occupying Prague.

After the defeat of the Germans, Czechoslovakia was reestablished; however, the Soviet Union exerted its influence on the young nation, and in 1948 the Communists seized power, establishing a government much like Joseph Stalin's in the Soviet Union. During the 1950s and early 1960s, the Communist Party ruled all areas of life, including the government, art, education, and culture.

The Prague Spring, 1968

In the 1960s, leaders such as Alexander Dubcek attempted to introduce modest political reforms. In this atmosphere of lessening repression, writers and artists came forward and asked for even more reforms to be quickly undertaken. In June 1967 Kundera himself addressed the Fourth Czechoslovak Writers Congress and called for open discussion and an end to repression and censorship. Many who spoke up at this meeting were punished.

This punishment did not put a stop to the push for reform. In January 1968, Dubcek became secretary of the party and attempted to make Czechoslovakian socialism more humane. The movement did not sit well with the Warsaw Pact nations, particularly the Soviet Union, which did not want any of its satellite nations to shift their orbits significantly.

The Soviet Invasion, August 1968

Consequently, in August 1968, troops from the U.S.S.R. and other Eastern Bloc nations invaded Czechoslovakia. The occupation resulted in Dubcek's removal and the end of the reform movement. The Soviets instituted a new Czechoslovakian regime that was both harsh and repressive. Writers such as Kundera lost their jobs and were prohibited from speaking publicly or publishing their works. For some seven years, Kundera was not allowed to travel to the West.

Conditions in Czechoslovakia remained largely the same until 1989, in spite of the growing reform movement in the Soviet Union inspired by President Mikhail Gorbachev. However, the fall of the Berlin Wall in 1989 opened the floodgates in Czechoslovakia as well. Ultimately, democracy was restored in Czechoslovakia but not without trouble. In the early 1990s, Slovakia, the eastern part of the country, wanted greater autonomy. Many Slovakians called for complete independence. At the same time, Czech nationalists also wanted their own country. Although President Havel strongly opposed the split, the people of the country voted in 1992 for candidates in favor of dividing the country. Consequently, in January 1993, Czechoslovakia became two independent nations, now known as the Czech Republic and Slovakia.

Critical Overview

When *The Unbearable Lightness of Being* appeared in 1984, it immediately became an international bestseller, garnering awards throughout the world, including a *Los Angeles Times* Book Award. Contemporary reviews of the novel were largely positive. Paul Gray, in a *Time* review, calls *The Unbearable Lightness of Being* "a triumph of wisdom over bitterness, hope over despair." Maureen Howard in the *Yale Review* writes, "*The Unbearable Lightness of Being* is the most rewarding new novel I've read in years." Thomas DePietro in *Commonweal* hones in on the heart of the book. He observes that *The Unbearable Lightness of Being* is a book of "burning compassion, extraordinary intelligence, and dazzling artistry." DePietro also notes the book "leaves us with many questions, questions about love and death, about love and transcendence. These are our burdens, the existential questions that never change but need to be asked anew."

Not all reviewers were enchanted with the book, however. Christopher Hawtree, in a *Spectator* review, faults Kundera for a "most off-putting" title and finds irksome the "elliptical structure" of the work. With faint praise, however, he acknowledges the novel is "a self-referential whole that manages not to alienate the reader." Wendy Lesser in the *Hudson Review* is even blunter, calling *The Unbearable Lightness of Being* "a bad novel." She particularly finds fault with Kundera's characterizations:

> The mistake Kundera makes is to treat his characters like pets. He thinks what he feels for them is love, whereas it's merely an excess of self. If it were really love, we would be able to push aside that gigantic authorial face that looms out of the pages of Kundera's novel . . . and find behind it the tiny, human, flawed faces of real novelistic characters. But they aren't there. Behind that leering, all-obliterating mask is nothing.

Scholarly interest in *The Unbearable Lightness of Being* continues unabated. Literary critics have found a variety of ways to read the novel. For example, John O'Brien in his book *Milan Kundera and Feminism* focuses on Kundera's representation of woman. He most notably studies the relationship between Tereza and Sabina, suggesting that Tereza

Juliette Binoche and Daniel Day-Lewis as Tereza and Tomas in the 1987 film adaptation of The Unbearable Lightness of Being

represents "weight" and Sabina represents "lightness." O'Brien next demonstrates how Kundera undermines such an easy dichotomy. Finally, he argues that it is in Sabina's painting that Kundera reveals his true focal point.

In *Terminal Paradox*, scholar Maria Nemcová Banerjee takes another tact, reading the novel as if it were a piece of music. Just as Tereza introduces Tomas to Beethoven's quartets, and thus to the seminal phrase *Es muss sein*, Kundera introduces the reader to a quartet of characters: "The four leading characters perform their parts in concert, like instruments in a musical quartet, each playing his or her existential code in strict relation to those of the others, often spatially separated but never imaginatively isolated in the reader's mind."

Finally, Kamila Kinyon in *Critique* uses the French critical theory of Michel Foucault and the notion of the "panopticon" to analyze the book. Panopticon literally means "all-seeing," and it suggests a kind of surveillance mechanism. As Kinyon argues, "Within Kundera's novel, in a system of totalitarian Marxism where 'God is dead,' [the terrifying mystery] of God's gaze is replaced by [the terrifying mystery] of the panopticon camera, which may be directed at the individual at any time and which thus controls behavior even at those times when it is physically absent."

Criticism

Diane Andrews Henningfeld

Henningfeld is a professor of English literature and composition who writes widely for educational and reference publishers. In this essay, Henningfeld argues that Sabina's paintings and Tereza's photographs call into question the "truth" of representational art.

The Unbearable Lightness of Being is a novel that functions on many different levels and consequently offers the scholar a host of literary theoretical positions to argue. The sheer number of ways the book has been read indicates this complexity. There are those who see it primarily as an exploration into the notion of love. Others see it as a dramatic account of the Russian invasion of Czechoslovakia. It is also possible to read the novel as a philosophical study, starting with Kundera's fascination with Fredriech Nietzsche and Parmenides. Still other literary critics focus on the novel's structure in that it emulates a musical composition such as a fugue or symphony, with its introduction and reintroduction of themes and events. Finally, many scholars find the oppositions in the novel worthy of close attention.

In his book *Milan Kundera and Feminism: Dangerous Intersections*, John O'Brien chooses to develop yet another reading, one asserting that

> Sabina's painting offers a clear alternative to oppositional thinking, and in this respect I believe Kundera presents Sabina's theory and practice of painting not only as a focal point of this novel, but also as a paradigm for understanding his work in general. Instead of reproducing surfaces that insist on a totalizing "intelligible lie," Kundera's novels, like Sabina's paintings, turn our attention to the deeper paradoxes, but . . . at the expense of the surface representations. In this insistence on and dramatization/staging of double vision, Kundera's novels do not just invite a deconstructionist perspective, but incorporate deconstructionist theory at the level of content.

Such a statement requires some unpacking. O'Brien's critical approach is to see Sabina's painting as metaphor for the entire structure of the novel. In so doing, he asserts that the novel is essentially "deconstructionist." Deconstruction is a critical theory that closely reads texts in order to demonstrate that texts do not generally mean what they appear to mean. In fact, deconstruction would argue that it is the nature of written language to both present and undermine "truth." Deconstructive writing often uses the device of metafiction (or fiction about fiction itself) to call attention to itself as a piece of writing, as opposed to reality. While these concepts may seem complicated, looking carefully at how Kundera uses Sabina's paintings as a metaphor may shed light on both the novel and the theory.

Sabina finds her characteristic style by accident. As an artist in a socialist country, she is both expected and required to embody social realism in her work. As the narrator notes, "art that was not realistic was said to sap the foundations of socialism . . . she had painted in a style concealing the brush strokes and closely resembling color photography." One day, Sabina spills red paint on a picture of a building site. She tells Tereza,

> At first I was terribly upset, but then I started enjoying it. The trickle looked like a crack; it turned the building site into a battered old backdrop, a backdrop with a building site painted on it. I began playing with the crack, filling it out, wondering what might be visible behind it. . . . On the surface, there was always an impeccably realistic world, but underneath, behind the backdrop's cracked canvas, lurked something different, something mysterious or abstract.

Sabina thus accidentally discovers the world behind the apparent world. While her paintings look superficially realistic, and appear to be of building sites and steelworks, they are really about the life hidden behind this realistic facade.

Eva Le Grand, in *Kundera: Or the Memory of Desire*, offers an idea that may prove useful in this exploration. She suggests that Kundera follows an "esthetic of the palimpsest." The word "palimpsest" is particularly apt. In the Middle Ages, because writing materials were so scarce, scribes would often wash the writing off a piece of parchment and use the parchment again and again. With new techniques of reading, contemporary scholars are able to read each level of the manuscript. Thus, while a manuscript will appear to be of a particular text, in reality there are many texts hidden behind the apparent one. Sabina's paintings then call to mind the notion of the palimpsest, the idea that there are other meanings hiding behind the apparent ones.

What Sabina accidentally discovers points to the essential problem of realistic representative art. It is dishonest in an insidious way. "Realistic" painting is not real; rather, it covers, hides, tricks the viewer through artifice to believe that what he or she sees is truth. For example, an artist will use the idea of perspective to create what seems to be a three-dimensional world. Thus, one object might appear to be farther away from the viewer than another object. In reality, both objects are exactly the same distance from the viewer. Modernist painters rebelled against realistic art for just this reason. In a very famous painting (*The Treason of Pictures*), the artist Rene Magritte painted a picture of a pipe with the words below it, "This is not a pipe." At first, this seems silly to the viewer: of course it is a pipe! Anyone would recognize it as such. At second thought, however, the viewer must admit that, no, what he or she is seeing is a picture, not a pipe at all. Thus, even the most realistic of paintings hides a host of other possible meanings behind its surface.

If painting is unable to depict the truth, what then of photography? Does it not faithfully capture the moment, preserving what really happened in the past? Kundera also explores this question in *The Unbearable Lightness of Being*, using Tereza's photography of the 1968 Soviet invasion as his example. He seems to be telling his reader that photographs *do* offer a way of revealing the truth of a situation. He writes,

> All previous crimes of the Russian Empire had been committed under the cover of a discreet shadow. The deportation of a million Lithuanians, the murder of hundreds of thousands of Poles. . . . remain in our memory, but no photographic documentation exists; sooner or later they will therefore be proclaimed as fabrications. Not so the 1968 invasion of Czechoslovakia, of which both stills and motion pictures are stored in archives throughout the world.

Kundera continues by describing the bravery of the Czech photographers, and their awareness of their responsibility of preserving this moment for the future. Nevertheless, later in the book Kundera reveals that even photographs are much more complicated than they might first appear. They serve to cover complexity rather than reveal it. Many chapters after the invasion, Tereza realizes that photographs of the invasion are being used by the new repressive regime to identify the dissidents and thus provide evidence for their punishment. What this reveals is the irrelevance of intention in the creation of an image. The truth the Czech photographers intend to preserve is not the same truth the government derives from the photos. All the good intentions in the world cannot change the fact that these same photographs become the primary means through which people are betrayed.

How then should a reader approach *The Unbearable Lightness of Being*? Sabina's paintings and Tereza's photographs reveal that Kundera's in-

> " How then should a reader approach *The Unbearable Lightness of Being*? Sabina's paintings and Tereza's photographs reveal that Kundera's intentions for his novel are probably irrelevant."

tentions for his novel are probably irrelevant. They also suggest that the smooth surface of the love story hides and distorts what happens beneath that story. Like a drip of red paint, Kundera's authorial intrusions constantly remind readers that the book in front of them is a book, not reality.

It would be comforting to stop here, to simply acknowledge that Kundera is warning his audience to look past the superficial kitsch of culture to ask the essential questions of existence. Deconstruction is not a comfortable theory, however, in that it reveals that all representation is just representation, not truth. In the case of *The Unbearable Lightness of Being*, Kundera provides so many levels that the reader thinks he or she must finally have arrived at meaning, if nowhere else than in the authorial intrusion, in which Kundera speaks directly to the reader. But is this Kundera speaking to the reader? Or is it yet just another representation, a representation of Kundera written by Kundera nearly two decades ago? And what of Sabina's paintings? Certainly the reader believes that the world revealed in the crack is the truth. But again, even the world behind the surface of Sabina's paintings is still more representation. Even more unsettling is this: Sabina's paintings do not exist in reality, no matter how clearly the reader envisions them. The surface painting and the painting below the surface are not paintings at all but black ink on white paper, words on the page, just as Magritte's pipe is not a pipe and Sabina's bowler hat is not a bowler hat. Kundera playfully reminds his reader with this enigmatic symbol that all representation is just representation, and, as it attempts to reveal, it necessarily conceals.

Source: Diane Andrews Henningfeld, Critical Essay on *The Unbearable Lightness of Being*, in Novels for Students, Gale, 2003.

> [Kundera] argues that he has invented a new method of writing a novel. His major works written since the 1980s consist of a series of texts which are bound together by a number of salient themes rather than by the narrative itself."

Jan Čulik

In the following essay, Čulik examines Kundera's work in the context of his life.

Milan Kundera is a major contemporary French/Czech writer who has succeeded in communicating the East European experience of life under totalitarian communism to a wide international public. Most recently, he has used his experience of life both in the East and in the West for commenting on contemporary Western civilization. Milan Kundera's knowledge of life in Czechoslovakia under Soviet rule has led him to important insights regarding the human condition of people living both in the East and in the West. Since Kundera moved to France in 1975, he has become an author of considerable international renown.

In Czechoslovakia after World War II, Kundera was a member of the young, idealist communist generation who were trying to bring about a "paradise on Earth," a communist utopia. It was not until their middle age that they realised that the communist regime had abused their idealism and that they had brought their nation into subjugation. This realisation resulted in a feeling of guilt which Milan Kundera has been trying to exorcise by his literary work in which, especially after leaving for the West, he has been able, by contrasting the Western and the East European experience, to elucidate important aspects of contemporary human existence. Kundera's mature work serves as a warning: the author argues that human perception is flawed and that human beings fall prey to false interpretations of reality. The primary impulse for this cognitive scepticism is undoubtedly Kundera's traumatic experience of his younger years when he uncritically supported communist ideology.

While he lived in Czechoslovakia, Kundera was always in the forefront of indigenous public debate on cultural issues. In the 1950s, he published lyrical poetry which while conforming to the demands of official communist literary style of "socialist realism" highlighted the importance of individual personal experience. Later, Kundera came to abhor lyricism and sentimentality.

In his own words, he "found himself" as a writer when, in the mid-1960s, he wrote short stories, later gathered in *Laughable Loves*. These are miniature dramas of intimate human relationships. Most of these short stories are based on bittersweet anecdotes which deal with sexual relations of two or three characters. Kundera believes that looking at people through the prism of erotic relationships reveals much about human nature. Sex and lovemaking is an important instrument for Kundera which enables him to delve into the minds of his characters in all his mature works.

Many Czech critics regard Kundera's first novel, *Žert* (*The Joke*) as his finest achievement. Here Kundera develops for the first time his most important theme: the warning that it is impossible to understand and control reality. The novel is a story of a young communist student, Ludvík Jahn, who, out of frustration that he cannot get a female-fellow student into bed, sends her a postcard in which he mocks her political beliefs. The postcard is intercepted and Ludvík is punished by being expelled from university and sent to work in the mines. Throughout his later life, Ludvík bears a grudge against all his former fellow students who voted for his expulsion. He plans an intricate revenge. However, it is impossible to enter the same river twice and Ludvík's plan misfires: although he prides himself on his intellectual capacity, his perception of reality is just as flawed as the perception of the "emotional" and "lyrical" women whom he despises. The structure of the novel is pluralist and polyphonic: the author compares and contrasts the testimonies of a number of different protagonists, thus forcing the reader to come to the conclusion that reality is unknowable. Most Western critics saw *The Joke* primarily as a criticism of Stalinist communism, yet Kundera rightly rejected such a simplistic interpretation.

Kundera further developed his writing style particularly in his novels *Kniha smíchu a zapomnění* (*The Book of Laughter and Forgetting*) and *Nesnesitelná lehkost bytí* (*The Unbearable Lightness of Being*), which made his name in the West in the 1980s. He argues that he has invented

---

Soviet troops march into Prague in September, 1968, to put an end to democratic reform movements formed during the Prague Spring

a new method of writing a novel. His major works written since the 1980s consist of a series of texts which are bound together by a number of salient themes rather than by the narrative itself. These themes are examined and analysed by means of variations, like in a musical composition.

In *The Book of Laughter and Forgetting*, a major theme when analysing people's insufficiencies in perceiving reality, is forgetting. One of the main characters of the novel, Czech emigré Tamina, who leads a meaningless and isolated existence in France, is trying desperately and unsuccessfully to reconstruct her life in Czechoslovakia with her now dead husband. In *The Unbearable Lightness of Being*, a work which was hailed in the West as a masterpiece, Kundera's preoccupations with insufficiencies of perception, lyricism, privacy and misunderstanding are re-examined in a polyphonic structure with a more traditional narrative line. It is a story of two Czech emigrés, Tomáš and Tereza who return to communist Czechoslovakia on an impulse and suffer the consequences.

In his later works, Kundera deals with various frustrating features of human behaviour, and again returns to the themes of privacy, individuality, perception and herd behaviour. *Immortality*, "a novel

of debate," is—among other things—a strong criticism of contemporary, superficial, Western civilisation in which commercial media and advertising images rule supreme and reduce everything to manipulated, meaningless drivel. Kundera here stands in awe over the mystery and authenticity of life and protests with all his might against its trite, consumerist simplification.

Source: Jan Čulik, "Kundera, Milan," in *Reference Guide to World Literature*, 3d ed., edited by Sara Pendergast and Tom Pendergast, Vol. 1, St. James Press, 2003, pp. 572–74.

Barbara Day

In the following essay, Day gives an overview of Kundera's work.

Milan Kundera's development as a writer has been strongly influenced by historical events. During World War II and in the brief, dynamic years which followed he was committed to the Communist cause; he later justified his enthusiasm with the explanation, "Communism enthralled me in much the way Stravinsky, Picasso and Surrealism had. It promised a great, miraculous metamorphosis, a totally new and different world" (New York Times Book Review). But in the 1960s, while still a member of the Communist Party, he became uneasy

> The predominant theme in Kundera's writing is that of identity: not simply the identity of the inner self, but with whom and with what a person identifies his or her self."

about its actual practice, including the policy concerning censorship. Kundera was one of a number of writers who refused to make changes in the articles they wrote and so ran the risk of remaining unpublished, but who eventually won greater freedom in the material which they did succeed in publishing.

The predominant theme in Kundera's writing is that of identity: not simply the identity of the inner self, but with whom and with what a person identifies his or her self. In the work Kundera completed while living in Czechoslovakia this theme has three strands: identification with (or commitment to) an ideology; identification with (or desire for) an idealised self-image; and identification with a history and a tradition.

In the mid-1950s Kundera was known to the Czech reading public as a poet, author of three collections: *Člověk zahrada širá* (Man: A Broad Garden), *Poslední máj* (The Last May), and *Monology* (Monologues). *Poslední máj* is particularly remarkable as an apparent sanctification of the Communist journalist Julius Fučík, who was executed by the Nazis.

Kundera's first published fiction, the short stories *Směšné lásky* (Laughable Loves), deal with the idealised self-image. The characters in the stories pride themselves on being able to manipulate the world around them and live out their self-images. In reality, however, they have no control over their lives; they can be humiliated by a simple chain of events or by another victim of chance. These hedonists are very different from the subject of Kundera's first full-scale work, *Umění románu: cesta Vladislava Vančury za velkou epikou* (The Art of the Novel: Vladislav Vančura's Road in Search of the Great Epic). (This is a different book from his 1987 work, *L'Art du roman*). Vančura had been a

member of the pre-war avant-garde, a writer and a Communist, who was executed by the Nazis at the end of the war. Kundera placed Vančura's work in the context of the world novel: of Henry Fielding, Sir Walter Scott, Leo Tolstoy, Honoré de Balzac, Gustave Flaubert, and Anatole France. Vančura, both in his commitment to Communism and his place in European culture, represented the antithesis of the ephemeral subjects of *Laughable Loves*.

Kundera's first play, *Majitelé klíčç* (The Owners of the Keys), also presents a contrast between material comfort and a commitment to history. The setting is a provincial town during the German occupation; the (positive) hero has to decide whether he will rejoin the (Communist) resistance—a decision which will mean the betrayal of his wife and her petit bourgeois parents to the Nazis. However, although the play was effective in dramatic terms, its content was conventional Socialist Realism. More significant was Kundera's first novel, *Žert* (The Joke), which tells the story of Communism in Czechoslovakia between the years 1948 and 1965. Through the experiences of its characters it traces the loss of idealism, the hopeless reliance on hollow images. Paradoxically, the character who remains inwardly most loyal to Communist ideals also values the folk traditions of the country's past.

Before August 1968, the Theatre on the Balustrade in Prague had commissioned a play from Kundera which was produced there in May 1969. *Ptákovina* (Cock-a-Doodle-Do) is set in a school staffed by cringing or sadistic teachers; the action is triggered by a crude practical joke played by the headmaster that eventually rebounds on him. The theme of the play is moral degradation in a society which has lost its values. *Jakub a pán* (Jacques and His Master), on the other hand, was written as an "homage to Diderot," a variation on Diderot's *Jacques le fataliste*. Kundera later claimed that when he wrote it, he saw the shadow of encroaching Asian hordes falling across the western world, and felt that he was trying to hold on to the disappearing civilisation of Diderot's world.

The subject of the novel *La Vie est ailleurs* (Life Is Elsewhere) is the degeneration which brought the West close to disintegration. The young poet, Jaromil—a precocious surrealist and Party hack poet—thinks of himself as an intellectual descendant of Arthur Rimbaud; to Kundera, he is a forerunner of the pretentious students revolting in the streets of Paris in May 1968. In *La Valse aux adieux* (The Farewell Party) the theme is death.

The action follows five days in the life of a popular jazz trumpeter who tries to persuade a young nurse to abort the child which she claims is his; it is a picture of a society in the grip of a life-denying force which seeks to suppress and condemn every natural, irrational or "mystical" experience.

In July 1967, during the run-up to the Prague Spring, Kundera, together with Ivan Klíma, Václav Havel, and Ludvík Vaculík (*qq.v.*), made a speech at the Congress of the Czechoslovak Writers' Union which was regarded by Party functionaries as a political outrage. Kundera appealed to writers to consider the role of literature in the wider context of Czech history. He described how the writers of the 19th century had helped to shape Czechoslovakia's destiny, and asked whether today's writers were prepared to let the decline into provincialism and officially sanctioned vandalism continue.

In Spring 1970, 18 months after the Russian occupation, the Communists embarked on a systematic humiliation of those considered to be in any way responsible. Early in 1970 Kundera lost his lectureship in world literature at the Prague Film Academy. At this time he did not expect to be published again in Czechoslovakia in his lifetime, and in 1975 accepted the post of Professor of comparative literature at the University of Rennes in France. Soon afterwards he was notified of the confiscation of his Czechoslovak citizenship. Ironically, the exile and the loss of his nationality led him to reassess his position, and to consider himself as a European rather than a Czechoslovak writer.

It was in France that Kundera wrote the two novels that enhanced his international fame—*Le Livre du rire et de l'oubli* (*The Book of Laughter and Forgetting*) and *L'Insoutenable Légéreté de l'être* (*The Unbearable Lightness of Being*). In these novels he abandons continuous narrative for a structure which resembles film collage. He juxtaposes one narrative with another, moves backward and forward in time, fictionalises historical characters, and treats fictional characters as real by bringing them into dialogue with the author-narrator. In *The Book of Laughter and Forgetting* the central character is Tamina, an exiled Czech working as a waitress in a provincial French town, who tries to remember her dead husband and to regain the diary and letters she left behind in Prague. In *The Unbearable Lightness of Being* Kundera contrasts the fate of two exiles, Tereza and Sabina: the one drawn back to her homeland and her death; the other who floats free and drifts to America. The novel weaves a web of chance encounters, uncertainties, and betrayals, both political and personal. The third member of the triangle is Tomas, husband of Tereza and lover of (among many other women) Sabina. Tomas is a surgeon who returns with Tereza to "normalised" Prague where, harassed by the secret police, he becomes a window cleaner. He and Tereza take "the only escape open to them," life in the countryside, where those who no longer have anything to lose have nothing to fear. They die together, when the weight of Tomas's badly main-tained truck crushes their bodies into the earth. Sabina, abandoning one lover in Geneva on her way to Paris, with a final destination of America, is aware of emptiness all around her: "Until that time, her betrayals had filled her with excite-ment and joy, because they opened up new paths to new adventures of betrayal. But what if the paths came to an end? One could betray one's parents, husband, country, love, but when parents, husband, country and love were gone—what was left to betray?"

The theme of identity powerfully re-emerges in Kundera's most recent novel, *L'Immortalité* (*Immortality*). It is not the immortal soul that Kundera is thinking of, but earthly immortality; as Laura says: "After all, we want to leave something behind!" only to be challenged by her sister Agnes's "sceptical astonishment." Although Agnes's life forms the axis of the novel, around it revolve other stories, fantasies, and feuilletons. Central to the theme is the story of Bettina von Arnim, who created her own immortality out of two or three meetings and an exchange of letters with Goethe. The structure of *Immortality* is built on echo and reflection, gesture and memory. Kundera contrasts the reality experienced by his grandmother in her Moravian village community with the "reality" seen by the average Parisian businessman on his evening TV news. Immortality is not in the roles we create for ourselves, the images we set up for posterity, but in the continuity of life and the fragile survival of our culture.

History is for Kundera the land and its traditions, which have shaped lives for generations. His exile from his country has shaped his awareness of the disintegration of European society. In his writing he tries to recapture and hold on to the last remnants of a vanishing western civilisation.

Source: Barbara Day, "Kundera, Milan," in *Contemporary World Writers*, 2d ed., edited by Tracy Chevalier, St. James Press, 1993, pp. 301–03.

Italo Calvino

In the following essay, Calvino explores how Kundera's "characters' stories are his first interest" in The Unbearable Lightness of Being.

When he was twelve, she suddenly found herself alone, abandoned by Franz's father. The boy suspected something serious had happened, but his mother muted the drama with mild, insipid words so as not to upset him. The day his father left, Franz and his mother went into town together, and as they left home Franz noticed that she was wearing a different shoe on each foot. He was in a quandry: he wanted to point out her mistake, but was afraid he would hurt her. So during the two hours they spent walking through the city together he kept his eyes fixed on her feet. It was then that he had his first inkling of what it means to suffer.

This passage from *The Unbearable Lightness of Being* illustrates well Milan Kundera's art of storytelling—its concreteness, its finesse—and brings us closer to understanding the secret due to which, in his last novel, the pleasure of reading is continuously rekindled. Among so many writers of novels, Kundera is a true novelist in the sense that the characters' stories are his first interest: private stories, stories, above all, of couples, in their singularity and unpredictability. His manner of storytelling progresses by successive waves (most of the action develops within the first thirty pages; the conclusion is already announced halfway through; every story is completed and illuminated layer by layer) and by means of digressions and remarks that transform the private problem into a universal problem and, thereby, one that is ours. But this overall development, rather than increasing the seriousness of the situation, functions as an ironic filter lightening its pathos. Among Kundera's readers, there will be those taken more with the goings-on and those (I, for example) more with the digressions. But even these become the tale. Like his eighteenth-century masters Sterne and Diderot, Kundera makes of his extemporaneous reflections almost a diary of his thoughts and moods.

The universal-existential problematic also involves that which, given that we are dealing with Czechoslovakia, cannot be forgotten even for a minute: that ensemble of shame and folly that once was called history and that now can only be called the cursed misfortune of being born in one country rather than another. But Kundera, making of this not "the problem" but merely one more complication of life's inconveniences, eliminates that dutiful, distancing respect that every literature of the oppressed rouses within us, the undeserving privi-leged, thereby involving us in the daily despair of Communist regimes much more than if he were to appeal to pathos.

The nucleus of the book resides in a truth as simple as it is ineludible: It is impossible to act according to experience because every situation we face is unique and presents itself to us for the first time. "Any schoolboy can do experiments in the physics laboratory to test various scientific hypotheses. But man, because he has only one life to live, cannot conduct experiments to test whether to follow his passion (compassion) or not."

Kundera links this fundamental axiom with corollaries not as solid: the lightness of living for him resides in the fact that things only happen once, fleetingly, and it is therefore as if they had not happened. Weight, instead, is to be found in the "eternal recurrence" hypothesized by Nietzsche: every fact becomes dreadful if we know that it will repeat itself infinitely. But (I would object) if the "eternal recurrence"—the possible meaning of which has never been agreed upon—is the return of the same, a unique and unrepeatable life is precisely equal to a life infinitely repeated: every act is irrevocable, non-modifiable for eternity. If the "eternal recurrence" is, instead, a repetition of rhythms, patterns, structures, hieroglyphics of fate that leave room for infinite little variants in detail, then one could consider the possible as an ensemble of statistical fluctuations in which every event would not exclude better or worse alternatives and the finality of every gesture would end up lightened.

Lightness of living, for Kundera, is that which is opposed to irrevocability, to exclusive univocity: as much in love (the Prague doctor Tomas likes to practice only "erotic friendships" avoiding passionate involvements and conjugal cohabitation) as in politics (this is not explicitly said, but the tongue hits where the tooth hurts, and the tooth is, naturally, the impossibility of Eastern Europe's changing—or at least alleviating—a destiny it never dreamed of choosing).

But Tomas ends up taking in and marrying Tereza, a waitress in a country restaurant, out of "compassion." Not just that: after the Russian invasion of '68, Tomas succeeds in escaping from Prague and emigrating to Switzerland with Tereza who, after a few months, is overcome by a nostalgia that manifests itself as a vertigo of weakness over the weakness of her country without hope, and she returns. Here it is then that Tomas, who would have every reason, ideal and practical, to remain in Zurich, also decides to return to Prague, despite an awareness that he is entrapping himself, and to face persecutions and humiliations (he will no longer be able to practice medicine and will end up a window washer).

Why does he do it? Because, despite his professing the ideal of the lightness of living, and despite the practical example of his relationship with his friend, the painter Sabina, he has always suspected that truth lies in the opposing idea, in weight, in necessity. "Es muss sein!" / "It must be" says the last movement of Beethoven's last quartet. And Tereza, love nourished by compassion, love not chosen but imposed by fate, assumes in his eyes the meaning of this burden of the ineluctable, of the "Es muss sein!"

We come to know a little later (and here is how the digressions form almost a parallel novel) that the pretext that led Beethoven to write "Es muss sein!" was in no way sublime, but a banal story of loaned money to be repaid, just as the fate that had brought Tereza into Tomas's life was only a series of fortuitous coincidences.

In reality, this novel dedicated to lightness speaks to us above all of constraint: the web of public and private constraints that envelops people, that exercises its weight over every human relationship (and does not even spare those that Tomas would consider passing *couchages*). Even the Don Juanism, on which Kundera gives us a page of original definitions, has entirely other than "light" motivations: whether it be when it answers to a "lyrical obsession," which is to say it seeks among many women the unique and ideal woman, or when it is motivated by an "epic obsession," which is to say it seeks a universal knowledge in diversity.

Among the parallel stories, the most notable is that of Sabina and Franz. Sabina, as the representative of lightness and the bearer of the meanings of the book, is more persuasive than the character with whom she is contrasted, that is, Tereza. (I would say that Tereza does not succeed in having the "weight" necessary to justify a decision as self-destructive as that of Tomas.) It is through Sabina that lightness is shown to be a "semantic river," that is to say, a web of associations and images and words on which is based her amorous agreement with Tomas, a complicity that Tomas cannot find again with Tereza, or Sabina with Franz. Franz, the Swiss scientist, is the Western progressive intellectual, as can be seen by he who, from Eastern Europe, considers him with the impassive objectivity of the ethnologist studying the customs of an inhabitant of the antipodes. The vertigo of indeter-

> In reality, this novel dedicated to lightness speaks to us above all of constraint: the web of public and private constraints that envelops people, that exercises its weight over every human relationship. . . ."

mination that has sustained the leftist passions of the last twenty years is indicated by Kundera with the maximum of precision compatible with so elusive an object: "The dictatorship of the proletariat or democracy? Rejection of the consumer society or demands for increased productivity? The guillotine or an end to the death penalty? It is all beside the point." What characterizes the Western left, according to Kundera, is what he calls the Grand March, which develops with the same vagueness of purpose and emotion:

. . . yesterday against the American occupation of Vietnam, today against the Vietnamese occupation of Cambodia; yesterday for Israel, today for the Palestinians; yesterday for Cuba, tomorrow against Cuba—and always against America; at times against massacres and at times in support of other massacres; Europe marches on, and to keep up with events, to leave none of them out, its pace grows faster and faster, until finally the Grand March is a procession of rushing, galloping people and the platform is shrinking and shrinking until one day it will be reduced to a mere dimensionless dot.

In accordance with the agonized imperatives of Franz's sense of duty, Kundera brings us to the threshold of the most monstrous hell generated by ideological abstractions become reality, Cambodia, and describes an international humanitarian march in pages that are a masterpiece of political satire.

At the opposite extreme of Franz, his temporary partner Sabina, by virtue of her lucid mind, acts as the author's mouthpiece, establishing comparisons and contrasts and parallels between the experience of the Communist society in which she grew up and the Western experience. One of the pivotal bases for these comparisons is the category of kitsch. Kundera explores kitsch in the sense of edulcorated, edifying, "Victorian" representation, and he thinks naturally of "socialist realism" and of political propaganda, the hypocritical mask of all horrors. Sabina, who, having established herself in the United States, loves New York for what there is there of "non-intentional beauty," "beauty by error," is upset when she sees American kitsch, Coca-Cola-like publicity, surface to remind her of the radiant images of virtue and health in which she grew up. But Kundera justly specifies:

> Kitsch is the aesthetic idea of all politicians and all political parties and movements. Those of us who live in a society where various political tendencies exist side by side and competing influences cancel or limit one another can manage more or less to escape the kitsch inquisition ... But whenever a single political movement corners power, we find ourselves in the realm of *totalitarian kitsch.*

The step that remains to be taken is to free one-self of the fear of kitsch, once having saved one-self from its totalitarianism, and to be able to see it as an element among others, an image that quickly loses its own mystifying power to conserve only the color of passing time, evidence of medi-ocrity or of yesterday's naïveté. This is what seems to me to happen to Sabina, in whose story we can recognize a spiritual itinerary of reconciliation with the world. At the sight, typical of the American idyll, of windows lit in a white clapboard house on a lawn, Sabina is surprised by an emotional real-ization. And nothing remains but for her to con-clude: "No matter how we scorn it, kitsch is an integral part of the human condition."

A much sadder conclusion is that of the story of Tereza and Tomas; but here, through the death of a dog, and the obliteration of their own selves in a lost site in the country, there is almost an ab-sorption into the cycle of nature, into an idea of the world that not only does not have man at its cen-ter, but that is absolutely not made for man.

My objections to Kundera are twofold; one ter-minological and one metaphysical. The termino-logical concerns the category of kitsch within which Kundera takes into consideration only one among many meanings. But the kitsch that claims to rep-resent the most audacious and "cursed" broad-mindedness with facile and banal effects is also part of the bad taste of mass culture. Indeed, it is less dangerous than the other, but it must be taken into account to avoid our believing it an antidote. For example, to see the absolute contrast with kitsch in the image of a naked woman wearing a man's bowler hat does not seem to me totally convincing.

The metaphysical objection takes us farther. It regards the "categorical agreement with being," an

attitude that, for Kundera, is the basis of kitsch as an aesthetic ideal. "The line separating those who doubt being as it is granted to man (no matter how or by whom) from those who accept it without reservation" resides in the fact that adherence im-poses the illusion of a world in which defecation does not exist because, according to Kundera, s—t is absolute metaphysical negativity. I would ob-ject that for pantheists and for the constipated (I belong to one of these two categories, though I will not specify which) defecation is one of the great-est proofs of the generosity of the universe (of na-ture or providence or necessity or what have you). That s—t is to be considered of value and not worthless is for me a matter of principle.

From this some fundamental consequences de-rive. In order not to fall either into vague sentiments of a universal redemption that end up by producing monstrous police states or into generalized and tem-peramental pseudo-rebellions that are resolved in sheepish obedience, it is necessary to recognize how things are, whether we like them or not, both within the realm of the great, against which it is useless to struggle, and that of the small, which can be mod-ified by our will. I believe then that a certain de-gree of agreement with the existent (s—t included) is necessary precisely because it is incompatible with the kitsch that Kundera justly detests.

Source: Italo Calvino, "On Kundera," in *Review of Con-temporary Fiction*, Vol. 9, No. 2, Summer 1989, pp. 53–57.

John Bayley

In the following essay excerpt, Bayley explores how Kundera balances lighter, more eternal ele-ments in his novel with the weight of reality and mortality.

Like most novelists of the present time Kun-dera is a theorist of his art, not only weaving ideas about it into the texture of the fiction he is invent-ing, but making the invention itself, and the char-acters produced by it, determined by his conception of where fiction can end and begin. From a casual sentence or two when we are getting on towards the end of *The Unbearable Lightness of Being* we discover that the hero and heroine (conventional terms which carry an unusual emphasis in this novel) were (or are to be) killed in a driving acci-dent shortly after the novel ends.

The confusion of tenses—were they killed, or are they to be killed?—shows the novelist drawing attention to a deliberate formal confusion: what is inside the fiction and what is outside it? The con-fusion can only be formal, of course, for anything mentioned in a novel belongs to that novel and nowhere else. The effect is none the less potent, how potent we can see if we imagine, for instance, that Henry James were to casually inform us, in *What Maisie Knew*, that something Maisie *didn't* know was that she would die of a chill and fever a few weeks after her story ends. James knew, as he put it in the Preface to *Roderick Hudson*, that "relations stop nowhere" and that the artists problem is to "draw the circle in which they shall happily appear to do so." The death of Roderick Hudson, as of Daisie Miller, indicates that the case under artistic examination has been closed, a conclusion or a diagnosis reached. But Maisie's case is just beginning; she has just acquired the knowledge to live in the world in which she will have to live, and a secret confidence in her own status as a moral judge. She is like James, entering upon living as James entered upon writing. The formal specification of her story, its drawn circle, includes her survival in a world which both she and her author can deal with.

Maisie was, but also is to be. By covering all tenses she has got outside the domination of time, as most novel characters do, including those whose existence is terminated inside the book, as a completion of its effect. Kundera has sought to combine the time-dominated bathos of contingent living and dying with the extra-temporal status normally assumed in novel characters. It is a curious paradox of the novel genre that we assume its characters live for ever, either by dying in it—a sure passport to immortality granted to Little Nell or Madame Bovary—or by surviving the novel, like Little Dorrit or Jane Austen's Emma Woodhouse, into some reassuringly permanent limbo of non-fiction. Kundera tries to get his hero and heroine outside the novel, but not into this aftermath world. By killing them off outside it he suggests they have never been in it, although their story has been told as if they were.

Like everything to do with the novel the device is hardly new. When Milton's Satan flies up out of Chaos he hits an air pocket. "Fluttering his pennons vain plumb down he drops," and "still had been falling" if the blast from a convenient volcano hadn't sent him back up again. Briefly the reader toys with the notion that the fallen Archangel might have been still going down, like a receding galaxy, at the moment when he reads these words, or when their first readers read them, or when they are read in time to come. In *The Old Wives' Tale* Arnold Bennett tells us that the papers Sophia secretes at the back of the top shelf of a hotel wardrobe may, for all he knows, still be there. By putting us momentarily outside it

such touches of course confirm the fictiveness of the tale, its truth—that is to say—as a tale.

But Kundera uses the device for a different purpose, a more dialectical one. For all its high-spirited vivacity (Kundera is a great admirer of Sterne) this masterpiece among his novels could not have been written by an Englishman, still less by a Frenchman. It is deeply, centrally European from the meeting-place of the Teutonic and Slav tradition, the tradition of Nietzsche in the spirit, and of Kafka's city of Prague, where neither Kafka nor Kundera can now be published. Kafka's heroes do not live in the world of fiction, and yet *The Castle* is one of the most completely realized fictional worlds that the art can show. Kundera sets about creating this paradox even more deliberately.

What is lightness of being? It is the normal state of consciousness, the condition in which we pass our time, a perpetual state of "once only" from which no story can develop and no identity be shaped, no happening acquire significance. It is the state referred to by the German proverb which says *Einmal ist keinmal*—one time is no time at all. Sexually speaking the state of lightness is a state of endless promiscuity, in which each sensation is abolished by its successor, each individual by the next one. The libertine speaks the truth in saying "it means nothing," that no importance or meaning can be attached to any of his goings on. They cannot be set up in a moral frame, the determined frame of an observed life.

Kundera does not set the actual or hypothetical present against the determined or storied past, as Milton and Arnold Bennett do in the examples I have given. He keeps everything in the present, but makes an antithesis between lightness of being, the non-fictional state in which all is forgiven because all is without meaning, and the weighted determined condition of life, story, or destiny which cannot be avoided or denied. Sex belongs to the first, love to the second. And, like the sophisticated technician of fictiveness that he is, Kundera suggests that two now time-honored ways of presenting the consciousness in fiction slot neatly into his antithesis: the sequential and determined narrative of the classic novelist, and the perpetually present envelope of awareness, which receives nothing but impressions. Inside his novel the technique of Balzac and Trollope confronts that of Virginia Woolf and Robbe-Grillet: the guidelines of concentration they set up for the reader become in Kundera a means of philosophic demonstration and debate, philosophy being contextualized as fiction

What Do I Read Next?

- Kundera's *The Art of the Novel* (1986) offers insight into Kundera's aesthetics of fiction and theories of the development of the novel.

- *Disturbing the Peace: A Conversation with Karel Hvizdala* (1990), by Karel Hvizdala and Vaclav Havel, offers a series of interviews Hvizdala conducted with playwright-turned-statesman Havel. Havel went from persecuted artist to president of Czechoslovakia. In this book, he offers his views of Czechoslovakia under communism, of the social and political role of art, and of the historic revolutions that brought democracy to Eastern Europe.

- Nancy Huston's novel *The Mark of the Angel* (1999) has been compared to Kundera's *The Unbearable Lightness of Being* for its similar writing style, content, and adherence to Nietzsche's concept of the eternal return. Huston's work follows the life and loves of a German girl working as a maid in post–World War II France.

- Tina Rosenberg's *The Haunted Land: Facing Europe's Ghosts after Communism* (1995) offers a reflection on guilt and punishment in postcommunist Eastern Europe. This book won both a Pulitzer Prize and a National Book Award.

by the nature of the antithesis itself. Doris Lessing did something similar in *The Golden Notebook*, creating an antithesis between novel creation and notebook creation, but her work is so humorless and laborious, that it fails either to delight the reader or to move him.

Naturally Kundera's hero and heroine themselves embody the antithesis he sets up. Tomas is a Prague surgeon, an insatiable womanizer, a once convinced communist who now has no belief at all in political or social solutions. Tereza, the heroine, is a waitress whom he happens to meet casually in a small town and who falls in love with him. Lightness encounters weight; consciousness meets destiny; the undefined casualness of being comes up against the experience of fictional definition. Being a modern novelist Kundera is not slow to point out the fictional provenance and function of two such characters, and to suggest in what sense they are characters.

> It would be senseless for author to try to convince reader that his characters had actually lived. They were not born of a mother's womb; they were born of a stimulating phrase or two from a basic situation. Tomas was born of the saying 'Einmal ist keinmal.' Tereza was born of the rumbling of a stomach.

Of course neither character is real, but each represents a different kind of fictiveness. With great

ingenuity Kundera makes use of his own highly contemporary proclamation of the fictiveness of all fiction to suggest that from this very fact can be demonstrated important truths about the nature of reality. From the antithesis of two fictive characters emerges an unexpected synthesis, with a new power to move and to convince us.

Tereza is born of the rumblings of a stomach—her own. She was overcome with shame because of the noise it made when Tomas first made love to her. In the excitement of traveling to meet him she had forgotten to eat anything, and she could do nothing about it. Neither of them can do anything about what is happening to them. Tomas, indeed, tries to continue his old life as if nothing has happened. He continues to make love to other women, to a circle of mistresses all of whom live as if everything was abolished as soon as it occurred. At night his hair smells of them, even though he has been careful to wash the rest of himself, and Tereza suffers from unbearable jealousy, which is not a weightless phenomenon.

Tomas, still light and adaptive, still living in the *Einmal*, gets a good job as a surgeon in Zurich, but his habits continue, and Tereza leaves him, goes back to Prague. This should be the moment at which lightness reasserts itself; Tomas might have been a prosperous and promiscuous surgeon in

Zurich; or he might have emigrated to America, as one of his weightless mistresses, Sabina, has done, and lived in the "once only" limbo of modern fiction. But his destiny is the other sort of novel, and Tereza, who "could never learn lightness."

Realizing he cannot live without Tereza he too returns to Prague, just in time for the Russian invasion. He loses his hospital job, becomes a window-cleaner, then a driver on a collective farm. With their dog, Karenin, he and Tereza stay together. They make love in order to sleep together (he has never been able to sleep with a woman before, only to make love to her). The dog, Karenin, of course reminds us of Tolstoy's novel, one of Kundera's many pointed jokes about the fictional form. In *Anna Karenina* the love of Vronsky and Anna can be seen, and by Tolstoy no doubt was seen, as representing what Kundera calls lightness of being. Tolstoy contrasts the weight and destiny of life, the things that matter, Kitty and Dolly and Levin and their children, with the sterile passion of Vronsky and Anna, their bogus menage. Kundera breaks this mould by making the union of Tomas and Tereza deliberately sterile, and by representing the weight between them in the name and person of their big dog, to whom they become increasingly attached, and who at last dies painfully of cancer. It is typical of Kundera's novel that what might be irritatingly knowing—the dog's name and the text it points to—is converted into the most directly, almost unbearably, moving sequence in the book.

Their helplessness, the death of their dog, their own death, news of which reaches us before the novel's tranquil ending—all emphasize the timeless nature of human life, suffering, destiny. Hero and heroine come to live as characters in an old-fashioned fiction might do, but the way in which their death is contrived outside its tranquillity reminds us of the unexpected ending of *King Lear*, when the calm of tragedy is dispelled by the wholly gratuitous death of Cordelia, and the abrupt extinction of Lear himself, wracked by delight at the illusion that she may still be alive.

What is so striking about *The Unbearable Lightness of Being* is the way in which Kundera has succeeded in making so schematic, even diagrammatic, a novel so unexpectedly human and moving. In this respect it has something in common with Lionel Trilling's novel *The Middle of the Journey*, which has in some ways a remarkably similar analytic pattern. Trilling also separates the weight of living from the lightness, associating the

latter with the world of politics and ideology and the former with love and death, and the individual's acceptance of them as determinants of his being. Trilling quotes with admiration E. M. Forster's statement that "Death destroys a man, but the idea of death saves him." The idea of death, like that of love, is incompatible with lightness of being.

And incompatible too with the new versions of Marxist man. One of the most effective satiric ploys in the novel, developing out of the way such satire is used in Kundera's previous novels and stories like *The Joke* and *The Book of Laughter and Forgetting*, is the relation between the political and social pretenses of a Marxist country like Czechoslovakia, and the new frivolous and negative attitudes towards them. The only escape from the congealed political *kitsch* of the regime is into the lightness of total irresponsibility. Kundera shows how the regime corrupts totally the private consciousness of the citizens; and this is more frightening and more desolating than the more simple-minded way (for it was not based upon his own actual experience) in which Orwell had seen opposition to Big Brother being inexorably destroyed until every dissident had learned to love Big Brother. That is a naive prediction of what happens, as is in its own way Trilling's more contemplative image of human privacy and dignity becoming disillusioned by the way the claims on Marxism push them aside. What really happens is for Kundera less dramatic, more depressingly banal. Communism in practice cannot conquer the private life, but makes it light and meaningless, weightless and cynical.

This, Kundera implies, is the final damnation of a frozen ideology. It destroys the instinctive and almost unconscious decencies and weighty rhythms which men and women have always lived by. No wonder Solzhenitsyn has claimed that there is no answer to Marxism except in other and more traditional kinds of spiritual authoritarianism, the old authority of Russian church and state. More empirically, Kundera shows what happens to the citizens of a country for whom total cynicism is the only defense against the hypocritical pretense of the regime that all are joyfully taking part in the grand march towards the gleaming heights of socialism. In the eastern bloc these ideals are now nothing but political kitsch, and kitsch, as Kundera observes, has become "the aesthetic ideal of all politicians." "The Brotherhood of Man will only be possible on a basis of kitsch."

Sabina, an artist and one of Tomas' many lovers, personifies the individual who has been

> Tereza and Tomas and their fated meeting, their clinging together in adversity, their dog's death, their own death, are deeply and unexpectedly moving, as moving as life and death in some old-fashioned novel, like *War and Peace*, or *The Old Wives' Tale*."

spiritually destroyed by the only way she can oppose the regime. She also destroys another lover, Franz, who loves her in the old-fashioned way and feels weighty emotions like jealousy, fidelity, despair, connubial devotion—emotions that fill Sabina with disgust because she logically but fatally identifies them with the propaganda of a communist regime. For her, weightlessness is the only answer, the only way out. Her life-style must express subversion of kitsch.

It amuses Kundera to display the ironies that arise from this. The authorities responsible for art have trained Sabina in the Socialist Realist manner, but she soon learned to practice a subterfuge which in the end became her own highly personal and original style, and which makes her rich and successful when she gets away to America. She produced a nice kitschy composition—children running on sunlit grass or happy workers handling girders—but then with the aid of a few apparently random drops of paint she evoked, as it were, in and beneath the scene a wholly unintelligible reality, a meaningless and therefore liberating lightness of being.

But of course the bogus, the congealed weight of a communist regime, a regime which spawns kitsch everywhere, has called up its oppositional counterpart in the west. Sabina is disgusted to find that her admirers in America mount an exhibition showing her name and a blurb against a tasteful background of barbed wire, and other corny symbols of oppression. This is ideological kitsch by other means, and Sabina protests that it is

not communism itself that she dislikes so much but the horrible aesthetic falsity it brings with it. True communist reality—persecution, suspicion, shortages of all kinds—she finds quite honest and tolerable. What she can't bear is its false idealism, its films, its art, its pretenses. Kundera himself, we may remember, was a professor of film technology before his escape to the west, and his pupils at that time produced a new wave in the Czech cinema.

Sabina, then, is in a subtle but profound sense wholly corrupted by her experience of communism, from which she cannot escape, even in the west. She is condemned to perpetual lightness of being, condemned to a rejection of all values, because every value seems to her compromised with and covered by the slime of ideological falsity. Were she a character in a Dostoevsky novel she would commit suicide. Being in a Kundera novel she merely shrugs it off, and goes on living in the only way she can; but the situation, the dialectic, is decidedly a Slavic one, and reminds us of the kind of tradition in which Kundera is writing. He is too expert a craftsman to make the pattern too clear. But the deepest irony in his book is that Tereza and Tomas unwittingly save themselves by returning to the oppression of Prague, which means disgrace, alienation, and finally a random death: while Sabina, for whom emigration means merely an accentuation of her former lifestyle, means success, affluence and as many lovers as she wants, remains a hollow shell of frivolity, a ghostly bubble. What she calls kitsch is not mocked; it wins out in the end, because in its horrible way it can still represent the enduring values of the human race, the Tolstoyan truths of what men live by.

Of course Kundera is very careful not to let all this become too visible. It is the merest implication in his novel, if that. There *is* a deep moral about suffering and love, but it is overlaid with something much more acceptable to the sophistication of contemporary and international novel-reading sensibility. Kundera's escape from the world of Socialist Realism, and its moral and aesthetic premises, is as complete and whole-hearted as Sabina's; all his writing shows a determination to be as brilliant and as frivolous as any author in the west. The point is obvious if we compare him with Solzhenitsyn, who has simply used the traditional methods of Socialist Realism for a purpose very different from that on which they are employed in their homeland. Solzhenitsyn remains a traditional Russian writer, while Kundera has reasserted for himself a complete European birthright, brought up to date and furnished with all the devices of modernist fiction. It remains to be seen whether his fiction is not too man-made, created by the fashion of the time and disappearing with it.

While both Kundera and Solzhenitsyn are wholly opposed to the state socialism of the eastern bloc, it is because they are technically such very different writers that their "messages" are also so different. Solzhenitsyn opposes communism with an ideal of Russian Christian orthodoxy which is equally authoritarian. Kundera is more intellectual, more metaphysical, more unexpected. He makes no simple East/West distinction, but transforms the symptoms and consequences of communist ideology into our overall modern consciousness, into consciousness as the novel today can present it. He reminds us that self-consciousness—"lightness of being"—is a permanent feature of the human state; and has always been opposed, since the days of the Greek philosopher Parmenides, to the determined aspect of our lives, to love, death, suffering, weight. His novel makes effective play with this ancient opposition by putting it in the framework of all that arises, ideologically speaking, from today's opposition between East and West.

In so doing Kundera reminds us too that the development of the novel form itself shows the same opposition. The novel is both the expression of ever-increasing self-consciousness and its antithesis or antidote. In so far as we have "lightness of being" we have neither future nor past, neither story nor character. Because in terms of lightness *Einmal ist keinmal*, all the bloody events of man's history "have turned into mere words, theories and discussions, frightening no one." They have turned into the light material of the modern novel. But the novel is also its own antidote because we escape lightness by representing ourselves in the weight of plotted and determined fictions. In Cartesian formula we think up characters: therefore we exist. And on the same basis we think up history, stories, morals; erecting them on the grave weight of human necessity, love, death, birth, etc.

By trying to make things ideologically, and thus spuriously "heavy," by emphasizing the Brotherhood of man and so forth, communism has only succeeded in making the consciousness of its subjects lighter, more cynical, more indifferent to everything except pleasure and advantage. Where fiction is concerned the instrument of the communist state is Socialist Realism, which produces its dead artificial kinds of weight, responsibilities, loy-

alties, moralities. The novelist can oppose the state, as Solzhenitsyn has done, by using its own method against it, by making Socialist Realism serve a different though equally "serious" moral outlook. Or it can be opposed by means of fantasy and irresponsibility, as Russian dissident writers—Sinyavsky, Dovlatov, Aksyonov—have lately been doing, and as Kundera has done in *The Unbearable Lightness of Being*. The drawback of this method is that you may throw out the baby with the bathwater, so to speak. By opposing lightness and humor to communist weight the novelist may himself become merely light and frivolous. The dialectical scheme of Kundera's novel recognizes and avoids this danger, but does so much more than dialectically. Tereza and Tomas and their fated meeting, their clinging together in adversity, their dog's death, their own death, are deeply and unexpectedly moving, as moving as life and death in some old-fashioned novel, like *War and Peace*, or *The Old Wives' Tale*.

Source: John Bayley, "Fictive Lightness, Fictive Weight," in *Salmagundi*, No. 73, Winter 1987, pp. 84–92.

Sources

Banerjee, Maria Nemcová, *Terminal Paradox: The Novels of Milan Kundera*, Grove Press, 1990, p. 206.

Bayley, John, Review of *The Unbearable Lightness of Being*, in *London Review of Books*, Vol. 6, No. 10, June 7–20, 1984, pp. 18–19.

DePietro, Thomas, "Weighting for Kundera," in *Commonweal*, May 18, 1984, pp. 297–300.

Doctorow, E. L., Review of *The Unbearable Lightness of Being*, in *New York Times Book Review*, April 29, 1984, p. 1.

Gray, Paul, "Songs of Exile and Return," in *Time*, April 16, 1984, p. 77.

Hawtree, Christopher, "Bottom Rung," in *Spectator*, June 23, 1984, pp. 29–30.

Howard, Maureen, "Fiction in Review," in *Yale Review*, Vol. 74, No. 2, January 1985, pp. xxi–xxiii.

Kinyon, Kamila, "The Panopticon Gaze in Kundera's *The Unbearable Lightness of Being*," in *Critique*, Vol. 42, No. 3, Spring 2001, pp. 243–51.

Le Grand, Eva, *Kundera; or, the Memory of Desire*, translated by Lin Burman, Wilfred Laurier University Press, 1999, p. 3.

Lesser, Wendy, "The Character as Victim," in *Hudson Review*, Vol. XXXVII, No. 3, Autumn 1984, pp. 468–82.

O'Brien, John, *Milan Kundera and Feminism: Dangerous Intersections*, St. Martin's Press, 1995, p. 116.

Further Reading

Brink, André, *The Novel: Language and Narrative from Cervantes to Calvino*, New York University Press, 1998.
Brink's book provides chapter-length analyses of a chronologically arranged series of novels. His chapter on *The Unbearable Lightness of Being* uses reader-response criticism to "explore the gaps."

Misurella, Fred, *Understanding Milan Kundera: Public Events, Private Affairs*, University of South Carolina Press, 1993.
Misurella's book is an excellent, accessible starting point for the student wanting to further study Kundera.

Petro, Peter, ed., *Critical Essays on Milan Kundera*, G. K. Hall, 1999.
This excellent collection of scholarly analyses and interviews with Kundera should prove valuable to those studying Kundera's work.

Under the Net

Iris Murdoch
1954

Under the Net, published in 1954 in London, was Iris Murdoch's first published novel. It relates the humorous adventures of Jake Donahue, a male protagonist who many critics believe is closely based on the author herself. Jake is described by Cheryl K. Bove in *Understanding Iris Murdoch* as a "failed artist and picaresque hero," a sentiment that Murdoch attributed to herself at the time she wrote this book. Although Murdoch was later embarrassed by *Under the Net* because she felt the writing was immature, other critics have hailed it as one of her best works. It is rated ninety-fifth on Random House's top 100 novels of the twentieth century, and it marked the beginning of a long and distinguished career for Murdoch, who went on to write twenty-five additional works of fiction, as well as several books on moral philosophy, one of her favorite topics. *Under the Net* can be read simply as a fascinating story of a crazy artist who loves serendipity or on a deeper level as an existential, absurd reflection on life.

Author Biography

Iris Murdoch was one of the "most productive and influential British novelists of her generation," writes Richard Todd in his book *Iris Murdoch*, and a "powerfully intellectual and original theorist of fiction." In other words, she could write a good story and also thoroughly understood the underlying concepts of her craft.

Iris Murdoch

Although Murdoch was born July 15, 1919, in Dublin, Ireland, to a family with a long history of Irish descent, she grew up in London and only returned to her homeland for holidays in her childhood. Her binational identity not only affected her personality it was also often reflected in her novels, which are known for their strong sense of place.

Murdoch was an only child. She has referred to her relationship with her parents and her memories of her youth as being very happy. Her father, Wills John Hughes, was a civil servant who was a cavalry officer in World War I. Her mother, Irene Alice Richardson, was a trained opera singer. In the 1930s, Murdoch attended Somerville College in Oxford and upon graduation worked in the Treasury Department as a civil servant. During this time, she wrote five novels, none of which were published.

During World War II, Murdoch left the Treasury and joined the United National Relief and Rehabilitation Administration. She was transferred to Belgium and then Austria, where she worked with war refugees. While in Belgium, she became fascinated with the existentialist movement, especially as professed by Jean Paul Sartre, the French philosopher and novelist. Sartre believed that the novel was, as Todd states, "a mode of human enquiry"; Mur-

doch's first published work, *Sartre: Romantic Rationalist*, is a study of Sartre's philosophy. Other writers who influenced Murdoch include Samuel Beckett and Raymond Queneau, who is fictionalized in Murdoch's novel *Under the Net* (1954).

At one time in her youth Murdoch was a member of the Communist Party and thus was refused a visa to visit the United States. She had earned a scholarship from Vassar and planned to study there, but instead she furthered her studies in London and eventually found a job teaching her favorite subject, moral philosophy. She taught first at St. Ann's College in Oxford and later at the Royal College of Art and at University College, both in London. In 1956 she married author and literary critic John Bayley whose own writing is said to have had an influence on her writing. Bayley taught English at Oxford and wrote a memoir, *Elegy for Iris* (1998), on which the movie *Iris* (2001) is based.

Murdoch's parents have claimed that Murdoch was a prolific writer as early as age nine. By the time of her death, she had produced twenty-six novels, the last of which was written in the early stages of Alzheimer's disease, which eventually took her life. *Under the Net* was her first published novel.

Murdoch won several awards in her lifetime. Her book *The Black Prince* (1973) won the James Tait Black Memorial Prize; *The Sacred and Profane Love Machine* (1974) was awarded the Whitbread Literary Award; and in 1978 *The Sea, The Sea*, which most critics agree is her best work, won the famed Booker Prize. In 1987, Murdoch was honored with the British title of dame. She was also made a Companion of Literature by the Royal Society of Literature in 1987, and awarded the National Arts Clubs (New York) Medal of Honor for literature in 1990. She died February 8, 1999, in Oxford.

Plot Summary

Chapters 1–5

Under the Net begins with protagonist James "Jake" Donahue returning to England to find his friend and almost constant companion Peter "Finn" O'Finney waiting to tell him the sad news that the two of them have been asked by Jake's current girlfriend, Magdalen "Madge" Casement, to leave their apartment. The two men have been living there for free. Madge has found a new boyfriend, Samuel "Sacred Sammy" Starfield, who has promised to make her famous.

Jake protests to Madge, but she insists that not only do they have to move, they must take everything with them that day. When Jake asks where he is supposed to go, Madge suggests he contact Dave Gellman, a philosopher friend of Jake's. The two men begrudgingly depart, taking almost every article they possess with them and wandering through the streets of London in search of a roof and a bed.

While Finn meanders over to Dave's place, Jake visits Mrs. Tinckham, the owner of a newspaper shop he often visits, seeking consolation from Mrs. Tinckham's straightforward statements; her willingness to listen and keep secrets; her watchful eye on Jake's meager possessions, which he often stows at her shop when he is between residences; and a shared drink of whiskey or brandy, which Jake provides and Mrs. Tinckham stores behind her counter. "People and money, Mrs. Tinck," Jake tells her. "What a happy place the world would be without them." Mrs. Tinckham concurs, adding, "And sex."

In chapter 2, Jake makes it to Dave's house, where he is reunited with Finn. Dave has told Finn that he can stay, but he tells Jake he must find someplace else to stay. "We must not be two nervous wrecks living together," Dave explains. Then he suggests that Jake find Anna Quentin, Jake's only admitted love. The thought throws Jake off guard. Once she has entered his mind, he cannot think of anything but Anna, and he is determined to find her though he has not seen her for several years.

In chapter 3, Jake encounters Anna at the Riverside Miming Theatre. She is the director of the theatre, and they share intimacies in her office before she abruptly leaves, informing Jake not to try to find her again. She says she will contact him when she is ready to see him again. She suggests that Jake contact her sister Sadie, who is in need of someone to house-sit her apartment. Jake spends the night in Anna's office.

Sadie is introduced in the next chapter. She is a successful actress and lives in a plush, third-floor flat. She tells Jake that she not only needs someone to stay in her home, she also needs a bodyguard to protect her from Hugo Belfounder, the head of the movie studio that employs Sadie. Hugo is a former friend of Jake's. At the mention of Hugo, Jake remembers the first time he met Hugo at a medical research laboratory, where he and Hugo were participants in a test for a new cold medicine. They spent several days there discussing philosophy. It was from these discussions that Jake

wrote his one and only published book. He felt so ashamed for never asking Hugo's permission that he ultimately avoided contact with Hugo. Hugo, according to Sadie, has fallen madly in love with her.

Jake returns to Madge's house in chapter 5 to retrieve his remaining belongings. While there, Sacred Sammy appears and suggests that he give Jake some money to better balance the situation, since Sammy feels Jake has been injured by Sammy taking Madge away from Jake. Jake, knowing that Sammy is a bookie, suggests Sammy place the offered money on a winning horse in that day's races. Sammy wins Jake quite a bit of money.

Chapters 6–10

In chapter 6, Jake sets himself up in Sadie's apartment. While she is out, he enjoys the luxurious food and drink he finds in her cabinets. While relaxing, he discovers a copy of his book *The Silencer* on Sadie's bookshelf. He has not seen a copy in years and is rather impressed with the writing, although he thinks about revising it. The book also stirs memories of Hugo, who coincidently calls Sadie's apartment, but hangs up when Jake identifies himself and asks if they can get together. This puts Jake in a frenzy, and he decides to go over to Hugo's house and confront him in person. He wants to finally confess to Hugo that he wrote a book about their shared thoughts and dialogues without asking his permission. However, he discovers to his dismay that Sadie has locked him inside the apartment, so he cannot get out. Finn and Dave show up at this time; Finn jimmies the lock, and the three men take a taxi to Hugo's place.

In chapter 7, the threesome arrives at Hugo's only to discover Hugo is not there. They go in search of him, basing their search on a note Hugo left to some unknown person that says he has gone to a pub. The men drink their way around a whole neighborhood of pubs without finding Hugo. They do, however, come across Lefty Todd, Dave's friend, who is active in a labor movement.

Chapter 8 includes Lefty's philosophy. Lefty invites Jake to write a political play that will help people understand labor-union issues. By the end of the chapter, the four men are very drunk, and they end up stripping and jumping into a river for a late-night swim.

In the morning, Dave remembers a letter he has for Jake. It is from Anna, who writes that she desperately needs to see Jake. When Jake arrives at the theatre, where she tells him she will meet him, he discovers that the theatre troupe is moving out and Anna is nowhere to be seen. She has left a small note, which tells him she could not wait any longer, having decided to take up some offer she does not define.

Chapter 10 begins with Jake wanting the copy of his book *The Silencer*, which he saw in Sadie's apartment. He returns to Sadie's place and as he climbs the back stairs, he overhears Sadie talking to Sacred Sammy. They are setting up a scheme that involves a manuscript, which turns out to be Jake's translation of Jean Pierre Breteuil's *The Wooden Nightingale*. Madge had given it to Sammy, and he and Sadie are preparing to ask another producer if he is interested in making a movie deal, something that Hugo was planning on doing. So in essence, Sadie and Sammy are scheming behind Hugo's back, wanting to make money in the deal.

Chapters 11–14

Jake learns from the conversation he overhears between Sadie and Sammy that the manuscript they are discussing is back at Sammy's place. Jake calls Finn, and the two of them break into Sammy's apartment. They cannot find the translation, but they do find Mister Mars, a German shepherd who is also a movie star. Jake refuses to leave Sammy's place empty-handed, so he decides to take the dog; however, he cannot figure out how to get the dog out of its locked cage. Finn and Jake carry the whole contraption, with the dog inside, downstairs and hail a cab.

In chapter 12, Jake decides to warn Hugo about Sammy and Sadie's plot. He goes to the movie studio and tricks a guard into letting him inside. Jake finds Hugo on a huge set that looks like a Roman amphitheater. In the center is Lefty Todd, rousing a huge crowd of people with his talk of unionization. Jake takes Hugo down to the floor in a wrestling move, in order to get his attention. As they begin to talk, a huge police squad enters the studio and mayhem breaks out. In the process, Jake is separated from Hugo but still has Mister Mars with him. In order to get past the police barricade without getting arrested, Jake tells Mister Mars to play dead, then carries him out, telling the police that his dog has been injured and he must get him to a vet. Once they are on the other side of the gates, Jake commands, "Wake up! Live dog!" to which Mister Mars responds, and a group of onlookers lets out a cheer.

In chapter 13, Dave, Finn, and Jake discuss what to do with Mister Mars. Jake wants to use the dog as ransom in exchange for his stolen manu-script. Dave points out that Sadie and Sammy have not really done anything illegal, whereas Jake has, by stealing Mister Mars. Jake feels hopeless until a telegram arrives. It is from Madge, who is in Paris and who offers Jake a free trip there if he will come immediately. She has a plan that involves him. Jake decides to go because he is curious about Madge's new plot, and because he has a feeling that Anna is in Paris and he hopes to see her.

Jake arrives in Paris in chapter 14. As he passes a bookstore window, he sees that Jean Pierre Breteuil, the French author for whom Jake has translated many books, has won a literary prize. This surprises Jake, who has always believed that Breteuil is not a very good writer. He feels betrayed in some odd way, as if Breteuil turned into a good writer behind Jake's back. He begins to think of Breteuil as a rival: "Why should I waste time transcribing his writings instead of producing my own?" He then promises himself that even if asked, he will not translate Breteuil's new novel.

When Jake finally arrives at Madge's hotel room, he is struck by how different Madge looks, more refined. She makes a proposal that will pay Jake a great deal of money for scripts for a shipping mogul, who wants to invest in the movie-making industry. As it turns out, Breteuil will be on the board of directors, and the first film will be an adaptation of his latest book. The job turns out to not really be a job, but what Jake refers to as a "sinecure," in which a person receives "money for doing nothing."

Madge tells Jake the new film company will be the demise of Hugo's studio. The new film studio has already purchased the rights to Breteuil's works, so Sadie and Sammy's plot is doomed to failure. Madge adds that Mister Mars has been retired, so his worth has been diminished to that of a household pet. Then Madge confesses that her whole scheme is just to get Jake back. In essence, she would be the one who is paying Jake, while she is being kept by the movie mogul.

Chapters 15–20

Jake thinks he sees Anna in a park while he is still in Paris, but the person turns out to be a stranger. Jake returns to London in chapter 16, and falls into depression. He spends many days in bed at Dave's place. In chapter 17, Jake decides to take a job as an orderly at the hospital located next to Dave's apartment. The routine helps get him out of his despair. While working one night, he sees a man brought in on a stretcher. It turns out to be Hugo, who has suffered a concussion after being hit over the head during a labor rally.

Jake is compelled to talk to Hugo. In chapter 18 he creates a plan. He will sneak back into the hospital after work and visit with Hugo after hours. Jake has questions only Hugo can answer. Once in his room, Jake asks questions about Anna, but Hugo instead talks about Jake's book. He tells Jake that he liked it. When Jake tells Hugo that he got most of the material from Hugo, Hugo has a hard time believing it. When they finally get around to the topic of Anna, Jake is terribly disappointed. It turns out that Anna is in love with Hugo. Hugo, on the other hand, is in love with Sadie, while Sadie is in love with Jake. Jake helps Hugo escape from the hospital.

Hugo told Jake that Anna had sent him letters, so Jake goes back to Hugo's apartment in chapter 19 and steals them. In the last chapter, Jake is with Mister Mars, heading back to Mrs. Tinckham's newspaper shop. He has a lot of mail to read, including a copy of Breteuil's new book and a request that Jake translate it. There is also a note from Finn telling Jake that he has gone back to Ireland. In a letter from Sadie, Jake discovers Sammy does not want Mister Mars back and says Jake can have the dog for seven hundred pounds. Jake writes out the check so Mister Mars can retire. Then he tells Mrs. Tinckham that he is going to find a part-time job. He also decides he is not going to translate other people's work. He is going to write his own.

Characters

Hugo Belfounder

Hugo Belfounder is a gentle soul who represents all that is good about people. He is a deep and profound thinker. He once worked in his parents' fireworks factory, where he made intricate displays that earned good money for his father's business. He could make the fireworks do fantastic things no one else could replicate. However, he tires of this profession and, upon inheriting the business, sells it and invests in a movie studio.

Hugo befriends the protagonist Jake while the two men are volunteering for medical research. They spend several days together in intense dialogue, which Jake transcribes and turns into a published book. Hugo falls in love with Sadie Quentin, Anna's sister. It is Anna, however, who falls in love with Hugo. Hugo allows Lefty to use his studio to talk to a crowd of people about labor unions. During one such talk, Hugo is hit over the head and is taken to the hospital where Jake works. It is in the hospital that Hugo answers many of Jake's questions.

Critics have noted that Hugo represents Murdoch's interpretation of either Ludwig Wittgenstein or his pupil Yorick Smythies. It is through Hugo that Murdoch expresses some of Wittgenstein's philosophical theories.

Jean Pierre Breteuil

Jean Pierre Breteuil is a French author who writes mediocre stories, which Jake gets paid to translate. Toward the end of the novel, Breteuil writes his best work and wins a literary prize. This prompts Jake to want to compete with Breteuil to prove that he is more than just a good translator; he is a good writer too.

Magdalen Casement

Magdalen (known as Madge) is living with Jake at the beginning of the novel, but she tells him he has to move out because Sammy is about to move in. Madge is in love with Jake, but Jake has refused to marry her. Madge later moves to France with a movie mogul with whom she has become involved. She finds that she has more money than she needs, so she offers to pay Jake a living wage without him needing to do much in return. She just wants Jake to be close to her.

James Donahue

James (known as Jake) is the protagonist of the story. He spends his life doing as little work as possible, living in other people's houses for free, and staying as clear of personal relationships as possible. He says his nerves are shattered. The closest he comes to being in love is his relationship with Anna, who has affection for him but is not in love with him; but her sister Sadie is in love with him. Jake temporarily moves in with Sadie to act as her bodyguard. It is through Sadie that Jake meets up with Hugo again after a long absence.

Jake is in many ways the antithesis of Hugo. Whereas Hugo is quiet and meditative, Jake hops around from situation to situation as quickly as one thought changes to another. His actions are completely spontaneous; he cannot have a concept in his mind without physically playing it out to see where it will lead him. When Dave mentions Anna, for example, Jake acts on impulse and goes in search of her immediately. Jake's buddies Finn and Dave like to follow him around as they know there will be adventure involved in whatever Jake does.

Jake also reflects many attributes of the author, leading many critics to believe that Murdoch chose a male first-person narrator both to remove herself from the character and as a vehicle through which she could present many personal details of her own life.

Jake shies away from jobs and makes a very basic living wage by translating books. He feels he is a writer and carries around several half-completed manuscripts but, until the end of the novel, does not sit down and take the time to work on them. He is shiftless all through the novel, flitting from one adventure to the next, never finding that which he is seeking. At the climax of the story, he finally has some issues resolved and is able to make a commitment to settle down, get a job, and find out if he is really as smart and capable as he thinks he is.

Finn

See Peter O'Finney

Dave Gellman

Dave Gellman is Jake's friend. He is not a close friend because he is in many ways too much like Jake, and they tend to get on one another's nerves. Dave teaches philosophy, but he is not so much the pure philosopher as Hugo is. Dave follows Jake around, seeking adventure, and provides some rationality and stability to Jake's life.

Jake

See James Donahue

Madge

See Magdalen Casement

Mister Mars

Mister Mars is a dog who just happens to have a movie contract. He has appeared in several films, and Jake steals him from Sammy's apartment in an attempt to persuade Sammy to give back a transcript Sammy has stolen from Jake. Mister Mars is getting old, however, and, unbeknownst by Jake, is about to be forced into retirement. Jake becomes attached to Mister Mars and in the end buys out his contract so that the dog can enjoy his final years as a non performer. Jake's attachment to Mister Mars marks the beginning of Jake's settling down.

Peter O'Finney

Peter (known as Finn) is Jake's friend. He does not say much, a quality that Jake likes. Finn follows Jake around and often gets Jake out of trouble. There is not much known about Finn, except that he is

from Ireland (in the end, he returns to his homeland) and that he has lived with Jake for a long time.

Anna Quentin

Anna is Sadie's sister, but the two sisters never encounter one another in the story. Anna was a folk singer when Jake first met her. She represents the closest relationship in which Jake has been involved. She flits around almost as much as Jake, often changing her mind about which profession she wants to follow and engaging in frequent relationships with a variety of men. Her actual presence in the story is only one chapter long, when Jakes bumps into her at the mime theatre. They have a brief encounter, and Anna promises to get back to him, but their paths never again cross. At the end of the story, Jake learns that Anna has fallen in love with Hugo. Some critics compare Anna to Murdoch, who also was very flighty in her early relationships and who was at one time a singer.

Sadie Quentin

Sadie is an actress and, according to Hugo, more intelligent than her sister Anna. She is a famous movie star in London, and she engages Jake to guard her from Hugo, who has become obsessed with Sadie. Sadie turns what little affection she has toward Jake. She does not trust Jake, however, or else she knows him too well, because when she leaves him at her apartment, she locks the door from the outside, so Jake cannot get out.

Sacred Sammy

See Samuel Starfield

Samuel Starfield

Sammy is a bookie who has made a lot of money. He is also a schemer. He becomes involved with Madge but drops her after Madge gives him a transcript that promises to make Sammy some more money. Sammy and Sadie plot against Hugo to gain a movie contract with another moviemaker. Their plot fails and Sammy drops out of the story.

Mrs. Tinckham

Mrs. Tinckham is probably the most stable person in this novel. She is a kind of earth-mother figure to whom everyone comes to be consoled. She is a great listener and never reveals the secrets with which people trust her. She owns an old, dusty newspaper shop that Jake often uses as a storage space whenever he is between residences. It is to her place that Jake goes both at the beginning of the story and at the conclusion.

Topics For Further Study

- Iris Murdoch is said to have been influenced by both Jean-Paul Sartre and Ludwig Josef Johann Wittgenstein. Choose one of these philosophers and analyze Murdoch's *Under the Net* in relation to his basic tenets. How does Murdoch demonstrate the philosopher's beliefs through her protagonist?

- What was the literary atmosphere in Europe and in the United States during the middle of the twentieth century? Which authors were winning literary prizes? What were the literary critics saying about the works contemporary to their times? What major literary movements were developing? Write a research paper that concludes with a reading list of novels prominent at the time.

- Research the activities of the Communist Party in London from the 1940s through the 1960s.

How did the Communist Party affect politics in England? How involved was it in the labor movement? Are there any remaining effects of the Communist Party on politics and social issues in London today?

- Research Alzheimer's disease and explain what it is, how it affects a person, what current research of the disease has revealed, and whether a cure is available.

- Read John Bayley's memoirs *Elegy for Iris* and *Iris and Her Friends: A Memoir of Memory and Desire*, and then write your own biography of Iris Murdoch for an audience of elementary-school children. Keep your language simple and the story interesting but uncomplicated. What elements of Murdoch's life do you think might most interest children of this age? Most inspire them?

Lefty Todd

Lefty is a socialist dedicated to unionizing workers. He probably represents Murdoch's involvement with the Communist Party, a party active in the promotion of unions. Lefty attempts to persuade Jake to write plays with a socialist theme, a proposition that Jake only momentarily considers.

Themes

Unrequited Love

Jake loves Anna, who loves Hugo, who loves Sadie, who loves Jake. Like a Shakespearian drama, unrequited love weaves through Murdoch's first novel. Jake, who claims that he does not like people and would rather stay clear of relationships, accidentally falls for Anna, and though she gives into him from time to time, she is forever elusive. Anna instead becomes enthralled with Hugo, whose mind is like a drug for Anna. His thoughts liberate and inspire her. She gives up singing (one

of the skills for which Jakes loves her the most) for Hugo, who then invests in creating a theatre dedicated to mime. In return, Anna loves Hugo, but Hugo finds Anna's sister Sadie more to his liking. Sadie is more intelligent, and Hugo becomes obsessed with capturing her. While he is aloof with Anna, he is clumsy with Sadie, to the point where Sadie fears for her safety. Sadie asks Jake to protect her from Hugo.

Silence

There are several allusions to silence. The name of the only book that Jake has published is called *The Silencer*, and it is based mostly on Hugo's thoughts and philosophy (who in turn reflects the concepts of Austrian philosopher Ludwig Josef Johann Wittgenstein, who professed the inability of language to express the deepest and most significant thoughts). The theme of silence is also apparent in Anna's mime theatre, where the actors do not speak and the audience is asked not to applaud. Jake likes his steady companion Finn because Finn hardly ever speaks. Even Mister Mars, the movie-star dog, never barks, not even when Jake and Finn are stealing him.

Jake, who makes a living translating French novels into English, finds himself unable to communicate when he goes to Paris, putting him into yet another form of silence. The value of silence is summed up in a conversation between Hugo and Jake when Hugo says, "For most of us, for almost all of us, truth can be attained, if at all, only in silence."

There is also the role that Jake plays out as a writer. Throughout the novel, he never speaks with his own voice in his work. Instead he translates the novels of another author, a man Jake criticizes for being a mediocre writer. Jake's only published work is another type of translation, as he all but transcribes conversations he had with Hugo. Jake is embarrassed about having published this book. He feels as if he has stolen the work from Hugo, since the basic tenets of the book are not his own. It is not until the end of the novel, after Jake has been challenged by the award that the French author Breteuil has won, that Jake attempts to create a voice of his own.

Artist versus Saint

Several critics have pictured the relationship between Jake and Hugo as one of artist versus saint. The role of the artist is to communicate ideas, to put them into some kind of form. The saint, on the other hand, is contemplative. Saints are the medium through which ideas are born. Jake and Hugo's most intimate relationship occurs while they are allowing themselves to be used as guinea pigs in medical experiments comparing new cold medicines. During this time they spend their days lost in theorizing and philosophizing. Hugo's concepts are stronger than Jake's. Hugo is the contemplative one. His concepts flow almost without an awareness that he is speaking, a point emphasized toward the end of the novel when Hugo does not even recognize his own thoughts when Jake asks him what he thinks about the book Jake wrote based on Hugo's ideas. When Hugo reads the book, he compliments Jake on his originality. He also states that some of the thoughts expressed in the book were a bit too deep for him.

Jake took Hugo's thoughts, rearranged them, and made them more accessible, much like the work he did for the French author Breteuil. Jake claims that Breteuil's work is clumsy, making it necessary for Jake to re-form it as he translates it from French into English. Jake even takes credit for improving Breteuil's work. Although he criticizes Breteuil's work, Jake himself does not sit

down to create an original work until the end of the novel. However, whereas Jake is compelled to put his thoughts on paper, Hugo has no aspiration to do so. At the end of the book, Hugo aspires only to learn how to make watches, possibly another form of meditation.

Style

First Person Narrative

Murdoch uses a first person narrator for *Under the Net*, but, rather than using a female voice, she relies on a male's perspective. Some critics believe that in so doing, she is able to write less self-consciously. The protagonist Jake is spontaneous, offering a quick pace to the story, as he hops from one thought and one reaction to another. Also, in using a first person narrator, Murdoch is able to develop the inner life of her protagonist by allowing readers to be privy to Jake's thoughts. This limits the scope of the other characters in the story, however, because everything that happens is seen through the eyes of only one person. Even the dialogue of the other characters is interpreted through Jake.

Setting

Setting always plays a large role in Murdoch's novels. *Under the Net* is no exception. Throughout the story, readers are aware that the characters are either in London or Paris, as Murdoch provides the precise names of streets. Jake even criticizes different parts of the city, stating that he prefers certain neighborhoods or sections of the city to others. The names of actual rivers and bridges, as well as the names of pubs, are often mentioned.

The Great Quest

From the opening lines of the first chapter, Murdoch sets up *Under the Net* as a great quest. Her protagonist is pushed out of his comfortable abode and must search for a new place to live. It is this initial action that leads to all the following actions, as Jake bumbles his way first to find a home, then to find an old lover, and then to locate an old book and, later, a stolen transcript. In the process, questions mount around him, questions that are not fully answered until the end of the book. This technique keeps the reader engaged in the story, curious about what might happen next. There are twists and secrets that beguile Jake, and, in turn, readers find they are pulled into the story, also wanting to find the answers.

Traditional Realism

After World War II, many artists wanted to break away from the confines of realism and move into abstraction and experimentation, as they tore old artistic forms into pieces and attempted to put them back together in new ways. Murdoch stood out in a group of her contemporaries for her determination to stay a realist. She preferred to look back to nineteenth-century English literature, which contained the traditional form of plot and rational point-of-view narration. Her novels are based in the real world, as opposed to fantasy. She is also exact in the naming of things and places. If she mentions that Hugo once worked in a fireworks factory, she provides the details of such an environment. She includes the riots between police and labor unions with a historic reference. Her work compares favorably to novelists like Jane Austen, George Eliot, and Sir Walter Scott.

Preliminary Writing

Murdoch was known to plot everything out before she began writing. She knew exactly what would happen and when, before she put pen to paper. She controlled her characters because she knew what they were supposed to do and why. She knew when the tension must rise at just the right place in the novel, as her protagonist becomes engulfed in emotions. Then the climax is reached at a precise moment, and everything is resolved. She was said to write preliminary notes, which usually included summaries of each chapter. The notes consisted of a variety of details, such as bits and pieces of dialogue she might use, descriptions of the characters, and possible beginnings and endings for each chapter. This outline was often revised several times before she actually sat down to write the book. Her outlines were written longhand, as was the actual writing of the full work, which was inked in notebooks, with writing on only one side of each page. The blank side of each page was left open for later revisions.

Historical Context

Philosophical and Literary Influences

Ludwig Josef Johann Wittgenstein (1889–1951) influenced many writers and philosophers at the turn of the twentieth century. Some people believe that he was possessed by the concept of moral and philosophical perfection. His most famous work is *Tractatus* (1921), which he himself later referred to as meaningless. In 1953 he totally rejected the concepts he had originally published in *Tractatus*. As a matter of fact, he eventually stated that what most philosophers have to say about life is nonsense, because language always imposes limitations on thought. What is most purely true cannot be put into words. He also suggested that the philosopher's role is to express what is possible, not what is conceivable. His philosophy is said to have affected Murdoch's attempts to put particulars into words, avoiding references to abstractions. Murdoch also believed, through Wittgenstein's influence, that life can only be shown, not explained.

Raymond Queneau (1903–1976) was a French author and precursor of the literary theory of postmodernism. His works are said to have been a link between the surrealists and the existentialists. He was very interested in language, and some of his novels were written phonetically rather than with proper spelling. Murdoch tried to translate one of his novels into English, but his use of colloquial language presented a challenge that she could not proficiently surmount. Some critics believe that Queneau's *Pierrot Mon Ami* (1942) was an inspiration for Murdoch's *Under the Net*. It is Queneau's book that Murdoch's narrator Jake takes with him when he must vacate his apartment at the opening of *Under the Net*. *Under the Net* is also dedicated to Queneau.

Jake is often referred to as a Sartre hero, in reference to France's philosopher and author Jean-Paul Sartre (1905–1980). Sartre was a proponent of existentialism, which stresses concrete individual experience as the source of all knowledge. This philosophy emphasizes the loneliness and isolation felt by individuals in a world of absurdities, a world in which there is no proof that a spiritual world exists beyond this one reality. Sartre's play *No Exit* is one of his most anthologized works. It tells the story of three people trapped in hell, and its message is that life can be controlled by a person's choices, a theme that Murdoch's narrator Jake plays out.

Another comparison that is made to Jake is the protagonist in Samuel Beckett's *Murphy*, a story about an alienated young man who cannot hold down a job except for a temporary position as a male nurse in a mental hospital. Like Jake, Murphy also has trouble involving himself in personal relationships. Samuel Beckett (1906–1989) is probably best known for his play *Waiting for Godot* (1953). Language in Beckett's work is somewhat useless, as most of his characters try in vain to express what is inexpressible, reminiscent of the thoughts of Wittgenstein. This concept is expressed throughout Murdoch's work.

Compare
&
Contrast

- **1950s:** Elizabeth II is crowned queen of England, and Winston Churchill, Anthony Eden, and Harold MacMillan, consecutively, are elected prime minister.

  Today: Elizabeth II continues as queen of England. Her reign has outlasted ten prime ministers, with Tony Blair serving in the post in the early twenty-first century.

- **1950s:** Existentialism, as espoused by Søren Kierkegaard and Martin Heidegger, is developed in France by Jean-Paul Sartre through his essays and novels.

  Today: Jacques Derrida, a Frenchman whose philosophical essays have inspired and influ-

enced literary criticism all over the world, espouses deconstruction and postmodern theories.

- **1950s:** Forgetfulness in old age is often referred to as a natural state of aging. Generic terms such as dementia or senility are applied to older people who display these symptoms.

  Today: After many years of research, Alois Alzheimer's theories have been accepted, and doctors and researchers have come to recognize the disease that is now referred to as Alzheimer's, an illness that affects over 4 million people in the United States alone.

Youths in Postwar Britain

Before World War II, Britain was a major world power, having gained riches from its policy of colonization. World War II, however, left the British government bankrupt. Shortly after the war, Winston Churchill lost his bid to remain prime minister, as the Labor Party gained strength. Harold MacMillan became the new prime minister in 1957, and he believed in change, which was interpreted as a dismantling of the old British Empire. Some historians believe that by changing the focus from an international one to a domestic one he appeased much of the population that was busy fending for themselves, recuperating from the war, and trying to create new definitions of themselves.

British youths in the 1950s were not as free as their counterparts in the United States. The war had left them with very few pleasures or dreams. They listened to music from the States, which spoke more directly to them than the music being produced in Britain. They could not afford expensive instruments, so their basement musical productions seemed pithy in comparison to the music they were importing. Then in the mid-1950s, a British youth named Lonnie Donegan began a trend. With one official musical instrument, a guitar, and some form of a rhythm base, which often was no more than a

washboard, Donegan caught the imagination of British teenagers. This musical trend gained momentum and soon there were many bands either copying Donegan or experimenting with their own forms of music.

By the 1960s, young people in Britain had a little more cash at hand than in the previous decade, and new bands seemed to appear everywhere. The most popular British bands in the United States were the Beatles and the Rolling Stones. Suddenly, youths in the States were looking to Britain for musical inspiration. London became the center of pop music and pop fashion, as Mary Quant, a designer whose mini skirts and model Twiggy (an extremely thin model) shocked the fashion world.

Youth gangs developed in the early 1960s in the seaside towns of southern England. The two most recognizable were the Mods, who favored stylish clothes and motorcycles and listened to American Motown music, and the Rockers, who liked to wear leather and listen to rock and roll.

Taboos on sexuality as ensconced by the Victorian era began to fall away in the 1950s and 1960s in Britain. This was first signified by a ruling by the courts that D. H. Lawrence's 1930 novel *Lady Chatterley's Lover* could finally be legally published. The ruling was so popular that over 2 million copies were eventually printed. Movies followed suit with more sexually revealing scenes; and musical lyrics became more sexually explicit as well. The women's movement also grew in strength around this same period.

Critical Overview

Under the Net was Murdoch's first published novel. She later felt somewhat embarrassed by this book, claiming it was juvenile. However, as Cheryl K. Bove in her study *Understanding Iris Murdoch* points out: "*Under the Net* foreshadows [Murdoch's] mature works with its fast-paced plot, closely detailed settings, fully developed characters, and attention to moral issues."

Under the Net marked the beginning of a long writing career for Murdoch, who also taught philosophy but only to the point it did not interfere with her writing schedule. Each of Murdoch's twenty-six novels was written longhand and, as John Russell explains in a *New York Times* article, she took each manuscript "to her publishers in London in a capacious paper bag." Her editors were never allowed to make any changes.

Peter J. Conradi, in his biography and study *Iris Murdoch: A Life*, takes great lengths to compare the life of Murdoch to the characters in her books. "It is no accident," Conradi writes, "that each of her first-person male narrators is the same age as Iris at the time of the novel's composition." It is her "first-person novels," Conradi states, that "are often among her best work" and it was through a male narrator that Murdoch was able to "liberate" her writing. Conradi, who notes that upon the publication of *Under the Net*, the *Times Literary Supplement* hailed Murdoch as a "brilliant talent that, despite a lack of 'fit' between characters and plot, promised great things." Conradi writes that author Kingsley Amis in the *Spectator* "admired her 'complete control of her material; [she was] a distinguished novelist of a rare kind.'" Conradi also observes that Asa Briggs, a noted British historian, "was struck by [Murdoch's] ability to turn common experience into poetry."

In a collection of critical reviews of Murdoch's works titled *Iris Murdoch*, Steven G. Kellman notes that a few critics find *Under the Net* to be Murdoch's best work: "Such critics tend to see *Under the Net* as her most successful work, as well as her most original, and her painstaking efforts at creating a fuller and more realistic world in her later

Raymond Queneau, a French author who influenced the writings of Iris Murdoch and to whom Murdoch dedicated Under the Net

books as an aberration, or a retreat into English bourgeois complacencies."

Criticism

Joyce Hart

Hart has degrees in English literature and creative writing and writes primarily on literary themes. In this essay, Hart explores the influence of Ludwig Wittgenstein's philosophy of truth on Murdoch's first novel.

Although she was never a student of the turn-of-the-century Austrian Ludwig Wittgenstein, Murdoch did once meet the philosopher and befriended Wittgenstein's star pupil, Yorich Smythies. Murdoch was also influenced by Wittgenstein's concepts, as many critics have noted, especially in her first novel, *Under the Net*. This influence begins with the title and carries through the story, in particular through her protagonist Jake Donahue.

One of the concepts that Wittgenstein professed in his most widely read philosophical treatise

> "Wittgenstein had tried to define truth, to explain it, or better yet, to explain that one cannot explain it. But he found that even that was ridiculous."

Tractatus (1921) is that the deepest truths, although people might conceive of them, can never be fully verbalized. Truths, he believed, become diminished by the limitations of language. Any attempt to talk about, to explain, or to write a truth is similar to placing a net over the truth, which in essence is to blur the image, to make the truth less than perfect, or, in other words, to hinder it. In choosing her title, Murdoch thus signals that she is incorporating the Wittgenstein theory into her work. To know this allows the reader to look for other ways in which Murdoch explores Wittgenstein's concepts. How might Murdoch have created her protagonist, for instance, to demonstrate Wittgenstein's ideas? How would this affect the rest of her characters? What would be the consequences? How might she symbolize the theory in her characters' actions?

Jake is introduced as he is walking down the street toward the house where he has been living with his close companion Finn (a man who seldom ever talks), and Jake's on-again, off-again girlfriend Madge. Finn greets Jake with the news that Madge has kicked them out. Jake and Finn are to pack their belongings and vacate the house that very day. Finn is disheartened, and Jake is a bit put-off by the sudden change of heart by Madge, but he is not totally surprised. He knows that Madge has wanted to get married. He had even considered it at one point, but he could not commit to such a relationship. Madge, on the other hand, just wants to get married. If she cannot have Jake, she will find someone else, like Sacred Sammy, the bookie. With this first scene, Murdoch demonstrates, on a somewhat simplistic level, the various layers of lies that are spoken in an attempt to express a truth. Wittgenstein believed that in verbalizing truths, only lies come forth. Madge, for instance, really does not want to marry Sammy. She wants to marry Jake. Jake, on the other hand, does not want to leave Madge, but he does not want to marry her either. The character Finn

here represents silence. Only in silence can one remain in truth, according to Wittgenstein.

Jake packs his bags, and his next stop is Mrs. Tinckham's newspaper shop. Mrs. Tinckham is the kind of woman with whom everyone likes to talk. She is a good listener. People come to her and tell her all kinds of personal stories, and they can count on her to keep all their secrets. This draws them to her. At one point, one of her customers becomes so frustrated with her unwillingness to share a secret about someone else that he shouts, "You are pathologically discreet!" In other words, Mrs. Tinckkam, like Finn, represents silence. Therefore she can be trusted. Mrs. Tinckham, with her gift of silence and thus trust, represents truth. "I suspect," states the narrator, "that this is the secret of Mrs. Tinckham's success." Then Jake tries to further describe Mrs. Tinckham, but he cannot quite figure her out. Is she very intelligent or very naïve? He has trouble defining her, just as one would have trouble defining truth. He concludes his observations of Mrs. Tinckham with the statement: "Whatever may be the truth, one thing is certain, that no one will ever know it." To know truth is to translate it, to put it into words. Truth is beyond knowing, according to Wittgenstein.

Jake travels on to Dave's house next, looking for a bed and a roof over his head. Dave is a philosopher, "a real one," Jake says. He also says that he used to like to talk to Dave about philosophy. "I thought that he might tell me some important truths." No matter how much Jake talks to Dave, he finds that they never get anywhere. Jake would present various philosophical concepts, say from Hegel or Spinoza, things that Jake did not fully understand. However, after Jake would submit his thoughts, Dave would tell him that he did not understand him. So Jake would repeat himself. "It took me some time," Jake says, "to realize that when Dave said he didn't understand, what he meant was that what I said was nonsense." This statement is very similar to one that Wittgenstein was known to make. He believed that all philosophers, including himself, could at best only write nonsense. Jake then offers one of Hegel's concepts, "Truth is a great word and the thing is greater still." This is another way of stating Wittgenstein's theory about the limitation of language. Jake finally concedes to Dave, or at least gives up trying to talk philosophy with him, because "Dave could never get past the word."

Jake must next find Anna. After Dave mentions Anna's name, Jake goes into a frenzy. He has not been with her for a while, but suddenly he has an uncontrollable impulse to see her. She is, he describes, someone who is "deep." She is also very elusive and the exact opposite of her sister Sadie. As he continues to describe her, Jake says that he has found her to be "an unfathomable being." The word *unfathomable* can mean either "mysterious" or "incomprehensible." Anna thus also symbolizes truth. Her sister Sadie, to further emphasize this fact, is an actress, someone who pretends. She is flashy and dazzling but not very real. She is a good con artist, and later in the story she actually becomes involved in a deceitful scheme with Sammy, as the two of them weave a web of lies in order to make some money. Jake ponders why Anna never became an actress. He feels that she could have been a good one. Then he concludes that it is because she has a lack of "definiteness": she could not be defined. All these statements about Anna (and her opposite, her sister Sadie) reinforce the idea that Anna represents truth as defined by Wittgenstein.

When Jake finds Anna, she is directing a theatre of mime. She works with performers who move on the stage in silence in order to portray their story. To exaggerate the silence, the audience is requested not to applaud. This silence is too heavy for Jake, which he says falls upon him like a "great bell." When he finally comes face to face with Anna, his first impulse is to turn away from her. He needs to collect his wits, he says. However, as soon as she speaks, Jake declares, "The spell was broken." This could imply that Jake is a seeker of truth, but the truth frightens him. He runs after it, but it is as elusive as Anna, who always seems to be slightly out of his reach. He runs after her until he catches her, and then he is afraid to confront her. When she speaks, she defines herself, and as Wittgenstein stated, this imposes a limitation; and as Jake discovers, when she speaks, the spell is broken. However, he is forever drawn to her "like the warm breeze that blows from a longed-for island bringing to the seafarer the scent of flowers and fruit."

Jake seems caught in a paradox. He appreciates silence, and that is why he likes to have Finn around him, a man who seldom speaks. But Jake abhors solitude. It makes him nervous. For him, silence is best found in a noisy pub, where he does not have to speak to anyone but also does not have to contemplate any of his own truths. He likes the distraction of busy sounds, even though he recognizes that words can break the spell, that one can become entrapped in words, like his friend Dave.

He has the desire to search for truth, but when he draws near it, he is afraid of it.

After Jake's encounter with Anna, he reminisces about Hugo, whom many critics believe represents Wittgenstein himself. Hugo used to work in his parents' fireworks factory, a place that fascinated him. He at one point tells Jake that what he likes most about fireworks is their impermanence and honesty. They were "an ephemeral spurt of beauty." Hugo also says in reference to fireworks: "You get an absolutely momentary pleasure with no nonsense about it. No one talks cant about fireworks." In other words, you do not have to define what you see. You do not have to talk about it. You just enjoy it, like Wittgenstein might have wanted to enjoy truth. Hugo's love of fireworks, however, is destroyed once they are shipped to the United States, where people begin to "talk" about them, to refer to them as pieces of art, to "classify them into styles."

Jake meets Hugo at a medical research hospital, where the two of them give themselves up as guinea pigs for a new cold remedy. They are roommates, and at first Jake fears that Hugo will bore him with endless chatter; but Hugo is completely silent for the first few days. When he does speak, Jake is fascinated by his intelligence. As with Anna, Jake is drawn to Hugo. Jake is always searching for something. He senses that Hugo might have some answers. With Hugo, Jake is comfortable enough to be "frank." Jake becomes so engrossed in their conversations that he enlists for a second medical experiment, and so does Hugo.

Jake describes Hugo as the most objective and "detached" person he has ever met. Hugo has little concept of self: this was not a condition to which Hugo aspired, but rather it was as if he had been born with it. He also has no general theories. Rather, he has separate theories of everything; when Jake tries to tie him down to something specific, he could not. In other words, Jake could not define Hugo. Then one night, Jake and Hugo begin a discussion of truth. "What if I try to be accurate?" Jake asks. "One can't be," Hugo responds. "The only hope is to avoid saying it." They are referring to emotions at the time of this conversation— the truth of one's feelings. The discussion is about defining feelings, which Hugo says is impossible. "Language just won't let you present it as it really was."

Jake goes on to record his conversations with Hugo. He edits them, changing them around, making some things clearer. Then he publishes them in a book he calls *The Silencer*, an ironic little twist, seeing that the book is a conversation about truth, which Wittgenstein stated could only be known in silence, and yet here Jake is trying to capture truth in words, only to call his creation *The Silencer*.

Of all Murdoch's characters in *Under the Net*, Hugo best represents truth. He does not like definitions, and when he finally reads Jake's book, he does not recognize the thoughts contained in the book as his own. He even congratulates Jake for his originality. He neither says anything about Jake having written down truths nor does he attempt to write his own book about them. It is understood that he believes this task to be impossible.

When Wittgenstein looked back on his own earlier writings about truth, he referred to the work as nonsense. Wittgenstein had tried to define truth, to explain it, or better yet, to explain that one cannot explain it. But he found that even that was ridiculous. Murdoch too, when she looked back at her first novel from the distance of several years, thought that *Under the Net* was a bit foolish. She, in her own way, had tried to explain what Wittgenstein believed could never be made clear.

Source: Joyce Hart, Critical Essay on *Under the Net*, in *Novels for Students*, Gale, 2003.

Howard German

In the following essay excerpt, German identifies and discusses the relevance of allusion in Under the Net.

In one of her essays, Irish Murdoch expresses her belief in the importance of details in the novel by citing a remark of Tolstoi's: "Strip the best novels of our time of their details and what will remain?" Miss Murdoch is convinced that the best novels are not neat symbolic works but those written in the manner of Sir Walter Scott, George Eliot and Tolstoi, novels which, while avoiding the purely journalistic, are still richly endowed with details. Her reason for praising this type of novel is not simply that such works can operate more powerfully upon the reader's imagination, but primarily that they are in accord with the nature of the world—contingent, messy, full of disorderly particulars. Consequently, Miss Murdoch's own novels are copiously endowed with details; however, these details are not selected solely to satisfy the demands of realism. For example, while eschewing the symbolic novel, she does use symbols, as the two bells in *The Bell* demonstrate. Moreover, her fiction is rich in details that serve as allusions: incorporated in each of her works is a background of material selected from earlier literary classics,

myths, biographies, and so forth. Since her novels seldom display an *extended* parallel with an earlier work, her practice is perhaps closer to that of Eliot in *The Waste Land* than to that of Joyce in *Ulysses*. In any case, perhaps because of her frequently expressed preference for realistic novels, these allusions have remained almost completely undetected. Since critical discussions of Eliot, Joyce and others have long since shown the value of such allusions in enabling a writer to achieve greater depth in a work or to provide a framework for judgment without entering into the novel in his own voice, my purpose here is not to defend the practice but rather to show the existence of some of the allusive material in Miss Murdoch's first five novels and to suggest the particular relevance of these details in each of the works.

The narrator of *Under The Net*, Jake Donaghue, states that his acquaintance with Hugo Belfounder is "the central theme" of the book: consequently, he spends considerable time in the novel describing Hugo's background, personality and ideas. The reader learns of Hugo's German ancestry; his prosperous family whose wealth came from armaments manufacture; his interest in music, films, and mechanical instruments; his plans for giving away all his wealth; and his powerful personality, which influences not only Jake but others, like Anna. Hugo impresses Jake not only by his honesty about himself but also by the novelty of his ideas. While interested in theories about everything, Hugo has a great distrust of generalities and of language, in particular of the use of language to describe one's emotions: for him, "the whole language is a machine for making falsehoods." Jake's book, *The Silencer*, a dialogue based upon his conversations with Hugo, supports Hugo's ideas. Inspired by Hugo's theories, Anna abandons her singing career and turns to pantomime, an art form uncorrupted by the distortions of language. Readers of Norman Malcolm's *Ludwig Wittgenstein: A Memoir* (London, 1958) will find that many details of Wittgenstein's life and personality are quite similar to those of Hugo described above. (Other less important resemblances such as a simplicity of dress and a passion for personal cleanliness might be noted.) The similarities in their ideas are also obvious. Wittgenstein, whose early work was a source of inspiration for the logical positivists (like David Gellman in the novel), was constantly striving for precision in language: his attitude can be summarized by a frequently quoted statement from the second paragraph of the Preface to the *Tractatus Logico-Philosophicus* (London, 1961): "What can be said at all can be said clearly, and what we cannot talk about we must consign to silence."

Clearly, *Under The Net* is not a *roman a clef* which provides intimate details about one of the twentieth century's most influential philosophers. The correspondence between Hugo and Wittgenstein is far from exact; indeed at the end of the novel, in describing Jake's ascetic living quarters and his career as a hospital orderly, Miss Murdoch is attributing elements from Wittgenstein's life to Jake, not Hugo. The justification for the allusions to Wittgenstein's life and ideas lies in their thematic appropriateness in a novel which is greatly concerned with the way in which life is inevitably distorted when reduced to a formula, when it is placed "under the net." Perhaps the best illustration in the novel of the way this falsification occurs can be seen in the fact that Hugo fails to recognize either himself or his ideas in Jake's book about him.

Another source of allusion for *Under The Net* is the *Aeneid*. Here are a few of the more obvious counterparts: Finn is Jake's *fides* Achates, the birds that defile Hugo's apartment are the equivalent of the Harpies, Miss Tinckham's store is the cave of the Cumaean Sibyl, Jake's refusal of Madge's offer is Aeneas' rejection of Dido, his search for Anna during the crowded Paris carnival is Aeneas' search for Creusa during the sacking of Troy, the fight on the Roman set in the film studio is the battle within the walls of Troy. That episodes in the novel are considerably modified from the originals in the *Aeneid* can be seen by examining the story of the Trojan horse. In Book II, lines 13–245, Laocoon is described warning the Trojans against the wooden horse while they are debating what to do with it; he throws his spear into the side of the horse, causing an ominous rumble from the hollow interior. But Laocoon is destroyed by the snakes; and Sinon, ragged and beaten, makes his appearance to dupe the Trojans into moving the horse within the walls. In the novel Jake appears at the theatre in a bloody shirt and muddy clothes after a night's revelry; outside the theatre he notices a large wooden board being carried away by some men, then jumps into a moving van where he finds a rocking horse, a stuffed snake, and a thundersheet. He rides "in the belly of the vehicle" for a while until he finds a note for him pinned on the side of the horse. Before jumping from the van, he strikes the thundersheet and produces an "uncanny sound" which astonishes the people in the street.

This example suggests the distance between the *Aeneid* and this novel and makes clear that the

> **Miss Murdoch is convinced that the best novels are . . . those . . . which, while avoiding the purely journalistic, are still richly endowed with details. Her reason for praising this type of novel is . . . that they are in accord with the nature of the world—contingent, messy, full of disorderly particulars."**

value of the allusions does not lie in detecting specific parallels such as these. Perhaps one of Miss Murdoch's reasons for using an archetype is heuristic; the search for modern equivalents may help to provide her with the mass of detail which she believes gives the novel its special merit. For the reader the value in this particular set of allusions lies in recognizing the parallel between Jake and Aeneas. Throughout the epic Aeneas is governed by his sense of destiny; when he occasionally forgets his goal, the gods remind him of his role as the founder of the Roman State. While Jake's acts parallel those of various figures in the *Aeneid*—in the van scene described above, his appearance and behavior follow that of Sinon, Laocoon, and the Greek warriors inside the horse—in general he is a counterpart to Aeneas. During the fight and the fire at the film studio, for example, he leads Mars around on a leash and then carries him off on his shoulder just as Aeneas leaves the burning city of Troy leading Ascanius by the hand and carrying Anchises on his shoulders. Jake, like Aeneas, is guided by an idea of fate, of inevitable acts and destiny; a romantic, he is always "expecting something," finding patterns in his life and declaring that events are written in heaven. The weaknesses in such a belief are seen as Jake succumbs to the temptation to publish his book without telling Hugo about it: "my only consolation lay in a dreadful fatalism—and the notion that I was still a free agent, and that the crime could still be avoided, was too

British rock progenitor Lonnie Donegan performing before a teenage audience in 1957

intensely painful to entertain." Although disagreeing with Vergil's emphasis upon a grand design for an individual, Miss Murdoch seems to have found the *Aeneid* an appropriate source for allusions.

Source: Howard German, "Allusions in the Early Novels of Iris Murdoch," in *Modern Fiction Studies*, Vol. XV, No. 3, Autumn 1969, pp. 361–77.

Raymond J. Porter

In the following essay, Porter examines Murdoch's use of leitmotiv—*the recurring blending of certain words, images, and symbols to convey a deeper, cohesive meaning—in* Under the Net.

Iris Murdoch, like many other twentieth-century novelists, began her literary career with a *Bildungsroman*. While commenting on *Under the Net* (1954), Miss Murdoch's first novel, a number of critics have pointed out that Jake Donaghue, the protagonist of the novel, is seeking a way to encounter the world and find himself. Jacques Souvage sees Jake striving for "self-fulfillment based upon self-knowledge"; Frederick Hoffman comments that Jake is constantly revising his conduct "to guarantee its freedom from theory"; and Malcolm Bradbury feels that Donaghue is "a writer or intellectual who is not sure how much one owes to the aesthetic and the social, with their contesting claims."

When we first meet Jake, he is in no way involved with life: he lives with friends, but wants no entangling relationships; he translates novels, but does no original work of his own. The root of his problem is hatred of "contingency"; at the beginning of the novel Jake states, "I want everything in my life to have a sufficient reason." As Hugo Belfounder says toward the end of the book, "The trouble with you, Jake, is that you want to understand everything sympathetically." As Donaghue comes to realize, what he thought he understood, he did not understand at all. He discovers he really has not known his friends but has projected upon them as objective reality his own inaccurate, subjective vision of reality.

During the week which the action of *Under the Net* covers, Jake comes to recognize his misjudgments of Peter O'Finney (Finn), Jean Pierre Breteuil, Anna Quentin, and Hugo Belfounder. Jake had always taken Finn for granted and had never taken seriously his plans to return to Ireland. When Finn does go, Jake "felt ashamed, ashamed of being parted from Finn, of having conceived things as I pleased and not as they were." Jake had translated several of Breteuil's novels, which he considered trash. When Jean Pierre produces a really good novel (it wins the *Prix Goncourt*), "It wrenched me, like the changing of a fundamental category. A man I had taken on as a business partner had turned out to be a rival in love ... Why should I waste time transcribing his writings instead of producing my own?"

But it is Jake's change of attitude toward Anna Quentin and Hugo Belfounder which is more important. In the big "recognition scene" of the novel (a midnight conversation between Donaghue and Belfounder in an unlighted hospital room), Jake discovers that his interpretation of events has been completely wrong: Hugo is not disgusted with him; Hugo does not love Anna, but Sadie, Anna's sister; the Mime Theatre was not Hugo's idea, but Anna's. Hugo also tells how Anna had developed a grand passion for him and pursued him around London. This really jars Jake: "I was struggling to recognize in this frenzied Maenad the Anna that I knew, the coolly tender Anna who was forever balancing the claims of her admirers one against the other with the gentle impartiality of a mother." The next day he thinks, "It seemed as if, for the first time, Anna really existed now as a separate being, and not as a part of myself." No longer suffering under the delusion that Anna is a sort of fairy-godmother to whom he can run for protection, Jake can begin to realize himself.

Most important, Jake frees himself from the influence of Hugo, an influence for which Jake, not Hugo, is responsible. In a flashback, we learn that a few years previous Jake had met Belfounder at a "cold-cure" institution and become fascinated with his ideas, particularly those on human communication. Hugo felt that one can not describe anything accurately: "The language just won't let you present it as it really was." During and after their stay at the institution, the two have long discussions on this topic, and Jake, "completely under Hugo's spell," begins to jot down and re-arrange the material. The result is a book in dialogue form, *The Silencer*. Jake recognizes that it was "from start to finish an objective justification of Hugo's attitude. That is, it *was* a travesty and falsification of our conversations." At this time, he stops seeing Hugo because he feels that his book is a betrayal of Belfounder. As mentioned above, Jake later discovers that Hugo had not recognized his ideas in *The Silencer*, just as he did not recognize his ideas as reflected in Anna Quentin's Mime Theatre.

Of course, this early experience with Hugo was what led Jake to stop creative writing and confine himself to translating: " ... it's like opening one's mouth and hearing someone else's voice emerge";

> " ... [B]oth the initial attitude Jake has toward life and the change he undergoes are not only dramatized through conversation and action but also woven into the very texture of the novel through the author's use of diction, image and symbol."

and to refrain from encountering things and people outside himself: "The substance of my life is a private conversation with myself and to turn it into a dialogue would be equivalent to self-destruction." But, as A. S. Byatt observes, this state of affairs is the product of an "obsession with Hugo's precise vision as an end in itself, the only permissible way of seeing." In the "recognition scene" referred to above, Hugo, himself, observes, "You think far too well of me, Jake." And by the end of *Under the Net*, Jake sees this too, and he slips "under the net" of theory, particularity, projected subjective vision, and is open to the "wonders" of life.

The critical commentaries that have been written on *Under the Net* have stressed the picaresque elements, the initiation theme, and the "philosophies" of the various characters in their relation to Jake Donaghue's development. Miss Murdoch's use of *leitmotiv* has not been explored. A close reading reveals that both the initial attitude Jake has toward life and the change he undergoes are not only dramatized through conversation and action but also woven into the very texture of the novel through the author's use of diction, image and symbol. The recurrence of particular words, phrases, images, and symbols throughout the book gives depth and imaginative force to the surface story of initiation and merges content with form.

Let us first consider Miss Murdoch's use of the motifs of "enchantment" and "reflection" to present Jake's earlier attitude toward people. As related above, Jake's hatred of contingency, his demand that everything in his life have a sufficient reason, leads him to project on others as objective reality his own inaccurate, subjective vision. This tendency is illustrated by the language and metaphors Jake uses to describe his reactions to and feelings for Anna Quentin and Hugo Belfounder. In Chapter Three, he encounters Anna for the first time in several years. They look at each other in silence before "The spell was broken." Shortly after, Jake describes Anna as lying in the prop-room of the Mime Theatre "amid the coloured debris like a fairytale princess." When the meeting ends, Anna says, " . . . don't come back here unless I summon you," and Jake stands "as one enchanted. . . ." This "enchantment" theme, associated with the fairytale, dominates the scene in which Jake pursues Anna through the Tuileries gardens (Chap. 15). She is described as having a "golden head," walking with a "dreamer's pace," and as "outlined against the forest like a lonely girl in a story." The Tuileries at night has the "dangerous charm of an enchanted garden," is an "unnatural garden" containing flowers "quiet as dream flowers." Jake picks up the shoes which Anna discards, and follows her; but the girl he encounters is not his Cinderella, and he leaves the spot in a nightmare-like flight, bumping into and recoiling from trees, statues, and whispering lovers.

"Enchantment" is also associated with Hugo. Commenting on his relationship with Belfounder, Jake says, "I was completely under Hugo's spell"; and in several places he comments that Hugo is his "destiny." Before breaking into the hospital during the night to visit his former friend, Donaghue reveals that his mind "was simply dominated by Hugo. It was as if from his bed in the hospital Hugo were holding the end of a cord to which I was attached, and from time to time I could feel it twitching." And as he touches the hospital room door, "It opened like a dream door. . . ." What follows is the all important conversation with Hugo which puts an end to Jake's fairy-tales and enchantments and opens his eyes to reality.

Miss Murdoch also makes use of images of "reflection" to underline the inaccuracy of Jake's subjective view of reality. The notion that there is a difference between a real thing and its reflected image is introduced in a scene in Chapter Four. Jake is in a beauty parlour talking with Sadie Quentin while looking at her through a mirror, when the thought occurs to him that " . . . if I were to look under the drier at the real face and not at the reflection, I should see there some terrible witch." Later in the book, the same image is used twice more; on these occasions the reflecting medium is

water. After unsuccessfully attempting to find Anna in Paris, Jake walks toward Notre-Dame until he can see "mirrored beneath it in the unflecked river a diabolic Notre-Dame, sketched there but never quite motionless, like a skull which appears in a glass as the reflection of a head." Shortly after, during the Bastille Day fireworks display, Jake spots Anna in the crowd on the opposite bank of the Seine. He tries to attract her attention by throwing a fragment from a Belfounder rocket into her image as he sees it reflected in the river. But, of course, he fails, since Anna from her location does not see what Jake sees from his. Here the image of "reflection" becomes part of a symbolic scene which embodies and gives expression to the principal problem of the novel—Jake's inability to view and accept things as they are.

One other prominent use of this image occurs during the night hospital conversation between Belfounder and Donaghue. Jake discovers that Hugo does not recognize his ideas as they were expressed in *The Silencer* and in Anna Quentin's Mime Theatre. Concerning the Theatre, Jake says:

> "That was just what was yours," I said. "It was you reflected in Anna, just as that dialogue [*The Silencer*] was you reflected in me."

> "I don't recognize the reflections," said Hugo. "The point is that people must just do what they can do. . . ."

Now let us return to a consideration of *leitmotiv* in relation to Jake's change. Miss Murdoch employs water symbolism and references to patterns and images breaking and reforming in such fashion that they seem to be, in the words of one reviewer, ". . . only the precise details that enrich a scene, a mood, yet which undeniably work upon the reader, preparing him for a future development which then seems inevitable. . . ." Water, with its associations of life and renewal, and breaking and reforming patterns are suitable elements for a novel of initiation.

Jake, a city dweller—though he frequently travels the waters between London and Paris—spends a good part of his time near the Thames and the Seine. After leaving the "old-cure" institution, he regularly met Hugo on Chelsea Bridge; and these two often carried on their conversations while pacing Chelsea embankment. In chapter Eight, he indulges in a night-swim in the Thames with Lefty Todd and Finn. In Paris, after refusing Madge's offer of a script-writing job, he seeks the Seine; then after unsuccessfully searching for Anna throughout the city, he again turns to the river. Later in London, before sneaking into the hospital to see Hugo,

What Do I Read Next?

- Often acclaimed as Murdoch's best work *The Sea, The Sea* (1978), a Booker Prize–winning novel, tells the story of Charles Arrowby, a tyrannical director-playwright, who decides to retire after a forty-year-long career in the theatre. He moves to a home by the sea and plans to write his memoirs about an old love affair. Things do not go as he had thought, as he is visited by people from his past (some of them no longer alive) and he learns a lot more about himself than he thought he wanted to know.

- *The Black Prince* (1973) is another of Murdoch's more reputed works. It is an experimental novel, and the story is told by Bradley Pearson, a self-conscious writer who is a perfectionist. He ends up in jail for a crime he did not commit.

- Jean-Paul Sartre introduced Murdoch to the philosophy of existentialism. She was most fond of his *Being and Nothingness* (1956), which began the existentialist movement and consists of essays on the topic of consciousness and free will. To live authentically, Sartre believed, one needs to be conscious of one's own acts. Existentialism was said to have heavily influenced *Under the Net*.

- Albert Camus, a contemporary and fellow existentialist of Sartre, wrote *The Stranger* (1946), considered one of the most widely read novels of the twentieth century. It tells the story of Meursault, a disaffected, amoral man who is alienated from society. Meursault, a young Algerian, ends up killing a man. His trial, however, reflects less on his crime than on his so-called deficient character.

- One of Murdoch's favorite authors was George Eliot, whose *The Mill on the Floss* (1860) relates the ordeals of a young woman, Maggie Tulliver, who has great difficulty adapting to her provincial world. Her intelligence is denied by all, except for one friend, whom her older brother eventually forbids her to see.

- Leo Tolstoy was another author whom Murdoch praised. His novel *The Death of Ivan Ilych* (first published in Russian in 1886) is a classic work, presenting Tolstoy's concerns about life, death, and religion. A mortal disease suddenly strikes down Tolstoy's protagonist, a man who has invested little emotion in his life, his family, and other people around him. His family soon tires of his complaints, and he is left to die with only one farmhand assisting him in his needs.

- The final novel of Fyodor Dostoevsky, another novelist whose writing Murdoch admired, is *The Brothers Karamazov* (1879), which is considered his masterpiece. It is the story of a love-hate relationship that exhibits Dostoevsky's astute understanding of psychology and spirituality. The story unfolds through a dramatic search for faith, which Ivan, one of the brothers, finally discovers is found not through the mind but through the heart.

- A good place to start examining Murdoch's philosophical ideas might be her *Existentialists and Mystics: Writings on Philosophy and Literature*, first published in the United States in 1998. This work is a collection of her thoughts on the connection between art and philosophy.

---

he goes to the Thames and, while standing on Hammersmith Bridge, gathers his thoughts.

However, it is during the night-swim episode that water is associated directly with Jake's problem and its eventual solution. The symbolism of this scene is emphasized in a heavy-handed manner when Jake, after emerging from the Thames, says, "A tension had been released, a ritual performed." But the significant statement of the episode is his observation that swimming depends upon "one's willingness to surrender a rigid and nervous attachment to the upright position." Already good at swimming, Jake later becomes good at living by applying the same principle to life and surrendering his demand for necessity.

This episode, with its obvious overtones of re-newal, is preceded and followed by scenes which also suggest rebirth. Before going to the Thames, Jake, Finn and Dave Gellman are led into a small enclosed garden, formerly the nave of St. Leonard Foster. This Eden-like enclosure, with its fig tree, high grass and Orion overhead, suggests a retrac-ing of steps, a going back in order to begin again. After swimming, the group partakes "joyously" of what can be taken as a Eucharistic meal of *pâté de foie gras*, biscuits and brandy, the last of which goes down "like divine fire."

After Jake refuses Madge's offer in Chapter Fourteen, water is again used in a passage which also contains the *motifs* of "reflection" and "pat-tern": "As I looked about me Paris recomposed it-self like a reflection that ceases to waver as the water becomes still. At last it was as still as glass. What *had* I done?" Toward the end of the novel, when Jake takes one last trip to Hugo's now-deserted apartment, an act which he considers the last of his old life, he says: "London passed before me like the life of a drowning man...." Finally, as Jake touches the manuscripts of his earlier attempts at creative writing, his hands tremble "like the hands of a water diviner."

Water, symbolizing life and renewal, is em-ployed artfully in *Under the Net*. It is present in many important scenes of the book, and referred to in a number of the key statements made by Jake Donaghue. This is equally true of the image of breaking and reforming patterns.

On two occasions Jake mentions his "pattern of life" is changing. Toward the end of the flash-back which tells of his break with Belfounder, Jake mentions that "gradually my life took on a new pat-tern and the powerful image of Hugo began to fade." Later, after rushing to the Mime Theatre to meet Anna only to find her gone, he says, "It was perfectly clear to me that my previous pattern of life was gone forever ... What new pattern would in due course emerge I had no means of telling."

In three other passages, we find allusions to breaking and re-forming images and patterns. Two of them were cited above in reference to other *mo-tifs:* the scene in which Jake, having refused a job as a script-writer, sees Paris recomposing itself; and the scene in which he throws the fragment from one of Belfounder's rockets into Anna's image re-flected in the Seine. The third passage is part of the "recognition scene" in the hospital. When Jake fi-nally realizes that it is Sadie Hugo loves, not Anna, he comments: "A pattern in my mind was suddenly

scattered, and the pieces of it went flying about me like birds."

During the course of *Under the Net*, Jake Don-aghue undergoes a change. When we first meet him, he hates contingency and has such a need for necessity that he unknowingly weaves false theo-ries to explain situations and people. But even at the beginning of the novel Jake is aware that things are shifting. In Chapter Two, when he is forced to leave Madge's apartment, he observes: " ... the Earls Court Road phase of my life was over, ... Madge had forced a crisis on me; well, I would ex-plore it, I would even exploit it. Who can tell what day may not inaugurate a new era?" At the end of the novel Jake inaugurates that new era. No longer attempting to impose false theories on things, he accepts the contingency of existence, the mystery and variety of life. "It was the morning of the first day," and the mixed breed of Maggie's newly-born litter of kittens cannot be explained—"It's just one of the wonders of the world."

In the process of developing and presenting this initiation, Iris Murdoch introduces us to stim-ulating characters and exposes us to thought-provoking, and sometimes highly amusing, situa-tions. But what gives distinction to *Under the Net* is Miss Murdoch's effective use of *leitmotiv*.

Source: Raymond J. Porter, "Leitmotiv in Iris Murdoch's *Under the Net*," in *Modern Fiction Studies*, Vol. XV, No. 3, Autumn 1969, pp. 379–85.

Sources

Bove, Cheryl K., *Understanding Iris Murdoch*, University of South Carolina Press, 1993, p. 36.

Conradi, Peter J., *Iris Murdoch: A Life*, W. W. Norton, 2001, pp. 380, 385.

Kellman, Steven, "Shakespearean Plot in the Novels of Iris Murdoch," in *Iris Murdoch*, edited by Harold Bloom, Mod-ern Critical Views series, Chelsea House Publishers, 1986, p. 89.

Russell, John, "Under Iris Murdoch's Exact, Steady Gaze," in the *New York Times*, February 22, 1990.

Todd, Richard, *Iris Murdoch*, Methuen, 1984, pp. 13, 16.

Further Reading

Antonaccio, Maria, *Picturing the Human: The Moral Thought of Iris Murdoch*, Oxford University Press, 2000.
    So much attention has been spent on Murdoch as a novelist that her philosophical contributions are of-

ten overlooked. This is one of the first books that has tried to fill that gap. Antonaccio explores the contributions to moral and religious philosophy that Murdoch fervently studied and presented.

Bayley, John, *Elegy for Iris*, St. Martin's Press, 1999.
Bayley wrote this book before his wife Iris Murdoch died. She was suffering from Alzheimer's disease at the time, and he recounts his memories of her and of their relationship together. The movie *Iris: A Memoir of Iris Murdoch* was taken from this book. Both the movie and the book received rave reviews.

————, *Iris and Her Friends: A Memoir of Memory and Desire*, W. W. Norton, 1999.
This is the second memoir written by Bayley about his wife. This one was written after her death, and many critics have highly recommended this book for its disclosure of a wonderfully warmhearted story of love.

Byatt, A. S., *Degrees of Freedom: The Novels of Iris Murdoch*, Chatto and Windus, 1965.
The philosophical ideas that influenced Murdoch's early novels are explored in this book, as Byatt examines how those ideas are used in her novels.

Kaufmann, Walter Arnold, ed., *Existentialism: From Dostoevsky to Sartre*, Meridian Books, 1984.
This has been hailed as an excellent introduction to the philosophy of existentialism. It includes a discussion of purely philosophical essays as well as the influence of existentialism on literary works. Such works discussed include Dostoevsky's *Notes from the Underground*, Camus's *The Myth of Sisyphus*, and Sartre's short story "The Wall." Philosophers include Kierkegaard and Nietzsche, among others.

A Very Long Engagement

Sébastien Japrisot

1991

Sébastien Japrisot's novel *A Very Long Engagement* was first published in France in 1991 and was translated into English and published in New York in 1994. Set in France during and after World War I, the plot revolves around the fate of five French soldiers who have been sentenced to death for shooting themselves in the hand to avoid military service. In January 1917 the men are marched to a frontline trench on the Somme, near Bouchavesnes. They are then pushed unarmed into no-man's-land between the French and German lines and abandoned to their fate. After the war, Mathilde Donnay, the fiancée of Manech, begins a long investigation into what happened to the five men. She hopes against hope that her fiancé is still alive. Through correspondence with the wives of the condemned men and with former military officers, as well as the placing of newspaper advertisements and the hiring of a private detective, she eventually discovers the truth about what happened.

A Very Long Engagement is an antiwar novel that exposes the cruelty and horror of trench warfare, and the official lies and corruption that allowed atrocities to take place. The novel is also a detective story, as Mathilde unravels the mystery of what happened to the five men. Finally, the novel is a moving love story, which shows that love can endure even when war destroys everything else that is valuable.

Author Biography

Jean Baptiste Rossi was born in 1931, in Marseille, France. Under the pseudonym Sébastien Japrisot, he is a mystery writer, film director, screenwriter, and translator. He lives in France.

Japrisot wrote and published his first novel in 1950, when he was eighteen years old. His first novel translated into English was *The 10:30 from Marseilles* (1963), which was published in its original French in 1962. The English translation was later published under a different title, *The Sleeping Car Murders* (1997). Drawing on the techniques of the police procedural novel, the story centers around a series of murders on a passenger train.

In Japrisot's novel *Trap for Cinderella* (original French edition published in 1964; English translation in 1964), two young women are burned in a house fire. The survivor is disfigured beyond recognition and suffers from amnesia. The mystery develops through a complex plot and descriptions of the same events from different points of view. The novel was awarded the Grand Prix de la Littérature Policiére.

Japrisot's psychological mystery *The Lady in the Car with Glasses and a Gun* (original French edition published in 1966; English translation in 1967) was awarded the Prix d'Honneur. It was followed by *Goodbye Friend* (original French edition published in 1968; English translation in 1969), in which a doctor returning from Vietnam is accused of murder. In *One Deadly Summer* (original French edition published in 1978; English translation in 1980), a daughter, conceived through her mother's rape, vows vengeance against her father, the rapist.

The English translation of *The Passion of Women* (original French edition published in 1986; English translation in 1990) was also published under the title *Women in Evidence*. It focuses on the death of a man falsely accused of killing a child. This novel was followed by *A Very Long Engagement* (original French publication in 1991; English translation in 1994), a tale of love and war, which won the literary Prix Interallia in 1991 and became a bestseller in France and abroad.

Japrisot's also penned *Rider in the Rain* (original French edition published in 1992; English translation in 1999), along with dozens of screenplays, some of them adaptations of his own novels, including *The Sleeping Car Murders* (1965), *Trap for Cinderella* (1965), and *One Deadly Summer* (1983). Negotiations were taking place in 2002 for a movie version of *A Very Long Engagement*,

although Japrisot declined the invitation to write the screenplay himself.

Plot Summary

Saturday Evening

A Very Long Engagement begins in January 1917, during World War I. Five French soldiers are being marched to the battlefront on the Somme. They are prisoners, having been condemned to death for shooting themselves in the hand to avoid military service. Their names are Kléber Bouquet (Eskimo), Francis Gaignard (Six-Sous), Benoît Notre-Dame (That Man), Ange Bassignano (Common Law or Nino), and Jean Etchervery (Manech, also known as Cornflower).

Bingo Crépuscule

In August 1919, Manech's fiancée Mathilde visits Daniel Esperanza, a former army sergeant who is dying in a hospital. He tells Mathilde everything he knows about what happened to the condemned men. He was in charge of escorting them to the frontline trench called Bingo Crépuscule. His orders were that the men were to be thrown over the trench, with their hands tied, into the no-man's-land between the French and German trenches. He arranged for the condemned men to send letters to their loved ones. Then they were sent over the trench. Esperanza does not know exactly what happened after that, since he was transferred to another regiment, but he heard that all five prisoners were killed.

The White Widow

The wheelchair-bound Mathilde studies the information that Esperanza left her. She reads the copies he made of the men's letters and also reads a letter from Captain Favourier to Esperanza dated Sunday, January 7, which says the five men are still alive and he hopes to receive an order to bring them back at nightfall. Mathilde tries to piece the puzzle together. From Aristide Pommier she gleans some information about Manech as he was awaiting trial. She sees Esperanza again and suspects he is withholding information from her. She suspects That Man's letter is not what it appears.

The Good Old Days

Mathilde writes to the wives of the dead prisoners. She meets Six-Sous's wife and receives letters from the village priest in That Man's town and Madame Conte, who is Tina Lombardi's godmother.

Conte says Tina received official notice that Common Law was killed in action January 7, 1917. Mathilde visits the bar owned by Little Louis, a friend of the Eskimo, who tells of how his friend was also declared killed in action. Louis tells of a quarrel between the Eskimo and his girlfriend Veronique Passavant, and between the Eskimo and one of his closest friends, a man known as Biscuit. Mathilde wants to believe that the Eskimo, a tough character, protected Manech and saved his life.

Queen Victoria's Tuppence

Pierre-Marie Rouvière has at Mathilde's request discovered more information. A casualty list dated Monday, January 8, 1917, lists all five men as dead. But there is no evidence they were killed in the manner Esperanza says, and the lawyer knows that there was an official pardon for the men on January 2. Even though Pierre-Marie tries to convince Mathilde that Manech is dead, she is not convinced. She publishes an advertisement in the newspapers, asking for information. She believes that a casualty list can be altered and that at dawn on Sunday, January 7, all five men were still alive.

The Mahogany Box

Mathilde receives a letter from Veronique Passavant, saying that she believes the Eskimo is still alive, although she has no evidence. The mother of Urbain Chardolet tells Mathilde that when her son saw the five men lying in the snow, one or perhaps two were not the person or persons he expected to find. This gives Mathilde hope. Benjamin Gordes's wife Elodie writes to say that Gordes was killed January 8, 1917, in a bombardment. Mathilde learns that Gordes is the man named Biscuit and that in 1916, Gordes and the Eskimo quarreled over a woman. Mathilde suspects that Gordes later had some influence on his former friend's fate.

The Woman on Loan

Elodie Gordes explains what happened between herself, her husband, and Eskimo in 1916. The war was hard on Benjamin Gordes. He told his wife that if they could have another child, making six in all, he would be discharged from the army. But alcohol had made him impotent. He suggested that she allow his friend Kléber, the Eskimo, to make love to her when he came home on leave. After Elodie and Kléber did this, the two men quarreled. Mathilde also guesses that Veronique Passavant, who was living with Kléber, walked out on him because of his affair with Elodie. Mathilde also learns from Pire, her private detective, that the five

men were buried by British soldiers and then interred two months later at a cemetery in Picardy.

The Mimosas of Hossegor

Mathilde and Manech first met in June 1910, when Mathilde was ten years old and Manech thirteen. Their love grew steadily, and Manech scratched the letters MMM in a poplar tree near the lake where they swam together. The letters stand for Manech's Marrying Mathilde.

In 1921, Mathilde buys the land on the shore of the lake, where her father builds her a large villa. The family makes a pilgrimage to Manech's grave. Mathilde receives an anonymous letter saying that Célestin Poux is dead.

The Terror of the Armies

Poux is convinced Manech was killed by machine-gun fire from a German plane, although he did not witness it personally. He describes the fates of the other men and the battle that took place that weekend. He asserts that the letter That Man wrote to his wife is in code, something Mathilde has suspected. They discuss Chardolet's comment that one or possibly two of the bodies were not who he expected. Poux believes that if any of them survived, it would have been That Man.

The Other Side of No-Man's-Land

Mathilde visits the former battlefield, which is now a huge freshly mowed field. At dinner, she meets Heidi Weiss, whose brother, a German soldier, was killed at the same trench at the same time as Manech. Weiss confirms that from what she was told, Manech was killed by fire from a German plane. Mathilde also hears via a newspaper report that Tina Lombardi has been executed for killing French military officers.

The Lovers of Belle de Mai

Mathilde receives a letter from Tina, written from Tina's prison cell. Tina explains that she killed the officers because they harmed her lover Nino. Like Mathilde, Tina had been searching for the truth of what happened to her lover. She provides information that fuels Mathilde's hope that Manech may still be alive.

The Sunflowers at the End of the World

With more information from Weiss, Mathilde is close to solving the mystery. She cracks the code That Man used in the letter he wrote to his wife. She finally finds That Man in a village called Bernay. He explains everything that happened, including how he managed to survive. He helped Manech away from the battlefield and thinks there is a good chance he survived.

Lieutenant-General Byng at Twilight

Mathilde learns that Manech is still alive, living under the name of Jean Desrochelles. He has amnesia and can remember nothing of the war. He lives with the mother of a soldier named Jean Desrochelles, who was killed in the war. The identity discs of the two men were switched. Desrochelles's mother went along with the deception, since her real son was dead and she needed someone to care for. Mathilde meets Manech, and although he does not recognize her, there are hints their romance will flourish again.

Monday Morning

Ten soldiers from Newfoundland arrive at the Bingo trench on Monday, January 8, 1917. They find the five dead soldiers and bury them.

Characters

Ange Bassignano

Ange Bassignano, also known as Common Law, is one of the five condemned French prisoners. He is twenty-six years old and handsome, but not of good character. He is regarded as sly, deceitful, and quarrelsome, and he has no occupation other than as a pimp. However, his girlfriend, the prostitute Tina Lombardi, is devoted to him. He was serving a five-year sentence for assault when he was plucked from prison and made to join the army. He is in the army for three months before he is condemned to death.

Bénédicte

Bénédicte is the wife of Sylvain. She helps to take care of Mathilde.

Biscuit

See Benjamin Gordes

Kléber Bouquet

Kléber Bouquet, nicknamed the Eskimo because he once went adventuring in Alaska, is the oldest of the five condemned French prisoners. He is thirty-seven and a carpenter from Paris. He was falsely accused of self-mutilation and has thus been condemned to death for something he did not do. He is close friends with Little Louis and Corporal Gordes, although he and Gordes quarrel fiercely because Kléber has an affair with Gordes's wife, which Gordes himself encouraged him to do. At Bingo, the Eskimo is killed by machine-gun fire from an enemy plane, but not before he brings the plane down with a grenade.

Urbain Chardolet

Urbain Chardolet is a corporal in the French army who escorts the condemned prisoners. He dies from injuries he receives in July 1918 in a battle at Champagne.

Common Law

See Ange Bassignano

Madame Veuve Paolo Conte

Madame Conte is Tina Lombardi's unofficial godmother and has known her since she was a baby. Madame Conte is just over fifty years old and not in good health. She writes to Mathilde from her home in Marseilles, telling of what she knows about Tina, whose whereabouts are unknown. She dies in 1923.

Cornflower

See Jean Etchervery

Jean Desrochelles

Jean Desrochelles is a corporal in the army who is killed at Bingo. Manech assumes Desrochelles's identity following the war.

Mathieu Donnay

Mathieu Donnay is Mathilde's rich father.

Mathilde Donnay

Mathilde Donnay was paralyzed by a fall at the age of three. She meets Manech when she is ten years old and their love blooms immediately. Mathilde comes from a wealthy family; she spends much of her time at her parents' vacation home in Capbreton, where she is cared for by Bénédicte and Sylvain. She is sixteen years old when Manech goes off to war, and seventeen when Manech faces his ordeal in no-man's-land. During the war, she teaches the children from a nearby town whose teacher has joined the army.

Mathilde is also a talented artist. She paints huge canvases of flowers, which after the war are exhibited in galleries across France. She loves cats and owns six of them.

After the war, Mathilde clings to the hope that Manech survived, even though all the evidence seems to suggest he did not. She is a resourceful woman and never gives up on her quest to find out what really happened that day. Like many women who lost their fiancés during World War I, Mathilde wants to marry Manech posthumously, although this feat proves impossible since Manech was too young to get married on his own.

Paul Donnay

Paul Donnay is Mathilde's older brother, for whom she has little affection.

The Eskimo

See Kléber Bouquet

Daniel Esperanza

Daniel Esperanza, a sergeant in the French army, was in charge of the five prisoners as they were taken to the front. He ends the war as a regimental sergeant-major and is awarded the Croix de Guerre. After the war, he contracts Spanish influenza. When Mathilde meets him, he is dying in a hospital. He is forty-three years old but looks sixty. He dies shortly after their meeting.

Jean Etchervery

Jean Etchervery, also known as Manech and Cornflower, is one of the condemned French prisoners. He is the fiancé of Mathilde and is nineteen years old. As a young man he was athletic and brave, a bit of a daredevil. In the army, he endured a traumatic experience when a torpedo exploded and he was drenched in another man's blood and scraps of flesh, leaving him fearful of the war. He deliberately gets himself shot in the hand because he wants a leave of absence to visit Mathilde. As a result of the injury, his right hand is amputated. By the time he is marched to the war front, he has almost lost his mind, and the expression on his face is a fixed smile. Once cast out into no-man's-land, he builds a snowman with his one hand.

Fancy Mouth

See Captain Etienne Favourier

Captain Etienne Favourier

Captain Etienne Favourier is also known as Fancy Mouth because of his colorful language. He does not approve of sending the prisoners into no-man's-land. He is killed during the battle at Bingo.

Francis Gaignard

Francis Gaignard, nicknamed Six-Sous, is one of the five condemned French prisoners. He is a corporal who has been reduced to the ranks. Six-Sous is a welder by trade, and he is also a passionate socialist and trade unionist. His views were influenced by an incident in 1908, in which he was wounded when cavalry attacked a group of striking workers. Six-Sous is a pacifist who hopes that one day the working men of all nations will refuse to fight in wars. When he is tossed into no-man's-land, he shouts to the Germans that war is a disgrace and everyone should put down their weapons. He is shot by a German soldier.

Théràse Gaignard

Théràse Gaignard is the wife of Six-Sous. After the war, she works as a laundress near Paris. She receives a pension and raises her two little daughters herself.

Benjamin Gordes

Benjamin Gordes is one of the two corporals who escort the condemned prisoners. He is also known as Biscuit. He is a quiet and decent man, rather sad but well thought of by others. At the age of twenty, Gordes becomes a widower with four adopted children. He has adopted one more child by the time he marries Elodie. He and Kléber have been friends since 1910 and are in the same regiment during the war. They quarrel over Gordes's wife Elodie. Gordes hates the war and takes to drinking. He is killed at Bingo going to aid his friend Kléber.

Elodie Gordes

Elodie Gordes is Benjamin Gordes's wife. Before she married Gordes, she had a daughter by a man who quickly deserted her. Elodie has an affair with Kléber, at the insistence of her husband, who wants her to have a sixth child so he can have permission to leave the army. But she does not become pregnant by Kléber.

Tina Lombardi

Tina Lombardi is the companion of Common Law (she calls him Nino), whom she has known since she was thirteen or fourteen. She had a difficult childhood. Her mother died while giving birth to her and her father was a drunkard. She became a prostitute. After the war, she searches for the truth of what happened to Nino. She hates all the military officers who had a part in his death, and she kills several of them. She is arrested, convicted, and executed.

Manech

See Jean Etchervery

Nino

See Ange Bassignano

Benoît Notre-Dame

Benoît Notre-Dame, nicknamed That Man, is one of the five prisoners condemned to death. A large, thirty-year-old farmer from the Dordogne, he is a loner who keeps his troubles to himself. He is a good soldier and does what is necessary to survive. On one occasion, he strangles an officer in his company. He is patient, obstinate, and cunning.

Mariette Notre-Dame

Mariette Notre-Dame is the twenty-year-old wife of That Man. When she hears that he has been killed, she sells their farm and moves away with her young son. She is seen in February 1917 when she rents a furnished room, but after that her whereabouts are a mystery.

Veronique Passavant

Veronique Passavant is the Eskimo's girlfriend. Eskimo refers to her in his letter as Véro. In 1916, after Kléber has an affair with Elodie Gordes, Veronique walks out on him and will not speak to him again. In spite of that incident, the love between them continues.

Germain Pire

Germain Pire is a private investigator hired by Mathilde to unlock the mystery of what happened to Manech.

Aristide Pommier

Aristide Pommier is a cook in Manech's regiment. He has known Manech since they were boys. Mathilde dislikes him. After the war, Pommier goes to live in Quebec and writes to Mathilde with some information about what happened to the five soldiers.

Célestin Poux

Célestin Poux is the young soldier known as the Terror of the Armies. He is known for his resourcefulness and determination in keeping his platoon supplied with food. He is extremely popular with his comrades. After the war, he serves as a corporal in the army of occupation across the Rhine, and then for a while he works at a garage. He loves his motorbike and does not like to stay in one place for too long. Eventually Mathilde makes contact with him and, during a long stay at her house, he tells her all that he knows about the events of the fateful weekend at Bingo.

Pierre-Marie Rouvière

Pierre-Marie Rouvière is the family lawyer who assists Mathilde in her investigation. He is skeptical that the incident with the prisoners ever happened but he agrees to investigate.

Lieutenant Jean-Baptiste Santani

Lieutenant Jean-Baptiste Santani is the medical officer who treats the five condemned prisoners. He is killed two days later in an enemy bombardment.

Six-Sous

See Francis Gaignard

Sylvain

Sylvain is a middle-aged man married to Bénédicte. The couple looks after Mathilde.

Louis Teyssier

Louis Teyssier is a friend of the Eskimo and a former boxer. He owns a bar, where Mathilde visits him. He gives her information about Veronique, the Eskimo, and Gordes.

That Man

See Benoît Notre-Dame

Heidi Weiss

Heidi Weiss is an Austrian woman whose brother was a German soldier killed at Bingo. She meets Mathilde and gives her information about what happened.

Themes

Love

The enduring nature of love is set against the destructiveness of war. Mathilde is so devoted to her fiancé that she tirelessly works to discover his fate and clings to the belief he is still alive. It is clear her love was reciprocated. During the seven months Manech was at war, Mathilde received sixty-three letters and postcards from him. She has read these so often she could recite them all word for word.

When Mathilde rediscovers Manech, although he does not recognize her because of his amnesia, his first words to her are exactly the same as those he spoke when they met as children: "You can't walk?" This is a significant moment. So much has been destroyed and yet here is a hint the two young

Topics For Further Study

- Investigate the causes of World War I. What was the immediate cause and what were the main underlying causes?

- Research the history of the use of poison gas in warfare, from World War I to the present. When was the use of poison gas banned internationally?

- Research the role of the United States in World War I. Why and when did the United States enter the war? What were the main battles fought by American troops?

- Were the men in the novel who shot themselves in the hand cowards, or were they justified in their desire to escape the conflict? Is a soldier always, without exception, obliged to follow the orders of his commanding officer? Why or why not?

- War leaves many victims other than those killed or wounded in battle. In the novel, who, other than the five prisoners, are victims of the war? What are the different ways in which these victims react to and cope with their losses?

---

people can start again, almost as if nothing has changed. Love can survive, even under such awful circumstances. They must rebuild and get to know each other again, but they can still have a future together. Although the author chooses not to elaborate on how their renewed relationship develops, the reference to Mrs. Desrochelles as Mathilde's future mother-in-law makes it clear that Mathilde and Manech do eventually marry. The same inference is conveyed by the narrator's comment, as Mathilde gazes at her fiancé: "Life is long and can still carry a great deal more on its back."

The love theme can also be seen in the story of Tina and Nino (Common Law), even though their story is much darker. It is like a reverse image of the idyllic love between the admirable Mathilde and Manech. Nino is a pimp and Tina a prostitute, but her love for him and her dedication to finding out the truth about what happened to him are no less than Mathilde's. It is implied that even though Tina and Nino led lives that most would regard as disreputable, the love they shared was no less valuable or intense than that of the other couple. There are all kinds of people and all kinds of love in the world, and it is love that is the antidote to war.

Antiwar

The antiwar theme is brought out on all levels. The war is presented as barbaric, cruel, and senseless. Common Law, for example, gives thanks

that he is not in the "first batch tossed into that meat grinder," an image that presents the soldiers as cattle being sent to the slaughterhouse. Daniel Esperanza, who was in the thick of the conflict, roundly condemns it and punctures any myths of the glory of war. He remarks on the photographs he possesses of soldiers showing "self-glorification for having captured a gun or an exhausted enemy soldier . . . self-satisfaction at the funeral of a fallen comrade."

The barbarity of the sentences meted out to the prisoners is also condemned by many of the characters. Esperanza's commanding officer, as he passes on his orders to Esperanza, says that in his opinion, "a good half of the high command should be sent off to the nuthouse." And yet when a pardon is received for the men, five days before they are pushed into no-man's-land, it is ignored. There is an official cover-up of the incident. No officers are allowed to sign any papers relating to the affair, and they are told to just forget about what happened. The official version, that the men were killed in action, is just one example of what the narrator scathingly refers to as "the lies called History." There are other examples of the narrator making his feelings known independently of the characters. When Mathilde visits the cemetery, she finds the grave of Six-Sous, who like the others died for no reason. The narrator comments on "the obscenity of a war that hadn't had one [a reason], aside from the egoism, hypocrisy, and vanity of a privileged few."

Style

Nonlinear Narration and Poetic Style

As befits a mystery novel, the plot does not unfold in a linear way. It jumps forward and backward in time, as the events of the weekend in which the prisoners were pushed over the trenches is retraced through the reminiscences and letters of a range of characters. The point of view remains that of Mathilde, and she acts as the unifying element and the fulcrum for the entire narrative, since it is through interviews with her, or letters addressed to her, that the truth of what happened unfolds gradually. The voice of the narrator is also heard occasionally, usually to deplore the stupidity of the war.

The style of the work is often poetic and somewhat wistful, as for example in the epitaph written by the Canadian patrol leader as he and others bury the bodies: "Here lie / five French soldiers, / who died with their shoes on, / chasing the wind, . . . where the roses fade, . . . a long time ago." The wistful, yearning tone can be seen again in the description of the painting on the back of the wooden sign from Bingo, showing a peaceful scene in which a British officer gazes into the distance where the sun is setting. It evokes the idyllic world of France that the war disrupted.

Through simple descriptions of nature, the novel also shows how some of that lost world can be recovered, as in the description of the site of the trench at Bingo, as it appeared several years after the war:

> The huge, freshly mown field has a lush green hill for its horizon, a little stream flowing quietly beneath a wooden bridge, and two truncated elms with leafy lower branches, their trunks ringed by suckers.

The same idea is contained in the figure of speech used by That Man in which life is personified as a traveler that can carry many burdens on its back and still continue. The idea occurs again in the evocative chapter title "The Sunflowers at the End of the World." The end of the world is where That Man says he now lives. The significance of the phrase is that in a sense the war was the end of the world. Not only must it have seemed that way to the men in the trenches, it literally put an end to the European world that existed until the guns started firing in August 1914. The end of the world where That Man lives is also the beginning of a new world, sym-bolized by the presence of That Man's son, whom Mathilde meets before she meets That Man himself. It also sets the scene for the peaceful idyll in which Mathilde meets Manech again, in the French village of Noisy-sur-Ecole. Perhaps Mathilde and Manech are the sunflowers, ready to bloom once more now that the clouds of war have passed.

Historical Context

World War I

World War I was one of the most devastating wars in human history. The number of casualties was huge. In the battle of Verdun, for example, which began in February 1916 and lasted for five months, the French suffered 350,000 fatalities as they repelled the German assault on a strategically important fort. The Germans had 300,000 fatalities. In the battle of the Somme, which began in July 1916, the British army suffered over 57,418 casualties, one-third of who were killed on the first day alone. By the time the battle petered out in November, the British had suffered about 400,000 dead and wounded men, the French nearly 200,000, and the Germans an estimated 500,000. For that price, the British and French allies had gained only a small amount of territory, no more than 125 square miles. Between October and November 1916, the battle for Verdun flared up again, and the French regained the forts of Douaumont and Vaux. This was the battle in the novel in which Common Law participated for fifty days and which he describes in this way:

> Fifty eternities of terror, second by second, horror by horror, to retake that ratrap stinking of the piss, [sh—], and death of all those on both sides who'd jerked one another around without quite managing to finish it off.

There are many nonfiction accounts of the peculiar horrors of World War I. Alan Lloyd, in his book *The War in the Trenches*, writes of Verdun:

> "We had never experienced its like," recalled a French sergeant. "Shells of all calibres kept raining on our sector. The trenches had disappeared, filled with earth. We crouched in shell holes, increasingly smothered by the mud from explosions. The air was unbreathable. Our blinded, wounded, crawling and shouting soldiers kept falling on top of us and died splashing us with their blood. It was living hell."

This is the background against which the twenty-eight French soldiers in the novel, including the five who are described in detail, decided to mutilate themselves in the early winter of 1916 rather than be exposed to this level of carnage.

Compare & Contrast

- **1914–1918:** Trench warfare is largely immobile. It involves large armies fighting for months to make very small territorial gains.

  Today: Trench warfare is a thing of the past, as are conventional wars in which large armies clash on battlefields. More common today are what are called asymmetrical conflicts, which involve large differences in military power between adversaries. Terrorist groups attacking larger powers such as the United States or Russia are examples of asymmetrical conflicts.

- **1914–1918:** Britain and France are bitter enemies of Germany.

  Today: Britain, France, and Germany are allies and members of the European Community.

- **1914–1918:** Poison gas is used by all sides in the conflict. An estimated 91,198 soldiers die as a result of poison-gas attacks and another 1.2 million are hospitalized. The Russian Army, with 56,000 deaths, suffers the most.

  Today: Since the Geneva Protocol of 1925, the use of poison gas has been banned. The 1993 Chemical Weapons Convention (CWC) is a global treaty that bans chemical weapons. One hundred and thirty-five countries, including the United States, have signed the treaty.

Trench Warfare

The battles of Verdun and Somme in 1916 were examples of trench warfare. The first trenches on what became known as the Western Front were built by the Germans in September 1914, only one month after the war began. The trenches were built so that the Germans could halt the advance of the British and French. The Allies, seeing they could not break through the German trenches, dug trenches of their own.

Because the Germans had built the first trenches, they were able to choose the most advantageous positions for them, generally on higher ground. The British and French had to build their trenches at a lower level, on land that in some cases was only a few feet above sea level. Water was usually found only two feet below the surface. This meant that building and maintaining a trench was a constant battle against water and mud.

There were three rows of trenches: frontline trenches, support trenches, and reserve trenches. There were also communication trenches, designed for the transportation of men and equipment. Frontline trenches were usually about seven-feet deep and six-feet wide. The front of the trench was known as the parapet, the top part of which would be packed with sandbags to absorb enemy fire. To enable troops to see over the trench, a ledge known as a fire-step was added.

Life in the trenches was hard. Not only was there the constant threat of being killed by enemy artillery or poison gas, there was the daily annoyance of rats, who flourished in the unsanitary conditions. Many of these rats were large and showed no fear of humans. They were bold enough to try to take food from a sleeping man's pocket. Body lice were another problem and proved impossible to eradicate. Lice carried the disease known as trench fever, which afflicted many soldiers. The condition known as trench foot was another hazard. It was an infection caused by cold and damp conditions, when men had to stand in waterlogged trenches for hours at a time. If it was not treated, trench foot could turn gangrenous and require amputation of the affected appendage.

Critical Overview

Reviews of *A Very Long Engagement* applaud Japrisot's skill in creating an intriguing mystery and the many ways in which he evokes the devastation caused by World War I. A *Publishers Weekly* critic praises Japrisot's "eloquently easy, almost

French soldiers keeping watch in a partitioned trench during World War I in Verdun, France

offhand style," and comments that his "re-creation of the nobility, futility and horror of trench warfare is harshly beautiful." The critic has one reservation, however, and that is the character Mathilde, whom the critic finds difficult to like.

Christine Donougher in the *Times Literary Supplement* admires the way in which the novel places ordinary people at the center of events. The effect, Donougher argues, is to make the reader aware that the noncombatant survivors of the war—wives, girlfriends, parents, children, and neighbors—were just as much victims of the war as the men who fought and died. Although Donougher feels the unsentimental tone of the novel is sometimes forced, she concludes that it is a "cleverly constructed detective novel, with strong elements of suspense and surprise, and, at the same time, it conveys the high price which was paid for a war that seemed to produce no victors."

A *New Yorker* contributor observes that "Japrisot writes with warmth, and has a gift for rendering almost every character instantly likable." Rachel Billington in the *New York Times Book Review* finds some elements of the plot unconvincing, but has high praise for the style exhibited by Japrisot and his translator Linda Coverdale, which is "deceptive, apparently without

flourishes but rich in imagery and daringly abbreviated rhythms."

Criticism

Bryan Aubrey

Aubrey holds a Ph.D. in English and has published many articles on twentieth-century literature. In this essay, Aubrey discusses trench warfare, shell-shock, self-inflicted wounds, indiscipline, and punishment in the British and French armies during World War I.

The reader of *A Very Long Engagement* needs to stay alert. Japrisot is a master at veiling the truth at the same time he half-reveals it. He readily drops physical clues such as a pair of German boots, a button from a British uniform, a unique postage stamp, or a red glove. He offers hints and offhand remarks that only reveal their significance later in the story; he creates subtle differences in the way various people relate the story about the events of that fateful weekend on the Western Front. Also, like any good mystery writer, Japrisot plants red herrings, like the hints that the men who survived, if anyone survived, might have been Common Law

What Do I Read Next?

- *Goodbye to All That* (1929), by Robert Graves, is a bitter autobiography by the British writer who served as an officer in the trenches during World War I. Graves participated in several battles and on one occasion was wounded and left for dead for twenty-four hours before receiving medical attention. Graves expresses nothing but contempt for the British army commanders and the British government that allowed such senseless slaughter.

- *Memoirs of an Infantry Officer* (1930), by Siegfried Sassoon, is a classic memoir of Sassoon's life in the trenches during World War I. It not only describes the horrors of trench warfare but also shows the emotional wounds of the survivors. Like Graves, Sassoon has only withering scorn for the British High Command.

- World War I produced an outpouring of memorable poetry. *The Penguin Book of First World War Poetry* (second revised edition, 1997), edited by Jon Silkin, is an excellent anthology that contains the works of thirty-eight British, European, and American writers.

- Sébastien Japrisot's *Women in Evidence* (2000) is another mystery novel. It is set in the years following World War II and describes a woman's quest for the identity of the man who killed her husband. Like *A Very Long Engagement*, the plot is complex and leaves the reader guessing until the end.

---

or the Eskimo. And he piles up the evidence that Manech really is dead, fooling the reader all the time (but not Mathilde) and only revealing the truth at the end.

But perhaps what remains most vividly in the reader's mind is not the skillfully plotted mystery, or the moving love affair between Manech and Mathilde, but the devastation of war. This is a mystery and a detective story set against the back-ground of "the war to end all wars," as World War I was known at the time.

A Very Long Engagement presents World War I as it was for the soldier at the front. In this aspect of the novel too, Japrisot uses his skills as a mystery writer. At various points in the novel, characters express disbelief that the French army could really have done something so callous as to toss their own men over the trenches to serve as shooting practice for the enemy. The reader wonders whether Japrisot invented the incident for the sake of telling a good story. This is, after all, a work of fiction. But near the end of the novel, the author very deliberately inserts a passage from the memoirs of General (later Field Marshall) Fayolle, a World War I commander. The memoirs were published in 1965 and include a record of a meeting of French generals in January 1915, during which General Pétain, later to become the French hero of Verdun, ordered that twenty-five French soldiers who had shot themselves in the hand should be bound and thrown over the trenches closest to the enemy. It is clear from Fayolle's comment about Pétain that he disagreed with the decision: "Character, energy! Where does character end and ferocious savagery begin!"

This insertion of a passage from a nonfiction memoir is almost as incongruous in a novel as a footnote might be; like a scholar documenting his sources, Japrisot provides the title, author, publisher, date of publication, and page number of his quoted material. Incongruous or not, the information hits home with the force of a barrage of artillery. The truth, unfortunately, is that acts of self-mutilation in order to avoid or terminate war service were not uncommon during World War I. Soldiers were exposed to a kind of warfare more hideous and terrifying in its squalor, deprivation, and danger than (many would agree) any country has a right to ask its young men to endure. And those who took drastic measures to avoid such horrifying conditions were punished.

In the British army, many soldiers hoped they would be wounded in battle, since this would be the equivalent of receiving a ticket to be sent home. Some soldiers took the logic of this further and inflicted wounds on themselves. This was an offense punishable by death. A total of 3,894 men in the British army were convicted of self-inflicted wounds. None were in fact executed, but all served periods in prison.

Other frontline soldiers committed suicide rather than endure the hell of the trenches. They would place the muzzle of their rifle to their head and squeeze the trigger with their big toe. There were also recorded instances when men driven beyond endurance would put their heads above the parapet and wait until they were shot by an enemy sniper. This is a variation of what Manech does in the novel, when he holds up his right hand above the parapet, clutching a lighted cigarette to guide the German sniper to the target. Manech hopes this will get him out of the trenches and sent home as an invalid.

Executions in the British army were carried out, if not for self-inflicted wounds then for other offenses, including desertion, being asleep or drunk on post, striking a superior officer, abandoning a position, and cowardice. There were 304 such executions in the British army during World War I; the vast majority were for offenses committed in the trenches at the Western Front. The executions were carried out by firing squads. It is clear from later statements of the soldiers who were ordered to shoot their own comrades that the executions aroused as much dislike and distaste as is shown by some of the French soldiers in the novel regarding the five men tossed over the trenches. In one case, a British soldier who faced a firing squad was injured by only one bullet that hit him in the side. Everyone in the nine-man firing squad was deliberately firing wide, so that they would not have the man's death on their conscience. (The poor victim was eventually dispatched with a bullet to the temple fired by the officer in charge.) Just as in the novel, such men were officially listed as killed in action.

Another common punishment for disobeying orders in the British army was called Field Punishment Number One. Among other measures, such as forfeiting pay and other perks, this punishment called for the offender to be attached to a fixed object for up to two hours a day and for a period up to twenty-one days. According to some reports, these men were sometimes placed within range of enemy shell-fire (although this was against official regulations). Many at the time regarded this aspect of Field Punishment Number One as a barbaric punishment.

The French army also had its problems with discipline. As Guy Pedroncini states in his article, "The French Armies: Recuperation and Recovery," about the time *A Very Long Engagement* takes place, in early 1917, there was much discontent in the ranks because of factors such as reductions in leave time, inadequate food at the front, and inadequate rest facilities at the rear of the front. Drunk-

"As far as living conditions were concerned, in addition to the ubiquitous rats, lice, and mud, there was the danger of being killed not only by the enemy but by your own side."

enness, insubordination, and desertions rose during the year, culminating in a mutiny of about 40,000 French soldiers in June. They refused to continue the kind of suicidal assaults on German lines that had produced large casualties and no results. The response of the French commanders was relatively mild. Five hundred and fifty-four men were sentenced to death, but only seven immediate executions took place. About half of the mutineers brought to court were granted extenuating circumstances, and one in eight was reprieved. Curiously, General Pétain, who had become the commander-in-chief of the French army, was in favor of leniency. "They are our soldiers," he reportedly said. This was the same Pétain who in 1915 had ordered the prisoners guilty of self-mutilation tossed over the trenches.

In most cases of indiscipline in the British and French armies, the problems were caused or exacerbated by the stresses of trench warfare. It is staggering for a modern reader to realize the extent of the system of trenches that crisscrossed Belgium and France during World War I. There were more than 12,000 miles of Allied trenches, and about the same number of German ones. It was almost possible to walk from Belgium to Switzerland entirely in trenches.

As far as living conditions were concerned, in addition to the ubiquitous rats, lice, and mud, there was the danger of being killed not only by the enemy but by one's own side. The passage in the novel where this is mentioned (Captain Favourier tells Esperanza about it) is not fiction. An estimated 75,000 British soldiers in the war were killed by British shells that had been intended for the Germans. The German and French armies also suffered casualties in this way.

One of the problems was that opposing trenches were very close together. In *A Very Long Engagement*, the trench known as Bingo Crépuscule is at its closest point only 120 meters (130 yards) from the German trench, and 150 meters (164 yards) at the farthest. The average distance in most sectors was about 230 meters (250 yards). The narrowest gap was at a place called Zonnebeke, where only 6 meters (7 yards) separated British and German soldiers.

The area between the trenches, known as no-man's-land, was full of hazards. In front of the trenches was barbed wire that was sometimes thirty meters deep. Elsewhere in no-man's-land there would be shell holes and craters that made any advance difficult. Ironically, it is these difficult conditions that give the five French prisoners in the novel their best chance of survival. In front of Bingo, according to Esperanza, there were plenty of shell craters that gave the men the possibility of finding at least temporary shelter.

It was the stresses of trench warfare, including sleep deprivation combined with the trauma of constantly being under fire, that was responsible for the thousands of cases of shell-shock. At first, the British authorities did not recognize the condition as genuine, which meant that some of the men who suffered from it were executed for cowardice or desertion. Today, the condition is sometimes known by the more general term, battlefield exhaustion. Symptoms in World War I ranged from the milder cases of giddiness and headaches to complete mental breakdown. In the novel, Manech is a victim of shell-shock after a shell explodes near him and he is covered with the blood and flesh of another soldier. It is this experience that costs him his sanity. Given the unmitigated horror of trench warfare, the wonder is not that men such as Manech went insane but that more men did not do so. In the face of such madness, madness might seem like a logical response.

Source: Bryan Aubrey, Critical Essay on *A Very Long Engagement*, in *Novels for Students*, Gale, 2003.

Sources

Billington, Rachel, "No Man's Land," in *New York Times Book Review*, September 12, 1993, p. 24.

Donougher, Christine, "A War without Victors," in *Times Literary Supplement*, January 21, 1994, p. 20.

Lloyd, Alan, *The War in the Trenches*, David McKay, 1976, p. 84.

Pedroncini, Guy, "The French Armies: Recuperation and Recovery," in *The Marshall Cavendish Illustrated Encyclopedia of World War I*, edited by Brigadier Peter Young, Vol. 8, Marshall Cavendish, 1984, pp. 2342–47.

Review of *A Very Long Engagement*, in *New Yorker*, Vol. 69, No. 31, September 27, 1993, p. 105.

Review of *A Very Long Engagement*, in *Publishers Weekly*, Vol. 240, No. 23, June 7, 1993, p. 51.

Further Reading

Fussell, Paul, *The Great War and Modern Memory*, Oxford University Press, 1975.

> Fussell examines World War I and how it has been assimilated, remembered, and mythologized by later generations. Chapter 2 gives an excellent account of life in the trenches.

Horne, Alistair, *The Price of Glory: Verdun 1916*, St. Martin's Press, 1963, reprint, Penguin, 1994.

> Originally written in the early 1960s, this remains the best account of the terrifying battle of Verdun, between the French and German armies. Over a period of ten months, there were a total of 1,250,000 casualties. Horne's research includes personal interviews with survivors of the battle.

Kakutani, Michiko, "Seeking Fiancé's Fate, and Finding Bigger Issues," in *New York Times*, September 21, 1993, p. C17.

> In this review, Kakutani views the novel as a gripping philosophical thriller and a meditation on the emotional repercussions of war.

Sixsmith, Major-General E. K. G., "Morale and Discipline," in *The Marshall Cavendish Illustrated Encyclopedia of World War I*, edited by Brigadier Peter Young, Vol. 8, Marshall Cavendish, 1984, pp. 2348–56.

> This is mainly a survey of discipline in the British army, which Sixsmith regards as generally excellent. He also discusses morale and discipline in the French, Russian, and German armies during World War I.

Waterland

Graham Swift
1983

British novelist Graham Swift's *Waterland* (London, 1983; New York, 1984) is a complex tale set in eastern England's low-lying fens region. It is narrated by Tom Crick, a middle-aged history teacher. Tom is facing a personal crisis, since he is about to be laid off from his job and his wife has been admitted to a mental hospital. He is a man who is keenly interested in ideas about the nature and purpose of history. Faced with a class of bored and rebellious students, he scraps the traditional history curriculum and tells them stories of the fens instead. These stories form the substance of the novel, which takes place mainly in two time frames: the present, and the year 1943, when Tom Crick is fifteen years old. The traumatic events of his adolescence reach forward in time to influence the present. The structure of the novel, which frequently moves back and forth in time, also suggests the fluidity of the interaction between past and present.

Tom's tale of the fens is sometimes lurid. It includes a family history going back to the eighteenth century and such lurid topics as murder, suicide, abortion, incest, and madness. These events are set against a background of some of the great events in history, such as World War I and World War II. The novel also includes digressions on such off-beat topics as the sex life of the eel, the history of land reclamation, the history of the River Ouse, and the nature of phlegm. At once a philosophical meditation on the meaning of history and a gothic family saga, *Waterland* is a tightly interwoven novel that entertains as it provokes.

Graham Swift

Author Biography

Graham (Colin) Swift was born May 4, 1949, in London, England, the son of Allan Stanley and Sheila Irene (Bourne) Swift. His father was a civil servant. Swift attended Dulwich College, in South London, from 1960 to 1967. He earned a bachelor of arts degree in 1970 from Queens' College, Cambridge, and a master of arts degree in 1975 from the same school. From 1974 to 1983 he worked part-time as a teacher of English.

Swift's first novel, *The Sweet-Shop Owner*, was published in 1980 and records the memories of a dying shopkeeper. It was followed by *Shuttlecock* (1981), which is also an analytical story about the past. A collection of Swift's short stories, *Learning to Swim and Other Stories* was published in 1982.

In 1983 Swift had a literary breakthrough with his novel *Waterland*. A commercial and critical success, it was nominated for the Booker Mc-Connell Prize and was awarded the *Guardian* Fiction Prize (1983), the Winifred Holtby Prize from the Royal Society of Literature (1984), and Italy's Premio Grinzane Cavour (1987). *Waterland* was adapted for film by Peter Prince and released by Palace Pictures in 1992. The novel was also a success in the United States, and since its publication,

Swift's earlier books have also been published in America.

Swift's third novel, *Out of This World* (1988), was followed a few years later by *Ever After* (1992). Like *Waterland*, each of these novels examines the interplay between the past and the present. *Ever After* was awarded France's Prix du Meilleur Livre Etranger in 1994. Swift's novel *Last Orders* (1996) won the James Tait Black Memorial Prize for best novel and the Booker Prize, both in 1996. *Last Orders* was adapted for film by Sony Pictures Classics in 2001, directed by Fred Schepisi and starring Michael Caine and Bob Hoskins. In 2003 Swift's novel *The Light of Day* is due to be published.

Plot Summary

Waterland begins with the narrator Tom Crick describing his childhood growing up in the low-lying fens area of eastern England. His father is a lock-keeper, and they live in a cottage by the River Leem. One day in July 1943, the drowned body of a local boy, Freddie Parr, floats down the river.

The story flashes forward to the present. Tom, having spent thirty-two years as a history teacher, is leaving his job because the school is eliminating the history department. The other reason he is leaving is because of a scandal involving his wife, who apparently has stolen a baby. No more details are given.

Crick abandons the history syllabus he is supposed to teach, deciding to tell his class stories of the fens instead. He describes the history of the fens and the persistent efforts over the centuries to drain the land. He also describes his ancestors, going back to Jacob Crick, who operated a windmill in the fens in the eighteenth century. His mother's ancestors were the Atkinsons, originally farmers from Norfolk.

After a scene in which the headmaster of the school, Lewis Scott, discusses Tom's dismissal with Tom, the narrative returns to 1943 and the discovery of the drowned body. Tom notices a bruise on the body, finds a telltale beer bottle in the rushes, and Tom's girlfriend Mary insists Freddie was killed by Dick, Tom's mentally retarded brother.

The narrator then embarks on one of his many explorations of the nature of history, before flashing back to a time in 1942 when Tom and Mary, both fifteen years old, first begin to explore each other sexually. They are careful to meet at times when they will not be discovered either by Freddie or Dick. After the death of Freddie, it transpires that Mary is pregnant, and Tom is unsure whether the baby is his or Dick's.

The narrative then returns to the distant past, as Tom relates the history of the Atkinson family and how they built their fortune through land-reclamation projects and a brewery business. One of the most significant events occurs in 1820, when Thomas Atkinson strikes his wife Sarah in a fit of unreasonable jealousy. She loses her mind as a result of the attack but lives another fifty-four years to become something of a local legend. The Atkinsons continue to prosper as the leading local family, the height of respectability and power. Arthur Atkinson is elected to Parliament in 1874, the same year that a great flood causes devastation throughout the area.

The story line goes back to 1943, and Freddie's death is ruled an accident. Freddie's father, unable to deal with his grief, attempts suicide but fails, thanks to the intervention of his wife. Mary goes into seclusion at her father's house for three years. It appears she never had her baby. Tom joins the army in 1945 and is stationed in Europe. In 1947 he returns home and he and Mary marry. They move to London, where he becomes a history teacher. For several decades they live a comfortable middle-class life. As the story reaches the present, Tom notices that his wife is becoming secretive. She has also become very religious. Then she announces, at the age of fifty-two, that she is going to have a baby. God has told her so.

Tom then launches another inquiry into the nature of history ("De la Révolution"), discussing the French Revolution. He debates the issues with his class, which includes a boy named Price, who questions everything Tom says.

After a digression about the attempts of man to divert the course of the River Ouse in the fens, the narrative returns briefly to the present, and then back again to describe the life of Tom's father, a World War I veteran who married the nurse who brought him back to health.

In the present day, Tom attempts a debate with Lewis Scott over the usefulness of history as a subject of instruction. They cannot agree on an answer.

Tom describes the life of his grandfather, Earnest Richard Atkinson, who perfected a special kind of ale and lived in seclusion after a failed bid to win a parliamentary seat. After another round of present-day disputation with Price, the narrative returns to 1911 and Atkinson's remarkable brew. In the celebrations for the coronation of George V, the whole town seems to become intoxicated. But there

Media Adaptations

- *Waterland* was adapted for film by Peter Prince and released by Palace Pictures in 1992. The film was directed by Stephen Gyllenhaal and stars Jeremy Irons and Sinead Cusack.

---

is a fire at the New Atkinson Brewery, and it burns to the ground.

The narrative returns to 1940 and the exploratory sexual games played by Tom, Mary, and their friends, including Freddie. Dick wins an underwater swimming contest, and there is sexual tension between him and Mary. Freddie puts an eel in Mary's panties, which prompts Tom, as narrator, to devote a chapter to the riddle of the birth and sex life of an eel.

In 1943, Tom puts the beer bottle he suspects was used by Dick to strike Freddie in Dick's room. He wants to see what Dick will do. Dick secretly returns the bottle to a mysterious locked chest in the attic.

Returning to the history of the Atkinsons, Tom describes how Earnest Atkinson becomes a recluse, falls in love with his daughter Helen, and lives with her as husband and wife. Helen becomes a nurse and wants to marry a wounded soldier, Henry Crick (Tom's father). Earnest Atkinson wants a child by Helen, and she agrees to his request on the condition that she can raise the child as if it is Henry's. The child, Dick, turns out to be mentally retarded. Earnest leaves a letter for Dick, hidden in the chest in the attic, to be opened on Dick's eighteenth birthday. The letter explains that Earnest is Dick's real father. After leaving the letter, Earnest shoots himself. Back in the present, Tom takes his argumentative pupil Price to a pub for a drink, where they discuss history and teaching.

The narrative now starts to swing more and more rapidly between time periods. In the early 1940s, Mary takes it upon herself to educate Dick about sexual matters. Tom believes it may be Dick who got Mary pregnant. Mary denies it and tells

Dick it is Freddie's baby, in order to protect Tom from what she fears might be Dick's jealousy.

In the present-day narrative, Tom returns from school to find his wife has snatched a baby from a supermarket. Back in the past, Tom's mother dies in the 1930s, when he is nine years old. In 1943 Mary tries unsuccessfully to abort her own baby, and then she and Tom go to a local woman, Martha Clay, who has a reputation as a witch. Martha performs a grisly abortion.

Present-day Tom insists to his wife that they return the stolen baby. They drive back to the supermarket and hand it back. They are both interviewed by the police. Back in 1943, Dick and Tom open their grandfather's chest. Tom reads Earnest Atkinson's letter and tries to explain to Dick his incestuous origin. Dick goes off on his motorcycle, heading for a dredger on the river.

Tom visits his wife in the mental institution. He is distressed and unable to sleep. At a school assembly, the headmaster makes a speech about Tom's departure. The narrative then describes the death of Tom's father in 1947. Finally, the story returns to 1943. Tom and his father chase after Dick. With two American servicemen, they take a boat out to the dredger but cannot stop Dick from leaping over the side to his death.

Characters

Alfred Atkinson

Alfred Atkinson is Thomas Atkinson's younger son. In 1832 he marries Eliza Harriet Bell, the daughter of a farmer. He and his brother George are extremely successful businessmen. They found the Atkinson Water Transport Company and build the New Atkinson Brewery. Alfred becomes mayor of Gildsey in 1848. In his later years, with his brother, he builds Kessling Hall, a rural family retreat.

Arthur George Atkinson

Arthur George Atkinson is the son of George Atkinson. In 1874 he becomes a member of Parliament for Gildsey.

Earnest Richard Atkinson

Earnest Richard Atkinson is the son of Arthur Atkinson. Born in 1874, he is Tom Crick's grandfather. Earnest experiments with the process of making beer and comes up with a recipe for a new ale, which he begins manufacturing in 1906. A

craze for the potent new beer spreads far and wide. Earnest stands for Parliament in 1909 for the Liberal Party but fails to win election. After the Atkinson brewery burns down in a fire in 1911, he goes into seclusion. He falls in love with his daughter Helen, who bears a child by him, Dick Crick.

George Atkinson

George Atkinson is Thomas Atkinson's elder son. In 1830 he marries Catherine Anne Goodchild, the daughter of a banker. He becomes mayor of Gildsey in 1864. Like his brother Alfred, with whom he partners, he is a highly successful businessman who brings industrial progress to the entire region.

Josiah Atkinson

Josiah Atkinson is Tom Crick's eighteenth-century ancestor. He is the first to establish the Atkinson business of selling beer.

Sarah Atkinson

Sarah Atkinson is the beautiful young wife of Thomas Atkinson. She is the daughter of a brewer, Matthew Turnbull. When she is thirty-seven, her husband strikes her in the face, and as she falls, she hits her head against a writing table. Although she lives for over fifty more years, her mind is completely gone as a result of the attack. During the long period of her insanity, local legends build up around her, including the idea that she has the gift to see and shape the future. She dies in 1874 at the age of ninety-two.

Thomas Atkinson

Thomas Atkinson is William Atkinson's son. He becomes rich from land-reclamation projects, during which time the Cricks first come to work for the Atkinsons. Thomas builds a malting house and furthers the family beer business. He is also a farmer who opens up the River Leem, formerly a swamp, for transportation of his produce. He becomes a prominent citizen known for his good works. He marries Sarah Turnbull, who is much younger than he, but in his later years he develops feelings of jealousy over her, although Sarah did nothing to justify them. In 1820, Thomas strikes Sarah in the face. As a result of an injury sustained in the attack, she loses her mind. Thomas spends the rest of his days in remorse. He dies in 1825.

William Atkinson

William Atkinson is Josiah Atkinson's son. An astute businessman, he further develops the family brewery business.

Bill Clay

Bill Clay is an old man who is about eighty in the early 1940s. He has lived in the fens all his life. In the winter, he makes a living by shooting ducks; in summer, he catches birds in snares and sells them locally but illegally, since he does not have a license.

Martha Clay

Martha Clay is the wife of Bill Clay. She is known locally as a witch. She lives in a rundown cottage in the fens. Mary and Tom go to her when Mary is pregnant, and Martha performs a crude abortion.

Dick Crick

Dick Crick is raised as the elder son of Henry Crick. He is born in 1923 and is mentally retarded. He receives only a minimum of education; he cannot read or write, or speak in coherent sentences. His job is to work on a dredger that removes silt from the bottom of the River Ouse. He is a diligent worker, tall and physically strong. He also has a knack with machinery; his hobby is working on his motorcycle. Dick becomes jealous of Freddie Parr because Mary tells him that Freddie is the father of her baby. Dick kills Freddie by hitting him on the head with a bottle and pushing him into the river. Dick later learns he is the product of an incestuous union between Earnest Atkinson and his mother, Earnest's daughter Helen. Henry Crick is not really his father. Distressed and confused by this information, he commits suicide by leaping from the dredger into the river.

Helen Crick

Helen Crick is the daughter of Earnest Atkinson. She trains as a nurse and nurses Henry Crick back to health after World War I. She marries Henry but cannot free herself from the incestuous attentions of her father, a relationship that produces the retarded Dick Crick, who is raised by Helen and Henry as the son of Henry Crick. Tom Crick is Helen and Henry's legitimate son. Helen dies of influenza in 1937, when Tom is nine years old.

Henry Crick

Henry Crick is Tom's father. He is a lockkeeper in the fens. He is also a superstitious man with a knack for telling stories. Henry was wounded in World War I and nursed back to health by Helen, whom he married in 1922. He does not know until Dick is eighteen that Dick is not really his son. Henry dies in 1947.

Jacob Crick

Jacob Crick is Tom Crick's eighteenth-century ancestor who operated two windmills in the fens.

Mary Crick

Mary Crick is the daughter of Harold Metcalfe. Her father has high hopes for her and sends her to a convent school. As a teenager, Mary is curious and sexually adventurous. She tries to educate Dick about sex and becomes pregnant by Tom. She tries to abort the baby herself and then goes to Martha Clay for an abortion. The abortion causes an injury that renders her unable to bear children. After some years of being married to Tom, she takes a job in a local government office concerned with the care of the elderly. She leaves her job during a troubled menopause and then becomes very religious, telling Tom that God has told her she is to have a baby. She eventually snatches a baby from a supermarket, and after Tom insists that they return it, she is committed to a mental institution.

Tom Crick

Tom Crick is the narrator of the novel. Born in 1927, he is the son of Henry and Helen Crick and the younger brother of Dick Crick. Unlike Dick, Tom is highly intelligent, and wins a scholarship to Gildsey Grammar School, where he first becomes interested in history. As an adolescent he later describes himself as timid and shy but still manages to get his girlfriend Mary pregnant in 1943, at the age of fifteen. In that same year, he discovers that the drowned Freddie Parr was murdered by Dick. For a while he is scared of his own brother. In 1945 Tom serves with the British Army on the Rhine, after the war has ended. He returns home in 1947, the year his father dies, to marry Mary. They move to London, and he teaches history in a school. The couple lives an uneventful, conventional life, although Mary, because of a botched abortion in 1943, cannot have children. But around 1979, Tom's life changes. Mary becomes mentally unstable and snatches a baby from a supermarket, and Tom's school terminates his employment because history is being phased out of the curriculum. Tom has not done his standing any good by abandoning the regular history syllabus and telling his class stories of the fens instead. Tom continually searches for the meaning of history, seeking to understand how the past impinges on the present. His present unhappy circumstances make this a necessary quest for him. He has a curious, questioning nature, always asking why things happened as they did.

Harold Metcalfe

Harold Metcalfe is Mary's father. He is a farmer, reserved and hardheaded. His wife dies less than two years after he marries her. Harold is devastated by Mary's teenage abortion and keeps her in seclusion for three years, only reluctantly giving her permission to marry Tom in 1947.

Freddie Parr

Freddie Parr is the son of Jack Parr and a friend of Tom Crick when they are teenagers. He is known as a gossip and is often drunk on whisky stolen from his father. He is also lecherous and has designs on Mary. Freddie dies at the age of sixteen when he is knocked on the head and pushed into the river by Dick. He cannot swim.

Jack Parr

Jack Parr is Freddie Parr's father. He is a signalman and guardian of the Hockwell level-crossing. He is known as a heavy drinker and exploits the wartime black market solely for the purpose of procuring alcohol.

Price

Price is a sixteen-year-old student in Tom Crick's history class. He questions the value of studying history.

Lewis Scott

Lewis Scott is the headmaster of the school where Tom Crick teaches. He and Tom do not see eye to eye. Lewis, who used to teach physics and chemistry, regards the teaching of history as of little value. He thinks education should be about the future, not the past.

Themes

The Nature of History

Tom Crick is obsessed with exploring the meaning and value of history, but the view he presents is not a comforting one. He rejects the naïve notion that we study history in order to learn from our mistakes and improve the present. He prefers instead a cyclical view of history that denies the idea of progress. Each step forward is followed by a step backward; there is no achievement without loss: "It [history] goes in two directions at once. It goes backwards as it goes forwards. It loops. It takes detours." Similarly, every benefit that has ever been granted to human society has been accompanied by

a corresponding regression. The invention of the printing press, for example, led not only to the dissemination of knowledge, but also the dissemination of propaganda and strife. All in all, Tom does not know whether the conditions of human life are any better now than they were the year zero.

History, in the view of Tom Crick, is an attempt to fight off the nothingness of existence, the essential meaninglessness of life. The idea of "nothing" continually recurs in the novel. Tom speculates that the feeling that everything in life really amounts to nothing haunted Tom's father in the World War I battlefield at Ypres; it also haunted his grandfather, Earnest Atkinson, which was why Earnest started drinking. The whole of civilization that looks so solid and immutable is in fact only a veil held across the face of nothing, and it easily collapses. But it is no less essential for its insubstantiality. It is essential, as is all of history, because it imposes an intelligible story on bare existence. Whether the story is true or not is less important than the fact that it exists. It is a way of making the emptiness seem full. "As long as there's a story, it's all right," says Tom. It is a way of driving out fear, and this is why all humans have the instincts of storytellers, whether they are professional historians or spinners of fairy tales.

Everything Tom says of the global history that forms the background of the novel (the French Revolution, the two world wars, the threat of nuclear annihilation during the Cold War) is true also of personal life, at least in Tom's view. For example, he regards the day-to-day details of his marriage to Mary as mere "stage-props," behind which lies "the empty space of reality." In Tom's view of life, children will grow up to be just like their parents, and in that sense there can be no such thing as progress.

But Tom does not abandon the study of history or the search for explanations. The reason he tells his class about the history of the fens is because he desperately needs to come to terms with his own present unhappiness. This has been prompted by the imminent loss of his job and his wife's insanity. In spite of his skepticism about traditional approaches to history, he knows he cannot understand his present situation except by delving into the past. In personal and in societal life, the past always fluidly interacts with the present. It is never buried, even when it appears to be; it lies in wait, ready to cast its pall over the present. This point is conveyed by Tom's 1943 discovery of the beer bottle in the river. His brother Dick threw the bottle away, but it did not vanish. It resurfaced, ready to tell its tale to anyone who would ask the relevant questions. The river in this example symbolizes the stream of the past and perhaps also the personal unconscious mind.

Asking questions is essential for the study of history, and it also happens to be, in Tom's view, one of the most fundamental human traits, related to innate curiosity. However, the question "Why?" that reverberates throughout the novel can never be finally answered. In the family saga of the Cricks and the Atkinsons there are plenty of alternative explanations bandied around regarding the interpretation of key events, just as there are always conflicting versions of history; no one can know with certainty the absolute, definitive truth of an event that lies in the past. Tom confesses that his investigation into the history of the fens yielded only "more mysteries, more fantasticalities, more wonders and grounds for astonishment than I started with." He concludes, "history is a yarn."

Be that as it may, history cannot be escaped. In the novel, the most dramatic moment that shows the past intersecting with the present comes almost immediately after the grim account of the abortion Mary had as a teenager. After a brief digression comes the sentence, "We take the baby to the car." For a brief moment the reader, having just read of the disposal of an aborted fetus, is unsure what is happening. Then it becomes clear that the narrative has returned to the present, to the baby who fifty-two-year-old Mary has just snatched from a supermarket, not the baby who was aborted nearly forty years earlier. This incident in itself seems to explain the necessity of history, whether personal or societal, since there is no other way of understanding Mary's bizarre action except in terms of what happened to her as a teenager, since the botched abortion prevented her from ever having children of her own.

Style

Metaphor

A metaphor is an implied comparison in which one item symbolizes a dissimilar item. For example, the process of land reclamation in the fens is a metaphor of the process of human history. Humans continually try to create substance and order (land) on the amorphous, slippery nature of life (the marshes and the water). Humans are always building dykes (histories, stories of all kinds) to keep the emptiness and nothingness of existence (the essential nature of water) at bay. And telling coherent stories

Topics for Further Study

- What aspects of human life have improved over the last one hundred years? What has stayed the same, and what if anything has got worse? Do you think that the sum total of human happiness today is more or less than it was in the past? Support your answers with details from your research.

- What, in your opinion, is the purpose of studying history? What value is there in learning about the history of one's nation or culture?

- Watch the 1992 movie version of *Waterland* and note whether it stays true to the story line of the novel. Does the novel easily lend itself to adaptation as a film? In the movie version, the location for the present-day sections is Pittsburgh, Pennsylvania, with flashbacks to the fens in England. What, if anything, is lost in such a switch?

- In what sense can a myth be as true as a historical narrative that sticks to known facts? Do myths teach us as much as history does? In what sense?

that satisfactorily explain the past is as difficult as the engineering projects that attempted to drain and stabilize the fens. Water is always striking back. It can never be fully defeated, just as behind the mask of history lies the terrifying prospect of naked existence, without story or explanation and so without comfort. The vast expanse and flat, featureless nature of the fens suggests such emptiness, which is why, according to Tom Crick, the people who dwell there are excellent storytellers. They need their stories to beat back the emptiness.

The eels that are so plentiful in the fens act as another metaphor. In the chapter "About the Eel," the narrator describes not only the mysterious sex life of the eel (for centuries no one knew how eels reproduced) but also the cyclical nature of the eels' lives. Apparently, the adult European eel, which spends years of its life in the fresh waters and estuaries of Europe and North Africa, eventually journeys back to the sea for the sole purpose of spawning before it dies. In other words, it returns to where it

Compare
&
Contrast

- **1943:** Abortion is illegal in Britain, and illegal abortions are performed by untrained people. Many women are seriously injured and about thirty die each year.

  1983: Abortion is legal if performed in the first twenty-eight weeks of pregnancy. This law was established by the 1967 Abortion Act.

  Today: Abortion in Britain is legal if performed in the first twenty-four weeks of pregnancy. The written permission of two doctors is required. In 2001 in England and Wales, 175,952 abortions are performed, with an additional 12,000 in Scotland.

- **1943:** The Allies begin to turn the tide against Nazi Germany in World War II.

  1983: The Cold War between two nuclear-armed superpowers, the United States and the Soviet Union, means that the world lives under the threat of nuclear annihilation.

  Today: One of the main global security problems is the proliferation of nuclear weapons and the threat of biological and chemical weapons. The fear that such nations as North Korea, Iraq, and Iran are close to producing or have produced nuclear and other weapons of mass destruction is perceived as a threat to Western nations such as the United States and Britain.

- **1943:** The teaching of history focuses mostly on political history.

  1983: The teaching of history has broadened and now includes the history of people and topics formerly ignored, such as women and minorities. There is a fierce debate in the history profession about methods of studying history.

  Today: Oral history has become an important part of the historian's arsenal. Oral history is the use of eyewitness accounts and oral narratives in the writing and presentation of history.

---

came from; it journeys in reverse. Crick calls this "Natural History ... Which doesn't go anywhere. Which cleaves to itself. Which perpetually travels back to where it came from." The implication in the novel is that human history may also, despite the frequent belief to the contrary, travel in a cyclical pattern. The very word "revolution," for example, implies the completion of a cycle, and the desire for progress is often accompanied by a desire for a return to a golden age that existed in a mythical past.

Historical Context

The English Fens

For centuries the fens of eastern England were vast desolate marsh areas. Patches of firm ground were interspersed with rivers, pools, and reedbeds. The rivers could be navigated only by shallow-bottomed boats. The fens harbored abundant bird life and sea life, especially eels (as *Waterland* makes clear).

The first attempts to drain the fens were made by the ancient Romans. In the sixteenth century, Queen Elizabeth I also wished to undertake the project to improve the region's agricultural yields. But it was not until the seventeenth century that drainage of the fens took place on a large scale. This was a massive engineering project that caused enormous ecological changes in the region and took several decades to accomplish. The impetus came from the Duke of Bedford and wealthy investors in London who wished to increase the value of the land they owned, which they could then sell at a profit.

The most important figure involved in the drainage project was Dutch hydraulic engineer Cornelius Vermuyden (1595–1683). Vermuyden became involved in drainage projects in England in the 1620s and had the confidence of King Charles I. During the 1640s, Vermuyden was the chief engineer when 40,000 acres of fen were drained. Vermuyden's methods included ditches (known as cuts), dykes, sluices, and windmills. The effect was to reclaim the rich peat soil that lay beneath the water. As the novel makes clear, however, not all the drainage projects were successful in the longterm. The fens were often resistant to the changes imposed on them. However, the initial intention of the drainers, to produce good summer grazing land, was fulfilled.

This success was in spite of the fact that the project was vigorously opposed by the local people, who had lived in the area for centuries and who feared the loss of their traditional hunting and fishing rights. They also resented the Dutch workers Vermuyden employed. (The narrator in *Waterland* mentions how the local fen dwellers cut the throats of the Dutch workers and threw their bodies into the very water they had been employed to drain.) Local opposition forced the authorities to agree to compensation for the native fen dwellers and also to employ only English workers.

The fens are flat and low-lying, and much of the area lies below sea level. The landscape is monotonous, "bare and empty," as Swift notes in *Waterland*, and observers often remark on the sense of isolation it produces. The nineteenth-century English poet John Clare wrote a descriptive poem called "The Fens" which contains the following lines:

> Oer treeless fens of many miles
> Spring comes and goes and comes again
> And all is nakedness and fen.

The poem concludes with a picture of the fens in winter:

> But all is level cold and dull
> And osier swamps with water full

The modern fens fall into four main categories: the settled fens, also known as the townlands, which include the long-established cities of Kings Lynn and Boston; the Peaty Fens or Black Fens, which were drained from the seventeenth through nineteenth centuries; the fens of southeastern Lincolnshire, which were originally one of Britain's richest wildlife habitats and were the last to be drained (little of the wildlife remains there in the twenty-first century); and the band of Wash Marshes, which were reclaimed from the Wash by the building of sea wall defenses.

Critical Overview

Waterland was shortlisted for Britain's most prestigious literary award, the Booker Prize. It received

Sinéad Cusack as Mary Crick and Jeremy Irons as Tom Crick in the 1992 film adaptation of Waterland

generous praise from critics. Peter S. Prescott, in *Newsweek*, is one of a number of reviewers who compare Swift to William Faulkner. Prescott praises the intricate design of the narrative, pointing out that it moves "as water in the fens does: a current flowing one way encounters eddies circling in others."

Alan Hollinghurst in the *Times Literary Supplement* notes the way Swift combines various literary traditions: the "family saga, the business saga, the novel of provincial life," including also "social history and adolescent love." Hollinghurst praises the novel's "vigorous and complex metaphorical life," by which he meant Swift's use of the constant process of land reclamation in the fens as a parallel to the attempts of humans to make sense of their past. Hollinghurst finds the novel's vision "appallingly bleak," noting it emphasizes the "circularity and repetitiousness of history" and creates through the central character of Tom Crick a "portrait of a man who is deeply disturbed, and who is vainly attempting to build a structure ... which will protect him from his childlessness, from his failure to create the future."

Few critics have anything but praise for the novel, although Michael Gorra in the *Nation*, while acknowledging the novel is "intellectually bold, provocative and challenging" finds fault with Swift's style. According to Gorra, the novel's "passion is all for history itself and not for the people who are affected by it."

Criticism

Bryan Aubrey

Aubrey holds a Ph.D. in English and has published many articles on twentieth-century literature. In this essay, Aubrey discusses the nature and purpose of history as presented in the novel.

Underlying the sometimes lurid story of murder, suicide, abortion, insanity, incest, and mental retardation are some central questions about the nature of history. What is history? What is the point of studying it? Can the past really be known? How does the past affect the present? As a schoolteacher, Tom Crick, the narrator, has a professional interest in history, and it is no coincidence that the present-day sections of the novel are set in 1979, during a time of great upheaval in the methods applied to the scholarly study of history. Tom Crick also faces an academic climate in which the study of history is considered expendable (his school is phasing out its history department). And he must deal with a troublesome though highly intelligent student named Price, who thinks history is a waste of time, a view shared by Lewis Scott, the school headmaster, who refers to history as "a rag bag of pointless information."

For a man of Crick's generation, the method of studying history that he would have learned in the 1940s and 1950s was very different from what it would later become and what it is today. Fifty years ago, history usually meant political history, the story of governments and their relations, of wars, international treaties, parliamentary legislation, and the like. The lives of ordinary people, including women, were not considered worthy of study, since ordinary people appeared not to exercise any power over historical events. In addition to the narrowness of historical study, the emphasis of historians was on what was called an empirical/analytic method. The facts were assembled, the historian studied them objectively and dispassionately, and wrote a narrative that purported to explain those facts. The explanation became history, and when practiced by the leading scholars in the field, it was generally considered a true account of what had happened in the past.

The voice of the traditional historian can be heard in Crick's mocking admonition, evoking "good, dry, textbook history":

> History, being an accredited sub-science, only wants to know the facts. History, if it is to keep on constructing its road into the future, must do so on solid ground. At all costs let us avoid mystery-making and speculation, secrets and idle gossip.

Of course, Crick himself does not believe any of this. Even when he was a child and first began to be bewitched by history, it was the myths and stories, the "fabulous aura" of history that attracted him, not the parade of facts. As a mature history teacher, he rejects the idea that history is studied in order to learn from the mistakes of the past, since if that were the case, history would be the record of inexorable progress, which it clearly is not. Nor does history reveal the meaning of the events it records and purports to explain. History in Crick's view is nothing more than a "lucky dip of meanings," even though this does not stop humans from perpetually searching for meaning.

Crick has clearly been influenced by the debate over the nature of history that swept through the intellectual community of historians during the 1960s and 1970s. Much of this was due to the influence of the movement known as postmodernism, which cast doubt on the reliability of the rational empirical method to interpret the meaning of the past. Historians began to ask questions such as, Is the meaning that the historian finds in history something that genuinely is inherent in the past, or is it something that the historian imposes on it? How does language shape meaning? Is there only one correct meaning in history, or might there be several competing interpretations and meanings, each with its own validity?

As history expanded with the study of women, minorities, gays, and cultures all taking their place alongside—and also challenging—old-style political history, the conclusion postmodernism pointed to was that there is really no such thing as objectivity. Just as a novelist or poet gives expression, knowingly or not, to a certain ideology often dictated by class or gender, so too does the historian. The interpretation of the facts before the historian is inevitably colored by his or her own subjectivity, biases, and cultural and intellectual assumptions. The historian is, in a sense, a partner with the past in an act of co-creation, rather than an objective chronicler of something entirely separate from him- or herself. This is why historians today often speak of "doing" history rather than "studying" it, of "constructing" a historical narrative rather than merely writing it. The newer terms help to convey the active role of the historian in shaping his or her material. Some radical postmodernists even express the view that it is impossible to "do" history at all, since what is known as history is in fact no more objectively true than a fairy tale. This is not unlike the view once expressed by the French philosopher and satirist Voltaire, who remarked in a letter that "History is after all nothing but a pack of tricks which we play upon the dead" (quoted in Durant's *The Story of Philosophy*).

In *Waterland*, Crick is clearly in sympathy with the postmodernist approach to history. Not only is history a "lucky dip" as far as meaning is concerned, it is also inherently and unavoidably incomplete, "the attempt to give an account, with incomplete knowledge, of actions themselves undertaken with incomplete knowledge." Crick's scrapping of the traditional curriculum and his decision to tell his students stories of the fens instead is also a radical attempt to revise what history is or should be. When challenged by Lewis Scott as to the value of this approach, Crick says, "Perhaps history *is* just story-telling," the implication being that the listener or reader can take whatever meaning he or she needs and wants from it. Certainly as Crick tells the family saga of the Atkinsons, he does not restrict himself merely to the facts that can be known. He also gives expression to local superstition and legend, of which the fens has much; they too are a part of the fabric of history, a history that Crick reconstructs more like a novelist than a historian. History, it seems, is more art than science, and like a great symphony or a great novel, it can afford many interpretations, none of which has a definitive claim on truth. The virtue is not so much in uncovering the facts, which are going to be colored anyway by how the historian thinks and writes about them, but in continuing to ask the questions. Questioning, always seeking if not always finding explanations, is humanity's saving grace, according to Crick. Curiosity is the quality that connects human beings to the web of life. When curiosity dies, then life (and history) dies with it.

There is one other way that history dies, and that is when people manage to live in what Crick calls the Here and Now, which he contrasts with living with an awareness of history. Normally, people live their lives enmeshed in and weighed down by the burden of history, both personal and societal, which increases over time. As Crick tells his class:

> And because history accumulates, because it gets always heavier and the frustration greater, so the at-

> Crick's scrapping of the traditional curriculum and his decision to tell his students stories of the fens instead is also a radical attempt to revise what history is or should be."

tempts to throw it off . . . become more violent and drastic. . . . As history becomes inevitably more massive, more pressing and hard to support, man . . . finds himself involved in bigger and bigger catastrophes.

It is this sense of the crushing weight of history that produces the tone of melancholy that pervades *Waterland*. It seems there is an inevitable paradox in human life, at least according to Crick. Humanity creates history, its collection of stories and explanations, in order to escape the grim, featureless face of naked existence, and yet that very construct that humans build serves only to burden them further, for the present cannot escape the weight of the past.

Unless, that is, humans can live in the Here and Now. This term carries several meanings in the novel. At one level, it simply refers to the urgent issues of the present day—whatever wars or other disturbances happen to be currently raging. The view advocated by Price, Crick's rebellious student, is that it is more important to tackle the Here and Now than to study the tortured upheavals of previous generations.

But Crick also means by the term the Here and Now, the times when an individual lives fully in the present moment, fully alive to the sensual reality of life and focused only on what the moment needs in terms of action and response. Thus in 1943, when he and Mary make love for the first time, they are in the Here and Now. The Here and Now is not necessarily a pleasurable experience, however, as when Tom, in the Here and Now, feels terror when he sees blood emerging from the drowned Freddie Parr's temple. The experience of the Here and Now, according to Crick, is a comparatively rare experience; only animals live fully and constantly in it; we humans are most often somewhere else, hoping for a future or pondering the past.

It is the concept of the Here and Now that underlies the curious passage in which Earnest Atkinson insists that his offspring by his daughter Helen will be the "saviour of the world." When the offspring turns out to be mentally retarded (Dick), the title his father bestowed on him appears absurd and ironic. And yet there is no irony in the following passage, which occurs as Dick goes through his last moments on board the dredger. The year is 1943, and the world is immersed in World War II:

> He's here. He knows his place. He knows his station. He keeps the ladder turning, the buckets scooping. The noise of the churning machinery drowns the fleeting aerial clamour of global strife. He hears no bombers, sees no bombers. And the smell of silt is the smell of sanctuary, is the smell of amnesia. He's here, he's now. Not there or then. No past, no future. He's the mate of the *Rosa II*.
>
> And he's the saviour of the world . . .

At this point, Dick is so focused on what he is doing in the Here and Now that history, either his own or the world's, does not touch him. In a curious way he is free, certainly freer than Tom Crick is ever to be. And there is a certitude and purposefulness about his actions that give him a kind of tragic dignity that he did not possess before. This can be seen in the description of his suicidal, self-sacrificial dive into the river, which takes place, significantly, in the glow of the setting sun behind him. As he dives "in a long, reaching, powerful arc," Tom observes his body "form a single, taut and seemingly limbless continuum, so that an expert on diving might have judged that here indeed was a natural, here indeed was a fish of a man."

In that moment Dick attains a kind of apotheosis that eludes every other character in the novel. Perhaps for a moment he *is* the savior of the world, at least the small world of the Cricks, since with his death the tragic folly of Earnest Atkinson is finally laid to rest.

Other aspects of the past, of course, are not so easily dispensed with. If the world can be, metaphorically speaking, saved only in the occasional moments when it is forgotten in the Here and Now, the Here and Now cannot keep history at bay for long, for when it passes from here and now to there and then, history claims it as its prize. Then the eternal question "Why?" rises up once more to beguile and haunt humans and to draw them back into the myths and stories of the past, where truth may or may not lie.

Source: Bryan Aubrey, Critical Essay on *Waterland*, in *Novels for Students*, Gale, 2003.

Cynthia Cameros

In the following essay, Cameros discusses Swift's work and the authorial intent that lies behind his novels.

"Can it be a kindness not to tell what you see? And a blessing to be blind? And the best aid to human happiness that has ever been invented is a blanket of soft, white lies?" asks one of the characters in *Out of This World*. These questions sound the central theme of Graham Swift's six novels: does human happiness depend on understanding or on feeling? While the question is asked as if for the first time in each novel, Swift's answer remains, with one exception, the same: "soft, white lies" are necessary to human happiness. In keeping with his belief that feelings matter more than understanding, Swift also adheres to a model of authorship that prioritizes self-expression above communication with readers.

The Sweet Shop Owner spans a single hot summer's day, the last day of the life of widowed shopkeeper Willy Chapman. Throughout much of the day Willy carries on an internal dialogue with his estranged daughter. He remembers his marriage to an unloving wife, Irene, who attempted to compensate by bearing him the child: "You were her gift." His scholarly daughter has forsaken her father, and, according to Mrs. Cooper, won't return. Refusing to accept this, Willy quietly kills himself in the hope of finally reuniting with his daughter. "Don't you see, you're no freer than before, no freer than I am? And the only thing that can dissolve history now is if, by a miracle, you come."

A single suspicion brings about the climax of *Shuttlecock*. Immobilized by the heroic figure of his war spy father, Prentis, a Dead Crimes Investigator, bullies his wife and two sons. The suspicion that his father may have been a traitor has multiple effects. It frees Prentis: "Something had collapsed around me; so I couldn't help, in the middle of the ruins, this strange feeling of release. I had escaped; I was free." The threat of the publicity of this suspicion also may have driven his father mad. The suspicion illustrates to Prentis the power—and the danger—of knowledge: "I stared again at the file. I thought of the number of times I'd opened the cover of *Shuttlecock* hoping Dad would come out; hoping to hear his voice. Was I afraid that the allegations might be true—or that they might be false? And supposing, in some extraordinary way, that everything Quinn told me was concocted, was an elaborate hoax—if I never looked in the file, I would never know. I read the code letters over and over again. C9/E. . . . And then suddenly I knew I wanted to be uncertain, I wanted to be in the dark." Rather than confirmation or denial of his father's betrayal, it is the suspicion—the "soft, white lies"—that ultimately proves more valuable because it preserves the possibility of a heroic man.

Like Charles Dickens's *Great Expectations*, *Waterland* is a *bildungsroman* about a young boy from the Fens of East Anglia. Unlike other Swiftian characters, Tom Crick, the history teacher protagonist, is drawn to face the truth of his family's tortured history: "I'm the one who had to ask questions, who had to dig up the truth (my recipe for emergencies: explain your way out)." But the price Tom pays for his knowledge is high. His wife abducts a child. His half-brother commits suicide.

The split between understanding and feelings structures *Out of This World,* which is narrated through the alternating monologues of photographer, Harry Beech, and his estranged daughter, Sophie. The latter has forbidden cameras (a metaphor for realist understanding) in her house. We learn that Sophie glimpsed Harry photographing the wreck of the car bombing of his own father: "I saw him first, then he saw me. He was like a man caught sleep-walking, not knowing how he could be doing what he was doing, as if it were all part of some deep, ingrained reflex. But just for a moment I saw this look on his face of deadly concentration. He hadn't seen me first because he'd been looking elsewhere, and his eyes had been jammed up against a camera." Appalled by her father's detachment, she has refused to speak to him for 10 years. At first Harry resists Sophie's point. Ultimately, Harry acknowledges that a lie reunited him with his estranged father. His father's lie, which shielded Harry from his wife's infidelity, demonstrated his father's love. Harry reciprocated by reaching out to his father: "We strolled to the end of the terrace. As we turned, I wanted to do that simple but rare thing and take his arm. . . . He said, 'I've never told you, have I?'"

The split between understanding and feelings also structures *Ever After,* which is narrated through the alternating monologues of Victorian Darwinist Matthew Pearce and widowed English professor Billy Unwin. Whereas the Victorian Pearce sacrificed his wife and family to remain faithful to his Darwinist beliefs, Unwin would sacrifice the few beliefs he holds to bring back his deceased wife. "I would believe or not believe anything, swallow any old make-believe, in order to have Ruth back. Whereas Matthew—Whereas this

> " Like Charles Dickens's *Great Expectations, Waterland* is a *bildungsroman* about a young boy from the Fens of East Anglia. Unlike other Swiftian characters, Tom Crick, the history teacher protagonist, is drawn to face the truth of his family's tortured history. . . ."

Pearce guy—" After a seduction plot momentarily tempts Unwin to forget the memory of his wife, life no longer appears to be worth living to the professor, who attempts suicide. His revival leads him to the discovery that it is the "soft, white lie" of the memories of his wife that gives him a reason for living.

Like Faulkner's *As I Lay Dying,* the polyphonic *Last Orders* is narrated through the friends and family of a recently deceased man on the burial journey. Londoners Ray Johnson, Lenny Tate, Vic Tucker, Vince Dodds, and Amy Dodds are bound to the recently deceased Jack Dodds through decades of love, friendship, and secrets. Vince is Jack's adopted son, who ran away as a teenager. Ray fought with Jack in World War II, and has been in love with Jack's wife, Amy, for as many years. Amy remembers the foundering of her marriage as Jack refused to acknowledge their mentally retarded daughter: "He won't mention June so I won't mention Ray. Fair dos. What you don't know can't hurt." Here the lies sometimes serve not only to protect, but also to create a better community. "So when Vince Pritchett, but forget the Pritchett, dropped into my lap, into our lap," says Amy, "I ought to have known it wouldn't help a bit, it wouldn't win him back. You can't make a real thing out of pretending hard." Regardless of her denial, it is through "pretending hard" that Amy has created a family: After years of resentment, Vince has reunited with his adopted parents.

The importance of "soft, white lies" is apparent in Swift's attitude towards authorship. Some authors write to communicate with their readers a

Laborers fill sandbags to form a blockade against surging waters

necessary piece of social criticism, a rationale which has its roots in the Realist tradition of social responsibility. Other authors write to express themselves, a rationale which has its roots in the Romantic tradition of self-expression. A quote from Swift expresses the Romantic tenet that deep feeling is the essential ingredient of art: "I am absolutely not a formalist, because what does matter to me are things as felt, and feeling seems at least to stand in opposition to form: form is to do with control and discipline, and feeling is to do with liberation. . . ."

While expressing himself may be Swift's intention as an author, it's suspect that this self-expression is "liberation." After all, what kind of "liberation" can obsessively rewriting the same plot be called? Immobilized by the excessive expectations of her parents, Irene in *The Sweet Shop Owner* could neither fully reject, nor fully participate in her family life. Immobilized by the heroic figure of his father, Prentis in *Shuttlecock* is freed by the revelation that his father may have been a traitor to the English. Immobilized by the expectations of her father to become like her sanctified mother, Mary in *Waterland* goes mad. Sense a pattern here? Regardless of which book by Swift one chooses, one meets the same plot: an adult frozen in childhood must free him- or herself from the overpowering

example of an idealized parent. The repetition of a single plot suggests that Swift has supported a rationale of writing as self-expression from necessity rather than from choice. Even if Swift had wanted to write for his audience, one wonders whether he could do so. As Swift has said, "I write a lot by sheer instinct, groping around in the dark."

Expressing himself may have been Swift's foremost aim, but communicating with his readers is a necessary aim of any author. Swift fails—as several reviewers' comments indicate—to communicate with his readers. Too many perspectives, none of which are authorized by the obfuscating narrator has been the frequent charge of reviewers. "Mr. Swift is so committed to seeing around perspectives, undermining his own assertions, squeezing the narrator between the pincers of the past and present, being ironic at the expense of what somebody didn't know but somebody now does, that the effect he creates is rather like a three-ring circus," a *New York Times Book Review* critic said of *Waterland*. "One yearns for a whiff of directness. . . ." Stephen Wall of the *London Review of Books* also protested that the multiple perspectives in *Ever After* were not resolved: "Despite its manifestly humane intentions, the different areas of narrative interest in *Ever After* disperse, rather than concentrate attention. Although its varying strands are conscientiously knitted together ... they don't seem significantly to cohere." In failing to organize the multiple viewpoints, Swift violates the assumption that the author will provide a "hierarchical organization of details." Instead, the reader is left alone to make meanings; a job she could have done without the reading of any of Swift's novels.

Why this refusal to guide his readers? An answer lies in Swift's admiration of "vulnerability." Swift's characters are often proud to say, "I don't know." In *Shuttlecock*, Prentis says: "'I don't know' ... It seemed to me that this was an answer I would give, boldly, over and over again for the rest of my life." According to Swift, when an author shows the reader his vulnerability, he gains the reader's trust: "An author ought to have authority ... It makes sure the reader trusts the writer ... Often that stems from the realization that the writer is prepared to show that vulnerability." When Swift has shown vulnerability, however, his reviewers have not trusted him. Just the opposite. Swift has said, "I am desperate to avoid a sense of power derived from form." His fear of authority is indeed evident in his novels.

Source: Cynthia Cameros, "Swift, Graham," in *Contemporary Novelists*, 7th ed., edited by Neil Schlager and Josh Lauer, St. James Press, 2001, pp. 959–61.

George P. Landow

In the following essay, Landow identifies Waterland *as a "self-reflexive text," focusing on the novel's treatment of the nature of storytelling, history, and the novel's relation to works by Dickens and Faulkner.*

> Children [are those] to whom, throughout history, stories have been told, chiefly but not always at bedtime, in order to quell restless thoughts; whose need of stories is matched only by the need adults have of children to tell stories to, of receptacles for their stock of fairy-tales, of listening ears on which to unload, bequeath those most unbelievable yet haunting of fairy-tales, their own lives.

Graham Swift's *Waterland* (1983), a novel cast in the form of a fictional autobiography, has much to tell us about the fate, even the possibility, of autobiography, in the late twentieth century. Although *Waterland* does not confuse personal with public history, it intertwines them, making each part of the other, for as Tom Crick, the secondary school teacher of history who is Swift's protagonist, seeks an explanation of how his life has turned out, he tells his story, but as he does so, he finds that he must also tell the stories of the fens and of his ancestors who lived there. In the course of telling his

> As a novel that questions the interrelated notions of self and story in Dickens's *Great Expectations* and Faulkner's *Absalom, Absalom!* at the same time that it draws upon them, *Waterland* appears a late-twentieth-century postmodernist rewriting of each."

story, their story, he questions why we tell stories to ourselves and our children, how the stories we tell relate to those found in literature and history, and what these stories tell us about selves, ourselves.

Waterland meditates on human fate, responsibility, and historical narrative by pursuing a mystery; so the book is in part a detective story. It is also the story of two families, of an entire region in England, of England from the industrial revolution to the present, of technology and its effects, and it is, finally, a meditation on stories and story-telling—a fictional inquiry into fiction, a book that winds back upon itself and asks why we tell stories.

As a novel that questions the interrelated notions of self and story in Dickens's *Great Expectations* and Faulkner's *Absalom, Absalom!* at the same time that it draws upon them, *Waterland* appears a late-twentieth-century postmodernist rewriting of each. In attempting to relate his own story, Tom Crick begins by questioning the purpose, truthfulness, and limitations of stories while at the same time making clear that he believes history to be a form of story-telling. These questionings of narrative within its narrative make *Waterland* a self-reflexive text.

The novel has as protagonist a history teacher who is about to be fired because history (his stories) are no longer considered of sufficient cultural value. He ruminates upon history in terms of the events of his own life, and he quickly runs up against the young, those without interest in the past, those who quite properly want to know why? why pay attention to what's over and done with? "You ask," the narrator tells his students, "as all history classes ask, as all history classes should ask, What is the point of history." They want to know, as we do, two things: What is the point of history as a subject; that is, why study the past? and what is the point of history itself, that is, does history, man's existence in public time, have any meaning, any pattern, any purpose?

This resistance to both notions of history by the young, who wish to live in the here and now, is embodied in Price, Tom Crick's student, who voices all the usual objections to paying attention to what has gone by. "Your thesis," Tom responds, "is that history, as such, is a red-herring; the past is irrelevant. The present alone is vital." Some of Tom's own statements about history and historiography suggest that Price might have a point. "When introduced to history as an object of Study ... it was still the fabulous aura of history that lured me, and I believed, perhaps like you, that history was a myth." Tom Crick confesses that he retained such pleasing, soothing notions of history

> Until a series of encounters with the Here and Now gave a sudden urgency to my studies. Until the Here and Now, gripping me by the arm, slapping my face and telling me to take a good look at the mess I was in, informed me that history was no invention but indeed existed—and I had become a part of it.

Concerned with saving the world from nuclear war, concerned that there may not be a future, Price thinks history is bunk: "I want a future . . . And you—you can stuff your past." As it turns out, Price's use of the second-person pronoun is correct, for this past, this history, that he rejects is precisely his—Tom's—past.

Price also makes a second appealing attack on history and historiography, namely, that it is a means of avoidance: "You know what your trouble is, sir? You're hooked on explanation. Explain, explain. Everything's got to have an explanation ... Explaining's a way of avoiding facts while you pretend to get near to them." To be against history is thus for Price anti-explanation, because according to him, both history and explanation evade life in the present—an attitude based on the assumption that the present is pleasant, nurturing, and not deadly.

Near the close of the novel Swift's protagonist answers the charge that people resort to history only as a means of evasion with the counter claim that curiosity and the explanations to which it leads are necessary and inevitable. They do not subvert life, claims Crick, nor do they bear responsibility for keeping us from engaging in important events like revolutions.

Supposing it's the other way round. Supposing it's revolutions which divert and impede the course of our inborn curiosity. Supposing it's curiosity—which inspires our sexual explorations and feeds our desires to hear and tell stories—which is our natural and fundamental state of mind. Supposing it's our insatiable and feverish desire to know about things, to know about each other, always to be sniff-sniffing things out, which is the true and rightful subverter and defeats even our impulse for historical progression.

Trying to understand why—trying to understand, that is, what has happened to him and his life—Crick retells the story of his life. By relating the events of his life in some sort of an order he makes it into a story. He constructs history—his story. He constructs himself, and in the course of doing so he recognizes that "Perhaps history *is* just story-telling": "History itself, the Grand Narrative, the filler of vacuums, the dispeller of fears of the dark." And he has examples of this in the historical legends told to him by his mother.

Before the murder of Freddie Parr, he and Mary lived outside of time and history, outside that stream of events he is trying to teach to his class. But with the discovery of Freddie's body floating in the canal lock, and with the discovery of a beer bottle, Tom and Mary fall into time and history. Previously, "Mary was fifteen, and so was I . . . in prehistorical, pubescent times, when we drifted instinctively." As Tom explains, "it is precisely these surprise attacks of the Here and Now which, far from launching us into the present tense, which they do, it is true, for a brief and giddy interval, announce that time has taken us prisoner."

This view accords with that of those philosophical anthropologists—Mircea Eliade and others—who emphasize that until human beings leave tribal, agricultural existence, they live in an eternal present in which time follows a cyclical pattern of days and seasons. Emphasizing that "from the point of view of a historical peoples or classes 'suffering' is equivalent to 'history,'" Eliade claims that archaic humanity has no interest in history or in the individuation it creates. Interest in the novel, the unique, the irreversible, appeared only comparatively recently. Tom Crick's whole existence in the novel instantiates Eliade's point that the "crucial difference" between tribal humanity and its descendants lie in the value "modern, historical man" gives to historical events—to the " 'novelties' " that once represented only failure and infraction. In tribal society, one becomes individual, one becomes *an* individual, only by botching a ritual or otherwise departing from some universal pattern. In such societies, one differentiates oneself, becoming an individual, only by sin and failure. The individual therefore is the man or woman who got wrong the planting or fertility ritual, the hunting pattern. Which is why the narrator explains: "What is a history teacher? He's someone who teaches mistakes. While others say, Here's how to do it, he says, And here's what goes wrong."

Therefore, writing history, like writing autobiography, only comes after a fall, for autobiography and other forms of history respond to the question "why," and people only ask that question after something has gone wrong. "And what does this question Why imply?" Crick asks his students. "It implies—as it surely implies when you throw it at me rebelliously in the midst of our history lessons—dissatisfaction, disquiet, a sense that all is not well. In a state of perfect contentment there would be no need or room for this irritant little word. History begins only at the point where things go wrong; history is born only with trouble, with perplexity, with regret." But, of course, were it not for trouble, perplexity, and regret we would not have autobiographies, and as the history of Victorian autobiography demonstrates, periods of trouble and perplexity, if not regret, produce self-histories galore, for in such circumstances autobiographers traditionally have offered their experiences, their survival, as exemplary.

Tom Crick's autobiographical project therefore centers on what went wrong. This whole novel, in fact, is an attempt to explain what went wrong—what went wrong with his own life and Mary's, with the lives of his parents, and with the lives of both their families, who represent the peasant and wealthy entrepreneurial classes of Britain from the seventeenth century to the present. *Waterland* begins, therefore, with the discovery of Freddie Parr's body in midsummer 1943, a discovery that comes all the more shockingly, unexpectedly, because Swift presents it within a fairy-tale landscape, for it was "a fairy-tale land, after all," in part because both his mother and father had a gift for making it such with their hand-me-down tales.

Waterland, in other words, to a large extent embodies the conventional Romantic pattern best known, perhaps, from "Tintern Abbey." Like the idealized Wordsworth who is the speaker of that poem, Tom Crick returns (though only in imagination) to the landscape of thoughtless youth, and like the poet, he concerns himself with the losses of innocence and with the corollary fall into time, self-consciousness, and social existence—into, that is, the world of adulthood, into "trouble . . . perplexity

. . . regret." Finally, like Wordsworth in "Tintern Abbey," Crick relates his meditations on his own life and its patterns in the presence of a younger audience, and like the poem's speaker, Crick also acts in the manner of a ventriloquist, obviously placing words in the mouths of that younger audience. The obvious difference between the two works, of course, appears in the fact that, unlike "Tintern Abbey," *Waterland* bravely refuses to find solace in some Romantic revision of Milton's Fortunate Fall.

Tom does, however, come to believe that all such explanatory narratives, function, however provisionally, as means of ordering our lives and thereby protecting us from chaos and disorder. And Swift's array of characters surely need such shelter, for some are victims of progress, technology, and the anti-natural (the Cricks of earlier generations lost their way of life as swamp people when the swamps were drained), and others victims of what the adult narrator considers purely natural (as are Mary, Tom, Dick, and Freddie, who were only following natural sexual urges); and yet others were victims of World War I (like Tom's father and uncle), or victims (like Tom's mother) of natural unnatural love, of the incest that produces Dick, his idiot half-brother. Story-telling, and history, and books like *Waterland* are these people's prime defences against fear: "It's all a struggle to make things not seem meaningless. It's all a fight against fear," Tom Crick tells his class. "What do you think all my stories are for . . . I don't care what you call it—explaining, evading the facts, making up meanings, taking a larger view, putting things in perspective, dodging the here and now, education, history, fairy-tales—it helps to eliminate fear."

In fact, Tom Crick argues, story-telling comes with time, with living in time, and story-telling, which distinguishes us from animals, comes with being human.

> Children, only animals live entirely in the Here and Now. Only nature knows neither memory nor history. Man man—let me offer you a definition—is the story-telling animal. Wherever he goes he wants to leave behind not a chaotic wake, not an empty space, but the comforting marker-buoys and trail-signs of stories. He has to go on telling stories. He has to keep on making them up. As long as there's a story, it's all right.

The problem, as this entire novel goes to show, is that the material of stories often refuses to be shaped by them, just as nature, unmediated nature, refuses to be shaped by the convenient story of progress within which Victorians tried to place it. (And, one must note in passing, this fact might cast into doubt all story-telling, particularly that of this novel, since narrative always involves some kind of progress.) Thus, Graham Swift's emphasis throughout the novel on two matters—the Fens and sexuality—that resist all ideological, narrative control, that refuse to be shaped by stories we tell. Putting together the two opposed forces that drive much of his tale, Tom claims "Children, there's something which revolutionaries and prophets of new worlds and even humble champions of Progress (think of those poor Atkinsons . . .) can't abide. Natural history, human nature." As Tom makes us realize, natural history is a paradox and an oxymoron—that is, a jarring placement together of contraries—because it is history of the antihistorical which has no order or is cyclical (nonhistorical) without individuating markers.

This whole novel, in other words, sets out to examine these ages—and their literary as well as religious and philosophical foundations—and finds them wanting. It examines various theories of history, such as that proposed by religion, progress, and hubris, and canvasses a wide range of subjects for history, such as political events from the Roman conquerors of Britain to the Bastille and World War I and II, the history of technology, including draining the Fens, the history of places, the history of families, the history of individual people, especially the narrator and Mary, and the history of a beer bottle.

Waterland, which is cast in the form of a fictional autobiography, probes the role of narrative and in so doing raises questions about the means and methods of autobiography. Like much recent theory and criticism, the novel looks skeptically at two aspects of narrative. First, it expresses suspicion of the way human beings gravitate towards folktales, myths, and other well-shaped narratives that falsify experience and keep us from encountering the world. Swift's narrator himself admits that his "earliest acquaintance with history was thus, in a form issuing from my mother's lips, inseparable from her other bedtime make-believe— how Alfred burnt the cakes, how Canute commanded the waves, now King Charles hid in an oak tree—as if history were a pleasing invention." Recent studies of nineteenth-century autobiography have pointed out the extent to which authors depend upon such conventional narrative patterns to create what Avrom Fleishman has termed a "personal myth" by which to tell their lives. As Linda H. Peterson has pointed out, however, conventional narratives, such as those drawn from scripture, create major problems for many would-be self-

historians, particularly women, who find that these narratives distort their stories or do not permit them to tell their stories at all.

Second, Swift's novel takes its skepticism about narrative further, for it not only points, like recent critics, to the falsifications created by particular stories, it is suspicious of all story-telling. *Waterland* questions all narrative based on sequence, and in this it agrees with other novels of its decade. Like Penelope Lively's *Moon Tiger* (1987), another novel in the form of the autobiography of an invented character, Swift's novel has a historian, Tom Crick, as his protagonist, and like Lively's character, Swift's relates the events of a single life to the major currents of contemporary history.

Using much the same method for autobiography as for history, Swift's protagonist would agree with Lively's Claudia Hampton, whose deep suspicion of chronology and sequence explicitly derive from her experience of simultaneity. Thinking over the possibility of writing a history of the world, Lively's heroine rejects sequence and linear history as inauthentic and false to her experience:

> The question is, shall it or shall it not be linear history? I've always thought a kaleidoscopic view might be an interesting heresy. Shake the tube and see what comes out. Chronology irritates me. There is no chronology inside my head. I am composed of a myriad Claudias who spin and mix and part like sparks of sunlight on water. The pack of cards I carry around is forever shuffled and reshuffled; there is no sequence, everything happens at once.

Like Proust's Marcel, she finds that a simple sensation brings the past back flush upon the present, making a mockery of separation and sequence. Returning to Cairo in her late sixties, Claudia finds it both changed and unchanged. "The place," she explains, "didn't look the same but it felt the same; sensations clutched and transformed me." Standing near a modern concrete and plate-glass building, she picks a "handful of eucalyptus leaves from a branch, crushed them in my hand, smelt, and tears came to my eyes. Sixty-seven-year-old Claudia . . . crying not in grief but in wonder that nothing is ever lost, that everything can be retrieved, that a lifetime is not linear but instant." Her lesson for autobiography is that "inside the head, everything happens at once." Like Claudia, Tom Crick takes historical, autobiographical narratives whose essence is sequence and spreads them out or weaves them in a nonsequential way.

Lively and Swift are hardly the first to suggest that narrative sequence falsifies autobiographical truth. Tennyson's *In Memoriam*, one of the most influential as well as most technically daring poems of the nineteenth century, embodies this postmodernist suspicion of narrative as falsifying. Arthur Henry Hallam's death in 1833 forced Tennyson to question his faith in nature, God, and poetry. *In Memoriam* reveals that the poet, who found that brief lyrics best embodied the transitory emotions that buffeted him after his loss, rejected conventional elegy and narrative because both falsify the experience of grief and recovery by mechanically driving the reader through too unified—and hence too simplified—a version of these experiences. Creating a poetry of fragments, Tennyson leads the reader of *In Memoriam* from grief and despair through doubt to hope and faith, but at each step stubborn, contrary emotions intrude, and readers encounter doubt in the midst of faith, pain in the midst of resolution. Instead of the elegiac plot of "Lycidas," "Adonais," and "Thrysis," *In Memoriam* offers 133 fragments interlaced by dozens of images and motifs and informed by an equal number of minor and major resolutions, the most famous of which is section ninety-five's representation of Tennyson's climactic, if wonderfully ambiguous, mystical experience of contact with Hallam's spirit.

Like Tennyson and most other nineteenth-century autobiographers, Tom Crick tells his story as a means of explaining his conversion to a particular belief and way of life. Unlike the great Victorian autobiographers, real and fictional, he does not relate the significant details about his life from the vantage point of relative tranquility or even complacency. Mill, Ruskin, and Newman, like the Pip of *Great Expectations* or the heroine of *Jane Eyre*, all tell the stories of their lives after *everything interesting* as already happened to them and they have at last reached some safe haven. Similarly, however tortured Tennyson's mind and spirit had been after the death of Hallam, and however little conventional narratives were suited to communicating that experience, by the close of *In Memoriam* the reader encounters an autobiographical speaker or narrator who stands on safe, secure, unchanging ground. In contrast, Tom Crick, unlike Pip and Jane, writes from within a time of crisis, for Tom, like his age, exists in a condition of catastrophe.

Such writing from within an ongoing crisis may well be the postmodernist contribution to autobiography, for whether or not one chooses to see such a narrative position as a pretentious pose—after all, people have always lived within crisis; the

Victorians certainly believed they did—this vantage point inevitably undercuts the traditional autobiographer's project, which entails showing himself and his survived crises as exemplary. Even though Newman, Mill, Ruskin, and Tennyson present themselves and their experiences as essentially unique, they nonetheless emphasize the representativeness and therefore relevance of their lives to their readers. They present themselves as living lessons for the rest of us. The approach to autobiography undertaken by Tom Crick, on the other hand, essentially deconstructs the potentially hopeful aspects of his narrative. By refusing the autobiographer's traditionally secure closing position, in other words, Swift's protagonist casts into doubt the world of the autobiographer, his autobiography, and narrative in general.

Waterland, as we have seen, is a book that winds back upon other books, for it is a descendent, an echo, and a qualification of both Dickens's *Great Expectations* and Faulkner's *Absalom, Absalom!* Swift's novel begins, for example, with an epigraph from *Great Expectations*, another work that opens in the fens, and it shares with Dickens's novel many elements other than their opening scenes of death and guilt. Both works, which combine autobiography and atonement, begin with the intrusion of a fearful reality into a young person's consciousness. Both, furthermore, tell of their protagonists' climb up the social ladder from working class to some form of shabby gentility, and both, for these reasons and others, could equally well bear the titles *Great Expectations* and *Expectations Disappointed*, for both end with far sadder, somewhat wiser narrators. Both novels relate the dark results of an adolescent passion, and both are haunted by the presence of an abused older woman, as Sarah Atkinson echoes and completes Miss Havisham—as do the breweries and flames that associate with each.

Waterland stands in a similar relation to a twentieth-century canonical work—Faulkner's *Absalom, Absalom!* Brian McHale's contrast of modernist and postmodernist fiction helps us place both *Waterland*'s attitudes toward narrative and its relation to Faulkner's novel. According to McHale, whereas epistemological concerns define the novels that embody modernism, ontological concerns characterize postmodernist fiction.

> That is, modernist fiction deploys strategies which engage and foreground questions such as . . . "How can I interpret this world of which I am a part? . . . What is there to be known? Who knows it?; How do they know it, and with what degree of certainty?;

How is knowledge transmitted from one knower to another, and with what degree of certainty?" . . . Faulkner's *Absalom, Absalom!* has been designed to raise just such epistemological questions. Its logic is that of a detective story, the epistemological genre *par excellence.*

In contrast to modernist fiction, which thus centers on questions of knowledge, postmodernist work is informed by ontological questions such as "What is a world?, . . . What happens when different kinds of world are placed in confrontation, or when boundaries between worlds are violated?; What is the mode of existence of a text, and what is the mode of existence of the world (or worlds) it projects?"

Although *Waterland* shares little of postmodernist fiction's aggressive, explicit destabilizing of the world and the self, the novel's intertextual relations with Faulkner differentiates it from both his work and from literary modernism. The clear parallels between *Waterland* and *Absalom, Absalom!* that reviewers have observed in fact serve to point up the differences between the two fictional worlds. As one anonymous review pointed out, "The Fens of east England serve novelist Graham Swift as Yoknapatawpha County served William Faulkner: less as a geographical setting than as an active force shaping people's lives . . . Mysteries ramify but ultimately lead, as in all Gothic novels (including Faulkner's) to a secret at the center of the family house." The two novels share other similarities as well: both take the form of family tragedies in which a male ancestor's hubris leads to terrible disaster, both emphasize violations of the family bond, and both employ as backgrounds cataclysmic wars that change their nations forever. Like Faulkner's *Absalom, Absalom!*, and like Dickens's *Great Expectations* (which the British reviewers don't mention), *Waterland* meditates on human fate, responsibility, and historical narrative by pursuing a mystery; so the book, like these others, is in part a detective story.

There is, however, one important difference: In true modernist fashion Quentin Compson and his Harvard roommate attempt to solve a mystery by detection and by imaginative re-creation. In true postmodernist fashion Tom Crick, who knew the identity of the murderer years before he began the story-telling that constitutes *Waterland*, creates a mystery (for us) where none exists.

In addition to *Waterland*'s very different, self-conscious use of mystery, its discussions of narrativity and narratology make it a late-twentieth century retelling of the works of both Faulkner and Dickens as do its postmodernist grotesqueries, play-

fulness, emphasis upon the erotic, and convoluted style that continually draws attention to itself. Another aspect of postmodernist fiction with particular significance for autobiography appears in Swift's creation of a textualized, intertextualized self.

Presenting Tom Crick as intertwined with so many other tales and selves, Swift presents the self in the manner of many poststructuralist critics and postmodernist novelists as an entity both composed of many texts and dispersed into them. In *Waterland* Swift textualizes the self, and that self matches the description of text that Roland Barthes advances in *S/Z* when he points out that entering a text is "entrance into a network with a thousand entrances; to take this entrance is to aim, ultimately . . . at a perspective (of fragments, of voices from other texts, other codes), whose vanishing point is nonetheless ceaselessly pushed back, mysteriously opened." Tom Crick's textualized self fulfills Barthes's description of the "ideal text" whose "networks are many and interact, without any one of them being able to surpass the rest; . . . it has no beginning; it is reversible." Therefore, we can say of the self-construction that Tom Crick offers us to read, that "we gain access to it by several entrances, none of which can be authoritatively declared to be the main one; the codes it mobilizes extend as far as the eye can reach, they are indeterminable." And that is why to record part of himself, Tom must also record so many other histories, for they all intertwine, echo, and reverbrate; causes, responsibilities, limits become difficult to locate.

In other words, as soon as Crick begins to tell his story he finds necessary expanding that story beyond his biological beginnings. On the one hand, *Waterland* seems a rigorously historicist presentation of selfhood; on the other, its self-conscious examination of the history that historicizes this self makes it appear that these narratives, like the historicism they support, are patently constructed, purely subjective patterns.

Tom Crick's autobiographical acts, in other words, turn out to be fictional analogues of the land reclamation whose presence dominates the novel. Provisional, essential, limited as they may be, telling stories can never adequately control reality or nature or what's out there or what Tom calls the Here and Now. Like the Fen waters, like the natural force it is, Mary's and Tom's and Dick's and, alas, Freddie's sexuality refuse to be contained by the canal walls and dams of human fairy stories and, instead, lead to Freddie's murder, Dick's suicide, Mary's abortion, and ultimately to her kidnapping an infant in a supermarket and subsequent commitment to a mental institution. That is why the Fen lands and Fen waters, which the Atkinsons and other commercial leaders of the Industrial Revolution try to fit into a human story, play such an important part in this novel. And that is why Tom, who explicitly takes draining the Fens to exemplify progressive theories of history, speaks in his imagination to his wife of their "Sunday walks, with which we trod and measured out the tenuous, reclaimed land of our marriage." Fen lands and waters represent the reality that won't fit into our stories (one can't call it nature or the natural because those terms refer to a reality that already has been placed in a story). "For the chief fact about the Fens," Crick emphasizes when he introduced them as the setting of his life history, "is that they are reclaimed land, land that was once water, and which, even today, is not quite solid."

Waterland examines and finds wanting the Neoclassical view of nature that takes it to be divine order, the Romantic one that takes it to be essentially benign and accommodated to our needs, and the Victorian one that takes it to be, however hostile or neutral, something we can shape to our needs and use for the material of a tale of progress.

Like John McPhee's *The Control of Nature*, *Waterland* takes land reclamation and man's battle against water as a heroic, absurd, all too human project that particularly characterizes modern Western civilization's approach to man, nature, and fate. Swift's novel presents both land reclamation and telling one's story as game, even heroic, attempts to shape the chaotic setting of human existence: marriage, nature, water, past time, memory, other literature. Within such a conception of things, telling one's own story takes the form of a similarly heroic, if absurd, reclamation from the destructions of nature and time, for autobiography, like land reclamation, takes the purely natural and after great self-conscious exertions makes it human. Of course, autobiography and history, like draining the fens, can never achieve more than temporary victories against the natural, for the simple reason that people carry out both these projects within time, and eventually, sooner or later, time wins. Time wears channels in the dykes, rusts machinery, makes a particular autobiographical act obsolete or irrelevant. None of these facts, of course, argue against reclaiming land nor do they argue against undertaking to write history and autobiography. But, as Tom Crick recognizes, they do cut such projects down to size. Suspicious of the idea of progress, Crick warns us that the world

does not really head toward any goal, and therefore "It's progress if you can stop the world from slipping away. My humble model for progress is the reclamation of land. Which is repeatedly, never-endingly retrieving what is lost. A dogged and vigilant business. A dull yet valuable business. A hard, inglorious business. But you shouldn't go mistaking the reclamation of land for the building of empires." Similarly, autobiographical acts (and fictional versions of them) provide brief, temporary, provisional living spaces for human beings.

Autobiographical acts, then, follow from a basic human need for order and meaning that relates intimately to the need to escape chaos and fear. Telling stories about ourselves, like telling stories about people of earlier times and about the natural world, derives from curiosity, that force that, according to Swift's narrator, weds us to both world and word—a force that drives sexuality, science, and story-telling. Swift raises the problem of the erotics of the text in the context of explaining his wife's curiosity as a fifteen year old back in that halcyon year, 1943. "Mary itched," Tom Crick explains. "And this itch of Mary's was the itch of curiosity. In her fifteen-year-old body curiosity tickled and chafed, making her fidgety and roving-eyed. Curiosity drove her, beyond all restraint, to want to touch, witness, experience whatever was unknown and hidden from her." This intense curiosity, which, according to Crick, defines the human, "is an ingredient of love. It is a vital force. Curiosity, which bogs us down in arduous meditations and can lead to the writing of history books, will also, on occasion, as on that afternoon by the Hockwell Lode, reveal to us that which we seldom glimpse unscathed (for it appears more often—dead bodies, boat-hooks—dressed in terror): the Here and Now." Despite the occasional encounters with terror that curiosity begets—which Swift instantiates by prompting our readers' curiosity to lead us to Dick's incestuous origins and Mary's horrific abortion—in *Waterland*, curiosity, the force of narrative, appears in Aristotelian fashion as an essentially life-giving drive. "Curiosity begets love. It weds us to the world." To be human we have to be curious, and curiosity produces story-telling.

As impossible as getting right these stories may be, attempting to shape a narrative, one's narrative, one's own novel, is all we have, and we must therefore all be historians. Like autobiography, "History is that impossible thing: the attempt to give an account, with incomplete knowledge, of actions themselves undertaken with incomplete knowledge. So that it teaches us no short-cuts to

Salvation, no recipe for a New World, only the dogged and patient art of making do."

> By forever attempting to explain we come, not to an Explanation, but to a knowledge of the limits of our power to explain. Yes, yes, the past gets in the way; it trips us up, bogs us down; it complicates, makes difficult. But to ignore this is folly, because, above all, what history teaches us is to avoid illusion and make believe, to lay aside dreams, moonshine, cure-alls, wonder-workings, pie-in-the sky—to be realistic.

However provisional, however reduced, however its narratives are fractured or dispersed, autobiography in the world of *Waterland* therefore remains essential and inevitable. One basic justification for history, narrative, and autobiography lies in the fact that it is something we as humans must do. As Crick explains to the members of his class, their very questioning of history provides one of its basic justifications:

> Your "Why?" gives the answer. Your demand for explanation provides an explanation. Isn't the seeking of reasons itself inevitably an historical process, since it must always work backwards from what came after to what came before? And so long as we have this itch for explanations, must we not always carry round with us this cumbersome but precious bag of clues called history? Another definition, children: Man, the animal which demands an explanation, the animal which asks Why.

Telling stories, particularly one's own story, turns out to be absurd and even comical when viewed by any cosmic scale, but for all that it is a necessary act, something that one does, as Carlyle put it, to keep our heads above water. Carlyle comes readily to mind when considering Tom Crick's willingness to face reality in reduced, bleak circumstances in part because, as Tom tells us, he read Carlyle's *French Revolution* during one crisis in his life and that work, which provides some of the narrator's facts and emphases, led to his vocation as a history teacher. But one thinks of Carlyle even more because Tom Crick also shares his general tone, his willingness to act in a bleak, barren world if only because that's all there is to do. Crick believes, finally, that

> All the stories once were real. And all the events of history, the battles and costume-pieces, once really happened. All the stories were once a feeling in the guts . . . But when the world is about to end there'll be no more reality, only stories. All there'll be left to us will be stories. Stories will be our only reality. We'll sit down, in our shelter, and tell stories to some imaginary Prince Shahriyar, hoping it will never . . . [ellipsis in original].

Source: George P. Landow, "History, His Story, and Stories in Graham Swift's *Waterland*," in *Studies in the Literary Imagination*, Vol. XXIII, No. 2, Fall 1990, pp. 197–211.

Judith Wilt

In the following essay excerpt, Wilt examines the concept of fatherhood in Waterland.

Waterland: *The Stream Flows Backwards*

Graham Swift's *Waterland* opens like a Gothic novel with a murdered body floating down the river that drains the English fenland. The narrator is a mysteriously spooked London history teacher whose fenland, paternal forbears were rural lock keepers and tale spinners, and whose maternal forbears were Victorian builders and brewers on the rise, in league with progress. Throughout the novel he addresses as his readers a class of adolescents who have suddenly rebelled against "the grand narrative"—history. The young people are spooked, too; they are pierced by nuclear fear, the recognition that the future, which is all that makes the past significant, may be foreclosed. Their challenge to the teacher, Tom Crick, culminates two other disasters. His headmaster, a no-nonsense technocrat with an airy faith in a future under the nuclear umbrella, has used the excuse of Thatcherite cuts in the budget to eliminate the history department and, by implication, Crick, too. And his wife, Mary, returning in her childless, early fifties to the Roman Catholic religion she had grown up in, began a "love-affair, a liaison . . . with God," whose issue was the kidnapping by the would-be, couldn't-be mother of another woman's baby from the supermarket.

The narrative is carried back from these present errors in rushes, oozes, and broken crosscurrents of self-interrupted musing, explaining, and reasoning, to the three deaths which at some profound level stopped the lives, the stories, of Tom Crick and Mary Metcalf, his wife. For, Crick warns his students in the obscure early pages of his rambling, "there is such a thing as human drainage, too, such a thing as human pumping." And the subsequent "pumping" of Mary and Tom, sexually, socially, intellectually, produces energies which drain continually back to the murder of Freddie Parr, found floating in the lock of the Leem River in 1943, the suicide (if it was such) of the murderer, and the pregnancy/abortion that caused and was caused by these.

Of the three mysteries these deaths involve, the first introduced is the most easily explained and the first illuminated. The narrator's brother, the mentally retarded "potato head," Dick Crick, killed Freddie Parr by getting him drunk on a bottle of his grandfather's famous Coronation Ale, then hitting him on the head and pushing him into the river. He did it because he was, in his dim but intense way in "lu—lu—love" with Mary Metcalf and believed that desire alone was sufficient to make him the father of the child the sixteen-year-old Mary was carrying. This naive belief runs in the family: brother Tom believed that desire alone is sufficient (and necessary) to fill "that empty but fillable vessel, reality" of which a woman's womb is "a miniature model." Mary's protest, protecting Tom, the real father, that their friend Freddie Parr was the father, thus outraged not only Dick's manhood but his very reality. For Dick is (more than he or we know at the moment) the child of the maternal Atkinson ancestors, a child of "progress" for whom the things that happen, are done, are made, *are* reality. Tom, on the other hand, is a child of their Crick ancestors, rural philosophers like Faulkner's Bundrens for whom events, deeds, are mere hallucinations in the everlasting flatland of vacancy, for whom "reality is that nothing happens."

The Atkinson vision thus privileges paternity as the ultimate sign of reality: Atkinsons seek fatherhood, invest it with godhood, be unable to relinquish it. But the Cricks have been "water people" for hundreds of years, living on its animals, sustaining and repairing its ravages, receiving its draining cargoes, and taking to heart its message: "For what is water, children, which seeks to make all things level, which has no taste or colour of its own, but a liquid form of Nothing?" For the Cricks, fatherhood is what it was to primitive peoples, man's hallucination, his favorite fiction, poignant attempt to raise on the flats of reality, in the empty womb of it, "his own personal stage, his own props and scenery—for there are very few of us who can be, for any length of time, merely realistic." A Crick will not believe his own fatherhood nor insist upon it, nor, on the other hand, will he be destroyed by it or by its lack.

This is what Tom Crick claims to understand of his own vision as he looks back beyond and around the conception and abortion of his only child, a primal scene reluctantly uncovered by the skittering narrative as a series of nightmarish snapshots. It started with "curiosity," a "vital force," an "itch," which drove the fifteen-year-old Mary to explore her own and Tom's bodies, an itch "beyond all restraint" whose verbal form, "those spellbinding words which make the empty world seem full," is (as it was in Faulkner's novel) the repeated phrase drained of reality, "I love—I love—love, love." It begins in a "little game of tease and dare" between the aggressive Mary and two boys, Tom

> **For the Cricks, fatherhood is what it was to primitive peoples. . . . A Crick will not believe his own fatherhood nor insist upon it, nor, on the other hand, will he be destroyed by it or by its lack."**

Crick and Freddie Parr, as to who will "show" what lies between the legs. Dick Crick, "potato head," several years older and more physically developed, suddenly makes himself a part of the game when Mary agrees to "show" to the boy who swims longest underwater. Experiencing an erection for the first time, Dick dives from the bridge and wins the game, the splash and swim itself serving as his act of intercourse with the river, with Mary, with the fillable vessel of reality. The whimsical and malignant Freddie Parr, seeing Dick, bewildered, fail to claim his trophy, initiates another game: he seizes an eel from the river trap and thrusts it into Mary's "knickers." And Dick, erection, dive, eel, and ejaculation combining in his rudimentary mind, begins a kind of courtship of Mary, bringing her an eel in an act which to him signifies his creativity, his fatherhood, his reality.

So the first fragment of mythic memory—Dick, ready, erect, on the bridge; Freddie in the water reaching for the eel; Mary, "impregnated"—contains all the elements of the second—Freddie, dead in the water from Dick's possessively paternal blow; and Mary, pregnant and, good Catholic girl that she is, "responsible," telling the terrified and shamed actual father, Tom, "I know what I'm going to do." Mary is frozen in guilt, "so inside herself she might never emerge again. And inside Mary who's sitting so inside herself, another little being is sitting there, too."

The abortion Mary plans is both her effort to emerge from herself, from her guilty self-imprisonment, and her effort to expiate one death with another, to punish in herself the sexual curiosity that led to Dick's murder of Freddie. It is a ritual of abasement and sacrifice which Swift's narrative connects with her Roman Catholicism: at the crisis of the abortion, "with a terrible involuntary persistence," comes the phrase from her school prayers, "Holy Mary Mother of God Holy Mary Mother of God Holy Mary Mother of—." Tom is excluded from this decision. It is Mary who first tries abortion by dislodgement: "She jumps. Her skirt billows; brown knees glisten. And she lands in what seems a perversely awkward posture, body still, legs apart, not seeming to cushion her fall but rather to resist it. Then, letting her body sink, she squats on the grass, clasps her arms round her stomach. Then gets up and repeats the whole process. And again. And again." Then, miscarriage begun but not completed, Mary makes the ultimate decision: "Little cramps—not so little cramps—in Mary's guts. And Mary says at last, because it's not working, it's not happening: 'We've got to go to Martha Clay's.'"

Martha Clay, fen dweller, "witch," living image along with her mate, Bill, of Tom's Crick ancestors, the water people, performs the abortion in a nightmarish evocation of the force that empties, drains, the vessel of reality:

> A pipe—no, a piece of sedge, a length of hollow reed—is stuck into Mary's hole. The other end is in Martha's mouth. Crouching low, her head between Mary's gory knees, her eyes closed in concentration, Martha is sucking with all her might. Those cheeks—those blood-bag cheeks working like bellows. . . . Martha appears to have just spat something into the pail. . . . In the pail is what the future is made of. I rush out again to be sick.

A figure from Tom's own kind of nightmare, Martha beckons him back into the circle, the decision from which Mary would have excluded him. After the long process of drainage, in the dawn, Martha orders him to empty the pail of "the future" into the water, the liquid form of nothing: "You gotta do it, bor. Only you. No one else. In the river, mind." So his seed is abandoned to the river, as was his brother Dick's in that first dive after his first erection. Tom Crick's vision of reality is sealed by that abortion, draining, flowing back, stopping. The whole superstructure of his subsequent life, love, and marriage with the abortion-injured and now barren Mary, the ever-filling "grand narrative" of history, the precarious "fatherhood" of the teacher with his students, is a gallant fiction extended over that fundamental fact. It collapses, paradoxically, when the fiction becomes intolerable for Mary and she opts for the madness of an alternate vision: that God has offered to her aged womb a child, like the patriarch of the Old

Testament did to Sarah, the patriarch of the New Testament to Elizabeth. Though her husband forces her to return the stolen child, as Martha had forced him to look on the reality which is drainage, she will never, Tom knows as he visits her in the "temporary" criminal asylum, submit to emptiness, will always grieve for the baby she believes she bore at age fifty-two, "the baby they took away from her and won't give back. That baby who, as everyone knows, was sent by God. Who will save us all."

With that phrase the story of Tom Crick's aborted fatherhood is linked with the messianic madness, the driven Atkinson pride, that produced empire, fueled war, sired Dick Crick, the mysterious elder brother whose attempts at lu—lu—love were behind the whole tragedy. Behind the tragedy of Dick's mental retardation is the Atkinson lu—lu—love (poignant, neurotic, incestuous) which begot him—a love timed by the "great narrative of history" to coincide with the Great War in which the Victorian dream of progress, of the March of Mind, of the primacy of energy over matter and of event and deed over reality, circled back upon itself and blew itself up (to quote an American tale of incest and the Great War, Fitzgerald's *Tender Is the Night*) "in a great gust of high explosive love."

The story of the "rise" of the Atkinson side of the narrator's family from Crick-like flatlanders and water people to hillside shepherds, barley farmers, then monopolist brewers, land reclaimers, transportation barons and heads of local government, is a story of "the tenacity of ideas" over/against "the obstinacy of water." It is also a story of powerful but blind patriarchs and haunted and haunting wives, of men who sought to control their women like their water. A blow struck out of psychotic jealousy by Thomas Atkinson in 1820 puts his beautiful wife, Sarah, in a waking coma for the next fifty-four years, and, despite his external activity, internally "history has stopped for him" at that moment, waters leveling once again the "unreclaimable internal land." And while his son and grandson maintain "the driving force of the Atkinson machine" through the century, the traumatized wife mutters or screeches three words, "smoke . . . fire . . . burning" at intervals, dives into the Ouse River "like a mermaid," according to local legend, just before her funeral, and, according to the same source, presides over the conflagration which destroys the Atkinson Brewery in the last moments of the long Edwardian summer, 1911.

Tom Crick possesses the journal of his grandfather (Sarah's great grandson), Ernest Atkinson, in whom the engine of progress finally strips its gears. The journals record Ernest's late Victorian doubts, financial and political failures. They follow his descent into a mysticism in which he brews a hallucinogenic, Coronation Ale, suffers and imposes an incestuous love upon his teenage daughter, Helen, and finally, despairing of humanity as his doubts and Sarah's ghostly prophecies have their culmination in World War, conceives the mad but tenacious idea that only beauty, a child of beauty, his own child begotten of his own Helen, can "become a Saviour of the World."

So Helen Atkinson, like Mary Metcalf thirty years later, becomes a ghostly emblem of Sarah Atkinson, "who, local lore has it, offers her companionship to those whose lives have stopped though they must go on living." Loving her father, seeing his diseased desire, Helen tried first to divert it. She helped him found an asylum for shell-shocked veterans: "Wasn't that a better plan? To rescue all these poor, sad cases, all of whom would be in a sense their wards, their children." But the father was adamant: both his Atkinson desire to control, possess, and materialize in his own deed, the idea, the "Saviour of the World," the son of beauty, and his counter-Atkinson despair at the secret failures of progress, drive him to this incest: "When fathers love daughters and daughters love fathers it's like tying up into a knot the thread that runs into the future, it's like a stream wanting to flow backwards."

The daughter's compromise, to marry the convalescing soldier Henry Crick but bear as his first child her father's projected saviour, frees her for a kind of future and triggers a last visit from the ghost of Sarah Atkinson as well as the suicide of the (next-to) last Atkinson: "Because on the same September evening that my father saw a will o' the wisp come twinkling down the Leem, Ernest Atkinson, whose great-grandfather brought the magic barley down from Norfolk, sat down with his back against a tree, put the muzzle of a loaded shotgun into his mouth and pulled the trigger."

The child of incest, "Saviour of the World," is Dick Crick, "potato head." This last Atkinson grows up like a Crick, deft handed, water drawn, apparently vacant brained. But as his brother, the narrator, noted, none of us, however apparently well-fitted for it, can be truly realistic—empty—all the time. In Dick's brain the disappearance (death) of his mother, Helen, becomes linked with his (putative) father's trips to the eel traps in the river, as well as with the substance (Ernest's last cache of

Coronation Ale) in the bottles his grandfather (who was really his father) left him in the chest with the journals that he couldn't read, though his brother Tom could. Out of this draught of his heritage, together with the sexual play with Mary and the eel which he witnessed and then took part in, Dick constructs a myth, incestuous in its turn, Oedipal, of a mother who will "rise up, wriggling and jiggling, alive—alive—o, out of the river"; who may consummate his earliest desire if he dives with force into the river, refuses to relinquish that desire. When he goes to the river after Tom's guilty and desperate revelation of his incestuous origin he is, Tom speculates, partly feeling that counter-Atkinson despair at the botch, the emptiness he is. But his dive has the look not of self-immolation but of search, another Atkinson push toward the idea, another gallant, if futile, move into the future which is, in reality, governed by the backward flow of the liquid form of nothing. It is a dive which kills him.

Source: Judith Wilt, "Abortion and the Fears of the Fathers: Five Male Writers," in *Abortion, Choice, and Contemporary Fiction: The Armageddon of the Maternal Instinct*, The University of Chicago Press, 1990, pp. 101–31.

Del Ivan Janik

In the following essay, Janik explores the interaction between history and the Here and Now in Waterland.

On one level, *Waterland* is a series of history lessons, the lessons Crick teaches in the last few weeks before he is forced into early retirement after thirty-two years. As such, they are often wildly inappropriate: the nominal topic of his class is the French Revolution, but he alludes to it rarely, only to illustrate a point about the family and personal events that form most of the narrative's substance. On another level, *Waterland* is a manifestation of man's need to tell stories to keep reality under control, and Crick can be seen in much the same light as Prentis, a man telling his story in an attempt to cope with its implications.

The novel's structure is rambling and recursive, intermixing episodes from three major elements. The first of these elements is a history of the Fenland and of the prominent entrepreneurial Atkinson family and the obscure, plodding Crick family, from the seventeenth century to the marriage of the narrator's parents after World War I. The second consists of events of the 1940s: Mary Metcalf's adolescent sexual experimentation with Tom, Crick and his "potato-head" half brother Dick (who in his demented father/grandfather's eyes is

> History is a matter of reflection, the attempt to retrieve or find or impose logic and order on what is neither logical nor orderly; it is the creation of public reality."

the "Saviour of the World"), Dick's murder of Freddie Parr, Mary's abortion, Tom's revelation of Dick's incestuous conception and Dick's consequent suicide by drowning, Tom's return from the war and his marriage to Mary. The final element involves events of 1980, the narrative present: Mary's religious visions, her kidnapping of a baby (whom she calls a "child of God") from a supermarket, her committal to a mental institution, and Tom's loss of his position as a history teacher. The structure is not chaotic, for each of these three major elements, as it comes to the forefront of the narrative, is treated more or less chronologically; but as a whole the novel conforms to Tom's characterization of history: "It goes in two directions at once. It goes backwards as it goes forwards. It loops. It takes detours" because "there are no compasses for journeying in time."

Tom Crick's stories, which would form a continuous narrative if they were rearranged chronologically, are also interrelated by a number of parallels that resemble in kind but far exceed in complexity the recurring images of confinement in *Shuttlecock*. One set of parallels involves the concept of history itself, with its emphasis on constructions like Rise and Fall or Revolution. Tom Crick occasionally returns, in his classes, to the subject of the French Revolution:

> Children, do you remember . . . how I explained to you the implications of that word "revolution"? A turning round, a completing of a cycle. How I told you that though the popular notion of a revolution is that of categorical change, transformation—a progressive leap into the future—yet almost every revolution contains within it an opposite if less obvious tendency: the idea of a return. A redemption; a restoration. A reaffirmation of what is pure and fundamental against what is decadent and false. A return to a new beginning. . . .

As Robespierre and Marat sought not a futurist utopia but a return to an idealized Rome, Crick's students demand his reinstatement when the headmaster acts out their spoken contempt for the subject of history; generations of Cricks devote themselves to reclamation of the land; the last Atkinson brewer seeks to reproduce the purity of his family's original ale; and Mary Metcalf tries in a Lewisham supermarket to regain the motherhood she had relinquished more than three decades before in a filthy Fenland cottage. The parallels are indirect and inexact, redolent not of literary contrivance but of Tom Crick's notion of history as a series of loops and detours in the journey through time.

The duality of History and the Here and Now that played an important role in Swift's first two novels comes to the forefront in *Waterland*, and virtually all of the elements of the novel contribute to Swift's exploration of this theme. Tom Crick's meditations lead him to define and redefine history, in ways that are sometimes contradictory but from which a pattern ultimately emerges. History is, in the first instance, an academic subject that is about to be retrenched at Crick's school because the headmaster considers it "a rag-bag of pointless information." While Crick admits that history is distinct from the usually much less eventful everyday reality, that it is "reality-obscuring drama," he nevertheless insists on its value in helping us to shape our responses to that reality: "even if we miss the grand repertoire of history, yet we imitate it in miniature and endorse, in miniature, its longing for presence, for feature, for purpose, for content."

Confronted by a rebellious class that doubts the value of history, that asks in effect "Why the past?," Crick at first resorts to the pat answer that the "Why?" itself is the reason for studying history, that man is "the animal which asks Why." But in the face of present reality—a job that is about to disappear, students who are convinced that history is about to end in nuclear holocaust, and a wife who has lost her sanity—he is less confident about history as explanation; perhaps it is only a matter of telling stories and *hoping* to find meaning through them. The study of history is also an attempt at reclamation, based on the desire to "discover how you've become what you are. If you're lucky you might find out why. If you're lucky—but it's impossible—you might get back to where you can begin again. Revolution." History is a matter of reflection, the attempt to retrieve or find or impose logic and order on what is neither logical nor orderly; it is the creation of public reality.

But as Tom Crick states early and keeps demonstrating, "history is a thin garment, easily punctured by a knife blade called Now." That other realm, the immediate life-transforming moment, the Here and Now, is history's mirror image: it is a matter of chance or impulse; its logic is the logic of madness or of nonsense; it is and creates the most intense kind of *private* reality. Price, the self-appointed leader of Crick's bored and rebellious students, introduces the term when he insists, "What matters is the here and now," setting Crick to wondering just what "this much-adduced Here and Now" really is:

> How many times, children, do we enter the Here and Now? How many times does the Here and Now pay us visits? It comes so rarely that it is never what we imagine, and it is the Here and Now that turns out to be the fairy tale, not History, whose substance is at least forever determined and unchangeable. For the Here and Now has more than one face. It was the Here and Now which by the banks of the Hockwell Lode with Mary Metcalf unlocked for me realms of candor and rapture. But it was the Here and Now also which pinioned me with fear when livid-tinted blood, drawn by a boat-hook, appeared on Freddie Parr's right temple.

The Here and Now is not simply present daily life, as Price would have it; "life includes a lot of empty space. We are one-tenth living tissue, nine-tenths water; life is one-tenth Here and Now, nine-tenths a history lesson." The Here and Now comes in "surprise attacks" that "bring both joy and terror" and "for a brief and giddy interval announce that time has taken us prisoner."

History and the Here and Now thus are not opposites but polarities, two aspects of experience. Both emerge out of the empty space of daily life. Making history, like the Atkinsons, and telling stories about it, like the Cricks, are two different ways to outwit the emptiness we glimpse (and fear) at the heart of reality; to "assure ourselves that . . . things are happening." It was a series of surprise attacks of the Here and Now in the summer of 1943—Freddie's murder, Mary's pregnancy and her abortion, Dick's suicide—that seriously involved Tom Crick in the study of history, which had seemed only a set of fairy tales:

> Until the Here and Now gave a sudden urgency to my studies. Until the Here and Now, gripping me by the arm, slapping my face and telling me to take a good look at the mess I was in, informed me that history was no invention but indeed existed—and I had become part of it.

The Here and Now—the moment of penetrating, inescapable reality in which one is poignantly alive and aware—thrusts one into history, the

What Do I Read Next?

- In Graham Swift's novel *Last Orders* (1996), which won a Booker Prize, four working-class English friends go on a day trip to honor a friend's last request that his ashes be dropped off Margate Pier. The men use the opportunity to review their lives and reflect on life and death.

- British playwright Caryl Churchill's play *Fen* (one of four Churchill plays in *Plays 2*, 1990) is about the plight of the fen inhabitants, who are presented as living hard lives dominated by religion and the traditions of their community, while being exploited by greedy landowners and land-buying conglomerates.

- *Master of Morholm: A Novel of the Fenland* (1987), by Timothy Wilson, is set in the eighteenth century in the fens. Wilson creates a complex story of romantic attachments that sheds light on class differences and morality.

- *East Anglia and the Fens* (2000), by Rob Talbot (photographer) and Robin Whiteman, is a pleasant and well-illustrated guide to the region in England that provides the setting for *Waterland*.

equally inescapable awareness that decisions are irrevocable and actions have consequences.

History and the Here and Now have the same sources, the most potent of which is curiosity. It was Tom's curiosity about his forebears, the Atkinsons and Cricks, his need for an explanation, that led to the stories he tells in *Waterland*, and it was Mary's sexual curiosity that led to the series of events that touched off the need:

> Curiosity which, with other things, distinguishes us from the animals, is an ingredient in love: It is a vital force. Curiosity, which bogs us down in arduous meditations and can lead to the writing of history books, will also, on occasion, as on that afternoon by the Hockwell Lode, reveal to us that which we seldom glimpse unscathed (for it appears more often—dead bodies, boat-hooks—dressed in terror): the Here and Now.

Curiosity is endangering, but it is also potentially redemptive. It is their lack of curiosity that most worries Crick about Price and his other students:

> Children [he warns them,] be curious. Nothing is worse (I know it) than when curiosity stops. Nothing is more repressive than the repression of curiosity. Curiosity begets love. It weds us to the world. It's part of our perverse, madcap love for this impossible planet we inhabit. People die when curiosity goes. People have to find out, people have to know.

Curiosity in its manifestation as the study of history contributes to the preservation of life and its value. Tom Crick explains to Price that he became a teacher of history because of his discovery, in the rubble of postwar Germany, that civilization is precious: "an artifice—so easily knocked down—but precious." History does not promise endless progress, in fact it tends to teach that "the same old things will repeat themselves," and it thereby offers a model of worthwhile human endeavor. A person, a generation, a people have been successful if "they've tried and so prevented things slipping. If they haven't let the world get any *worse*." Crick expands on this idea when he addresses the school on the occasion of his forced retirement:

> There's this thing called progress. But it doesn't progress. It doesn't go anywhere. Because as progress progresses the world can slip away. My humble model for progress is the reclamation of land. Which is repeatedly, never-endingly retrieving what is lost. A dogged and vigilant business. A dull yet valuable business. A hard, inglorious business. But you shouldn't go mistaking the reclamation of land for the building of empires.

The *Rosa II*, the silt-dredger where Dick Crick works and dies, is a reclaimer of land, performing the work of staying even, the unglamorous but essential business of "scooping up from the depths this remorseless stuff that time leaves behind." The student of history has the same task: to keep scooping up the detritus of time in the attempt, if not to get ahead, at least not to leave things worse than they were. In his last confused, drunken hours on the dredger Dick unconsciously acts out that imperative:

> He's here. He knows his place. He knows his station. He keeps the ladder turning, the buckets scooping.... And the smell of silt is the smell of sanctuary, is the smell of amnesia. He's here, he's now. Not there or then. No past, no future. He's the mate of *the Rosa II*.
>
> And he's the saviour of the world....

Considering the nature of Dick's work, the valediction is only partially ironic. In two of *Waterland's* crucial event—Dick's death and the return of the child Mary kidnapped—the Here and Now and the principles of history meet and clash, with uncertain results. The "Saviour of the World" drowns himself, and the "child of God" is restored to his natural mother and an ordinary life. The world cannot afford saviors, cannot support them. The only salvation is in the continual task of reclamation of the land.

Source: Del Ivan Janik, "History and the 'Here and Now': The Novels of Graham Swift," in *Twentieth Century Literature*, Vol. 35, No. 1, Spring 1989, pp. 74–88.

Sources

Clare, John, *John Clare: Selected Poetry and Prose*, edited by Merryn and Raymond Williams, Methuen, 1986, pp. 150–53.

Durant, Will, *The Story of Philosophy*, Simon & Schuster, 1926, p. 241.

Gorra, Michael, Review of *Waterland*, in *Nation*, March 31, 1984, p. 392.

Hollinghurst, Alan, "Of Time and the River," in *Times Literary Supplement*, October 7, 1983, p. 1073.

Prescott, Peter S., "Faulkner in the Fens," in *Newsweek*, April 30, 1984, pp. 74–75.

Further Reading

Higdon, David Leon, "Double Closures in Postmodern British Fiction: The Example of Graham Swift," in *Critical Survey*, Vol. 3, No. 1, 1991, pp. 88–95.
> Higdon analyzes Swift's use of closure (that is, how he ends his novels) in *Waterland* and other works. He concludes that Swift synthesizes traditional endings with a postmodernist open-endedness.

Hutcheon, Linda, *A Poetics of Postmodernism: History, Theory, Fiction*, Routledge, 1988.
> Hutcheon includes an analysis of *Waterland*, concluding that the narrative strategy of the novel is designed to question modern concepts of history and to explore the processes of historiography.

Janik, Del Ivan, "History and the 'Here and Now': The Novels of Graham Swift," in *Twentieth Century Literature*, Vol. 35, No. 1, Spring 1989, pp. 74–88.
> Janik discusses the relationship between history and the present in Swift's first three novels.

Landow, George P., "History, His Story, and Stories in Graham Swift's *Waterland*," in *Studies in the Literary Imagination*, Vol. XXIII, No. 2, Fall 1990, pp. 197–211.
> Landow discusses Swift's emphasis on history and storytelling in *Waterland*, classifying the novel as a late-twentieth-century example of fictional autobiography.

When the Legends Die

Hal Borland
1963

Hal Borland's *When the Legends Die*, published in 1963, immerses the reader in two worlds, that of the wild West and that of wild nature, two topics with which Borland was quite familiar. Written in 1963, around the height of Borland's writing career, the story follows a young Native American boy as he struggles not only with the rite of passage to manhood but also with the harsh realities of the clash of his native culture and the modern white society. Having been raised in the traditional ways of his Ute ancestors, the protagonist of the story must first learn the "new ways" of the white people who dominate his world before he can create a clear identity of who he is and where he fits in his environment.

The novel was well received and eventually was produced by Twentieth Century Fox as a movie in 1972. *When the Legends Die* is often compared to Jack London's *Call of the Wild* (1914), which takes up the theme of the wilderness, and Conrad Richter's *The Light in the Forest* (1953), which deals with the clash of cultures in the West. All three books explore rite of passage or coming of age themes, and all three were produced as movies.

The story of Thomas Black Bull, the protagonist of Borland's novel, is one of constant transformation as a young boy searches for an identity. Symbolizing this most clearly is the fact that, throughout the story, Thomas's name is changed several times. He receives the name Little Black Bull from his parents, which is changed to Thomas Black Bull when a white minister baptizes him.

Then, as he nears puberty, Thomas gives himself the name of Bear's Brother. When he becomes popular on the rodeo circuit, his fans dub him with the moniker Killer Tom. As he works out his frustration and anger from losing his parents before reaching puberty, being forced to enter a school to learn white society's ways, being used by swindlers and crooks as well as by people who need heroes, Thomas tries on many personas, but, in the end, he finds his way back home and is finally able to define his own identity.

Author Biography

Harold Glen (Hal) Borland was born on May 14, 1900, in Sterling, Nebraska, to William A. Borland (whose family had arrived in Nebraska via covered wagon) and Sarah Clinaburg Borland. The family later moved to eastern Colorado and settled on an arid, hostile, and isolated homestead.

Between 1918 and 1920, Borland attended the University of Colorado, but he dropped out of school to become an associate editor for his father's newspaper, *Flagler News*. After one year of working for this small newspaper, Borland set out for the big cities, stopping in New York City for a couple of years, then moving on to Salt Lake City, Fresno, San Diego, Philadelphia, and finally returning to New York. Along the way, he developed his writing skills, working variously as a reporter, editor, copyreader, publisher, and eventually taking on the role of columnist. Borland, a prolific writer, also honed his talents through a steady stream of longer works, with almost forty titles of collected essays, personal narratives, poetry, and novels to his name. He also wrote folk stories, book reviews, short stories, articles for encyclopedias, lyrics for songs, and scripts for radio, film, and stage. He states, in a brief biography published in *World Authors, 1950–1970*:

> Early engineering training taught me to respect facts and logic. Newspaper years taught me to write straight sentences and build logical paragraphs, and fostered my work habits. A bent toward poetry gave me a sense of words and language that helped shape my style.

Borland's first book to be published, *Heaps of Gold* (1922), was a collection of poems. Then, in the 1930s, he wrote a few light-hearted Western novels under his pseudonym Ward West. During the following decades, Borland's fictional writing took a more serious bent as his subject matter fo-

cused on the harsh realities of pioneer life on the Great Plains. Included in this period was the publication of his *When the Legends Die* (1963), a novel that takes place at the turn of the century and tells the story of a young Native American boy's coming-of-age trials.

Some of Borland's most celebrated works were his autobiographical narratives, the award-winning *High, Wide and Lonesome* (1956), which recounts his youth in Colorado, and its sequel *Country Editor's Boy* (1970).

In 1945, Borland moved to New England, where he eventually bought a one-hundred-acre Connecticut farm that had, at one time, been the site of an ancient Indian village. This country setting inspired many of his subsequent nonfiction essays on nature. Borland's nature writings are often said to reflect a Thoreau-like quality. He was a self-taught naturalist who was interested in extracting, from his country surroundings, a philosophy about life.

Borland was twice married. His first marriage produced two sons. In 1945, he married his second wife, Barbara Ross Dodge, who shared Borland's interest in writing and contributed articles with him to several magazines. Both Borland's and his wife's writings are collected at the Beinecke Library of Yale University. Borland died in Sharon, Connecticut, on February 22, 1978.

Plot Summary

Part I: Bessie

When the Legends Die begins in the company town of Pagosa, Colorado, where the protagonist's father, George Black Bull, a Native American of the Ute tribe, works at a sawmill. George enters the scene running. He is being sought after because he has killed Frank No Deer, a common thief. George is afraid that he will be put in jail, so he tells his wife where he is going in the wilderness and tells her to follow him after dark. His wife, Bessie, when asked by the sheriff if she knows where her husband is, denies knowing. As she waits for nightfall, Bessie thinks back on how she and her husband and son ended up in Pagosa. Then, in the middle of the night, she packs a few belongings, wakes her young son, and takes a circuitous route to the location of the planned rendezvous with her husband.

In the wilderness, George and Bessie return to their traditional ways, capturing meat, finding seeds, and picking berries for food. They make clothes and a shelter from the natural materials that they gather. They sing songs and tell stories that their grandparents had taught them. At the end of the first year, before the winter has ended, George is trapped and killed in an avalanche.

Before the next winter, Bessie takes Thomas back to Pagosa to buy supplies. Bessie is an expert basket maker and trades her wares for the winter clothing and the utility items that she needs. She worries that the sheriff is still looking for her husband and might take her son away from her. A while later, when she returns to town, she feels more confident and asks the shopkeeper for details about the sheriff. Jim Thatcher tells her that the sheriff has decided that her husband acted in self-defense and that her family is free to return to the town.

Another winter comes, and Bessie becomes sick and dies. Thomas befriends the animals around him, including a small, orphaned grizzly bear cub. He becomes what he believes to be the bear's brother. One summer, Thomas ventures back into Pagosa, with the bear trailing behind him. When some of the citizens of the town threaten to shoot the bear, Jim Thatcher stops them.

Blue Elk, a man who one character states would sell anything to make a profit, including his own grandmother, befriends Thomas, who does not speak English, only to betray him. Blue Elk strikes a deal with the local minister, who believes that Thomas is not fit to live on his own and must be taken to the nearby Indian school, a place where Thomas can learn the ways of the white men. To get Thomas to agree to leave his wilderness lodge, Blue Elk tells Thomas that the other Native American children at the school need to learn the traditional songs and old ways of the Ute people. He suggests that Thomas go with him to Ignacio, the center of the Ute reservation, to teach the children the things that Thomas has learned. The bear cub tags along.

Part II: The School

Once he arrives at the school, Thomas quickly discovers that he has been tricked. His bear is chained and caged. Thomas is roomed with Luther Spotted Dog, a boy close to his age but who lives in world totally different from the one that Thomas is used to. Thomas dislikes the bed he is told to sleep on, the clothes he is told to wear, and the food he must eat. He lashes out in anger at almost everyone who demands that he must change.

The bear must be gotten rid of, so once again it is Blue Elk who schemes to get Thomas to re-

Media Adaptations

- *When the Legends Die* was made into a film in 1972 by Twentieth Century Fox. The movie starred Frederick Forrest and Richard Widmark and was billed as a sensitive story about two friends (making reference to Thomas Black Bull's and Red Dillon's relationship.)

turn the bear to its natural surroundings. Thomas, who believes Blue Elk is taking him home, agrees to go with Blue Elk. However, once they arrive in the vicinity where Thomas used to live, Blue Elk blackmails Thomas by threatening to leave the bear chained to a tree to starve unless Thomas returns to the school.

Upon his return, Thomas does not fare much better than he had before. After a fight, he is put on restriction and locked in a small room. One night, he escapes and returns on his own to the lodge in the wilderness. When he arrives, little remains of his former dwelling. Blue Elk has ransacked his home, taking everything he can use or sell and burning the rest. Thomas, after discovering that Benny Grayback, one of the counselors from the school, has followed his trail, returns to the school, resigned to his fate.

In the next episodes, Thomas dons the white man's clothes, has his braids cut off, and tries to learn the skills of farming and the language of his oppressors. He learns to ride horses and herd and sheer sheep, skills that will be of benefit to him in the future. One day, while visiting a nearby city to sell sheepskins, a cowboy tries to tease Thomas by promising to give him money if he can find his horse and ride it into town, knowing that his horse does not like strange riders. Thomas, thinking that the moneymaking proposition sounds easy, follows the man's instructions and rides the horse. Disbelieving that the boy can repeat his success, the cowboy offers Thomas more money to bring yet another horse to him. The next horse is even meaner than the first, but Thomas is successful.

Red Dillon, an old bronco cowboy who has followed the rodeo circuit, sees a promising financial future in Thomas. Red promises to teach the boy to ride bronco style and takes him to his cabin in New Mexico.

Part III: The Arena

Once they arrive at the cabin, Red introduces Thomas to Meo, a Mexican cowboy who has been somewhat crippled by his rodeo-riding days. The two men teach Thomas everything he has to know about riding wildly erratic horses. Soon, Red believes that Thomas is ready to go to the small rodeo held in the nearby town of Aztec.

Red has big plans for Thomas, but those plans do not always match the ideas that Thomas has conceived. For instance, Red tells Thomas when he is to win certain matches and when he is to lose them. Red knows that Thomas is good enough to win almost all of the events in which he participates, but, to increase the gambling odds in Red's favor, he has Thomas purposefully foul out of certain matches. Although their winnings are small, Red is encouraged by Thomas's potential. Meanwhile, Thomas learns how to cheat. Some of their plans do not always meet Red's expectations: Thomas is tired and loses matches because he cannot concentrate; sometimes the people who lose money on their bets suspect that Red has cheated them, and Red and Thomas must quickly run out of town.

Thomas often wins, and at one point he rides one horse so hard that the horse dies in the arena. This makes Thomas feel sick. Red offers Thomas alcohol to ease his pain. Most of Red's winnings are spent on alcohol. The little money left over buys food and cheap hotel rooms.

The pace increases, and Thomas ends up riding in a rodeo at least once a week and then riding his own horse to the next town. He gets hurt and feels exhausted. After one big win, Red and Thomas decide to go home and rest until the following spring.

Two years down the road, Red sets Thomas up for a big rodeo event. The stakes are high, and Red is anticipating taking home pockets full of money. In the final round of this rodeo, however, Thomas's horse breaks its neck and then falls, trapping Thomas beneath him. Thomas's leg is broken. Having anticipated winning, Red has bought an old Cadillac. Drunk, Red drives Thomas home. In the fall, Thomas and Red are at it again.

During this time, Thomas has grown into a young man. He quarrels with Red more often, un-

afraid of the repercussions because he knows he can take care of himself. He decides that he is no longer going to throw any rides. He is going to ride them clean and win all that he can. He and Red part.

Thomas does well on his own, but he gains a reputation for riding his horses so hard that he often kills them. When he rides, Thomas feels like he wants to punish the horses, trying to seek revenge for some unrealized pain. One day when he returns to the cabin, Meo tells Thomas that Red is in town, sick and almost dead. Thomas goes to get him, but it is too late. A few rodeos later, Thomas again returns to find out that Meo, too, has died.

Thomas's reputation as a mean rodeo rider grows. He is known by several different nicknames. One of them is Killer Tom; another is Devil Tom. All of them refer to his vicious riding. During a rodeo at Madison Square Garden in New York City, Thomas is crushed by his horse and ends up in the hospital. He has a broken pelvis, several cracked ribs, a broken thighbone, punctured lungs, and a concussion. He spends six weeks in the hospital convalescing. His nurse, Mary Redmond, pays special attention to Thomas, half hoping that he will come home with her to complete his recovery. Thomas heals faster than expected and leaves New York, Nurse Redmond, and the hospital behind. He decides to gain his strength back in the Colorado mountains.

Part IV: The Mountains

Thomas travels back to Pagosa. While eating lunch at a cafe, he coincidentally runs into a man who needs someone to herd his sheep. The sheep are grazing in the mountains where Thomas used to live. Thomas needs time, fresh air, and some way to earn a living while he is recuperating, so he and the man strike a deal.

While in the mountains, memories slowly creep back into Thomas's consciousness. When a grizzly bear attacks his sheep, Thomas's anger builds, and he is driven to hunt the grizzly down and kill it. Thomas waits for the bear to reappear, and when he sees it and raises his rifle to shoot it, something happens inside of Thomas that makes him stop. Through a series of dreams, Thomas realizes that all along the thing that has driven him to kill horses and try to kill this bear is really a subconscious urge to kill something inside of him. He goes on a fast and a vision quest. Finally, he recognizes that it is the pain and anger inside of him of which he wants to rid himself. With this new vision, he realizes that he has come home, not only to the land and to his beginnings but to himself.

Characters

Bear's Brother
See Thomas Black Bull

Killer Tom Black
See Thomas Black Bull

Bessie Black Bull
Bessie is Tom's mother. After her husband runs to the mountains to escape jail, she waits until the middle of the night, then packs up a few items of clothing and utensils, takes her young son, and follows her husband into the wilderness. When her husband dies, she teaches Tom all the old stories and songs of his native culture.

Bessie gathers seeds and berries for food. She also is a basket maker and sells her wares in town in exchange for blankets and winter clothing. During one winter, Bessie becomes sick. When her condition worsens, she tells Tom to "Sing the song for going away." She dies shortly thereafter.

George Black Bull
George Black Bull is Tom's father. In the beginning of the story, he gets into trouble for having killed the thief Frank No Deer. Afraid that he would be sent to jail, George tells his wife to follow him; then he runs into the wilderness. In the mountains, George builds a lodge and lives off nature, providing his family with food, shelter, and clothes made from animal skins. One winter while hunting, he is killed in an avalanche.

Little Black Bull
See Thomas Black Bull

Thomas Black Bull
Thomas is the protagonist of the story. He is the son of George and Bessie, who take their son to the wilderness and raise him there until their deaths. Although barely a teenager, Thomas is able to physically provide for himself upon his parents' deaths. However, he is forced to go to the nearest Indian Service school to learn the ways of the white people.

Thomas spends most of his youth learning what other people think is best for him. In the process, he becomes a man who has little awareness of his own identity. He endures many hardships and abuses along his path to physical maturity and learns to suppress his emotions. Of all his emotions, anger is the first to express itself, and it comes out in deadly bursts of energy. As a rodeo cowboy, he takes out his frustrations on the horses, many of which die in their efforts to throw Thomas off their backs. Thomas does not escape his own wrath, as his body suffers from multiple bone fractures, punctured lungs, and concussions.

When his body reaches the point at which it cannot endure the physical abuse that Thomas's riding demands, he is subconsciously led back to his emotional source, the wilderness. At first Thomas barely remembers what it felt like to live in nature, but something holds him there. Slowly, as his body heals, so do his mind and his emotions. He learns to reflect on the events of his life, untangle the feelings that he has been hiding, and make decisions that are based on his welfare.

Blue Elk
Blue Elk is a Native American man who makes a living swindling other people, mostly people of his own tribe. His famous line, which is often repeated in defense of others, is "my people do not lie." Blue Elk, however, lies all the time.

Blue Elk is responsible for George and Bessie Black Bull ending up in the sawmill town of Pagosa. Probably paid off by the sawmill boss, he was responsible for George and Bessie's owing money to the tribal council for hunting without permits. He then lies to them, promising that if they work for the sawmill, they will soon be out of debt and have plenty of money left over. However, the sawmill owners make sure that George and Bessie stay in constant debt to them so they will never be able to leave.

After George kills Frank No Deer, Blue Elk later lies again, telling them that it was because of him that George no longer is a wanted man. He tells Bessie that she owes him something for this favor. When she refuses to pay him, he steals from her. After Bessie and George die, Blue Elk misleads Tom into believing that the people at the Indian Service school of Ignacio need Tom to teach them the "old ways," to get him to leave his life in the wilderness and go to the school. For his efforts, Blue Elk receives a few dollars. Later, Blue Elk lies to Tom again to get Tom to take his bear cub off the school grounds and leave the bear in the wilderness. When Blue Elk does not get paid for his efforts, he returns to Tom's lodge in the woods and steals everything that Tom has left there.

Red Dillon

Red is a former circuit rodeo rider who likes to gamble and swindle people. When he sees Tom ride a horse for the first time, he realizes the potential Tom has for making money at the rodeos. So he takes Tom away from the school and teaches him how to ride at his squatter cabin in New Mexico.

Red sets up bets at each of the rodeo events, telling Tom when to win and when to fake a loss. He does this to increase the odds in his favor and is often run out of town when the bettors discover that they have been swindled. He feeds and clothes Tom but seldom gives him any of their winnings.

As Tom grows older, stronger, and more skilled, he tells Red that he is going to win as many events as he can. Tom had grown tired of losing on purpose. Red, an alcoholic, does not take the news well, and Tom must bail Red out of jail. A few months later, Meo and Tom hear that Red is in the nearby city of Aztec. He is dying. Tom goes to get him, but Red dies in the hotel bed.

Rowena Ellis

Rowena is an English teacher at the Indian Service school. She is in her forties and acts as a surrogate mother to the children who live at the school. Rowena speaks several of the Native languages and is able to communicate with Tom in Ute. She tells him that he must learn the new ways. When Tom returns to the school after having sent the bear back to the wilderness, Rowena suggests that Tom be given a private room. She describes Tom as "an unusual boy, exceptionally reserved and self-sufficient."

Benny Grayback

Benny is a thirty-year-old Ute who lives at the school. He is a vocational instructor. Benny wears his hair short and dresses in the white man's style, but he still remembers how to speak his native tongue, so he translates for Tom. Thereafter, Benny tries to condition Tom for his life in the world of white people. In one attempt to discipline Tom, Benny locks Tom in a small room.

Charley Huckleberry

Charley is a council member on the Southern Ute Reservation in Arboles, Colorado. The fact that Charley belongs to the council makes Tom's mother and father trust that when they go fishing and hunting without the required official permits, they will not get into trouble. However, Blue Elk reports them

all to the council, and they are forced to pay a penalty. Since they have no money, they are tempted into going to work at the sawmill. That is how Bessie and George Black Bull end up being trapped in the town of Pagosa, perpetually in debt to the owners of the mill. Charley tried to warn them not to go, but the money they were promised sounded too good.

Albert Left Hand

Albert is the owner of a herd of sheep, and Tom is sent to him as an assistant. Albert is described as a short, fat man who constantly berates Tom for being lazy. It is when Albert takes Tom to Bayfield to sell his sheepskins that Tom meets Red Dillon, who takes him away from the school and into the world of rodeos.

Meo

Meo works at Red Dillon's place. He is an old man by the time Tom meets him, but Meo used to ride in the rodeos. Meo cooks and tends the garden. He also helps Red teach Tom to ride horses. Several years later, when Tom returns to the cabin, he notices that the garden is run over with weeds. He goes into town and discovers that Meo has died.

Frank No Deer

This is a minor character; however, he plays a pivotal role. He often stole money, food, and other things from Tom Black Bull's father, pushing him to the point of getting into a serious fight in which Frank No Deer ends up dead. It is because of this death that Tom Black Bull's father, George, runs into the wilderness, with his family eventually following him.

Mary Redmond

Mary is a nurse in the New York hospital where Tom is taken after he suffers a very serious fall during a rodeo in Madison Square Garden. She is described as a plump woman in her thirties who has a strong urge to nurture and take care of people.

Mary is single, and it is implied that she would like to take Tom home with her to help him recuperate. She is a good healer, but Tom suspects that she, like everyone else in his life before, will force him to live his life the way she wants him to, not the way that is best for him. Mary encourages Tom's healing, but she also tries to thwart his progress in order to keep him dependent on her longer.

Luther Spotted Dog

Luther is Tom's first roommate at the Indian Service school. He is fourteen and wants to grow up to be like Benny Grayback. Tom and Luther get into many fights, and eventually Tom kicks Luther out of the room they share. Later, Luther joins in with other students to tease Tom, calling him a girl because he is very good at weaving baskets.

Neil Swanson

Neil is a teacher at the Indian Services school. He tries to teach Tom how to farm. When Tom gets into a fight with some of the other students, Neil beats him. This causes Tom to run away. It is through Neil's efforts, however, that when Tom comes back to school, he learns to ride horses and herd and shear sheep.

Jim Thatcher

Thatcher is a store owner who befriends Bessie and Tom. He tells Bessie not to worry about the sheriff because George is no longer being hunted as a murderer. He also offers Bessie decent prices for her basketry. He is honest and often generous with her. When Tom brings the grizzly bear cub to town, Thatcher stops the other townsmen from shooting it.

Themes

Alienation

From the very beginning of the story, the theme of alienation is apparent. George Black Bull is on the run from the law. From that point until the conclusion of the novel, the underlying theme is one of isolation.

Thomas's family is forced to leave the community and find their way in the wilderness. The family finds peace in the forest, but, by a twist of fate, Thomas is yanked from this environment and is forced into another strange setting. Again Thomas feels alienated. He is not comfortable with his new surroundings, and because of his unusual background, he becomes estranged from the people around him. Everything about the new people he must live with is different from Thomas: their language, clothes, beliefs and visions of the world, and even the type of food they eat. His life follows this pattern, taking him from one strange environment to another. In each new environment, he always feels like the stranger, the alienated one.

In the end, it is Thomas's alienation from himself that he must face. Although he seeks out his homeland on a subconscious level, it takes him awhile to remember that this is the place of his roots. At first, he believes that he has come home

to recuperate from his accident. Slowly, it dawns on him that he has truly come home. In the last moments of the novel, Thomas learns to bridge the alienation that exists in his own head.

Dishonesty

One of the main causes of the underlying theme of alienation in this story is the dishonesty of the people around Thomas. Blue Elk, a fellow Ute, pretends to befriend Thomas and his family in the beginning of the story. However, Blue Elk's intentions are always selfish and usually mercenary. Blue Elk first leads Thomas's family to Pagosa's sawmill and away from the reservation by filling their heads with the idea that they would make a lot of money. Instead, the family becomes ensconced in chronic debt. Blue Elk lies to Thomas to get the boy to leave his wilderness lodge. Blue Elk then steals all the boy's possessions.

Red Dillon is also dishonest. He teaches Thomas to throw rodeo events so that he can up the ante on bets. His cheating often causes the two of them to get into trouble such that they must strategically hide their horses for sudden getaways from the small Western towns in which Thomas rides in rodeos.

Rites of Passage

The other overall theme of this novel is the rite of passage. This is portrayed through Thomas, who must learn to negotiate his way from childhood to adulthood down some very complicated roads. First, Thomas learns to find his way through the wilderness. He becomes completely self-sufficient in nature, learning not only to kill for his food and to make his own clothes but to communicate with the wild creatures there.

Then Thomas must learn to deal with his peers. He is not very successful in this arena. The only way he can deal with them is to isolate himself from them or to beat them up. The school environment in which he must face his peers is also a challenge because it is ruled by the ways of the white society. This means that Thomas must surrender his traditional ways, even though his peers are fellow Utes. He does eventually acquiesce to the school environment, accepting the clothes and food and trying to learn farm skills.

Thomas's rites are not over, however. He has more things to learn before he reaches manhood. He is taken in by Red Dillon and is taught how to ride tough horses. He learns how to take falls. He becomes very familiar with constant, physical pain.

Topics For Further Study

- Controversy surrounds contemporary rodeo shows. Research the history of rodeos up to current times, including all the pros and cons of this contentious topic, then organize a class discussion. Be prepared, being as objective as possible, to stimulate the dialogue with interesting and well-examined data and anecdotes.

- Study the history of the Ute tribe. Then present your findings using graphs, maps, and transparencies. Cover a variety of topics, such as the tribe's loss of land, the spiritual and cultural rituals, and the effects of the U.S. government's attempts at assimilating these people to white society.

- Research the contemporary topic of multiculturalism, with a strong focus on cultural assimilation. How have the techniques, the philosophies, and the effects changed since the beginning of the twentieth century? Subjects that you might want to research are bilingualism, the surge in the publication of multicultural literature, and current discussions of multiculturalism in the nation's public educational system.

- Borland's *When the Legends Die* encompasses the story of a young man finding his way through the challenges of maturing from a dependent boy to a self-sufficient man. Write a short story about one of the contemporary challenges that a young boy or girl might face as she or he experiences her or his own rite of passage to adulthood. The story does not have to be fictionalized. It could be written as a memoir.

- Research three or more of the state lottery systems that are in current use. Do an analysis of how the money that the states collect is used. What are the benefits of using a lottery? Which income bracket of the population most often supports the lottery? What other choices are available to states to create revenue? Conclude your paper with an examination of the effects of gambling caused by the lottery on the population.

He also learns how to cheat. Eventually, he gains enough confidence to free himself from Red.

The effects of all the hardships that Thomas has endured stay with him as he continues down his road toward maturity. He takes his anger out on the horses, torturing them, as he has been tortured. He is filled with anger and frustration. His final lessons begin when he is crushed under the weight of a fallen horse. During his recuperation, Thomas experiences the final rite, the passage which forces him to face himself.

Culture Clashes

There are two different types of culture clashes going on in this novel. First, there is the clash between the Native American culture and that of the white people. Then there is the clash between the traditional and nontraditional Indians.

The clash between the Native American culture and the white people is evident in the way that Thomas and his family must live on the Ute reservation. They are not allowed to go fishing or hunting when they are hungry without first receiving permits. This system, although supervised by the Bureau of Indian Affairs (BIA), is the direct result of having had their land confiscated by the U.S. government and then partially reissued as reservation land, with strict boundaries and prohibitive rules.

The other aspect of this clash between the divergent cultures is demonstrated at the school to which Thomas is sent. The school is run by white people, whose philosophy demands that Native children must look and act like white people to get along in the world.

The clash between traditional and nontraditional Native people is shown in the way many of the Utes look at the Black Bull family when they return to town, dressed in their native clothes. It is also seen in the attitudes of the Native American children when they react to what seems strange to them, as when Thomas refers to the ancient songs and stories of the Ute people. The nontraditional Native Americans are only vaguely aware of these traditions, if they are aware of them at all. Thomas's relationship to nature, in particular to the bear cub, is yet another unusual aspect that the nontraditional Native Americans do not understand.

Style

Setting

When the Legends Die takes place in the West at the turn of the twentieth century. It begins in Pagosa, Colorado, a real-life, small-town location that currently boasts of its tourist attraction of healing spring waters. At the time of this novel, however, the town was not much more than a sawmill town, probably with only the Native Americans being aware of the healing springs.

The story then moves to Ignacio, Colorado, the heart of the Ute reservation in southern Colorado. In creating the school to which Thomas is sent, Borland could be making reference to the Indian school that once was housed at Fort Lewis near the boundaries of Ignacio. The fort was set up in an attempt to "control" the Native American population. Part of this effort concentrated on educating the Native American children in the ways of the white settlers, thus stripping them of their traditional culture.

While Thomas travels the rodeo circuit, his home base is in Red Dillon's cabin that sits on land outside of Aztec, New Mexico, another actual small town in the West. Most of the small towns that sponsored the rodeos at the time of the novel still hold these annual events today.

The wilderness area to which Thomas's family retreats, and later to which Thomas returns, is land in the San Juan Mountain Range. It is through these mountains that the Piedra River runs, the same river that is mentioned when Bessie and George first run away from Pagosa. This area was part of the traditional home of the Ute tribe, and artifacts can still be found there. Evidence of Native American camps in the San Juan Range are estimated to go back to 6000–2000 B.C. Today, much of this land is still uncultivated and belongs to the U.S. forest system. Thomas's family probably built their lodge somewhere between seven and eleven thousand feet in elevation.

Narration

The story is told from the point of view of an omniscient narrator. This narrator is privileged to see the unfolding of the tale through several different characters. This gives the story a well-rounded but sometimes shallow perspective. Though the reader is witness to many variations of opinions, none of the characters is revealed in depth.

The omniscient narrator tells the story in a very straightforward manner. There is only one flashback and that occurs in the beginning of the story; the rest is told in a linear time line. The narration is simple, with minimal descriptions offered about the landscape, the way people look, the colors of clothing, or, on a nonphysical level, the way people feel.

There is very little use of symbol or metaphor in the narration. Rather, the tale unfolds through a series of actions, with almost half of the story involved with the activity at rodeos.

Historical Context

The Utes

The people known as the Utes once inhabited most of the land of present-day Utah (which takes its name from the Utes), Colorado, and New Mexico. They were a hunter-gatherer society and were comprised of seven different groups, or bands, in ancient times. They lived in temporary shelters and moved with the seasons, following the animals and the harvesting time of the wild fruits and nuts that were their staple foods.

The history of the Utes is filled with their struggle for land and their desire to maintain their traditional living. The Spanish were the first Europeans to make contact with the Utes in the 1630s. With the Spanish came horses, a factor that would change the lifestyle of the Utes. Horses allowed them to hunt buffalo, evade their enemies, transport goods, and go farther to hunt for food. Because of these advantages, the Utes ceased their practice of breaking the tribe into smaller family groups, and, in its place, they created larger, more permanently settled units that were then ruled by powerful leaders.

Amidst battles with the Spanish as well as intertribal battles with other Native Americans, the Utes fought to maintain their rights to food and land. With the approach of the white pioneers, the trappers, the gold miners, and the inevitable U.S. military, the Ute people and their land began to dwindle. Between 1859 and 1879, the Ute population decreased from an estimated eight thousand to

Compare & Contrast

- **1800s:** Cowboys show their skills at roping calves and riding wild horses during the large spring roundup of cattle out on the plains.

  1900s: Cowboys follow a rodeo circuit across North America that includes over two thousand shows a year. Most performers belong to an organized group called the Cowboys Turtle Association (CTA).

  Today: Cowboys have a large following of fans (estimated at over 13 million) who either watch them perform live at rodeo arenas across the United States and Canada or see them on weekend broadcasts on television.

- **1800s:** The Ute Indians roam the San Juan Mountains in search of food and stop at the Pagosa (which is Ute for "healing waters") springs to cure themselves of the pains of rheumatism and other health problems.

  1900s: The U.S. government sets up a fort near the Pagosa springs and a white settlement called Pagosa Springs is incorporated. Cattlemen and lumberjacks soon roam through the mountains.

  Today: Tourism is the largest industry of Pagosa Springs. The small town of a little over two thousand residents is the starting point for white-water rafting, fishing, and backcountry camping expeditions. Median income of its residents is $19,000. Median price of a home is a little less than $200,000.

- **1800s:** Legalized gambling in the United States sees the emergence of government-sponsored lotteries to help finance local and national projects. However, due to many scandals, such as sponsors absconding with the money collected, gambling is outlawed in all but three states.

  1900s: The Great Depression causes a resurgence of gambling. Looked at as a way to stimulate the economy, states rescind their antigambling laws. Capitalizing on a crackdown on illegal gambling, Nevada and New Jersey are the first to welcome gambling with the construction of gaming houses. State lotteries soon follow.

  Today: To help combat the chronic poverty on many reservations, over one hundred Native American tribes build gambling casinos on their reservation land. Many states argue about how to tax the tribal gambling earnings, which some estimate to be between $2 and $8 billion a year.

---

two thousand people. The cause of this decrease was blamed on disease and a lack of food. Ute land was taken away in huge chunks. By 1868, the whole tribe was confined to the western third of Colorado. In 1873, they were forced to concede another fourth of their land. In 1880, the tribe was living on a reservation that measured fifteen miles wide and one hundred miles long. Having access to smaller and smaller areas of land, the Utes eventually became dependent on the military, who rationed food to them.

Education of Native Americans

Up until the 1960s, numerous Native American children were taken from their homes and their parents and placed in boarding schools to be trained in the "new ways" of American white culture. Often under the auspices of the Bureau of Indian Affairs (BIA), social workers, who may have believed they were doing the right thing for these children by assimilating them to modern society, were in fact making many of the children miserable. Many of these children died from diseases against which they had no natural immunity. Some people claim that other children died of heartbreak. Even the children who survived the schools often discovered, upon graduation, that they neither fit into their old traditional way of life, because they had changed too much, nor into the white society, because they had not changed enough—white people still looked at them as nonwhites, no matter how well educated they were.

Not all schools were this miserable; some schools were even established on the reservations with the blessing of the tribes. There was also the Indian Reorganization Act of 1934, which encouraged the teaching of Native history and culture in BIA-sponsored schools. Much later, in the 1970s, after a period of cultural upheaval in the United States that included the fight for civil rights among the Native American population, Congress passed the Indian Self-Determination and Education Act of 1975 and the Education Amendments Act of 1978, which together gave more power to Native American tribes to operate and determine the type of education their children would receive in all BIA and reservation schools.

Fort Lewis, the school to which Thomas was most likely taken in Borland's *When the Legends Die*, began as a military post from which the U.S. government hoped to control the Utes. It was first located in Pagosa but later moved closer to the center of the Ute reservation in Ignacio. The fort eventually was converted to a boarding school for the Ute children and in 1911 became the state high school of agriculture. The school continued to evolve, becoming a junior college, and, in 1962, it began to offer a four-year liberal arts degree program. Today, it honors its roots by offering free tuition to all Native Americans.

Rodeos

The term *rodeo* is a derivative of the Spanish word *rodear* (pronounced "ro-day-are"), which means "to surround." The Spanish occupied most of the Western lands of the United States at one time, and it was they who brought the horses and cattle into that part of the nation. As pioneers and homesteaders began pressing into the West, the new American cowboys learned their skills from the Spanish.

Before fences crisscrossed the Western lands, cattle roamed wide expanses of land and were only rounded up once a year, at which time they were branded and taken to large stockyards where they were slaughtered. It was during these large roundups that cowboys would gather together in camps on the open plains, and, after their work was done, they would demonstrate their skills in impromptu competitions.

In the latter part of the 1800s, it is guessed that the first official rodeo took place in Cheyenne, Wyoming. As trains and other modern inventions eliminated the need for the large roundups, cowboys, still anxious to show off their skills, began performing in front of small audiences. The custom caught on, and the audiences, as well as the prize money, grew. Thus, the modern tradition of rodeos was born.

Today, rodeos are often protested by animal activist groups, who contend that the sport causes unnecessary and cruel punishment for the cattle and horses involved in these events. Instead of riding wild horses, bronco riders sit atop horses that have flank straps wrapped around their groins and pulled tight enough to cause irritation. Cowboys are also allowed to wear spurs on their boots. This further increases the bucking of the horse, as the star-shaped wheels on the spurs are dug into the horse's sides.

Veterinarians attending rodeo animals have claimed to see injuries such as broken necks and backs, broken legs and ribs, as well as internal hemorrhaging. Despite these reports, rodeos continue to draw large audiences, both at live performances and on television.

Critical Overview

Although not seen as a classic work of literature, Borland's examination of the effects of white culture on the life and psychology of a young Native American man has been used in studies of the problems of assimilation and culture clash in the United States. Recently, Borland's book became the focus of a study compiled by Dr. Mitch Holifield, a professor in the Department of Educational Administration and Secondary Education at Arkansas State University. In his article "When the Legends Die: A Point beyond Culture," published in *Education*, Holifield states that Borland's novel "realistically portrays the deculturalization of Native Americans." Holifield, using Edward T. Hall's *Beyond Culture* (1977), analyzes *When the Legends Die*, concluding that an understanding of this story and the effects upon the protagonist, Thomas Black Bull, could significantly change the way educators deal with the challenges of multiculturalism in American society. He writes, "Understanding Tom's metamorphosis suggests questions and answers for helping America's schools be a more positive force for humane treatment for all people and for the positive coexistence and appreciate of diverse cultures."

When Borland's novel *When the Legends Die* was first published, it was received without much

Frederic Forrest (front) as Tom Black Bull and Richard Widmark as Red Dillon in the 1972 film adaptation of When the Legends Die

fanfare. Although sometimes criticized for his overly sentimental tone in relationship to Native American culture, Borland, as a writer, is often commended for his overall philosophy of living simply with a respect for nature, a theme that prevails throughout this novel as well as most of his other writings.

Criticism

Joyce Hart

Hart has degrees in English literature and creative writing and writes primarily on literary themes. In this essay, Hart examines the mother figure in Borland's novel as portrayed by his four female characters.

Borland's *When the Legends Die* is mostly a man's story, in that the main focus of the novel is on the development of a young boy into manhood, and, in the process of his growth, the main voices heard are masculine. However, there are minor female characters. The least significant of these female roles are the flirtatious young women or

prostitutes who are used mainly to indicate to Thomas that he has emerged from puberty. More noteworthy are four more prominent women who represent various aspects of mother figures. Each of these four women appears in a well-defined and separate time frame and reflects the various stages of maturity as the protagonist Thomas Black Bull progresses from youth to full adulthood.

The first chapter of *When the Legends Die* is titled "Bessie," referring to the biological mother of Thomas Black Bull. Bessie is a strong woman. She is also a Native American who is familiar with the traditional ways of her tribe. Although she has adjusted to reservation life, as well as to life in a small white community, she is capable of self-sufficient living in the wilderness. Bessie raises Thomas in his earliest years in an environment that is affected by a mixture of Native American culture and white society. However, when Thomas's father gets into trouble with the law, Bessie teaches Thomas how to live in nature without the benefit of relying on others to provide him with the rudimentary elements of physical survival, such as food and warmth, or without the more light-hearted enjoyment of psychological pleasures, such as social education and entertainment. Thus Thomas learns to hunt and gather wild berries in order to satisfy his hunger, to build a protective lodge and maintain a fire to endure the bitter cold, to memorize the ritual songs and stories of his ancestors to improve his mind, and to make friends with the animals to provide a sense of kinship.

Bessie nurtures Thomas both physically and emotionally. She creates his foundation. By teaching him to survive in nature, she has given him a home to which he can always return. Bessie has also provided Thomas with a history, a connection to the past. Through the songs and the stories that she teaches him, Bessie provides Thomas with roots that give him a sense of self. Thomas's mother also teaches Thomas respect for life. Through her, Thomas learns to honor the plants and animals that provide him with nourishment. To waste life frivolously, Bessie shows him, is the worst crime of all. Bessie is his birth mother. She establishes in Thomas a sense of self, his first identity.

Unfortunately for Thomas, Bessie dies while he is still very young. Although he is more capable of taking care of himself than most young people his age, the elders who live in the social communities around Thomas believe that the young boy needs guidance. Whether it is because the men do not themselves know how to survive in the wilderness or because they want the boy to conform to the society in which they live, the men conspire to take Thomas from his wilderness home and bring him back to the enclave dominated by white society. Although Thomas is self-sufficient, he is not physically strong enough to rebel against these men, nor is he savvy enough to understand their motives. With his mother gone, Thomas has no one to explain these new developments to him. So he is cast into a world of men who want to socialize and baptize him, as well as to capitalize on him.

Thomas is taken to a school organized by white people to educate, and thus control, the native population. He is tricked into coming to this school by Blue Elk, a fellow Ute tribesman, who tells Thomas that the children and other people at the school need and want to learn the traditional ways that Thomas's mother taught him. When Thomas arrives at the school, of course he discovers that this is not true. The school is there solely to teach Native American children how to exist in white society. Thomas's anger explodes in fistfights with anyone who comes near him. His world has been quickly transposed from one of balance and mutual respect to one of aggression and common distrust. On a symbolic level, he is taken from the feminine and forced into the masculine.

The world of the school is not devoid of women. There is one teacher, Rowena Ellis, who is Thomas's English teacher. She is one of the few people at the school who speaks Thomas's native language. Rowena, the narrator states, is also the supervisor of the girls' dormitory. She is described as unmarried, gray-haired, plump, and in her forties, and she represents an "unofficial mother to every shy, homesick boy and girl in the school." In other words, Rowena is the universal surrogate mother. Her full figure and gray hair even push her into the realm of grandmother, a sort of double-cast mother figure.

Connecting Rowena more strongly to a mother figure, Borland, in one of the first few words that Rowena and Thomas share, has Rowena encouraging Thomas to learn English by saying, "Your mother would tell you to learn these things." A few sentences later, Rowena asks Thomas to tell her about his mother. During a conference with some of Thomas's other teachers, Rowena is the only one who acknowledges Thomas's emotions. While the men see a defiant child, Rowena tells them that Thomas is doing well, learning more than he lets on. She also tells them that he is an "unhappy boy and hard to reach, but he learns fast."

Thomas rebels even more drastically, and eventually he runs away from the school. Once he arrives at his old lodge in the mountains, he discovers that Blue Elk has burnt his place to the ground. All that remains of Thomas's past is ashes. He returns to the school resigned to his fate in the world of white people. Upon reentering Rowena's class, she notices a change in him and praises his determination to learn the language of the white people. It is through Rowena that Thomas is given the most important tool in dealing with the new world around him. As his mother taught him how to "talk" with nature, Rowena teaches him how to talk with the society that has taken over his world. She has given him the skills that allow him to communicate with the men who will soon introduce him to yet another world. Whereas Bessie introduces Thomas to the natural world and to the world of his ancestors, Rowena prepares Thomas to enter into the social world and into the world of the dominant culture.

Thomas next enters the rodeo world, a place that his mother, Bessie, would be diametrically opposed to. In this world, not only does Thomas learn to cheat and swindle, he becomes very abusive toward animals. His actions go against the natural world. The horses he rides are not naturally mean or wild; they are frustrated and hurt. They harbor feelings similar to the ones that stew inside of Thomas. His mother taught Thomas to love and respect the natural world, but the rodeo, as well as the cattle industry behind it, is about money, oppression, and greed. This is a mean world, and Thomas is forced to leave it a broken man.

At the end of his career as a bronco rider, Thomas suffers a terrible accident. He wakes up in a hospital under the care of the nurse Mary Redmond, who becomes the third mother figure. Mary is also plump, as was Rowena, a description that Borland uses to imply a motherly figure. Her personality is bubbly and her first impulse upon Thomas's regaining consciousness is to get him to eat, a typically maternal act. Mary is a healer. She helps Thomas regain the feelings in his body. She massages his limbs, encouraging the flow of blood. Symbolically, Mary attempts to restore Thomas's humanity. Thomas has become numb in more ways than just physically. His emotions, like his body, have been stomped on, kicked, bruised, and battered. The more cheerful Mary is, the more despondent Thomas becomes. He resents her because she makes him aware of his need for her. He cannot eat unless she brings him food. He cannot clean himself. He cannot get out of bed unless she helps him.

> "It is through the All-Mother that Thomas is able to reclaim not only his childhood but his heritage and his culture, everything that his real mother had presented to him, everything that all the mother figures along his path had taught him."

Although Borland portrays Mary as a mother figure, he also hints that she has something else on her mind. Mary is a caretaker, but she would like to have Thomas need her so much that he will come home with her when he is well enough to leave the hospital. This makes Mary a type of crossover female figure. She is both mother and temptress, mother and potential lover. However, Thomas is not attracted to her. He is forced to accept her help as a healer, but he feels suffocated by her need for a lover. Thomas deals with Mary only on the mother level, but even that gets old, as Mary, unlike Thomas's real mother, does not encourage him to be strong. Mary would rather that Thomas remain dependent upon her. She believes that this is the only way she can keep a man. So, once again, Thomas rebels. He quickly moves beyond the parameters that Mary sets for him and heals himself on a schedule that is more efficient, more to his own liking. As soon as he is capable of walking, he leaves the hospital and Mary and, without knowing why, heads home to the place where he last saw his real mother.

Thomas goes back to the wilderness. He thinks he is going there to recuperate from the physical beatings he has endured while working the rodeo circuit. His plan is to find an easy way to earn a living that allows him to be outdoors. By coincidence, he meets a man who needs a sheepherder, and Thomas takes the job. One day while tending the sheep, a grizzly bear attacks and carries away one of the lambs. This angers Thomas, who feels that the bear has personally stolen something from him. Shortly thereafter, Thomas seeks revenge.

As if having completely forgotten everything about his childhood, even the close relationship that Thomas had with a grizzly cub when he himself was a child, Thomas hides and waits for the bear's return. Thomas has a rifle in his hands and the bear's death on his mind. At this point, Thomas still believes that he is in the mountains only to heal himself so that he will be strong enough to return to bronco riding. His mind remains in a fog, not knowing for sure who he is and not caring to find out.

While awaiting the bear, Thomas falls asleep but is awakened by an awareness of another being's presence. At first he thinks it is the bear, but it is not. What Thomas sees is a woman. He cannot see her clearly, "but he knew, something deep inside him knew, who she was. She was the mother, not his own mother but the All-Mother, the mothers and the grandmothers all the way back to beginning." This mirage of woman, this archetype of motherhood, begins to chant, much like Thomas's real mother had done. Thomas chants, too. Then he recognizes the chant. It is the bear chant, and that is when he sees the bear.

While chanting, Thomas tries to shoot the bear, but he cannot. Every time he tries, he asks himself, why? Why does he feel this need to kill the bear? When he finally realizes that it is not the bear that he wants to kill, he, through this vision of the All-Mother, knows that he must go on a vision quest. He has questions that must be answered, and only through the traditional ways that his mother has taught him will he know how to answer them.

Thomas goes on a fast. He climbs to the top of a mountain and settles himself in a cave, where, out of hunger, thirst, and fatigue, he has several dreams. In one of them, he tells himself that he has forgotten who he is. He also admits that what he has been trying to kill is not the bear but rather his past. Before the dream ends, the mountain asks Thomas who he is. Thomas is incapable of answering. That is when he hears a voice. It is the voice of the All-Mother, who tells the mountain, "He is my son."

Thus, the journey of Thomas is complete. Although throughout the story Thomas's biological mother is not there to guide him, Borland creates other mother figures to nurture Thomas during his passage from boyhood to maturity. Each mother has a specific goal. Each goal, when reached, teaches Thomas something new about the world and about himself. The mother figures give Thomas skills to deal with life. They also give him reasons to reflect on the meaning of his life. In the end, Borland sums up all the mothers by creating a spiritual figurehead. She, the All-Mother, is the one who brings Thomas back to himself. She makes him feel at home. It is through the All-Mother that Thomas is able to reclaim not only his childhood but his heritage and his culture, everything that his real mother had presented to him, everything that all the mother figures along his path have taught him.

Source: Joyce Hart, Critical Essay on *When the Legends Die*, in *Novels for Students*, Gale, 2003.

Mitch Holifield

In the following essay, Holifield interprets Tom's maturation in Borland's When the Legends Die.

Hal Borland's novel *When the Legends Die* vividly portrays the evolution and resolution of an identity crisis. The protagonist Tom Black Bull, a Ute Indian, finds himself caught between the old Ute culture and that of white America seeking the assimilation of Indians. Tom undergoes a somewhat circular metamorphosis by moving from a child's notion of his identity as a Ute, to a repression of that identity as a survival response, and ultimately to a reaffirmation of his Indian heritage.

Although Edward T. Hall's *Beyond Culture* is not a literary explication of Borland's novel, at the crux of Tom's identity crisis lurk several covert elements of culture as described in Hall's book, which expose an array of these universal, cultural elements. In what might serve as a thesis statement, Hall writes, "Beneath this clearly perceived, highly explicit surface culture there lies a whole other world which when understood will ultimately radically change our view of human nature." This "other world" is so subtly interwoven into cultural fabrics that its discovery necessitates a treacherous journey into the nether regions of Freudianism, sociology, and biology. Being so integrally founded upon these elements of this other world, cultures have paradoxically become blind to their forceful presences.

The more notable subsurface forces impacting Borland's protagonist concern what Hall defines as synchronous movement in monochronic and polychronic time systems, bureaucratic irrationality, cultural bases of education, and the cultural identification syndrome. These forces exert tremendous tensions against Tom, who must in response ask the ageless question, "who am I" or, as Hall might put it, "to what should I attend."

In order to point out the tension inherent in Tom's identity crisis, we must first come to a basic, elementary understanding of the old Ute cultural concept of time which Hall describe's as polychronic. A polychronic time system is not lin-

ear, segmented, or dependent on rigid adherence to arbitrarily set schedules and is characterized by many things happening at once. Such a system is demonstrated when a group of Utes, including Tom's family, leaves the reservation and the confines of the cornfields to fish and hunt:

> They stayed there a week. Then they went up the river another day and found a place where there were more berries, more fish. And the men killed two fat deer which had come down to the river to drink. The venison tasted good after so much fish, and the women told the men to go up on Horse Mountain and get more deer and they would dry it, the old way, for winter. There were many deer on Horse Mountain and they made much meat. Nobody remembered how long they were there because it didn't matter. When they had made meat for the winter, they said, and had smoked fish and dried berries for the winter, they would go back to the reservation.

In this context, the activity and inter action, not time, are valued.

The Ute culture's notion of time and one's part in nature can be further explored in "the roundness-of-life" motif, a key cultural gestalt. Nature is cyclical as demonstrated in the rhythms of day and night, seasonal changes, birth and death, the regular "path of the stars," lunar phases, etc. Such contextual rhythms serve as the basis of the Utes' concept of time continuance and determine collective tribal activities and perception. Being in sync with this system is viewed with more importance than that given it by the white culture. The Utes are not as far removed or extended from their immediate dependence on nature by the implements of progress which demands that the tribal members not only act in sync with one another but with the cosmic clock of nature as well.

Borland demonstrates this synchronization symbolically in the guise of the Ute chants. The chant seems to be a microcosmic interaction of the Indians' culture, personality, intellect, and even intuition with the mystical forces and laws of nature. Trivial as well as monumental occurrences are experienced within the "magic" of the chants. For example, after Tom, his mother Bessie, and his father George escape from the sawmill, George, using a bow and arrows, goes on an unsuccessful deer hunt. Bessie reminds him that they had not sung the deer chant. After singing the chant the following afternoon, George kills a doe. The chant, then, seems to be a key in affecting a union with an underlying harmony and subsequently to invoking providence.

Additionally, the Indians' perception of one's part in the "roundness of life" and this underlying

Group of Ute Indians

harmony is much like the Bergsonian intuitional view of duration or "stream of life." This is at least implied in Borland's use of Bessie's metaphorical explanation of the chipmunk stripes:

> These stripes, she said, were the paths from its eyes, with which it sees now and tomorrow, to its tail, which is always behind it and a part of yesterday ... They are the ties that bind man to his own being, his small part of the roundness.

In contrast to the polychronic time system in the "roundness of life" as perceived by the Utes, the American white culture into which Tom is forced mainly functions according to what Hall labels as monochronic or M-time. Ruled by meta-phors of saving, spending, wasting, running out of, and making up time, M-time systems implement and religiously adhere to rigid schedules which have as side effects segmentation and narrower per-ceptions. Hall explains:

> M-time can alienate us from ourselves and deny us the experience of context in the wider sense. That is M-time narrows one's view of events in much the same way as looking through a cardboard tube nar-rows vision, and it influences subtly and in depth how we think—in segmented compartments

Such a time system is not necessarily con-ducive to personal creativity and biorhythms, for at the core of M-time is scheduled attendance to one thing at a time as exemplified by the schedule and curriculum at the reservation school. The window to which Tom withdraws from class participation graphically symbolizes the narrowness and segmentation. In this case, the institution literally "boxes him in."

Tom's first memorable introduction into the cultural paradigm of American white bureaucracy is initiated by the well-meaning preacher who discovers that the boy he once christened as Tom Black Bull is now living in the old Ute fashion as Bear's Brother. Fulfilling what he interprets as his Christian duty, the preacher pays Blue Elk to take the boy to the reservation school, a prime exemplar of what Hall designates as institutional irrationality.

Hall views institutions as self-serving in order to nourish their own existences: "Established to serve mankind, the service function is soon forgotten, while bureaucratic functions and survival take over." For Tom, the reservation system is inherently evil in that its purpose is primarily to imprison, conditionally modify, and assimilate the Indians—all for the good of the white culture. If in this context Hall's thesis concerning bureaucratic irrationality is given credibility, one can then deduce that the reservation's bureaucratic survival is maintained even to some degree at the expense of the service it is to yield the white culture. To compound the matter, the bureaucracy is inherently more sensitive to the goals of white culture than to the Utes. Hence, the Indians are doubly jeopardized.

Tom's best interests are interpreted within the perspective of the institution; he is "served" whether he shares in this point of view or not for the bureaucracy "knows best" and must control. In the chapter "Cultural and Primate Bases of Education," Hall writes the following bias:

> Another guiding principle is that the American system of education is assumed to be the best in the world and equally applicable to all people and must therefore be imposed upon them . . . without regard to their own culture.

This principle is stereotypically mandated by the Indian agent's judgmental sentencing when he orders, "He (Tom) will go to school here and learn the things he should know." Tom reconciled to such imposition with the archetypical lament, "I do not need these things."

The methodology and curriculum at the school seem to support Hall's notion that America's educational system is over-structured, is basically geared to teach who is boss, and limits man's

innate need for physical activity with "sacred" schedules and confinement to desks. Tom is forced into a cultural context much in the same manner that a square peg is whittled to fit a round hole. He is imprisoned in the dormitory, corporally punished, mocked by peers, forced to forsake his pet bear whom he considers a brother, and robbed of his possessions by Blue Elk, who loots and burns his lodge.

Furthermore, nature and Tom's mother are replaced as instructors by Indian teachers already acclimated to the expectations of the culture and the institution. The curriculum emphasizing nature, practical arts, and the "roundness of life" is usurped by the school's highly compartmentalized three R's: woodworking, sheep herding, and basket-weaving. In the different cultural paradigm, new aspects demand Tom's attention; and intelligence is judged primarily in regard to how well and exhaustively that attention was given.

Regarding methodology, Hall believes that one of the primate bases of education is that man is a "playing animal" but that many educational practices contradict and frustrate this basic nature. Ironically, Tom, while playing yet breaking the school rules against riding the unbroken horses in the herd, gains the skills of what later is to be his occupational "claim to fame" as a rodeo bronco rider. The acquisition of these skills makes leaving the reservation system possible.

Borland uses Luther Spotted Dog, who remains in the system, as an example of the product or output of the reservation school. Upon returning to Pagosa to recuperate after his rodeo accident, Tom finds Luther, his one-time roommate, sitting on the curb and looking like a "skid-row character." The contrast between Tom and Luther seems to echo Hall's premise that education is ". . . a game in which there are winners and losers, and the game has little relevance to either the outside world or to the subject being taught." The conclusion drawn from the contrast is perhaps that by eventually leaving the school via Red Dillon's greedy intent to use Tom in the rodeo circuit in gambling schemes Tom achieves more "success" than did Luther, who remained. Such is Borland's comment on what Hall deems as bureaucratic irrationality.

As previously noted, Tom's transition from the Ute culture is abruptly violent. In the new environment Tom eventually denies his inner-being nurtured by the Ute cultural heritage, for only in the denial and disassociation does he find a tolerable degree of ease from tensions inherent in the

What Do I Read Next?

- *Rising Voices: Writings of Young Native Americans* (1992) is a collection of poems and essays written by young Native Americans about their identity, their families, the rituals that have been passed down to them, and the difficulties of their daily lives.

- N. Scott Momaday is an award-winning and very respected Native American author. His book *House Made of Dawn* (1968) tells the story of a young man who feels lost and displaced in white America. The novel follows his journey through many difficult challenges, ending with his gaining some insights into his self-proclaimed identity.

- *Talking Leaves: Contemporary Native American Short Stories* (1991) is a good place to find an introduction to many of the most celebrated contemporary Native American authors. Included are Louis Erdrich, Michael Dorris, N. Scott Momaday, James Welch, and many others.

- A collection of myths and legends of various Native American cultures has been put together by Paula Gunn Allen in *Spider Woman's Granddaughters: Traditional Tales and Contemporary Writing by Native American Women* (1989). The collection includes tales that are both traditional and contemporary and focus on the lives of Native American women.

- *Lame Deer, Seeker of Visions* (1972) tells the life story of John Fire Lame Deer, a traditional medicine man who was a respected elder of his Lakota tribe. The book is a must-read for those interested in exploring the philosophy and spiritual beliefs of the Lakota people. Many people outside of the Native American community have found this book helpful in their own spiritual quests, regardless of their culture.

- James Welch is a talented writer who focuses on Native American culture. In his *Fools Crow* (1986), he tells the story of the effects of white encroachment on the Blackfoot tribe in Montana during the latter part of the nineteenth century. The main character of this story is a young man who chooses a spiritual path, eventually becoming a medicine man of his people.

- Borland's *The Amulet* (1957) was written six years prior to his *When the Legends Die* and shares a similar Western tone. This story of young love is set on the plains of Missouri during the Civil War.

- Borland is most famous for his collections of essays. Included in this genre are his books *The Enduring Pattern* (1959), *Sundial of the Seasons: A Selection of Outdoor Editorials from the "New York Times"* (1964), and *Borland Country* (1971). Borland, a self-taught naturalist, often writes about the environment and reflections of his life in the countryside. His essay writing has been described as Thoreau-like.

---

change of cultural context. Upon returning to the school after having escaped only to find his lodge looted and destroyed, Tom begins to conform by cutting his braids, wearing the school uniform, uninterestedly attending classes, and perhaps most significantly speaking only English.

Yet, Tom's ultimate submission occurs after he must, in order to save it from being shot, drive off his bear when it returns to the school after hibernation. The bear by this point has become a symbol of Tom's Ute identity:

The boy backed away. "I do not know you!" he cried. "You are no longer my brother. I have no brother! I have no friends!"

"Go away," the boy said. "Go or they will kill you. They do not need guns to kill ..."

Triggered by the repression and denial, Tom enters Hall's cultural identification syndrome. Hall writes:

Part of the frustration can be traced to anger at oneself for not being able to cope with a dissociated aspect of one's personality and at the same time to defeat from being denied the experience of an important part of the self.

Being denied his Ute way of life and disassociating himself from the behavior patterns implicit in that life style prompt Tom's frustration. From the rhythms of the "roundness of life," Blue Elk betrays him into the structure of the reservation system where Tom's denial of his heritage begins as a response to the tension exerted by being between cultures. The denial continues as Tom tries Red Dillon's way in the rodeo circuit within which Tom's life settles into the pattern or segmentation of hopping from one town to the next, from one gambling spoof to another—all the while with Red being the boss. But perhaps the denial deepened when Tom rebels and leaves Red to become the legendary Killer Tom Black, the killer of rodeo horses.

The horses become symbols for all the hurts Tom had experienced at the hands of Blue Elk, Red Dillon, and school personnel such as Benny Grayback, Neil Swanson, and Rowena Ellis. To the amazement but sadistic thrill of the crowd, he rides the horses to their deaths to be the boss over all the memories he sought to kill. Tom's mania is symptomatic of the identification syndrome in that he views the loss of self as purposed by forces or personalities outside himself. The most intense segment of his daily life is the ten-second mastery over the horse. This is monochronic time fragmentation and narrowness of perspective epitomized to the point of mania.

Still, Tom can not totally deny his Ute heritage. During his recuperation on Horse Mountain, Tom finally confronts the grizzly which had once been his pet. Here he plans the ultimate denial of his heritage by killing the bear symbolizing the old Ute ways. Yet, when the "moment of truth" comes, Tom can not kill the bear; instead comes the reaffirmation of his heritage:

> He closed his eyes, fighting with himself. I came to kill the bear! His throbbing pulse asked, Why? He answered, I must! And again his pulse beat, Why? He answered, To be myself: And the pulse asked, Who . . . are . . . you? He had no answer. The pulse kept beating the question at him. Angrily he said, This bear has made trouble: The question beat back, To . . . whom? And his own bitter answer, To me! Then the question, as before, Who . . . are . . . you? (italics in original) And he, having no answer he could face, said, whispering the words aloud, "This bear did not make trouble. The trouble is in me." And he lowered the rifle.

Upon realizing that the trouble is in himself, Tom takes the first step in resolving the identity

> *The horses become symbols for all the hurts Tom had experienced at the hands of Blue Elk, Red Dillon, and school personnel such as Benny Grayback, Neil Swanson, and Rowena Ellis.*"

crisis. In the chronology following this insight, Tom subjects himself to various Ute rituals for purification. Finally in the last of a series of dreams, he rediscovers his part in the roundness. The All-Mother, symbolizing not only all the mothers in Ute history but nature as well, claims Tom as her son.

By understanding himself, he can now understand and accept others. Hall writes:

> The paradoxical part of the identification syndrome is that until it has been resolved there can be no friendship and no love—only hate. Until we can allow others to be themselves, and others to be free, it is impossible to truly love another human being; neurotic and dependent love is, perhaps possible, but not genuine love, which can be generated only in the self.

This explains why Tom cannot accept Mary Redmond's friendship offered before his reaffirmation of himself as a Ute and viewed as another form of entrapment. After this reaffirmation, Tom plans a return to Pagosa to learn what happened to Blue Elk and what motivated his betrayal of the Utes. Tom also wants to visit the reservation school and try to understand the system. However, he has no need to return to the rodeo arena because the legendary Killer Tom Black was no more; the person rediscovered on Horse Mountain is Tom Black Bull, a Ute.

In summation, reading Hall's *Beyond Culture* as a companion book to Borland's *When the Legends Die* reveals cultural axioms that provide some explanation as to the causes and resolution of Tom's identity crisis which to some extent can be a paradigm. In Hall's exposure of monochronic and polychronic time systems, bureaucratic irrationality, the cultural bases of education, and the cultural identification syndrome is found clarification of man's response to his finitude in that these very gestalts are in part the parameters of that finitude.

Source: Mitch Holifield, "*When the Legends Die*: A Point beyond Culture," in *Education*, Vol. 120, Issue 1, Fall 1999, pp. 93–98.

Sources

Holifield, Mitch, "*When the Legends Die*: A Point beyond Culture," in *Education*, Vol. 120, No. 1, Fall 1999.

Wakeman, John, ed., *World Authors, 1950–1970*, H. W. Wilson, 1975.

Further Reading

Bass, Rick, *The Lost Grizzlies: A Search for Survivors in the Wilderness of Colorado*, Houghton Mifflin, 1997.
Rick Bass, a gifted writer of novels, short stories, and nature essays, tackles the mystery of the grizzly bears in the San Juan Mountains of Colorado. Many people continue to claim they have seen grizzlies in these mountains where the bears have been officially declared extinct. Through his lyrical prose, Bass recounts his adventures in an attempt to finally put the questions to rest.

Borland, Hal, *Country Editor's Boy*, Lippincott, 1970.
This book recounts Borland's life story as he matures into a young man. Borland tells the story by describing his relationships with his parents, friends, and neighbors.

———, *High, Wide and Lonesome*, Lippincott, 1956.
This is an autobiography about Borland's youth. It is told through Borland's constant vision of the landscape around him.

Brown, Dee, *Bury My Heart at Wounded Knee: An Indian History of the American West*, Holt, Rinehart & Winston, 1970.
This highly praised account of the Western expansion as witnessed by Native Americans is a powerful testimony to the fortitude of the native peoples of America. Brown covers such controversial and sorrowful topics as the Long Walk of the Navahos, the constant struggle and fight over the last herds of buffalo, and the founding of the Bureau of Indian Affairs.

Eisler, Kim Isaac, *Revenge of the Pequots: How a Small Native American Tribe Created the World's Most Profitable Casino*, Simon & Schuster, 2001.
Eisler tells the story of how the descendents of the Pequots, a small tribe in southern Connecticut, turned oppression into advantage by using the laws that the U.S. government had created to ensure their financial success, becoming the wealthiest Indian tribe in the history of North America. The irony of this story surrounds the fights that ensued when rights of the Pequots to claim themselves as an official tribe were challenged, something that no one bothered to argue until this tribe was about to reap the benefits of a profitable gambling casino.

Hirschfelder, Arlene, ed., *Native Heritage: Personal Accounts by Native Americans, 1790 to the Present*, Macmillan, 1995.
The book contains a collection of personal essays, written or told during two hundred years of transition in Native American culture. The stories focus on the effects of these changes on Native American families, language, land, education, traditions, and spirituality.

Wroth, William, *Ute Indian Art and Culture: From Prehistory to the New Millennium*, Colorado Springs Fine Arts Center, 2001.
This is a beautiful collection of photographs and essays on the Ute culture, an often overlooked or totally ignored subject. Wroth, a former curator of the Colorado Springs Fine Arts Center, has brought together an assembly of old clothing, jewelry, and other artifacts in an attempt to tell the story, through pictures and words, of the history of these people.

Glossary of Literary Terms

A

Abstract: As an adjective applied to writing or literary works, abstract refers to words or phrases that name things not knowable through the five senses.

Aestheticism: A literary and artistic movement of the nineteenth century. Followers of the movement believed that art should not be mixed with social, political, or moral teaching. The statement "art for art's sake" is a good summary of aestheticism. The movement had its roots in France, but it gained widespread importance in England in the last half of the nineteenth century, where it helped change the Victorian practice of including moral lessons in literature.

Allegory: A narrative technique in which characters representing things or abstract ideas are used to convey a message or teach a lesson. Allegory is typically used to teach moral, ethical, or religious lessons but is sometimes used for satiric or political purposes.

Allusion: A reference to a familiar literary or historical person or event, used to make an idea more easily understood.

Analogy: A comparison of two things made to explain something unfamiliar through its similarities to something familiar, or to prove one point based on the acceptedness of another. Similes and metaphors are types of analogies.

Antagonist: The major character in a narrative or drama who works against the hero or protagonist.

Anthropomorphism: The presentation of animals or objects in human shape or with human characteristics. The term is derived from the Greek word for "human form."

Antihero: A central character in a work of literature who lacks traditional heroic qualities such as courage, physical prowess, and fortitude. Antiheroes typically distrust conventional values and are unable to commit themselves to any ideals. They generally feel helpless in a world over which they have no control. Antiheroes usually accept, and often celebrate, their positions as social outcasts.

Apprenticeship Novel: See *Bildungsroman*

Archetype: The word archetype is commonly used to describe an original pattern or model from which all other things of the same kind are made. This term was introduced to literary criticism from the psychology of Carl Jung. It expresses Jung's theory that behind every person's "unconscious," or repressed memories of the past, lies the "collective unconscious" of the human race: memories of the countless typical experiences of our ancestors. These memories are said to prompt illogical associations that trigger powerful emotions in the reader. Often, the emotional process is primitive, even primordial. Archetypes are the literary images that grow out of the "collective unconscious." They appear in literature as incidents and plots that repeat basic patterns of life. They may also appear as stereotyped characters.

Avant-garde: French term meaning "vanguard." It is used in literary criticism to describe new writing that rejects traditional approaches to literature in favor of innovations in style or content.

B

Beat Movement: A period featuring a group of American poets and novelists of the 1950s and 1960s—including Jack Kerouac, Allen Ginsberg, Gregory Corso, William S. Burroughs, and Lawrence Ferlinghetti—who rejected established social and literary values. Using such techniques as stream of consciousness writing and jazz-influenced free verse and focusing on unusual or abnormal states of mind—generated by religious ecstasy or the use of drugs—the Beat writers aimed to create works that were unconventional in both form and subject matter.

Bildungsroman: A German word meaning "novel of development." The *bildungsroman* is a study of the maturation of a youthful character, typically brought about through a series of social or sexual encounters that lead to self-awareness. *Bildungsroman* is used interchangeably with *erziehungsroman,* a novel of initiation and education. When a *bildungsroman* is concerned with the development of an artist (as in James Joyce's *A Portrait of the Artist as a Young Man*), it is often termed a *kunstlerroman*. Also known as Apprenticeship Novel, Coming of Age Novel, *Erziehungsroman,* or *Kunstlerroman*.

Black Aesthetic Movement: A period of artistic and literary development among African Americans in the 1960s and early 1970s. This was the first major African-American artistic movement since the Harlem Renaissance and was closely paralleled by the civil rights and black power movements. The black aesthetic writers attempted to produce works of art that would be meaningful to the black masses. Key figures in black aesthetics included one of its founders, poet and playwright Amiri Baraka, formerly known as LeRoi Jones; poet and essayist Haki R. Madhubuti, formerly Don L. Lee; poet and playwright Sonia Sanchez; and dramatist Ed Bullins. Also known as Black Arts Movement.

Black Humor: Writing that places grotesque elements side by side with humorous ones in an attempt to shock the reader, forcing him or her to laugh at the horrifying reality of a disordered world. Also known as Black Comedy.

Burlesque: Any literary work that uses exaggeration to make its subject appear ridiculous, either by treating a trivial subject with profound seriousness or by treating a dignified subject frivolously. The word "burlesque" may also be used as an adjective, as in "burlesque show," to mean "striptease act."

C

Character: Broadly speaking, a person in a literary work. The actions of characters are what constitute the plot of a story, novel, or poem. There are numerous types of characters, ranging from simple, stereotypical figures to intricate, multifaceted ones. In the techniques of anthropomorphism and personification, animals—and even places or things—can assume aspects of character. "Characterization" is the process by which an author creates vivid, believable characters in a work of art. This may be done in a variety of ways, including (1) direct description of the character by the narrator; (2) the direct presentation of the speech, thoughts, or actions of the character; and (3) the responses of other characters to the character. The term "character" also refers to a form originated by the ancient Greek writer Theophrastus that later became popular in the seventeenth and eighteenth centuries. It is a short essay or sketch of a person who prominently displays a specific attribute or quality, such as miserliness or ambition.

Climax: The turning point in a narrative, the moment when the conflict is at its most intense. Typically, the structure of stories, novels, and plays is one of rising action, in which tension builds to the climax, followed by falling action, in which tension lessens as the story moves to its conclusion.

Colloquialism: A word, phrase, or form of pronunciation that is acceptable in casual conversation but not in formal, written communication. It is considered more acceptable than slang.

Coming of Age Novel: See *Bildungsroman*

Concrete: Concrete is the opposite of abstract, and refers to a thing that actually exists or a description that allows the reader to experience an object or concept with the senses.

Connotation: The impression that a word gives beyond its defined meaning. Connotations may be universally understood or may be significant only to a certain group.

Convention: Any widely accepted literary device, style, or form.

D

Denotation: The definition of a word, apart from the impressions or feelings it creates (connotations) in the reader.

Denouement: A French word meaning "the unknotting." In literary criticism, it denotes the resolution of conflict in fiction or drama. The *denouement* follows the climax and provides an outcome to the primary plot situation as well as an explanation of secondary plot complications. The *denouement* often involves a character's recognition of his or her state of mind or moral condition. Also known as Falling Action.

Description: Descriptive writing is intended to allow a reader to picture the scene or setting in which the action of a story takes place. The form this description takes often evokes an intended emotional response—a dark, spooky graveyard will evoke fear, and a peaceful, sunny meadow will evoke calmness.

Dialogue: In its widest sense, dialogue is simply conversation between people in a literary work; in its most restricted sense, it refers specifically to the speech of characters in a drama. As a specific literary genre, a "dialogue" is a composition in which characters debate an issue or idea.

Diction: The selection and arrangement of words in a literary work. Either or both may vary depending on the desired effect. There are four general types of diction: "formal," used in scholarly or lofty writing; "informal," used in relaxed but educated conversation; "colloquial," used in everyday speech; and "slang," containing newly coined words and other terms not accepted in formal usage.

Didactic: A term used to describe works of literature that aim to teach some moral, religious, political, or practical lesson. Although didactic elements are often found in artistically pleasing works, the term "didactic" usually refers to literature in which the message is more important than the form. The term may also be used to criticize a work that the critic finds "overly didactic," that is, heavy-handed in its delivery of a lesson.

Doppelganger: A literary technique by which a character is duplicated (usually in the form of an alter ego, though sometimes as a ghostly counterpart) or divided into two distinct, usually opposite personalities. The use of this character device is widespread in nineteenth- and twentieth-century literature, and indicates a growing awareness among authors that the "self" is really a composite of many "selves." Also known as The Double.

Double Entendre: A corruption of a French phrase meaning "double meaning." The term is used to indicate a word or phrase that is deliberately ambiguous, especially when one of the meanings is risqué or improper.

Dramatic Irony: Occurs when the audience of a play or the reader of a work of literature knows something that a character in the work itself does not know. The irony is in the contrast between the intended meaning of the statements or actions of a character and the additional information understood by the audience.

Dystopia: An imaginary place in a work of fiction where the characters lead dehumanized, fearful lives.

E

Edwardian: Describes cultural conventions identified with the period of the reign of Edward VII of England (1901-1910). Writers of the Edwardian Age typically displayed a strong reaction against the propriety and conservatism of the Victorian Age. Their work often exhibits distrust of authority in religion, politics, and art and expresses strong doubts about the soundness of conventional values.

Empathy: A sense of shared experience, including emotional and physical feelings, with someone or something other than oneself. Empathy is often used to describe the response of a reader to a literary character.

Enlightenment, The: An eighteenth-century philosophical movement. It began in France but had a wide impact throughout Europe and America. Thinkers of the Enlightenment valued reason and believed that both the individual and society could achieve a state of perfection. Corresponding to this essentially humanist vision was a resistance to religious authority.

Epigram: A saying that makes the speaker's point quickly and concisely. Often used to preface a novel.

Epilogue: A concluding statement or section of a literary work. In dramas, particularly those of the seventeenth and eighteenth centuries, the epilogue is a closing speech, often in verse, delivered by an actor at the end of a play and spoken directly to the audience.

Epiphany: A sudden revelation of truth inspired by a seemingly trivial incident.

Episode: An incident that forms part of a story and is significantly related to it. Episodes may be either self-contained narratives or events that depend on a larger context for their sense and importance.

Epistolary Novel: A novel in the form of letters. The form was particularly popular in the eighteenth century.

Epithet: A word or phrase, often disparaging or abusive, that expresses a character trait of someone or something.

Existentialism: A predominantly twentieth-century philosophy concerned with the nature and perception of human existence. There are two major strains of existentialist thought: atheistic and Christian. Followers of atheistic existentialism believe that the individual is alone in a godless universe and that the basic human condition is one of suffering and loneliness. Nevertheless, because there are no fixed values, individuals can create their own characters—indeed, they can shape themselves—through the exercise of free will. The atheistic strain culminates in and is popularly associated with the works of Jean-Paul Sartre. The Christian existentialists, on the other hand, believe that only in God may people find freedom from life's anguish. The two strains hold certain beliefs in common: that existence cannot be fully understood or described through empirical effort; that anguish is a universal element of life; that individuals must bear responsibility for their actions; and that there is no common standard of behavior or perception for religious and ethical matters.

Expatriates: See *Expatriatism*

Expatriatism: The practice of leaving one's country to live for an extended period in another country.

Exposition: Writing intended to explain the nature of an idea, thing, or theme. Expository writing is often combined with description, narration, or argument. In dramatic writing, the exposition is the introductory material which presents the characters, setting, and tone of the play.

Expressionism: An indistinct literary term, originally used to describe an early twentieth-century school of German painting. The term applies to almost any mode of unconventional, highly subjective writing that distorts reality in some way.

F

Fable: A prose or verse narrative intended to convey a moral. Animals or inanimate objects with human characteristics often serve as characters in fables.

Falling Action: See *Denouement*

Fantasy: A literary form related to mythology and folklore. Fantasy literature is typically set in non-existent realms and features supernatural beings.

Farce: A type of comedy characterized by broad humor, outlandish incidents, and often vulgar subject matter.

***Femme fatale*:** A French phrase with the literal translation "fatal woman." A *femme fatale* is a sensuous, alluring woman who often leads men into danger or trouble.

Fiction: Any story that is the product of imagination rather than a documentation of fact. Characters and events in such narratives may be based in real life but their ultimate form and configuration is a creation of the author.

Figurative Language: A technique in writing in which the author temporarily interrupts the order, construction, or meaning of the writing for a particular effect. This interruption takes the form of one or more figures of speech such as hyperbole, irony, or simile. Figurative language is the opposite of literal language, in which every word is truthful, accurate, and free of exaggeration or embellishment.

Figures of Speech: Writing that differs from customary conventions for construction, meaning, order, or significance for the purpose of a special meaning or effect. There are two major types of figures of speech: rhetorical figures, which do not make changes in the meaning of the words, and tropes, which do.

***Fin de siecle*:** A French term meaning "end of the century." The term is used to denote the last decade of the nineteenth century, a transition period when writers and other artists abandoned old conventions and looked for new techniques and objectives.

First Person: See *Point of View*

Flashback: A device used in literature to present action that occurred before the beginning of the story. Flashbacks are often introduced as the dreams or recollections of one or more characters.

Foil: A character in a work of literature whose physical or psychological qualities contrast strongly with, and therefore highlight, the corresponding qualities of another character.

Folklore: Traditions and myths preserved in a culture or group of people. Typically, these are passed on by word of mouth in various forms—such as legends, songs, and proverbs—or preserved in customs and ceremonies. This term was first used by W. J. Thoms in 1846.

Folktale: A story originating in oral tradition. Folktales fall into a variety of categories, including legends, ghost stories, fairy tales, fables, and anecdotes based on historical figures and events.

Foreshadowing: A device used in literature to create expectation or to set up an explanation of later developments.

Form: The pattern or construction of a work which identifies its genre and distinguishes it from other genres.

G

Genre: A category of literary work. In critical theory, genre may refer to both the content of a given work—tragedy, comedy, pastoral—and to its form, such as poetry, novel, or drama.

Gilded Age: A period in American history during the 1870s characterized by political corruption and materialism. A number of important novels of social and political criticism were written during this time.

Gothicism: In literary criticism, works characterized by a taste for the medieval or morbidly attractive. A gothic novel prominently features elements of horror, the supernatural, gloom, and violence: clanking chains, terror, charnel houses, ghosts, medieval castles, and mysteriously slamming doors. The term "gothic novel" is also applied to novels that lack elements of the traditional Gothic setting but that create a similar atmosphere of terror or dread.

Grotesque: In literary criticism, the subject matter of a work or a style of expression characterized by exaggeration, deformity, freakishness, and disorder. The grotesque often includes an element of comic absurdity.

H

Harlem Renaissance: The Harlem Renaissance of the 1920s is generally considered the first significant movement of black writers and artists in the United States. During this period, new and established black writers published more fiction and poetry than ever before, the first influential black literary journals were established, and black authors and artists received their first widespread recognition and serious critical appraisal. Among the major writers associated with this period are Claude McKay, Jean Toomer, Countee Cullen, Langston Hughes, Arna Bontemps, Nella Larsen, and Zora

Neale Hurston. Also known as Negro Renaissance and New Negro Movement.

Hero/Heroine: The principal sympathetic character (male or female) in a literary work. Heroes and heroines typically exhibit admirable traits: idealism, courage, and integrity, for example.

Holocaust Literature: Literature influenced by or written about the Holocaust of World War II. Such literature includes true stories of survival in concentration camps, escape, and life after the war, as well as fictional works and poetry.

Humanism: A philosophy that places faith in the dignity of humankind and rejects the medieval perception of the individual as a weak, fallen creature. "Humanists" typically believe in the perfectibility of human nature and view reason and education as the means to that end.

Hyperbole: In literary criticism, deliberate exaggeration used to achieve an effect.

I

Idiom: A word construction or verbal expression closely associated with a given language.

Image: A concrete representation of an object or sensory experience. Typically, such a representation helps evoke the feelings associated with the object or experience itself. Images are either "literal" or "figurative." Literal images are especially concrete and involve little or no extension of the obvious meaning of the words used to express them. Figurative images do not follow the literal meaning of the words exactly. Images in literature are usually visual, but the term "image" can also refer to the representation of any sensory experience.

Imagery: The array of images in a literary work. Also, figurative language.

In medias res: A Latin term meaning "in the middle of things." It refers to the technique of beginning a story at its midpoint and then using various flashback devices to reveal previous action.

Interior Monologue: A narrative technique in which characters' thoughts are revealed in a way that appears to be uncontrolled by the author. The interior monologue typically aims to reveal the inner self of a character. It portrays emotional experiences as they occur at both a conscious and unconscious level. Images are often used to represent sensations or emotions.

Irony: In literary criticism, the effect of language in which the intended meaning is the opposite of what is stated.

J

Jargon: Language that is used or understood only by a select group of people. Jargon may refer to terminology used in a certain profession, such as computer jargon, or it may refer to any nonsensical language that is not understood by most people.

L

Leitmotiv: See *Motif*

Literal Language: An author uses literal language when he or she writes without exaggerating or embellishing the subject matter and without any tools of figurative language.

Lost Generation: A term first used by Gertrude Stein to describe the post-World War I generation of American writers: men and women haunted by a sense of betrayal and emptiness brought about by the destructiveness of the war.

M

Mannerism: Exaggerated, artificial adherence to a literary manner or style. Also, a popular style of the visual arts of late sixteenth-century Europe that was marked by elongation of the human form and by intentional spatial distortion. Literary works that are self-consciously high-toned and artistic are often said to be "mannered."

Metaphor: A figure of speech that expresses an idea through the image of another object. Metaphors suggest the essence of the first object by identifying it with certain qualities of the second object.

Modernism: Modern literary practices. Also, the principles of a literary school that lasted from roughly the beginning of the twentieth century until the end of World War II. Modernism is defined by its rejection of the literary conventions of the nineteenth century and by its opposition to conventional morality, taste, traditions, and economic values.

Mood: The prevailing emotions of a work or of the author in his or her creation of the work. The mood of a work is not always what might be expected based on its subject matter.

Motif: A theme, character type, image, metaphor, or other verbal element that recurs throughout a single work of literature or occurs in a number of different works over a period of time. Also known as *Motiv* or *Leitmotiv.*

Myth: An anonymous tale emerging from the traditional beliefs of a culture or social unit. Myths use supernatural explanations for natural phenomena. They may also explain cosmic issues like creation and death. Collections of myths, known as mythologies, are common to all cultures and nations, but the best-known myths belong to the Norse, Roman, and Greek mythologies.

N

Narration: The telling of a series of events, real or invented. A narration may be either a simple narrative, in which the events are recounted chronologically, or a narrative with a plot, in which the account is given in a style reflecting the author's artistic concept of the story. Narration is sometimes used as a synonym for "storyline."

Narrative: A verse or prose accounting of an event or sequence of events, real or invented. The term is also used as an adjective in the sense "method of narration." For example, in literary criticism, the expression "narrative technique" usually refers to the way the author structures and presents his or her story.

Narrator: The teller of a story. The narrator may be the author or a character in the story through whom the author speaks.

Naturalism: A literary movement of the late nineteenth and early twentieth centuries. The movement's major theorist, French novelist Emile Zola, envisioned a type of fiction that would examine human life with the objectivity of scientific inquiry. The Naturalists typically viewed human beings as either the products of "biological determinism," ruled by hereditary instincts and engaged in an endless struggle for survival, or as the products of "socioeconomic determinism," ruled by social and economic forces beyond their control. In their works, the Naturalists generally ignored the highest levels of society and focused on degradation: poverty, alcoholism, prostitution, insanity, and disease.

Noble Savage: The idea that primitive man is noble and good but becomes evil and corrupted as he becomes civilized. The concept of the noble savage originated in the Renaissance period but is more closely identified with such later writers as

Jean-Jacques Rousseau and Aphra Behn. See also Primitivism.

Novel of Ideas: A novel in which the examination of intellectual issues and concepts takes precedence over characterization or a traditional storyline.

Novel of Manners: A novel that examines the customs and mores of a cultural group.

Novel: A long fictional narrative written in prose, which developed from the novella and other early forms of narrative. A novel is usually organized under a plot or theme with a focus on character development and action.

Novella: An Italian term meaning "story." This term has been especially used to describe fourteenth-century Italian tales, but it also refers to modern short novels.

O

Objective Correlative: An outward set of objects, a situation, or a chain of events corresponding to an inward experience and evoking this experience in the reader. The term frequently appears in modern criticism in discussions of authors' intended effects on the emotional responses of readers.

Objectivity: A quality in writing characterized by the absence of the author's opinion or feeling about the subject matter. Objectivity is an important factor in criticism.

Oedipus Complex: A son's amorous obsession with his mother. The phrase is derived from the story of the ancient Theban hero Oedipus, who unknowingly killed his father and married his mother.

Omniscience: See *Point of View*

Onomatopoeia: The use of words whose sounds express or suggest their meaning. In its simplest sense, onomatopoeia may be represented by words that mimic the sounds they denote such as "hiss" or "meow." At a more subtle level, the pattern and rhythm of sounds and rhymes of a line or poem may be onomatopoeic.

Oxymoron: A phrase combining two contradictory terms. Oxymorons may be intentional or unintentional.

P

Parable: A story intended to teach a moral lesson or answer an ethical question.

Paradox: A statement that appears illogical or contradictory at first, but may actually point to an underlying truth.

Parallelism: A method of comparison of two ideas in which each is developed in the same grammatical structure.

Parody: In literary criticism, this term refers to an imitation of a serious literary work or the signature style of a particular author in a ridiculous manner. A typical parody adopts the style of the original and applies it to an inappropriate subject for humorous effect. Parody is a form of satire and could be considered the literary equivalent of a caricature or cartoon.

Pastoral: A term derived from the Latin word "pastor," meaning shepherd. A pastoral is a literary composition on a rural theme. The conventions of the pastoral were originated by the third-century Greek poet Theocritus, who wrote about the experiences, love affairs, and pastimes of Sicilian shepherds. In a pastoral, characters and language of a courtly nature are often placed in a simple setting. The term pastoral is also used to classify dramas, elegies, and lyrics that exhibit the use of country settings and shepherd characters.

Pen Name: See *Pseudonym*

Persona: A Latin term meaning "mask." *Personae* are the characters in a fictional work of literature. The *persona* generally functions as a mask through which the author tells a story in a voice other than his or her own. A *persona* is usually either a character in a story who acts as a narrator or an "implied author," a voice created by the author to act as the narrator for himself or herself.

Personification: A figure of speech that gives human qualities to abstract ideas, animals, and inanimate objects. Also known as *Prosopopoeia*.

Picaresque Novel: Episodic fiction depicting the adventures of a roguish central character ("picaro" is Spanish for "rogue"). The picaresque hero is commonly a low-born but clever individual who wanders into and out of various affairs of love, danger, and farcical intrigue. These involvements may take place at all social levels and typically present a humorous and wide-ranging satire of a given society.

Plagiarism: Claiming another person's written material as one's own. Plagiarism can take the form of direct, word-for-word copying or the theft of the substance or idea of the work.

Plot: In literary criticism, this term refers to the pattern of events in a narrative or drama. In its simplest sense, the plot guides the author in composing the work and helps the reader follow the work. Typically, plots exhibit causality and unity and have a beginning, a middle, and an end. Sometimes, however, a plot may consist of a series of disconnected events, in which case it is known as an "episodic plot."

Poetic Justice: An outcome in a literary work, not necessarily a poem, in which the good are rewarded and the evil are punished, especially in ways that particularly fit their virtues or crimes.

Poetic License: Distortions of fact and literary convention made by a writer—not always a poet—for the sake of the effect gained. Poetic license is closely related to the concept of "artistic freedom."

Poetics: This term has two closely related meanings. It denotes (1) an aesthetic theory in literary criticism about the essence of poetry or (2) rules prescribing the proper methods, content, style, or diction of poetry. The term poetics may also refer to theories about literature in general, not just poetry.

Point of View: The narrative perspective from which a literary work is presented to the reader. There are four traditional points of view. The "third person omniscient" gives the reader a "godlike" perspective, unrestricted by time or place, from which to see actions and look into the minds of characters. This allows the author to comment openly on characters and events in the work. The "third person" point of view presents the events of the story from outside of any single character's perception, much like the omniscient point of view, but the reader must understand the action as it takes place and without any special insight into characters' minds or motivations. The "first person" or "personal" point of view relates events as they are perceived by a single character. The main character "tells" the story and may offer opinions about the action and characters which differ from those of the author. Much less common than omniscient, third person, and first person is the "second person" point of view, wherein the author tells the story as if it is happening to the reader.

Polemic: A work in which the author takes a stand on a controversial subject, such as abortion or religion. Such works are often extremely argumentative or provocative.

Pornography: Writing intended to provoke feelings of lust in the reader. Such works are often condemned by critics and teachers, but those which can be shown to have literary value are viewed less harshly.

Post-Aesthetic Movement: An artistic response made by African Americans to the black aesthetic movement of the 1960s and early '70s. Writers since that time have adopted a somewhat different tone in their work, with less emphasis placed on the disparity between black and white in the United States. In the words of post-aesthetic authors such as Toni Morrison, John Edgar Wideman, and Kristin Hunter, African Americans are portrayed as looking inward for answers to their own questions, rather than always looking to the outside world.

Postmodernism: Writing from the 1960s forward characterized by experimentation and continuing to apply some of the fundamentals of modernism, which included existentialism and alienation. Postmodernists have gone a step further in the rejection of tradition begun with the modernists by also rejecting traditional forms, preferring the anti-novel over the novel and the antihero over the hero.

Primitivism: The belief that primitive peoples were nobler and less flawed than civilized peoples because they had not been subjected to the tainting influence of society. See also Noble Savage.

Prologue: An introductory section of a literary work. It often contains information establishing the situation of the characters or presents information about the setting, time period, or action. In drama, the prologue is spoken by a chorus or by one of the principal characters.

Prose: A literary medium that attempts to mirror the language of everyday speech. It is distinguished from poetry by its use of unmetered, unrhymed language consisting of logically related sentences. Prose is usually grouped into paragraphs that form a cohesive whole such as an essay or a novel.

***Prosopopoeia*:** See *Personification*

Protagonist: The central character of a story who serves as a focus for its themes and incidents and as the principal rationale for its development. The protagonist is sometimes referred to in discussions of modern literature as the hero or antihero.

Protest Fiction: Protest fiction has as its primary purpose the protesting of some social injustice, such as racism or discrimination.

Proverb: A brief, sage saying that expresses a truth about life in a striking manner.

Pseudonym: A name assumed by a writer, most often intended to prevent his or her identification as the author of a work. Two or more authors may work together under one pseudonym, or an author may use a different name for each genre he or she publishes in. Some publishing companies maintain "house pseudonyms," under which any number of authors may write installations in a series. Some authors also choose a pseudonym over their real names the way an actor may use a stage name.

Pun: A play on words that have similar sounds but different meanings.

R

Realism: A nineteenth-century European literary movement that sought to portray familiar characters, situations, and settings in a realistic manner. This was done primarily by using an objective narrative point of view and through the buildup of accurate detail. The standard for success of any realistic work depends on how faithfully it transfers common experience into fictional forms. The realistic method may be altered or extended, as in stream of consciousness writing, to record highly subjective experience.

Repartee: Conversation featuring snappy retorts and witticisms.

Resolution: The portion of a story following the climax, in which the conflict is resolved. See also *Denouement.*

Rhetoric: In literary criticism, this term denotes the art of ethical persuasion. In its strictest sense, rhetoric adheres to various principles developed since classical times for arranging facts and ideas in a clear, persuasive, appealing manner. The term is also used to refer to effective prose in general and theories of or methods for composing effective prose.

Rhetorical Question: A question intended to provoke thought, but not an expressed answer, in the reader. It is most commonly used in oratory and other persuasive genres.

Rising Action: The part of a drama where the plot becomes increasingly complicated. Rising action leads up to the climax, or turning point, of a drama.

Roman a clef: A French phrase meaning "novel with a key." It refers to a narrative in which real persons are portrayed under fictitious names.

Romance: A broad term, usually denoting a narrative with exotic, exaggerated, often idealized characters, scenes, and themes.

Romanticism: This term has two widely accepted meanings. In historical criticism, it refers to a European intellectual and artistic movement of the late eighteenth and early nineteenth centuries that sought greater freedom of personal expression than that allowed by the strict rules of literary form and logic of the eighteenth-century neoclassicists. The Romantics preferred emotional and imaginative expression to rational analysis. They considered the individual to be at the center of all experience and so placed him or her at the center of their art. The Romantics believed that the creative imagination reveals nobler truths—unique feelings and attitudes—than those that could be discovered by logic or by scientific examination. Both the natural world and the state of childhood were important sources for revelations of "eternal truths." "Romanticism" is also used as a general term to refer to a type of sensibility found in all periods of literary history and usually considered to be in opposition to the principles of classicism. In this sense, Romanticism signifies any work or philosophy in which the exotic or dreamlike figure strongly, or that is devoted to individualistic expression, self-analysis, or a pursuit of a higher realm of knowledge than can be discovered by human reason.

Romantics: See *Romanticism*

S

Satire: A work that uses ridicule, humor, and wit to criticize and provoke change in human nature and institutions. There are two major types of satire: "formal" or "direct" satire speaks directly to the reader or to a character in the work; "indirect" satire relies upon the ridiculous behavior of its characters to make its point. Formal satire is further divided into two manners: the "Horatian," which ridicules gently, and the "Juvenalian," which derides its subjects harshly and bitterly.

Science Fiction: A type of narrative about or based upon real or imagined scientific theories and technology. Science fiction is often peopled with alien creatures and set on other planets or in different dimensions.

Second Person: See *Point of View*

Setting: The time, place, and culture in which the action of a narrative takes place. The elements of setting may include geographic location, characters' physical and mental environments, prevailing cultural attitudes, or the historical time in which the action takes place.

Simile: A comparison, usually using "like" or "as", of two essentially dissimilar things, as in "coffee as cold as ice" or "He sounded like a broken record."

Slang: A type of informal verbal communication that is generally unacceptable for formal writing. Slang words and phrases are often colorful exaggerations used to emphasize the speaker's point; they may also be shortened versions of an often-used word or phrase.

Slave Narrative: Autobiographical accounts of American slave life as told by escaped slaves. These works first appeared during the abolition movement of the 1830s through the 1850s.

Socialist Realism: The Socialist Realism school of literary theory was proposed by Maxim Gorky and established as a dogma by the first Soviet Congress of Writers. It demanded adherence to a communist worldview in works of literature. Its doctrines required an objective viewpoint comprehensible to the working classes and themes of social struggle featuring strong proletarian heroes. Also known as Social Realism.

Stereotype: A stereotype was originally the name for a duplication made during the printing process; this led to its modern definition as a person or thing that is (or is assumed to be) the same as all others of its type.

Stream of Consciousness: A narrative technique for rendering the inward experience of a character. This technique is designed to give the impression of an ever-changing series of thoughts, emotions, images, and memories in the spontaneous and seemingly illogical order that they occur in life.

Structure: The form taken by a piece of literature. The structure may be made obvious for ease of understanding, as in nonfiction works, or may obscured for artistic purposes, as in some poetry or seemingly "unstructured" prose.

Sturm und Drang: A German term meaning "storm and stress." It refers to a German literary movement of the 1770s and 1780s that reacted against the order and rationalism of the enlightenment, focusing instead on the intense experience of extraordinary individuals.

Style: A writer's distinctive manner of arranging words to suit his or her ideas and purpose in writing. The unique imprint of the author's personality upon his or her writing, style is the product of an author's way of arranging ideas and his or her use of diction, different sentence structures, rhythm, figures of speech, rhetorical principles, and other elements of composition.

Subjectivity: Writing that expresses the author's personal feelings about his subject, and which may or may not include factual information about the subject.

Subplot: A secondary story in a narrative. A subplot may serve as a motivating or complicating force for the main plot of the work, or it may provide emphasis for, or relief from, the main plot.

Surrealism: A term introduced to criticism by Guillaume Apollinaire and later adopted by Andre Breton. It refers to a French literary and artistic movement founded in the 1920s. The Surrealists sought to express unconscious thoughts and feelings in their works. The best-known technique used for achieving this aim was automatic writing—transcriptions of spontaneous outpourings from the unconscious. The Surrealists proposed to unify the contrary levels of conscious and unconscious, dream and reality, objectivity and subjectivity into a new level of "super-realism."

Suspense: A literary device in which the author maintains the audience's attention through the buildup of events, the outcome of which will soon be revealed.

Symbol: Something that suggests or stands for something else without losing its original identity. In literature, symbols combine their literal meaning with the suggestion of an abstract concept. Literary symbols are of two types: those that carry complex associations of meaning no matter what their contexts, and those that derive their suggestive meaning from their functions in specific literary works.

Symbolism: This term has two widely accepted meanings. In historical criticism, it denotes an early modernist literary movement initiated in France during the nineteenth century that reacted against the prevailing standards of realism. Writers in this movement aimed to evoke, indirectly and symbolically, an order of being beyond the material world of the five senses. Poetic expression of personal emotion figured strongly in the movement, typically by means of a private set of symbols uniquely identifiable with the individual poet. The principal aim of the Symbolists was to express in words the highly complex feelings that grew out of everyday contact with the world. In a broader sense, the term "symbolism" refers to the use of one object to represent another.

T

Tall Tale: A humorous tale told in a straightforward, credible tone but relating absolutely impossible events or feats of the characters. Such tales were commonly told of frontier adventures during the settlement of the west in the United States.

Theme: The main point of a work of literature. The term is used interchangeably with thesis.

Thesis: A thesis is both an essay and the point argued in the essay. Thesis novels and thesis plays share the quality of containing a thesis which is supported through the action of the story.

Third Person: See *Point of View*

Tone: The author's attitude toward his or her audience may be deduced from the tone of the work. A formal tone may create distance or convey politeness, while an informal tone may encourage a friendly, intimate, or intrusive feeling in the reader. The author's attitude toward his or her subject matter may also be deduced from the tone of the words he or she uses in discussing it.

Transcendentalism: An American philosophical and religious movement, based in New England from around 1835 until the Civil War. Transcendentalism was a form of American romanticism that had its roots abroad in the works of Thomas Carlyle, Samuel Coleridge, and Johann Wolfgang von Goethe. The Transcendentalists stressed the importance of intuition and subjective experience in communication with God. They rejected religious dogma and texts in favor of mysticism and scientific naturalism. They pursued truths that lie beyond the "colorless" realms perceived by reason and the senses and were active social reformers in public education, women's rights, and the abolition of slavery.

U

Urban Realism: A branch of realist writing that attempts to accurately reflect the often harsh facts of modern urban existence.

Utopia: A fictional perfect place, such as "paradise" or "heaven."

V

Verisimilitude: Literally, the appearance of truth. In literary criticism, the term refers to aspects of a work of literature that seem true to the reader.

Victorian: Refers broadly to the reign of Queen Victoria of England (1837-1901) and to anything with qualities typical of that era. For example, the qualities of smug narrowmindedness, bourgeois materialism, faith in social progress, and priggish morality are often considered Victorian. This stereotype is contradicted by such dramatic intellectual developments as the theories of Charles Darwin, Karl Marx, and Sigmund Freud (which stirred strong debates in England) and the critical attitudes of serious Victorian writers like Charles Dickens and George Eliot. In literature, the Victorian Period was the great age of the English novel, and the latter part of the era saw the rise of movements such as decadence and symbolism. Also known as Victorian Age and Victorian Period.

W

Weltanschauung: A German term referring to a person's worldview or philosophy.

Weltschmerz: A German term meaning "world pain." It describes a sense of anguish about the nature of existence, usually associated with a melancholy, pessimistic attitude.

Z

Zeitgeist: A German term meaning "spirit of the time." It refers to the moral and intellectual trends of a given era.

Cumulative Author/Title Index

Cumulative
Nationality/Ethnicity Index

African American

Angelou, Maya
  *I Know Why the Caged Bird
    Sings:* V2
Baldwin, James
  Go Tell It on the Mountain: V4
Cleage, Pearl
  *What Looks Like Crazy on an
    Ordinary Day:* V17
Ellison, Ralph
  Invisible Man: V2
Gaines, Ernest J.
  *The Autobiography of Miss Jane
    Pittman:* V5
  A Gathering of Old Men: V16
  A Lesson before Dying: V7
Haley, Alex
  *Roots: The Story of an American
    Family:* V9
Hurston, Zora Neale
  Their Eyes Were Watching God: V3
Kincaid, Jamaica
  Annie John: V3
Morrison, Toni
  Beloved: V6
  The Bluest Eye: V1
  Song of Solomom: V8
  Sula: V14
Naylor, Gloria
  Mama Day: V7
  The Women of Brewster Place: V4
Shange, Ntozake
  Betsey Brown: V11
Toomer, Jean
  Cane: V11
Walker, Alice
  The Color Purple: V5

Wright, Richard
  Black Boy: V1

Algerian

Camus, Albert
  The Plague: V16
  The Stranger: V6

American

Alcott, Louisa May
  Little Women: V12
Alexie, Sherman
  *The Lone Ranger and Tonto
    Fistfight in Heaven:* V17
Allison, Dorothy
  Bastard Out of Carolina: V11
Alvarez, Julia
  *How the García Girls Lost Their
    Accents:* V5
Anaya, Rudolfo
  Bless Me, Ultima: V12
Anderson, Sherwood
  Winesburg, Ohio: V4
Angelou, Maya
  *I Know Why the Caged Bird
    Sings:* V2
Auel, Jean
  The Clan of the Cave Bear: V11
Banks, Russell
  The Sweet Hereafter: V13
Baum, L. Frank
  The Wonderful Wizard of Oz: V13
Bellamy, Edward
  Looking Backward: 2000–1887:
    V15

Bellow, Saul
  Herzog: V14
Borland, Hal
  When the Legends Die: V18
Bradbury, Ray
  Fahrenheit 451: V1
Bridal, Tessa
  The Tree of Red Stars: V17
Brown, Rita Mae
  Rubyfruit Jungle: V9
Butler, Octavia
  Kindred: V8
Card, Orson Scott
  Ender's Game: V5
Cather, Willa
  My Ántonia: V2
Chandler, Raymond
  The Big Sleep: V17
Chopin, Kate
  The Awakening: V3
Cisneros, Sandra
  The House on Mango Street: V2
Clavell, James du Maresq
  Shogun: A Novel of Japan: V10
Cleage, Pearl
  *What Looks Like Crazy on an
    Ordinary Day:* V17
Clemens, Samuel
  *The Adventures of Huckleberry
    Finn:* V1
  The Adventures of Tom Sawyer: V6
Conroy, Frank
  Body and Soul: V11
Cooper, James Fenimore
  The Last of the Mohicans: V9
Cormier, Robert
  The Chocolate War: V2
  I Am the Cheese: V18

South African

Gordimer, Nadine
July's People: V4
Paton, Alan
Cry, the Beloved Country:
V3
Too Late the Phalarope:
V12

Spanish

Saavedra, Miguel de Cervantes
Don Quixote: V8

Swiss

Hesse, Hermann
Demian: V15

Uruguayan

Bridal, Tessa
The Tree of Red Stars: V17

West Indian

Kincaid, Jamaica
Annie John: V3

Subject/Theme Index

Look Homeward, Angel: 96–98,
103–104, 110–113
Tom Jones: 167–168, 171,
177–178
*The Unbearable Lightness of
Being:* 199–200, 204,
206–207, 217, 219–221
A Very Long Engagement:
244–247, 250–255
Waterland: 258–260, 263–264,
267–268, 275, 277, 279–281,
283–284
When the Legends Die: 287–288,
294–295, 299
Deceit
Tom Jones: 166, 175–176, 179
Description
I Am the Cheese: 67, 71
Sense and Sensibility: 120, 123,
128
Tom Jones: 181–183, 189, 191,
194
Dialogue
Sense and Sensibility: 121, 128
Under the Net: 225, 230–231,
239–240
Dishonesty
When the Legends Die: 291
Drama
Under the Net: 225, 229
Dreams and Visions
I Am the Cheese: 69, 71, 73
Sons and Lovers: 157–158,
161–164
Under the Net: 238–240
Duty and Responsibility
Sense and Sensibility: 137–139,
143

E

Emotions
Daughter of Fortune: 3, 8, 12, 17
Dracula: 46, 48
I Am the Cheese: 56, 59, 64–65,
67–68, 72–73
A Long and Happy Life: 76
Look Homeward, Angel: 103,
110–113, 116
Sense and Sensibility: 119, 125,
127, 135–138, 141–143
Sons and Lovers: 145, 148, 150,
154–157, 160
*The Unbearable Lightness of
Being:* 202, 204, 215–216,
220
Under the Net: 231, 235
Waterland: 275
When the Legends Die: 296–297
Eternity
Dracula: 34–35
*The Unbearable Lightness of
Being:* 219

Europe
Dracula: 22–24, 30–32, 34–35,
39–42, 44–46, 48–49
Sense and Sensibility: 122, 125,
127–130, 132–133
Sons and Lovers: 145, 147,
152–153
Tom Jones: 166–171, 176–178,
181–184, 189–195
*The Unbearable Lightness of
Being:* 197, 199–200,
202–203, 205–206, 210–215,
217–220
Under the Net: 223–227,
230–233, 236–240, 242
A Very Long Engagement: 244,
251–252
Waterland: 257–259, 263–265,
271, 273–274, 276
Evil
Dracula: 39–43
I Am the Cheese: 69–73
Sense and Sensibility: 140
Tom Jones: 171–172, 180–181,
185
Existentialism
Under the Net: 223, 231–232

F

Family Life
Sense and Sensibility: 130
Sons and Lovers: 157, 163
Tom Jones: 190, 194
Farm and Rural Life
I Am the Cheese: 53–58, 60–61
A Long and Happy Life: 76–77,
81–83
Sons and Lovers: 147–148,
152–153
Tom Jones: 177
Fate and Chance
Daughter of Fortune: 14–17
I Am the Cheese: 63–65, 67, 72,
74
A Long and Happy Life: 90–91,
93
Sense and Sensibility: 121, 123,
125, 127, 129
*The Unbearable Lightness of
Being:* 214–215, 217–221
Under the Net: 237
A Very Long Engagement: 244,
246–247, 249
Waterland: 271–272, 275–278
Fatherhood
Waterland: 278–280
Fear and Terror
Dracula: 23, 25, 29–32
I Am the Cheese: 67–70, 73–74
A Very Long Engagement: 244,
251–253
Waterland: 273, 275, 277

Feminism
Daughter of Fortune: 1, 10–11
Film
A Long and Happy Life: 92, 94
Under the Net: 225–226, 230, 233
Folklore
Dracula: 36–37, 41
Forgiveness
Tom Jones: 176
Free Will
Sons and Lovers: 150
Freedom
Daughter of Fortune: 15, 17
Sense and Sensibility: 125,
129–130

G

Ghost
Look Homeward, Angel:
111–113, 116–117
Tom Jones: 184–185
Gothicism
Dracula: 23, 30, 32, 38
Grief and Sorrow
Sense and Sensibility: 136–138,
140

H

Happiness and Gaiety
Sense and Sensibility: 136–140,
143
Tom Jones: 168–170, 172
Hatred
Dracula: 41–44, 47
I Am the Cheese: 69–72
Sons and Lovers: 145, 147,
150–151
Tom Jones: 184
A Very Long Engagement: 250,
252, 254–255
Waterland: 277
Heroism
Dracula: 38, 46, 48
Look Homeward, Angel: 114–117
Sense and Sensibility: 125,
127–128, 131–134, 136–137,
139–140
Sons and Lovers: 158, 160, 162,
164
Tom Jones: 166, 168, 175–176,
178
*The Unbearable Lightness of
Being:* 216–219
History
Tom Jones: 181–182, 184–185
Under the Net: 232–233
A Very Long Engagement:
250–251
Waterland: 257–259, 262–268,
271–274, 276–278, 281–284